Charles F. Goldfarb's
XML
Handbook™
Fifth Edition

The Charles F. Goldfarb Definitive XML Series™

Descriptions of the series books can be found on page 1134.

005·4 GOL

Titles in this series are produced using XML, SGML, and/or XSL. XSL-FO documents are rendered into PDF by the *XEP Rendering Engine* from RenderX: www.renderx.com

About the Series Editor
Charles F. Goldfarb is the father of XML technology. He invented SGML, the Standard Generalized Markup Language on which both XML and HTML are based. You can find him on the Web at: www.xmlbooks.com

About the Series Logo
The rebus is an ancient literary tradition, dating from 16th century Picardy, and is especially appropriate to a series involving fine distinctions between markup and text, metadata and data. The logo is a rebus incorporating the series name within a stylized XML comment declaration.

Charles F. Goldfarb's
XML
Handbook™

Fifth Edition

- Charles F. Goldfarb
- Paul Prescod

Prentice Hall PTR
Upper Saddle River, NJ 07458
www.phptr.com

Library of Congress Cataloging-in-Publication Data

Goldfarb, Charles F.
    Charles F. Goldfarb's XML Handbook / Charles F. Goldfarb, Paul Prescod.—5th ed.
        p. cm.—(The Charles F. Goldfarb Definitive XML Series)
    ISBN 0-13-049765-7
    1. XML (Document markup language). I. Prescod, Paul. II. Series.

    QA76.76.H94 G65 2001b
    005.7'2—dc21

Editorial/Production Supervisor: *Faye Gemmellaro*
Editor-in-Chief: *Mark L. Taub*
Editorial Assistant: *Noreen Regina*
Marketing Manager: *Chanda Leary-Coutu*
Manufacturing Buyer: *Maura Zaldivar*
Cover Designer: *Anthony Gemmellaro*
Cover Design Director: *Jerry Votta*
Series Designer: *Gail Cocker-Bogusz*

PRENTICE
HALL
PTR

© 2004 Charles F. Goldfarb
Published by Pearson Education, Inc.
Publishing as Prentice Hall PTR
Upper Saddle River, NJ 07458

**Prentice Hall PTR offers discounts on this book when ordered in quantity for bulk purchases
or special sales. For more information, please contact: U.S. Corporate and Government Sales,
1-800-382-3419, corpsales@pearsontechgroup.com. For sales outside of the United States, please
contact: International Sales, 1-317-581-3793, international@pearsontechgroup.com.**

Company and product names mentioned herein are the trademarks or registered trademarks of their
respective owners.

Printed in the United States of America

First Printing
Text printed on recycled paper.
ISBN 0-13-049765-7

Pearson Education Ltd.
Pearson Education Australia Pty. Limited
Pearson Education Singapore, Pte.Ltd.
Pearson Education North Asia Ltd.
Pearson Education Canada, Ltd.
Pearson Educación de Mexico, S.A. de C.V.
Pearson Education—Japan
Pearson Education Malaysia, Pte. Ltd.

involve risk and uncertainties including, without limitation: risks of intellectual property litigation; risks in technology development and commercialization; risks in product development and market acceptance of and demand for the company's products; risks of downturns in economic conditions generally and in the markets for Web, Internet, and intranet software and services markets specifically; risks associated with competition and competitive pricing pressures; risks associated with foreign sales and higher customer concentration; and other risks detailed in each company's filings with the Securities and Exchange Commission.

To Linda – With love, awe, and gratitude.

Charles F. Goldfarb

For Lilia – Your support makes it possible and
your love makes it worthwhile.

Paul Prescod

Overview

Contents

Preface

When Paul Prescod and I wrote the first edition of this book – six years and over 100,000 copies ago – XML was brand new and the subject of extraordinary hype. It promised to provide universal data interchange, revolutionize publishing on the Web, and transform distributed computing.

Those claims were amazing in the extent of their promised impact, but even more so in the diversity of the areas affected. More amazing yet, the claims have been fulfilled – even exceeded as XML has lept from the server to the desktop to appear in every office suite. With the support of the entire computer industry, an XML-based infrastructure is being constructed for modern computing; indeed, for modern business itself.

In many ways, though, the construction site resembles the Tower of Babel. The professionals in the areas affected by XML tend to talk and write about it in their own way, from each area's unique perspective, and in its specialized jargon.

But not in *The XML Handbook*!

From the first edition, our aim has been to integrate and unify the teaching of XML so that any tech industry professional can learn it, regardless of background. And by "learn it" we mean not just the technical details but the way that XML is used. Specifically:

- We use a unified standards-based vocabulary consistently. We explain when particular disciplines or industries use terms in conflicting or ambiguous ways.
- We explain all technical concepts as we introduce them, even the basics, but we don't indulge in "simplification by distortion". We clarify without sacrificing accuracy.
- We describe major trends, applications, and product categories objectively, employing the unified vocabulary, so you can see clearly how they relate to one another and to XML technology.

As a result, developers with diverse backgrounds found they could get the full picture of XML from *The XML Handbook*. Moreover, they also found they could encourage management to read the book and learn why XML is so important to the enterprise.

XML in an instant

HTML – the HyperText Markup Language – made the Web the world's library. XML – the Extensible Markup Language – is its sibling, and it is making the Web the world's commercial and financial hub.

In the process, the Web is becoming much more than a static library. Increasingly, users are accessing the Web for "Web pages" that aren't actually on the shelves. Instead, the pages are generated dynamically from information available to the Web server. That information can come from databases on the Web server, from the site owner's enterprise databases, or even from other websites.

And that dynamic information needn't be served up raw. It can be analyzed, extracted, sorted, styled, and customized to create a personalized Web experience for the end-user. To coin a phrase, Web *pages* are evolving into Web *services*.

For this kind of power and flexibility, XML is the markup language of choice. You can see why by comparing XML and HTML. Both are based on SGML – the International Standard for structured information – but look at the difference:

In HTML:

```
<p>P200 Laptop
<br>Friendly Computer Shop
<br>$1438
```

In XML:

```
<product>
<model>P200 Laptop</model>
<dealer>Friendly Computer Shop</dealer>
<price>$1438</price>
</product>
```

Both of these may appear the same in your browser, but the XML data is *smart* data. HTML tells how the data should *look*, but XML tells you what it *means*.

With XML, your browser knows there is a product, and it knows the model, dealer, and price. From a group of these it can show you the cheapest product or closest dealer without going back to the server.

Unlike HTML, XML allows custom tags that can describe exactly what you need to know. Because of that, your client-side applications can access data sources anywhere on the Web, in any format. New "middle-tier" servers sit between the data sources and the client, translating everything into your own task-specific XML.

But XML data isn't just smart data, it's also a smart document. That means when you display the information, the model name can be in a different font from the dealer name, and the lowest price can be highlighted in green. Unlike HTML, where text is just text to be rendered in a uniform way, with XML text is smart, so it can control the rendition.

And you don't have to decide whether your information is data or documents; in XML, it is always both at once. You can do data processing or document processing or both at the same time.

With that kind of flexibility, it's no wonder that we're starting to see a new Web of smart, structured information. It's a "Semantic Web" in which computers understand the meaning of the data they share.

Your broker sends your account data to Quicken using XML. Your imaging software keeps its templates in XML. Everything from math to multimedia, chemistry to commerce, wireless to Web services, is using XML.

The XML Handbook will help you use it too!

What about SGML?

This book is about XML, which is a simplified subset of SGML. However, you won't find feature comparisons to SGML, or footnotes with nerdy observations like "the XML empty-element tag does not contradict the rule that every element has a start-tag and an end-tag because, in SGML terms, it is actually a start-tag followed immediately by a null end-tag".[1]

Nevertheless, it is worth addressing the question of how XML and SGML relate. Eliot Kimber, who was a member of both the XML and SGML standards committees, says:

> There are certain use domains for which XML is simply not sufficient and where you need the additional features of SGML. These applications tend to be very large scale and long term; e.g., aircraft maintenance information, government regulations, power plant documentation, etc.

> A single model of commercial aircraft, for example, requires some four million unique pages of documentation that must be revised and republished quarterly. Multiply that by the number of models produced by companies like Airbus and Boeing and you get a feel for the scale involved.

I agree with Eliot. I invented SGML, I'm proud of it, and I'm awed that such a staggering volume of the world's mission-critical information is represented in it.

I'm gratified that SGML made the Web possible and that the Society for Technical Communication awarded joint Honorary Fellowships to the Web's inventor, Tim Berners-Lee, and myself in recognition of the synergy.

But I'm also proud of XML. I'm proud of my friend Jon Bosak who made it happen, and I'm glad that the Web is now becoming XML-based.

SGML still keeps the airplanes flying, the nuclear plants operating safely, and the defense departments in a state of readiness. You should look into it if you produce documents on the scale of an Airbus or Boeing. For the rest of us, there's XML.

---

1. Well, yes, I did just make that nerdy observation, but it wasn't a footnote, was it?

About our sponsors

With all the buzz surrounding a hot technology like XML, it can be tough for a newcomer to distinguish the solid projects and realistic applications from the fluff and the fantasies. It is tough for authors as well, to keep track of all that is happening in a field expanding as rapidly as this one.

In this case, the solution to both problems was to seek support and expert help from friends in the industry. I know the leading companies in the XML arena and know they have experience with both proven and leading-edge applications and products.

In the usual way of doing things, had we years to write this book, we would have interviewed each company to learn about its strategies, products and/or application experiences, written some chapters, asked the companies to review them, etc., and gone on to the next company. To save time and improve accuracy, we engaged in parallel processing. I spoke with each sponsor, agreed on subject matter for a chapter that would fit the book plan, and asked them to write the first draft.

I used their materials as though they were my own interview notes – editing, rewriting, deleting, and augmenting as necessary to achieve my objective for the chapter in the context of the book. I used consistent standards-based terminology and an objective factual style. All sponsored chapters are identified with the name of the sponsor, and usually with the names of the experts who contributed to it. I'd like to take this opportunity to thank them for being so generous with their time and knowledge.

We are grateful to our sponsors just as we are grateful to you, our readers. Both of you together make it possible for *The XML Handbook* to exist. In the interests of everyone, we make our own editorial decisions and we don't recommend or endorse any product or service offerings over any others.

How to use this book

The XML Handbook has twenty-four parts, consisting of 69 chapters, that we intend for you to read in order.

Well, if authors didn't have dreams they wouldn't be authors.

In reality, we know that our readers have diverse professional and technical backgrounds and won't all take the same route through a book this large and wide-ranging. Here are some hints for planning your trip.

To start, you can get the best feel for the subject matter by reading the Table of Contents and the introductions to each part. The introductions are less than a page long and usually epitomize the subject area of the part in addition to introducing the chapters within it.

Part One contains introductory tutorials and establishes the terminology used in the remainder of the book. Please read it first.

Parts Two through Twenty-three cover different application domains. The chapters are application discussions, case studies, and tool category discussions, plus some introductory discussions and tutorials. You can read them with only the parts that precede them (especially Part One) as background, although technical readers may want to complete the remaining tutorials first.

Those can be found in Parts Eighteen through Twenty-three. We strove to keep them friendly and understandable for readers without a background in subjects not covered in this book. Tutorials whose subject matter thwarted that goal are labeled as being a tad tougher so you will know what to expect, but not to discourage you from reading them.

Part Twenty-four contains resources: a catalog of public XML vocabularies, an acronym dictionary, and guides to the other books in this series and to the CD-ROMs.

There is an extensive index that also serves as a glossary. Pages where an index entry is defined are listed separately from the entry's other pages. I believe that the meaning of a term is best understood in context – in several contexts if they add to understanding, or the term has multiple meanings.

Acknowledgments

The principal acknowledgment in a book of this nature has to be to the people who created the subject matter. In this case, I take special pleasure in the fact that all of them are friends and colleagues of long standing in the SGML community.

Tim Bray and C. Michael Sperberg-McQueen were the original editors of the XML specification, later joined by Jean Paoli. Dan Connolly put the project on the W3C "to-do list", got it started, and shepherded it through the approval process.

But all of them agree that, if a single person is to be thanked for XML, it is Jon Bosak. Jon not only sparked the original ideas and recruited the team, but organized and chaired the W3C XML Working Group.

As Tim put it: "Without Jon, XML wouldn't have happened. He was the prime mover."

But before there could be an XML, or even an SGML, there had to have been ML. I continue to be grateful to Ed Mosher and Ray Lorie, my co-inventors – and namesakes – of the first markup language, IBM's GML.

Acknowledgment is due also to Norm Scharpf and the Graphic Communications Association (now called IDEAlliance) for their support and community-building efforts on behalf of XML, a continuation of their "from day one" support of SGML.

Regarding the content of the book, Paul and I would like to thank Jean Paoli, Jon Bosak, G. Ken Holman, Bob DuCharme, Eliot Kimber, Andrew Goldfarb, Lars Marius Garshol, Lilia Prescod, and Steve Newcomb for contributing great material; Bryan Bell, inventor of MIDI, education video producer, and information system architect, for his advice and support; Steve Pepper and Bob DuCharme for talent-spotting; Priscilla Walmsley for her insights into XML Schema and Microsoft Office; and G. Ken Holman for his encyclopedic knowledge of XSLT, XSL-FO, and DSSSL.

Prentice Hall PTR uses Adobe FrameMaker and other Adobe graphic arts and publishing software to produce most of its books. We thank Jennifer Stern of Adobe for providing Paul and me with copies.

Paul and I designed, and Paul implemented, an SGML-based production system for the book. It uses James Clark's Jade DSSSL processor, FrameMaker, and some ingenious FrameMaker plug-ins designed and implemented by Doug Yagaloff of Caxton, Inc. We thank Doug, and also Randy Kelley, for their wizard-level FrameMaker consulting advice.

But a great production system is nothing without a great production team. Faye Gemmellaro supervised the project for the publisher; we thank her for her dedication, attention to detail, and unfailing kindness and patience. We also appreciated her excellent rapport with the cover artist, Anthony Gemmellaro, who responded to our constantly changing complex requirements with inspired designs.

Special thanks also to Peter Snell for his efforts on our two CD-ROMs; Dmitry Kirsanov, for his remarkable combination of artistic talent coupled with expertise on XML and XSLT 2.0; Ann Salinger for her great work on the index; and Audrey and Ron Turner and their Soph-Ware Associates team, distinguished XML consultants, developers, and trainers with whom I've worked on many projects over the years.[2]

I owe a very special thank you to Andrew Goldfarb who once again has been like a son to me in our work together on this book.[3] He served as

2. In fact, they co-wrote the first book in my Prentice Hall series, *ReadMe.1st: SGML for Authors and Editors*, among many other books and articles.
3. And in other respects as well!

Managing Editor, with responsibility for the sponsorship program and other editing and production tasks, plus art director and artist-on-demand.[4]

Mark Taub, our Editor-in-Chief at Prentice Hall PTR, first proposed that I edit a book series on markup languages in 1993, long before markup became cool. I thank him again for his continued help, encouragement, and guidance, for both the series and *The XML Handbook*.

I'd also like to acknowledge a major debt to four people who supported and encouraged my efforts to develop and popularize markup languages. They epitomize vision and leadership in technical management. Norm Pass and Bobby Lie were my managers at IBM during most of the 25 years that I worked on GML and SGML. Yasufumi Toyoshima and Charles Brauer, then of Fujitsu Network Communications, were my consulting clients for six years following my retirement from IBM in 1994. They saw the potential for a Web-friendly, grammatically simple SGML subset long before I did – or anyone else I know.

As the senior author, I gave myself this preface to write. I'm senior because Paul's folks were conceiving him about the same time that I was conceiving SGML. In return, Paul got to write the history chapter, because for him it really is history.

This gives me the opportunity to thank Paul publicly for the tremendous reservoir of talent, energy, and good humor that he brought to the project. The book benefited not just from his XML knowledge and fine writing skills, but from his expertise in SGML, Jade, and FrameMaker that enabled us to automate the production of the book (with the previously acknowledged help from our friends).

Thanks, Paul.

Charles F. Goldfarb
Saratoga, CA
November 26, 2003

---

4. Andrew was once a best-selling author in his own right. For a brief period his *The Ballad of a Slow Poisoner* outranked both Stephen King and The Bible on the Barnes and Noble e-book best-seller list. Check out his non-XML art at: `http://www.slowpoisoners.com/flyers`

XML everywhere!

■ By Jean Paoli
Product Unit Manager, XML Technologies
Microsoft Corporation
Co-editor of the W3C XML Recommendation

■ *Redmond, April 24, 1998*

Foreword

When HTML came onto the scene it sparked a publishing phenomenon. Ordinary people everywhere began to publish documents on the Web. Presentation on the Web became a topic of conversation not just within the computer industry, but within coffeehouses. Overnight, it seemed as though everyone had a Web page.

I see the same phenomenon happening today with XML. Where data was once a mysterious binary blob, it has now become something ordinary people can read and author because it's text. With XML, ordinary people have the ability to craft their own data, the ability to shape and control data. The significance of this shift is difficult to overstate, for not only does it mean that more people can access data, but that there will undoubtedly be more data to access. We are on the verge of a data explosion. One ignited by XML.

By infusing the Web with data, XML makes the Web a better place for people to interact, to do business. XML allows us to do more precise searches, deliver software components, describe such things as collections of Web pages and electronic commerce transactions, and much more. XML is changing not only the way we think about data, but the way we think about the Web.

And by doing so, it's changing the way we think about the traditional desktop application. I have already witnessed the impact of XML on all types of applications from word processors and spreadsheets to database managers and email. More and more, such applications are reaching out to the Web, tapping into the power of the Web, and it is XML that is enabling them to do so. Gone are the days of the isolated, incompatible application. Here are the days of universal access and shared data.

I joined Microsoft in the summer of 1996 with great faith in the Standard Generalized Markup Language (SGML) and a dream that its potential might one day be realized. As soon as I arrived at Microsoft, Jon Bosak of Sun Microsystems and I began discussing the possibility of creating an XML standard. Jon shared my enthusiasm for a markup language such as XML, understanding what it could mean to Web communication.

My goal in designing an XML standard was to produce a very simple markup language with as few abstractions as possible. Microsoft's success is due in no small part to its ability to develop products with mass-market appeal. It is this mass-market appeal that I wanted to bring to XML. Together with Jon and other long-time friends from the SGML world, C.M. Sperberg-McQueen, James Clark, Tim Bray, Steve DeRose, Eve Maler, Eliot Kimber, Dave Hollander, Makoto Murata, and Peter Sharpe, I co-designed the XML specification at the World Wide Web Consortium (W3C). This specification, I believe, reflects my original goals.

It was truly an exciting time. For years, we had all been part of a maverick band of text markup enthusiasts, singing its praises every chance we had, and before us was an opportunity to bring XML into the mainstream, maybe even into the operating system. At last, we were getting our chance to tell the World of the thing we had been so crazy about for all this time.

By the fall of 1996, many groups inside Microsoft, including Office, the Site Server Electronic Commerce Edition, the Data Access Group, to cite a few, were searching for an open format to enable interoperability on the Web. It was then that I began working with the managers of Internet Explorer 4, with the passionate Adam Bosworth, with Andrew Layman, with Thomas Reardon, to define the Channel Definition Format (CDF). CDF, the first major application of XML on the Web, became an immediate and incredible success, and XML started catching on like wildfire across the Web.

I remember those weeks and months that followed as a time where it seemed that every day another new group within Microsoft began coding applications using XML. Developers, left and right, were turning on to XML. They frenetically began to develop applications using XML, because XML gave them what they wanted: an easy-to-parse syntax for representing data. This flurry of activity was so great that by October of 1997, almost a year after my arrival at Microsoft, Chairman Bill Gates announced XML as "a breakthrough technology." Since that time we've never looked back.

This book is an excellent starting point where you can learn and experiment with XML. As the inventor of SGML, Dr. Charles F. Goldfarb is one of the most respected authorities on structured information. Charles has had a very direct influence on XML, as XML is a true subset of SGML, and he clearly understands the impact that XML will have on the world of data-driven, Web-based applications.

Charles and I share a common vision, that the most valuable asset for the user or for a corporation, namely the data, can be openly represented in a simple, flexible, and human-readable form. That it can easily travel from server to server, from server to client, and from application to application, fostering universal communication with anyone, anywhere. This vision can now be realized through XML.

Enjoy the book!

Jean Paoli
Product Unit Manager, XML Technologies, Microsoft Corporation
Co-editor of the XML Recommendation
Redmond, April 24, 1998

XML: Looking back and looking forward

- By Jon Bosak
  XML Architect, Sun Microsystems
  Chair, W3C XML Coordination Group
- *Los Altos, August 1999*

Prolog

The World Wide Web is a medium that gained acceptance where earlier attempts had failed by providing the right combination of simplicity and fault tolerance. Now it faces the job of reinventing itself as a scalable, industrial-strength infrastructure strong enough to carry both human communication and electronic commerce into the new century. The story of XML and its companion standards is the story of that reinvention.

XML arose from the recognition that key components of the original Web – HTML tagging, simple hypertext linking, and hardcoded presentation – would not scale up to meet future needs. Those of us involved in industrial-strength SGML-based electronic publishing before the Web came into existence had learned the hard way that nothing substantially less powerful than SGML would work over the long run.

We also realized that any solution not based on SGML – the only formal International Standard that addresses this problem – would likely employ a proprietary binary format that would require special proprietary tools. XML is the creation of a small group of SGML experts who were motivated in large part by a desire to ensure that the Web of the future would not be dominated by standards controlled by a single vendor or nation. Its adoption by the world's largest computer software and hardware companies marks a significant turning point in the struggle to keep data free.

XML is a tremendous victory for open standards. It is freely extensible, imposing no limits on the ability of users to define markup in any combination of the world's major natural languages; it is character-based and human-readable, which means that XML documents can be maintained using even the most primitive text processing tools; and it is relatively easy to implement, so users can look forward to an abundance of inexpensive commercial XML processing tools and an ever-growing number of free ones.

Most importantly, XML provides a standard framework for making agreements about communication. It allows people sharing a common data exchange problem to work out an open solution to that problem – without interference from third parties, without dependence on large software vendors, without bindings to specific tools, without language restrictions, and in a way that lets anyone with a similar problem use the same solution. While the task of defining such standards within each industry and user community still lies before us, the framework for doing so is now in place.

Nevertheless, we must not lose sight of the larger goal. True interoperability requires not just interoperable syntax, but interoperable semantics. This ultimate goal cannot be achieved with anything less than the standardization of meaning itself, at least in those areas in which we wish to achieve automatic interoperability.

The coming standardization of domain-specific element types and attributes will establish the semantically meaningful labeling of content in particular industries, but it cannot address the behavioral aspect. While interoperable behavior can always be specified using a platform-neutral programming language like Java, such a powerful tool is often disproportionate to simple tasks. Just as we cannot ask our airline pilots to be aircraft engineers, we cannot require every creator of meaning to also be a programmer.

In the areas of hypermedia linking and presentation of rendered data, we can and must establish standardized techniques for behavioral specification that are declarative enough to be usable by nonprogrammers and yet powerful enough to get the job done in industrial contexts of unlimited scale. In both areas we are being held back by early superficial successes with simple mechanisms that are easy to learn but place unacceptable limits on what can be done, just as the early success of HTML held back the adoption of extensible markup.

The parallels to be drawn among the recent histories of markup, linking, and presentation are striking.

- In all three cases, early visionaries went much farther than the majority of adopters were ready to follow.
- In all three cases, breakthroughs in public consciousness were made by relative newcomers whose major contribution was to radically simplify the early, more advanced techniques in a way that made them accessible to the first wave of implementors.
- In all three cases, the original work is now being reconsidered, as those who understand the essential coherence of the original, larger view labor patiently to reconstruct mechanisms adequate for the demands of the future.
- And in all three cases, the biggest roadblock to deployment of the more advanced solutions is the success of the limited ones that got the Web off the ground.

I have no doubt that we will eventually succeed in replacing today's anemic realization of hypertext with something closer to the ideal articulated by the visionaries of the 1960s and worked out in the research projects of the 1970s and 1980s. I also have no doubt that we will eventually achieve interoperability of formatting behavior in a way that preserves the delivery of textual semantics to Web clients while simultaneously enabling the level of typographic control associated with printed newspaper and magazine publishing. My certainty is based not on a logical analysis of the future but simply on the same from-the-trenches understanding of basic needs that motivated me to begin the XML project in the first place.

What is not clear is how long it will take for Web implementors to realize the limitations of their existing conceptions of hyperlinking and style specification in the way that the more advanced among them now understand the limitations of HTML markup. But whether it takes two years or ten, the next steps are as necessary as was the first step to XML.

The XML Handbook can help us take those steps.

Jon Bosak
XML Architect, Sun Microsystems
Chair, W3C XML Coordination Group
Los Altos, August 1999

The Who, What, and Why of XML

- Why XML?
- Just enough XML
- XML in the real world
- XML and your browser
- XML and e-business
- The XML Jargon Demystifier

Part One

This part is the essential introduction to everything else in the book, which is why we named it Part One! Please read it from beginning to end because each chapter builds on the preceding ones.

For example, Chapter 2's *Just enough XML* tutorial relies on insights and markup fundamentals presented in their historical and business contexts in Chapter 1. That knowledge lets Chapter 3 tackle the most fundamental issue for XML: the relationship between documents and data and what that means for applications and products.

By Chapter 4 we've covered enough to understand XML's impact on people, over the Web and on the desktop, and then, in Chapter 5, how it enables computer-to-computer communication. Chapter 6 reveals some of the mysteries of XML software development that even non-programmers need to know.

Finally, in Chapter 7 we can apply what we have learned to an examination of the most important terms related to XML – the ones that people misuse the most! You'll learn what they really mean, and how to decipher the intended meaning when others get them wrong.

Reading this part will prepare you for the application and tool discussions in Part 2 through Part 17. High-tech readers may want to complete the tutorials in Part 18 through Part 23 first, but others can just dip into the tutorials on a need-to-know basis.

Why XML?

- What is XML, really?
- Origins in document processing
- Abstraction vs. rendition
- Documents and data

T he success of the Extensible Markup Language is extraordinary: in just five years it has changed the way software is written, sold and used. All of the major software companies are enthusiastic about XML. New industry standards based upon it are released daily.

As you may have noticed, the XML book rack has grown from *The XML Handbook*™ and a couple of others to hundreds of books on every imaginable technical variation and combination. Where did this language come from and why has it become so important?

The computer world's excitement can be summarized in two words: *information interchange*. XML is about making computer systems work together through the exchange of everything from simple numbers to elaborate data structures and human-readable texts.

For instance, to make Web browsers compatible with drawing tools like Corel Draw and Adobe Illustrator, the World Wide Web Consortium created an XML-based language called the Scalable Vector Graphics language (SVG).

Similarly – but in a totally different domain – a group of accounting software vendors defined an XML-based language called Open Financial Exchange (OFX).[1] There are similar languages for virtually every industry.

Each allows information interchange between potentially varied hardware, software, and operating system combinations. If you need to get two computer programs to talk about anything, experts agree that XML is a fundamental building block.

Analysis   XML is a framework for any project that involves moving information from place to place, even between different software products and platforms.

Once computers can interchange information, they can work together. This in turn allows people to work together more efficiently. It does not matter whether you are buying and selling, writing a manifesto or collecting data on the fertility rates of fruit flies – XML can be used for any kind of information interchange.

Many of the most influential companies in the software industry promote XML as the next step in the Web's evolution. How can they be so confident about something so new? More important: how can *you* be sure that your time invested in learning and using XML will be profitable?

We can all safely bet on XML because its technology is in fact very old and has been proven effective over several decades and thousands of projects. The easiest way to understand the central ideas of XML is to go back to their source, the *Standard Generalized Markup Language* (SGML).

XML is, in fact, a streamlined subset of SGML, so SGML's track record is XML's as well. SGML enables information interchange within and between some of the world's largest companies. SGML was first used for document processing but as time goes by it has become increasingly clear that with the extensible markup technology of SGML and XML, data processing and document processing are the same thing! If you understand where it all comes from, you'll understand where it – and the Web – are going.

---

1. If you're going to work with XML, you'll need to get used to contrived acronyms with the letter "X" in them. For help, see Chapter 67, "The XML Handbook Acronym Guide", on page 1120.

1.1 | Text formatters and SGML

XML comes from a rich history of text processing systems. *Text processing* is the sub-discipline of *computer science* dedicated to creating computer systems that can automate parts of the document creation and publishing process. Text processing software includes simple word processors, advanced news item databases, hypertext document presentation systems and other publishing tools.

The first wave of automated text processing was computer typesetting. Authors would type in a document and describe how they would like it to be formatted. The computer would print out a document with the described text and formatting.

We call the file format that contained the mix of the actual data of the document, plus the description of the desired format, a *rendition*. Some historically important rendition notations include *troff*, *Rich Text Format* (*RTF* – used in some Microsoft software), and *LaTeX*.

The system would convert the rendition into something physically perceivable to a human being – a *presentation*. The presentation medium was historically paper, but eventually electronic display.

Typesetting systems sped up the process of publishing documents and evolved into what we now know as desktop publishing. Newer programs like *Microsoft Word* and *Adobe PageMaker* still work with renditions, but they give authors a nicer interface to manipulate them. The user interface to the rendition (the file with formatting codes in it) is designed to look like the presentation (the finished paper product). We call this *What You See Is What You Get* (*WYSIWYG*) publishing. Since a rendition merely describes a presentation, it makes sense for the user interface to reflect the end-product.

1.1.1 *Formatting markup*

The form of typesetting notation that predates WYSIWYG (and is still in use today) is called *formatting markup*. Consider an analogy: you might submit a manuscript to a human typesetter for publication. Imagine it had no formatting, not even paragraphs or different fonts, but rather was a single continuous paragraph that was "marked up" with written instructions for how it should be formatted. You could write very precise instructions for layout: "Move this word over two inches. Bold it. Move the next word beside it. Move the next word underneath it. Bold it. Start a new line here." and so forth. It might look like Figure 1-1.

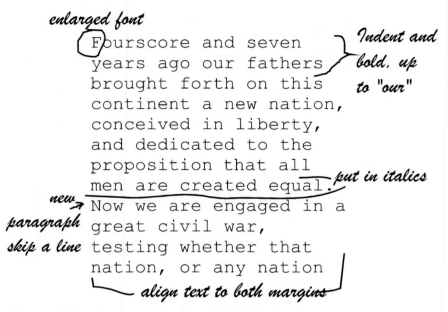

Figure 1-1   A manuscript "marked up" by hand

Formatting markup is very much the same. We "circle" text with instructions called *tags* or *codes* (depending on the particular formatting markup language). Here is an example of markup in one popular formatting markup language called TeX.

Example 1-1. A document with formatting markup

This is a marked up document. It contains words that are italicized because they are in a foreign language {\it oo la la} and bold-faced because they are {\bf important}.

In this markup language, the curly braces describe the extent of the formatting. So the italics started with the \it command extend until the end of the second word "la" and only the word "important" is affected by the

\bf command. Because the markup uses only ordinary characters on typical keyboards, it can be created using existing plain text editors instead of special word processors (which came later).

1.1.2 *Generalized markup*

This process is adequate if your only goal is to type documents into the computer, describe a rendition and then print them. Around the late sixties, people started wanting more from their documents. In particular, IBM asked a young researcher named Charles Goldfarb (the name may sound familiar) to build a system for storing, finding, managing, and publishing legal documents.

Goldfarb found that there were many systems within IBM that could not communicate with each other. They could not interchange information! Each of them used a different command language. They could not read each other's files, just as you may have had trouble loading *WordPerfect* files into *Word* and vice versa. The problem then, as now, was that they all had a different *representation* (sometimes also called a *file format*) for the information.

In the late sixties, Goldfarb and two other IBM researchers, Ed Mosher and Ray Lorie, set out to solve this problem. The team recognized (eventually) that the language would need to support three basic features:

Common data representation: markup
Various computer programs and systems would need to be able to read and write information in the same representation.

Markup should be extensible
There are an infinite variety of different types of information that must be exchanged. The markup language must be extensible enough to support them all.

Document types need rules
There must be a mechanism for formally describing the rules shared by documents of a common type.

These principles are important far beyond the exchange of traditional documentation. In fact they underlie the exchange of any form of information whatsoever.

1.1.3 *Common data representation*

The need for a common data representation is easy to understand. Tools cannot interchange information if they do not speak the same language. As an analogy, consider the popularity of Latin terms in describing chemical and legal concepts and categories. To a certain extent, chemists and lawyers have chosen Latin as a common language for their fields. It made sense in the text processing context that the common language should be some form of markup language, because markup was well understood and very compatible with existing text editors and operating systems. Markup is like a common language shared by many disciplines.

Before SGML and XML there was no standardized data representation. Every organization or project would invent its own from scratch. This meant that many programmers spent a significant portion of their life just writing the software that understands (*parses*) all of these different representations.

1.1.4 *Customized document types*

Second, the three realized that the common format should be *specific* to legal documents while at the same time being general enough to be used for things that are completely unrelated to the law. This seems like a paradox but it is not as impossible as it sounds!

This is a little more subtle to grasp, but vital to understanding XML. The team could have invented a simple language, perhaps similar to the representation of a standard word processor, but that representation would not have allowed the sophisticated processing that was required. Lawyers and scientists both use Latin, but they do not use the same terminology. Rather they use Latin words as building blocks to create domain specific vocabularies (e.g. "habeas corpus", "ferruginous"). These domain specific vocabularies are even more important when we are describing documents to computers. Markup is the lingua franca but it must be customized (extended!) for each community, consortium or problem domain.

Just as Latin can be used to describe anything under the sun, XML can be used for legal and scientific projects, for electronic business and also for poetry. XML is great for everything from long, complicated academic documents to the business transaction documents that allow commerce to flow around the planet: purchase orders, requests for quotation, bills of lading and so forth. Because XML is so expressive, the business transaction documents can be created and consumed by computers; increasingly, they can transact business with little or no human intervention.

1.1.4.1   Computers are dumb

They are not very good at working with documents unless we provide additional information about the documents' properties. Even then, they would be hard put to search our hard disk for a document that is a "memo" type document, that is *to* "Martha" and that is *about* "John Smith's will". Even though this example is much simpler than something a lawyer or chemist would run into, the fundamental problems are the same.

Most people recognize that the computer is completely incapable of understanding the concepts of "memo", "Martha" or "a will". Instead we might tell it to search for those words, and hope that we had included them all in the document. But what would happen if the system that we wanted to search was massive? It might turn up hundreds of unrelated documents. It might return documents that contained strings like "Martha, will you please write me a memo and tell me how John is doing?"

The fundamental problem is that the computer does not in any way understand the text. The solution is to teach the computer as much about the document as possible. Of course the computer will not understand the text in any real sense, but it can pretend to, in the same way that it pretends to understand simple data or decimal numbers.[2] We can make this possible by reducing the complexity of the document to a few structural *elements* chosen from a common vocabulary.

The elements that we use are not chosen just for the computer but also because they have significance to people and our sociological systems. We

---

2. We hope we haven't disillusioned anyone here. Computers may seem to know everything about math, but it is all a ruse. They are only manipulating zeros and ones.

can choose elements that closely mirror the components of established, real-world document types.

One important example of this is in electronic commerce vocabularies. If corporate policy or national law requires a certain form of document be produced in order to conduct a certain kind of business, then XML allows that document type to be moved directly into a digital representation. The system can move from a manual process to a digital one without breaking any laws or corporate policies.

1.1.4.2   Computers can be trained

Once we "teach" computers about structured information, we can also program them to do things they would not have been able to otherwise. Using their new "understanding" they can help us to navigate through large documents, organize them, and automatically format the documents for publication in many different media, such as hypertext, print or tape.

In other words, we can get them to process text for us! The range of things we can get them to do with the documents is much wider than what we would get with WYSIWYG word processors or formatting markup. In the world of transaction documents, the computer typically rips the documents apart and can do a variety of things with the pieces: store them in databases, perform financial computations or anything else necessary to a business process.

Let us go back to the analogy of the typesetter working with a document marked up with a pen on paper to see why this is so powerful.

Imagine if we called her back the next day and told her to "change the formatting of the second chapter". She would have a lot of trouble mentally translating the codes for presentation back into high level constructs like sections and paragraphs.

To her, a title would only look like a line of text with a circle around it and instructions to make it italicized and 18 point. Making changes would be painful because recognizing the different logical constructs would be difficult. She probably could eventually accomplish the task by applying her human intuition and by reading the actual text. But computers do not have intuition, and cannot understand the text. That means that they cannot reliably recognize logical structure based totally on formatting. For instance they cannot reliably distinguish an italicized, 18 point title from an italicized, 18 point warning paragraph.

Even if human beings were consistent in formatting different types of documents (which we are not) computers would still have trouble. Even in a single document, the same formatting can mean two different things: italics could represent any kind of emphasis, foreign words, mathematical notations, scholarly citations or other types of data elements.

Note that this all comes back to our theme of information interchange, but in a subtle way. The human being has information about a document that may not show up in any particular rendered print-out of the document. The author knows which documents are memos and which are not. The author knows which words are foreign and which are emphasized for rhetorical effect. A markup language can serve as a vehicle for the human to transmit this information *to the computer*.

We'll see that in some applications we can use markup to let computers talk to computers also! In fact, we can build systems in which each participant does not know or care whether its conversation partner is mechanical or biological.

1.1.4.3   Abstractions and renditions

Computers are not as smart as we are. If we want the computer to consider a piece of text to be written in a foreign language (for instance for spell checking purposes) then we must label it explicitly `foreign-language` and not just put it in italics! We call "foreign language" the *abstraction* that we are trying to represent, and we call the italics a particular rendition of the abstraction.

Formatting information has other problems. It is specific to a particular use of the information. Search engines cannot do very interesting searching on italics because they do not know what they mean. In contrast, the search engine could do something very interesting with `citation` elements: it could return a list of what documents are cited by other documents.

Italics are a form of markup specific to a particular application: formatting or printing. In contrast, the citation element is markup that can be used by a variety of applications. That is why we call this form of structural markup *generalized markup*. Generalized markup is the alternative to either formatting markup or WYSIWYG (lampooned by XML users as What You See is *All* You Get). Generalized markup is about getting more.

Because of the ambiguity of formatting, XML users typically do not bother to capture the document's presentational features at all, though

XML would allow it. We are not interested, for instance, in fonts, page breaks and bullets. This formatting information would merely clutter up our abstract document's representation. Although typographic conventions allow the computer to print out or display the document properly, we want our markup to do more than that. As you can imagine, removing all ambiguity is especially important in commerce applications, where millions of dollars may hinge on the proper completion of a transaction.

1.1.4.4   Stylesheets

Of course, if you are using XML for publishing, you must still be able to generate high quality print and online renditions of the document. Your readers do not want to read XML text directly. Instead of directly inserting the formatting commands in the XML document, we usually tell the computer how to generate formatted renditions *from* the XML abstraction.

For example in a print presentation, we can make the content of TITLE elements bold and large, insert page breaks before the beginning of chapters, and turn emphasis, citations and foreign words into italics. These rules are specified in a file called a *stylesheet*. The stylesheet is where human designers can express their creativity and understanding of formatting conventions. The stylesheet allows the computer to automatically convert the document from the abstraction to a formatted rendition.

We could use two different stylesheets to generate online and print renditions of the document. In the online rendition, there would be no page breaks, but cross-references would be represented as clickable hypertext links. Generalized markup allows us to easily produce high-quality print and online renditions of the same document.

We can even use two different stylesheets in the same medium. For instance, the computer could format the same document into several different styles (e.g. "New York Times" style vs. "Wired Magazine") depending on the expressed preferences of a Web surfer, or even based on which Internet service provider they use.

We can also go beyond just print and online formatting and have our document be automatically rendered into braille or onto a text-to-speech machine. XML is highly endorsed by those who promote the *accessibility* of information to the visually impaired.

Generalized markup documents are also "future-proof". They will not have to be redone to take advantage of future technologies. Instead, new stylesheets can be created to render existing documents in new ways.

Future renditions of documents might include three-dimensional virtual reality worlds where books are rendered as buildings, chapters as rooms and the text as wallpaper! Once again, the most important point is that these many different renditions will be possible without revising the document. There are millions of SGML documents that predate the Web, but many of them are now published on it.

Typically, they were republished in the Web's Hypertext Markup Language (HTML) without changing a single character of the SGML source's markup or data, or editing a single character of the generated HTML. All of the reorganization and reformatting can be done by computer programs instead of through months of re-typing. The same will be true of the relationship between XML and future representations.

The key is abstraction. SGML and XML can represent abstractions, and from abstractions you can easily create any number of renditions. This is a fact well-known to the world's database programmers, who constantly generate new renditions – reports and forms – from the same abstract data. In this sense, XML brings some of the rigor of the database world to the document world, where it has typically been lacking.

In the electronic commerce world, stylesheets can be used to make an information-dense computer-to-computer message into a visual rendition fit for human consumption. Perhaps your company policy is to require purchase orders beyond some limit to be considered by an executive. A stylesheet could turn an abstract XML document full of business process data into a familiar rows-and-columns purchase order that can be printed, touched and stapled to a wall. If some executives are comfortable working online, a different stylesheet could turn it into a transient computer window with the purchase order information at the top and two buttons: "Accept" and "Reject" at the bottom. The same information can have different renditions depending on your corporate policies and systems of the day.

1.1.4.5   Transformations

Stylesheets allow different people to consume the same information in many different ways. Sometimes computer programs also need to work

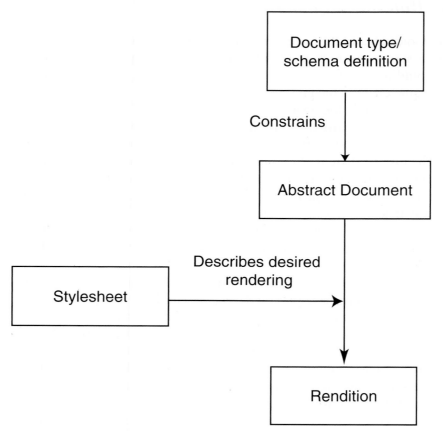

Figure 1-2   Rule-based markup

formatting such a letter, a stylesheet would typically not do a good job with it. In fact, it might crash, as some word processors do when they try to load corrupted documents. The document type definition protects us from this.[3]

The rigor of a formal document type is just as important when the creator of the document is a computer (e.g. a purchasing system) and the receiver is also a computer (e.g. a delivery system). If your company lives and dies by its supply of widgets, you cannot afford a miscommunication

---

3. Of course, computer programmers will always invent new excuses for crashing software.

that could cause a purchase to fail. You need both parties to know in advance what they should provide as requests and what they should expect back as responses. You need seamless interchange.

1.2 | XML markup

Enough hype about generalized markup! You probably want to know what it looks like. To mark up a memo, we could identify its components like this:

Example 1-2. A simple memo

```
<memo>
<to>Martha Mason</to>
<from>Joan Joplin</from>
<re>John Smith's will</re>
<p>John Smith wants to update his will.</p>
<p>Another wife left him.</p>
</memo>
```

This text is a short XML document. The markup identifies components, called *elements*, of the document in ways that the computer can understand. The start-tag "<to>" marks the beginning of a to element and the end-tag "</to>" marks the end of that element.

Each element is an instance of an *element type*: memo, to, from, re, or p. There are two instances of p and one instance of each of the others.

If you use an XML-aware word processor, you may never work with markup at the textual tag level, but you would still annotate sections of the document in this way (using the graphical interface that the tool provides).

Instead of each element type describing a formatting construct, each one instead describes the logical role of its elements – the *abstraction* it represents. The goal is for the abstraction to be descriptive enough and suitably chosen so that particular uses of the document (such as printing, searching and so forth) can be completely automated as computer processes acting on the elements.

For instance, we can search for a document that is "to" Martha, about ("re") John Smith's will. Of course the computer still does not understand the human interaction and concepts of sender and receiver, but it does know enough about the document to be able to tell me that in a "to" element of this particular document, the word "Martha" appears. If we expanded the memo a little to include addresses and so forth, we could also use an appropriate stylesheet to print it as a standard business memo.

1.2.1   *Documents and databases*

We can make our memo example even more precise and specific:

Example 1-3. Another memo

```
<memo>
<to>marthac@thelegaleagles.com</to>
<from>joanj@thelegaleagles.com</from>
<regarding>
<document-retrieval-request>will</document-retrieval-request>
<customer-name>John Smith</customer-name>
<customer-number>802-31348-5749</customer-number>
</regarding>
<comment>John Smith wants to update his will. Another wife left
him.</comment>
</memo>
```

XML does not require this level of detail, but it allows it. If you are familiar with databases, you might recognize that this looks database-ish in the sense that the customer number could be stored in a special index and you could easily search and sort this document based on customer number, document retrieval request, and so forth.

But you can only do this sort of thing if your memo processing system understands your company's concepts of customer-numbers and your documents consistently provide the information. In other words, you must define your own vocabulary of element types just as the IBM team did.

In fact, many people have noticed that XML documents resemble traditional relational and object database data in many ways. Once you have a language for rigorously representing documents, those documents can be treated more like other forms of data.

But the converse is also true. As we have described, XML documents have many features in common with databases. They can preserve the abstract data and prevent it from being mingled with rendition information.

Furthermore, you can actually use generalized markup to represent data that is not what we would traditionally think of as documents, but too complex to be directly handled in conventional databases. In this brave new world, DNA sequences are documents, and so are molecular diagrams and virtual reality worlds. A document is just an interchangeable form of data! In other words, generalized markup allows us to blow the doors off the word "document" and integrate diverse types of data. This database-ization of documents and document-ization of data is one of the major drivers of the XML excitement. Prior to XML, the Web had no standard data interchange format for even moderately complex data.

Only a few people could see 30 years ago that markup languages might one day change the entire world of databases and electronic commerce. But XML's unique usefulness as a data interchange representation is a direct consequence of the IBM team's three fundamental concepts:

- Markup as a common data representation
- Extensibility through document types (vocabularies)
- Verification that documents follow rules (document type/schema definitions).

XML isn't magic. Building XML-based systems can be easy or difficult, depending on the complexity of the problem at hand. XML eases the difficulty by allowing you to concentrate on the important aspects of your problem and ignore the irrelevant ones. Thanks to its common data representation, projects that use XML can avoid a tedious process of inventing a new data representation. That allows you to concentrate on choosing or creating a vocabulary tailored to your problem. Finally, XML has schema and DTD languages that allow you to clearly and precisely define the rules of your vocabulary.

Beyond XML, there are many related standards for stylesheets, transformations, linking and so forth. Each standard exists to help you to focus on the essential points that make your vocabulary unique. The associated standards allow you to avoid reinventing wheels.

1.3 | Road to XML

In 1969, the IBM team developed a language that could implement their vision of markup that would allow the construction of sophisticated, robust systems that integrate many applications on many different operating systems. They called it the *Generalized Markup Language* (which, not coincidentally, has the same initials as the names Goldfarb, Mosher and Lorie).[4]

However, it wasn't until 1974 that Goldfarb proved the concept of a "validating parser", one that could read a document type definition and check the accuracy of markup, without going to the expense of actually processing a document. As he recalls it: "At that point SGML was born – although it still had a lot of growing up to do."

Between 1978 and 1986, Goldfarb acted as technical leader of a team of users, programmers and academics that developed his nascent invention into the robust International Standard (ISO 8879) they called the *Standard Generalized Markup Language*.

That team, with many of the same players still involved, is now ISO/IEC JTC1/SC34, which continues to develop SGML and related International Standards. Three of the most important are *HyTime*, which standardizes the representation of hyperlinking features, *Topic Maps*, which standardize the representation of information navigation features, and *DSSSL*, which standardizes the creation of stylesheets.[5]

The SGML standard took a long time to develop, but arguably it was still ahead of the market when it was created. Over those years, the basic concepts of GML were broadened to support a very wide range of applications. Although GML was always extensible and generalized, the SGML standard added many features and options, many intended for niche markets. But the niches had to be catered for: some of the niche users have document collections that rival the Web in size!

By the time it was standardized in 1986, SGML had become large, intricate and powerful. In addition to being an official International Standard, SGML is the de facto standard for the interchange of large, complex docu-

---

4. In fact, Goldfarb coined the term "markup language" for the purpose.
5. Knowing the full names probably won't help much, but just in case, HyTime is short for "Hypermedia/Time-based Structuring Language" and DSSSL (pronounced "dis-sal") is short for "Document Style Semantics and Specification Language". We warned you that it wouldn't help much.

ments and has been used in domains as diverse as programming language design and airplane maintenance.

1.3.1 *HTML and the Web*

In 1989, a researcher named Tim Berners-Lee proposed that information could be shared within the CERN European Nuclear Research Facility using hyperlinked text documents. He was advised to use an SGML-ish syntax by a colleague named Anders Berglund, an early adopter of the new SGML standard. They started from a simple example document type in the SGML standard[6] and developed a hypertext version called the *Hypertext Markup Language* (HTML).

Relative to the 20 year evolution of SGML, HTML was developed in a hurry, but it did the job well. Tim called his hypertext system the *World Wide Web* and today it is the most diverse, popular hypertext information system in existence. Its simplicity is widely believed to be an important part of its success. The simplicity of HTML and the other Web specifications allowed programmers around the world to quickly build systems and tools to work with the Web.

HTML exhibits some important strengths of SGML. With a few exceptions, its element types are generalized and descriptive, not formatting constructs as in languages like TeX and Microsoft Word. This means that HTML documents can be displayed on text screens, under graphical user interfaces, and even projected through speakers for the sight impaired.

HTML documents use SGML's simple angle bracket convention for markup. That means that authors can create HTML documents in almost any text editor or word processor. The documents are also compatible with almost every computer system in existence.

On the other hand, HTML only uses a fixed set of element types. As we discussed before, no one document type can serve all purposes, so HTML only benefits from the first of GML's revelations, that document representations must be standardized. It is not extensible and therefore cannot be tailored for particular document types, and it was not very rigorously defined

---

6. That DTD was based on the very first published DTD, from a 1978 IBM manual written by Goldfarb, derived in turn from work that he and Mosher had done in the early 70's.

until years after its invention. By the time HTML was given a formal DTD, there were already thousands of Web pages with erroneous HTML.[7]

1.3.2 *HTML gets extended – unofficially!*

As the Web grew in popularity many people started to chafe under HTML's fixed document type. Browser vendors saw an opportunity to gain market share by making incompatible extensions to HTML. Most of the extensions were formatting commands and thus damaged the Web's interoperability. The first golden rule – standardization – was in serious danger.

For instance the Netscape browser introduced a CENTER element that cannot be "pronounced" in a text to speech converter. A BLINK element cannot be rendered on some computers. Still, this was a fairly understandable reaction to HTML's limitations.

One argument for implementing formatting constructs instead of abstractions is that there are a fixed number of formatting constructs in wide use, but an ever growing number of abstractions. Let's say that next year biologists invent a new formatting notation for discussing a particular type of DNA. They might use italics to represent one kind of DNA construct and bold to represent another. In other words, as new abstractions are invented, we usually use existing formatting features to represent them. We have been doing this for thousands of years, and prior to computerization, it was essentially the only way.

We human readers can read a textual description of the meanings of the features ("in this book, we will use Roman text to represent...") and we can differentiate them from others using our reasoning and understanding of the text. But this system leaves computers more or less out of the loop.

For instance superscripts can be used for trademarks, footnotes and various mathematical constructs. Italics can be used for references to book titles, for emphasis and to represent foreign languages. Without generalized markup to differentiate, computers cannot do anything useful with that information. It would be impossible for them to translate foreign languages, convert emphasis to a louder voice for text to speech conversion, or do calculations on the mathematical formulae. Over time, the Web became more

---

7. Today there are millions with misleading or downright erroneous informational content, so perhaps bad HTML markup is not that big a problem in the overall scheme of things.

and more optimized for a single delivery platform: whichever Web browser had the most market share on a particular day. Handhelds, braille printers and other alternative devices became marginalized.[8]

1.3.3 *The World Wide Web reacts*

As the interoperability and diversity of the Web became more and more endangered by proprietary formatting markup, the World Wide Web Consortium (headed by the same Tim Berners-Lee) decided to act. They attacked the problem in three ways. First, they decided to adopt the GML method for specifying the formatting of documents – the stylesheet.

They invented a simple HTML-oriented stylesheet language called *Cascading Style Sheets* (CSS) that allowed people to attach formatting to HTML documents without filling the HTML itself with proprietary, rendition-oriented markup.

Second, they invented a simple mechanism for adding abstractions to HTML. We will not look at that mechanism here, because XML makes it obsolete. It allowed new abstractions to be invented but provided no mechanism for constraining their occurrence. In other words it addressed two of GML's revelations: it brought HTML back to being a single standard, more or less equally supported by the major vendors, and it allowed people to define arbitrary extensions (with many limitations).

But they knew that their stool would not stand long on two of its three legs. The (weakly) extensible HTML and CSS are only stopgaps. For the Web to move to a new level, it had to incorporate the third of GML's important ideas, that document types should be formally defined so that documents can be checked for validity against them.

Therefore, the World Wide Web Consortium decided to develop a subset of SGML that would retain SGML's major virtues but also embrace the Web ethic of minimalist simplicity. They decided to give the new language the catchy name *Extensible Markup Language* (XML). They also decided to make related standards for advanced hyperlinking and stylesheets.

The first, called the *Extensible Linking Language* (XLink), is inspired by HyTime, the ISO standard for linking SGML documents, and by the Text Encoding Initiative, the academic community's guidelines for applying SGML to scholarly applications.

---

8. Although, thanks to XML, that is starting to change, as we shall see.

The second, called the *Extensible Style Language* is a combination of ideas from the Web's Cascading Style Sheets and ISO's DSSSL standard. There have been many new XML-related standards added to the World Wide Web Consortium scripture since XML was published. We will discuss these as we go along.[9]

Since then many other standards have been built on top of XML. Schema languages have been designed to augment the abilities of DTDs, query and addressing languages have been invented, and XML has become the foundation for Web services standards and even an ambitious effort to create a sort of hive mind called the *Semantic Web*.

XML was specifically designed to enhance reliable interchange on the Web. At about the same time, the Internet became popular as a place to do business: to buy and sell things. People saw that in the future, computers would do the buying and selling completely independently of human beings. They would also need a robust, sophisticated information interchange language. In other words, electronic business needed XML.

1.4 | EDI, EAI and other TLAs

By 1998, many understood that XML was not just a tool for Web servers sending information to Web browsers. Many people who had previously considered their problem domains to be separate came to see them as really variations on the same things.

Each of these domains is known by a *Three Letter Acronym (TLA)*. When you combine these with the various XML-world specs and standards the result is a terminological alphabet soup. Pick up your spoon, we'll help you through!

---

9. This description necessarily presented as linear, straightforward, and obvious a process that was actually messy and at times confusing. It is fair to say that there were many people outside the World Wide Web Consortium who had a better grasp on the need for XML than many within it, and that various member corporations "caught on" to the importance of XML at different rates.

1.4.1 *Electronic data interchange (EDI)*

One of the first groups to sense the coming convergence between documents and data was the electronic data interchange (EDI) community. EDI is the technology that large companies typically use to buy, sell and interchange information with each other.

Most people agree that XML is easier to work with and more extensible. Where EDI only scratched the surface of the business world, XML-based e-commerce should penetrate down even to small companies. The thing that differentiates this sort of e-commerce from the kind you can find on any old website is that it is *integrated*.

With *integrated e-commerce (IEC)*, your system is integrated directly or indirectly with your partner's system so that transactions can be verified and logged automatically in your internal systems. In contrast, buying a book (even this book!) from Amazon's website is not integrated e-commerce because there is no way that the purchase could be automatically entered into your local accounting system or sent to your boss for approval. Amazon, of course, uses a great deal of IEC when buying from *its* suppliers.

The venture capital world has chosen to embrace the somewhat confusing term "business to business e-commerce"(B2B) for this application. We consider the term confusing because one business could buy products from another business through a Web storefront and it would not typically be termed B2B, even though it was "business to business" and "e-commerce". What the pundits (fund-its?) really mean is *integrated* e-commerce.

So if buying from Amazon isn't IEC, what would be? Imagine if you bought a thousand widgets and your computer system automatically generated and delivered a purchase order and then updated your inventory while the receiving system automatically entered the order into its order system. Whew! That's a lot of automation! The opportunity to automate things is the fundamental strength of integrated e-commerce.

Integration wasn't invented with XML. Rather, XML allows corporations and consortia to rapidly negotiate standards that make it feasible to integrate disparate computer systems economically. Without standards, each business must negotiate with every other business individually and the costs quickly spiral out of control. A much more *scalable* solution is to negotiate a standard with all potential partners at once. XML provides the framework for this negotiation and thus for integrated e-commerce.[10]

The integrated solution allows a new class of *Business Process Automation (BPA)* software. BPA software allows businesses to describe their business process workflows in terms of the steps necessary to complete the process. Where human oversight is necessary, BPA software routes the information to the right person and solicits approval or input. BPA extends the concept of workflow by allowing processes to go beyond the boundaries of an organization. Of course this depends on standards – and most of these standards will be based upon XML.

There will also be a role for intermediaries that help businesses find each other and conduct transactions. Depending on their features, you can think of them as brokers or exchanges. Fortunes will be made and lost in this new application domain.

1.4.2 *Enterprise Application Integration (EAI)*

The next TLA that we will tackle is Enterprise Application Integration (EAI). We have described how XML helps businesses to communicate with each other. It is just as good at helping the parts of a business to communicate. This area of XML use is termed Enterprise Application Integration (or just Application Integration).

EAI is important because it is necessary before integrated e-commerce can really begin to save money. The accounting system must be integrated with inventory. Inventory must be integrated with delivery systems. Deliveries must be integrated with billing, which is a part of accounting and so forth. "The thigh bone's connected to the leg bone, the leg bone's connected to the ankle bone..." XML is today's choice for the cartilage between the bones in your organizational skeleton.

XML can be directly generated by many large-scale enterprise accounting, Enterprise Resource Planning (ERP), Customer Relationship Management (CRM), Supply Chain Management (SCM) and related packages. Even systems that do not natively "speak" XML can be made to do so through third-party or in-house extensions. When the vocabularies do not exactly match up (in other words, before there is a widely adopted standard vocabulary for a particular task) we can *transform* XML from one vocabulary into another.

---

10. Negotiation, however, is a slow process and frankly the B2B market has not taken off to the extent that many expected. Little by little the job is being done but not at the heady pace of the late nineties.

In a sense, EAI and integrated e-commerce are two sides of the same coin. EAI is a kind of integration within your corporate boundaries in order to present better information to employees and systems. Integrated e-commerce is a form of integration that spans corporate boundaries in order to improve the flow of information and products among partners. EAI is a much easier nut to crack because the level of agreement necessary to get something done is much lower. All IT professionals in a business report to a single CIO but there is no such role for a whole industry or for an entire economy. Within a business, security issues are fairly manageable. Across enterprise boundaries it is harder to establish the trust necessary for sharing vital information.

1.4.2.1   Acronym Hell!

BPA, EAI, EDI, B2B, IEC, ERP: XML touches every business acronym and has spawned scores of its own, like XSL, DOM, WebDAV, WSDL etc. In Chapter 67, "The XML Handbook Acronym Guide", on page 1120 we explain hundreds of acronyms that have appeared in editions of The XML Handbook.[11] And in Chapter 66, "Public XML vocabularies", on page 1094 we identify hundreds of XML vocabulary projects – almost all of which are guilty of spawning even more.

1.5 | Conclusion

XML is likely to be the basis for most information interchange in the future. If you buy a car on the Web, your browser will signal your decision with an XML document in one vocabulary. The auto dealer will replenish its stock of cars from the car company through another XML document using another vocabulary. The auto manufacturer will buy parts from its suppliers by sending out an automated request for quotes in XML in an e-business auction vocabulary and suppliers will respond in XML. In other words, whenever two computers need to communicate with each other, there is a role for XML.

---

11. Only four created by us, we hasten to add!

In many ways, none of this is new. Ancients used documents to communicate around their kingdoms and across centuries. Cavemen used documents (also known as wall paintings) to communicate their hopes and fears. XML allows computers to get into the conversation.

Analysis   Now we've seen the origins of XML, and some of its key ideas. Unlike lots of other "next great things" of the high-tech world, XML has solid roots and a proven track record. You can have confidence in XML because the particular subset of SGML that is XML has been in use for twenty years.

Just enough XML

- Elements
- Entities
- Markup
- Document types
- Stylesheets

I n this chapter we will explore the fundamental concepts of XML documents and XML systems. If XML were a great work of literature then this chapter would be the Cliff notes. The chapter will introduce the ideas that define the language but will avoid the nitty-gritty details of the *syntax* in which the constructs are expressed.

This early presentation of these ideas will allow you to see XML's "big picture". We will do this by walking through the design process for an XML-like language. Hopefully by the end of the process, you will understand each of the design decisions and XML's overall architecture.

Our objective is to equip you with "just enough" XML to appreciate the application and tool discussions in the following parts of the book, but being over-achievers we may go a little too far. Feel free to leave at any time to read about XML in the real world.

2.1 | The goal

First we should summarize what we are trying to achieve. In short, "What is XML used for?" XML is for the *digital representation* of documents. You probably have an intuitive feel for what a document is. We will work from your intuition.

Documents can be large and small. Both a multi-volume encyclopedia and an invoice can be thought of as documents. A particular volume of the encyclopedia can also be called a document. XML allows you to think of the encyclopedia whichever way will allow you to get your job done most efficiently. You'll notice that XML will give you these sorts of options in many places. XML can even represent the message from a police department's server to a police officer's handheld computer that reports that you have unpaid parking tickets.

When we say that we want to *digitally represent* documents we mean that we want to put them in some kind of computer-readable notation so that a computer can help us store, process, search, transmit, display and print them. In order for a computer to do useful things with a document, we are going to have to tell it about the structure of the document. This is our simple goal: to represent the documents in a way that the computer can "understand", insofar as computers can understand anything.

XML saves money by allowing programmers to reuse a piece of code called an XML *processor* or *parser*. The former term is used in the XML spec, but the latter is more often used in discussions. The processor parses (interprets) the markup and passes the data to whatever application the programmer is writing. It figures out which parts of the document are there just to get the document from point A to point B and which are the real information that the programmer needs to deal with. There are processors available for almost every programming language on every platform and most of them are available freely on the Web![1]

XML allows a standardized syntax to be used with many different vocabularies. Without it there would be a unique syntax for every type of data and programmers would need to create unique parsers for each one of them. Parser writing is difficult and extremely error prone. For most data, most of the time, it is somewhat of a waste of effort. XML allows programmers to skip that step and go directly to solving real problems. But more

---

1. You can find some on the CD-ROMs that accompany this book.

important, it takes the ability to create customized languages out of the hands of a small elite with a strong background in computer science and makes it available to the masses just trying to get their jobs done.[2]

XML documents can include pictures, movies and other multimedia, but we will not usually represent the multimedia components as XML. If you think of representation as a translation process, similar to language translation, then many multimedia components are the parts that we will leave in their "native language" because they have no simple translation into the "target language" (XML). We will just include them in their native formats as you might include a French or Latin phrase in an English text without explicit translation.

Most pictures on the Web are files in formats called GIF or JPEG and most movies are in a format called MPEG. However, if a graphic is made up mostly of lines, boxes, arcs, fades and other, similar geometric shapes, we call it a *vector graphic*.

In other words, vector graphics are graphics that are created in terms of structured components by a graphic artists. In contrast, many *bitmap graphics* are photographs of things in the real world. XML is often used to represent vector graphics but seldom used to represent bitmap graphics, recorded audio or movies. Nevertheless, XML can easily integrate those types of data by reference.

2.2 | Elements: The logical structure

Before we can describe exactly how we are going to represent documents, we must have a model in our heads of how a document is structured. Most documents (for example books and magazines) can be broken down into components (chapters and articles). These can also be broken down into components (titles, paragraphs, figures and so forth). And those components can be broken down into components until we get to the textual data itself – words and sentences. At this point we would typically stop breaking the document into components unless we were interested in linguistic research.

---

2. We did say that XML is revolutionary. Information workers of the world, unite!

It turns out that every document can be viewed this way, though some fit the model more naturally than others. In fact all information can be viewed this way...with the same caveat!

In XML, these components are called *elements*. Each element represents a logical component of a document. Elements can contain other elements and can also contain the words and sentences that you would usually think of as the text of the document. XML calls this text the document's *character data*. This hierarchical view of XML documents is shown in Figure 2-1.

Markup professionals call this the *tree structure* of the document. The element that contains all of the others (e.g. Book, Article or Memo) is known as the *root element*. This name captures the fact that it is the only element that does not "hang" off of some other element. The root element is also referred to as the *document element* because it holds the entire logical document within it. The terms *root element* and *document element* are interchangeable.

The elements that are contained in the root are called its *subelements*. They may contain subelements themselves. If they do, we will call them *branches*. If they do not, we will call them *leaves*.

Thus, the Chapter and Section elements are branches (because they have subelements), but the Paragraph and Title elements are leaves (because they only contain character data).[3]

Elements can also have extra information attached to them called *attributes*. Attributes describe properties of elements. For instance a CIA-record element might have a security attribute that gives the security rating for that element. A CIA database might only release certain records to certain people depending on their security rating. It is somewhat of a judgement call which aspects of a document should be represented with elements and which should be represented with attributes, but we will give some guidelines in Chapter 52, "Creating a document type definition", on page 792.

Real-world documents do not always fit this tree model perfectly. They often have non-hierarchical features such as cross-references or hypertext links from one section of the tree to another. XML can represent these structures too. In fact, XML goes beyond the powerful links provided by HTML. More on this in 2.9, "Hyperlinking", on page 50.

---

3. This arboreal metaphor is firmly rooted in computer science. However, markup experts have recently extended it with the term "grove". This term recognizes that a single document may best be viewed as multiple trees.

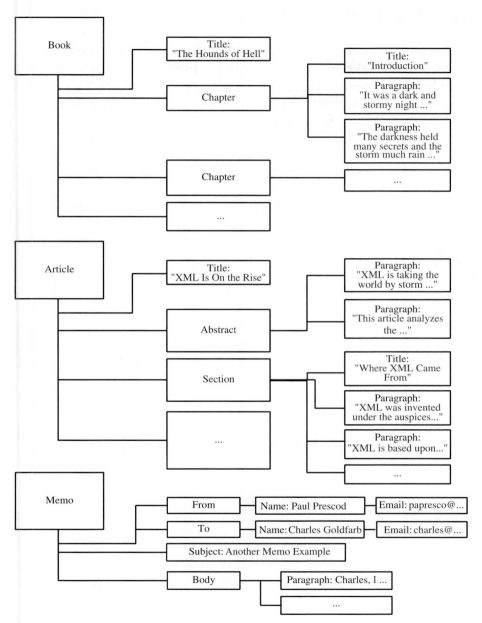

Figure 2-1 Hierarchical views of documents

2.3 | Unicode: The character set

Texts are made up of characters. If we are going to represent texts, then we must represent the characters that comprise them. So we must decide how we are going to represent characters at the bits and bytes level. This is called the *character encoding*. We must also decide what characters we are going to allow in our documents. This is the *character set*.

If you are a native English speaker you may only need the fifty-two upper- and lower-case characters, some punctuation and a few accented characters. The pervasive *7-bit ASCII character set* caters to this market. It has just enough characters (128) for all of the letters, symbols, some accented characters and some other oddments. ASCII is both a character set *and* a character encoding.

XML's character set is *Unicode*, a sort of ASCII on steroids. Unicode includes thousands of characters from languages around the world.[4] However the first 128 characters of Unicode are compatible with ASCII and there is a character encoding of Unicode, *UTF-8* that is compatible with 7-bit ASCII. This means that at the bits and bytes level, the first 128 characters of UTF-8 Unicode and 7-bit ASCII are the same. As if by magic, every ASCII document is automatically a Unicode document. This feature of Unicode allows authors to use standard plain-text editors to create XML immediately.

2.4 | Entities: The physical structure

An XML document is defined as a character string. An XML processor starts at the beginning and works to the end, parsing the text. XML provides a mechanism for allowing text to be organized non-linearly and potentially in multiple pieces. The processor reorganizes it into the linear structure.

The "piece-of-text" construct is called an *entity*. An entity could be as small as a single character or as large as all the characters of a book.

---

4. Some are quite esoteric. There are sections of Unicode dedicated to "Japanese dentistry symbols", "Dingbat ornamental brackets", "Recycling symbols" and "More recycling symbols". Even "Klingon" from *Star Trek*™ was considered, but eventually rejected.

Entities have *names*. Somewhere in your document, you insert an *entity reference* to make use of an entity. The processor replaces the entity reference with the entity itself, which is called the *replacement text*. It works somewhat like a word processor macro expansion (and for that reason is sometimes called *entity expansion*).

For instance you could define your product version number as an entity and, by changing the entity text when you produce the manual for a new version, you could update all occurrences of it automatically. An entity called "introduction-chapter" could be a chapter in a book. You would refer to the entity at the point where you wanted the chapter to appear.

The feature of XML that allows documents to be broken into many physical files is called the *external entity*.[5] An XML document can be broken up into many files on a hard disk or objects in a database; each would be an entity in XML terminology. Entities could even be spread across the Internet. Whereas XML elements describe the document's logical structure, entities keep track of the location of the chunks of bytes that make up an XML document. We call this the *physical structure* of the document.

The units of XML text that we will typically talk about are the entity and the document. Documents are composed of one or more entities. You may be accustomed to thinking about files, but entities do not have to be stored as files. For instance, entities could be stored in databases or generated on the fly by a computer program. Some file formats (e.g. a *zip* file) even allow multiple entities to reside in the same file at once. The term that covers all of these possibilities is entity, *not* file. Still, on most Web sites each entity will reside in a single file so in those cases external entities and files will functionally be the same. This setup is simple and efficient, but will not be sufficient for very large sites.

External entities help to break up large files to make them editable, searchable, downloadable and otherwise usable on the ordinary computer systems that real people use. Entities allow authors to break their documents into workable chunks that can fit into memory for editing, can be downloaded across a slow modem and so forth.

---

5. External entities are often referred to merely as entities, but the meaning is usually clear from context.

Without entities, authors would have to break their documents unnaturally into smaller documents with only weak links between them (as is commonly done with HTML). This complicates document management and maintenance. If you have ever tried to print out one of these HTML documents broken into a hundred HTML files then you know the problem. Entities allow documents to be broken up into chunks without forgetting that they actually represent a single coherent document that can be printed, edited and searched as a unit when that makes sense.[6]

Non-XML objects are called *unparsed entities*. We think of them as *data entities* because there is no XML markup in them that will be noticed by the XML processor. Data entities include graphics, movies, audio, raw text, PDF and anything else you can think of that is not XML (including HTML and other forms of SGML).[7] Each data entity has a *notation* that indicates whether the entity is a GIF, JPEG, MPEG, PDF, etc.

Because data entities aren't parsed as XML, they can only be referenced by means of attribute values. Users therefore often bypass the entity mechanism and simply use HTML-style `href` attributes to access non-XML objects.

Entities are described in all of their glorious (occasionally gory) detail in Chapter 54, "Entities: Breaking up is easy to do", on page 842.

2.5 | Markup

We have discussed XML's conceptual model (the tree of elements), its strategy for encoding characters (Unicode), and its mechanism for managing the size and complexity of documents (entities). We have not yet discussed how to represent the logical structure of the document and link together all of the physical entities.

---

6. That said, the HTML linking syntax is very familiar and popular. In the years since XML's standardization, entities have never caught on to the same extent. A specification in development called *XInclude* is attempting to take the best ideas from HTML's linking syntax and apply them to the problem of segmenting documents, albeit at the cost of intermixing a document's logical and physical structures. (See 54.10, "XML Inclusions (XInclude)", on page 865.)

7. Actually, a data entity could even contain XML, but it wouldn't be treated as part of the main XML document.

Although there are XML word processors and programmer's editors, one of the design goals of XML was that it should be possible to create XML documents in plain text editors, which are supplied with every operating system. Even users of XML-based word processors may depend on plain text editors to "debug" their documents if the word processor makes a mistake, or allows the user to make a mistake. The only way to allow authors and programmers convenient access to both the structure and data of the document in plain text editors is to put the two right beside each other, "cheek to cheek".

As we discussed in the introduction, the stuff that represents the logical structure and connects the entities is called markup. An XML document is made up exclusively of markup and character data. Both are in Unicode. Collectively they are termed *XML text*.

This last point is important! Unless the context unambiguously refers to data, as in "textual data", when we say "XML text", we mean the markup and the data.

Caution   The term XML text refers to the combination of character data and markup, not character data alone. Character data + markup = text.

Markup is differentiated from character data by special characters called *delimiters*. Informally, text between a less-than (<) and a greater-than (>) character or between an ampersand (&) and a semicolon (;) character is markup. Those four characters are the most common delimiters. This rule will become more concrete in later chapters. In the meantime, Example 2-1 shows a small document to give you a taste of XML markup.

The markup starting with the less-than and ending with the greater-than is called a *tag*. A processor looking at the document would recognize the characters <QUESTION> to be a start-tag, and would know that they signaled the start of a QUESTION element.[8]

---

8. You may be familiar with other languages that use similar syntax. These include HTML and other SGML-based languages.

Example 2-1. A small XML document

```
<Q-AND-A>
<QUESTION>I'm having trouble loading a WurdWriter 2.0 file into
WurdPurformertWriter 7.0. Any suggestions?</QUESTION>
<ANSWER>Why don't you use XML?</ANSWER>
<QUESTION>What's XML?</QUESTION>
<ANSWER>It's a long story, but there is a book I can
recommend...</ANSWER>
</Q-AND-A>
```

2.6 | Document types and schemas

The concept of a document type is fairly intuitive. You are well aware that novels, bills of lading and telephone books are quite different, and you are probably comfortable recognizing documents that conform to one of these categories. No matter what its title or binding, you would call a book that listed names and phone numbers a phone book. So, a document type is defined by its element types. If two documents have radically different element types or allow elements to be combined in very different ways then they probably do not conform to the same document type.

A set of element types is called a *vocabulary* and every document type, of course, has one. Or perhaps more than one. Just as in English, there are no hard and fast rules in XML about where one vocabulary ends and another begins.

2.6.1 *Defining document types*

This notion of a document type can be formalized in XML. A *document type definition* (*DTD*) or *schema definition* consists of a set of definitions for element types, attributes, entities and notations. XML has a built-in mechanism for expressing DTDs called *DTD declarations*.

Schemas are a newer, more sophisticated (and also more complicated) arrival to the party. Schemas and document types share concepts, so at a high level the terms can be used interchangeably. Of course when we get down to the details, schema definitions and DTDs look quite different, even though the underlying concepts are similar.

A DTD or schema definition declares which element types, etc., are legal within the document and in what places they are legal. A document can claim to conform to a particular DTD in its *document type declaration.*[9] It can be associated with a schema by means of specialized attributes.

DTDs and schemas are powerful tools for organizational standardization in much the same way that forms, templates and style-guides are. A very rigid design that only allows one element type in a particular place is like a form: "Just fill in the blanks!". A more flexible design is like a style-guide in that it can, for instance, require every list to have two or more items, every report to have an abstract and could restrict footnotes from appearing within footnotes.

DTDs and schemas are critical for organizational standardization, but they are just as important for allowing robust processing of documents by software. For example, a letter document with a chapter in the middle of it would be most unexpected and unlikely to be very useful. Letter printing software would not reliably be able to print such a document because it is not well defined what a chapter in a letter looks like.

Even worse is a situation where a document is missing an element expected by the software that processes it. If your mail program used XML as its storage format, you might expect it to be able to search all of the incoming email addresses for a particular person's address. Let us assume that each message stores this address in a from element. What do we do about letters without from elements when we are searching them? Programmers could write special code to "work around" the problem, but these kinds of workarounds make code difficult to write.

By taking on much of the responsibility for checking input validity, DTDs and schemas simplify the construction of software. This is analogous to the way that XML processors take over responsibility for parsing!

DTDs and schemas also serve as a sort of agreement or contract between information creators and consumers. You can hammer them out using any reasonable mechanism (a consortium, an ad hoc meeting or even through old-fashioned coercion). Once you have a schema or DTD, you can use it as a formal and objective definition of which documents are valid within the system and which are not.

The XML world has both DTD notation and schema languages because they were developed with different user requirements in mind. In fact, the

---

9. The document type declaration is usually abbreviated "DOCTYPE", because the obvious abbreviation would be the same as that for document type definition!

requirements are diverse enough that at least three different schema languages have achieved popularity, for a total of four languages:

DTD notation
The DTD language is part of the W3C XML Recommendation itself. It was designed to represent any kind of information, particularly long publications with complex structures.

XML Schema definition language (XSDL)
The "official" W3C schema language is powerful but verbose. Its design was driven by the need for XML to interwork with relational databases.

RELAX NG
This language is famous for achieving simplicity and elegance at the cost of omitting some features of XML that some users loathe (but others love).

Schematron
This language is quite different in philosophy and syntax from the other three. It is intended to complement them.

Recognizing the differing user requirements and the strengths and weaknesses of the different language designs, the International Organization for Standardization (ISO) is developing a "framework" standard called Document Schema Definition Languages (DSDL). It allows a single document to be validated against multiple DTDs and/or schemas in multiple languages. It also confers International Standard status on RELAX NG and Schematron.

2.6.2 *HTML: A cautionary tale*

HTML serves as a useful cautionary tale. It actually has a fairly rigorous structure, defined in SGML, and available from the World Wide Web Consortium. But everybody tends to treat the rules as if they actually came from the World Wrestling Federation – they ignore them.

The programmers that maintain HTML browsers spend a huge amount of time incorporating support for all of the incorrect ways people combine the HTML elements in their documents. Although HTML has an SGML DTD, very few people use it, and the browser vendors have unofficially sanctioned the practice of ignoring it. Workarounds are expensive, time consuming, boring and frustrating, but the worst problem is that there is no good definition of what these illegal constructs mean. Some incorrect constructs will actually make HTML browsers crash, but others will merely make them display confusing or random results.

In HTML, the `title` element is used to display the document's name at the top of the browser window (on the title bar). But what should a browser do if there are two titles? Use the first? Use the last? Use both? Pick one at random? The HTML standard does not allow this construct. It certainly does not specify a behavior! Believe it or not, an early version of Netscape's browser showed each title sequentially over time, creating a primitive sort of text animation. That behavior disappeared quickly when Netscape programmers realized that authors were actually creating invalid HTML specifically to get this effect! Since authors cannot depend on nonsensical documents to work across browsers, or even across browser versions, there must be a formal definition of a valid document of a particular type.

In XML, the DTD or schema provides a formal definition of the element types, attributes and entities allowed in a document of a specified type. If this seems important for documents intended for human reading, consider the absolute importance of clear standards and tight validation in computer-to-computer e-commerce applications!

There is also a more subtle, related issue. If you do not stop and think carefully about the structure of your documents, you may accidently slip back into specifying them in terms of their formatting rather than their abstract structure. We are accustomed to thinking of documents in terms of their rendition. That is because, prior to GML, there was no practical way to create a document without creating a rendition. The process of creating a DTD or schema definition gives us an opportunity to rethink our documents in terms of their structure, as abstractions.

2.6.3 *Declaring a DTD*

Example 2-2 shows examples of some declarations that are used to express a DTD. Example 2-3 shows the equivalent DTD as a schema definition.

Example 2-2. Markup declarations

```
<!ELEMENT Q-AND-A (QUESTION,ANSWER)+>
<!-- This allows: question, answer, question, answer ... -->
<!ELEMENT QUESTION (#PCDATA)>
<!-- Questions are just made up of textual data -->
<!ELEMENT ANSWER (#PCDATA)>
<!-- Answers are just made up of textual data -->
```

Example 2-3. Schema definition

```
<schema xmlns='http://www.w3.org/2001/XMLSchema'
        xmlns:qa='http://www.q.and.a.com/'
        targetNamespace='http://www.q.and.a.com/'>
 <element name="Q-AND-A">
 <complexType>
  <sequence minOccurs="1" maxOccurs="unbounded">
   <element ref="qa:QUESTION"/>
   <element ref="qa:ANSWER"/>
  </sequence>
 </complexType>
 </element>
<!-- This allows: question, answer, question, answer ... -->
 <element name="QUESTION" type="string"/>
<!-- Questions are just made up of textual data -->
 <element name="ANSWER" type="string"/>
<!-- Answers are just made up of textual data -->
</schema>
```

Caution   A document type or schema is a concept. A document type definition (DTD) or schema definition is the expression of that concept. The distinction is important because that expression can be created in several ways. You can use markup declarations (for DTDs), or any of several schema definition languages. However, the distinction is rarely made in normal parlance. In this book we make it only when needed for clarity.

Some XML documents do not have a schema definition or document type declaration. That does not mean that they do not conform to a document type. It merely means that they do not claim to conform to some formally expressed schema (or DTD).

If the document is to be useful as an XML document, it must still have some structure, expressed through elements, attributes and so forth. When you create a stylesheet for a document you will depend on it having certain elements, on the element-type names having certain meanings, and on the elements appearing in certain places. However it manifests itself, that set of things that you depend on is the document type.

You can formalize that structure in a DTD or schema. In addition to or instead of a formal computer-readable definition, you can also write out a prose description. You might consider the many HTML books in existence to be prose definitions of HTML.

Finally, you can just keep the document type in your head and maintain conformance through careful discipline. If you can achieve this for large, complex documents, your powers of concentration are astounding! Which is our way of saying: we do not advise it. We will discuss DTDs more in Chapter 52, "Creating a document type definition", on page 792 and schemas in Chapter 63, "XML Schema (XSDL)", on page 1030.

2.7 | Well-formedness and validity

Every language has rules about what is or is not correct in the language. In human languages that takes many forms: words have a particular correct pronunciation (or range of pronunciations) and they can be combined in certain ways to make valid sentences (grammar). Similarly XML has two different notions of "correct". The first is merely that the markup is intelligible: the XML equivalent of "getting the pronunciation right". A document with intelligible markup is called a *well-formed* document. One important goal of XML was that these basic rules should be simple so that they could be strictly adhered to.

The experience of the HTML market greatly informed the development of XML. Much of the HTML on the Web does *not* conform to even the simplest rules of an HTML specification. This makes automated processing of HTML quite difficult.

Because Web browsers will display ill-formed documents, authors continue to create them. In designing XML, we decided that XML processors should actually be prohibited from trying to recover from a *well-formedness* error in an XML document. This was a controversial decision because there were many who felt that it was inappropriate to restrict XML implementors from deciding the best error recovery policy for their applications.

The XML equivalent of "using the right words in the right place" is called *validity* and is related to the notion of document types. A document is *valid* if it declares conformance to a DTD in a document type declaration and actually conforms to that DTD.[10]

Documents that do not have a document type declaration are not really *invalid* as there is no known DTD for them to violate. But neither are they valid, because there is also no known DTD to which they conform.

If HTML documents with multiple titles were changed over to use XML syntax, they would be *well-formed* and yet *invalid* because they would not conform to the DTD (known as XHTML). If we remove the document type declaration, so that they no longer claim to conform to the XHTML DTD, then they would become merely well-formed but neither valid nor invalid.

Caution   For most of us, the word "invalid" means something that breaks the rules. It is an easy jump from there to concluding that an XML document that does not conform to a DTD is free to break any rules at all. This is not so. Well-formed documents are at least still XML even if they do not conform to the DTD.

You should think carefully before you decide to make a document that is well-formed but not valid. If the document is one-of-a-kind and is small, then making it well-formed is probably sufficient. But if it is to be part of any kind of information system (even a small one) or if it is a large document, then you should write a DTD or schema definition for it and validate whenever you revise it. When you decide to build or extend your information system, the fact that the document is guaranteed to be consistent will make your programming or stylesheet writing many times easier and your results much more reliable.

---

10. There is a similar concept for schemas.

2.8 | Namespaces

There is a problem that arises when you allow anybody to pick names as XML does. The problem is that different people in different places will invariably use the same names for different things. This makes it very difficult to build systems that work with documents from multiple independent sources because a publisher could use the element-type name PAR to mean paragraph while a military vocabulary could use an element type with the same name to mean paratrooper. A mathematician might use an element type with that name to label paradoxes!

2.8.1 *The homonym problem*

Recall that a vocabulary is just a set of element types. XML has no formal construct for "vocabulary" that would allow a computer to resolve this homonym problem. Indeed, it is inherent in our human languages. A "trunk" is one thing to a baggage handler and quite another to an elephant keeper.

So even using full names as element-type names would not help to avoid name clashes. Two different e-business frameworks might mean slightly different things by the term purchase_order. This slight misunderstanding is just as dangerous to a computer program as a more drastic mistake. If an XML system misinterprets an element type then it will launch the wrong processing, expect the wrong elements to be in particular places and otherwise just mess up.

Yet it is becoming more and more necessary to mix and match element types invented by different groups in different places. If you need to include math formulas in your technical reports, it makes no sense to reinvent element types for them when you can use the MathML vocabulary. The problem is, how can you tell which names in your document come from MathML?

2.8.2 *Prefixes*

There is a standard known as *Namespaces in XML* that addresses this problem. A *namespace* is a scope within which a name always has the same meaning wherever it is used. A vocabulary is a namespace and so is a document. The standard lets you mix vocabularies in a document by creating vocabulary nicknames that you can prefix to element-type names.

For example, you might choose to prefix names from a meteorological information vocabulary with `met:`. So a document might have elements such as `met:temperature`, `met:humidity` and so forth. It could also have `health:temperature`, from a different vocabulary. To the computer, `met:temperature` and `health:temperature` are clearly different names.

Of course, this solution appears to create its own problem: How can you be sure that different XML designers will use `met` to refer to the same vocabulary? The short and happy answer is: They don't have to!

That's because within your document `met` – which, remember, is just a nickname – is associated with an unambiguous identifier of the vocabulary. That identifier is based on a Web address and could look something like `http://www.weatherworld.com`. Other documents might use a different prefix for that vocabulary or use `met:` to prefix a different vocabulary. In practice, though, vocabulary developers recommend prefixes and people tend to use the recommended ones.

2.9 | Hyperlinking

You probably do not need to be convinced of the importance of hyperlinking. It is a cornerstone of the Web. One thing you might not know, however, is that the Web's notions of hyperlink are fairly tame compared to what is available in the best academic and commercial hypertext systems. XML alone does not correct this, but it has an associated standard called *XLink* that goes a long way towards making the Web a more advanced hypertext environment.

The first deficiency of today's Web links is that there are no standardized mechanisms for making links that are external to the documents that they are linking from. Let's imagine, for example that you stumble upon a Web page for your favorite music group. You read it, enjoy it and move on. Imagine next week you stumble upon a Web page with all of the lyrics for all of their songs (with appropriate copyrights, of course!). You think: there should be a link between these two pages. Someone visiting one might want to know about the other and vice versa.

What you want to do is make an *external link*. You want to make a link on your computer that appears on both of the other websites. But of course you do not have the ability to edit those two documents. XLink will allow this external linking. It provides a representation for external links, but it does not provide the technology to automatically publish those links to the world. That would take some kind of *link database* that would track all of the links from people around the world. Needless to say this is a big job and though there are prototypes, there is no standardized system yet.

You may wonder how all of these links will be displayed, how readers will select link sheets and annotations, how browsers will talk to databases and about other operational issues. The simple answer is: "nobody knows yet."[11]

Before the first Web browser was developed there was no way to know that we would develop a convention of using colored, underlined text to represent links (and even today some browsers use other conventions). There was also no way to know that browsers would typically have "back" buttons and "history lists". These are just conventions that arose and browser features that became popular. We expect that this same process will one day occur with external links.[12]

Another interesting feature of XML extended links is that they can point to more than one resource. For instance instead of making a link from a word to its definition, you might choose to link to definitions in several different dictionaries. The browser might represent this as a popup menu, a tiny window with the choices listed, or might even open one window for each. The same disclaimer applies: the XML Link specification does not tell browsers exactly what they must do. Each is free to try to make the most intuitive, powerful user interface for links. XML brings many interesting hypertext ideas from university research labs and high-tech companies "to the masses." We still have to work out exactly how that will look and who will use them for what. We live in interesting times!

---

11. But we've got some ideas. See Chapter 34, "Extended linking", on page 546.

12. It is taking longer than most of us expected. XLink was standardized in mid-2001 and implementations are still thin on the ground. But as they say, patience is a virtue. We still expect some day to have a standardized user interface to apply external link sheets and a mechanism to find link sheets related to a document on the Web. XLink moves us toward that goal by providing a notation for representing the links.

2.10 | Stylesheets

To a certain extent, the concerns described above are endemic to generalized markup. Because it describes structure, and not formatting, it allows variations in display and processing that can sometimes disturb people.

However, as the Web has evolved, Web developers have become less and less tolerant of having browser vendors control the "look and feel" of their documents. An important part of all communication, but especially modern business communication, is the idea of style. Stylesheets allow us to attach our own visual style to documents without destroying the virtue of generalized markup. Because the style is described in a separate entity, the stylesheet, software that is not interested in style can ignore it.

For instance most search engines would not care if your corporate color is blue or green, so they will just ignore those declarations in the stylesheet. Similarly, software that reads documents aloud to the sight-impaired would ignore font sizes and colors and concentrate on the abstractions – paragraphs, sections, titles and so forth.

The Web has a very simple stylesheet language called *Cascading Style Sheets* (CSS), which arose out of the early battles between formatting and generalized markup in HTML. Like any other specification, CSS is a product of its environment, and so is not powerful enough to describe the formatting of document types that are radically different in structure from HTML. It is, however, lightweight enough for on-the-fly formatting of Web pages.

More powerful formatting usually needs to be done statically, meaning that pre-formatted documents are stored on the server and downloaded on demand. The Adobe Acrobat *Portable Document Format* (PDF) is widely used for this purpose. Document developers can use a variety of publishing, graphics, and word processing products to create PDF documents.

There is even a W3C stylesheet language that can be used for that purpose, the *Extensible Stylesheet Language* (XSL). XSL takes many features from CSS, but also borrows major ideas from ISO's DSSSL stylesheet language. Its formatting model uses the page-oriented structure and sophisticated graphic arts techniques of high-quality printed materials.

There are two parts to XSL. *XSL Formatting Objects* (XSL-FO) does the actual formatting, while *XSL Transformations* (XSLT) can reorganize and manipulate the document before the formatting takes place.

In fact, XSLT can take any type of XML document and transform it into any other type. For formatting, the result type could be HTML or XHTML as well as XSL-FO. XSLT has proven to be so useful that it has taken on a life of its own, independent of XSL-FO and formatting, and is now pretty much essential to any XML installation.

2.11 | Conclusion

There are a lot of new ideas here to absorb, but we'll be repeating and re-emphasizing them as we move along. At this point, we're ready to look at the spectrum of XML usage in the real world.

The XML usage spectrum

- Real-world concepts
- Documents vs. data
- Machine-oriented messaging (MOM)
- People-oriented publishing (POP)

Chapter

3

L ike the Jets and the Sharks, the factions never mixed.[1]
On the one hand there were the document-heads armed with word processors and formatters. On the other, the data-heads from the relational database world. It's time for a truce – no, an alliance. XML finally makes clear an internal truth: documents and data are the same thing. To be precise, documents are the interchangeable form of data!

3.1 | Is XML for documents or for data?

What is a document?
The dictionary says:

> "Something written, inscribed, engraved, etc., which provides evidence or information or serves as a record".

---

1. Depending on your cultural proclivities, these are either athletic teams or the rival gangs in *West Side Story*.

Documents come in all shapes and sizes and media, as you can see in Figure 3-1. Here are some you may have encountered:

- Long documents: books, manuals, product specifications
- Broadsides: catalog sheets, posters, notices
- Forms: registration, application, etc.
- Letters: email, memos
- Records: "Acme Co., Part# 732, reverse widget, $32.50, 5323 in stock"
- Messages: "job complete", "update accepted"

An e-commerce transaction, such as a purchase, might involve several of these. A buyer could start by sending several documents to a vendor:

- Covering note: a letter
- Purchase order: a form
- Attached product specification: a long document

The vendor might respond with several more documents:

- Formal acknowledgment: a message
- Thank you note: a letter
- Invoice: a form

The beauty of XML is that the same software can process all of this diversity. Whatever you can do with one kind of document you can do with all the others. The only time you need additional tools is when you want to do different kinds of things – not when you want to work with different kinds of documents.

And there are lots of things that you can do.

3.2 | A wide spectrum of application opportunities

Sorry about that, we've been reading too many marketing brochures. But it's true, nevertheless.

Figure 3-1 Documents come in all shapes and sizes.

At one end of the spectrum we have the grand old man of generalized markup, *POP* – People-Oriented Publishing. You can see him in Figure 3-2.

At the other end of the spectrum is that darling of the data processors, *MOM* – Machine-Oriented Messaging. She smiles radiantly from Figure 3-3.

Let's take a closer look at both of them.

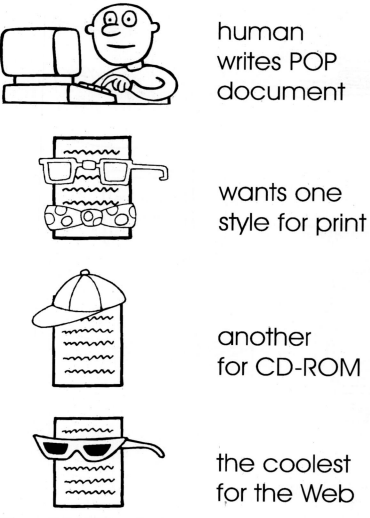

Figure 3-2   POP application.

3.2.1 *People-oriented publishing*

POP was the original killer app for SGML, XML's parent, because it saves so much money for enterprises with Web-sized document collections.

POP documents are chiefly written by humans for other humans to read.

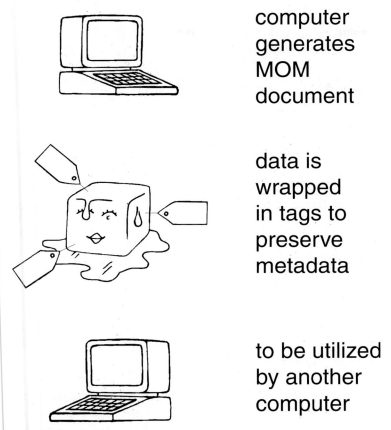

computer
generates
MOM
document

data is
wrapped
in tags to
preserve
metadata

to be utilized
by another
computer

Figure 3-3   MOM application.

Instead of creating formatted renditions, as in word processors or desktop publishing programs, XML POP users create unformatted abstractions. That means the document file captures what is *in* the document, but not how it is supposed to look.

To get the desired look, the POP user creates a stylesheet, a set of commands that tell a program how to format (and/or otherwise process) the document. The power of XML in this regard is that you don't need to choose just one look – you can have a separate stylesheet for every purpose.[2] At a minimum, you might want one for print, one for CD-ROM, and another for a website.

POP documents tend to be (but needn't be) long-lived, large, and with complex structures. When delivered in electronic media, they may be interactive. How they will be rendered is of great importance, but, because XML is used, the rendition information can be – and is – kept distinct from the abstract data.

3.2.2 *Machine-oriented messaging*

MOM is the killer app – actually, a technology that drives lots of killer apps – for XML on the Web.

The software that processes the messages is called *middleware*.[3] As you might suspect from the name, it is software that comes between two other programs. It acts like your interpreter/guide might if you were to visit someplace where you couldn't speak the language and had no idea of the local customs. It talks in the native tongue, using the native customs, and translates the native replies – the messages – into your language.

MOM documents are chiefly generated by programs for other programs to read.

Instead of writing specialized programs (clients) to access particular databases or other data sources (servers), XML MOM users break the old two-tier client/server model. They introduce a third tier, the "middle tier", that acts as a data integrator. The middle-tier server does all the talking to the data sources and sends their messages to the client as XML documents.

That means the client can read data from anywhere, but only has to understand data that is in XML documents. The XML markup provides the *metadata* – information about the data – that was in the original data source schema, like the database table name and field names (also called "cell" or "column" names).

The MOM user typically doesn't care much about rendition. He *does* care, though, about extracting the original data accurately and making

---

2. We know that all office suites offer some degree of stylesheet support today, but XML (well, GML) did it first, and still is the only way to do it cleanly.

3. In fact the MOM acronym has long been used in the industry – and in previous editions of this book – to mean *message-oriented middleware*. We prefer the new meaning because it puts the emphasis on the data, rather than the software, some of which still hasn't caught on to using XML.

some use of the metadata. His client software, instead of having a specialized module for each data source, has a single "XML parser" module. The parser is the program that separates the markup from the data, just as it does in POP applications.

And just like POP applications, there can be a stylesheet – a set of commands that tell a program how to process the document. It may not look much like a POP stylesheet – it might look more like a script or program – but it performs the same function. And, as with POP stylesheets, there can be different MOM stylesheets for different document types, or to do different things with message documents of a single document type.

There is an extra benefit to XML three-tier MOM applications in a networked environment. For many applications, the middle-tier server can collect all of the relevant data at once and send it in a single document to the client. Further querying, sorting, and other processing can then take place solely on the client system. That not only cuts down Web traffic and overhead, but it vastly improves the end-user's perceived performance and his satisfaction with the experience.

MOM documents tend to be (but needn't be) short-lived, non-interactive, small, and with simple structures.

3.3 | Opposites are attracted

To XML, that is!

How is it that XML can be optimal for two such apparently extreme opposites as MOM and POP? The answer is, the two are not really different where it counts.

In both cases, we start with abstract information. For POP, it comes from a human author's head. For MOM, it comes from a database. But either way, the abstract data is marked up with tags and becomes a document.

Here is a terminally cute mnemonic for this very important relationship:

Data + Markup = DocuMent

Aren't you sorry you read it? Now you'll never forget it.

But XML "DocuMents" are special. An application can use three different processing techniques with one:

- *Parse it*, in order to extract the original data. This can be done without information loss because XML represents both metadata and data, and it lets you keep the abstractions distinct from rendition information. Once extracted, the data can be manipulated as needed by the application.
- *Render it*, so it can be presented in a physical medium that a human can perceive. It can be rendered in many different ways, for delivery in multiple media such as screen displays, print, Braille, spoken word, and so on.
- *Hack it*, meaning "process it as plain text without parsing". Hacking might involve cutting and pasting into other XML documents, or scanning the text to get some information from it without doing a real parse.

The important revelation here is that data and documents aren't opposites. Far from it – they are actually two states of the same information. The real difference between the two is this:

- When data is in a database, the metadata about its structure and meaning (the schema) is stored according to the proprietary architecture of the database.
- When data is in a document, the metadata is stored as markup.

A mixture of markup and data must be governed by the rules of some *notation*. XML and SGML are notations, as are RTF and Word file format. The rules of the notation determine how a parser will interpret the document text to separate the data from the markup.

Notations are not just for complete documents. There are also *data object notations*, such as GIF, TIFF, and EPS, that are used to represent such things as graphics, video (e.g., MPEG), and audio (e.g., MP3). Document notations usually allow their documents to contain data objects, such as pictures, that are in the objects' own data object notations.

Data object notations are usually (not always) in *binary*; that is, they are built-up from low-level ones and zeros. Document notations, however, are frequently *character-based*. XML is character-based, which is why it can be hacked.[4]

Since databases and documents are really the same, and MOM and POP applications both use XML documents, there are lots of opportunities for synergy.

Figure 3-4   Dynamic servers: The MOM and POP store.

3.4 | MOM and POP – They're so great together!

Classically, MOM and POP were radically different kinds of applications, each doing things its own way with different technologies and mental models. But POP applications frequently need to include database data in their document content – think of an automotive maintenance manual that has to get the accurate part numbers from a database.

Similarly, MOM applications need to include human-written components. When the dealer asks for price and availability of the automotive parts you need, the display might include a description as well.

---

4. In fact, a design objective was to support the *desperate Perl hacker* – someone in a hurry who writes a script to scan XML without parsing it. Note that the term "hacker" had none of the "cracker" stigma implied by the popular press. The only security compromised by the desperate Perl hacker is his job security, for leaving things to the last minute!

With the advent of generalized markup, the barriers to doing MOM-like things in POP applications began to disappear. Some of the POP-like applications you'll read about later in the book appear to have invented the middle tier on their own. And now, with the advent of XML, MOM applications can easily incorporate POP functionality as well.

What is now emerging is a new generation of composite systems, dynamically serving both persistent POP information and dynamic MOM data. They use databases to store information components so they can be controlled, managed, and assembled into end-products in the same way as components of automobiles, aircraft, or other complex devices. Think of them as the MOM and POP store (Figure 3-4).[5]

In fact, we'd go so far as to say there is no longer a difference in kind between the two, only a difference in degree. There really is "an endless spectrum of application opportunities". It is a multi-dimensional spectrum where applications need not be implemented differently just because they process different document types. The real differentiators are other document characteristics, like persistence, size, interactivity, structural complexity, percentage of human-written content, and the importance of eventual presentation to humans.[6]

At the extremes, some applications may call for specialized (or optimized) techniques, but the broad central universe of applications can all be implemented similarly. Much of the knowledge that POP application developers have acquired over the years is now applicable to MOM applications, and vice versa. Keep that in mind as you read the application descriptions and case studies.

That cross-fertilization is true of products and their underlying technologies as well. All of the tool discussions in this book should be of interest, whether you think of your applications as chiefly being MOM or being POP. It is the differences in functionality and design that should cause you to choose one product over another, not their marketing thrust or apparent orientation. As you read the tool category discussions, you'll find remarkable similarities among tools that were developed for entirely different purposes.

---

5. Generations ago the Mom and Pop store (grocery, convenience, etc.) was the achievement of the entrepreneurial couple who'd lifted themselves out of the working class. Today they'd have an e-commerce website!

6. The relationship between documents and data is explored further in 7.11, "Documents and data", on page 152.

3.5 | Conclusion

We've covered the key concepts of XML itself in previous chapters and the spectrum of its uses in this one. Along the way we've discovered that:

- Documents are the interchangeable form of data
- MOM data is (usually!) made by machines
- POP data is (usually!) made by people
- MOM apps deliver MOM (and/or POP!) data to machines
- POP apps deliver POP (and/or MOM!) data to people

In the next two chapters, we'll look at the key application concepts at both ends of the spectrum.

XML for people

- Beyond HTML
- Metadata
- Personalized information delivery
- Alternative delivery platforms
- Office tools
- Drawing and diagramming

Chapter

4

I n this chapter we look at POP applications – those that prepare
information for delivery to people. The information itself, as
we saw in Chapter 3, could come from both people and machines.

The World Wide Web has become a major information delivery vehicle
for people. And despite the fact that HTML still governs the browser interface, XML has begun to affect the Web dramatically.

XML has also begun to impact desktop productivity applications, often
with many of the same technologies used on the Web. We'll look at those as
well.

4.1 | Beyond HTML

XML was originally conceived as a big brother to HTML. As its name
implies, XML can be used to extend HTML or even define whole new languages completely unlike HTML.

4.1.1 *Table fables*

For instance, a company might want to offer technical manuals on the Web. Many manuals have a formatting style for tables (e.g. a table listing a software product's supported languages) and repeat the formatting on several tables in the manual (perhaps once per program in a package). The formatting of these tables can be very intricate.

The rows, for example may be broken into categories with borders between them. The title of each column and row might be in a particular font and color. The width of the columns might be very precisely described. The final row ("the bottom line") might be colored. HTML could provide the formatting markup that the layout would require, but it would entail a lot of duplication. In fact, it would be such a hassle that most companies would choose to use a graphic or an *Adobe Portable Document Format* (PDF) file instead.

4.1.1.1   An HTML table

To demonstrate how XML can help, we will use a sample table (adapted from the specification for HTML tables), shown in Table 4-1. The XML solution will be shorter (in number of characters) and easier to read than the HTML source in Example 4-1.

If there are many of these tables the cumulative effort of doing this manual work can add up to a large burden, especially since it must be maintained as products change. Even with an HTML editing tool, you will probably have to do the layout manually, over and over again. As if this internal expense was not disturbing enough, every person who reads the annual report over the Web must download the same formatting information row after row, column after column, table after table, year after year. Right thinking Web page authors will understand that this situation is not good. The repetition leads to longer download times, congested servers, dissatisfied customers and perhaps irate managers.

Table 4-1   Rendered Table

Code Page ID	Name	Windows NT 3.1	Windows NT 3.51	Windows 95
1200	Unicode (BMP of ISO 10646)	X	X	
1250	Windows 3.1 Eastern European	X	X	X
1251	Windows 3.1 Cyrillic	X	X	X
1252	Windows 3.1 US (ANSI)	X	X	X
1253	Windows 3.1 Greek	X	X	X
1254	Windows 3.1 Turkish	X	X	X
1255	Hebrew			X
1256	Arabic			X
1257	Baltic			X
1361	Korean (Johab)			X

Example 4-1. HTML markup for Table 4-1

```
<TABLE>
<COLGROUP align="center">
<COLGROUP align="left">
<COLGROUP align="center" span="3">
<THEAD valign="top"><TR><TH>Code<br>Page<br>ID<TH>Name
<TH>Windows<br>NT 3.1<TH>Windows<br>NT 3.51<TH>Windows<br>95
<TBODY>
<TR><TD>1200<TD>Unicode (BMP of ISO/IEC-10646)<TD>X<TD>X<TD>
<TR><TD>1250<TD>Windows 3.1 Eastern European<TD>X<TD>X<TD>X
<TR><TD>1251<TD>Windows 3.1 Cyrillic<TD>X<TD>X<TD>X
<TR><TD>1252<TD>Windows 3.1 US (ANSI)<TD>X<TD>X<TD>X
<TR><TD>1253<TD>Windows 3.1 Greek<TD>X<TD>X<TD>X
<TR><TD>1254<TD>Windows 3.1 Turkish<TD>X<TD>X<TD>X
<TR><TD>1255<TD>Hebrew<TD><TD><TD>X
<TR><TD>1256<TD>Arabic<TD><TD><TD>X
<TR><TD>1257<TD>Baltic<TD><TD><TD>X
<TR><TD>1361<TD>Korean (Johab)<TD><TD><TD>X
</TABLE>
```

4.1.1.2   An XML table

The XML solution would be to invent a simple extension to HTML that is customized to the needs of the manual. It would have table elements that would only require data that varies from table to table. None of the redundant formatting information would be included. We would then use a stylesheet to add that information back in. The beauty of the stylesheet solution is that the formatting information is expressed only in one place. Surfers only have to download that once. Also, if your company decides to change the style of the tables, all of them can be changed at once merely by changing the stylesheet. Example 4-2 shows what that might look like.

Example 4-2. XML version of Table 4-1

```
<CODE-PAGE-TABLE>
<CP NUM="1200" NAME="Unicode (BMP of ISO/IEC-10646)"
   PLATFORMS="NT3.1 NT3.51"/>
<CP NUM="1250" NAME="Windows 3.1 Eastern European"
   PLATFORMS="NT3.1 NT3.51 WIN95"/>
<CP NUM="1251" NAME="Windows 3.1 Cyrillic"
   PLATFORMS="NT3.1 NT3.51 WIN95"/>
<CP NUM="1252" NAME="Windows 3.1 US (ANSI)"
   PLATFORMS="NT3.1 NT3.51 WIN95"/>
<CP NUM="1253" NAME="Windows 3.1 Greek"
   PLATFORMS="NT3.1 NT3.51 WIN95"/>
<CP NUM="1254" NAME="Windows 3.1 Turkish"
   PLATFORMS="NT3.1 NT3.51 WIN95"/>
<CP NUM="1255" NAME="Hebrew"
   PLATFORMS="WIN95"/>
<CP NUM="1256" NAME="Arabic"
   PLATFORMS="WIN95"/>
<CP NUM="1257" NAME="Baltic"
   PLATFORMS="WIN95"/>
<CP NUM="1261" NAME="Korean (Johab)"
   PLATFORMS="WIN95"/>
</CODE-PAGE-TABLE>
```

The difference between this XML version and the HTML version is not as dramatic as in some examples, but the XML version is clearer, has fewer lines and characters, and is easier to maintain. More importantly, the stylesheet can choose to format this in many different ways as time goes by and tastes change. All the XML version represents is the actual information about Windows code pages, not the tabular format of a particular presentation of it. The markup is also clearer (to someone interested in code pages!) because the element type names (CODE-PAGE-TABLE, CP) and attribute names (NAME, PLATFORMS, NUM) relate directly to the world of code pages and not to the world of HTML tables. A table is just one way to display this data today! We may choose another way tomorrow.

One thing to note is that the extra download of a stylesheet does take time. It makes the most sense to move formatting into a stylesheet when that formatting will be used on many pages or in many parts of the same page. The goal is to amortize the cost of the download over a body of text.

A similar caveat applies to the time it takes to make the stylesheet and design the table elements. Doing so for a single table would probably not be cost effective. Our example above basically shifts the complexity from the document to the stylesheet, on the presumption that there will probably be many documents (or at least many tables) for every stylesheet.

4.1.2 *Extensible HTML (XHTML)*

You can get some of XML's benefits "on the cheap" – without creating your own DTD or schema – with *XHTML*. XHTML is a version of HTML that uses XML syntax. The element types are all identical to those in ordinary HTML, so you do not have to learn new ones.

XHTML's major benefit is the availability of XML parsers. HTML's definition has always been very loose. Major browsers do not offer a way to validate documents. They often accept non-conforming HTML-like text as if it were really HTML. XHTML disallows this practice. XHTML documents must always be well-formed and valid.

Because of this "cleanliness", XHTML is much easier to work with than old-fashioned HTML. XHTML is also extensible so that you can add a few of your own element types to the standard XHTML mix.

4.1.3 *Specialized XML*

XHTML is fine as a generic Web display language but there are real benefits to being able to store and interchange information using XML markup that was designed for the purpose. We'll look first at some examples, and then discuss the benefits of using them.

4.1.3.1   Some examples

As the Web was originally invented in a physics laboratory for communication among physicists, we'll look at a few scientific vocabularies. Then we'll show you where to find hundreds of vocabularies and document types for all sorts of industries and applications.

4.1.3.1.1   MathML

Despite the Web's scientific origin, it never developed into a great system for communicating mathematical formulae. Markup for mathematics is more complex than it seems at first to non-mathematicians. Nevertheless, The World Wide Web Consortium has created an XML-based language called *MathML*.

A rendition of a mathematical formula is shown in Figure 4-1. Its MathML markup is illustrated in Example 4-3.

$$x^2 + 4x + 4 =$$

Figure 4-1   Rendition of a mathematical formula

4.1.3.1.2   Other sciences

The *Chemical Markup Language (CML)* is an XML-based language for describing the management of molecular information on computer networks. Using a Java viewer, users are able to view and manipulate molecules in two and three dimensions.

Bioinformatic Sequence Markup Language is a standard for representing DNA, RNA and protein sequence information. One day your doctor may download your DNA into XML and then upload it into a Petri dish to make a mini-you. We hope you'll be well-formed!

4.1.3.1.3   Other industries

There are literally hundreds of public initiatives that are developing specialized vocabularies of element types and attributes, and even full-blown

Example 4-3. MathML markup for the formula in Figure 4-1

```
<mrow>
  <mrow>
    <msup>
      <mi>x</mi>
      <mn>2</mn>
    </msup>
    <mo>+</mo>
    <mrow>
      <mn>4</mn>
      <mo>&invisibletimes;</mo>
      <mi>x</mi>
    </mrow>
    <mo>+</mo>
    <mn>4</mn>
  </mrow>
  <mo>=</mo>
  <mn>0</mn>
</mrow>
```

DTDs and schemas. We categorize and describe over 300 of them in Chapter 66, "Public XML vocabularies", on page 1094.

4.1.3.2   Productivity benefits

When you move from XHTML or HTML to a full-fledged industry- or company-specific XML document type, you can sometimes realize more radical productivity gains than you first intended. That's because your documents, like your database, now hold abstract data – not rendered.

Imagine that you use XML tables to publish the financial information in your company's annual report. Your accountants may be able to use their software's report writing feature to directly transfer accounting information into the XML table. This can eliminate one more opportunity for typos: between the accountants' printout and the Web author's keyboard.

There might also be opportunities for automation at the other end of the spectrum. Other software might transform the XML table directly into a format required for submission to some government agency.

Of course none of this automation comes for free. You still need to connect the XML-based systems so they can communicate (usually using Internet protocols).[1] You still need to design or obtain a DTD or schema. In order to render and visualize the data you will need a stylesheet.

All of this is an investment up-front but over the long term it is much cheaper than manual processes or ad hoc integration mechanisms. We will talk more about these sorts of machine-to-machine processes in Chapter 5, "XML for machines", on page 102.

4.2 | Database publishing

The last discussion suggests how XML can interact with systems that are not typically associated with documentation. As documents become abstractions, they can become integrated with the other abstract data in an organization. Some of the same techniques can be used to create them (such as report writing software or custom graphical user interfaces) and some of the same software is able to read them (such as spreadsheets and database software). One popular application of XML is the publishing of databases to the Web.

Consider for instance a product database, used by the internal ordering system of a toy manufacturer. The manufacturer wants the database to be available on the Web so that potential customers would know what was available and at what price. Rather than having someone in the Web design department mark up the data again, they build a connection between their Web server and their database using the data piping features typically built into Web servers.

The designers then beautify the product list using a stylesheet. Pictures of the toys are supplied by the database. In essence, the Web site is merely a view of the data in the database. As toys get added and removed from the database, they appear and disappear from the view on the website.

This mechanism gives the website maintainer the freedom to update the "look and feel" of the website without dealing with the database or the plumbing that connects it to the Web server! Publishing information from a database to the Web is pretty well understood these days, but XML allows standardization, rigor, and a separation of the tasks of programmers and Web designers.

XML is also an important tool for interchange of database information. Databases have typically interchanged information using simple data for-

---

1. In technology as in diplomacy, *protocols* are rules for communicating. We explain them in 6.4, "Protocols", on page 135.

mats like *comma-separated values (CSV)*: one record per line with commas between the fields.

CSV is not sufficient for the new object-oriented information being stored and generated by databases.[2] XML can represent objects by using elements and attributes to provide a common representation for transferring records between databases.

For example, one database might produce an XML document representing all of the toys the manufacturer produces. That document could be directly loaded into another database either within the company or at a customer's site. Unlike the beautified POP document intended for humans to read, this document is a MOM document, produced by and for computer software.

One is shown in Example 4-4. For the full details, you'll want to read Part 9, "Databases", on page 446.

Example 4-4. A products database in XML

```
<TOYS>
<ITEM>
<TITLE>GI John</TITLE>
<MANUFACTURER>War Toys Inc.</MANUFACTURER>
<PRICE>50.95</PRICE>
<IN-STOCK>3000</IN-STOCK>
</ITEM>
<ITEM>
<TITLE>Leggo!</TITLE>
<MANUFACTURER>Grips R US</MANUFACTURER>
<PRICE>64.95</PRICE>
<IN-STOCK>2000</IN-STOCK>
</ITEM>
<ITEM>
<TITLE>Hell On Wheels</TITLE>
<MANUFACTURER>Li'l Road Warriors</MANUFACTURER>
<PRICE>150.95</PRICE>
<IN-STOCK>3200</IN-STOCK>
</ITEM>
</TOYS>
```

---

2. Objects must have internal structure and links between them. We explain objects in 6.1, "Object-oriented", on page 127.

4.3 | Graphics and multimedia

XML is strongly associated with character data but it is increasingly being used to represent graphical images. After all, if a picture is worth a thousand words, it ought to be worth a few tags as well!

The W3C *Scalable Vector Graphics (SVG)* Recommendation allows vector graphics to be represented entirely in XML, as shown in Example 4-5.

Example 4-5. Diagram represented in SVG

```
<!DOCTYPE svg PUBLIC "-//W3C//DTD SVG August 1999//EN"
  "http://www.w3.org/Graphics/SVG/SVG-19990812.dtd">
<svg width="4in" height="3in">
<desc>Two groups, each of two rectangles</desc>
<g style="fillcolor:red">
  <rect x="100" y="100" width="100" height="100" />
  <rect x="300" y="100" width="100" height="100" />
</g>
<g style="fillcolor:blue">
  <rect x="100" y="300" width="100" height="100" />
  <rect x="300" y="300" width="100" height="100" />
</g>
</svg>
```

Vector graphics are described in terms of *vectors* (straight lines and curves), *shapes* (groups of vectors), and *formulas* (transformations of vectors). In contrast, most graphics on the Web are *bitmaps*. That is, they are lists of bits that correspond to individual *pixels* (picture elements) of different colors.[3]

For many types of graphics, bitmaps are inefficient. For example, a bitmap would individually describe the color of every pixel in a rectangle, whereas the vector graphic in Example 4-5 just says: "There is a 100x100 pixel rectangle and it is red".

Vector graphics are much more efficient for images that are fundamentally made up of lines and shapes, such as logos, diagrams, characters, maps, charts, icons and drawings. You could say that a single SVG element is worth a thousand pixels!

---

3. This distinction is explored at length, with illustrations, in 18.1, "Computer graphics notations", on page 313.

On the other hand, bitmaps are more efficient for photographic images. SVG will not replace the popular JPEG and TIFF file formats.

Vector graphics are said to be *scalable* because vectors can be zoomed in or out easily. If you zoom in on a logo represented as a JPEG or GIF bitmap, the curves get jagged or *pixelated*. If you zoom into a vector graphic, the computer redraws the lines according to their formulas. As a result, a single map could be useful at the neighborhood, city or national level. And the same image can look equally sharp on a PDA or a movie theater screen!

SVG can support animations of vectors. It accomplishes this by building on the *Synchronized Multimedia Integration Language (SMIL)*. SMIL is an XML document type for scripting multimedia presentations. When used within SVG, SMIL allows the animation of vectors and gradients. SMIL can also be used on its own for sequencing of audio, video, text and graphic components.

SVG and SMIL could be used for animating charts and graphs. Think of the possibilities: pie charts that rotate and bar charts that stretch. SVG and SMIL are also a perfect fit for those ubiquitous animated banner advertisements. They would not be any less annoying but they would download more quickly!

SVG also has support for interactivity. For example, an SVG graphic can allow end-users to customize the view. A map might allow viewers to turn layers on and off to include or exclude roads, railway tracks, cities, etc. A bar graph might allow a user to choose the scale units. These business applications are interesting, but over time SVG's animation and interactivity will probably be used for more important tasks, such as video games on cell phones!

SVG has other important applications. For instance, it is increasingly easy to move graphics between software products like *Adobe Illustrator*™ and *CorelDraw*™ using SVG. It is also possible on some operating systems to use SVG to create desktop icons that look correct on any size screen.

4.4 | XML-based forms

The Web is not a read-only medium. It is quite common for Web users to submit information ranging from their credit card numbers to *weblogs* (*blogs*) full of their thoughts and feelings. This information is duly processed by a server and is either saved in a database for later retrieval or served up as more Web content to be delivered to other surfers. The Web collects this information through HTML forms. Even discussion groups are populated by information entered into forms.

4.4.1 *Problems with HTML forms*

Despite the incredible success of HTML's forms mechanism, it leaves a great deal of room for improvement.

4.4.1.1   Hierarchical structure

HTML forms do not deal well with hierarchically structured data. HTML forms display a single level of named fields and therefore they only collect simple lists of named values. They cannot support lists of lists, let alone lists of lists of lists, etc.

4.4.1.2   Abstraction vs. rendition

HTML forms also intermingle the purpose of a form with the form's display characteristics. Therefore, if the display must change for an alternative device (such as a voice recognition system), the entire form must be redesigned from scratch.

4.4.2 *XML to the rescue!*

The W3C has developed the XForms specification to solve these problems. An XForms form design includes a schema (and other constraints) for the form and a set of initial data values for the form fields.

4.4.2.1   Hierarchical structure

When a user completes a form, an XML document instance conforming to the form schema is submitted to the host (as opposed to HTML's list of field names and values). The XML instance can be as deeply structured as the schema calls for. Form fields can be represented as either elements or attributes.

4.4.2.2   Abstraction vs. rendition

The rendition of a form is like the user interface to an application, as it is used for data collection as well as display. When rendered by a browser, the XForms user interface objects are roughly the same as those provided by standard HTML: check boxes, radio buttons, text fields. But there are two major differences in the XForms interface design:

- It is completely separate from the form design.
- Its elements, called *form controls*, are abstractions, not renditions. The form control `select1`, for example, could be rendered either as two radio buttons by a Web browser, or as a voice prompt with two choices by a telephony application.

4.5 | Semantic Web

The W3C vision of the *Semantic Web* is one where the data and the relationships among the data are well understood by the machines that process it. That will allow the machines to do more than simply display requested Web pages to humans. In what may be the ultimate MOM/POP application merger, software will be able to analyze and process *metadata* – data about the data – to find the best pages to display to a particular user, or deliver to another machine.

4.5.1 *Platform for Internet Content Selection (PICS)*

The first standardized metadata specification for the Web was developed before XML and is called the *Platform for Internet Content Selection (PICS)*. PICS allows the filtering of inappropriate material from computer screens based on external descriptions of content.

The "violent content" label on a video tape is a perfect example of metadata. The data provided, "violent content" describes the contents of the tape – it is data about data. PICS is an electronic version of that label.

Parts of the PICS family of standards are based upon XML. It took almost two years to get PICS into the XML world. This is because on the way to developing PICS the W3C created an intermediate layer called *Resource Description Framework (RDF)*.

4.5.2 *Resource Description Framework (RDF)*

RDF is not a document type: it is a convention for designing XML documents so that they can more easily be interpreted as metadata.[4]

RDF's central concept is the "property". An RDF document can associate many properties with documents on the Web. Some of those properties can be from the PICS vocabulary. However, there are other vocabularies used with RDF that are unrelated to content filtering, as illustrated by the (imaginary) "bibliography" vocabulary used in Example 4-6.

Example 4-6. Describing the author of a document in RDF

```
<rdf:RDF xmlns:bib="http://bibliography.dummy.org">
  xmlns:rdf="http://www.w3.org/1999/02/22-rdf-syntax-ns#">
  <rdf:Description about="http://www.bar.com/some.doc">
    <bib:author rdf:resource="http://bibliography.dummy.org/author">
      <bib:name>John Smith</bib:name>
  <bib:email>john@smith.com</bib:email>
  <bib:phone>+1 (555) 123-4567</bib:phone>
    </bib:author>
  </rdf:Description>
</rdf:RDF>
```

In one sense, this sounds very complicated: PICS is based on RDF which is based on XML. But on the other hand, it is not so complicated in prac-

---

4. At least that is what it looks like from an XML user's point of view. A metadata user would say that RDF is a model for metadata and XML is a particular way of representing that model. We discuss RDF from that viewpoint in Chapter 36, "RDF: Metadata description for Web resources", on page 582.

tice. PICS has a set of element types that are applied according to the XML syntax described in this book. RDF, the middle layer, is only visible to the wizards who invent new ways of cataloging, describing and organizing information – the librarians of the future.[5]

RDF is discussed in Chapter 36, "RDF: Metadata description for Web resources", on page 582.

4.5.3 *Topic maps*

A related development comes from the *International Organization for Standardization (ISO)*. *Topic maps* are a specific type of metadata designed to allow the construction of logical "maps" of information. Topic maps are designed to help us navigate through the massive amounts of information on the Web. You can think of topic maps as a very sophisticated indexing mechanism for online information. We think of them as the Global Positioning System (GPS) for the Web![6]

One aspect of topic maps' sophistication is the idea of *scoping*. With scoping, you can label a particular characteristic (roughly, an index entry) as only being applicable within a certain context.

For example, if you label characteristics as being applicable only in a particular language, a query for information on a topic would only return occurrences in your native tongue. If you labeled characteristics as being either "biological" or "psychological", then a search for the word "evolution" would return only biological topics or only psychological ones, depending on your query.

Tip   There is a friendly tutorial on topic maps in Chapter 35, "Topic maps: Knowledge navigation aids", on page 562 and you can see how they are used in Chapter 35, "Topic maps: Knowledge navigation aids", on page 562.

---

5. Luckily, the librarians of the present are very much involved in these standardization efforts.
6. The exact relationship between RDF and topic maps is somewhat unclear to everybody concerned. Formally, they are unrelated but it seems like there is some opportunity for cooperation in the future. The experts are looking into this even as you read!

4.5.4 *Web Ontology Language (OWL)*

The *Web Ontology Language* (OWL) is a companion specification to RDF. Whereas RDF describes individual Web resources and other objects, OWL describes classes of objects and the characteristics ("properties") of all members of ("instances of") a class.

You may recall from Philosophy 101:

1. All men are mortal;
2. Socrates is a man;
3. Therefore Socrates is a mortal.

In that famous syllogism, "men" is a class and "Socrates" is an instance of the class (a man). "Mortality" is a property which, as a member of the class, Socrates exhibits.

There are also subclasses. Greek men are a subclass of men (every Greek man is a man). A collection of these statements about classes, subclasses and properties is termed an *ontology*.

A syllogism allows one to leap from two or more facts (one about men being mortal, and one about Socrates being a man) to a third (Socrates being mortal). The relationship is called *entailment*. The first two statements *entail* the third.

With entailment, a set of facts can be more than the sum of its parts. A "mere" database can become a knowledge base.

With the connectivity provided by the Web, knowledge bases from around the world can, in theory, be merged into one – a true *Semantic Web*.

On the other hand, entailment could be considered just a weak form of artificial intelligence. You can build up pretty impressive towers of entailment, with one thing entailing another entailing another. But as powerful as the prospect appears, it is quite fragile, so do not worry about the computers becoming our overlords very soon. As any Star Trek fan knows, the computer can be thrown off by the simplest metaphor, inaccuracy, or disagreement.

Socrates lives on in our hearts and minds so perhaps he is not mortal. Or perhaps he lives on in some Greek afterlife. How do we know Socrates was a man and not a visiting alien. (He certainly seemed smarter than most men you'll meet!)

The human mind weighs all of these possibilities and chooses an interpretation that seems most reasonable. But, as the Star Trek fan will tell you, the computer will start to overheat and eventually explode – or at least report a logic error.

4.5.5 *Whither the Semantic Web?*

The sum of the Semantic Web will not be accurate and consistent, no more than the whole Web is completely accurate and consistent. The hope is that we will be able to write programs (*agents*) that gather information from trustworthy sources (where trustworthiness is determined by human beings) and ignore untrustworthy ones.[7]

The Semantic Web project is incredibly ambitious and we would be tempted to write it off entirely if it were not for previous experience with markup-related grand visions. After all, neither the World Wide Web, Web services, nor markup languages themselves have yet achieved – and likely never shall achieve – the goals originally set by their designers.

Nevertheless, all of them are based on a solid core of technologies that have returned substantial benefits to their users.[8]

4.6 | Personalized information delivery

At the beginning of the Internet revolution, knowledge workers were like kids in a candy store. The information they needed became easily available. Now the stomach-ache is setting in. The information that they need is buried in gigabytes of information they do not need.

4.6.1 *Portals*

Enter the *portal*: a website designed to help users find their way through information.

---

7. For some, this is nothing more than a rehashing of the artificial intelligence dreams of the 1980s (which in turn were a rehashing of the artificial intelligence dreams of the 1960s).
8. In the case of the Semantic Web, we discuss that solid core in Part 11, "Semantic Web", on page 546 and Part 12, "Topic Map Applications", on page 592.

The first portals only helped people to find other websites. Then public portals started to add interactive features such as stock quotes and weather reports. Later, they started to allow users to build customized "home pages" including their favorite stock quotes, local weather reports and other information specific to them. This trend is termed *personalization*.

In addition to public portals like Yahoo™, there are also many portals used within large companies. These are termed *Enterprise Information Portals* (EIPs) or *digital dashboards*. We discuss EIPs in detail in Part 6, "Portals", on page 326.

XML serves as a fundamental building block for personalized portals. XML can be used to bring various information resources into one common structure. From there, XML tools such as parsers, search engines and transformation engines can slice and dice the information into bite-sized pieces applicable to the user. The vocabulary details of the information returned by various enterprise systems may vary, but they can be transformed into a common vocabulary using any programming language or the XSLT transformation language.

In a sense, an Enterprise Information Portal serves as a friendly user interface to the unified system that results from Enterprise Application Integration (EAI).[9] EAI systems use XML because it is good for integrating various data sources. An EIP adds another feature of XML: XML documents can easily be formatted for presentation to a human being using stylesheets.

We'll say it again: XML brings the worlds of document and data processing together.

4.6.2 *Content packaging and syndication*

As portals evolved to become personalized information consoles, it became necessary to find efficient ways to acquire a user's requested information content, and to keep that content up-to-date. Content syndication has emerged as the solution.

Content syndication is about using metadata to move information, such as news articles, from place to place. It is a problem domain that is tailor-made for XML because when you put XML and the Internet together you have a powerful information distribution infrastructure.

---

9. See 1.4, "EDI, EAI and other TLAs", on page 26.

4.6.2.1　News aggregation with RSS

Various news and discussion sites syndicate themselves using the lightweight, popular RSS XML vocabulary.[10] Example 4-7 shows a single news item from an RSS feed.

Example 4-7. News item from an RSS feed

```
<item>
<title>Man bites dog</title>
<link>http://...com/dogstory.html</link>
<description>Once the very definition of a newsworthy event, now
(possibly because of a depressed economy or increased cultural
diversity) it has become increasingly common ... </description>
<category>Enterprise</category>
<guid isPermaLink="true">http://rss.com.com/2110-1012896.html</guid>
<pubDate>Tue, 03 Jan 2006 16:43:00 PDT</pubDate>
</item>
```

Like HTML before it, RSS is a markup language that has spawned a new category of software. An RSS *news aggregator* can collect everything from the latest articles in your favorite national newspaper to the ramblings of your second cousin in his weblog.

According to Dave Winer, CEO of the weblog site *Radio Userland*, a news aggregator is "software that periodically reads a set of news sources, in one of several XML-based formats, finds the new bits, and displays them in reverse-chronological order on a single page."

In other words, it's kind of a cross between a portal and a news reader. There are even implementations that handle email as well.

You can often find out if a publication supports RSS by looking for an orange button labeled "XML" on the Web page.

---

10. The RSS world is very political: so much so that there is no consensus on what RSS stands for, nor on the precise details of the vocabulary itself. Nevertheless, the idea is so useful that the language thrives even amidst the bickering.

4.6.2.2   Other syndication standards

The alphabet soup of competing and cooperating standards is too long to cover in depth, but we can name a few of the key ones:

- *ICE* is the *Information Content and Exchange* specification from the vendor and user consortium of the same name. It is described in detail in Chapter 31, "Syndicating content with Web services", on page 504.
- *PRISM (Publishing Requirements for Industry Standard Metadata)* is an extensible XML metadata standard for syndicating, aggregating, post-processing and re-purposing content from publications, news feeds, and similar sources. It also provides a set of controlled vocabularies with which to describe the content being interchanged. PRISM is illustrated in 16.3.1, "Associating metadata", on page 285.
- *NewsML* is a packaging and metadata format for news content, similar to PRISM and RSS. NewsML is developed by the International Press Telecommunications Council (IPTC), a consortium of news providers, mostly in the print and wire-service industries. As NewsML deals only with packaging and metadata, it is complementary to syndication protocols like ICE.

4.6.3   *Instant messaging*

Many people these days find their inboxes so cluttered with spam, junk and (worst of all!) work that they are afraid to look at it. Auxiliary communications mechanisms are starting to catch on. These mechanisms use XML pervasively.

For instance, there is an emerging standard for instant messaging called Jabber. All Jabber data is sent as XML. In fact a Jabber session consists of one long XML document that starts when you open the Jabber client application in the morning and ends when you close the application at night.

4.7 | Alternative delivery platforms

One of the original benefits of generalized markup was its ability to make information available to new delivery devices. When the Web was young, some of the first serious content providers were established SGML users. Information that predated the Web by years could easily be served as HTML through an automated conversion. Now the Web-as-we-know-it is the legacy platform (not paper) and new devices such as electronic books and hand-held computers are the up and coming, new, new thing.

4.7.1 *XML goes wireless*

As you may have heard, desktop Web browsers are already passé. The next wave is wireless. And your new surfboard is the *Wireless Application Protocol (WAP)*. WAP is the term for the collection of standards that is driving the move to Internet access over handheld computers, mobile telephones, wrist watches and other go-anywhere technologies. Not all of the WAP standards are based on XML. The main XML specifications are *WBXML* and *WML*.

4.7.1.1 WBXML

WBXML, is, as you might have guessed, a schema for television shows on the Warner Brothers Network. Okay, not really. WBXML is *WAP Binary XML*. The philosophy behind WBXML is that small machines typically have very slow connectivity to the Internet. WBXML documents are compressed XML files that can be more efficiently sent back and forth over tiny little Internet pipelines.

4.7.1.2 WML

Wireless Markup Language (WML) is a markup language for small devices.

The central concept of WML is the *card*. Cards are to WML what pages are to the Web's HTML. One big difference is that many cards may reside in the same XML document. This means that the WML browser in the cell-phone or handheld computer does not have to constantly download new documents across the network.

Example 4-8 is an example of a document made up of two cards. The example is not very interesting: it just allows the user to bounce back and forth between the two cards.

Example 4-8. Two-card WML example

```xml
<?xml version="1.0"?>
<!DOCTYPE wml PUBLIC "-//WAPFORUM//DTD WML 1.1//EN"
   "http://www.wapforum.org/DTD/wml_1.1.xml">
<wml>

   <card id="card1" title="My Wap Page">
     <p>
      Hello world - welcome to my first wap card!
     </p>
     <p>
      <a href="#card2">Go to the second card</a>
     </p>
   </card>

   <card id="card2" title="Second Card">
     <p>
      Welcome to my second wap card!
     </p>
     <p>
      <a href="#card1">Go back to the first card</a>
     </p>
   </card>

</wml>
```

OpenWave™ has an application that allows testing of WAP applications on ordinary desktop computers. It actually emulates various kinds of cellular telephones. Figure 4-2 shows the rendered version of Example 4-8.

WML also supports forms to send information back to the server, client-side scripts to add interactivity, hyperlinks to jump from card to card and document to document and so forth. Form fields are entered one at a time rather than in a screenful as in HTML. Example 4-9 is a single card with a form for subscribing to a service. It causes separate screens to be rendered for each field, as shown in Figure 4-3 and Figure 4-4.

Figure 4-2   Two-card WML example rendered

Example 4-9. WML subscription card

```
<?xml version="1.0"?>
<!DOCTYPE wml PUBLIC "-//WAPFORUM//DTD WML 1.1//EN"
    "http://www.wapforum.org/DTD/wml_1.1.xml">
<wml>
  <card id="card1" title="Subscribe">
    <p>E-mail login:<br/>
      <input name="login" title="E-mail login"/>
    </p>
    <p>Password:<br/>
      <input name="pwd" type="password" title="Password"/>
    </p>
  </card>
</wml>
```

4.7.1.3   Concerns with WAP

Not everyone believes that WAP is destined for great success. The first complaint about WAP was that it is designed to present the so-called "wireless Web" on cell phones. But many people claim that cell phone users do not want the Web as much as they want instant messaging. In other words, they are much more interested in using cell phones to communicate with each other than to browse Web sites. WAP supports this form of communication but not to the same extent as it does browser-style applications.

Figure 4-3   Rendered login screen

Figure 4-4   Rendered password screen

The other major issue with WAP is that it does not build strongly enough on Web standards. For instance WBXML is very much like XML, but it is not pure XML – it uses a WAP-specific compression mechanism.

The WAP specifications are controversial to some technologists but what concerns some business analysts are the business issues. Many WAP implementations are closed systems with no connectivity to other WAP systems. Many WAP implementations are very expensive and inefficient in terms of connection times.

It is possible that these issues will be worked out over time. As phones become more powerful and Internet-connected, they become increasingly able to directly support Web standards like XHTML and SVG.

4.7.2 *Device-specific content*

Earlier we described how PICS builds on RDF to ensure that Web surfers download age-appropriate data. Similarly, a specification called *Composite Capabilities/Preferences Profile (CC/PP)* uses RDF to ensure that users get device-appropriate data.

In some cases it makes perfect sense to send exactly the same Web pages to handheld devices as to desktop computers. In others, it makes more sense to send device-specialized representations of the pages. For instance a city map being sent to a PDA might have greatly reduced detail to improve bandwidth usage and readability. A Web page about the city might remove vertical frames that would not fit on the screen properly.

CC/PP allows devices to communicate with servers to tell them what capabilities they have. For instance a cellular phone might declare "I am a cellular phone and my screen is 400 pixels high and 200 pixels wide. I can deal with Unicode data. I can display 4 colors. I know how to deal with JPG but not MPEG." Using this description, an information provider can deliver the most appropriate representation of the content to the device.

4.7.3 *Beyond voice mail*

It is all very well and good to surf the Web on a cell phone but that does not change the fact that there are some serious limitations to the reach of WAP technology. Not everyone has a cell phone. Not all cell phones are WAP enabled. Many people do not consider number keys and small LCD screens a good user interface.

There is another technology that is well-established without any of these limitations. Press 1 if you know what technology we are speaking of. Press 2 if you do not. Then say your name after the tone.

The computers that answer telephones are known to most people as "answering machines" But they do not have much in common with the old tape-based devices. As you have probably noticed, the most interesting change is that it is now possible to navigate many of these services using your voice rather than the keypad. This is due to advances in a technology known as *speech recognition*. Speech recognition is maturing at exactly the same time that XML is gaining popularity and the Web is expanding to other devices.

The merger of these technologies permits the development of XML-based *Interactive Voice Response (IVR)* applications. The W3C is developing the *VoiceXML* specification for this purpose. What HTML is to Web pages and WML to the wireless Web, VoiceXML is to voice-based applications. Example 4-10 has an example.

Example 4-10. VoiceXML example

```
<menu>
  <prompt>Welcome home. Say one of: <enumerate/></prompt>
  <choice next="http://www.sports.example/vxml/start.vxml">
     Sports
  </choice>
  <choice next="http://www.weather.example/intro.vxml">
     Weather
  </choice>
  <choice next="http://www.stargazer.example/voice/astronews.vxml">
     Stargazer astrophysics news
  </choice>
  <noinput>Please say one of <enumerate/></noinput>
</menu>
```

Unfortunately we cannot show you the output of this example as easily as we could with WML but you can imagine one of those robotic generated computer voices. It would ask you to say one of the phrases "Sports", "Weather" or "Stargazer astrophysics news". Once you selected one, it would launch a new VoiceXML document and either ask you some more questions or read you some information. Note that the tinny robotic voice is not a requirement. You can use VoiceXML with pre-recorded voices. VoiceXML creates a whole new market for voice actors!

We let VoiceXML speak for itself in Part 16, "Voice", on page 706.

4.7.4 *Downloading the library*

It is great to be able to surf your stock quotes while you are on the run, but what about when you want to curl up by the fire with a novella? Futurists have promised us electronic books for almost as long as they have promised us flying cars. Business interests are starting to believe that electronic books are now feasible and worth research and investment. We should all have one any day now. No word yet on the flying cars.

The Open eBook Forum creates and maintains standards relating to electronic books. The forum is made up of hardware and software companies, electronic book publishers and related organizations. Common standards for electronic books allows those books to work on systems as diverse as laptop computers, text-to-speech readers and PDAs.

The Forum's principal specification is called the *Open eBook Publication Structure (OEBPS)*. It is not so much an invention as a standardized combination of specifications defined elsewhere: XHTML, the Web's Cascading Style Sheet (CSS) language, and a metadata vocabulary known as Dublin Core.

4.8 | Office suites

Someday our non-technical relatives and co-workers will email us XML documents without thinking they are doing anything special. When that day arrives, it will likely be the result of XML being supported in popular productivity suites.

A giant step in that direction was taken by the 2003 edition of the 800-pound gorilla of office suites, *Microsoft Office®*. That product made a major commitment to XML that we cover at length in Part 8, "Desktop XML", on page 414. In this section, we consider MS Office XML features briefly, along with the XML features of the competition.

4.8.1 *In the beginning was the word processor*

XML was designed to be used with textual documents and that is still a core domain. We foresee a future in which every magazine article, business report, obituary, and high school essay is stored in XML. In this future world it will be much easier for programmers to extract information from XML documents, transform documents into a variety of forms, and move them between competing and cooperating software applications.

4.8.1.1   Microsoft Word

The dominant application in the word processing market is, of course, *Microsoft Word®*. Its native file format is DOC, which contains a binary representation of a rendered document.

Microsoft has never encouraged developers to work directly with DOC files. Instead, it offers a plain text notation, called *Rich Text Format (RTF)*, that is supposed to be the character-based equivalent of DOC. All Word products and versions support RTF, as do (we suspect) all the other word processors in the world. It is the closest thing we have to a word processing interchange standard.

And now a third format has been added. Every version of Word 2003 can import and create an XML vocabulary that Microsoft calls *Word Markup Language (WordML)*. Example 4-11 illustrates the WordML markup for a sentence with a footnote.

Example 4-11. Sentence with footnote in WordML

```
<w:p xmlns:w=
       "http://schemas.microsoft.com/office/word/2003/2/wordml">
  <w:r><w:t>A sentence ending with a footnote</w:t></w:r>
  <w:r>
    <w:rPr><w:rStyle w:val="FootnoteReference"/></w:rPr>
    <w:footnote>
      <w:p>
        <w:pPr><w:pStyle w:val="FootnoteText"/></w:pPr>
        <w:r>
          <w:rPr><w:rStyle w:val="FootnoteReference"/></w:rPr>
          <w:footnoteRef/>
        </w:r>
        <w:r><w:t>The actual footnote</w:t></w:r>
      </w:p>
    </w:footnote>
  </w:r>
</w:p>
```

Note that there aren't element types named `FootnoteText` or `FootnoteReference` as there would be in a normal document type. Those are names of a paragraph style (`w:pStyle`) and a character style (`w:rStyle`), respectively. WordML, like RTF and DOC, represents the rendition-oriented structure of Word documents. Its element types include paragraphs (w:p), "text runs" (w:r), text string components of a run (w:t), and their properties (respectively, w:pPr, w:rPr and (w:tPr).

This lack of abstract structure is perhaps the major flaw in WordML, as it is in RTF. But, unlike RTF, the WordML syntax is XML and is easily parsed, transformed, and integrated into other applications. Moreover, professional editions of Word also support custom abstract schemas, as we'll see in 4.8.1.4, "XML editing: Style comes second!", on page 97.

In short, WordML is a big step forward. We'd like to see it replace DOC as the default file format for Word!

4.8.1.2   Competitors to Word

Microsoft's competitors have embraced XML aggressively.

We use the term "competitors" advisedly. It is well-known that Microsoft has such an overwhelming share of the word processing market that there is little commercial competition.

Open source products have stepped into this void that commercial vendors tend to shy away from. Because open source products do not have to justify their development in terms of revenues, they can survive for as long as their communities' enthusiasm holds out, even if the market is very small.

Those enthusiasts do believe that eventually there will be a mainstream market for the open source tools, but they are not in as big a hurry as a commercial company would be. They have no shareholders and they believe that if they keep working at it, they will one day find a market because their programs will be indisputably better, cheaper, and more open.

Because open source products tend to be newer and have smaller installed bases, they have moved quickly to use XML and other standards in their data representations.

4.8.1.2.1   *OpenOffice*

The open source office suite *OpenOffice* has used XML for its native data representation since 1999. In fact, XML is part of the OpenOffice project mission statement.[11] The word processor is called *Writer*.

---

11. An enhanced version of the OpenOffice suite is marketed by Sun as *StarOffice*.

All products in the OpenOffice suite use the same file format. It is being standardized by the OASIS industry consortium under the slightly different name *Open Office.*[12]

Caution   Technically, a data representation (or data format) is a character or bit string that is interpreted according to the rules of some notation. A file format is a packaging of one or more data representations for storage. XML is a notation for data representation and has nothing to do with files, but we'd still like to have a nickel for each time someone calls it a "file format". We try to keep the terms straight in this book.

The Open Office file format is a ZIP archive containing one or more compressed XML documents and possibly files in other data representations (e.g. graphics). You can access the XML within an Open Office file using normal unzipping software.

4.8.1.2.2 K Desktop Environment (KDE)

The *K Desktop Environment (KDE)* is one of the two major desktop environments for Linux and other Unix-like operating systems. Its integrated office suite is called *KOffice* and its word processor (predictably) is called *KWord*.

Like OpenOffice Writer, KOffice KWord uses compressed XML documents as its native file format. There is a strong possibility that KWord will migrate to the Open Office file format.

4.8.1.2.3 Gnome desktop

AbiWord is the word processor for the competing *Gnome* desktop for Linux and Unix. AbiWord was one of the first word processors to use XML for its data representation back in the late 1990s. It is still going strong and has partial support for the OASIS Open Office file format.

---

12. Yes: OpenOffice is an office suite. Open Office is a file format. A space makes all the difference. Ask any cubicle dweller about the importance of office space!

4.8.1.3   Too many XML representations?

Word processor data representations are renditions, rather than abstractions, and as such they reflect the processing abilities of their products. For that reason, product vendors may never agree on a single interchange standard. Why make your product development a hostage to the standards process, especially if you have 200 or 300 million users!

Is it a problem that there are a variety of different XML word processor formats: WordML versus OASIS Open Office versus AbiWord's XML and so forth?

End users may find that interchanging files with users of other word processors isn't an error-free process. Developers certainly find that it takes extra effort to write applications that support all the formats. But thanks to XML, the problem is much less severe than in the past.

XML makes writing import and export filters for another product's data representations substantially easier. Word processing developers are now treating their file formats, not as proprietary trade secrets, but as open, documented, public contracts. Thanks to XML, there is a public expectation that the data in the document should be open and available to all processes, rather than exclusively owned by the application that created it.

So even in a worst case scenario where there is no adoption of multi-vendor interchange standards, an XML-enabled future is better than the binary, private-format past.

4.8.1.4   XML editing: Style comes second!

An XML editing application is different from an ordinary word processor. It is designed so an expert or power-user can customize it to work with a particular schema or DTD. Most importantly, it is designed to preserve the abstract data and keep it from getting mixed up with style information.

XML editing reflects the original vision going back even before SGML, to GML:

- Users should be able to define their own document types, specific to their needs.
- Tools should conform to the needs of people, rather than vice versa.

Historically, XML editing has been the domain of specialized products. These tools are extremely flexible and configurable. They may be designed to interface with content management systems in which each element is managed like a record in a database.

The rendition of the data that users work with is determined by stylesheets. A user can't simply click on a "bold" button and change the font of a word.

The Office Professional Edition of Word is now crossing the boundary between a traditional word processor and an XML editing application. It can create documents that conform not just to WordML but to any schema. It can let users save the abstract data only, ignoring any clicks of the "bold" button.

Word is not yet a complete substitute for those specialized products for high-end uses involving complicated schemas and highly customized user interfaces. But neither can those products touch Word's familiarity and ubiquity. The market should have a place for both.

4.8.2 *Software in a new form!*

Word is not the only one of Microsoft's office tools that is bending categories.

InfoPath™ (nee *XDocs*) is a cross between a word processor, an XML editor, and a form design and completion tool. It is available in the Professional Enterprise Edition of the Office suite and individually.

InfoPath is intended for data collection for Web services and enterprise data stores. It tries to provide the flexibility of a word processing user experience, while still maintaining the rigorous control needed for completing a form.

As a form-like technology, InfoPath competes with tools based on XForms,[13] and forms interfaces provided by database management systems. But in InfoPath, the data collected is determined by a custom schema, and display of the form is specified by XSLT stylesheets.

Just as with a form-completion tool, the user is constrained by a structure that is built into the form design. But when the schema allows multiple occurrences of an element or group of elements, the "form" can grow like a word processor table and have sections added to it. However, just as with an

---

13. See 4.4, "XML-based forms", on page 77.

XML editor, you will need to configure InfoPath to work with your schema using its design mode, scripts, and other customizations.[14]

4.8.3 *Between the spreadsheets*

The second traditional anchor of an office suite, along with the word processor, is a spreadsheet program. In the right hands a spreadsheet can take columns of numbers and turn them into revenue projections or departmental budgets. Today's generation of spreadsheets can store those projections and budgets in XML.

Microsoft Excel®, like Word, has a native XML representation. It is called *XML Spreadsheet (XMLSS)*. And, like Word, Office Professional Editions of Excel can work with custom schemas as well.

The OpenOffice spreadsheet is known as *Calc*. It recognizes that a spreadsheet is a specialized form of table, which makes it easy to paste spreadsheets into word processing documents. The fact that Calc and Writer share the same file format helps!

Gnome Office's *Gnumeric* has its own XML representation, as does KOffice's *KSpread*.

4.8.4 *Drawn-out solutions*

In 4.3, "Graphics and multimedia", on page 76 we saw that pictures are represented either as bitmaps or vectors. As XML doesn't help much with bitmaps, the paint and photo programs that use them don't usually use XML.

That leaves the vector graphics programs, which come in several varieties: general-purpose drawing programs and specialized diagramming and presentation programs. All three have basic vector graphics support, but a diagramming program has extended capabilities for drawings – such as flowcharts and organization charts – that consist primarily of shapes joined by lines. Presentation programs add facilities for managing and presenting sequences of drawings, plus animations, videos, and other media.

---

14. We cover InfoPath in detail in Chapter 26, "Flexible data capture with structured forms", on page 430.

Let's look at the XML support trends in these categories, bearing in mind that details are subject to change over time.

4.8.4.1   General-purpose drawing

Modern office suites recognize that most people are visual creatures. We often prefer to create drawings to explain ideas. Many suites have vector-based drawing programs for drawing logos and other pictures. Some are stand-alone programs; others are integrated into the word processor or other suite components

The Gnome Office drawing program is called *Sodipodi*. It uses SVG as its native representation.

The OpenOffice *Draw* program uses the integrated Open Office format, but SVG is under consideration as a replacement for the graphic portion.

The KOffice *Karbon* drawing program has a very simple SVG-like XML vocabulary. Karbon can import and export SVG.

4.8.4.2   Diagramming

Microsoft bought the market-leading *Visio* diagramming software in 1999. It now has its own XML data representation, called VDX. Visio can also import SVG drawings as shapes and export complete diagrams in SVG. It is also possible to attach XML data in any schema to objects in a Visio diagram.

The Gnome Office diagramming program is called *Dia*. As with Visio, Dia shapes can be defined in SVG and Dia diagrams can be exported as SVG.

OpenOffice *Draw* is also a diagramming program, as it incorporates the defining feature of diagramming software, the so-called *smart connector*. Smart connectors are lines that stretch and shrink as needed when the shapes they join are moved around.

KOffice includes *Kivio*, which is modeled after Visio. It uses XML, but not SVG.

4.8.4.3   Presentation

Once you have developed your business plan it is time to take it on the road. To convince anyone that your numbers are real you need to put them in a flashy presentation with distracting animations. XML is up to the task! Several presentation packages are XML-based.

The OpenOffice presentation program is called *Impress*. Predictably, it uses the unified Open Office format.

The KOffice presentation program, *KPresenter* has its own XML vocabulary.

Apple has a presentation package called *Keynote* that is reputed to be so cool that some people are switching to Macintoshes to use it! Apple calls the XML vocabulary it uses Apple Presentation XML (APXL). It is almost like SVG, but not quite.

Microsoft PowerPoint® doesn't presently use XML, but Microsoft is making major investments in XML-based graphics and animation technologies. These could influence future PowerPoint versions.

4.8.5   *Working together*

Before XML it was common for desktop software developers to take the position: "Our data is for our application. You can use it if you can figure it out." Now developers are coming to understand that they live in an ecology of complementary and competing products so their files should be clear, easy to read, properly documented and, where possible, based upon industry standard vocabularies.

Consequently, it is becoming increasingly easy for desktop users to interchange data with one another without worrying which applications they use. We still have a long way to go but we are making definite progress in the right direction.

4.9 | Conclusion

In the next chapter we'll talk about MOM applications that dispense with people. Computers talk to one another to automatically accomplish tasks that have traditionally been labor-intensive and error prone.

XML for machines

- Electronic commerce and EDI

- Commerce frameworks

- Vertical applications

- Registries and repositories

- Web services

Chapter

5

A t one end of the XML spectrum are the people-oriented publishing (POP) applications designed primarily for human consumption. This chapter addresses the other end of the spectrum: the MOM applications, wherein computers talk to one another with minimal human intervention.

5.1 | Integrated electronic commerce (IEC)

There are many machine-oriented applications, but the most complicated and difficult tend to involve buying and selling products. Nevertheless, despite the difficulty, companies are swarming into the *integrated e-commerce* (IEC) business: the XML-based merger of the Web and electronic document interchange (EDI).

As a notorious criminal said when asked why he robbed banks: "That's where the money is". Many companies dream of getting a small cut of the billions of dollars that flow between corporations every day.

There are many different standards under development in this area. They sometimes overlap, compete and maybe even contradict each other. That's partly because we are in the early days of XML-based e-business; even the experts are just feeling their way in the dark, trying to find the model that works best. But it's also because there's lots of competition for that "small cut".

We'll try to help you sort out the competition!

5.1.1 *Automating the supply chain*

When you buy a television set, you are really buying a bundle of parts that one company bought from other companies to assemble for you. Those parts are made up of raw materials that were bought from somewhere else. Some company sold the service of removing the waste materials from these processes. Every company in this *supply chain* also had to buy desks, paper clips, and overhead projectors.

In the future, the vast majority of these products will be bought through the Internet. The vision of integrated e-commerce is that a large subset will be bought automatically, without human intervention, through XML-based systems. When the warehouse runs low on staples, a computer will recognize this situation in the inventory and order more.

In a particularly futuristic vision, before a plant runs short of steel its computer will order some from the day's lowest-priced supplier, perhaps even negotiating some of the terms of the purchase agreement.

5.1.2 *EDI was first!*

The original machine-processed documents weren't great works of fiction, or even technical manuals. They were the *business documents* that accompany commercial transactions: purchase orders, invoices, and the like.

The first computer applications for these were POP applications: the computer helped a human create a purchase order, which was then printed and mailed to another human, who read it. For many – perhaps most – companies, it is still a POP application today.

But for the last 25 years or so big businesses have converted purchasing and other supply chain processes into MOM applications, by means of *electronic data interchange (EDI)*. EDI allows the computers of a buyer and a seller to communicate sets of documents representing agreed transactions. EDI provides great efficiency and huge cost savings for the largest enterprises; they are completely dependent on it.

But EDI isn't perfect!

5.1.2.1 Problems with EDI

EDI is wonderful for big businesses but it has never appealed to small or medium sized organizations for a variety of reasons.

private network costs
> The first problem is that EDI is typically conducted over expensive private networks known as *Value Added Networks* (VANs). The EDI standards predate the public Internet by many years. VANs are in many ways still better than the public Internet. They are very secure and are better at quickly and reliably delivering information. But VANs are also too expensive and proprietary to appeal to small businesses.

excessive customization
> The second problem with EDI is that it is typically always "customized" for every communication between two corporations. This is very expensive for a small corporation with many big partners. Each big partner will demand the small company use the big guy's own variant of EDI.

complex document representation
> Finally, EDI is considered to be too complicated because it uses a somewhat confusing pre-XML representation.

5.1.2.2 From EDI to IEC

EDI would not have been successful with its large customers if it did not have some important benefits. Embedded within EDI is a great deal of knowledge about how businesses work in terms of processes and policies.

The challenge of the new XML-based commerce is to take the virtues of EDI forward into a more open environment based on Web standards. Ideally the new XML-based specifications will be just as useful to a small emu rancher as to a large airplane manufacturer.

Note   We discuss the details of EDI and its problems, plus its metamorphosis into integrated e-commerce, in Part 3, "E-commerce", on page 200.

5.1.3 *Frameworks and libraries*

Several industry organizations, including vendor consortia, are developing standardized Web-based approaches to business automation. They consist of a mix of XML vocabulary libraries, best practice recommendations, and markup conventions. There may also be a framework for connecting these parts together.

The word *framework* is deliberately vague. It is an environment in which to frame other work: not something directly usable by itself. XML could be considered a framework!

You cannot simply download an e-commerce framework and begin to work. Rather you use it as guidance in designing the details of your document types and software. If many document types adhere to the same framework then some portion of your implementation code can be reused between document types.

We describe some of the leading framework and library projects in this section.

5.1.3.1   ebXML

Getting all of the world's computers to talk to and negotiate with each other will not be easy. Consider the variety of international human languages. Even within a country, there are huge variations in terminology and process between and within industries. Someone needs to standardize terminology, message structures, and product and business codes.

The United Nations and OASIS have created a framework to tackle this problem. It is known as *ebXML*. Because ebXML has the formal support of the United Nations, it is likely to become a very important standard internationally. According to the founders:

The goal of ebXML is to facilitate open trade between organizations regardless of size by enabling XML to be used in a consistent manner to exchange electronic business data.

5.1.3.1.1 *Messaging*

The ebXML framework includes a messaging infrastructure based upon an XML protocol called *SOAP*. The SOAP spec defines a standardized carrier document, like an envelope, in which another document – the *payload* – is transported. ebXML's messaging extends SOAP with features for guaranteeing the reliability of transmission.[1]

In ebXML messages, the payload is a business document (such as a purchase order or invoice) which is conceptually composed of *core components*. A core component is an aggregation of business information items that are related to a single concept. An example would be bank account identification, which consists of account number and account name. Components can themselves be aggregated into larger components (possibly including additional information items), and eventually into complete documents.

5.1.3.1.2 *Core components*

The core components are among the trickiest parts of the ebXML system to get right because they are most directly linked to the wide variety of business processes in the real world. The core components specification has to deal with the wide variance in terminology and practice around the world.

Note that the core components are conceptual; they don't define XML representations of the information items. Other standards provide those vocabularies.

For example, the *XML Common Business Library (xCBL)* is an XML component library for business-to-business e-commerce. It is currently developed by an industry consortium and distributed free of charge. xCBL components can be combined into custom document types by users, and schemas for a library of standardized document types have been developed by the consortium.

Other projects are developing similar libraries. Some try for the same universality as xCBL, while others are specialized for a particular industry. We discuss one of the latter in 5.1.3.4, "RosettaNet", on page 109.

---

1. We discuss SOAP in more detail in 6.4.4, "Slippery SOAP", on page 139.

Although the xCBL components don't correspond completely to ebXML core components, they are evolving in that direction because of a newer development, the *Universal Business Language (UBL)*.

5.1.3.2   Universal Business Language (UBL)

The Universal Business Language is a modestly-named specification with an equally modest goal. It is to be the default XML vocabulary used by anybody doing business anywhere. Whereas ebXML is a framework and its core components are concepts, UBL is an actual XML vocabulary, with schemas for element types and document types.

ebXML message payloads are supposed to be XML documents, but the ebXML specification does not provide schemas for them. That is what UBL is for.

The UBL Charter requires development of UBL "by mutually agreed-upon changes to xCBL 3.0 based on industry experience with other XML business libraries and with similar technologies such as Electronic Data Interchange." As a result, many of the UBL components already developed are equivalents of those in xCBL, but UBL currently lacks the depth and breadth of xCBL.

Over time, as UBL continues to develop, xCBL will migrate to the new standard. New UBL components will replace their xCBL equivalents in future releases of xCBL. The xCBL consortium predicts that most existing xCBL components, and many of the xCBL document types, will eventually be replaced by UBL equivalents.

5.1.3.3   BizTalk Framework

The BizTalk™ Framework is an electronic business framework from Microsoft. There is also the BizTalk Server, which is Microsoft's implementation of the framework.

The BizTalk Framework is a set of guidelines for XML best practices. The framework describes how to publish schema definitions in XML and how to use XML messages to integrate software programs together in order to build new solutions.

Like ebXML, the framework defines an envelope that manages message routing, workflow and security. Also like ebXML, BizTalk has no pre-defined payload document types. Those would likely be defined by ebXML or another industry consortium.

The BizTalk envelope is a little more descriptive than the sort of envelopes we use in the paper world. It describes the sender and receiver of the message, how it should be delivered, whether a return receipt is required, what sort of processing deadlines are in force and other, similar *quality of service (QoS)* details.

5.1.3.4 RosettaNet

RosettaNet is an non-profit consortium that develops and deploys standard electronic business interfaces. RosettaNet exists to combat the problem of "supply chain misalignments" in the information technology industry. In the information technology business, the supply chain would include everything from silicon to chips to parts to software.

A supply-chain misalignment is an inefficiency caused by poor information flow between organizations in a supply chain. As a child you may have played the game "telephone" where information was relayed from person to person, getting more and more garbled as it traveled. A supply chain has the same problems. These problems are particularly severe in the computer hardware industry because things change so rapidly and margins are very thin. A small company that makes too many or too few computer chips may not have an opportunity to correct its mistake.

RosettaNet is the name of the organization and also of the electronic business framework developed by the consortium. Partners use RosettaNet specifications to align their internal business processes and create inter-company information flows. The RosettaNet framework includes dictionaries of common computer and business terminology. RosettaNet also defines many standardized business processes, known as *Partner Interface Processes (PIPs)*.

RosettaNet has developed a dictionary of thousands of IT products. The group has also created dozens of XML-based PIPs. These guidelines amount to dialogs between computers conducted entirely in XML. The PIPs enable manufacturers, distributors, resellers, customers and other supply chain members to execute those processes in a standard fashion. Existing PIPs cover basic supply chain functions such as distributing new product information, transferring shopping carts, managing purchase orders and querying technical information. Others are under development.

Examples of PIPs include "Request Quote", "Query Price and Availability" and "Change Basic Product Information". These standards form a common integrated e-commerce language. They align processes between supply chain partners on a global basis, rather than using individually or bilaterally developed methods.

5.2 | Vertical applications

There are hundreds of organizations adapting XML to particular industries. These are termed *vertical applications* or *verticals*. It is not possible to discuss them all here.[2] Instead, we will focus on a few successful verticals that can serve as models for other, similar activities.

5.2.1 *Open Financial Exchange (OFX)*

Remember, about banks being where the bucks are? The Open Financial Exchange is the name of a technical specification created by Intuit, Check-Free and Microsoft. OFX allows financial institutions (banks, brokerages and billers) to communicate with one another and their clients about account transactions.

OFX is one of the most mature uses of markup languages in the consumer software world, having originated as an SGML application. It is supported on the client side by accounting packages such as *Microsoft Money* and Intuit's *Quicken*, and on the server side by numerous financial institutions.

OFX supports four major kinds of services: banking, bill presentment and payment, investing, and tax forms.

5.2.1.1   Banking

Using the OFX banking services, your client software can communicate directly with your bank. That means that your banking transactions can appear in your accounting software automatically. Bad news: covering up

2. There's a helpful catalog, including website links, in Chapter 66, "Public XML vocabularies", on page 1094.

the trail left by transfers into the "poker money" account is about to get tricky.

Information can flow the other way also. Using an OFX-based accounting program, you could transfer money from account to account instead of through a separate website (or, heaven forbid, a branch office). Now your spouse can transfer the poker money back into the "university fund" account without leaving the house!

Customers can even schedule transfers in advance so that the disputed money is sent to the university account (or the university!) as soon as the paycheck clears. All of these features apply both to regular accounts and to credit card accounts. Spending money has never been so easy!

5.2.1.2   Bill presentment and payment

With OFX-based bill payment, your accounting software can direct the bank to pay your bills automatically when they arrive. You can specify which bills should be paid automatically and which should be done manually. Bill presentment allows billers (typically utility companies) to deliver their bills directly to your accounting software.

5.2.1.3   Investing

Although OFX does not currently allow customers to buy and sell investments through their accounting software, it does allow you to download information about your transactions, balances, and positions for entry into your accounting package. It is possible to manage 401(k) accounts as well as cash, margin and short accounts. OFX cannot guarantee that your investments grow but it can ensure that you are always aware of exactly where they stand.

5.2.1.4   Tax Forms

OFX version 2 allows U.S.-based accounting software to download 1099 and W2 forms from financial institutions and payroll processors. These XML element types closely mimic the equivalent print forms. As the tax forms change, the XML specifications have to change to follow them. (This is the only part of OFX that is US-specific.)

5.2.2   *eXtensible Business Reporting Language*

The *eXtensible Business Reporting Language (XBRL)* is an XML vocabulary for representing financial statements, accounting records and other financial information. An XBRL financial statement includes everything an accountant would expect of a printed financial statement, including a balance sheet, an income statement, a statement of equity, a statement of cash flows, notes to the financial statements, and an accountant's report.

XBRL is quite different from OFX. Where OFX is used for individual transactions (buy this, sell that), XBRL is used for reporting on the overall effect on the company's finances (we made money this year, we lost money last year).

Those of us who are not accountants can think of XBRL as a standardized XML representation of the tables and fine print from a company's annual report. Once the information has been represented in XML, it is much easier for potential investors or regulators to do calculations based upon the information, compare it to results for other companies, and generally determine the health of a company's bottom line.

In the wake of the accounting scandals of the last few years, many hope that XBRL will bring some transparency to accounting. Of course if someone is determined to perpetrate fraud they will find a way around whatever system stands in the way!

Nevertheless, XBRL should reduce the workload of accountants and regulators by automating more of their work. We hope they will use their free time to look at the books a little more closely!

5.2.3   *Health Level Seven (HL7)*

Health Level Seven (HL7) is an industry consortium for healthcare information standardization, founded in 1987. It is an ANSI-accredited Standards Developing Organization for clinical and administrative data in the healthcare industry.

HL7 has been working with XML since 1996. In September 2000, the HL7 membership ratified Version One of the Clinical Document Architecture, which defines an XML architecture for exchange of clinical documents.

The most widely used HL7 specification is the Application Protocol for Electronic Data Exchange in Healthcare Environments. This is a messaging standard that enables health care applications to exchange data within and between organizations. Version Three of the HL7 specifications uses XML extensively.

HL7 standards are designed for systems that cannot be permitted to fail. They remind us that XML is used in life and death applications. Those of us who develop XML specifications and tools must take this responsibility seriously and keep reliability as a major focus.

5.3 | Repository stories

As you can see, there are hundreds of schemas, DTDs, frameworks and other specifications swirling around XML like leaves in a storm. This is as it should be. XML is a building block. There can never be one or ten or one hundred "definitive" XML document types. New ones will be invented all the time, as new situations arise.

As we come to understand the human genome, we will need genome markup languages. When we send robotic probes to other planets, NASA may well deliver the results of experiments to the Web in various appropriate markup languages. Believe it or not, there is already a Spacecraft Markup Language![3]

Fortunately, organizations have begun to establish websites to catalog these vocabularies. The sites come in a few flavors (some are swirls!) which, for the rest of this chapter, we'll define informally as follows:

directory
> a catalog in which things may be listed with or without their owners' overt participation (or even knowledge!)

---

3. It might be presumptuous to predict that XML would be the basis for communication at Federation Headquarters. The aliens may already have their own GML (Galactic Markup Language)!

registry
> a catalog whose participants must request participation, either explicitly or as a by-product of organization membership, legal action, etc.

repository
> a place where things are stored, often in conjunction with a registry or directory

5.3.1 *ebXML*

Let us pretend that you are the president of Crazy Kazoos Incorporated. You need to find business partners, such as customers and suppliers. There are two parts to this task.

- You want to publish your contact information so potential partners can find you.
- You want to browse other companies' contact information to look for potential partners.

In both cases you need some form of registry.

ebXML has defined standards for creating interoperable registries and repositories. While registries consist of entries with a known uniform structure, repositories can hold more complicated informational files and free form documents. The ebXML repository allows organizations to publish specifications, schema definitions and other business documents for public consumption.

An ebXML registry entry includes a *Business Profile*. It contains the business' contact information and industrial classification. It also describes the business processes supported by the business.

The business' technical capabilities are represented by a *Collaboration Protocol Profile (CPP)*. It describes what protocols the business intends to use, what URI to use as the end-point, what security features the business uses, and so forth.

When two companies find each other through the registry, the two determine (either automatically or manually) what protocols they support in common. They do this by comparing their Collaboration Protocol Profiles and merging them into a *Collaboration Protocol Agreement (CPA)*. In other words, the CPA is the intersection of the capabilities of the two business partners.

5.3.2 *xml.org*

xml.org is a project of the *Organization for the Advancement of Structured Information Standards (OASIS)*. Its website incorporates a content management system, which allows the site to serve as both a registry and a repository for DTDs, schemas and other standards documents. Groups and individuals who create such documents can store them at the xml.org site.

The repository does not require any particular schema language or adherence to a particular framework. This is good in that it maximizes contributor freedom and opportunity to innovate. The downside is that all of these specifications may not work together nicely because there are no published guidelines for making them work together.

OASIS wants xml.org to become more than a standalone repository. It wants the site to become an index to a variety of other, technically compatible repositories. In other words, it should one day be able to delegate queries to affiliated repositories run by other companies.

5.3.3 *Directories*

Some sites are primarily directories for schemas stored elsewhere. These sites are older than the ones we've just discussed, and in some domains they are more complete.

The first such site was Robin Cover's. Robin has cataloged markup-related information since the earliest SGML days, before there was even a Web as we know it. His Web pages have come to be known as the *Cover Pages*. (Get it?)

In addition to vocabularies, Robin's pages track software, Web pages, printed books, and everything else pertaining to XML and SGML. The Cover pages are one-stop shopping for consumers of XML news and information.

Our Australian friend, James Tauber, runs a directory with the imaginative name `schema.net`. Well, okay, the name itself is rather obvious; the imagination was in grabbing the domain name before anyone else saw the importance of schemas!

5.4 | Web services

If you are involved with information technology – and haven't spent the last five years installing Wi-Fi access points on Mars – you've heard of Web services.

In fact, you may have heard of it in breathless terms as a "revolution". The last time there was so much revolutionary talk in the air, there was also tea in Boston harbor.

5.4.1 *Communication protocols*

You can understand the hype if you look back at recent history. Before the Web, it was very difficult to distribute information so that anybody could access it using any computer system. The Web standards made computer-to-human communication easy and automatic. In this chapter we've seen that XML is starting to make computer-to-computer communication easier as well.

Web services is trying to go further in this direction. It is a term for services supported by a new set of XML-based protocols intended to make computer-to-computer communications not just easy, but standardized and automatic.[4]

The Web services protocols use XML as the data representation. They use Web communication protocols such as HTTP to move the XML around the Internet, but offer additional functions. The SOAP messaging protocol that we discussed in 5.1.3.1.1, "Messaging", on page 107 is an example.[5]

SOAP is the protocol beloved of large software companies. For many, the use of SOAP is implied by the term "Web services", but others do without it. We'll look at two well-known Web services, one SOAPless and one SOAPy.

---

4. These services are sometimes known as *XML Web Services* to distinguish them from the general class of Web-based services – such as online psychic readings! However, the IT industry, with its usual aversion to the precise use of English, seems happy with *Web services* alone. So despite the ambiguity, we too use the shorter term.

5. SOAP is considered a Web services protocol even though it has other uses and actually pre-dates the Web services hype by several years.

5.4.2 *Amazon.com*

Amazon's Web service has an interesting business model. The service is free to use; it earns its money by increasing Amazon's sales. It is essentially a search service for Amazon's product line, but because the line in many areas is comprehensive, the service has research value as well: "How many books did Paul Prescod write? Did he ever record a DVD?"

5.4.2.1   Amazon Associates

Amazon has long had a model whereby "associates" can earn money by directing book buyers to the Amazon site. Amazon's Web service allows these vendors to integrate more tightly with Amazon's underlying databases.

Some even set up their own virtual store-fronts, selling books as if they were full-service retailers but allowing Amazon to do the actual fulfillment and billing. Entrepreneurial developers have created software that allows anyone to build a virtual storefront on top of the Amazon Web service in hours.

One innovative associate allows people to choose things from Amazon and then purchase them using currencies that Amazon does not support. The associate does the appropriate currency trading for you behind the scenes.

Everyone benefits from the Web service. The associates make more money by selling more products. The Web service gives them very accurate and timely information. When Amazon changes a price, they know quickly. Amazon makes a profit on most books it sells, so it benefits from giving the associates the tools they need to build their storefronts and sell books.

5.4.2.2   Why not HTML?

From the earliest days of the Amazon associates program, Amazon supplied HTML graphics and search boxes for associates to include on their Web pages. The links created by that HTML markup caused HTML pages to be displayed. That was o.k. for end users who wanted to buy books, but it was a nuisance for programmers who needed to integrate Amazon search results into complex Web pages or other applications.

In a nutshell: Amazon delivered renditions when the programmers needed abstractions!

Amazon's browser style is pretty elaborate, as you can see from the search results page in Figure 5-1. It shows that the most popular book about the keyword "genome" is called "Genome" and is by "Matt Ridley". It costs $11.20 at Amazon.

Figure 5-1   Amazon.com search results in a Web browser

It follows from the elaborate formatting that the corresponding HTML source is pretty elaborate as well, as you can see in Example 5-1. A programmer looking for the facts about the top search result has to ignore things in the HTML pages that are helpful to people but irrelevant to computers, such as fonts, tabular layouts, line breaks, and so forth.

A program that analyzes a rendition to find abstract data is said to be *screen scraping*. Such programs are difficult to write because there is no guaranteed pattern of formatting markup. Worse yet, the program might break any time that Amazon decides to change the layout of the search results.

Example 5-1. Partial HTML source of Figure 5-1

```
<table border=0 cellpadding=3 width=100%>
<tr valign=top> <td> <font size=-1><b>1.</b></font></td>
<td align=center width=60>
<font face=verdana,arial,helvetica size=-1>
<a href=/exec/.../sr=2-1/ref=sr_2_1/103-5013077-5501429>
<img src="http://...PIt.arrow,TopLeft,-1,-17_SCTHUMBZZZ_.jpg"
     width=42 height=66 align=left border=0></a>
</font>
</td>
<td width=100% valign=top>
<font face=verdana,arial,helvetica size=-1>
<a href=/exec/.../sr=2-1/ref=sr_2_1/103-5013077-5501429>
<b>Genome</b></a>
-- by Matt Ridley (Author); Paperback
<br>
<span class=small>
<a href=/exec/.../ref=sr_2_1/103-5013077-5501429>
Buy new</a></span>: <b class=price>$11.20</b>
--
<a
href=http://.../all/ref=sr_pb_a/103¬5013077-5501429>
Used & new from</a>: <b class=price>$3.95</b>
 
</font>
</b>
```

5.4.2.3   The Amazon Web service

The Amazon Web service eliminates the need for screen scraping by returning abstract XML documents. That makes it easy for programs to find the desired information elements.

Using the Web service, it is possible to construct queries similar to those that Amazon's user interface allows: search by author, search by ISBN, search by keyword, and so forth.

Example 5-2 shows the Web service query for books about "genome". You can actually type this query in a browser's address pane and see a rendition of the XML document that the service would return to a program.[6]

If you ask the browser to "View Source", you will see the XML source of the search result, as shown in Example 5-3.[7]

---

6. Well, you once could have. As we went to press, Amazon changed its Web service interface and now requires a "developer's token" in its queries.

Example 5-2. Web service query (split into two lines to fit page width of this book)

```
http://rcm.amazon.com/e/cm?t=encyclozine&l=st1
&search=genome&mode=books&pk102&o=1&f=xml
```

Example 5-3. Partial XML source of Example 5-2 search result

```
<?xml version="1.0" encoding="ISO-8859-1"?>
<catalog>
<keyword>genome</keyword>
<product_group>Books</product_group>
  <product>
    <ranking>1</ranking>
    <title>Genome</title>
    <asin>0060932902</asin>
    <author>Ridley, Matt</author>
    <image>
      http://images.amazon.com/images/P/0060932902.01.MZZZZZZZ.jpg
    </image>
    <small_image>
      http://images.amazon.com/images/P/0060932902.01.TZZZZZZZ.jpg
    </small_image>
    <our_price>$11.20</our_price>
    <list_price>$14.00</list_price>
    <release_date>20001003</release_date>
    <binding>Paperback</binding>
    <availability> </availability>
    <tagged_url>http://www.amazon.com:80/exec/obidos/redirect?
      tag=encyclozine&amp;creative=9441&amp;camp=1793
      &amp;link_code=xml&amp;path=ASIN/0060932902</tagged_url>
  </product>
  -- more products here --
</catalog>
```

As you can see, Example 5-3 yields much of the same information as Example 5-1. The top-ranked book about the keyword "genome" is called "Genome" and is by "Matt Ridley". It costs $11.20 at Amazon which is a few dollars cheaper than its $14.00 list price. But unlike the HTML, this XML is about as straightforward as you could hope for.

This Web service is SOAPless; Amazon offers a SOAPy version as well, which returns a substantially more complex document. We'll look at a SOAP-based service next, but instead of Amazon we'll use the equally famous Google.

---

7. Note that in reality the content of `tagged_url` has no white space. It was broken into three lines in order to fit this book's page width.

5.4.3 *Google*

The Google Web service allows programmers to treat Google as if it were a massive database of information about the Web. Or to be more precise, they now have access to the real database that underlies the Google search engine. Now, for example, a programmer can write a program that compares the change in popularity of different slang terms from day to day.

Google provides three different operations:

search

performs a traditional Google search

spelling

checks the spelling of a word and returns a suggestion if it is misspelled: Did you mean "handbook"?

cache

returns the version of a page that Google stored the last time its spider crawled the Web

Example 5-4 illustrates the result of a search query for "XML Handbook". The `return` element is the payload of a SOAP message. It contains the Google search result.

Example 5-4 is clearly not the poster child for XML's simplicity and elegance. But computers have an easier time reading it than do humans.

For example, if you examine the document carefully you can see an `estimatedTotalResultsCount` element containing the number of hits for this query. A program or XPath expression can find it much more easily than you can. Still, the complexity required by SOAP has somewhat tarnished a mostly positive reaction to Google's service.

And yet Google's result format is considered simple for a SOAP-based service. So why get involved with SOAP's complexity in the first place? We'll explore that question next.

5.4.4 *Service discovery*

One of the more advanced ideas underpinning Web services is that of *service discovery*. At present, humans generally decide with whom a program

Example 5-4. Google query result

```
<?xml version='1.0' encoding='UTF-8'?>
<SOAP-ENV:Envelope
  xmlns:SOAP-ENV="http://schemas.xmlsoap.org/soap/envelope/"
  xmlns:xsi="http://www.w3.org/1999/XMLSchema-instance"
  xmlns:xsd="http://www.w3.org/1999/XMLSchema">
<SOAP-ENV:Body>
<ns1:doGoogleSearchResponse
  xmlns:ns1="urn:GoogleSearch"
  SOAP-ENV:encodingStyle=
    "http://schemas.xmlsoap.org/soap/encoding/">
  <return xsi:type="ns1:GoogleSearchResult">
    <documentFiltering
      xsi:type="xsd:boolean">false</documentFiltering>
    <estimatedTotalResultsCount
      xsi:type="xsd:int">120000</estimatedTotalResultsCount>
    <directoryCategories
      xmlns:ns2="http://schemas.xmlsoap.org/soap/encoding/"
      xsi:type="ns2:Array"
      ns2:arrayType="ns1:DirectoryCategory[0]">
    </directoryCategories>
    <searchTime xsi:type="xsd:double">0.071573</searchTime>
    <resultElements
      xmlns:ns3="http://schemas.xmlsoap.org/soap/encoding/"
      xsi:type="ns3:Array"
      ns3:arrayType="ns1:ResultElement[0]">
    </resultElements>
    <endIndex xsi:type="xsd:int">0</endIndex>
    <searchTips xsi:type="xsd:string"></searchTips>
    <searchComments xsi:type="xsd:string"></searchComments>
    <startIndex xsi:type="xsd:int">0</startIndex>
    <estimateIsExact
      xsi:type="xsd:boolean">false</estimateIsExact>
    <searchQuery
      xsi:type="xsd:string">xml handbook</searchQuery>
  </return>
</ns1:doGoogleSearchResponse>
</SOAP-ENV:Body>
</SOAP-ENV:Envelope>
```

should share information. The purchasing agent for Miracle Cleanser tells his computer that the order for the "free if you act now" scrub brushes should be sent to the High-on-the-Hog Bristle Company.

Some believe that with Web services, that won't be necessary. The purchasing program can search for a supplier using an elaborate registry system called *Universal Description, Discovery, and Integration (UDDI).*[8] A UDDI registry contains three classes of information:

white pages
> They contain general contact information about organizations.

yellow pages
> These list organizations by business category or location.

green pages
> These include the technical aspects of conducting business, including Web service descriptions and schemas.

The green page Web Service descriptions are expressed in XML conforming to the *Web Services Description Language (WSDL).*

A WSDL service description in turn affects the structure of the SOAP messages that are used in conjunction with the service. It indicates the operations that the service performs, the message structure for requesting each operation, and the message structures that the operation returns.

This dynamic interaction between SOAP and WSDL is what makes this model of service discovery possible. (We discuss UDDI and WSDL in detail in Chapter 40, "Web services technologies", on page 628.)

5.4.5 *Web services for the REST of us!*

SOAP is not without its critics, who argue that it doesn't do enough to warrant its complexity and attendant costs. They observe that in most SOAP services the HTTP Web protocol is doing the heavy work of moving data from place to place, and XML is describing the data that is being moved. Although SOAP does contribute, the value of that contribution is somewhat difficult to discern.

Worse yet, they point out that SOAP doesn't use HTTP and XML in the way they were designed to be used. Instead of treating XML documents as

---

8. Given the problems that even humans have in evaluating service offerings and providers – plus the many intangibles often involved in a decision – some skepticism may be warranted. Full realization of service discovery would seem to require both artificial intelligence from the computer and genuine faith from the humans!

persistent resources with Web addresses (URIs), SOAP treats them as transient messages sent to objects that are completely outside the Web or XML framework.

A second generation of Web services is now being developed that is integrated with the architecture of the Web: Web URIs address XML documents that can be retrieved via the Web's HTTP. This architecture has been named *REST*. (You don't want to know why.)[9]

Developers who use REST techniques say it is a more productive way to build Web Services because it builds on techniques that are known to work. It also integrates better with XML technologies like XLink, and Semantic Web technologies like RDF and OWL.

Users seem to agree. The Amazon.com Web service is available in both the REST form that we discussed earlier and in a SOAP version. At the time of writing, Amazon reports that the REST service gets 85% of the use!

Analysis   For some, Web services conjures up nightmare visions of computers taking over the world. For others it suggests extraordinary opportunities for universal commerce. Either way, you can see why it is arousing enormous interest. We discuss Web services at length in Part 13, "Web Services", on page 618. But as Web services is gradually pervading the entire XML world, it is pervading the rest of The XML Handbook as well.

5.5 | Conclusion

The first wave of the Internet revolution made access to information easier than it had ever been before. The second wave made commerce between individuals and businesses easier. Now the third wave will eliminate vast amounts of paperwork and inefficiency in processes that are conducted between businesses. XML is a key enabler of this more integrated business

---

9. Web pages are *representations* of resources. An application changes *state* as it traverses links to *transfer* from one page to another, hence *Representational State Transfer (REST)*. We warned you that you didn't want to know why!

world. It serves as the foundation for industry-neutral frameworks, industry-specific verticals, and the Web services that bind them together.

In the next chapter, we visit Geek World to look at some of the underlying technology that makes all these wonders possible. We'll try not to go native. We'll just explain some of the key concepts at a high level so you'll know what the buzzwords mean when you hear them.[10]

---

10. Fellow geeks, please bear with us. Tourism is good for the economy!

Secrets of the XML programmers

Introductory Discussion

- Object-oriented
- Parsers
- APIs
- Protocols

Chapter

6

T his chapter may seem intimidating if you are not a programmer – possibly even if you are! But we are just going to take a high-level view of a few constructs that will be helpful in understanding the chapters that follow. These aren't really secrets – they just seem that way because programmers tend to speak in code as much as they write it. We'll cover the XML geek-speak Top Term List: object-oriented, parsing, APIs, and protocols.

6.1 | Object-oriented

One of the favorite marketing epithets in high tech – right up there with reliability, availability, scalability, and security – is *object-oriented*. Like most marketing epithets, there is no guarantee (some would say no hope!) that it is always applied correctly. But unlike some, "object-oriented" at least has a precise factual origin.

It comes from the term *object-oriented programming*. Historically, programs were *procedural*; that is, they were designed in terms of the data and steps – or *procedures* – needed to accomplish a computing task. Today, however, the dominant mode of thinking about software problems is in terms of *objects*.

6.1.1 *What is an object?*

An object in a computer may be a model of an object in the real world. An object has characteristics, called *properties*, and capabilities, called *methods*. You can send a *message* to an object to change the value of its properties. You can also send a message asking the object to do something; that is, to *invoke a method*.

For example, anything from a bank account to an entire bank could be modeled as an object. You could change the "interest rate" property of an account, or add money by invoking the account's "make deposit" method.

An object exists in computer memory while a program is working with it. If it is to *persist* between program sessions, it must be stored permanently; for example, in a file, a database, or an XML document.

Some properties and methods are private, or *encapsulated*, available only to the object's own methods. Encapsulation means that a program that wants to read and update the data can't do so directly. Instead, it invokes one of the object's methods to do the job. Before doing it, the method checks that the change would leave the object in a state that makes sense (for example, that the purchase order total isn't less than zero).

Properties and methods intended for public use are said to be *exposed*, the opposite of encapsulated. The means of invoking the exposed methods, and the format of the data they receive and return, are part of the *interface* to the object.

The things you can do with an object, then, depend completely on the interface. Methods aren't limited to reading and updating, but could involve complex operations on the data. For example, you could open a new account by invoking the bank object's "create account" method.

6.1.2 *Inter-object communication*

Most modern programming languages provide some way of building objects. Such objects are represented by a data structure in the computer's memory. Each programming language does it differently.

Just like the real world objects they represent, computer objects need to communicate with one another. In our example, it is the bank object that sends the message to the account object to change the latter's "interest rate" property. Messages themselves are modeled as objects, so in general there is a requirement for interchanging objects among programs.

Inter-object communication mechanisms have been developed to meet this need. They are known as *inter-object protocols*.[1] They are designed for use by programs implemented in different programming languages, and even on different operating systems and computer architectures. Programs on Windows™ systems typically employ the Component Object Model (COM) while among Unix™, Linux, and other systems, CORBA is widely used.

The objects communicated by these protocols are represented as strings of binary digits. To find a specific part of a binary object, a program needs to count the bits. For example, bits 21-50 might be the new interest rate in our example message. Counting is a very fast way for a computer to find things. But if the sending program made a mistake in the object, or a bit got dropped during transmission, the receiving program might pick up bits that aren't a valid interest rate. That in turn could cause the program – or even the operating system – to crash.

For that and other reasons, binary inter-object protocols have never caught on for communicating between machines. Developers have shown a clear preference for text-based inter-machine communication mechanisms. And, inevitably, they have begun to show a clear preference for XML.

Since XML can represent any information, the objects can be modeled as XML elements and represented as text instead of bit strings. This means that the messages can be inspected with standard textual tools and safely processed with any programming language.

6.2 | Parsing

Great as XML is for representing data, eventually that data has to be processed, which requires the use of one or more programs. One of the nice

---

1. In technology as in diplomacy, *protocols* are rules for communicating. We explain them in 6.4, "Protocols", on page 135.

things about writing XML applications is that there is an abundance of reusable component and utility software available to help.

6.2.1 *Basic parsing*

All great programmers try to reduce their work! If every programmer reinvented the wheel when it came to basic processing of XML, no programmer would ever get around to building applications that *use* XML. Instead of implementing basic XML processing over and over again, programmers tend to download or buy packages that implement various types of XML services.

The most basic reusable service is *parsing*. Parsing is about ripping apart the textual representation of a document and turning it into a set of conceptual objects.

For example, a parser looking at the document in Example 2-1 would recognize the characters <QUESTION> to be a start-tag, and would know that it signaled the start of a QUESTION element. The tag is part of the representation; the element is the conceptual object.

6.2.2 *Type validation*

The W3C XML Recommendation defines more than just the parsing of XML documents, hence it refers to the software that parses as an *XML processor*.

Every XML processor, while parsing, checks that a document is well-formed, as set forth in the XML 1.0 (or 1.1) Recommendation. Some also *validate* the XML document; that is, test whether the document conforms to additional constraints that are imposed on documents of its type.

For example, if a processor were validating the document in Example 2-1 according to the DTD in Example 2-2, it would make sure that an ANSWER element followed the QUESTION element.

Initially, document type definitions (DTDs) were the only method of defining these additional constraints, which primarily affect the structure, element types, and attributes of a document. Because DTDs are a fundamental part of the XML recommendation, validation against a DTD is performed by the XML parser itself. Parsers that can validate are called – with astounding clarity for high tech nomenclature – *validating parsers*.

Other methods of element and datatype validation have been introduced, using XSDL, RELAX NG, *Schematron*, or other schema definition languages to express the constraints. They require software in addition to the XML processor.

Analysis   As a human being, you do parsing unconsciously. Because you've learned about elements and attributes, when you look at XML text you can think about the document in those conceptual terms.

But without an XML processor, a computer program can only see the characters. It's sort of the micro version of not seeing the forest for the trees. Without some form of parsing, an XML application cannot see the tree because of all of the characters!

6.3 | APIs

There are many good XML processors out there for use with many different programming languages. There are so many that it is hard to choose. An application developer would hate to pick one and be wedded to it forever. The programmer might want to change some day to a faster or cheaper one, or from a non-validating processor to a validating one.

Switching processors is easy if the two "look" the same to an application. You can plug in different brands and types of light bulbs into the same socket because of the standardization of the socket. The equivalent concept in software components is the standardization of *Application Processing Interfaces (APIs)*.

6.3.1   *Categories of XML API*

XML parsing transforms a document from a string of Unicode characters into a data structure that an application can access conveniently. Processor APIs can be classified in terms of those data structures. There are two kinds: *event-based* and the ever-popular *object-oriented*.

6.3.1.1   Event-based

As a processor parses an XML document it produces a stream of *parser events*. These events reflect the markup and data in the order found in the document. For an event-based API, that stream is the data structure that is presented to the application. The Simple API for XML (SAX) is the most popular example.

6.3.1.2   Object-oriented

For an object-oriented API, the event stream isn't presented to the application. Instead, the processor uses it to construct an object with a tree structure. The tree corresponds to the conceptual hierarchical document represented by the nested start- and end-tags of the XML text string. In principal, two kinds of object can be built:

generic XML object
> The nodes of its tree structure are XML constructs of the conceptual document, such as elements and attributes. The dominant example is the W3C Document Object Model (DOM) API, which provides an interface for accessing and manipulating the tree.

application-specific object
> The nodes of its tree structure are application-defined constructs, such as `Buyer`, `Shipper`, and `LineItem` in a purchase order application. The process of producing an application object API is known as *data binding*.

6.3.2 *Popular XML APIs*

Let's take a look at three popular APIs in more detail: DOM, SAX, and application objects.

6.3.2.1   The DOM

The DOM is a generic object-oriented API standardized by the World Wide Web Consortium. It has been available in Web browsers since version 5. If you write code for Microsoft's *DOM* implementation, it should be relatively easy to make that code also work on Mozilla's or Opera's DOM.

But the DOM is not only for use in browsers. You can use the DOM to read, write and transmit XML on your Web server and in desktop applications. DOM-based programs can talk to some XML content management systems.

The DOM is very popular for general XML processing. It has been implemented, for example, for use with Python and Perl scripts and with the C++ and Java™ programming languages, among others. In fact, DOM toolkits ship with recent releases of all major operating systems.

6.3.2.2   SAX

The DOM is popular and useful but it is not the be-all and end-all of XML processor APIs. It is a little bit like putting a plane on automatic pilot. You point your DOM-building processor at an XML document and it returns you an object tree based on the structure of the document.

But if the document is five hundred megabytes of text and resides on the "other side" of the Internet, your program will just wait. And wait. And wait. When you finally get the data it will fill your computer's memory and some of its disk space. If you are having a bad day it might fill up everything and then crash the computer.

In a situation like this, you would rather just get tiny bits of the data as they come in. An *event-based API* allows this mode of operation. Event-based APIs let your application work on the bit of the data that the parser finds at each "event" in the document.

For example, each XML start-tag causes a "start element" event. Each end-tag causes an "end element" event. Data characters and other constructs cause other parser events. The event-based XML API tells the application what the parser sees in the document as if through a peep-hole. It does not try to reveal the larger picture to the application. An event-driven API is more efficient even for small documents, but it is not as convenient as an object-oriented API.[2]

The most popular event-based API is the *Simple API for XML*. *SAX* was developed by XML processor users and developers in an open discussion group called *XML-DEV*. Despite the name, SAX is not actually much simpler than the DOM. It is much more efficient and low-level, however. The price for efficiency is convenience. The API only provides you with a peep-hole view, so if your application needs more than that, you'll need to write your own code to present an API with the "big picture" of the parsed document. We'll discuss that next.

6.3.3 *Application objects*

The DOM API is said to present *generic XML objects* because its data structure and methods reflect constructs that occur in every XML document: elements, attributes, textual data, etc. Alternatively, the parser event stream could be used to create application-specific data structures. These too could be objects – *application objects* – with methods created for the particular application rather than generic DOM methods. Programs could use these methods to operate on the data structure in terms of application constructs, rather than XML constructs.

For example, the DOM provides methods that allow reading and updating of elements, but knows nothing about the meaning of the element types. In contrast, an application-specific data structure could be encapsulated as a "purchase order" object, with methods to calculate shipping and taxes.

This process of binding data to application objects, called *data binding*, requires *data mapping*; that is, making a correspondence between components of the XML document and components of the application-specific data structure. There are programming tools for simplifying the process; for example, by automatically generating application-specific mappings from schema definitions.

---

2. If you concluded from this description that a processor in effect uses an event-based API as it constructs the DOM, you are right.

6.4 | Protocols

Computers are like humans in that they cannot communicate with each other except by means of a shared language. Just like humans, they also cannot communicate if both parties speak at the same time. There must be some concept of back and forth, send and receive, talk and listen. The specification of how this happens is termed a *protocol*.

XML is not a protocol. XML is the shared language; it helps you to define what the terms of discussion are. But XML does not itself say anything about who speaks first, what they may say, what is appropriate in response, and other requirements of transmission.

Once again we are visiting the domain of programmers, but we'll try to keep the conversation at a level that will be meaningful to others – a diplomatic protocol discussion, so to speak!

6.4.1 *The protocol stack*

Protocols are like salted peanuts: You seldom use just use one. They build on one another, as shown in Figure 6-1.

At the lowest level, your computer's network interface card speaks the Ethernet protocol and your modem uses protocols with cryptic names like ITU-T V.32, V.42, V.32bis, and V.42bis. Wireless devices use IEEE protocols like 802.11b and 802.11g. Protocols at this level just let the bits go back and forth. They are known as *wire protocols*, although nowadays the wires are optional!

Above this physical level of communication, protocols typically organize the bits into *packets* or *messages*. For example, to communicate over the Internet, the TCP/IP protocol directs packets of bits to specific "IP" addresses. However, it doesn't say anything about the meaning of the packets. For that, you need a higher-level protocol.

Those protocols come into play during activities like email or Web browsing. Email uses the POP and SMTP protocols. The Web uses the HTTP protocol, which transmits HTML documents. These protocols let you have a "conversation" about specific subjects; they define what is in the packets.

If you want two computers to have a new sort of conversation, you need to invent a new protocol. For instance to get computers to talk about net-

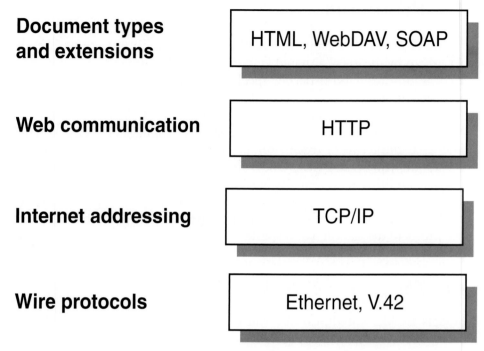

Figure 6-1   Protocol stack

work management, the Internet Engineering Task Force invented the Simple Network Management Protocol (SNMP).

The HTTP protocol can also transmit XML documents. That provides a convenient base for creating more specialized protocols, simply by defining them as document types. We'll look at three protocols built on HTTP: one extension (WebDAV) and two document types (XML-RPC and SOAP). We'll even explain what the acronyms mean![3]

6.4.2 *Writing the Web (WebDAV)*

The early Web allowed little more interactivity than following links. Later, it became possible to build real, interactive Web applications. This is a

---

3. At least the most important and less-known ones; the rest are in Chapter 67, "The XML Handbook Acronym Guide", on page 1120.

quantum leap but it still does not go as far as Tim Berners-Lee had hoped. He wanted Web publishing to be so easy that anyone could do it with any software package whenever they felt like it. We are not there yet.

The problem is that the protocol used to communicate between Web clients and servers (HTTP) is only really designed to retrieve information. The early Web designers never got around to finishing the half of the specification that would standardize writing back to the Web. A variety of half-solutions have arisen. Some people use the older File Transfer Protocol (FTP). Some use product-specific protocols like Microsoft's *FrontPage Extensions*. Neither of these is a true, standardized Web protocol.

Another half-solution is to allow publishing through a small "text entry box" on a Web page. Some bulletin-board websites use this technique. If you have ever edited more than a few lines in this environment, you will know how inconvenient it is – like mowing the lawn with hand-clippers.

Finally we have a real Web protocol for writing to Web sites. It is called *WebDAV* because it allows *Web-based Distributed Authoring and Versioning*.

WebDAV is an extension to HTTP that uses XML extensively to represent complex, structured values that can be associated with documents for searching and management. WebDAV is already supported by the Microsoft Office software products and the Apache Web server. That means it has already passed a significant milestone: most people buying new computers will have WebDAV-enabled content creation capability and most people deploying new Web servers will have free access to a WebDAV implementation. Even so, it takes time for these technologies to become ubiquitous and popular. WebDAV promises to one day correct a long-acknowledged limitation of the World Wide Web.

6.4.3 *Remote procedure call (XML-RPC)*

A procedure is a basic unit of program behavior. In many languages, computer programs are made by stringing together calls from one procedure to another. A *Remote Procedure Call (RPC)* protocol extends this paradigm to calls between computers.

You can do remote procedure calls in XML using a protocol called XML-RPC. Example 6-1 is the XML portion of an XML-RPC message that invokes a procedure called `calculateTax`. The `methodCall` element invokes the procedure. The `methodName` element names the procedure to be called. The `param` elements provide the information that the calculation requires.

Example 6-1. XML-RPC method call

```
<?xml version="1.0"?>
<methodCall>
  <methodName>calculateTax</methodName>
  <params>
    <param><value><i4>Alaska</i4></value></param>
    <param><value><i4>41</i4></value></param>
  </params>
</methodCall>
```

Example 6-2 shows the response to the remote procedure call in Example 6-1. The Alaskan sales tax is $1.87.

Example 6-2. XML-RPC method response

```
<?xml version="1.0"?>
<methodResponse>
  <params>
    <param><double>1.87</double></param>
  </params>
</methodResponse>
```

The primary virtue of XML-RPC is that the programmer does not need to think about this stuff at all. In many programming languages, one can just call a procedure, using traditional procedure call syntax, and all of the remote procedure stuff happens automatically.

Some programmers consider this approach heresy and would rather control the details of the transmission themselves. Neither side is right or wrong. Suffice to say that the right approach depends on a variety of factors including how fast and secure your network is and how much time you have available to solve a problem![4]

---

4. XML-RPC is quick and dirty. The details of its specification leave quite a bit to be desired. For instance it has poor support for the character sets needed for languages other than English. Nevertheless, if you have to connect two disparate systems and are willing to accept some limitations, you cannot find a much easier protocol to use than XML-RPC.

There is a subtle but important difference between WebDAV and XML-RPC. WebDAV is designed to do exactly one thing: allow you to manage content over the Internet. XML-RPC is more of a meta-protocol. Just as XML is a language for defining new computer-processable languages, XML-RPC is a protocol that allows you to define new protocols.

In Example 6-1, we invented a tax calculation protocol. We could use XML-RPC to create protocols that talk about anything we like – the price of tea in China or the odds in Vegas. XML-RPC is really more of a *protocol framework* than a single, domain-specific protocol like WebDAV. If WebDAV were invented today it might be built on top of XML-RPC. Or more likely on top of a newer specification that has more corporate backing, SOAP.

6.4.4 *Slippery SOAP*

We've looked at the SOAP protocol in connection with Web services, but SOAP actually started life years earlier as a sibling to XML-RPC.[5] Versions 1.0 and 1.1 were created by a Microsoft-led consortium, but SOAP 1.2 is an official W3C Recommendation.

SOAP is one of the few things that Microsoft, IBM and Sun all agree is useful. It is even becoming popular in the Linux world, which tends to be suspicious of Microsoft-sponsored technologies. That's all good news.

The bad news is that over the years SOAP has morphed into something quite different from the RPC protocol it started as. RPC is now just one possible SOAP configuration. So even though large software vendors agree strongly that SOAP should be used, there is quite a bit of disagreement about the best way to use it!

Let's look at some of the issues.

---

5. The name originally stood for "Simple Object Access Protocol" – an attempt to profit from association with the all-important object paradigm. However, the acronym has since been abandoned, along with the pretense that SOAP has anything to do with objects.

6.4.4.1   The customizer isn't always right!

Like XML-RPC, SOAP is a meta-protocol; it allows you to define new protocols based on it. The big difference between the two is in how this is accomplished.

XML-RPC is restricted to a fixed set of XML element types; you customize it by changing the elements' data content. There is a *SOAP RPC style* that works the same way.

However, there is also the *SOAP document literal style*, which allows SOAP messages to include element types that you define, even those with complex hierarchical structures. Many feel that such custom vocabularies are an unnecessary complexity that adds to the difficulty of using SOAP.

6.4.4.1.1   *The ice cream is delayed*

If you go to an ice cream store to buy some ice cream, you expect to receive it immediately. That is a *synchronous* transaction.

On the other hand, if you order a tub of specialty ice cream over the phone (or the Internet!) you expect it to arrive later. That's an *asynchronous* transaction.

A protocol is an *asynchronous protocol* if the person making the request does not wait around for a response but rather expects it to arrive some time later. SOAP can be used as an asynchronous protocol.

SOAP's creators feel that asynchronous messaging is much more appropriate for high volume systems than is RPC. But many developers feel that SOAP's asynchronous messaging capability is outweighed by RPC's ease of use: it resembles a programming language procedure call.

6.4.4.1.2   *The natives are REST-less*

Some developers argue that SOAP should be used in a fashion that is more compatible with the Web as we know it. They believe URIs should be used to address documents served as XML and that SOAP should use standard Web security techniques and protocols.

They cite WebDAV as a protocol that, like SOAP, carries an XML payload, yet uses the REST development techniques that maintain Web principles. This issue is most heated in the area of Web services; we discuss it in 5.4.5, "Web services for the REST of us!", on page 123.

6.5 | Conclusion

We have examined some of the key programming technologies and concepts that support the implementation of XML applications. Even if you are not a developer, you now know the "secrets" of the XML programmers – even some of the dirtier ones![6]

In the next chapter, we'll look at the most important terms in the XML lexicon: the ones that people misuse the most often!

---

6. Secrets, that is – not programmers!

XML Jargon Demystifier™

- Structured vs. unstructured
- Tag vs. element
- Document type, DTD, and markup declarations
- Schema and schema definitions
- Notations and characters
- Documents and data

Chapter

7

> "When I use a word," Humpty Dumpty said, in a rather scornful tone, "it means just what I choose it to mean, neither more nor less." – Lewis Carroll, *Through the Looking Glass*

O ne of the problems in learning a new technology like XML is getting used to the jargon. A good book will hold you by the hand, introduce terms gradually, and use them precisely and consistently.

Out in the real word, though, people use imprecise terminology that often makes it hard to understand things, let alone compare products. And, unlike authors,[1] they sometimes just plain get things wrong.

For example, you may see statements like "XML documents are either well-formed or valid." As you've learned from this book, that simply isn't true. *All* XML documents are well-formed; some of them are also valid.[2]

In this book, we've taken pains to edit the application and tool chapters to use consistent and accurate terminology. However, for product literature and other documents you read, the mileage may vary. So we've prepared a handy guide to the important XML jargon, both right and wrong. Think of it as middleware for XML knowledge.

---

1. We should be so lucky!
2. So does that mean a merely well-formed document is "invalid"? No, for the reasons described in 2.7, "Well-formedness and validity", on page 47. Hey, we didn't promise to justify XML jargon, just to explain it.

7.1 | Structured vs. unstructured

Structured is arguably the most commonly used word to characterize the essence of markup languages. It is also the most ambiguous and most often misused word.

There are four common meanings:

structured = abstract

XML documents are frequently referred to as structured while other text, such as renditions in notations like RTF, is called *unstructured.* Separating "structure from style" is considered the hallmark of a markup language. But in fact, renditions can have a rich structure, composed of elements like pages, columns, and blocks. The real distinction being made is between "abstract" and "rendered".

structured = managed

This is one of the meanings that folks with a database background usually have in mind. Structured information is managed as a common resource and is accessible to the entire enterprise. Unfortunately, there are also departmental and individual databases and their content isn't "structured" in quite the same sense.

structured = predictable

This is another alternative for relational database people. Structured data is captured from business transactions, comes in easily identified granules, and has metadata that identifies its semantics. In contrast, *freeform data* is normally buried in reports, with no metadata, and therefore must be "parsed" (by reading it!) to determine what it is and what it means. If an essentially freeform document has islands of structured data within it, the document might be termed *semi-structured.* See 7.11, "Documents and data", on page 152 for more on this.

structured = possessing structure

This is the dictionary meaning, and the one used in this book. There is usually the (sometimes unwarranted) implication that the structure is fine-grained (rich, detailed), making components accessible at efficient levels of granularity. A structure can be very simple – a single really big component – but nothing is unstructured. All structure is well-defined and "predictable" (in the sense of consistent), it just may not be very granular.

These distinctions aren't academic. It is very important to know which "structured" a vendor means.

What if your publishing system has bottlenecks because you are maintaining four rendered versions of your documents in different representations? It isn't much of a solution to "structure" them in a database so that modifying one version warns you to modify the others.

You'll want to have a single "structured" – that is, abstract – version from which the others can be rendered. And if you find that your document has scores of pages unrelieved by sub-headings, you may want to "structure" it more finely so that both human readers and software can deal with it in smaller chunks.

Keep these different meanings in mind when you read about "structured" and "unstructured". In this book, we try to confine our use of the word to its dictionary meaning, occasionally (when it is clear from the context) with the implication of "fine-grained".

7.2 | Tag vs. element

Tags aren't the same thing as elements. Tags describe elements and delimit them.

In Figure 7-1 the pet carrier, metaphorically speaking, is an element. The contents of the carrier is the *content* of an element. It is bounded by two tags.

The start-tag, at the left, describes the element. It contains three names:

- The *element-type name* (dog), which says what type of element it is.
- A *unique identifier*, or id (Spike), which says which particular element it is.
- The name of an attribute that describes some other property of the element: weight="8 lbs".

Figure 7-1   Tags aren't elements!

The end-tag, at the right, marks the end of the element. It repeats the element-type name.

When people talk about a *tag name*:

1. They are referring to the element-type name (in this case, dog).
2. They are making an error, because tags aren't named.

And when they talk about an *element name*:

1. They are again referring to the element-type name.
2. They are again making an error, because an element is named by its unique identifier (in this case, Spike).

7.3 | Content

We know that formally the *content* of an element is what occurs between the start-tag and the end-tag. Therefore, the content of a document is what occurs between the first start-tag and the last end-tag of the document.

So when people say that "XML separates content from presentation", they really mean that XML lets you separate abstract data (in the document) from rendition information (in a stylesheet).

When they say "an XML document has content and structure", they mean it has data and structure.

People also refer to "content" or "XML content" as a commodity: "Our website has dynamic, involving, interactive, rich, multimedia XML content". We do that as well in this book when the context is clear (but without the adjectives!).

Some people – not us – also use the term "content" when making a principled distinction between POP data intended for people ("content") and MOM data intended for machines ("data").

7.4 | Document type, DTD, and markup declarations

A *document type* is a class of similar documents, like telephone books, technical manuals, or (when they are marked up as XML) inventory records.

A *document type definition* (*DTD*) is the set of rules for using XML to represent documents of a particular type. These rules might exist only in your mind as you create a document, or they may be written out.

Markup declarations, such as those in Example 7-1, are XML's way of writing out DTDs.

Example 7-1. Markup declarations in the file `greeting.dtd`.

```
<!ELEMENT greeting (salutation, addressee) >
<!ELEMENT salutation (#PCDATA) >
<!ELEMENT addressee  (#PCDATA) >
```

It is easy to mix up these three constructs: a document type, XML's markup rules for documents of that type (the DTD), and the expression of those rules (the markup declarations). It is necessary to keep the constructs separate if you are dealing with two or more of them at the same time, as when discussing alternative ways to express a DTD. But most of the time, even in this book, "DTD" will suffice for referring to any of the three.

7.5 | Schema and schema definition

The programming and database worlds have introduced some new terminology to XML.

We now speak of a document type as a kind of *schema*, a conception of the common characteristics of some class of things. Similarly, a DTD is a *schema definition*, the rules for using XML to represent documents conforming to the schema.

Schema definitions are invariably written out in a notation called a *schema definition language*, or simply a *schema language*. And as with DTDs, the word "schema" can serve for all these purposes when there is no ambiguity.

7.6 | Document, XML document, and instance

The term *document* has two distinct meanings in XML.

Consider a really short XML document that might be rendered as:

Hello World

The *conceptual document* that you see in your mind's eye when you read the rendition is intuitively what you think of as the document. Communicating that conception is the reason for using XML in the first place.

In a formal, syntactic sense, though, the complete text (markup + data, remember) of Example 7-2, is the *XML document*. Perhaps surprisingly, that includes the markup declarations for its DTD (shown in Example 7-1).

The XML document, in other words, is a character string that *represents* the conceptual document.[3]

In this example, much of that string consists of the markup declarations, which express the greeting DTD. Only the last four lines describe the conceptual document, which is an instance of a greeting. Those lines are called the *document instance*.

Example 7-2. A greeting document.

```
<?xml version="1.0"?>
<!DOCTYPE greeting SYSTEM "file://greeting.dtd">
<greeting>
<salutation>Hello</salutation>
<addressee>World</addressee>
</greeting>
```

That term gets flipped around when schema languages are involved. Unlike DTD declarations, schema languages are XML-based, so a schema definition must be stored as an XML document in its own right (a *schema document*). That means an instance of a schema definition is a separate document, so it is known as an *instance document*.

7.7 | What's the meta?

Nothing. What did you think was the meta?[4]

There are two "meta" words that come up regularly when computer types talk about XML: metadata and metalanguage.

---

3. After a program parses the string it usually keeps an *object model* in memory so that it can navigate and access data directly in terms of the conceptual document structure. During processing it usually updates the object model, then *serializes* it as the result XML document.
4. Sorry about that!

7.7.1 *Metadata*

Metadata is data about data. The date, publisher's name, and author's name of a book are metadata about the book, while the data of the book is its content. The DTD and markup tags of an XML document are also metadata. If you choose to represent the author's name as an element, then it is both data and metadata.

If you get the idea that the line between data and metadata is a fluid one, you are right. And as long as your document representation and system let you access and process metadata as though it were data, it doesn't much matter where you draw that line.

Be careful when talking to database experts, though. In their discipline "metadata" typically refers only to the schema.

7.7.2 *Metalanguage*

You may hear some DTDs referred to as languages, rather than document types. HTML is a prominent example. There's nothing special about them, it is just another way of looking at the way a markup language works.

Remember that an XML document is a character string that represents some conceptual document. The rules for creating a valid string are like the rules of a language: There is a *vocabulary* of element type and attribute names, and a *grammar* that determines where the names can be used.

These language rules come from the DTD or schema, which in turn follows the rules of XML. A language, such as XML, which you can use to define other languages (such as DTDs), is called a *metalanguage*. XML document types are sometimes called *XML-based languages*.

7.8 | Notations and characters

Normally, the characters in a document are interpreted one at a time. They are given the meaning assigned by the document character set, which for XML documents is Unicode. So the character a is interpreted as the letter "a" and the character < is interpreted as the mathematical symbol "less-than".

A character-based *notation* is a set of rules for interpreting a *sequence* of characters at once, and giving the sequence a meaning that is different from the character-set meaning of the individual characters. The HTML notation, for example, interprets `<a name=b>` as the start-tag of an "a" element.

Computer languages (including markup languages and languages defined by markup languages), document and data formats like RTF and JPEG, and the string representations of datatypes, are all examples of notations.

The distinction between various kinds of notations can be rather esoteric. The important thing is that characters don't have their usual meaning. You need a *parser* to figure out what that meaning is. But XML is simple enough that, after reading Part 18, "XML Core Tutorials", you should be able to parse XML documents yourself.

7.9 | Coding, encoding, and markup

People refer to computer programs as *code*, and to the act of programming as *coding*.

There is also the word *encoding*, which refers to the way that characters are represented as ones and zeros in computer storage. XML has a declaration for specifying an encoding.

You'll often see (in places other than this book) phrases like "XML-encoded data", "coded in HTML", or "XML coding".

But using XML isn't coding. Not in the sense of programming, and not in the sense of character encoding. What those phrases mean are "XML document", "marked-up in HTML", and "XML markup".[5]

7.10 | URL and URN and URI and URI reference

"U R kidding!", U might think, but we R not!

---

5. Although dynamic HTML pages contain so much scripting that the phrase "HTML coding" is sometimes warranted.

There really are four different things that look like URLs, and act like them as well. We explain the differences and their significance in 64.2, "Uniform Resource Identifiers", on page 1058. But unless we make a point of the difference in a specific context, you can safely treat them as equivalent when reading the book.

Now when you see *URI* in the text, you'll know that it isn't a typo.

7.11 | Documents and data

We presented the easy illustrated guide to the documents and data relationship in Chapter 3, "The XML usage spectrum", on page 54, but it's worth summarizing the high points here.

7.11.1 *It's all data!*

In an XML document, the text that isn't markup is data. You can edit it directly with an XML editor or plain text editor. With a stylesheet and a rendering system you can cause it to be displayed in various ways.

In a database, you can't touch the data directly. You can enter and revise it only through forms controlled by the database program. However, rendition is similar to XML documents, except that the stylesheet is usually called something like "report template".

The important thing is that, in both cases, the data can be kept in the abstract, untainted by the style information for rendering it. This is very different from word processing documents, of course, which normally keep their data in rendered form.

7.11.2 *Data-centric vs. document-centric*

Documents, data, and processes are sometimes characterized as "data-centric" in contrast to "document-centric". Since all XML documents (except empty ones) contain data, these terms are actually a misleading shorthand. Worse, they are applied in two very different contexts:

■ how much the XML resembles relational data; and,

■ whether you have to deal with the whole document at once.

7.11.2.1   How relational is it?

The *data-centric* misnomer is common among database hackers trying to describe structures that map easily onto relational tables and primitive datatypes. Structures that don't are called *document-centric*.

The intended meaning of data-centric is that the document structure – really element structure, since a document is essentially just the largest element – is *strongly predictable*.

An element has a *strongly predictable structure* if it (and its subelements, if any) are constrained to contain either:

■ type-sequenced elements (e.g., a sequence of elements of the types: `quantity`, `itemNum`, `description`, `price`),
■ data characters only (i.e., #PCDATA), or
■ nothing at all.

Strongly predictable elements can easily be visualized as forms. A business transaction document such as a purchase order is more likely to be strongly predictable than a memo.

In addition to "data-centric", the misnomer *highly structured* is sometimes used. However, *highly predictable* is a more precise term, particularly as many documents that don't meet our definition of "strongly predictable" are still much more predictable than they are freeform.

7.11.2.2   How granular is it?

Another (mis)use of *data-centric* is to characterize the storage and/or access of documents at the level of individual elements, rather than the entire document at once (*document-centric*). Once again, the usage is misleading because what it describes has nothing to do with data per se, and because it implies a contradiction between data and documents that does not exist.

7.11.3 *Document processing vs. data processing*

While "data-centric" and "document-centric" aren't rigorous terms for characterizing information, they are quite meaningful when applied to processing. XML, however, because it can preserve abstract data (like a database) but still be interchanged and processed as a character string (like a document), is starting to break down the historic separation of the two paradigms. Applications can now intermix data processing and document processing techniques to get the job done.

7.11.4 *Comparing documents to data*

Since documents contain data, what are people doing when they compare or contrast documents and data?

They are being human. Which is to say, they are using a simplified expression for the complex and subtle relationship shown in Table 7-1. They are comparing the typical kind of data that is found in XML and word processing (WP) documents with business process (BP) transactional data, which usually resides in databases.

Table 7-1   (typical data in) **Documents and** (business process) **Data**

	XML data	**BP data**	**WP data**
Presentability	Abstraction	Abstraction	Rendition
Source	Written	Captured	Written
Structure	Hierarchy+ links	Fields	Paragraphs
Purpose	Presentation	Processing	Presentation
Representation	Document	Database	Document

Note that the characteristics in the table are typical, not fixed. For example, as we've shown many times in this book, XML data can be a rendition and WP data can be an abstraction. In addition, XML data could:

- Be captured from a data entry form or a program (rather than written);
- Consist of simple fields like those in a relational table (rather than a deeply nested hierarchy with links among the nodes); and
- Be intended for processing (rather than presentation).

In casual use, the term "document" connotes the data characteristics shown in Table 7-1 for "XML data" or "WP data", whichever is being referred to.

When "data" is contrasted with "document", it means the "BP data" column of the table. However, in other contexts, it could refer to "XML data" or all data.

We are more specific whenever a different meaning is intended in this chapter (and elsewhere in the book).

Caution   The true relationship between documents and data isn't as widely understood as it ought to be, even among experts. That is in part because the two domains existed independently for so long. This fact can complicate communication.

7.12 | And in conclusion

The matrix in Figure 7-2 ties together a number of the concepts we've been discussing.

The top row contains two conceptual documents, as they might appear in your mind's eye. Actually, they are two states of the same document, the one we saw in Example 2-1.[6]

---

6. But for clarity only the second pair of QUESTION and ANSWER elements is shown here.

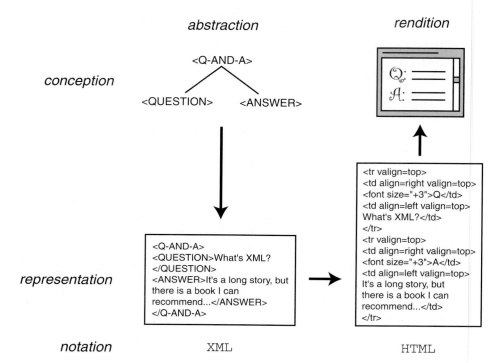

Figure 7-2   A rendition can be generated from an abstraction

The left column shows the document in its abstract state, while the right column shows it rendered.

The bottom row shows the computer representations of the abstraction and the rendition. The abstraction uses the XML notation while the rendition uses HTML. The horizontal arrow indicates that the rendition was generated from the abstraction.

The diagram illustrates some important points:

- Abstraction and rendition are two *presentability* states that a document can be in. Renditions are ready to be presented; abstractions aren't.
- Renditions can be generated from abstractions automatically.
- Markup languages can represent both abstractions and renditions; "structuring in XML" is no guarantee that you'll get an abstraction.

■ The *computer representation* of a document incorporates two ideas: presentability and notation. In other words, the representation of a document is either an abstraction or a rendition, and is either in an XML-based language or some other notation.

Hint   The road ahead diverges at this point. If your main interest is in what XML can do for you, rather than what makes it tick, proceed with the application and tool discussions in Part 2 through Part 17. On the other hand, if you took clocks apart as a child, you may first want to read the tutorial chapters, beginning with Part 18, "XML Core Tutorials", on page 764, before continuing.

Three-tier Applications

- Content aggregation
- Middle-tier servers
- Data sources

Part Two

The advent of the personal computer (PC) popularized a two-tier networking model called *client/server*. Servers are typically large computers that control proprietary databases and act as *data sources*. They "serve" that data to end-users whose software, running on PCs (the "clients"), requests it.

Both client and server have to understand the proprietary representation in which the data is interchanged. And if a client needs data from several data sources, it has to deal with multiple servers and be able to understand the proprietary data formats of all of them.

XML is changing all that because it is a universal data representation. XML facilitates a *three-tier* model, in which a single *middle-tier* server can be an intermediary that aggregates data from multiple sources and presents all of it at once to the client.

In this part, we look at three-tier Web applications from all three sides. First we see the end-user's perspective from the client side, then take a closer look at how a middle-tier application works. Finally, we'll examine how remote data sources can deliver XML to the middle tier.

Personalized frequent-flyer website

Introductory Discussion

- Three-tier XML Web application
- Client/server Web model has changed
- Website personalization

Contributing experts: Dianne Kennedy of XMLXperts Ltd.,
http://www.xmlxperts.com, and Bruce Sharpe

> If the original frequent-flyer website model had been the ultimate in doing business on the Web, then business on the Web would never have taken off. This chapter explains how the middle tier can help keep a business flying!

I f you travel by air, you have probably stopped by your favorite airline frequent-flyer website. Let's consider how that experience would have been in the early days of the Web.

It might have been fun to find the site and to see all the last minute bargains offered for frequent flyers. Perhaps those specials were initially enough to motivate you to return to the site, if only to dream of taking a vacation in the middle of your biggest project!

8.1 | Client/server frequent-flyer sites

Beyond viewing the posted specials, perhaps you interacted with the site in a limited way, by entering your frequent flyer number to see your current point balance. But during heavy traffic hours on the Web, such interactions might have taken quite a long time.

And once you knew how many points you'd accumulated, what about the whole series of new questions it stimulated for which the website couldn't provide an answer. At that point, you had to resort to calling the toll-free number to learn more about your award options and eventually book a flight.

Bottom line: once the novelty wore off, that Web experience, like countless others, was less than satisfying.

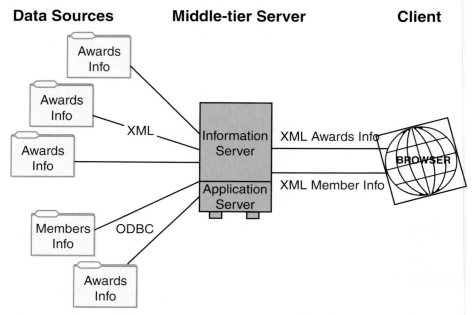

Figure 8-1   Three-tier XML processing architecture.

8.2 | What's wrong with this Web model?

The original Web model that we've described here is a "client/server" model. In this model, any personalized interaction takes place on the Web server you have contacted. As a result, there is little of it.

Instead, the Web pages you saw were static brochures rendered in HTML to provide eye-appealing display. In fact, some of the websites that were rated highest in that early market were those that provided multi-media sizzle – heavy on graphics, streaming media, animation, and sound. Personalized content, while an increasingly important consideration, had not yet become the primary distinguishing characteristic of a successful website. But as the Web continued its shift from simply providing entertainment value to facilitating business transactions, it became clear that personalization was the way to win customers.

In an airline frequent-flyer website, there is a great deal of HTML information that the customer can view. If this information and its associated links changes daily, the website becomes more interesting and is more likely to generate return visits. Likewise, interactivity generates more site traffic.

But in the two-tier client/server model, interactivity requires lengthy periods where the customer must be connected to remote servers. Queries from the customer go to the server, and resulting responses are shipped back to the customer for viewing in HTML. Unfortunately, a Web server can handle only a limited number of connections at one time.

Every time a new piece of information is requested, a transaction between the client's Web browser and remote Web servers is required. Sooner or later the number of transactions slows the server and the customer experiences lengthy time-outs when queries are processed and data is transferred back to the browser.

8.3 | A better model for doing business on the Web

Today, XML has enabled a new breed of Web server software, one that allows the Web developer to add a new *middle-tier server* to the Web model. This new three-tier Web architecture is illustrated in Figure 8-1.

Remember, in the old Web model, the customer using a browser on the client interacted directly with data sources on remote servers. The client maintained its connection throughout the interactive session. Each query was sent a response in HTML which could be directly viewed by the client browser. Maintaining the connection between the client and server was critical.

In the new three-tier Web model, the information that fits the profile of the customer is retrieved at once from remote data sources by software on the middle tier, either as XML documents or through a direct database connection such as ODBC. From that point, continued interaction with the remote data sources is no longer required. The connection to the remote servers can be, and is, terminated.[1]

Once all information that fits the customer profile has been assembled by software on the middle tier, it is sent in XML to the client. Now the requirement for further interaction between the client and the middle-tier server is eliminated as well.

Figure 8-2   "Welcome to *Softland Air*"

Rich XML data, directly usable by client applications and scripting languages like *JavaScript*, has been delivered to the client. The connection

---

1. Incidentally, the term "three-tier" is a relative one. Any of the remote data sources could itself be the client of a three-tier application, so if you are actually counting tiers between the end user and the farthest data source, the number could be much higher than three. Nevertheless, the architectural model remains three-tiered.

between the client and middle-tier server can now be terminated. At this point, all computing becomes client-based, resulting in a much more efficient use of the Web and a much more satisfying customer experience.

To understand the new three-tier Web model better, one must understand the role XML plays as an enabling technology. One must also understand how efficient delivery of structured abstract data to the client makes all the difference.

8.4 | An XML-enabled frequent-flyer website

Initially, differences between the *Softland Air* XML-enabled frequent-flyer website shown in Figure 8-2 and those early sites may not be apparent. Both provide a pleasing HTML-rendered site brochure. Both enable you to select the services you wish to use. But here the similarities end. New business functions, not possible with non-XML sites, quickly become apparent.

Figure 8-3   "Members, sign in here"

From the initial *Softland Air* screen you can select the "frequent flyer" option, which causes the page in Figure 8-3 to be displayed. The frequent-flyer page asks you to enter your membership identification number.

Once you have entered your membership number, a personalized, interactive Web experience begins. The next screen that is displayed (Figure 8-4) not only returns your number of frequent flyer points, but shows you destinations for which you have already qualified for awards. This screen will vary from member to member, based upon the points a member has in the frequent-flyer database and other personal information the database holds, such as city of origin.

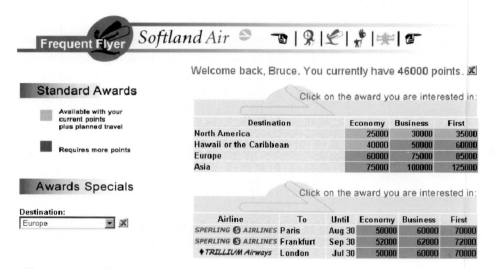

Figure 8-4   Personalized frequent-flyer information

In addition to showing you the awards you have already earned, the *Softland Air* website enables you to select destinations of interest. You can see that you have 46,000 points and are qualified to go anywhere in North America in economy through first class. You can also go to Hawaii or the Caribbean by economy class. You do not qualify to go to Europe, but you can see that you nearly have enough points for a European trip.

Suppose you are interested in going to Europe. To learn more about options to get there, you would select a destination on the "Awards Specials" part of the screen. This destination information is added to your profile, along with your city of origin and the number of points you currently have. It will be used to personalize the ensuing transactions.

Once you have selected a destination, the Web page in Figure 8-5 shows you awards, both on *Softland Air* and on partner airlines, that fit the destination you have selected. From this screen you can see what destinations in Europe most nearly fit with the number of award points you hold. As you do not currently qualify for a trip to Europe, you can use the "Planned Trips" portion of the screen to determine what trips you can take by this summer in order to qualify for the award you want.

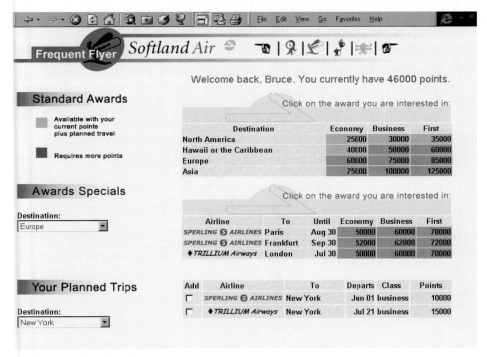

Figure 8-5   Trip planning

Using the screen in Figure 8-5, you can plan trips and even book tickets. In this way you can put enough miles in the bank to be able to earn the award to Europe.

Notice how the entire transaction is personalized for the client interacting with the website. It is also important to note that aside from logging on to enter your membership number and select the frequent-flyer transaction, all other transactions occurred on the PC in your home or office. Because the middle-tier server can aggregate data from remote sources, package it as XML documents, and send it to the client, a continuous connection to the data source servers is not required.

This model is one that leading business sites on the Web have striven for and can now achieve. And XML, working with an information server in the middle tier, is the reason.

8.5 | Understanding the *Softland Air* scenario

When you connect to the *Softland Air* website you first sign in with your membership ID. Your membership number is used to extract your name, the number of award points you have earned, and your city of origin from the "member information" database. This information is sent from remote data sources to the middle-tier server, which combines it into an XML document (see Example 8-1). Once the data is in XML, the member name, city of origin, and number of award points can be addressed and used by middle-tier and client applications.

Example 8-1. XML document generated from member information database

```
<CUSTOMER
  MEMBERID="1AB345"
  FIRST="Bruce"
  LAST="Sharpe"
  POINTS="46000"
  CITY="Vancouver"/>
```

At this point, the middle-tier software knows who signed on. It can request all relevant awards information from both its own awards database and the remote databases maintained by its partner airlines. Example 8-2 shows the XML data for award specials items from remote awards databases. Note that because this data is in XML, we can easily see the number of points required for each award, the partner airline name, the city of origin, the destination, and the dates the special runs. Again, this information is available for use by both middle-tier and client-side processing based on member queries.

Example 8-2. XML document generated from award specials database

```
<special_item
  economy="50000"
  business ="60000"
  first   ="70000"
  partner_name="Sperling Airlines"
  from_city="Vancouver"
  to_city="Paris"
  start   ="02/Apr/1998"
  end   ="Aug 30"/>
<special_item
  economy="52000"
  business ="62000"
  first   ="72000"
  partner_name="Sperling Airlines"
  from_city="Vancouver"
  to_city="Frankfurt"
  start   ="02/Apr/1998"
  end   ="Sep 30"/>
<special_item
  economy="50000"
  business="60000"
  first="70000"
  partner_name="Trillium Airways"
  from_city="Vancouver"
  to_city="London"
  start="01/Apr/1998"
  end="Jul 30"/>
```

The middle-tier server can also request all planned flight point earnings from all remote flight information databases, as shown in Example 8-3. We can easily see the number of points that would be earned from each flight, the partner airline name, the city of origin, the destination, and the date of flight and class of service. This information is available for use by middle-tier and client-side processing.

The information that is sent to the middle tier is compact, personalized, and precise. It differs from HTML because it contains the actual abstract data, not the look of the screen. Middle-tier software acts to assemble and deliver the right information at the right time, minimizing Web traffic and providing a higher degree of user interaction and satisfaction.

Example 8-3. XML document with flight point earnings

```
<flight
   points="10000"
   partner_name = "Sperling Airlines"
   from_city = "Vancouver"
   to_city = "New York"
   depart="Jun 01"
   flightclass="business"/>
<flight
   points="15000"
   partner_name = "Trillium Airways"
   from_city = "Vancouver"
   to_city = "New York"
   depart="Jul 21"
   flightclass="business"/>
```

8.6 | Towards the Brave New Web

The World Wide Web continues to evolve rapidly. Today the hottest entertainment websites are still those that provide multimedia sizzle. But for business sites, dynamic personalized content is increasingly important.

XML allows the website developer to add a new middle-tier server to the Web model. It is this middle tier that enables business transactions in a way that was simply not possible before XML.

The *Softland Air* scenario shows how a middle-tier server, using XML as a structured information interchange representation, enables personalized data aggregation and organization from multiple remote data sources, and interactive delivery to client browsers based upon end-user requirements.

Building an online auction website

Application Discussion

- Three-tier Web application
- Dynamic generation of XML documents
- Extracting data from XML documents
- Creating a user interface
- Demo on CD-ROM

Sponsor: Microsoft Corporation, http://msdn.microsoft.com/xml
Contributing expert: Charles Heinemann

Chapter

9

An online auction is the epitome of a complex real-time interactive application – not to mention being the hottest business-to-consumer (B2C) business model on the Web! This chapter describes a realistic *Auction Demo* that shows that even complex applications can be based on straightforward use of the three-tier Web architecture.

T he *Auction Demo* is a three-tier Web application that simulates an online auction using technologies that have been available since *Internet Explorer 5.01* (IE 5.01). It allows you to view the items available for auction, place bids on those items, and monitor the bids placed by fellow bidders.

Like other three-tier Web applications, the *Auction Demo* has data sources on the back end, a user interface on the client, and a Web server in the middle. We'll see how it was developed, using just three permanent Web pages:

userInterface.htm

This page uses *Dynamic HTML* (DHTML) to allow the Web browser to present the auction information to the user. It contains scripts that collect or update data on the middle tier by requesting *Active Server Pages* (ASP).

auction.asp

This page is an ASP file. When userInterface.htm requests this page, the scripts in it are executed on the server. The scripts generate auction.xml, an XML document that contains the latest auction data, which is delivered to the client.

makebid.asp

This page is requested by userInterface.htm when the user wants to make a bid. It is executed on the middle tier, causing the data source to be updated with the new bid information.

The user interface (UI) for the *Auction Demo* is shown in Figure 9-1. It is the rendition of the userInterface.htm *Dynamic HTML* page, which is downloaded to the client when the user clicks on a link to the auction.

That page has scripts within it that handle all the client-side activity. That includes requesting data from the middle tier in order to display the most current values of the items and bids. We'll see later how the UI page does its thing, but first let's look at how the middle tier collects and transmits the data. It does so by packaging the data as XML documents.

9.1 | Getting data from the middle tier

The role of the middle tier in a Web application is to gather information from data sources and deliver it in a consistent manner to clients. In the *Auction Demo* we start with a single data source, an ODBC-compliant database. (Later we'll see how multiple data sources of different kinds can be accessed.)

The "Auction" database used for the *Auction Demo* is a relational database with two tables, an "Item" table and a "Bids" table. The "Item" table contains data about each of the items up for auction. It is shown in Figure 9-2.

For the sake of clarity, we'll just cover the "Item" table in this chapter (the "Bids" are handled similarly). You can see the full demo in the Microsoft folder on the CD-ROM. We want to deliver the data in that table in the form of an XML document, so the client's user interface page won't have to know anything about the actual data source.

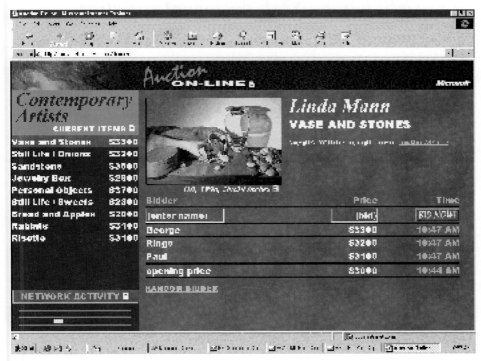

Figure 9-1   The *Auction Demo* user interface.

Title	Artist	Dimensions	Materials	Year
Vase and Stones	Linda Mann	20x30 inches	Oil	1996
Still Life / Onions	Linda Mann	20x30 inches	Oil	1997
Sandstone	Linda Mann	20x30 inches	Oil	1995
Jewelry Box	Linda Mann	20x30 inches	Oil	1994
Personal Objects	Linda Mann	20x30 inches	Oil	1995
Still Life / Sweets	Linda Mann	20x30 inches	Oil	1994
Bread and Apples	Linda Mann	20x30 inches	Oil	1995
Rabbits	Linda Mann	20x30 inches	Oil	1996
Risotto	Linda Mann	20x30 inches	Oil	1995

Figure 9-2   The *Auction Demo* item table.

9.1.1   *Defining the XML document structure*

The key to creating useful XML documents is the proper structuring of the data. For the *Auction Demo*, that means deciding how a record in the "Item" table will be represented as an ITEM element in XML. There is a straightforward mapping, shown in the data-less element in Example 9-1.

Example 9-1. Template for an ITEM element

```
<ITEM>
  <TITLE></TITLE>
  <ARTIST></ARTIST>
  <DIMENSIONS></DIMENSIONS>
  <MATERIALS></MATERIALS>
  <YEAR></YEAR>
</ITEM>
```

For each field in the "Item" table, there is a corresponding subelement of the ITEM element.

To generate XML documents with these ITEM elements, the *Auction Demo* uses ASP files.

9.1.2   *Using ASP files to generate XML documents*

XML can be generated on the middle tier using *Active Server Pages*. ASP offers an environment in which Web authors can create documents dynamically by intermixing markup languages with in-line scripts. The scripts can be written in a variety of scripting languages, including *JScript* and *VBScript*, and can invoke server-side components to access databases, execute applications, and process information.

When a browser requests an ASP file, it is first processed by the server, which delivers a generated Web page containing standard markup.

In an ASP file, commands and scripts are delimited by "<%" and "%>". Everything not so delimited is markup or data that will appear in the generated page. For example, consider the trivial ASP file in Example 9-2.

Example 9-2. Sample ASP file

```
<%@ LANGUAGE = VBScript%>
<%DIM Total = 2%>
<AMOUNT><%=Total%></AMOUNT>
```

The file, after establishing that the scripting language is *VBScript*, creates the variable "Total" with the value "2". The following line generates an XML AMOUNT element whose content is generated by executing the small script, which in this case retrieves the value of "Total".

When the browser requests this file, it will actually receive the XML document that is generated from the file, as shown in Example 9-3.

Example 9-3. XML document generated by sample ASP file

```
<AMOUNT>2</AMOUNT>
```

Note that the ASP syntax (<%...%>) does not cause an XML parsing error. That is because the ASP file is not itself an XML document. The ASP file is processed on the server and only the generated XML document is returned to the client.

In the case of the *Auction Demo*, the file auction.asp is used to access the "Auction" database and generate XML containing the data within the "Item" and "Bids" tables. The ability to generate XML on the middle tier makes it possible to provide the Web application with content that can be manipulated on the client and refreshed without having to refresh the entire user interface.

In Example 9-4, auction.asp begins like the ASP file in Example 9-2, by declaring the scripting language. The next two lines are the XML declaration and the start-tag of the root element (AUCTIONBLOCK) of the XML document to be generated, which we will call "auction.xml".

Example 9-4. Start of auction.asp

```
<%@ LANGUAGE = VBScript %>
<?xml version="1.0"?>
<AUCTIONBLOCK>
```

Next, a connection to the "Auction" database is established and that connection is opened:

Example 9-5. Connecting to the database

```
<%
Set Conn = Server.CreateObject("ADODB.Connection")
Conn.Open "Auction","Auction","Auction"
%>
```

A "record set" variable (ItemRS) is now established to contain each record of the "Item" table as it is accessed, and a "Do While" loop is begun to perform the access.

Example 9-6. Preparing to access the "Item" records

```
<%
Set ItemRS = Conn.Execute("select * from item")
Do While Not ItemRS.EOF
%>
```

Next, the template in Example 9-1 is used to create the XML ITEM element that will be generated. Just as in Example 9-2, a small script is inserted as the content of each subelement of ITEM within auction.asp. In this case, the script extracts the corresponding field's data from the record set.

Example 9-7. Markup and scripts to generate an ITEM element

```
<ITEM>
  <TITLE><%=ItemRS("Title")%></TITLE>
  <ARTIST><%=ItemRS("Artist")%></ARTIST>
  <DIMENSIONS><%=ItemRS("Dimensions")%></DIMENSIONS>
  <MATERIALS><%=ItemRS("Materials")%></MATERIALS>
  <YEAR><%=ItemRS("Year")%></YEAR>
</ITEM>
```

After an ITEM element is generated, the script moves to the next record in the record set. The loop is then repeated. Once all of the records have been run through, the root element is ended.

Example 9-8. Repeating the loop and ending the document

```
<%
  ItemRS.MoveNext
Loop
%>
</AUCTIONBLOCK>
```

The complete auction.asp file is in Example 9-9.

Example 9-10 is an abridged version of the XML document (auction.xml) generated by the auction.asp file in Example 9-9.

9.1.3 *Generating XML from multiple databases*

One powerful reason to generate XML documents on the middle tier is that they can contain data that is sourced from multiple independent databases. The technique is similar to what we've already seen. The only difference is that multiple database connections are made instead of one.

The ASP file in Example 9-11 does just this, generating a single XML document with data from the databases "Gallery1" and "Gallery2".

Example 9-9. The complete auction.asp file

```
<%@ LANGUAGE = VBScript %>
<?xml version="1.0"?>
<AUCTIONBLOCK>
<%
Set Conn = Server.CreateObject("ADODB.Connection")
Conn.Open "Auction","Auction","Auction"
Set ItemRS = Conn.Execute("select * from item")
Do While Not ItemRS.EOF
%>
  <ITEM>
    <TITLE><%=ItemRS("Title")%></TITLE>
    <ARTIST><%=ItemRS("Artist")%></ARTIST>
    <DIMENSIONS><%=ItemRS("Dimensions")%></DIMENSIONS>
    <MATERIALS><%=ItemRS("Materials")%></MATERIALS>
    <YEAR><%=ItemRS("Year")%></YEAR>
  </ITEM>
<%
  ItemRS.MoveNext
Loop
%>
</AUCTIONBLOCK>
```

Example 9-10. Abridged auction.xml document generated by auction.asp

```
<?xml version="1.0"?>
<AUCTIONBLOCK>
  <ITEM>
    <TITLE>Vase and Stones</TITLE>
    <ARTIST>Linda Mann</ARTIST>
    <DIMENSIONS>20 X 30 inches</DIMENSIONS>
    <MATERIALS>Oil</MATERIALS>
    <YEAR>1996</YEAR>
  </ITEM>
  <ITEM>
  . . .
  </ITEM>
  . . .
</AUCTIONBLOCK>
```

The XML generated by the ASP file in Example 9-11 looks structurally just like Example 9-10, an AUCTIONBLOCK element with multiple ITEM children. However, the data content originates from two different data sources.

Also notice that, for the DIMENSIONS, MATERIALS, and YEAR elements, the source fields in the "Gallery2" database are actually labeled differently from

Example 9-11. Generating one XML document from two databases

```
<%@ LANGUAGE = VBScript %>
<?xml version="1.0"?>
<AUCTIONBLOCK>
<%
'Connect to the Gallery1 database data source
Set Conn = Server.CreateObject("ADODB.Connection")
Conn.Open "Gallery1","Gallery1","Gallery1"
Set ItemRS = Conn.Execute("select * from item")
Do While Not ItemRS.EOF
%>
  <ITEM>
    <TITLE><%=ItemRS("Title")%></TITLE>
    <ARTIST><%=ItemRS("Artist")%></ARTIST>
    <DIMENSIONS><%=ItemRS("Dimensions")%></DIMENSIONS>
    <MATERIALS><%=ItemRS("Materials")%></MATERIALS>
    <YEAR><%=ItemRS("Year")%></YEAR>
  </ITEM>
<%
  ItemRS.MoveNext
Loop
'Connect to the Gallery2 database data source
Set Conn = Server.CreateObject("ADODB.Connection")
Conn.Open "Gallery2","Gallery2","Gallery2"
Set ItemRS = Conn.Execute("select * from item")
Do While Not ItemRS.EOF
%>
  <ITEM>
    <TITLE><%=ItemRS("Title")%></TITLE>
    <ARTIST><%=ItemRS("Artist")%></ARTIST>
    <DIMENSIONS><%=ItemRS("Size")%></DIMENSIONS>
    <MATERIALS><%=ItemRS("Medium")%></MATERIALS>
    <YEAR><%=ItemRS("Date")%></YEAR>
  </ITEM>
<%
  ItemRS.MoveNext
Loop
%>
</AUCTIONBLOCK>
```

the corresponding fields in "Gallery1." One benefit of consolidating the data on the middle tier is that the semantics can be identified consistently, and therefore made more easily accessible.

9.1.4 *Generating XML from both databases and XML data sources*

The middle tier can source data of different kinds, not just databases. In Example 9-12, the ASP file, as in previous examples, first accesses data from "Gallery 1", an ODBC compliant database. However, it then adds data from "Gallery 3", a source of XML documents.

The Gallery3 XML document is processed by the *MSXML* parser (details below), which allows access to the document's data content. Note that there is no way – and no need – to tell whether Gallery3 is a persistent document, or was generated by another middle-tier application.

9.2 | Building the user interface

The user interface is critical to the success of any application. It must allow the user to interact with the application in an efficient and straightforward manner. The user interface for the *Auction Demo* was built using DHTML.

DHTML is a set of features introduced in *Internet Explorer 4.0* for creating interactive and visually interesting Web pages. It is based on existing HTML standards and is designed to interoperate with applications, *ActiveX* controls, and other embedded objects.

With DHTML a developer can create a robust and efficient UI without additional support from applications or embedded controls, or even return trips to the server. A *Dynamic HTML* page is self-contained, using styles and scripts to process user input and directly manipulate the HTML markup and other text within the page.

Let's see how userInterface.htm creates the *Auction Demo* interface by using scripts and the W3C Document Object Model. Two basic techniques are employed: procedural scripts and descriptive binding.

9.2.1 *Using procedural scripts*

Internet Explorer 5.01 includes the *MSXML* parser, which exposes the parsed XML document as a Document Object Model. Once exposed, scripts can access the data content of the XML elements and dynamically insert the data into the user interface.

Example 9-12. Generating one XML document from a database and another XML document

```
<%@ LANGUAGE = VBScript %>
<?xml version="1.0"?>
<AUCTIONBLOCK>
<%
'Connect to the Gallery1 database data source
Set Conn = Server.CreateObject("ADODB.Connection")
Conn.Open "Gallery1","Gallery1","Gallery1"
Set ItemRS = Conn.Execute("select * from item")
Do While Not ItemRS.EOF
%>
  <ITEM>
    <TITLE><%=ItemRS("Title")%></TITLE>
    <ARTIST><%=ItemRS("Artist")%></ARTIST>
    <DIMENSIONS><%=ItemRS("Dimensions")%></DIMENSIONS>
    <MATERIALS><%=ItemRS("Materials")%></MATERIALS>
    <YEAR><%=ItemRS("Year")%></YEAR>
  </ITEM>
<%
  ItemRS.MoveNext
Loop
'Connect to the Gallery3 XML document data source
Set XML = Server.CreateObject("MSXML2.DOMDocument")
XML.setProperty("ServerHTTPRequest",true)
XML.load("http://datasource3/Gallery3.xml")
Set Items = XML.documentElement.childNodes
For I = 0 to Items.length - 1
  Set Item = Items.childNodes.item(I)
%>
  <ITEM>
    <TITLE><%=Item.childNodes.item(0).text%></TITLE>
    <ARTIST><%=Item.childNodes.item(1).text%></ARTIST>
    <DIMENSIONS><%=Item.childNodes.item(2).text%></DIMENSIONS>
    <MATERIALS><%=Item.childNodes.item(3).text%></MATERIALS>
    <YEAR><%=Item.childNodes.item(4).text%></YEAR>
  </ITEM>
<%
Next
%>
</AUCTIONBLOCK>
```

The userInterface.htm code in Example 9-13 applies *MSXML* to auction.xml, the XML document generated by auction.asp. That creates an *ActiveX* object representing the parsed document.

Example 9-13. Creating the auction document object

```
var auction = new ActiveXObject("MSXML2.DOMDocument");
auction.load("http://Webserver/auction.asp");
```

In Example 9-14, the script next retrieves the root element. It then navigates the tree until it locates the TITLE element within the first ITEM element of auction.xml. The innerText property is used to insert the data content of TITLE into the user interface as the value of the item_title attribute, which appears on a DIV element.

Example 9-14. Extracting data from the auction document object

```
var root = auction.documentElement;
var item0 = root.childNodes.item(0);
var title = item0.childNodes.item(0).text;
document.all("item_title").innerText = title;
<DIV ID="item_title"></DIV>
```

One of the benefits of using procedural scripts to display XML documents is that you can manipulate the data content of an XML element before you display it. For example, if you wanted to display the dimensions of each painting using the metric system, rather than feet and inches, your script could simply convert the content of the DIMENSIONS element from inches to centimeters.

9.2.2 *Using descriptive data binding*

The *XML Data Source Object* (XML DSO) is a declarative alternative to the procedural scripts described in the last section. It enables the data of XML elements to be bound as the content of HTML documents.

Example 9-15. An *XML Data Source Object*

```
<XML ID="auction" SRC="auction.asp"></XML>
```

An XML DSO is shown in Example 9-15. It is an XML element that assigns the ID "auction" to the data source "auction.asp", which causes auction.xml to be generated on the middle tier. A persistent XML data source could also have been used.

In Example 9-16, data binding is used to populate the part of the user interface that shows the painting and the caption beneath it. No scripting is needed. Instead, the SPAN elements identify the "auction" DSO as the pointer to the data source and the XML element type name as the DATAFLD to be bound.

Example 9-16. Data binding with the XML DSO

```
<TD>
  <DIV STYLE="margin-left:16px;margin-top:16px;margin-right:16px">
    <DIV ID=pict></DIV>
    <DIV CLASS="details">
      <SPAN DATASRC="#auction" DATAFLD=MATERIALS></SPAN>,
      <SPAN DATASRC="#auction" DATAFLD=YEAR></SPAN>,
      <SPAN DATASRC="#auction" DATAFLD=DIMENSIONS></SPAN>
    </DIV>
  </DIV>
</TD>
```

One advantage of displaying XML with the XML DSO is that the XML document is processed asynchronously to the rendering of the page. Therefore, if the inventory of paintings were very large, the initial elements of the XML document could be displayed even before the last elements were processed.

9.3 | Updating the data source from the client

We have seen how userInterface.htm on the client obtained data to display to the user by invoking auction.asp on the middle tier. It can also enable the user to make his own bid by invoking another middle tier page, make-bid.asp.

In the *Auction Demo*, the user bids by overwriting the price and bidder name in the first row of the bid table. A bid therefore consists of the "title" of the item currently displayed, the "price" of the new bid, and the name of the new "bidder".

These data items must be passed as parameters to makebid.asp, which executes a script to process them and update the database. The script returns to the client a "return message" XML document: a single element containing information about the status of the processing.

The script in userInterface.htm (see Example 9-17) begins by assigning the title of the current item up for auction to the "title" variable, the value of the "price" text box to the "price" variable, and the value of the "bidder" text box to the "bidder" variable.

It then creates the return message document object, which will state whether makebid.asp successfully updated the database. The three variables are passed as parameters to the ASP file when it is invoked.

Example 9-17. Sending a new bid to makebid.asp

```
var title = current_item.childNodes.item(0).text;
var price = price.value;
var bidder = bidder.value;
var returnMsg = new ActiveXObject("MSXML2.DOMDocument");
returnMsg.load("http://auction/makebid.asp?title=" +
  title + "&price=" + price + "&bidder=" + bidder;
```

In Example 9-18, makebid.asp (called by userInterface.htm in Example 9-17) assigns the values of the parameters "title", "price", and "bidder" to variables with the same names.

The "BidRS" record set object is then created and a connection to the "Auction" database is made. Note that the connection is made for both reading and writing. The "Bids" table is then opened and the new information is added to the record set, after which the connection is closed. The process is much the same as it was for auction.asp, except that the database is written to instead of just being read.

Finally, makebid.asp generates the return message document with the status of the update.

Example 9-18. The makebid.asp file updates the database

```
<%@ LANGUAGE = VBScript %>
<%
title = Request.QueryString("title")
price = Request.QueryString("price")
bidder = Request.QueryString("bidder")

Set BidRS = Server.CreateObject("ADODB.RecordSet")
connect = "data source=Auction;user id=sa;password=;"
BidRS.CursorType = 2
BidRS.LockType = 3   ' read/write
BidRS.Open "Bids", connect

BidRS.AddNew
BidRS("item") = title
BidRS("price") = price
BidRS("bidder") = bidder
BidRS.Update
BidRS.Close
%>
<STATUS>OK</STATUS>
```

9.4 | Conclusion

The entire *Auction Demo* was built using the methods described above. Although newer implementation technologies continue to emerge, the principles of middle-tier interactive application design remain timeless.

XML enables Web applications by providing dynamic, accessible content that can be navigated and manipulated on the client. In addition, it enables the updating of content without having to refresh the entire user interface. This ability saves time by reducing round trips to the server for information that already exists on the client.

With XML, users can manage data over the Internet just as they presently do on their local machines. As a result, the Web is made a more interactive and interoperable medium. As the information superhighway has transformed itself into the data superhighway, Web applications similar to the *Auction Demo* are allowing far better utilization of the vast resources made available by the Web.

Analysis   The Auction Demo clearly illustrates the architecture of a three-tier application. It uses the middle tier as a transient data aggregator and normalizer. In the next chapter we take a closer look at how data sources can generate XML for use by middle-tier servers.

Enabling data sources for XML

▌ InetPurchasing.Com

▌ Dynamic data sources

▌ Catalog creation and dissemination

Contributing expert: Jeff Davison

Chapter

10

One of the toughest jobs for developers of middle-tier applications is accessing and converting data from a multitude of sources. XML helps, of course, but even with XML there are challenges of data conversion and dissimilar vocabularies. Here's how one company was able to shift that burden onto the data sources, with happy results for all concerned.

Middle-tier servers deliver to clients information that the servers aggregate from multiple data sources. At some point in that process, the data is converted to XML if it wasn't that way from the start. Even if it was, it might have used a different vocabulary, in which case the aggregation process would include converting it to the vocabulary of the aggregated information.

10.1 | XML data sources

In our examples so far, the data sources have either been relational databases or XML documents. That tends to be true in the real world as well, but "XML document" offers a lot of scope for variety. That's because the document doesn't have to be a persistent one. It could be generated by the data source to deliver information produced in real time by a complex process.

10.1.1 *Dynamic data sources*

We've seen plenty of websites that present weather information to readers. But consider a situation where an application program needs to get the outside temperature in order to accomplish some particular function. For instance, a program that is supposed to shut down some piece of machinery if the outside temperature is too high or too low.

Traditionally, to get the current outside temperature into a program, the programmer would have to interface with a sensor of some sort. That would entail a direct hardware hookup, replete with interface cabling and driver software.

How much more convenient it would be if the application programmer could get the temperature in a similar way to the end user, with a URL. The program could just link to the network location of an XML document that contains the desired information, download it via HTTP, and parse it to get the temperature values.

Several websites actually provide such a service. They offer various XML documents describing real-time temperature, humidity, and forecasts for many cities and regions.

10.1.2 *Converting to XML*

There is no question that such services free the data consumer of a major effort, hooking up temperature and humidity sensors. The current temperature (along with any other XML data item on the Web) is available as a service to any program that wishes to use it (and if necessary, pay for it). The fact that the temperature data is maintained by a website in a different state, or even a different country, is immaterial to the consuming program. The only thing that is relevant is that an XML document containing the local area weather can be pulled from the Web and easily parsed.

That leaves just one critical question: How does the service provider convert the sensor data to XML in the first place? In most cases, the first step in this or similar data capture situations is to store the data in a relational database. The database would probably have a simple schema, with each sensor reading stored as a record with fields for `date`, `time`, `location`, `temperature`, and so on.

We saw in the previous chapter how a middle-tier application can convert such database records to XML documents by using scripts in a Web page. The process is called *data binding*. In this case, the provider of the weather service wants to make things easier for its customers by performing the data binding itself. It may also want to publicize the service so others can find it.

Many tools are available for these purposes; we'll look at one shortly. But first, let's consider a burning question.

10.1.3 *Is this a Web service?*

As the chapter started, we were discussing "the delivery of XML documents". At this point we're talking in terms of "a service of collecting weather data, which is delivered in the form of XML documents". We've shifted the focus to the creation of the documents, but in other respects there is no real difference.

A website like *Weather.com*, for example, is similar in that it also offers a weather data collection service, except that it delivers its output as HTML pages rather than XML. In other words, Web-based services are as old as the Web itself.

But *Web services*, the idea that is getting all of the hype of late, is slightly different. If you recall our introduction to the subject in 5.4, "Web services", on page 116, the newer, hyped Web services concept involves more standardization of the way in which service providers and service requestors communicate. There is also more emphasis on the discovery of services through a third party, called a *service broker*, also by means of standardized descriptions and protocols.

The ultimate vision for the new Web services is universal discovery and purchase of services from previously unknown providers, a very different world from what we have today, on or off the Web. But even as the industry promotes and begins to implement that vision, the classic Web-based services continue. Other XML-based techniques are providing simpler deployment and access options for smaller companies and narrower communities of interest.

For these situations, the benefits of the new Web services standards – universal reach and service anonymity – aren't needed and don't justify their cost and complexity. We discuss the vision, and the underlying reality, in detail in Part 13, "Web Services", on page 618. But for now, let's look at simpler means to achieve a less ambitious – but sufficient – result. We'll use the experience of a real company to illustrate.

10.2 | InetPurchasing.Com

InetPurchasing.Com provides Web based buying services for state government agencies in the U.S. To do this, it collects product and pricing information for all sorts of stuff: from paper clips, to computer systems, to jet fuel. It is a Web-based service for buying things over the Web, tailored for the requirements of government purchasing.

10.2.1 *Data acquisition*

The company needs to acquire product information from large numbers of different types of vendors. It must aggregate this information into a single relational database so that product characteristics, prices, availability, and delivery options can be compared and alternatives presented to its end users: government buyers.

There is an obvious problem: How does it get all the product, price and delivery information from all suppliers into its database? This data must be acquired in near real-time since prices and availability are subject to change for each supplier. Suppliers were willing to cooperate to a fair degree, since it improved their chances of getting orders.

Three methods of getting the product information were considered. Let's look at them.

10.2.1.1   Email

One possibility was to have each vendor email its product catalogs in a specific file representation, such as a particular spreadsheet format. The idea was rejected because it would have required an army of people to load the spreadsheet data into the database. A system that utilized this approach would not even be close to a real-time system.

10.2.1.2   HTML

Another approach was to collect URLs of product catalogs in HTML that each vendor made available on its own website. So-called *screen scraping* programs would parse the HTML and extract the data.

This technique was actually implemented. It had the benefit of near real-time update, but suppliers had to conform to rigorous layout standards in constructing their HTML-based catalogs. For example, product data had to be entered as a five-column table and no other markup could be used. That's because InetPurchasing.Com's software needed *abstract* product data, while HTML is designed to describe *rendered* Web pages.

10.2.1.3   XML

Ultimately, the company asked suppliers to create XML documents describing their products, and to submit URLs for those documents. This approach achieved the same near real-time availability as HTML. However, instead of rendition-oriented elements like `table` and `row`, the XML documents contained meaningful abstract elements, such as `item`, `description`, and `price`.

10.2.2   *Implementing the middle tier*

InetPurchasing.Com needed XML middleware to aggregate the product information from the vendors and make it available to the buyers.

10.2.2.1   System architecture

Figure 10-1 shows the system architecture. There are three major components – aggregator, directory, and vendors.

aggregator
  The content aggregator, labeled *XML Portal*, is shown in the upper center. Its role is to search the directory for relevant URLs and retrieve the XML documents from the vendor data sources. In this particular application, the aggregator loads the aggregated XML documents into a relational database that the buyers' client software can manipulate directly. It also creates HTML renditions of the aggregated data.

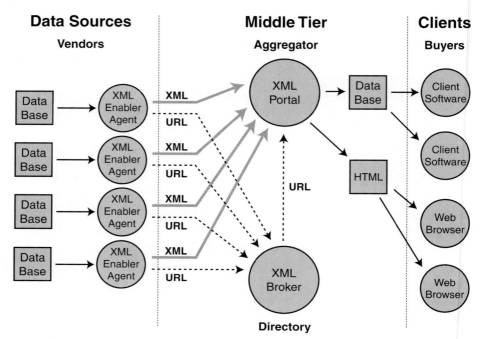

Figure 10-1   InetPurchasing.Com three-tier Web application

directory

Vendors register the URLs of their product catalogs with a directory, shown at the lower center. The directory software, labeled *XML Broker*, is a search engine that receives the URLs and performs some validation of the documents.

vendors

Each vendor must create one or more product catalogs in XML, place them at a website, and submit the catalog URLs to the directory. To facilitate this, each vendor utilizes the software labeled *XML Enabler Agent*, an adaptation of an HTTP server with tools for XML data binding and for registering URLs with directories.

10.2.2.2   System flow

To summarize the flow in Figure 10-1, multiple vendors convert database data into XML product catalogs and register the catalog URLs with the directory. The aggregator searches the directory for the documents, retrieves them directly from the vendors, and loads their data into a relational database. The net result is that many separate databases, under the control of different vendors, are aggregated into a single database.

Although the aggregator and the directory could have been implemented as a single program, there is value in their being distinct. The job of the directory is to collect URLs into a search engine database, whereas the job of the aggregator is to collect and process actual XML data. This division enhances scalability of the system.

Moreover, it is possible to mix-and-match directory sites and aggregator sites. Any directory can feed URL information to many different aggregators, and each aggregator can search the URLs from many different directories.

Finally, note that the aggregator produces two outputs:

- A relational database containing the aggregated data, to allow product comparisons and direct access by client software.
- HTML pages to display the aggregated data in a browser.

As a result, the *XML Portal* simultaneously supports the aggregator as both a Web shopping portal for humans and as a Web-based service for purchasing software implemented by the buyers on their own systems.

10.2.3 *Enabling the data sources*

The InetPurchasing.Com system is unusual in placing the burden of data binding on the vendors, rather than on the middle-tier aggregator. Each vendor is obliged to produce a catalog in XML that conforms to a DTD that the aggregator can accept. The vendors also have the responsibility of registering their catalog URLs with the directory.

The vendors are motivated to participate in the system because they want the increased business that will result. But there is a limit to the resources they can invest and, for smaller vendors, to the complexity they can handle. The process had to be as simple and inexpensive as possible for them.

The company's solution was to give each vendor a copy of *XML Enabler Agent*.

10.2.3.1   *XML Enabler Agent* functions

The vendor interface of the product is shown in Figure 10-2. The vendors used it to perform the following functions:

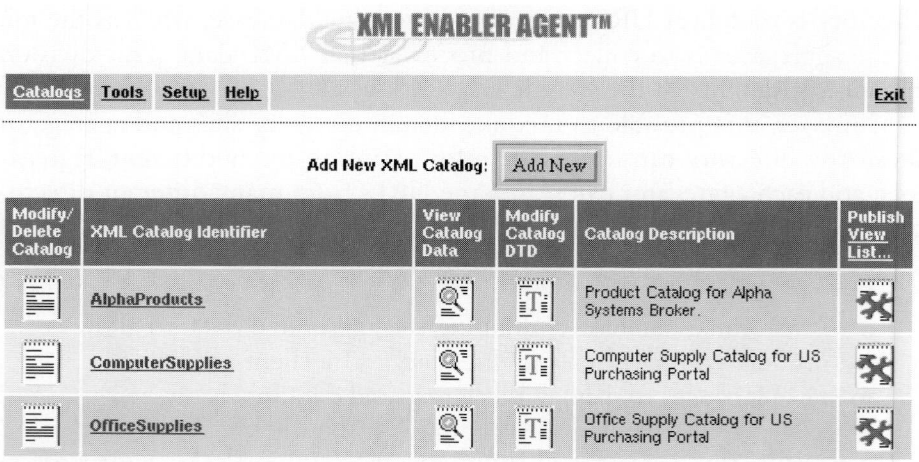

Figure 10-2   *XML Enabler Agent* vendor interface

catalog creation

The program accesses data from a relational database and generates an XML document, including a DTD and XSDL schema definition. A unique URL is assigned to the catalog document.

catalog registration

A wizard guides the vendor in registering a catalog in the directory.

catalog de-registration
> There is a tool for removing a registered ("published") URL from the directory.

support functions
> There are also tools to set up database drivers, authorize access to the system, and perform general-purpose queries on the database.

There was an added benefit for the vendors. The product is capable of creating multiple catalogs from the same database, each satisfying the requirements of a specific directory or aggregator, and each conforming to a different DTD. As a result, vendors could make their product information available to customers other than InetPurchasing.Com.

10.2.3.2   Conflict resolution

In some cases, vendor databases and the final aggregate database used different field names or datatypes. To resolve such conflicts, the *XML Enabler Agent* provides a Web-based client interface that allows InetPurchasing.Com employees to change the XML markup of catalogs generated for its use. Although the vendor continues to own the data, it does not need to get involved in data binding details for individual customers.

10.3 | Conclusion

The InetPurchasing.Com system is successful because its vendors find it simple enough to participate. They are willing and able to generate the necessary XML catalogs and publish them to the Web. Even small companies were able to take part, which allowed them to compete in the e-commerce arena along with their larger competitors. The result was increased choices for InetPurchasing.Com's customers and a higher perceived level of satisfaction with the service.

E-commerce

- Electronic data interchange (EDI)
- Business-to-business (B2B)
- Supply chain integration
- Trading exchanges
- Integrated e-commerce (IEC)

Part Three

E-commerce is all about the elimination of manual procedures among trading partners. The eventual goal is to have each partner's system exchange information directly with all the others.

The most visible manifestations of e-commerce are *Web storefronts* – websites where an online catalog replaces a paper catalog and mailed-in order forms. These sites enter transactions directly into the vendor's system, but the purchaser must do everything manually.

Historically, though, business supply chain automation, in the form of electronic data interchange (EDI), has been the major driver of e-commerce. EDI is vital to those companies rich enough to have implemented it, but for smaller trading partners it is unattainable.

In the following chapters, we'll see why traditional EDI has reached its limit and how XML and the Web can help it realize its full potential. The key to the value of EDI is its *integration* into the business systems of all trading partners, something that the storefront does not accomplish. With XML-based EDI, a truly integrated e-commerce is now possible, for partners of all sizes.

From EDI to IEC: The new Web commerce

Introductory Discussion

- Electronic data interchange (EDI)

- Integrated e-commerce (IEC)

- Leveraging XML and the Internet for EDI

- Supply chains and supply webs

Contributing expert: Mike Hogan

Chapter

11

XML and the Internet are dramatically altering the electronic data interchange (EDI) landscape. By driving down costs and complexity, they are creating a revolutionary form of business-to-business integrated e-commerce (IEC) that complements EDI and vastly extends its reach. IEC is becoming a truly ubiquitous technology that is reshaping business as we know it. This chapter introduces EDI and explains its evolution to IEC.

O ver the past several decades, corporations have invested trillions of dollars in automating their internal processes. While this investment has yielded significant improvements in efficiency, that efficiency is only beginning to be extended to external processes.

In effect, companies have created islands of automation that are isolated from their vendors and customers – their trading partners. The interaction among companies and their trading partners remains slow and inefficient because it is still based on manual processes.

11.1 | What is EDI?

Electronic data interchange (EDI) has been heralded as the solution to this problem. *EDI* is defined as the exchange of data between heterogeneous systems to support transactions.

EDI is not simply the exportation of data from one system to another, but actual interaction between systems. For example, Company B is a supplier to Company A. Instead of sending purchase orders, bills and checks in hard copy form, the two might connect their systems to exchange this same data electronically.

In the process they could benefit in many other ways, including faster turnaround on orders, better inventory control, reduced financial float, complete real-time information about orders and inventory for improved decision-making, reduced costs for manual data input, and more. Companies that have implemented EDI rave about the various benefits.

In fact, these benefits can be expanded to a chain of suppliers. For example, Company C might be a supplier to Company B above. If companies B and C implement EDI, then Company A gains the additional benefits of superior integration with its entire *supply chain* of suppliers.

11.1.1 *Extranets can't hack it*

There is a significant gap between the business benefits described above and the actual implementation of EDI. This is because the actual implementation of "traditional EDI" is fundamentally flawed. It is difficult and costly to implement and, even worse, it requires a unique solution for each pair of trading partners. This situation is analogous to requiring a unique telephone line to be wired to each person to whom you wish to speak.

Many people falsely proclaimed the Internet as the solution to this problem. By implementing EDI over a single network, our problems would be solved. This "solution" was so exciting it was even given its own name, the extranet. Unfortunately, a network with a common protocol is still only a partial solution.

This is because the systems implemented in each company are based on different platforms, applications, data formats (notations), protocols, schemas, business rules, and more. Simply "connecting" these systems over the Internet does not, by itself, solve the problem. To use the phone system analogy again, this is analogous to wiring each business into the global phone network, only to realize that each company's phone system is unique, and incompatible with every other phone system.

And given the trillions of dollars companies have invested in automation, they are not simply going to replace these systems with new "compatible" solutions, assuming such things existed.

11.1.2 *XML can!*

There are a number of reasons why XML provides a solution for EDI over the Internet. XML is a universal notation (data format) that allows computers to store and transfer data that can be understood by any other computer system. XML maintains the content and structure, but separates the business rules from the data. As a result, each trading partner can apply its own business rules. This flexibility is critical to creating a complete solution for EDI.

There are additional technologies that are also part of the complete solution. Security, for example, is critical to EDI. Transactional integrity, connection stability, authentication and other services are also critical to implementing a complete solution. These requirements are addressed by technologies that are layered on top of the Internet. We refer to them generically as *Internet-based services*.

The final piece of the EDI solution is data storage. XML introduces a unique set of requirements for hierarchical naming and structure. It also requires rich relationships and complex linking. XML's use in EDI adds further requirements for metadata and versioning. These requirements levy heavy demands on database technology.

11.1.3 *Integrated e-commerce*

By combining XML, the Internet, Internet-based services and database connectivity, we have a complete solution for universal *integrated e-commerce (IEC)*. IEC, which complements and extends EDI, is changing our entire business landscape. EDI is metamorphosing from a handful of unique interconnections, defined by the supply chain, into a "supply web". The supply web is an intelligent common fabric of commerce over the Internet. Trading communities and exchanges are examples of supply webs.

According to Metcalfe's Law – formulated by Robert Metcalfe, the inventor of *Ethernet* – the value of a network is roughly proportional to the square of the number of users. Imagine what this means when your EDI "network" expands from a one-to-one proposition to a true network that encompasses practically every company in the world. Suddenly, the trillions of dollars companies have invested in internal automation increase in value by several factors. By the same token, this information can also be extended to customers, adding significant value to the vendor-customer relationship, thereby enhancing customer loyalty.

This is a pivotal time in the history of technology. With the emergence of XML, all of the pieces are available to create a universal mechanism for EDI. The Internet provides the transport. XML provides the flexible, extensible, structured message format. Various Internet-based services provide solutions for security, transactional integrity, authentication, connection stability, network fail-over and more.

Add to this sophisticated data storage and you have all of the pieces necessary to unite corporate islands of automation into a single coherent fabric of electronic commerce. IEC has already achieved dramatic improvements in efficiency, cost-savings, superior access to real-time data for analysis and decision-making, superior inventory management, and more.

Integrated e-commerce will have a profound impact on business-to-business (B2B) and business-to-consumer (B2C) relationships. The many problems with current implementations of EDI have relegated it to large enterprises and selected industries. However, the combination of the Internet, Internet-based technologies, and XML is opening up EDI – as enhanced by IEC – not only to small-to-medium enterprises (*SMEs*), but also to individuals (Example 11-1).

IEC will experience growth and market penetration that will rival the email market. It has already begun to blossom on the Web and become an everyday part of our lives. It will eventually usher in a new era in computing. The Internet will complete its metamorphosis from a transport for Web pages into a ubiquitous and seamless foundation for every imaginable transaction. In the future, IEC will touch every aspect of computing.

We will be examining these propositions in detail, and the technology that makes them possible.

11.2 | The value of EDI

While traditional EDI is very costly and difficult to implement, the potential benefits are very significant. Companies that have implemented EDI rave about benefits like improved efficiency, vendor management, cost savings, superior access to information for decision making, tighter inventory control, customer responsiveness, and it is a competitive advantage that can be marketed to attract new customers.

Example 11-1. The value of data interchange.

Mike opens his company expense report, and in the microsecond it takes to launch, he reminisces about the old days when he had to fill out these things himself. Now the computer does it for him. Mike recently took a trip to Utah to close a major deal. In the process he purchased a plane ticket, a rental car and various meals. In the old days, he used to enter all of these charges manually into an expense program...not any more.

Mike uses a corporate American Express card for these purchases. When he opens the expense report, it automatically connects to American Express and presents a list of new charges. Mike selects the charges that are appropriate for this expense report.

American Express sends this data to Mike's computer, which automatically formats the data into his expense report. Mike then clicks the send button and the expense report is sent to his manager to approve. Then the company's bank instantly wires the money to Mike's bank account.

Behind the scenes, all these companies are establishing connections, as needed, to share information in a secure and reliable manner using XML and the Internet. But Mike doesn't concern himself with what goes on behind the scenes; he's off to close another big deal in Washington.

EDI was initially implemented to improve efficiency by enabling companies to eliminate costly and slow manual methodologies, like the processing of purchase orders and bills. It was thought that by allowing the computers of two or more companies to share this information, they could achieve dramatic improvements in efficiency.

However, the largest savings are derived from a complete shift to EDI that allows companies to completely eliminate their hard copy processes. The traditional 80/20 rule applies in reverse to EDI, meaning that it is the last 20% of your trading partners to convert to EDI who account for 80% of the potential savings.

This is because even with 80% of your trading partners using EDI, you must still maintain the same manual processes for the remaining 20% who don't. While most companies have not been able to completely convert from hard copy processes to EDI, the 20% savings companies have realized have still been very significant. With integrated e-commerce enabling companies to completely eliminate their manual processes, the savings will improve dramatically.

With EDI, companies are also able to manage their supply chains much more efficiently. Through EDI, companies have been able to reduce the average time from issuance of an order to receipt of goods from several weeks, to a matter of days. By improving inventory control, companies are able to minimize their investment in costly inventory, while still being able to address spikes in business. For industries where inventory costs are a significant part of their business, like manufacturing, this represents a significant cost savings.

EDI also reduces the financial float by eliminating the typical order generation, delivery and processing, by 5-7 days. By combining EDI with electronic funds transfer (EFT) companies can also reduce the financial float by 8-10+ days. Based on the amount of money involved, this can represent a significant savings.

EDI also provides companies with superior real-time information upon which to base decisions. Everyone recalls stories of companies who simply didn't have the data to realize how bad things were, until it was too late. With EDI, companies have access to complete data in real-time. The ability to collect, manipulate and measure information about your relationships with vendors and customers can be critical to your company's success.

Customer responsiveness is becoming increasingly important. Many companies have leveraged technology to dramatically improve customer responsiveness. A good example of this is Federal Express, who pioneered the concept of a website where customers can track the status of their packages.

The site is possible only because of FedEx's end-to-end dedication to EDI. By capturing information about the package status at each step in the process, and making this information accessible to customers, they have made themselves leaders in customer support. This is critical to building and growing businesses, especially in the Internet age.

Some companies who have implemented EDI with one customer, have gone on to market this capability to other potential customers, as a unique selling point. This has enabled them to grow their businesses. As IEC becomes more ubiquitous, the tide could even shift to the point where companies will not accept vendors who are not IEC-capable. That is because of the dramatic savings that vendors can achieve by a complete conversion to EDI.

11.3 | Traditional EDI: Built on outdated principles

EDI is a process for exchanging data in electronic format between heterogeneous applications and/or platforms in a manner that can be processed without manual intervention.

11.3.1 *The history of EDI*

EDI dates back to the 1970s, when it was introduced by the Transportation Data Coordinating Committee (TDCC). The TDCC created transaction sets for vendors to follow in order to enable electronic processing of purchase orders and bills.

At the time, the technology landscape was very different from what it is today. Lacking ubiquitous powerful CPUs, a common transport, and a file format that allows for flexibility, they defined strict transaction sets. These transaction sets addressed the needs for data content, structure and the process for handling the data. In other words, the business rules were embedded into the transaction set.

The incorporation of business rules into the definition of the transaction set causes many problems, because:

1. Business rules vary from company to company;
2. Business rules for one size company may be completely inappropriate for companies of another size;
3. Business rules are subject to change over time according to changes in market dynamics.

In short, the use of fixed and rigid transaction sets, while necessary at the time, have limited the value of EDI, and therefore stunted its growth.

11.3.2 *EDI technology basics*

Traditional EDI transaction sets are defined by standards bodies such as the United Nations Standard Messages Directory for Electronic Data Interchange for Administration, Commerce and Transport (*EDIFACT*), and the

American National Standards Institute's (ANSI) Accredited Standards Committee X12 sub-group.

Transaction sets define the fields, the order of these fields, and the length of the fields. Along with these transaction sets are business rules, which in the lexicon of the EDI folks are referred to as "implementation guidelines".

To actually implement EDI, the trading partners would follow these steps:

1. Trading partners enter into an agreement, called a trading arrangement.
2. They select a Value Added Network (VAN).
3. The trading partners typically either contract for, or build themselves, custom software that maps between the two data set formats used by these trading partners.
4. Each time a new trading partner is added, new software would have to be written to translate the sender's data set for the recipient. In other words, you start from scratch with each new trading partner.

Transaction sets are typically transmitted over expensive proprietary networks, which generally base charges on a mixture of fixed fees and message lengths. These fees can become quite substantial, but they are typically overshadowed by the cost to build and maintain the translation software. The VANs provide value-added services such as:

1. Data validation (compliance) and conversion
2. Logging for audit trails
3. Customer support
4. A secure and stable network
5. Accountability
6. Transaction roll-back to support uncommitted transactions

It is important to note that EDI is not simply the exportation of data from one system to another, but a bidirectional mechanism for interaction between systems. Because these disparate systems typically employ different file formats (data notations), schemas, data exchange protocols, etc., the process of exchanging data is very difficult.

11.3.3 *The problems of traditional EDI*

Traditional EDI suffers from many problems that have limited its growth. One of the most significant problems is the fact that it is based on the transfer of fixed transaction sets. This rigidity makes it extremely difficult to deal with the normal evolution necessary for companies to introduce new products and services, or evolve or replace their computer systems.

In addition, these transaction sets include strict processes for handling the data. These processes are not universally acceptable to companies in various industries and of various sizes. This problem is compounded by a standardization process that is too slow to accommodate the accelerating pace of business today.

In addition, the high fixed costs of implementation have been too much to justify for SMEs. In short, there are a host of problems which, despite the benefits of EDI, have prevented its universal adoption.

11.3.3.1 Fixed transaction sets

EDI is currently built on transaction sets that are fixed in nature. For example, a contact field might include the individual's name, title, company, company address and phone number. However, the company does not have the flexibility to add or subtract fields.

Why is this important?

Companies cannot be frozen in time by a fixed transaction set. This prevents them from evolving by adding new services or products, changing their computer systems and improving business processes. This inflexibility inherent in the current custom solutions required to map data between each trading partner pair is untenable, despite the significant benefits of EDI (Example 11-2).

11.3.3.2 Slow standards evolution

EDI standards are defined by standards bodies that are structurally ill-equipped to keep up with the rapid pace of change in the various business environments they impact, as illustrated by Example 11-2.

These standards accommodate many companies with very different needs. They also encompass not just the ontology, but the associated busi-

Example 11-2. Problems of traditional EDI: Healthcare

The transaction sets created for the healthcare system were defined for the traditional indemnity model, where the insurance company pays the doctor on a per visit basis. However, the movement toward managed care was not foreseen in this transaction set. Since managed care pays the doctor a set fee per patient, but does not reimburse on a per visit basis, the standard transaction set simply doesn't work.

The typical doctor sees a mixture of patients, some having managed care insurance and others with indemnity insurance. In order to accommodate this scenario, the doctor is forced to create a false "per visit" fee for managed care patients. This false fee, which is required in order to "complete" the transaction set, creates havoc with the doctor's other billing systems, which EDI was supposed to help.

Rigid transaction sets that enforce process as well as content are simply not flexible enough to address the ever-changing business environment.

---

ness processes. As a result, it is very slow and difficult, if not impossible, to develop one-size-fits-all solutions.

The current process for defining standards for transaction sets can take years. This simply will not work in today's business environment, which is characterized by accelerated change and increased competition. However, in an effort to jump-start the creation of industry ontologies in the form of DTDs for XML, the work of the traditional EDI standards bodies could be enormously valuable.

Historically, technology standards that are defined and managed in a top-down fashion, like EDI standards, have been replaced by bottom-up standards that allow for independent and distributed development. In other words, technologies like XML, that support greater flexibility and diversity, while providing compatibility between implementations, typically replace inflexible managed solutions like fixed transaction sets.

11.3.3.3   Non-standard standards

Despite the perception of standardization, there remains some flexibility in the interpretation of traditional EDI standards. The simple fact of the matter is that companies have unique needs, and these needs must be translated into the information they share with their trading partners.

In practical terms, the customer is at a significant economic advantage in defining these "standards", vis-a-vis the supplier. As a result, suppliers are forced to implement one-off solutions for each trading partner. In many of the industries where EDI is more prevalent, the suppliers also tend to be the smaller of the two partners, which makes the financial proposition even worse.

Because of the various informational needs of companies, it is impractical to expect that EDI standards can be a one-size-fits-all proposition. The variables of company size, focus, industry, systems, etc. will continue to create needs that are unique to each company. As evidence, consider the amounts companies spend on custom development and customization of packaged applications.

11.3.3.4 High fixed costs

While large companies tout the financial and operational benefits of EDI, these same benefits have eluded the SMEs. That is because of the high fixed costs of implementation, which must be balanced against savings that are variable.

Depending on the level of automation, implementing EDI for a large enterprise is not substantially more expensive than it is for SMEs. In fact, it can be more expensive for the SMEs. Larger companies can often implement a single EDI standard, while the SMEs must accommodate the various standards of their larger partners. This can be very expensive.

Yet, ironically, the benefits are variable. So, if savings are 2% of processing costs, this might not be a substantial number for the manufacturer of car seat springs, but it can be a huge number for GM, Ford or Chrysler. SMEs simply do not have the scale to compensate for the high fixed costs of traditional EDI.

Because of this some of the SMEs that claim to implement EDI are actually printing a hard copy of the data feeds and re-typing them in their systems. The reason they implemented this faux-EDI is to meet customer requirements, because they simply do not have the transactional scale to justify the investment in traditional EDI. Something had to be done to bring down those costs (Example 11-3).

Example 11-3. Problems of traditional EDI: Retail

One large retailer requires its vendors to implement EDI in order to qualify as a vendor. However, like all traditional EDI implementations, the data set is unique to the retailer.

For small companies, implementing this system can be quite an investment. Retail is a very fast-paced industry, because it is forced to cater to ever-changing customer demands. As a result, some suppliers to this retailer have implemented this costly technology, only to later lose their contract with the retailer. In fact, because of the significant investment in technology these companies were forced to make, they have sued the retailer.

If this technology were universally applicable, the vendor's investment in a single customer would be eliminated, as would the retailer's legal liability.

11.3.3.5   Fixed business rules

Business rules are encapsulated in the definition of the transaction sets as implementation guidelines. However, business rules are not something that can be legislated, nor can they be rigid.

Business rules that are applicable for a large enterprise, may be completely inappropriate for an SME. To make matters worse, business rules for a medium-sized enterprise may be wholly inappropriate for a small enterprise.

These business rules will also vary between industries. Even companies of the same size that are in the same industry will implement different business rules. What's more, business rules change over time. The earlier healthcare example demonstrates this point.

Traditional EDI focuses too much on process as an integral part of the transaction set. This is a fatal flaw. New technologies, like XML, support the separation of process, or business rules, from the content and structure of the data. Achieving this separation is critical to widespread adoption of EDI.

The linkage between transaction sets and business rules creates additional problems. The real-life implementation of EDI typically requires custom solutions for each trading partner pair. This creates havoc when trying to implement or modify global business rules.

For example, if your company changed business policy to begin accepting purchase orders, which you had refused to accommodate in the past, you would have to manually change the individual software for each trading partner. You could not make these changes on a global basis using traditional EDI.

This problem also impacts your ability to upgrade or replace your internal systems, since they are uniquely woven into the EDI software in place. In essence, you can become locked into systems that may become obsolete by the time you actually implement the total solution.

11.3.3.6   Limited penetration

EDI penetration has been very limited, when compared to the penetration rates of other automation technologies. Yet the majority of the value of EDI is derived by complete elimination of the hard-copy processes EDI is meant to replace.

As mentioned above, EDI benefits do not follow the 80/20 rule, because converting the first 80% of your vendors to EDI results in only 20% of the potential cost savings. The remaining 80% of the costs remain, since the company is forced to maintain all of the old manual process in tandem with the electronic processes. The most significant savings come only from completely replacing all manual processes with EDI.

The real value of any network is in its adoption by users. Remember Metcalfe's Law: The value of any network is roughly proportional to the number of users squared.

But EDI, in its current state, is *not* a single interlinked network. On the contrary it is a series of one-to-one chains of data flow. As a result, it is vulnerable to alternative "networked" solutions like those enabled by XML, the Internet, Internet-based services, and database connectivity.

11.4 | Leveraging XML and the Internet

Now that we've established the tremendous benefits of EDI, and the structural problems of traditional EDI, the obvious question is: "How can we fix the problems?"

Fortunately, new technologies are coming together to completely reshape the EDI landscape. Today, EDI is currently implemented in a 1-to-1 manner between trading partners. These partnerships can then be extended through tiers to create a supply chain.

This is all changing!

The new paradigm is the *supply web*. The supply web is based on utilization of XML, the Internet, Internet-based services and database connectivity to create a network, or "web", of trading partners.

Implementation and operational costs are plummeting, trading partners are able to implement one-size-fits-all solutions, and adoption is skyrocketing. And the benefits will not be limited to the trading partners, they will be driven down to end-users as well. EDI will become as commonplace as email.

In short, EDI will dramatically alter the business computing landscape, moving the world forward from our current islands of automation toward a single fabric of commerce tying together businesses and end-users.

Traditional EDI is based on the technologies that existed in the 1970s. Now it is time to build a new EDI architecture on current technologies like XML, the Internet, Internet-based services and database connectivity.

- XML provides the ability to separate the data and structure from the processes.
- The Internet provides the ubiquitous connectivity upon which a Web of interconnected trading partners can flourish.
- Internet technologies provide a layer of security, authentication, transactional support and more, to support the needs of EDI.
- Database connectivity means that XML data, and the business rules that interact with that data, can be communicated among disparate systems by means of middle-tier data filters and aggregators.

Together, these technologies are removing the barriers that prevented widespread adoption of EDI. By leveraging these technologies, EDI functionality is becoming more flexible, more powerful, and less expensive – and integrated e-commerce will ultimately become ubiquitous.

11.4.1 *XML*

XML is closely related to HyperText Markup Language (HTML), the original document representation of the World Wide Web, as both are based on SGML. While HTML enables the creation of Web pages that can be viewed on any browser, XML adds tags to data so that it can be processed by any application. These tags describe, in a standardized syntax, what the data is, so that the applications can understand its meaning and how to process it (Example 11-4).

For example, in HTML a product name and a price might be somewhere in the text. But the computer only knows that there is a collection of characters and numbers. It cannot discern that this data represents a product name and price. As a result, little can be done with the data.

With XML, however, the product name is tagged (e.g. `product_name`), as is the product price (e.g. `product_price`). More importantly, there is an association between the product price and the product name.

This information results in significant additional value. For example, a user can now search for the best price on a specific product.

Example 11-4. XML insulates applications from diversity: Customer record

The following example demonstrates one of the values of XML. Below are three different types of message documents from three different companies (A,B and C). Each describes its respective company's customer data:

Company A:
```
<Person name="Mike Hogan" phone="6502864640"
        email="mph@poet.com" />
```
Company B:
```
<Person name="Mike Hogan" street address="999 Baker Way"
        city="San Mateo" zip="94404" phone="6502864640"/>
```
Company C:
```
<Person name="Mike Hogan" phone="6502864640"/>
```

The XML parser parses, or disassembles, the messages to show the `person` element, which has associated attributes (`name`, `phone`, etc.). These attributes, as you can see, differ in content and organization.

However, if your application was written to extract a person's name and phone number, it could work equally well with each of these document types without modification. In fact, if these companies evolve their data to include additional information, your application continues to function without modification. This flexibility is one of the benefits of XML.

XML documents must be "well-formed", which means that most document-type information – grammar and hierarchy – can be embedded in the tags that "mark up" the individual document. There can also be an associated *document type definition* (DTD) or schema definition containing additional meta-information that describes the data.

In either case, XML is self-describing. As a result, applications can be very flexible in their ability to receive, parse and process very diverse sets of information. This enables companies to write a single application that will work with diverse sets of customers. In fact, such a system is even capable of processing information from new trading partners in an ad hoc fashion. This capability completely changes the dynamics of EDI.

Using XML, companies can separate the business rules from the content and structure of the data. By focusing on exchanging data content and structure, the trading partners are free to implement their own business rules, which can be quite distinct from one another. Yet, using templates, companies can work with legacy EDI, non-XML datatypes as well (as we will see in Chapter 12, "XML and EDI: Working together", on page 224).

11.4.2 *The Internet*

Many companies heralded the cost savings and ubiquity of the Internet as the death knell for VANs. However, this future has not come to pass...yet.

The boldest of these claims was based on the notion that the extranet would redefine the new computing paradigm. What these pundits failed to realize was that the Internet alone does not address the needs of the EDI community.

The EDI community is generally limited to the largest enterprises. EDI is mission critical, and requires a dependable network. It also requires a level of security that couldn't be found on the Internet. To put it simply, the savings were not sufficient to justify the switch.

Furthermore, connectivity is only a small part of the problem, the largest issue is the exchange of data in a universal fashion.

All these issues have now been addressed.

- Technology is now available to provide connectivity services to support the Internet in addressing up-time and throughput for mission critical information.
- Security has improved dramatically.

- The use of XML has broadened the EDI customer base to include SMEs and individuals. This new group of customers is much more price-sensitive, so they are inclined to seek an Internet-based solution.
- The ability to exchange data in a more democratic and ad hoc manner is causing an explosion in the average number of EDI connections.

The average number of traditional EDI trading partners, for those companies who utilize EDI at all, is *two*. Building EDI solutions based on XML, and operating this over the Internet, which offers a low-cost ubiquitous transport, is dramatically expanding the value of EDI, according to Metcalfe's Law.

11.4.3 *Internet technologies*

Internet technologies have improved, and continue to improve dramatically, now providing a critical mass of technologies that is capable of replacing the services of VANs. Consider the following list of VAN services, each followed by the Internet-based alternatives that offer greater functionality and flexibility:

Data validation and conversion
XML DTDs and schemas, XML validation, templates, and structure-based data feed interpretation.

Intermediary-based logging for audit trails
XML-savvy repositories employed by all trading partners enables rich logging for audit trails. Combining these with electronic signatures ensures system and company identification.

Consulting, customer service and customer support
This function could be handled by VANs capable of making the transition to Internet technologies, or by the other legions of consultants.

Security and accountability

Public key cryptography, certificate authorities, digital signatures can assure secure transactions.

Connection reliability, stability

New technologies in bandwidth allocation, general improvement in the stability of the Internet and alternative fail-over solutions like dial-up continue to move the Internet toward supporting critical real-time data flow. (Remember, it was originally designed to withstand nuclear attack!)

Trading partner negotiation

Directories (X.500, LDAP, NDS, Active Directory), certificate authorities, digital signatures, email, Internet versions of the Better Business Bureau, etc., can support this function.

Transactional support (roll-back, etc.)

The improvements in remote messaging systems and transaction processing monitors provide a layer of transaction support that is capable of adding transactional integrity even on unstable networks.

11.4.4 *XML data storage*

In other technological transitions, data storage has been a moot point, since the data could be mapped more-or-less directly into relational tables or file systems. More recently, object-oriented database management systems became available for this purpose.

XML data, however, occurs in self-describing information elements that are richly linked, and that utilize a hierarchical structure and naming mechanism. These qualities enable new data-access capabilities based on the tree structure, such as context-sensitive queries, navigation, and traversal.

XML-based support for these new capabilities can be provided by a content management layer above a relational DBMS, and by native XML databases.

11.4.5 *Data filtering*

The source of the vast majority of EDI-related information is currently in mainframes and relational databases. This data will be marked-up on the fly with XML tags. XML data will also come from data sources such as:

- XML content management systems
- Various Internet resources
- EDI-XML documents, both full documents like purchase orders and short inter-process messages
- Result sets from applications, also in XML

These diverse sources must be communicated with by a middle-tier "data filter" that can speak to each source in a manner that the source will recognize. The data must then be filtered in source-dependent ways, based on one's confidence in the data, application of consistent business logic, resolution of the various element-type name ontologies, response mechanisms, security, caching for performance, etc. Only then can the application address the data in a consistent manner and receive consistent responses from the middle tier, as shown in Figure 11-1.

The middle tier could maintain valuable meta-information that would add structure and context to the data stream. Such information could include:

- Routing for the query, response, etc.
- Source of the information (to indicate credibility, etc.)
- Time stamps
- Data, DTD/schema, and markup normalization
- Context and navigation aids

Further details on XML content management and the use of storage systems in the management of XML data can be found in Part 5, "Content Management", on page 266 and Part 9, "Databases", on page 446.

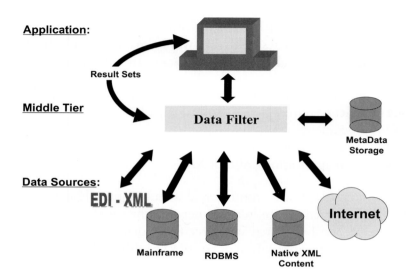

Figure 11-1   Data filter in an XML-based EDI system

11.5 | Conclusion

After decades of investment in corporate data centers, we have created islands of automation inside companies. Their isolation from trading partners limits the value companies can recognize from these systems.

EDI offers the ability to change all of this. EDI offers benefits like:

- improved efficiency
- supply chain management
- real-time data and metrics
- better planning
- superior execution
- control systems
- resource management
- cost savings
- superior access to information for decision making
- customer responsiveness

However, traditional EDI is very difficult and expensive to implement. Because of problems like rigid transaction sets that embed business rules, slow standards development, high fixed costs, and limited market penetration, EDI has not achieved broad adoption. Fortunately, XML-based technology is now available to address these problems and, in the process, reshape the use of EDI.

XML, the Internet, Internet-based services and database connectivity are combining to complement EDI and enhance commerce, in the form of integrated e-commerce. Instead of forcing companies to adapt their systems and business processes to the EDI data, this data can now adapt dynamically to the companies' existing systems.

Where traditional EDI was isolated to certain industries and to the largest enterprises, integrated e-commerce will become as ubiquitous as email. Trading communities have evolved from EDI's one-to-one supply chain to IEC's richly interconnected web of trading partners forming the supply web.

This supply web is resulting in dramatic improvements in efficiency. Companies are slashing costs, while improving access to critical information. This information will be pushed all the way to the end-user, providing superior customer support as well.

XML and EDI: Working together

Introductory Discussion

- Approaches to e-commerce
- Traditional-EDI and XML e-commerce compared
- Leverage existing EDI with XML

Contributing experts: Jeffrey Ricker and Drew Munro

Chapter

12

Large companies have invested millions in their existing successful EDI systems. XML can enhance that investment by extending them to a Webful of EDI-less trading partners. This chapter explains how traditional EDI and XML can work together.

I n a few short years, the Internet has changed the fundamental rules for conducting business.

Now consider EDI: Large companies have been using it with their major trading partners for nearly 20 years. But, as we have seen, traditional EDI commerce has proven itself to be too complicated and expensive for most small and many midsize companies. As a result, EDI has never been adopted widely enough to cause any such fundamental change.

Now, however, there is an e-commerce that all companies can afford. The Internet and XML have lowered the barriers to e-commerce, in both cost and complexity. But they are not replacing EDI, they are extending it to bring e-commerce to small and midsize companies. XML complements EDI and, in so doing, finally turns the vision of EDI into the reality of integrated e-commerce.

12.1 | What is integrated e-commerce?

In traditional commerce, each customer and vendor may be automated internally, but they are individually isolated. They traverse the gulf between their systems by manual processes such as mail, email, fax, meetings and phone calls. This *manual gulf* between "islands of automation" is illustrated in Figure 12-1.

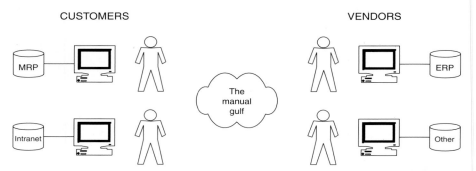

Figure 12-1   A manual gulf separates trading partners in traditional commerce

The objective of *integrated e-commerce (IEC)* is to bridge that manual gulf; that is, to eliminate manual trade processes by allowing the internal applications of different companies to exchange information directly.

Not all e-commerce is integrated e-commerce, but a lot of it is. At present, there are three major approaches, which vary in the extent to which they fully realize this goal.

12.1.1   *Web storefronts*

Web storefronts provide a Web interface to a vendor's catalog of products or services, as illustrated in Figure 12-2. Customers can place orders directly into a vendor's internal system through a Web storefront. Famous examples include Amazon.com and Dell.

Web storefronts have proven immensely popular with customers, and they clearly can achieve economic and other objectives for vendors. How-

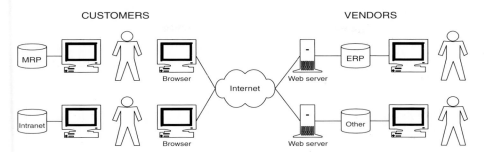

Figure 12-2 Web storefronts automate only one side of trading

ever, in terms of achieving the full potential of integrated e-commerce, they are unilateral.

Nothing is automated on the customer's side. He must go to each web-site separately and manually search through the catalogs. He must also enter orders manually through a Web form and simultaneously update his internal ERP system or intranet application.

For a large manufacturer with 40,000 suppliers, Web storefronts are not much of an improvement over printed catalogs and telephones.

12.1.2 *E-commerce portals*

Some companies have proposed *e-commerce portals* to automate both vendors and customers. With e-commerce portals, customers go to only one website – the portal website – to view vendor catalogs and place orders. Vendors go to the same portal to view and respond to orders (see Figure 12-3).

E-commerce portals bridge the manual gap better than Web storefronts, and can offer the convenience and quick ramp-up of an outsourced solution. However, there are tradeoffs to be considered in this approach:

- Both vendors and customers must update their ERP systems from the portal. Can this task be automated?
- A company's e-commerce data resides outside that company on the portal website. Is the security risk acceptable?
- E-commerce portals may charge a subscription fee and may also charge for every transaction. In essence, they are charging

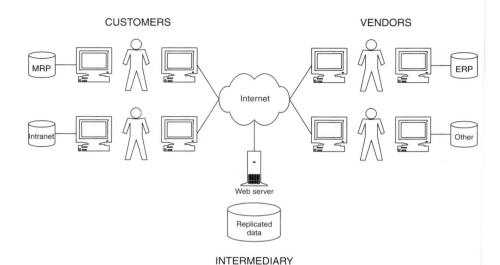

Figure 12-3   E-commerce portals rely on an intermediary

companies to access their own information. Would another approach be more cost-effective?

Caution   *E-commerce portals are a type of application service provider (ASP). They should not be confused with the popular types of information portal that are discussed in Part 6, "Portals", on page 326.*

12.1.3 *Integrated e-commerce*

EDI was the first attempt at integrated e-commerce. Although its users reap great benefits from it, there are only about 300,000 of them worldwide. The reasons for this were explored in Chapter 11, "From EDI to IEC: The new Web commerce", on page 202.

The basic premise of EDI, however, is right on track. EDI eliminates manual processes by allowing the internal applications of different companies to exchange information directly.

Today, thanks to XML, there are business-to-business e-commerce systems that accomplish the original goal of allowing the internal applications of trading partners to share information directly, as illustrated in Figure 12-4.

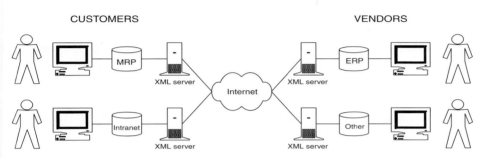

CUSTOMERS   **VENDORS**

Figure 12-4   **XML-based integrated e-commerce bridges the manual gulf**

Intranets are ubiquitous today. Most, if not all, ERP systems have Web-based interfaces, which makes them intranets. Midsize and small companies that do not have ERP systems also have intranets. With XML-based EDI, any company can view its trading partners through its own corporate intranet, rather than through its hundreds of suppliers' individual websites or a third-party website.

The financial services industry has been a leader in bringing the benefits of integrated e-commerce to individuals. Its offerings reflect the approaches to e-commerce we have discussed here. When you go to your broker's website to execute trades and examine your statement, you are using a Web storefront. But when your broker sends the information to *Quicken* and you execute trades from your ledger, that's integrated e-commerce.[1]

---

1. We use the term "integrated e-commerce" in preference to "business-to-business (B2B)" e-commerce because not all B2B e-commerce is integrated into internal applications. Also, as seen in this example, integrated e-commerce isn't limited to businesses.

12.2 | Traditional EDI and XML compared

The stark differences between traditional EDI e-commerce and XML e-commerce stem from the basic characteristics of the two technologies, as compared in Table 12-1.

The creators of EDI were very concerned about size of their messages. Bandwidth for EDI networks is very expensive even today. EDI messages are therefore very compressed and use codes to represent complex values. For the same reason, all the metadata is stripped from the messages, which makes them very hard to read and debug.

The complexity of EDI makes EDI programmers hard to train and expensive to keep, which in turn makes EDI applications expensive to buy and maintain. Complexity drives cost.

Table 12-1   EDI and XML e-commerce solutions compared

Traditional EDI	XML e-commerce
Optimized for compressed messages	Optimized for easy programming
Requires dedicated EDI server costing $10,000 to $100,000	Requires Web server costing $0 to $5000
Uses value-added network (VAN) charging $1 to $20 per message or more	Uses your existing Internet connection
EDI message format takes months to master	XML message format learned in hours
Requires costly program development	Requires only scripts and stylesheets

12.2.1   *Message formats*

EDI comes in two distinct flavors, X12 and EDIFACT. X12 is the American standard that evolved over the years from the most basic attempts at exchange in the 1960s to full-blown billion-dollar networks. EDIFACT is the international standard, endorsed by the United Nations and designed from the ground up beginning in 1985. Both flavors have several version releases of their message formats. Compatibility between versions is not always straightforward.

XML e-commerce is currently even more diversified, with proposed standards that use XML only and others that are XML-EDI hybrids. Some of the most important are discussed in Chapter 5, "XML for machines", on page 102.

Example 12-1 and Example 12-2 provide a comparison between traditional X12 EDI and XML. To demonstrate the difference to yourself, try to find the purchase order number in each document.

Example 12-1. Sample X12 EDI purchase order

```
ISA*00*     *00*  *08*61112500TST      *01*DEMO WU000003
*970911*1039*U00302000009561*0*P?
GS*PO*6111250011*WU000003 *970911*1039*9784*X*003020
ST*850*397822
BEG*00*RE*194743**970911
REF*AH*M109
REF*DP*641
REF*IA*000100685
DTM*010*970918
N1*BY*92*1287
N1*ST*92*87447
N1*ZZ*992*1287
PO1*1*1*EA*13.33**CB*80211*IZ*364*UP*718379271641
PO1*1*2*EA*13.33**CB*80211*IZ*382*UP*718379271573
PO1*1*3*EA*13.33**CB*80213*IZ*320*UP*718379271497
PO1*1*4*EA*13.33**CB*80215*IZ*360*UP*718379271848
PO1*1*5*EA*13.33**CB*80215*IZ*364*UP*718379271005
CTT*25
SE*36*397822
GE*1*9784
IEA*1*000009561
```

Example 12-2. Sample XML purchase order

```
<?xml version="1.0" ?>
<?xml:stylesheet?>
<purchase-order>
<header>
    <po-number>1234</po-number>
    <date>1999-02-08</date><time>14:05</time>
    </header>
<billing>
    <company>XMLreSolutions</company>
    <address>
        <street>601 Pennsylvania Ave. NW</street>
        <street>Suite 900</street>
        <city>Washington</city>
        <st>DC</st><postcode>20004</postcode>
        </address>
    </billing>
<order items="1" >
    <item>
        <reference>097251</reference>
        <description>Widgets</description>
        <quantity>4</quantity>
        <unit-price>11.99</unit-price>
        <price>47.96</price>
        </item>
    <tax type="sales" >
        <tax-unit>VA</tax-unit>
        <calculation>0.045</calculation>
        <amount>2.16</amount>
        </tax>
    ...
```

12.3 | An XML-EDI trading system

Traditional EDI works. You can rely on it. There is no greater accolade for a technology. Large companies have spent millions on their EDI systems, which are mission-critical and unlikely to be abandoned. The objective now should be to leverage this sound base and extend it to more trading partners.

Simply sending EDI X12 or EDIFACT messages over HTTP – the Web transport protocol – won't do the job. Although EDI's transport system is primitive, it is not EDI's governing limitation.

The expense of EDI is rooted in its complexity, and its complexity is based in its compressed, cryptic message formats. XML can overcome this complexity by storing the metadata within the text of the message. And XML also happens to be designed for HTTP.

Traditional EDI users can extend their electronic trading base by installing XML-EDI translators on their Web servers, as shown in Figure 12-5. The translation must go both ways: XML to EDI for messages starting from the small company and EDI to XML for messages starting from the large company traditional EDI user.

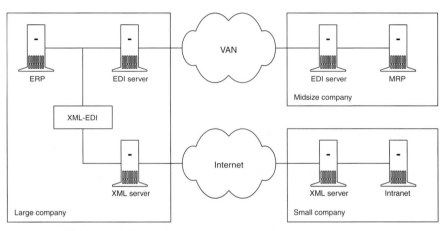

Figure 12-5   An XML-EDI trading system

12.3.1 *XML to EDI*

XML-EDI translators are already available, many relying on proprietary technology and unique scripting languages. Others use XSLT to specify the transformation, as shown in Figure 12-6.

Although XSLT is most commonly used to transform XML into HTML for presentation, it is perfectly well-suited to transform XML into any representation, including EDI. And as it is an open standard, it is likely to benefit from the availability of free and open-source implementations and a large body of skilled developers.

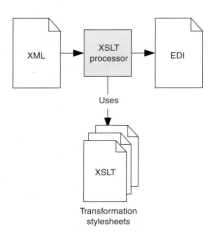

Figure 12-6   XSLT is well-suited for transforming XML into EDI

12.3.2 *EDI to XML*

XSLT cannot be used directly for the inverse conversion, as it can only transform from XML. The problem is well-known from the long experience in SGML and XML systems of having to convert word processing documents to generalized markup. The solution is also well-known: an intermediate trivial translation from the foreign notation to the markup language. A translation, in other words, that changes only the representation of the document, not the meaning. Then XSLT can be applied to accomplish more powerful transforms.

This technique is illustrated in Figure 12-7, which shows an EDI parser as the intermediate translator. The EDI parser has an application programming interface (API) very similar to the XSLT processor (and the XML parser for that matter). The EDI parser makes an XML message out of the EDI message by replacing EDI codes with their full names and making XML elements out of the EDI segments and elements. This process preserves the X12 taxonomy when translating to XML.

Once the EDI message is a well-formed XML document, XSLT can transform it into various XML-EDI message standards, such as those described in Chapter 5.

Because there are many kinds of XML and many kinds of EDI, an XML-EDI translator is not a one-to-one system but rather a many-to-many

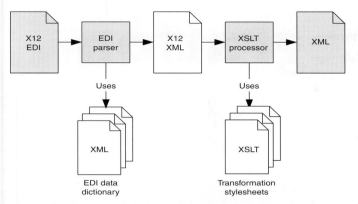

Figure 12-7   Transforming EDI to XML requires an intermediate step

system. Such a translator can therefore also serve as an XML to XML translator and an EDI to EDI translator.

12.4 | The future of e-commerce

The objective of integrated e-commerce is to eliminate manual processes by allowing the internal applications of different companies to exchange information directly. Stated more generically, *integrated e-commerce* is systems integration that crosses the boundary of the enterprise.

That definition encompasses more than just the automation of supply chain paperwork. It envisions a future framework that also automates business processes and workflow between trading partners, and that accommodates those few trading partners that might never automate as well.

XML and EDI working together is the first step toward that future.

Integration

- Enterprise application integration (EAI)
- Low-cost integration
- Unified business integration

Part Four

Integrating applications that know nothing of one another is a challenge, even when they are internal to a single enterprise. So it may seem strange that the earliest integration success – EDI – was external integration. (Perhaps it's because internal projects frequently abandon loosely-coupled application integration in favor of a tightly-coupled ERP system, an option not open to external trading partners.)

We saw in Part 3 how XML is changing EDI. In this part we'll see how XML message formats and inexpensive Web transport protocols are starting to change all forms of integration, even between websites and internal legacy applications.

We'll also examine the convergence of external and internal integration into a single *business integration* problem space. Think of it as the integration of integration!

Application integration with Web and email

- Legacy applications

- Integration of outsourced website with internal system

- Email as XML data transport

Contributing experts: Tim Browne and Sasha Epstein

If your sales leads come from your outsourced
website, and your sales tracking is done on your
internal legacy system, how do you integrate the two?
XML, as we have seen, solves the data representation
aspects of the problem. But how will the XML
documents be transported from the outsourced
system to yours? For one company there was an easy
answer: You get mail!

The long history of software development has left a legacy of
ancient but vital applications, each written in a vacuum. Modern business needs require that these programs now cooperate,
not just with one another, but with the newest programs and technologies.
We'll explore how one company solved the problem, but first let's see
where the problem came from.

13.1 | Legacy applications

In the 1950s, all the data that a program needed was represented in a manner that was integral to the program (*hard-coded*). Each computer system
required its own special forms of program code and data representation.
And each individual programmer was free to use these instructions and formats in a unique way.

By the 1960s, data was separated from programs and stored in ASCII flat
files. However, there was still an integral tightness maintained between programs and their data, both input and output. While standardized languages
and coding styles were starting to be established within the programming

community, the data to be manipulated by the programs was still generally represented in completely arbitrary ways, according to the preferences of the programmer and not in conformance to any standardized rules.

By the late 1970s, nearly all newly-designed systems took advantage of data modeling techniques, along with storage and representation in formal database management systems. Languages, grammars, and program analysis methods coalesced as the foundation of a software engineering discipline. In particular, the relational model for representing and accessing data became the dominant approach and *Structured Query Language (SQL)* became the pervasive standard for formulating queries of data stored in the relational form.

Today, many of the programs and systems created in the 60's and 70's are still operating (!) and constitute the *legacy applications* that may comprise the vital core of an organization's daily activities. However, the competitive environment in most sectors has changed substantially over the past few years. Enterprises can – and, in fact, must – tolerate the existence of legacy applications because it is either too expensive or too risky to replace or rewrite them. However, they cannot tolerate the rigidity that was assumed when those legacy applications were originally written.

13.2 | Enterprise application integration (EAI)

Commercial applications of computing have evolved from straightforward production of payroll checks to the pervasive, and vital, role of controlling the enterprise central nervous system. It would seem obvious that "the right hand should know what the left hand is doing." Surprisingly, though, the central nervous system metaphor suffers a breakdown when subjected to that simple test.

Despite the fully fifty years of commercial computing, most intra-enterprise – and nearly all inter-enterprise – computing applications do not communicate effectively or efficiently with one another.

Today, businesses must adapt quickly to changing circumstances or they will die. Everything about modern business is volatile, from interest rates to technology innovations to competitor strengths and weaknesses. For example, among many other things, businesses need to:

- modify the partners in their supply chains,
- collaborate with their partners,
- limit or expand information provided to their distribution channel,
- modify the prices that they charge to customers as groups or as individuals,
- bundle or unbundle packages of products or services.

All of these activities require interaction among different computer systems, platforms and applications. These interactions proceed more or less smoothly as a function of the degree of communication among the various components.

Historically, enterprises attempting to improve this communication have seen it as two separate problem domains:

- Internal, or intra-enterprise;
- External, or inter-enterprise.

13.2.1 *Internal integration*

Intra-enterprise system integration projects have almost always resulted in the design and implementation of enterprise resource planning (ERP) or materials resource planning (MRP) systems. These are based on a single vendor's proprietary schemes for writing applications and representing data. Unfortunately, these efforts have not always produced the net economic benefits that, in the original investment analysis, justified going forward.

Moreover, many of these efforts were undertaken at different times, by different departments, and utilizing different vendors. At the end of the day, therefore, most corporations have an intra-enterprise computing system apparatus that resembles a Rube Goldberg contraption. This jumble of computing applications, with its *ad hoc* and jerry-built connections, is typically what is really meant by the euphemism *legacy applications*.

13.2.2 *External integration*

The inter-enterprise integration and connectivity picture is hardly much prettier, if not actually worse. Typically, independent business partners who wish to share data electronically have to use either

- electronic data interchange (EDI);
- *ad hoc* electronic file transfer; or
- electronic mail.

EDI is both secure and predictable, but very expensive. As we saw in Chapter 11, "From EDI to IEC: The new Web commerce", on page 202, the realization of its potential benefits requires:

- a point-to-point real or virtual private network;
- compatible systems on both ends of the communication link;
- absolute compliance with X.12 or EDIFACT transaction and semantic rules; and
- custom programming for each document type to be transferred, on a per-business-partner basis.

To evaluate the other methods, we need to separate the media from the messages.

Ad hoc electronic file transfer and email are not as expensive as EDI, but neither are they as secure, reliable, or predictable.[1]

However, these weaknesses as transport mechanisms are surmountable, and are getting better all the time. The real problem is that both custom code and one-off translation/interpretation may be required to make sense of the data being transferred.

A thousand years ago, during the Middle Ages, crusaders and traders from many nations found themselves along the eastern shore of the Mediterranean Sea with a similar problem. They needed to communicate but had no common language. A kind of simplified pidgin language or jargon, called *lingua franca*, grew up to enable simple business transactions. In modern times, the term is applied to any common or commercial language or mechanism for communication among diverse peoples or systems.

---

1. Sneaker-net transmission of electronic files by manual delivery of tapes or disks may be, but just isn't fast enough, even with the coolest sneakers!

SQL is a modern *lingua franca*, but it has limitations. It assumes that the data to be queried, retrieved, or manipulated is stored and represented in conformance to the relational model.

XML, however, makes no such assumptions. It is rapidly becoming the *lingua franca* for everything else. Let's see how a company solved an external integration problem by combining XML with inexpensive transport mechanisms.

13.3 | Subject Software Company

Subject Software Company is a fictional name for a real software publisher. The company maintains a website on which it offers free trials of its products. Interested visitors complete a "trial software download form", which is an important source of sales leads.

13.4 | The challenge

Like many companies, Subject Software manages its own internal system for sales force automation, customer support, order entry, and other business-unit applications, as well as enterprise email. However, its website is operated by its Internet service provider (ISP) and is not connected to its internal system.

As a result, the sales leads from the trial software downloads had to be imported manually from the outsourced website. This was done on a weekly basis, using a *comma-separated values (CSV)* text file. Subject Software needed to integrate its website with its internal system, as shown in Figure 13-1.

The company was able to accomplish this goal using a message-oriented middleware solution. It uses XML documents and the Internet email infrastructure to move the sales lead information quickly from the website to the internal sales systems. Lead processing is now automatic, and occurs almost immediately after a person downloads trial software from the outsourced website.

Let's take a closer look at the new system.

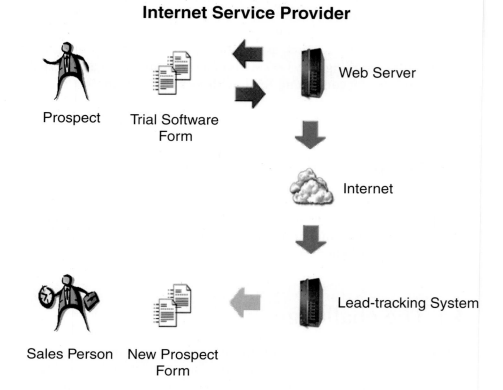

Internet Service Provider

Prospect   Trial Software Form   Web Server

Internet

Sales Person   New Prospect Form   Lead-tracking System

In-house System

Figure 13-1   Integrating sales leads generated at an outsourced website

13.5 | The solution

The architecture of the new system is illustrated in Figure 13-2. An XML document contains information collected at the outsourced website. It is transmitted to the internal *Notes/Domino* sales-tracking system using the Internet email infrastructure as the transport.

The process consists of three parts:

1. Create and send XML email
2. Receive and verify XML email

3. Process XML email and update database

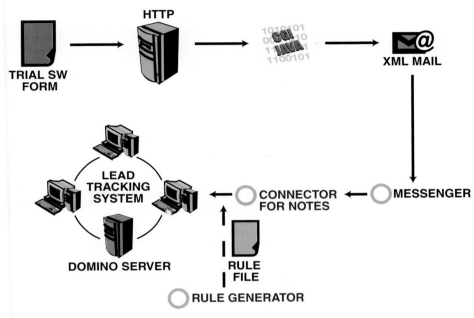

Figure 13-2   Lead-tracking system architecture

13.5.1 *One: Create and send XML email*

When a user fills out a form to download a trial version of software from the outsourced website, a RegisterUser.CGI script is invoked. That script calls the Send_XML_Lead subroutine, an excerpt from which is shown in Example 13-1.

Send_XML_Lead creates a Download XML document, like that shown in Example 13-2. It incorporates the document in an email message and calls the SendMail component of the Web server operating system to send the message to the lead-tracking inbox on the internal system's mail server.

Example 13-1. Excerpt from Send_XML_Lead subroutine

```
sub send_xml_lead {
  if ($FORM{'email'} ne '') {
  open (LEAD, ">$leadtemp") || die "Can't open $leadtemp!\n";
  print LEAD "To: SalesLeads\@subjectsoftware.com\n";
  print LEAD "From: TrialSite <website@subjectsoftware.com>\n";
  print LEAD "Reply-To: website\@subjectsoftware.com\n";
  print LEAD "Content-Transfer-Encoding: 7bit\n";
  print LEAD "Content-Type: text/plain\n";
  print LEAD "Subject: $fullname ($product $edition) \n\n";
  print LEAD "<\?xml version=\"1.0\" encoding=\"UTF-8\"?>\n";
  print LEAD "<Download>\n";
  print LEAD "<Person>\n";
  print LEAD "  <FirstName>$FORM{'fname'}</FirstName>\n";
  print LEAD "</Person> \n";
  ...
  print LEAD "</Download>\n";
  close (LEAD);
  system("$convprog -SJ $leadtemp|$mailprog -t");
  }
}
```

Example 13-2. XML document created by CGI Script in Example 13-1

```
<Download>
<Person>
  <FirstName>Robert</FirstName>
  <LastName>Blacken</LastName>
  <FullName>Robert Blacken</FullName>
  <MailAddress>rblacken@hotprospect.com</MailAddress>
  <JobTitle>CIO</JobTitle>
</Person>
<Company>
  <CompanyName>HotProspect</CompanyName>
  <OfficeAddress>900 Cummings Center</OfficeAddress>
  <OfficeCity>Beverly</OfficeCity>
  <OfficeState>Massachusetts</OfficeState>
  <OfficeZip>01915</OfficeZip>
  <OfficeCountry>United States</OfficeCountry>
  <OfficePhone>978-922-4029</OfficePhone>
</Company>
<Other>
  <Comment>Evaluating software for new app</Comment>
  <Categories>Download - iPEX for Solaris</Categories>
</Other>
</Download>
```

13.5.2   *Two: Receive and process XML email*

The second part of the process is handled inside the company's firewall, on its internal system. The `Download` XML documents containing the sales leads are stored in a mail queue on the company's Lotus *Domino* mail server.

Message-oriented middleware (labeled *MESSENGER* in the figure) pulls the email into a working directory, using the IMAP4 protocol. It verifies the sender's email address and the document type of the XML documents (in this case, `Download`).

The XML document is then processed according to the business rules defined for the particular sender and document type. The rules can cause invocation of DOS batch (.BAT) files or executable programs (.EXE). They also cause the internal system database to be updated with data extracted from the XML document, as we'll see shortly.

The behavior of the middleware is configurable by the configuration tool shown in Figure 13-3. That figure illustrates some of the settings that were used for this application. The program was set to run at one minute intervals and to use `D:\SalesLead\XML` as the working directory.

The configuration tool supports multiple categories of XML email in one or more email queues. It does so by allowing different behaviors to be specified for different XML document types and/or sender's email addresses.

13.5.3   *Three: Update database*

Because Subject Software's internal system uses Lotus *Notes*, the middleware uses the appropriate connector software to update the lead-tracking database. That tool includes a graphical interface for defining the rules for extracting data from XML elements and updating the corresponding database fields. The defined rules are represented in XML.

Example 13-3 shows a subset of the XML *rule* document used in this application. It maps the element types of a `Download` document onto the fields of the `Person` form in the *Domino* lead-tracking system.

Although Subject Software's system uses Lotus *Notes* and *Domino*, the principles apply to any email system and to any database management system.

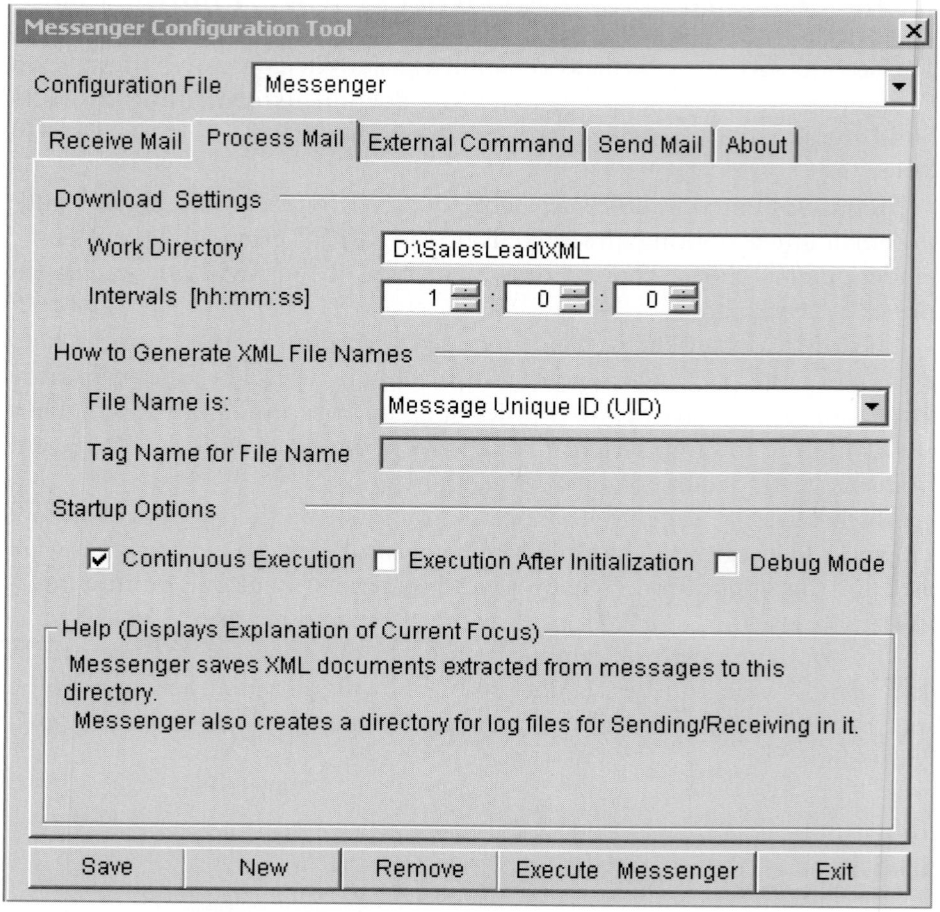

Figure 13-3 *MESSENGER* Configuration Tool

Example 13-3. Excerpt from `rule` document

```
<rule:rule
  xmlns:rule=
    "http://www.xmlns.org/system/jp/co/subjectsoftware/rule/"
  xmlns:notes=
    "http://www.xmlns.org/system/jp/co/subjectsoftware/tdf/notes/"
  default-space="strip"
  indent-result="yes">
<rule:template
  match="/database/table[@name=&quot;Person&quot;]/record">
  <Download>
  <Person>
    <FirstName>
      <rule:apply-templates
        select="field[@name=&quot;FirstName&quot;]"
        mode="_Download_Person_FirstName_.text."/>
    </FirstName>
    <LastName>
      <rule:apply-templates
        select="field[@name=&quot;LastName&quot;]"
        mode="_Download_Person_LastName_.text."/>
    </LastName>
    ...
  </Person>
  ...
  </Download>
</rule:template>
</rule:rule>
```

Business integration

- Partner connectivity
- Application connectivity
- Data transformation
- Process management
- Software and services

Contributing expert: Greg Olsen, Ph.D.

Chapter

14

In the quest for efficient operation and increased customer satisfaction, enterprises seek greater integration of their business processes with those of their partner suppliers and customers. Unfortunately, their independent software gets in the way. But thanks to XML, independent software can cooperate while remaining independent, and the desired business integration can be achieved.

P erhaps the earliest form of business integration is traditional *electronic data interchange (EDI)*, which allows members of a supply chain to conduct business electronically. With the rise of the Internet and the expansion of e-business, other areas have become targets for integration.

Caution   Acronym alert! This chapter contains an Alphabet Soup of Initialisms and Acronyms (ASIA). Please don't be put off by them. They're not for understanding the chapter, so if you don't know them, ignore them. If you know them, you'll see how they fit in the framework that the chapter describes. (They are all defined in Chapter 67, "The XML Handbook Acronym Guide", on page 1120.)

14.1 | Integration domains

Integration efforts have traditionally been categorized as either internal or external.

Internal integration occurs within an organization. Some examples are:

- Integration of application packages from different vendors.
- Integration of legacy systems with newer packaged applications.
- Coordination of data between business applications and data marts and data warehouses.
- Development of custom-distributed software applications.

External integration occurs among separate organizations. Domains include:

Supply chain integration
Sharing information with suppliers, customers, distributors, outsourced providers of fabrication or assembly services, etc.

Business unit integration
For example, post-merger coordination of independent business units.

Market integration
Procurement activities brokered through a market exchange would be an example.

For years, these two types of integration problem were considered independent of one another. Different groups within a company would manage the relevant activities separately and might apply completely different technology approaches to their solutions. Figure 14-1 shows an oversimplified view of the development of business integration.

E-business has progressed to the point where these separate integration efforts, which go by names like *Enterprise Application Integration (EAI)* and *Business to Business Integration (B2Bi)*, have converged into a single *business integration* problem space. The terms *eBusiness Integration (eBI)* and *Enterprise Business Integration (EBI)* are often used to describe the convergence.

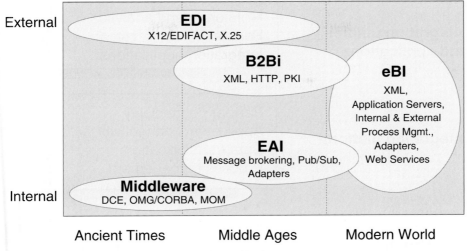

Figure 14-1 A brief history of business integration

By "convergence" we mean that software and service providers are addressing these formerly independent problems holistically. It also means that the problem space can be described through a single set of layered components, the business integration stack.

14.2 | The business integration stack

Business integration is a complex activity that is built from several layers of technology. Figure 14-2 shows a high-level view of the business integration stack.

14.2.1 *Infrastructure*

The infrastructure technologies on which business integration relies are, of necessity, pervasive. They therefore tend to emanate from highly influential sources:

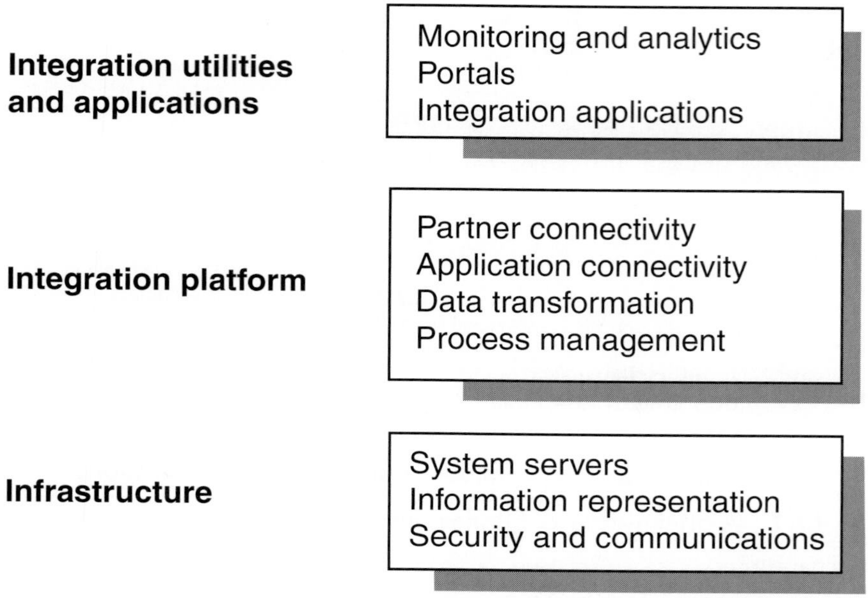

Integration utilities
and applications

> Monitoring and analytics
> Portals
> Integration applications

Integration platform

> Partner connectivity
> Application connectivity
> Data transformation
> Process management

Infrastructure

> System servers
> Information representation
> Security and communications

Figure 14-2   The business integration stack

- major software infrastructure vendors (e.g. IBM, Microsoft, Oracle, and Sun),
- open source initiatives,
- formal standards organizations (e.g. ISO, IEEE, ANSI), and
- industry consortia (e.g. W3C, IETF, OASIS, RosettaNet).

They fall into three major categories that we'll now examine.

14.2.1.1   System servers

Application servers have emerged as the focal point for runtime management and a variety of brokering functions used in integration solutions. Reliable messaging systems are also a fundamental component of nearly all integration solutions, as are information repositories.

While some products in the integration platform layer may incorporate facilities like these, developers increasingly expect them to be available as part of the infrastructure of a system.

14.2.1.2   Information representation

XML has emerged as the primary information representation for both internal and external integration requirements. It is an important ingredient in all the integration platform components at the next layer, as well as being employed in other infrastructure components.

In addition to the base XML Recommendation and related W3C standards such as XSLT and XLink, the infrastructure layer includes industry standards based on XML. Many consortia (e.g. RosettaNet and OAG) are developing common vocabularies that can be used in both internal and external integration contexts. While XML is clearly the preferred information representation approach some EBI vendors have yet to convert from proprietary information representations.

14.2.1.3   Security and communications

Recent years have seen a dramatic improvement in the technologies available in this category, for both internal and external integration needs. They include public key infrastructure (PKI), data compression, a diverse set of communication protocols (e.g. TCP/IP, HTTP, RMI, IIOP, SOAP), message and channel security standards, and directory infrastructure standards (e.g. LDAP, UDDI).

14.2.2   *Integration platform*

The integration platform layer builds upon the infrastructure just described. Its components are obtainable from a variety of integration product and service vendors.

It is important to keep in mind that the word "integration" refers only to the business result. At the software level, a better term would be "coordination". Individual application programs need not be rewritten; they can be totally unaware of one another.

Instead, the integration platform allows them to share data, and schedules their operation so as to achieve the desired result. Developers refer to this remote coordination of programs, when running on multiple computers, as *distributed computing*.

The integration platform components are shown in Figure 14-3. We'll discuss them in the following sections.

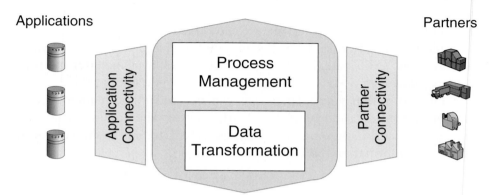

Figure 14-3   Integration platform components

14.2.2.1   Partner connectivity

Even with the advances in the available security and communications infrastructure, external communications (communications across organizational boundaries) are still a primary focus at the integration platform level. That is because of the diverse set of partners, and corresponding diverse partner connectivity requirements, that any good-sized organization is likely to have.

Typical requirements for partner connectivity include the need to support multiple communication protocols and security models, diverse approaches to message "envelopes", and multiple techniques for error recovery and other communication details.

14.2.2.2   Application connectivity

Integration platforms accomplish their magic by creating a "normalized" view of the applications with which they interact. This view includes the representation of the data that will be interchanged with the application, the protocols for requesting services from the application, and the means by which the application can initiate communications with the platform. This normalized view relies heavily on XML.

Unfortunately, the applications typically don't share this view. They have their own way of doing things that may have served them for years, even decades!

The primary method for bridging these conflicting views is through the use of software *adapters* (also called *connectors*). Adapters provide a bridge between the interfaces presented by applications and the normalized view of the integration platform.

Ideally, application adapters should require little or no custom coding. Vendors may supply wizards that can automatically configure an adapter by accessing a repository of application interface descriptions and metadata. This wizard-based approach not only simplifies initial installation but also provides significant advantages for long-term solution manageability.

14.2.2.3   Data transformation

Data transformation has probably the longest history as an integration function. Prior to XML it was inseparable from partner and application connectivity because there was no neutral representation technology. The structure and meaning of the information (semantics) could not be processed without understanding the proprietary notation (syntax) used by the originating application and/or external communication protocol.

XML, however, enables a clean separation. Connectivity adapters can transform the structure and semantics of the data to and from the XML notation. Data transformation functions can then operate on the data without regard to its origin or eventual destination. For example, a purchase order conforming to an internal DTD could be transformed to one that is used by a partner, which might require different element type names ("vendor" rather than "supplier") or a different sequence of elements.

An integration platform might increase efficiency for high-demand specialized transformations (e.g. among XML, X12, and EDIFACT) by retaining tight coupling between the semantics and syntax.

14.2.2.4   Process management

Coordination of activity can take many forms, from complex sequencing of interactions among applications and business partners to simple routing rules. Workflow and rules-based solutions allow high-level representation of dependencies and other logic.

An integration platform typically uses a process engine as a master controller. It reads the rules and controls the invocation of other platform components, such as data transformation components and adapters.

It is important for a platform to distinguish between external (public) processes that span multiple organizations from internal (private) processes. Doing so facilitates lifecycle and change management, which are ultimately the most difficult challenges facing large-scale integration solutions.

14.2.3   *Integration utilities and applications*

An integration platform, in addition to performing its primary function of coordinating independent applications, can support a variety of additional facilities. These include utilities that provide information about the system, portals that allow human access to data processed by the system, and applications built on top of the integration platform.

14.2.3.1   Monitoring and analytics

Much useful information can be gleaned from watching and recording the behavior of an integration platform. Metrics can be supplied to support a range of activities.

For vital signs monitoring, for example, data could include system load, throughput, and similar health metrics. For business-oriented analysis, data could help answer questions like:

- Which partners are performing best?
- Where are supply chain bottlenecks?
- What are the highest-value activities?
- What processes are most error prone?

14.2.3.2 Portals

Integration platforms may need to support user interaction, not just for the operation and monitoring of the system, but for access to the data processed by the applications under its control. Interaction among users, as well as between users and the system, may be supported.

The systems that provide such access are called *portals*. They can be thought of as being attached to the integration platform, rather than on top of it, as they may share the platform's infrastructure components (e.g. application server, information repository, and security infrastructure).

14.2.3.3 Integration applications

In the same way that business applications are built on relational database infrastructures, new categories of software are being built on top of integration platforms. These *integration applications* are actually composite applications, in the sense that they are built from the applications controlled by the platform.

As composites, integration applications tend to focus on inter-organizational tasks. Some examples are collaborative order management, collaborative forecast management, and collaborative design management.

14.3 | Deploying business integration

Business integration solutions can be implemented in the obvious manner by installing and configuring the appropriate software components at a customer site. However, it is also possible to obtain full business integration capabilities through service providers.

A combination of the two can also be employed. Some possible scenarios are shown in Figure 14-4, Figure 14-5, Figure 14-6 and Figure 14-7.

The classic integration service provider is the *Value-Added Network (VAN)* that supports traditional EDI. The idea behind the VAN is that integration capabilities are provided in the network, outside the firewall, instead of within a company's own IT environment.

Integration service providers today are known by a variety of other names as well, such as *Managed Service Provider (MSP)*, *Application Service Pro-*

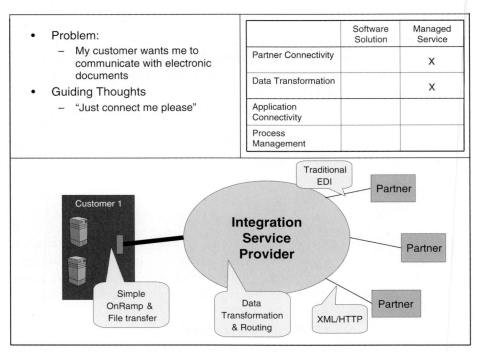

Figure 14-4   Integration solution: Connectivity

vider (ASP), or *Business Service Provider (BSP)*. In the following sections we'll look at their offerings for the components of an integration platform.

14.3.1   *Partner connectivity services*

The original EDI VANs provided basic connectivity prior to the existence of Internet-based options. These private networks continue to be used today and new forms of private networks, built on Internet infrastructure, have arisen. The range of external communications services that can be provided is broad and includes:

- basic data movement;
- guaranteed levels of service;
- numerous security services; auditing, tracking, and monitoring; and

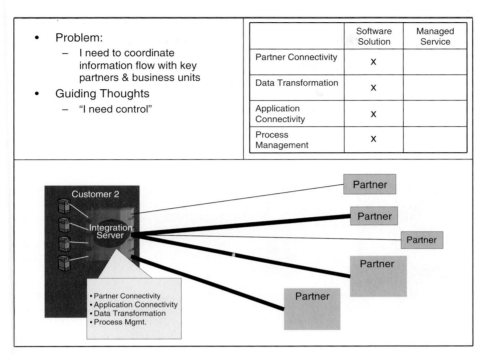

	Software Solution	Managed Service
Partner Connectivity	X	
Data Transformation	X	
Application Connectivity	X	
Process Management	X	

Figure 14-5   Integration solution: Process management

    ■   partner directory services.

Service providers can bridge diverse and asymmetric external communications requirements on a very large scale. The partners of any single company may collectively employ a great many security and communication options. These can include traditional EDI VAN traffic, batch direct dial-up, SNA networks, and a wide variety of Internet-based protocols and security approaches. A service provider can consolidate support for large numbers of communications options in one place and can gateway customers from one communication method to another.

14.3.2 *Application connectivity services*

It is less common for service providers to supply application connectivity than other components of an integration platform. However, companies

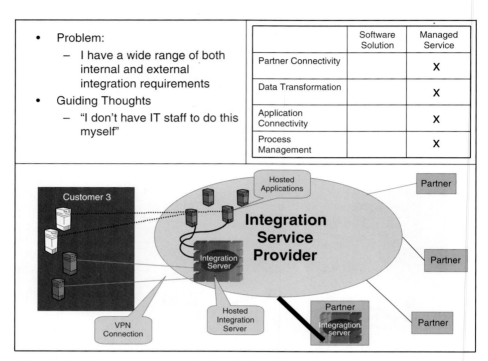

	Software Solution	Managed Service
Partner Connectivity		X
Data Transformation		X
Application Connectivity		X
Process Management		X

- Problem:
  - I have a wide range of both internal and external integration requirements
- Guiding Thoughts
  - "I don't have IT staff to do this myself"

Figure 14-6   Integration solution: Managed service

can grant application access to a provider over a virtual or physically private network, and let the service provider develop and maintain the adapters. This strategy allows application connectivity expertise to be consolidated by the provider, who can then offer client companies a very low maintenance solution.

14.3.3 *Data transformation services*

Service providers can enable very high performance bulk data transformation through access to high-end hardware environments.

A service provider can also centralize creation and maintenance of the maps used in transformations from one data representation vocabulary to another (as discussed in 14.2.2.3). These could include, for example, transformations from one DTD to another or between a data dictionary and a DTD or schema.

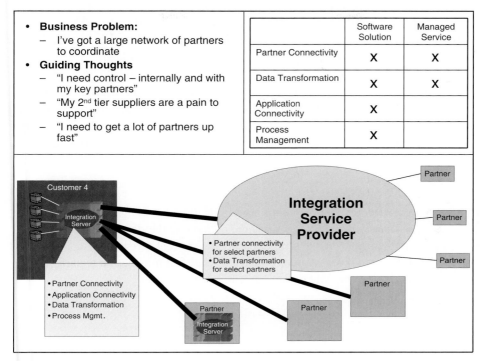

	Software Solution	Managed Service
Partner Connectivity	X	X
Data Transformation	X	X
Application Connectivity	X	
Process Management	X	

- **Business Problem:**
  - I've got a large network of partners to coordinate
- **Guiding Thoughts**
  - "I need control – internally and with my key partners"
  - "My 2nd tier suppliers are a pain to support"
  - "I need to get a lot of partners up fast"

Customer 4 — Integration Server

- Partner Connectivity
- Application Connectivity
- Data Transformation
- Process Mgmt.

Integration Service Provider

- Partner connectivity for select partners
- Data Transformation for select partners

Partner — Integration Server

Partner

Partner

Partner

Partner

Partner

Figure 14-7 Integration solution: Network management

14.3.4 *Process management services*

Many smaller companies are not equipped to maintain process management software on their sites. Service providers can help companies manage both internal and external processes. To do so, simple stateless linkages are maintained between the customer and the service provider, and the service provider is responsible for the management of state coordination and failure recovery.

14.4 | Conclusion

Many factors have led to the convergence of independent integration activities into the unified domain of business integration that we have been discussing. However, the emergence of the Internet and XML are the most significant. Unlike data representations such as ANSI X12, ASN.1, and SQL, XML has succeeded in providing a data model of sufficient flexibility and ease of use that it can be used as a common foundation for a broad spectrum of integration problems.

Of all the integration platform components, process management has emerged as the major differentiator among integration solutions. It is primarily in the definition of process rules that the business logic of integration is captured, and there that difficult change and lifecycle management issues are most visible.

Analysis   Like content processing, business integration – and its counterpart, application coordination – is the dominant motivation of many XML applications and tool categories. And, as also occurs with content processing, that fact may not be explicit and the term "integration" may not even be used.

Content Management

- Multi-national translation and distribution
- Content systems in detail
- Component management for text and graphics

Part Five

Content is king!

Whether it's a website, your car's owner's manual, or a newspaper, the style may get your attention but the content is why you are there and why you will (or won't) return.

And the demand for new content – and new ways of packaging and delivering it – is growing by leaps and bounds. This calls for increased efficiency in the creation, processing, and delivery of content.

As a result, enterprises are increasingly realizing that content is a valuable corporate asset, one that needs to be managed with the same care as other valuable property.

In this part we'll look at the systems that have been developed for content management. We'll set the stage with a classic application, then look at the full scope of a content system that is built around a content management. Finally we'll look at the key XML value-add: component management, for both text and graphics.

"World" class content management

Case Study

- Tweddle Litho Company
- Automotive manuals in 30 languages
- XML content management
- Natural language translation

Contributing experts: Jon Parsons and Judy Cox

Chapter

15

For the perfect introduction to content management and its benefits, you need look no further than the glove box of your car – and the manuals in the language of whichever of 60 countries you bought it in. It is literally a "world" class application. This chapter will show you how that miracle of logistics is accomplished.

When you lease or buy an automobile, you become dependent on documentation.

You know that the glove box will contain an owner's manual, a maintenance schedule, a warranty maintenance book, and a book that describes your radio and/or CD player. You expect them to completely and accurately describe the car you are in. What's more, when you take the car in for service, you rely on the service technician having the information needed for the model and year of your car in a language he or she can read – no matter where in the world you are.

Ensuring that the information is there and available when needed is literally a "world" class task, a task made achievable by XML and a content management system. Let's look at how that task is accomplished at Tweddle Litho Company, producer of more than half of the world's automotive owner and glove box documentation.

15.1 | Auto manufacturing is large-scale publishing

For a successful worldwide launch of a new car, the manufacturer needs a full range of publications. The owner's guide, audio guide, and warranty material must be present in each vehicle. A service manual must be available to the service providers in every country.

These documents must be translated into as many as 30 different languages. Each document must be modified to conform to the national regulations for each country that imports the car. Cars shipped to Mexico, for example, must include jumper cables, and the documentation must reference this.

Producing those documents for a single new vehicle launch is a huge undertaking. Producing them for all of a manufacturer's models is a monumental one.

And one that compounds over time, because each model changes to a greater or lesser degree each year. And for each of the models, in each of the years, in each of the languages, the information must be available in print, on the Web, and on CD-ROM. Figure 15-1 illustrates the complexity.

Many auto manufacturers choose to outsource these projects to a full-service technical publishing house such as Tweddle Litho Company of Clinton Township, Michigan.

Founded in 1954 as a small printing company, Tweddle Litho pioneered computerized photocomposition and typesetting. As technologies changed, the company seized the opportunity to move further upstream from publishing to encompass the entire data management cycle, including writing, translation, and other related services.

Today, with customers such as Ford Motor Company, General Motors, Chrysler, Nissan, and Volvo, Tweddle Litho produces approximately 55 percent of all the automotive owner's literature worldwide.

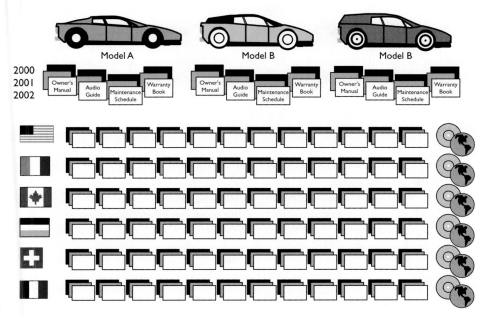

Figure 15-1   Auto documentation for multiple models, model years, languages, and delivery formats

15.2 | Global markets, global information

As Tweddle's business grew, so did the requirements for internationalizing the information it managed for its customers. It soon became acquainted with the difficulties of the translation process:

- Passing information to translation houses, communicating about what was really meant, and answering questions about context
- Tracking the status and progress of the translations underway – and what had been returned
- Retranslating what had already been translated – and hadn't changed – when only a small portion of a document was modified

Managing the process manually was time consuming and prone to error. It also required a large editorial staff.

As a result, Tweddle undertook to find and apply a technology that would strategically position it to solve the large-scale problems of its customers. Tweddle knew it had to be prepared to support a vehicle release in 30 languages in 60 countries simultaneously. It needed to support 40 vehicle lines with a total of 6000 books. The information management team defined a number of objectives:

- Designing a friendlier more appealing visual style for the owner's manuals
- Creating a global, culturally neutral style
- Meeting local regulations (engineering, regulatory, safety, environmental)
- Reducing time to produce the information
- Reducing overall cost
- Increasing usability of the information
- Anticipating future uses of the information
- Managing artwork

Not everything on their list could be addressed by software, but the issues of time, cost, and reuse of the information could. They concluded that proper management of their information assets required generalized markup and a component-based information management system that could handle it.

15.3 | Needed: An XML component management system

By delimiting and labeling each of the individual elements of a document, XML enables both people and software to manipulate information as units useful for the purpose at hand. No longer is it necessary to deal with a whole document or even a complete chapter when only a small piece – perhaps only one or two paragraphs, a table, or step or two in a procedure – changes.

These units of information are called *components*. Figure 15-2 shows how XML identifies them.

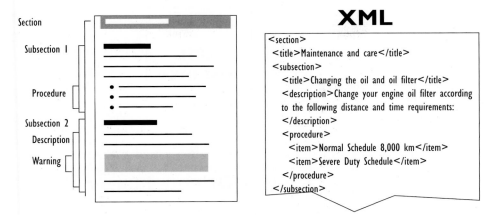

Figure 15-2   XML supports the use of document components

By managing these units separately and combining them into larger chunks of information – sections or chapters or books – only when needed, Tweddle could give only those units that changed to the translators. That level of precision enormously reduces redundant work.

In addition to providing the focus they needed for translation, a component management approach also let them reuse information in multiple documents. They could write a piece once, use it in several different places, and when changes occurred, update the component only once and have the changes replicated in each place it was used.

Even more, a component-based management system allowed them to build different views of the data. For example, a technical writer may be focusing on air conditioning or braking systems for a given auto model. The writer can look into the database and find all the procedures for that kind of system. Another writer, creating a view for a different model, might find that it included many of the same procedures because the systems were similar in both autos.

The architecture for component storage is shown in Figure 15-3.

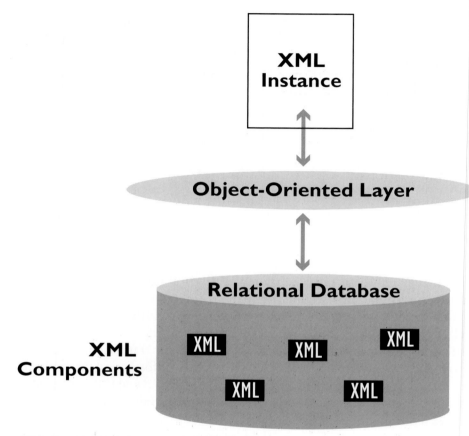

Figure 15-3   Component storage

15.4 | Improving the translation process

Component management allowed translation to be focused on revised components only, a concept illustrated in Figure 15-4.

The translation workflow at Tweddle is based upon the use of in-country translators; that is, native speakers of a language living in the country for which the information is destined. In this workflow, there is a significant exchange of information at arm's length between Tweddle and the translators. A key aim in managing the translation process is to preserve context so that the translator has sufficient information to make sound decisions about which word to choose in rendering one language into another.

When changes are made to a previously translated document, *Content@* creates a translation package for the translator that includes a proof version that shows how the component looked in the last printed book, the previous XML source file for the component, the revised XML source file, and a list of differences. The package provides the context the translator needs.

The system creates the translation package automatically, triggered by the changes made when the revised component is returned to the repository. It is checked out for translation and the translation package is delivered electronically to the translator. Once the translation is complete, the revised translation component is checked back into the database and its status is automatically noted by the workflow manager.

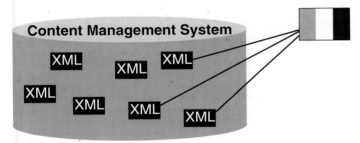

Figure 15-4   Only revised components are sent to the translator.

A further advantage of component management is the ability to coordinate parallel work on the same document. For example, one of the European car manufacturers writes some parts in German while Tweddle continues to write other parts in English. They can still maintain the common use of data.

15.5 | One source, multiple delivery formats

A key advantage of using XML is that markup reflects the structure of an element, totally apart from how it is to be rendered. This separation of abstract content from rendered format allows delivery of the information in multiple formats from a single source.

15.5.1 *Printed delivery*

When all revisions and translations are complete, the system assembles a complete version of the book from its components. This XML instance is then sent to an XML publishing system that automatically composes and paginates the XML instance into finished documents.

Where it had taken up to six months to deliver a translated book, Tweddle is now getting the same results in three weeks and is even able to support the release of a foreign language document prior to release of the domestic English version.

Tweddle has been setting up remote printing facilities around the world in response to a growing need for on-demand printing. One of its European customers routinely has it prepare service literature in 22 languages and then prepare deliverables in both print and CD-ROM formats. Instead of shipping a large quantity of bulky books, Tweddle sends the files electronically to be printed in Belgium for European distribution, in Singapore for Asian distribution, and so on.

15.5.2 *Online delivery*

Owner's literature may stay a paper-based product for some time because inside a car, at present, there are few practical alternatives for viewing it electronically. However, with the advent of more on-board electronics and touch screen panels, the ability to deliver owner information in an electronic form as well as in print will become essential. XML provides the way. A few of the auto manufacturers have already eliminated paper deliverables completely for documents other than the owner's manuals.

Another big trend is the move away from paper toward electronic files for customer assistance representatives. Rather than sorting through one hundred manuals, each 1,400 to 2,000 pages long, the customer service representative is able to access a searchable database to find the appropriate procedure for a specific problem.

15.6 | Conclusion

XML enables solutions to complex information management problems such as Tweddle's because:

- XML can enforce the strict separation of abstract content from rendered format.
- XML enables the management and manipulation of small units of data that can be reused and assembled into multiple documents.
- XML can represent the structure of the abstract content, which is the same regardless of the natural language of the text.

Together with a component management system that supports and uses these advantages, XML solves immediate business problems while preserving a flexible and open foundation for whatever changes technology may bring.

Content systems

Application Discussion

- Acquisition
- Enrichment
- Management
- Collaboration
- Distribution

Contributing experts: Mark A. Hale, Ron Daniel Jr., and Jack Jia

> As businesses move more of their operations to the Web they become increasingly aware of the importance of their multitude of information content assets. These must now be made available as website content, in addition to their conventional use in reports and printed publications. To do it right, you need a robust content system, with content management at its core.

A large enterprise can have millions of information content assets, routinely produced by thousands of people. Those assets include everything from the graphs and figures that go into your year-end analysis report, to the operating instructions in your product manuals, to the business process data captured in your ERP or legacy systems.

As the Web looms ever larger in the business world, there is an increasing need to aggregate and exploit that content. And there is also an increasing recognition of just how complex and difficult a problem it is.

16.1 | The content challenge

All businesses, regardless of size, begin to appreciate the broad scope of content in day-to-day operations when they attempt to collect content for their first website. Even a single Web page may display information assets from many sources, as we see in Figure 16-1. That page contains graphics and text from the file system, output of applications, and data from databases. Clearly, many people contributed to this one Web page alone. Moreover, the form of the content varies significantly, ranging from static text strings to data generation on-demand.

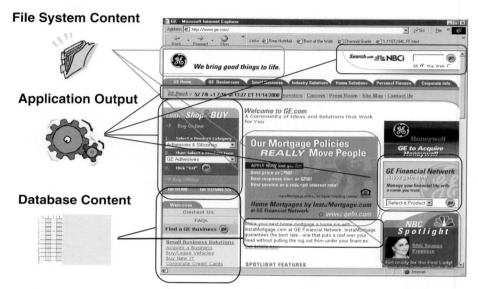

Figure 16-1   Content of a Web page

This diversity of content types and sources is now the norm for production websites. It presents a challenge to the Web designers who must integrate the content to produce the final pages. They must cope with:

- Large numbers of interdependent contributors and information assets.
- A wide variety of continuously revised assets, from sources such as office applications, data collection forms, databases, and internal communications.
- Content delivery not just on the company website, but via printed documentation, wireless phones, handheld PDAs, portals, syndication, and other means.

These requirements can be met by aggregating and processing content as an enterprise resource, independently of its original sources or the uses to which it may eventually be put. XML makes this approach possible. You can think of it as building an XML-based *content infrastructure* for the enterprise. It would support five functional areas:

- Acquisition: Collecting content from diverse sources
- Enrichment: Adding value to content to maximize returns
- Management: Storage, versioning, and access control
- Collaboration: Working on content with other contributors
- Distribution: Making content available to users

Although it is convenient to speak of these areas as sequential processing steps, in practice there is overlap, concurrency, and recycling among them.

Let's look more closely at each area, using a media relations application as an example. We'll develop a simple press release.

16.2 | Acquisition

In order to maximize the use of content, it must be represented in XML. However, that phrase accommodates a number of approaches:

- Create an XML document from scratch.
- Convert a non-XML document to XML.
- Encapsulate a non-XML document in an XML wrapper.

Regardless of the approach, consideration must be given to the circumstances of acquisition and the skills and culture of the people involved. User interfaces should be provided that allow contributors to contribute content in the manner that is least obtrusive in their day-to-day work.

16.2.1 *Creating XML documents*

XML application designers may be willing to face XML markup head-on. They may even prefer it, because it guarantees that no software is distorting what they see. Such folks can use ordinary text editors or specialized XML development tools to create their XML documents.

For other document creators, XML-aware publishing and word processing tools may be best. These usually provide a rendered view of the data that conceals the XML markup. However, the markup can be examined when desired. These tools can support richly-structured complex documents.

However, for capture of structurally-simple business process data, the long-standing favorite user interface has been the form. Unlike the forms in HTML, though, a form in an XML content system is actually a rendition of an XML template. That is, an XML document with markup but no data.

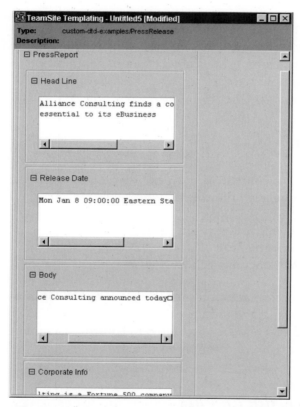

Figure 16-2   Rendered XML template capturing press release in Example 16-1

Figure 16-2 shows the XML template for our press release rendered into a form by an XML content system. A contributor has entered data into the form fields, which causes creation of the XML document shown in Example 16-1.

Example 16-1. Press release in XML

```
<PressReport>
  <Headline>
    Alliance Consulting finds a content infrastructure
    essential to its eBusiness
  </Headline>
  <ReleaseDate>
    Mon Jan 8 09:00:00 Eastern Standard Time 2001
  </ReleaseDate>
  <Body>
    Alliance Consulting announced today...
  </Body>
  <CorporateInfo>
    Alliance Consulting is a Fortune 500 company...
  </CorporateInfo>
</PressReport>
```

16.2.2 *Acquiring non-XML documents*

All content will undergo transformations in a content system as it is prepared to be placed on a website. XML content is easiest to operate on because its structure is explicit and its notation is standardized. However, there is a significant amount of content in non-XML form that businesses use every day that must be acquired for the content system.

Both document representation issues and user interface issues should be considered when planning this aspect of a content system.

16.2.2.1 User interface considerations

Contributing content should be made as unobtrusive as possible for the many content creators. They should be allowed to focus on what they do best: create meaningful content.

To achieve this goal, a content system could support transparent access from popular document creation tools such as *Microsoft Office*® and *Adobe® Acrobat®*. For example, on systems that use the WebDAV protocol, users could create documents in these applications and upload them to a content system straightforwardly by using the standard File Save function.

A content system could also allow users to import and export through a virtual file system view. Such a facility would allow users, for example, to import pictures from a photo CD by simply dragging them into a folder on the desktop. The cost-effectiveness is compelling, considering the number of users who create files and who are familiar with this common user interface.

16.2.2.2   Document representation

The basic distinction here is between converting data to XML or merely encapsulating it in an XML tracking document.

16.2.2.2.1 *Conversion*

Acquiring legacy content is an important component of publishing large catalogs in electronic commerce. Businesses find that they are exchanging a large number of content assets with their partners and customers. Conversion to XML provides a mechanism for automating catalog content generation and reuse for channel delivery.

Many tools are available for automatically or semi-automatically converting from non-XML notations to XML. There are also outsourcing services with specialized expertise and the capacity to handle large-volume projects that might be burdensome for in-house resources.

Some conversions are relatively trivial. Simple data structures such as comma-delimited text files exported from database systems, for example, can easily be converted using XSLT.

16.2.2.2.2 *Encapsulation*

Encapsulation is the simplest technique for implementing the file system interface. An XML tracking document is created for each non-XML asset, with elements that record metadata about its representation, access rights, external links, etc.

The non-XML document could physically be encapsulated as a CDATA section within the tracking document. More conveniently, it could be associated logically as an external unparsed data entity.

16.3 | Enrichment

In producing a website or other final publication, designers aggregate content collected from XML templates, office applications and other sources.

These designers aren't necessarily domain experts for the content they manipulate. To guide them in using content effectively and accurately, creators can associate metadata with content.

Example 16-2. PRISM metadata for press release

```
<rdf:RDF xmlns:prism="http://prismstandard.org/1.0#"
  xmlns:rdf="http://www.w3.org/1999/02/22-rdf-syntax-ns#"
  xmlns:dc="http://purl.org/dc/elements/1.1#">
  <rdf:Description about="release22.xml">
    <dc:title>Alliance Consulting finds a content infrastructure
              essential to its eBusiness</dc:title>
    <dc:creator>Alliance Consulting</dc:creator>
    <prism:releaseTime>2001-01-08T09:00:00Z-05
    </prism:releaseTime>
    <prism:creationTime>2001-01-05T10:51:17-08:00
    </prism:creationTime>
    <prism:modificationTime>2001-01-05T10:51:17-08:00
    </prism:modificationTime>
    <dc:format>text/xml</dc:format>
    <prism:category rdf:resource="#pressRelease" xml:base=
       "http://prismstandard.org/vocabularies/1.0/category.xml"/>
  </rdf:Description>
</rdf:RDF>
```

16.3.1 *Associating metadata*

Metadata consists of information like:

asset metadata
> Description of a content asset. It includes familiar properties such as file permissions, creation dates, etc.

subject metadata
> Controlled vocabularies of descriptive properties of the content, such as film type for photographs and drug classifications for prescriptions.

similarity metadata
> Information applicable to multiple content assets, such as similarity of subject matter or color.

at the beginning of the listing and the property request follows in XML. The `prop` element contains an empty element for each requested metadata property.

Example 16-4. WebDAV client request for press release metadata

```
PROPFIND /pressreleases/alliance.xml HTTP/1.1
Content-Type: text/xml
Depth: 1

<propfind xmlns="DAV:">
  <prop>
    <href/>
    <displayname/>
    <creationdate/>
    <getlastmodified/>
    <getcontenttype/>
  </prop>
</propfind>
```

The response from the server is shown in the listing in Example 16-5. Content has been supplied for the requested metadata property elements.

16.3.4 *Finding content*

In addition to finding metadata, a content system needs to provide tools for finding content assets themselves. It is particularly helpful for a contributor to know about related content during preparation of an asset, as it could improve the quality and accuracy of his work.

Metadata can make this possible. For example, consider a content system containing drug description documents. A user interface could be created for a doctor with two forms side-by-side. As he entered prescription information in one, related drugs could be shown in the other so that drug interactions can be assessed. The relationships, of course, are captured in the metadata in the drug descriptions.

usage metadata
> Content performance measures, such as number of downloads and geographic locations.

link metadata
> References to related content. For example, a paint selection guide could have link metadata that references home improvement and interior decorating catalogs that use the guide.

Example 16-2 is an RDF description of our press release utilizing metadata properties from the PRISM vocabulary. PRISM itself incorporates element types from other vocabularies, identified by the namespace prefix in the tags: `rdf` for RDF itself and `dc` for Dublin Core.

16.3.2 *Automated metadata creation*

A content system could supply tools that simplify a contributor's creation of metadata by generating it automatically from the asset. Such software is aware of appropriate metadata vocabularies and analyzes content for relevant data.

For example, in our press release, software could determine that Alliance Consulting is listed on the New York Stock Exchange. From the listing record, the company's Standard Industry Classification (SIC) code, 8748, could also be determined. Using the SIC code, further metadata about the industry classification could be obtained, as shown in Example 16-3. The `pcv` namespace prefix indicates that the PRISM Controlled Vocabulary is used.

Example 16-3. Generated metadata for the press release (excerpt)

```
<rdf:Description
   about="http://www.osha.gov/cgi-bin/sic/sicser2?8748">
   <pcv:label>Business Consulting Services,
```

Example 16-5. WebDAV server response to Example 16-4

```
HTTP/1.1 207 Multi-Status

<multistatus xmlns="DAV:">
  <response>
    <propstat>
      <prop>
        <href>/pressreleases/alliance.xml</href>
        <displayname>/alliance.xml</displayname>
        <creationdate>2001-01-05T10:51:17-08:00</creationdate>
        <getlastmodified>2001-01-06T18:51:17-08:00</getlastmodified>
        <getcontenttype>text/xml<getcontenttype/>
      </prop>
      <status>HTTP/1.1 200 OK</status>
    </propstat>
  </response>
</multistatus>
```

Such interfaces are called *recommendation systems*. While a user is working in one part of the user interface, queries are executed in one (or more) other parts. Systems can allow users to create such queries explicitly. They can also "learn" from a user's previous activities and generate appropriate queries automatically.

16.4 | Management

Management facilities are responsible for ensuring across-the-board consistency of all assets, users, platforms, applications, and storage facilities within a content system. They must be scalable to cope with potentially enormous numbers of assets, and reliable to assure high availability.

Management functions include:

- Providing a repository for storage of assets
- Maintaining multiple versions of assets and editions
- Asset-locking for safe collaboration
- Asset comparison to determine differences among assets or versions
- Conflict resolution through merger of jointly-created content
- Providing user and role-based access control and user authentication

- Maintaining relationships for document composition
- Managing risk: backup, archiving, maintenance, etc.

Content management is the heart of a content system. Let's look at two key aspects in detail: storage and versioning.

16.4.1 *Storage*

A content repository holds all of the assets acquired for the system, whether original or converted XML, or encapsulated non-XML data. Once assets are brought into a repository, they are subsequently managed uniformly using the functions just described, such as versioning, merging, and locking.

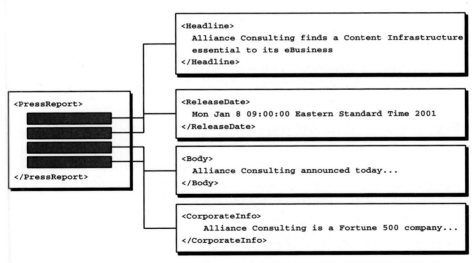

Figure 16-3   Components of press release

XML documents offer the added capability of being stored in *components*. That is, each of the document's constituent elements and fragments of data can be stored as individual assets. In Figure 16-3, our press release is divided into the components Headline, ReleaseDate, Body, and CorporateInfo, each consisting of an element of the original document.

16.4.2   *Versioning*

Version management is the content system facility that tracks and accesses the revision history for the assets managed by the system. The benefits and capabilities of versioning include:

- Tracking of individual assets

  All operations a user performs with respect to an asset are tracked. Content changes are therefore always accountable.

- Navigation of asset history

  Users can manage content development and revert to previous versions if needed.

- Parallel development and update of assets

  Users can try new ideas or start a new project from an existing one.

- Persistence in the event of system failure

  Content always keeps its integrity.

16.5 | Collaboration

As content is acquired from various sources, attention must be given to how the numerous interactions with the content can be coordinated. Some issues are the degree of interactivity of creators with their content and the relationship among diverse users.

    The keys to managing this complexity are:

- organizing the content;
- coordination through workflow; and
- virtualized testing.

16.5.1 *Organization of content*

One approach is to organize the content by projects, each corresponding to a significant deliverable publication, such as a library of manuals for a product, a top-level feature on a website, or even a complete website. For example, one project could be created for a company's website on the public Internet and a separate project for its internal intranet, which would allow contributors to easily distinguish which information will be published inside or outside the corporate firewall.

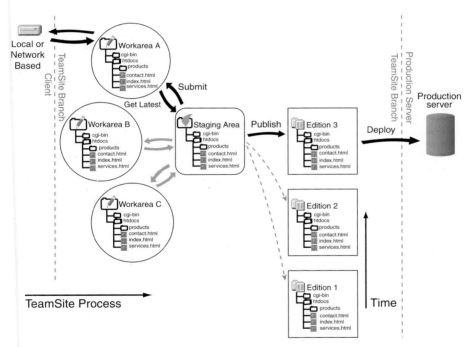

Figure 16-4   Content organization for collaboration

Figure 16-4 shows a project in the Interwoven *TeamSite* content infrastructure system. At the left are work areas for each contributor to the project. Contributors can be individual contributors and/or departments, such as marketing, engineering, and sales. A work area is a directory in which a contributor collects content for the portion of the project for which he is responsible. That content could contain links to content outside the work area.

Content ultimately works its way from the work areas into deliverable publications. To facilitate this process, content is first collected from contributors in a "staging area", where a designer can merge contributions together and sort out conflicts.

Because content can change over time, the publications change as well. At the right the project diagram shows successive editions of the publication. The latest, at the top, is deployed on the production server for distribution.

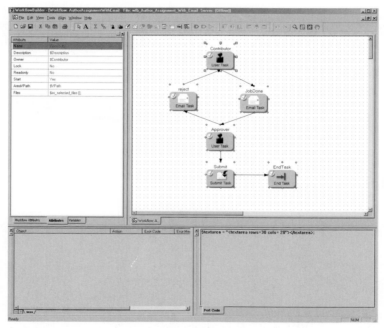

Figure 16-5   Workflow coordinating press release

16.5.2   *Coordination through workflow*

Workflow is used to coordinate contributor activities as they collaborate to publish an edition. In our press relations example, the activities range from entering press contacts to publishing final releases to syndicates. Figure

16-5 depicts the workflow that governs a reporter ("Contributor") and manager ("Approver") in the tasks of approving a press release and submitting it for distribution.

Workflow can be represented in XML, as shown in Example 16-6. The elements corresponding to the various task types (user, submit, email, etc.) are easily identified in the listing.

Example 16-6. XML representation of workflow in Figure 16-5

```
<workflow name="AuthorAssignmentWithEmail">
  <usertask name="Contributor" >
    <successors>
      <succ v="JobDone"/>
    </successors>
  </usertask>
  <emailtask name="JobDone">
    <successors>
      <succ v="Approver"/>
    </successors>
  </emailtask>
  <usertask name="Approver">
    <successors>
      <succ v="reject"/>
      <succ v="Submit"/>
    </successors>
  </usertask>
  <emailtask name="reject" >
    <successors>
      <succ v="Contributor"/>
    </successors>
  </emailtask>
  <submittask name="Submit">
    <successors>
      <succ v="EndTask"/>
    </successors>
  </submittask>
  <endtask name="EndTask"/>
</workflow>
```

16.5.3 *Virtualized testing*

There is an underlying complexity that businesses face when accommodating a large number of contributors. A contributor only has control over a single work area, but the final publication incorporates content from other work areas as well. How then can a content contributor test individual content modifications before they have been deployed to a production server?

Consider for example, a standard corporate statement appended to the end of our press release example. This XML element may belong to the legal department and exist in that department's work area. However, the press release is in the work area of its author.

The solution lies in *virtualization*, automatically resolving references to content assets located outside the work area. During test, a contributor proceeds to aggregate content as though constructing a new edition of the final publication. As it would be prohibitive to replicate complete databases for individual testing needs, the current version of the specific content referenced is displayed from the staging area.

16.6 | Distribution

The final step in content development is to deploy the edition whose content has been tested and approved in a production environment. This process is shown in Figure 16-6.

In our media relations example, the press releases are frozen as an edition and distributed to a syndicate. In turn, the syndicate caches the releases for high volume distribution to news agencies. If a database provides some of the content, the database is also distributed.

All references are resolved for the published edition and optimized for delivery performance on production sites. For XML content, this includes reconstructing XML documents from their stored components.

The figure also shows some of the advanced capabilities of a distribution network. Distribution networks can be configured so that content can be distributed worldwide and replicated in server farms for fast access. Syndication permits rules, schedules, profiles, and transformations to be defined on the server so that subscriptions can effectively be managed for content delivery to users, partners, and suppliers.

16.6.1 *Preparing content for delivery*

Content today must be distributed not just in printed form or conventional website delivery, but through such means as Web services, personalization,

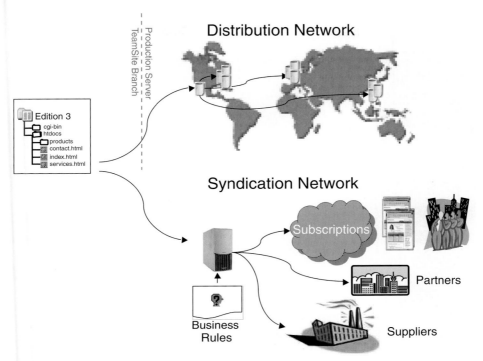

Figure 16-6 Content distribution and syndication

portals, wireless devices such as PDAs and cellular phones, and syndicates. This is called *multi-channel delivery* and businesses that adopt it are preparing their content for new products and markets.

As channels differ in their physical presentation capabilities, the content must be rendered appropriately for each one. A formatting program will process the edition and a suitable stylesheet to produce a rendition. Depending on the channel, the rendition may be represented in XML, as for many wireless devices, or may be in other notations, such as electronic data interchange (EDI).

For example, Figure 16-7 shows how a summary of our press release might appear on a cellular phone. Data is delivered to the phone using the Wireless Markup Language (WML), an XML document type.

To produce the summary, the XSLT stylesheet in Example 16-7 is used to govern the processing of the press release in Example 16-1. Elements in

Figure 16-7   Press release on a wireless device

the xsl namespace are instructions to the processor. The other elements are included unchanged in the generated output.

Note that if an instruction element returns data, the data is also included in the generated output. In our example, the first xsl:value-of instruction generates the data of the press release Headline element. The second generates the data of the ReleaseDate element.

16.6.2 *Distribution protocols*

Many of the emerging distribution channels use XML to transport content over many of the Internet protocols. We discussed the benefits of using XML in this way in 6.4, "Protocols", on page 135. In Example 16-8, you can see how our press release could be transmitted as email using ebXML (namespace prefix eb) for the routing header and manifest. ebXML in turn uses a SOAP envelope (namespace prefix SOAP-ENV).

Example 16-7. Stylesheet to generate press release summary in WML

```
<xsl:stylesheet
  xmlns:xsl="http://www.w3.org/1999/XSL/Transform"
  version="1.0">
  <xsl:output omit-xml-declaration="yes"/>
  <xsl:template match="/">
<wml>
    <card id="card1" title="Alliance Press Release">
      <p>
        <b>Headline: </b>
        <xsl:value-of select="PressReport/Headline" /><br/>
        <b>Date: </b>
        <xsl:value-of select="PressReport/ReleaseDate" /><br/>
      </p>
    </card>
  </wml>
  </xsl:template>
</xsl:stylesheet>
```

Email is represented in a non-XML notation called MIME. In a multi-part email such as this one, the parts are separated by a boundary string ("111Boundary" in the example), much as XML uses tags to bound elements.

16.7 | Conclusion

We've seen our sample press release work its way through all parts of a content system. XML was critical in each step of the process. Some of the highlights:

- The press release was captured in XML without the user having to mark up the XML explicitly.
- Metadata about the release was captured in XML.
- The press release was stored in components that can be maintained and reused independently.
- XML documents represented and drove the workflow by which the release was eventually sent for publication.
- XSLT stylesheets were used to format the press release for multi-channel delivery.

Example 16-8. ebXML message to distribute press release

```
Content-type: multipart/related; boundary="111Boundary";
              type="text/xml"; start=" <ebxmlheader@interwoven.com>"
--111Boundary
Content-ID: <ebxmlheader@interwoven.com>
Content-Type: text/xml;
<SOAP-ENV:Envelope
  xmlns:SOAP-ENV='http://schemas.xmlsoap.org/soap/envelope/'
  xmlns:eb='http://www.ebxml.org/namespaces/messageHeader'>
  <SOAP-ENV:Header>
    <eb:MessageHeader SOAP-ENV:mustUnderstand="1" eb:version="1.0">
      ...
    </eb:MessageHeader>
  </SOAP-ENV:Header>
  <SOAP-ENV:Body>
    <eb:Manifest SOAP-ENV:mustUnderstand="1" eb:version="1.0">
      ...
    </eb:Manifest>
  </SOAP-ENV:Body>
</SOAP-ENV:Envelope>
--111Boundary
Content-ID: <ebxmlheader@interwoven.com>
Content-Type: text/xml
<PressReport>
  <Headline>
    Alliance Consulting finds a content infrastructure
    essential to its eBusiness
  </Headline>
  <ReleaseDate>
    Mon Jan 8 09:00:00 Eastern Standard Time 2001
  </ReleaseDate>
  <Body>
    Alliance Consulting announced today...
  </Body>
  <CorporateInfo>
    Alliance Consulting is a Fortune 500 company...
  </CorporateInfo>
</PressReport>
--111Boundary--
```

Components:
Key to content management

Tool Discussion

- Content management defined
- Document components
- Information reuse
- Custom document assembly

Contributing experts: Sean Baird, Wil Shaw, Carol Houtz, Brad Chang, Willie Lim, Grant Vergottini, and Frazer Robinson

> Document management is about managing documents as a whole, regardless of what is inside them. *Content* management, on the other hand, gets deep down inside and so is far more powerful. The key to content management is XML's ability to let you work with the bits and pieces of a document – its *components*.

Technical publications are critical in today's corporation. Behind these documents are the writers, artists, and editors who develop and maintain the massive amounts of documentation that keep a company running. Now, both publication managers and corporate directors are looking for better ways to exploit this wealth of data for higher returns throughout the enterprise.

Many enterprises benefit from managing document content as *components*, rather than as entire publications. This practice is called *content management*, in contrast to *document management*. Middle-tier Web applications, in particular, benefit from the ability to assemble components with other data for delivery to the client.

17.1 | Components are everywhere

From new cars to software, components are the way we make things today.

In manufacturing industries as much as 80% of products now consist of components drawn from a company's parts library or purchased from suppliers. Product designers routinely tap into internal databases and online parts warehouse services in the course of drafting and specifying new models.

In software, most new code is being written as objects, self-contained bundles of information and operations with the ability to send and receive messages in standard ways. Programs can be created by assembling a bunch of these object components and making them exchange information and services with each other.

17.1.1 *Components in publishing*

And now components are becoming the trend in publishing as well. That's because in publishing, as in other endeavors, components simplify complexity and increase flexibility for adapting to change. Consider these general advantages of components and how they come into play in a content management publishing environment.

17.1.1.1   System simplification

Components make it possible to break down complex systems into pieces that are easier to understand and work with. For publishing groups this means that teams of writers and editors can work on components for the same document simultaneously. Users can more easily locate specific information since components can be searched for individually.

17.1.1.2   Easier revision

When something needs to be revised or customized, changes can be made to just the components affected, without having to redesign the whole document. If a single paragraph in a document needs to be revised, the author can check out just that paragraph from the content management system rather than the whole document. Or, if it's important to see the change in context, the author can check out the section the paragraph appears in. After editing, when the section is checked back in, versioning information is applied only to the paragraph that has changed.

17.1.1.3 Efficient collaboration

Studies show that at least 30% of the content created by technical publishing groups is reusable – or would be, if people could find the information. Typically, it's buried in documents, scattered here and there in file systems on various desktop systems and servers. Content management eliminates the need to redo work by providing a universal repository for managing published and in-progress documents. The ability to unlock content from structured documents so that individual components of information can be independently accessed, tracked, and versioned enables writers and editors to immediately focus on exactly what they're looking for. With larger documents, since authors are able to work on small sections, multiple authors can work simultaneously on the same document.

17.1.1.4 Less routine editing

A huge amount of the editing process involves checking documents for consistency and correcting them to maintain a standardized style. Content management minimizes editing time and tedium by enabling editors to maintain glossaries as collections of components. This information can be added to or revised rapidly, every day if necessary, with the new material instantly available to all users.

17.1.1.5 Automated assembly and delivery

Component-level management means that new documents may be created and customized by changing only what is unique about them. This approach allows content management systems to automate the assembly and delivery of highly personalized documents, specific to new market or customer, based upon specific interests and requirements. By automating these processes, content management systems are able to deliver this level of personalized content delivery through dynamic Web sites.

17.1.1.6 Universal updates

Each information component exists in the content management repository as a single object. When authors want to reuse a component, instead of

copying it, they simply create a pointer to the object. This approach eliminates the redundant work of trying to find all places where the information
appears and updating them independently. Instead authors can revise the
component in the repository once, and it will be automatically updated in
all documents that incorporate it.

17.1.1.7 Streamlined translations

Translators typically work with a moving target, a source document that
continues to change while translation is occurring. Translated versions then
have to be returned to translators for a laborious manual process of identifying, changing, and checking new material. Content management can speed
this process by providing translators with only those document components
that are new, along with information about what has changed and exactly
where the revisions should be inserted in the document.

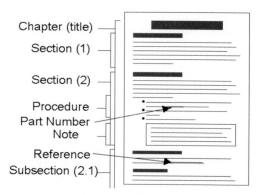

Figure 17-1 Document components described with XML

17.1.1.8 Flexible distribution

Content management makes it easy to reuse content for different media.
Users can assign custom attributes to a particular component. For example,
an attribute of an element could tell the software whether or not the element should be included when exporting a document for the Web, as

opposed to printing it. Users can therefore automate document assembly, including adjustments for target media.

17.1.2 *XML makes components*

XML allows information to be broken into small components. The smaller and more specific the component is, the more addressable and reusable it is.

For example, the document in Figure 17-1 uses descriptive element type names to identify the components and structure of the document. A component is a piece of information that can be used independently, such as a paragraph, chapter, instructional procedure, warning note, part number, order quantity, graphic, side-bar story, video clip, or one of an infinite variety of additional information types.

When managed by a content management system (Figure 17-2), these pieces can be controlled, revised, reused, and assembled into a variety of new documents.

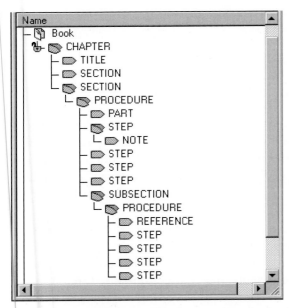

Figure 17-2   Hierarchical structure shown in content management system

Another way XML adds value to information is through attributes that describe additional metadata. The attributes let users describe the information more richly for reuse.

A user can assign an attribute to a particular component, for example, to specify whether or not to include it when publishing the document for the Web, as opposed to printing it. When the document is published, the content management system will make the proper adjustments for the target medium.

Metadata can also be used to identify the intended audience for specific components. In Example 17-1, for example, a "beginner" requires more information than an "expert". Multiple attributes may be used to create a matrix of possible document combinations. The content management system can then assemble and publish a document that matches these criteria.

Example 17-1. Metadata can identify the intended audience

```
<step audience="beginner">
Keep the engine running and park car on level ground.
</step>

<step audience="expert">
Keep the engine running.
</step>
```

17.1.3 *Applications for content reuse*

Reuse, the most compelling feature of content management, allows content within any document to be used elsewhere in the repository. Reuse means writing the information once and linking to it from other documents. This can be very useful when multiple documents contain standard "boilerplate" information. This reuse of information saves users rework and duplication of effort, as shown in Figure 17-3.

Applications for information reuse are everywhere. Reuse can be as simple as finding a description from one document and linking it into a new document. Common content creates an "information pool" of reusable pieces available to individuals or groups inside the company. Linked reuse, instead of copying, ensures consistency of information, makes updates more efficient and reduces redundant storage.

Organizations that maintain common glossaries of business terms can benefit from reuse. When glossary information stored in a content manage-

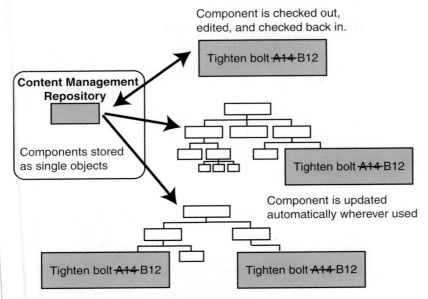

Component is checked out,
edited, and checked back in.

Tighten bolt A14 B12

Content Management
Repository

Components stored
as single objects

Tighten bolt A14 B12

Component is updated
automatically wherever used

Tighten bolt A14 B12

Tighten bolt A14 B12

Figure 17-3   Component reuse

ment system changes, the information is revised only one time. All of the documents incorporating that information are automatically updated.

Because commonly-used procedures, warnings, and cautions usually require careful wording, organizations strive for uniformity across all documents. Manually locating and changing dozens of these elements in hundreds of contexts can consume countless hours and is error-prone. Content management solves that problem by allowing XML documents to reuse content across documents.

For global business processes, linked reuse simplifies the translation process, helping organizations get to market faster around the world. By identifying the newly revised information in a repair manual, only the new information will be translated into the target languages, saving valuable time and money.

17.2 | A content management implementation

To better understand what content management systems provide, it is helpful to look at an actual product in action. A component-based *content* management system attempts to provide value beyond that of generalized *document* management systems. It does so by managing the content of the document as a set of components (see Figure 17-4).

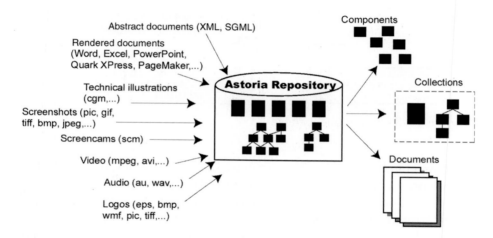

Figure 17-4   A component-based repository

Some of the product's off-the-shelf capabilities are described in the following sections. Customization for specialized requirements is possible through public APIs.

17.2.1   *Revision tracking*

The product automatically collects revision information at each check-in, indicating time, date, author, revision number, and an optional comment. Past versions are available for republishing or to provide an audit trail (see Figure 17-5).

For XML documents, revision history is detected and maintained at the component level, not just at the document level. A differencing engine is used to apply revision information to only the content that changes during an editing session.

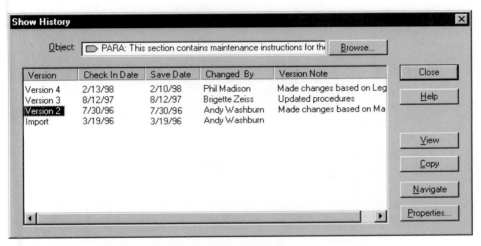

Figure 17-5   Revision history of a paragraph

At important milestones such as release dates and the beginning of review cycles, users can formalize document versions into editions. The document state can then be recreated for that point in time by opening the appropriate edition.

17.2.2 *Search*

Search options let users locate documents created in common applications. Advanced indexing enhances search by looking for various forms of the word (e.g., plural, tenses, root). Matching documents can be selected for viewing and editing.

Custom attributes can automatically be created from XML metadata. In addition to custom attributes, document structure, data content, and version information can be used in queries (see Figure 17-6).

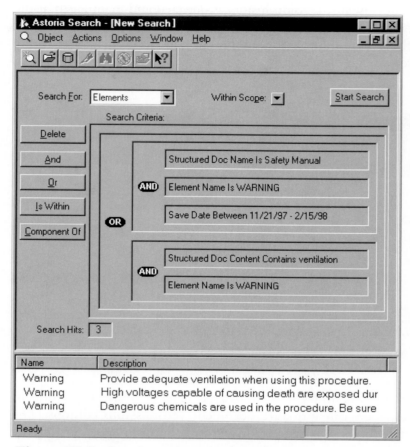

Figure 17-6   Search results refined with XML structure and metadata

Another form of search, where-used queries, locates content that is reused in multiple XML documents. Users can determine whether changes to that content are appropriate in all contexts before committing to the change.

17.2.3 *Dynamic content assembly and delivery*

One of the compelling benefits of managing documents at the component level is that users can effectively create an information pool from which new documents may be created.

Content creators define the associations between the attributes of individuals visiting the Web site and the metadata stored within the content. As visitors log into a Web site, the product creates and delivers personalized Web pages to them, as shown in Figure 17-7.

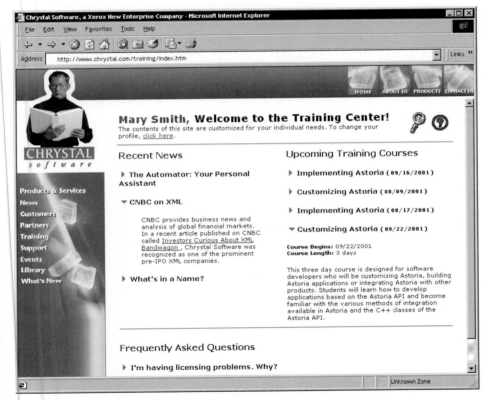

Figure 17-7   A custom document assembly

Components for graphic content

Application Discussion

- Computer graphics notations

- Graphic components

- WebCGM

- Hyperlinking graphic components

Contributing expert: Kevin O' Kane

Chapter

18

There is a widely used graphic image notation called *TIFF*, for *Tagged Image File Format*. Unfortunately, its tags are binary and are meaningful only to TIFF processors. But what if graphics could be tagged with XML, organized into components, and hyperlinked to and from the text of documents? That pretty picture is the subject of this chapter.

Graphics are more like text than you might think.

Consider Figure 18-1 for example. Unless you're an auto mechanic, it's probably not the kind of picture you customarily look at. But even a non-mechanic can see that the suspension assembly it depicts is made up of many different components.

Interestingly, that is true of the computer representation of the picture as well. In fact, it is possible to use XML to represent the component structure, thereby bringing to graphics the benefits of component management that we have been discussing. Before we look at how to accomplish that, we need a quick course in graphic representation.

18.1 | Computer graphics notations

The concepts of abstraction and rendition are critical to XML and have been discussed throughout this book.[1] It is relatively easy to see how they

---

1. For a refresher, see 7.12, "And in conclusion", on page 155.

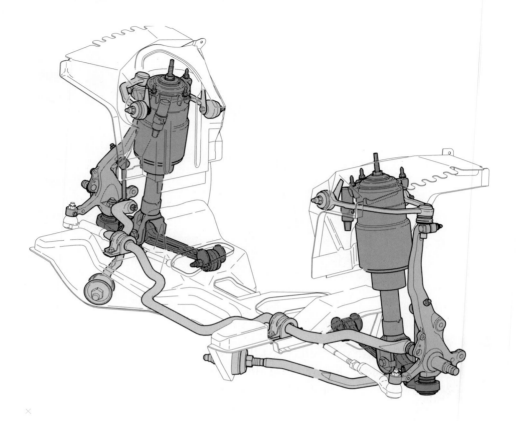

Figure 18-1   Automobile suspension assembly

apply to text (formatted vs. unformatted). What is less obvious is that graphics have abstract and rendered representations as well.

The abstract notations use rich geometric formulas and are typically termed *vector graphics*. Some examples are CGM, SVG, and EPS.

The rendered notations use arrays of points and are usually called *raster graphics* or *images*. Some image notations are JPEG, TIFF, and GIF.

18.1.1   *Raster is for rendition*

When you see a graphic on a physical medium, such as a printed page or computer screen, you are viewing a presentation of a raster rendition of the graphic.

Technically speaking, a raster image is actually another geometric representation, and the process of generating it is a geometric transformation. However, the geometric model of a raster image is rather impoverished. It is limited to points, called *pixels* (picture elements), which are X, Y coordinates in two-dimensional space.

Just as with text, the rendition of graphics loses abstract information. Consider the magnified image in Figure 18-2, in which each square represents a pixel. The image is round, but because the abstract information is lost, it is no longer possible to determine if the content was a circle, the number "0", or the letter "O".

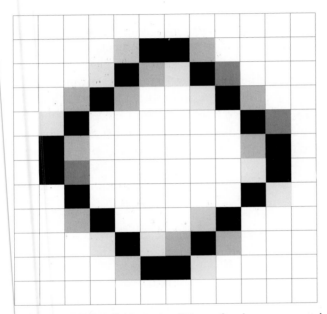

Figure 18-2   Raster rendition of unknown round abstraction

The raster geometric representation is almost identical to the model used by a computer display system. It can therefore be presented on a computer screen very quickly, which is why JPEG and GIF are so much favored for Web pages. But this speed comes at a price:

- There is no abstract content, as we just saw, nor is there abstract structure.

- A high quality image has a large memory footprint.

  For example, 500 characters of text might require as much as 7KB when rendered as a JPEG.

- Images are not easy to edit, which limits reuse.
- The scale of an image cannot be changed without introducing visual distortions.

18.1.2   *Vectors allow variation*

Vector graphics employ a much richer geometric model.

In addition to points, a vector graphic document may contain geometric elements, such as lines, circles, ellipses, curves, and shapes – possibly in a three-dimensional coordinate system to represent solid objects.

A vector graphic, using equations for these geometric elements, is an abstract representation of graphic objects. Rather than representing a circle with a list of pixels, we can specify the center point and a radius for a circle element. When it is time to render the circle, the computer, either in software or hardware, can apply a transform to generate the list of pixels that would be "covered" by the circle, and would then color the pixels accordingly.

A vector graphics representation does not have the limitations of a raster image:

- By applying a scale factor to the radius of the circle we can dynamically zoom in or zoom out of an image without distortion.
- If we change the coordinates of the center point, we can easily edit the circle to change its location in the picture.
- The number of bytes required to store the circle remains relatively constant, no matter how big or small the circle becomes.

18.1.3   *Structural elements*

If you've used a vector graphics drawing program, you may be familiar with the grouping command, which allows you to combine several geometric elements into a larger object. Groups may themselves be grouped, and so on.

A group is an example of a graphic *structural element*. Whereas a *geometric element*, such as a circle or polygon, contains the formula for drawing the shape, a structural element combines geometric elements and other structural elements but does no drawing of its own.

Most modern graphic notations include structural elements to model the abstract structure; for example, a circle and some lines might be grouped to form a wheel. A graphics notation with a structural element can be modeled using XML and integrated into the component structure of an XML document.

18.2 | Representing graphic components

XML-based content management systems typically support graphics, but they treat an entire graphic as a single component. This approach is less than optimal, since a complex graphic like that in Figure 18-1 is made up of multiple components. It would be desirable to manage those components in the same way as text components, with individual versioning, checkin/checkout, reuse, and other content management facilities. It would also be useful to have hyperlinks among the graphic components and between them and the text components.

In a nutshell, what is needed is the integration of graphics at the component level into the XML document, as shown in Figure 18-3.

The key to component management for graphics is the use of XML. Two approaches can be taken:

- Use an XML-based graphics notation to represent geometric and structural elements.

  The W3C has developed Scalable Vector Graphics (SVG) for this purpose, which we discuss in 4.3, "Graphics and multimedia", on page 76. As it is an XML document type, utilization in a component management system is straightforward and won't be discussed further here.

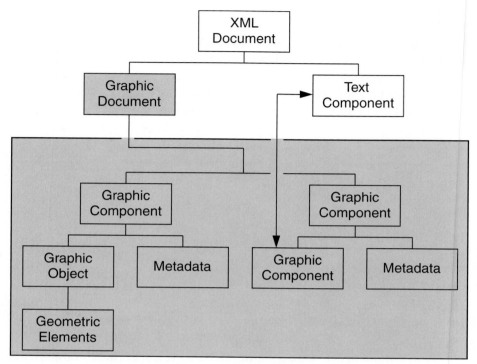

Figure 18-3   Graphic components in an XML document

■ Use a binary graphics notation that has a structural element, but echo its structure in XML.

The W3C has created WebCGM – a Web-optimized profile of the Computer Graphics Metafile (CGM) International Standard – that can be used in this way. It is of particular interest because it is compatible with the vast majority of existing CGM graphics, which therefore have a high probability of being rendered accurately in WebCGM-enabled software.

18.2.1 *WebCGM*

CGM is a stable graphics format of long standing.[2] The WebCGM profile supports almost all CGM graphic elements, plus several raster image notations, including JPEG and PNG.

Most importantly, WebCGM uses *CGM Application Structures (APS)* as a structural element for creating graphic components.

18.2.2 *Inside a graphic component*

It is common for XML content management systems (CMS) to create an XML tracking document for a non-XML component, such as a graphic. The graphic component document includes a pointer to the actual graphic object, plus metadata that describes access rights and other properties.

Systems for XML graphic content management take a similar approach, except that their graphic component documents have a detailed internal structure. It echoes the structure of graphic objects right down to the geometric element level.

Example 18-1 shows the WebCGM definition of a `grobject`, what we've been calling a *graphic component*.

A component can exhibit several attributes. They specify metadata for:

identification
   `id` and `name`

description
   `screentip`

viewer control
   `region` and `viewcontext`

hyperlinking
   `linkuri`

---

2. CGM's history parallels that of markup languages. It became an ISO standard in 1987, the year after SGML. Its WebCGM profile for the World Wide Web became a W3C Recommendation in 1999, the year after XML, which is SGML's profile for the Web.

Example 18-1. WebCGM definition of graphic component (`grobject`)

```
<!ELEMENT grobject (grobject | para | gdata)* >
<!ATTLIST grobject
  id              ID        #REQUIRED
  region          CDATA     #IMPLIED
  viewcontext     CDATA     #IMPLIED
  linkuri         CDATA     #IMPLIED
  screentip       CDATA     #IMPLIED
  name            CDATA     #IMPLIED
>

<!ELEMENT gdata EMPTY >
<!ATTLIST gdata
  cgmprim         ENTITY    #REQUIRED
>
```

The structure of a component is hierarchical because it can include other components. It can also include `para` and `gdata` elements, which have no data content; they serve as references to the graphic objects of components, which we'll examine next.

18.2.3 *Graphic objects*

A *graphic object* is created when a structural element is used to group geometric elements. Collectively, the geometric elements form the geometric representation of an object, such as the objects in the four components shown in Figure 18-4.

Example 18-2 shows a graphic object as it might be represented in an XML-aware component-based graphic drawing product.

It is possible for a component's object to have several geometric representations, each referenced by a separate `gdata` element. For example, the representation of a manufactured object can start as a 3-D solid model, be transformed into a 3-D polygon mesh, and collapsed to a 2-D view using shapes. All of them would be managed together as part of the component.

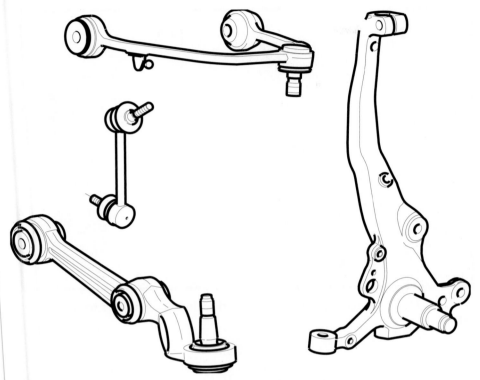

Figure 18-4   Components of an automobile suspension

Example 18-2. Graphic object represented in XML

```
<graphic_object>
  <circle>....</circle>
  <spline>....</spline>
  <rect>......</rect>
</graphic_object>
```

18.3 | Reusing graphic components

Reusing graphic components offers the same benefits as reusing text components, but introduces some unique technical considerations.

Consider the graphic in Figure 18-5. It contains several instances of the graphic components from Figure 18-4, but note that they have different

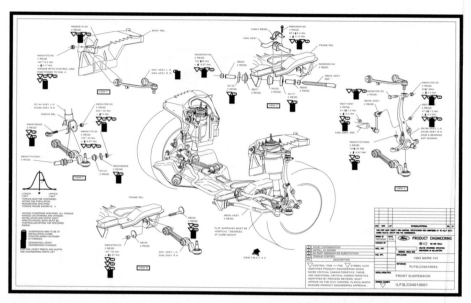

Figure 18-5   Assembly with rotated and scaled components from Figure 18-4

sizes and orientations. The component's metadata was used to reconcile the rotation and scale of the component with respect to those of the full graphic.

18.4 | Hyperlinking graphic components

Hyperlinking is possible both to and from graphic components. Hyperlinking *from* a component is done with the `linkuri` attribute of the `grobject` element. Hyperlinking *to* a component is done with a *URI reference*, which can address file fragments, as shown in in Example 18-3.

The URI portion of the reference addresses the "auto13.cgm" file. The fragment identifier portion begins with the #. It is an XPointer that addresses the graphic component named "123" within that file. The viewer

Example 18-3. URI reference to a WebCGM graphic component

```
<a xlink:href="auto13.cgm#name(123)">
  <text x="12" y="437" style="fill:blue">
    Automatic Transmission Drive Chain Assembly
  </text>
</a>
```

would normally center and zoom into the view window defined by the component's `viewcontext` attribute.

In Figure 18-6 the graphic components are both sources ("hotspots") and targets of hyperlinking. They are bi-directionally linked to the parts list on the left of the HTML page in which both the list and graphic are framed.

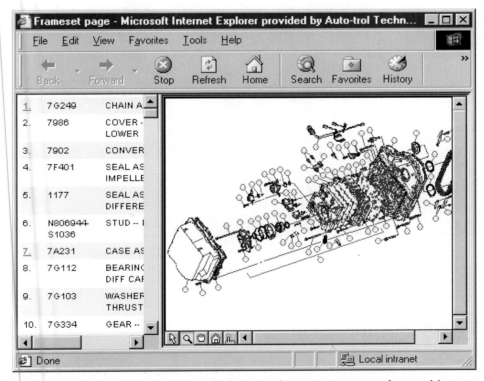

Figure 18-6   Parts list hyperlinked to graphic components of assembly

Figure 18-7 shows the result of navigating from the parts list to the "chain" component of the WebCGM graphic. The graphic was scaled and positioned to the view region specified by the component's `view_context` attribute.

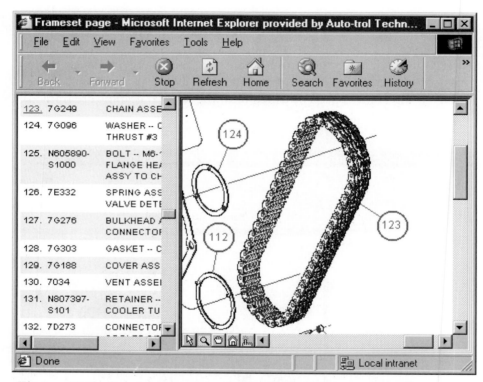

Figure 18-7   Result of navigating in Figure 18-6 from a part number to its graphic component

18.5 | Conclusion

It is possible to integrate reusable graphic components into an XML document by using XML to model the abstract structure of graphic documents represented in a binary notation. The graphic notation must have a structural element that can group geometric elements and metadata in a hierarchical structure; WebCGM has this facility.

Once the abstract structure is modeled, the components of the graphic document can be used in bi-directional links among themselves and non-graphic components of XML documents.

Portals

- Doorways to information
- Enterprise information portal (EIP)
- Coherent view of multiple data sources
- A portal for your Doctor!

Part Six

A portal is a doorway, and in the language of the World Wide Web, a "portal site" is one that users visit first. It acts, literally, as the user's doorway to all of the resources of the Web.

Now organizations are constructing their own portals – not all-encompassing sites for the masses, like traditional Web portals, but *enterprise information portals* (EIP). An EIP is a doorway to a focused set of resources, intended for a specific audience, like the employees, customers, and suppliers of a business. Most importantly, an EIP can serve as a single coherent view of information aggregated from disparate sources by e-commerce systems and integration servers.

In this part, we'll explore the reasons for EIPs and the systems needed to build them. We'll also look at an EIP in detail: an imaginary but possible portal that you'll wish your doctor had.

Portal servers for e-business

Tool Discussion

- Portal server requirements
- Architecture of an e-business portal server
- Other portal server facilities

Contributing expert: Bryan Caporlette

In today's e-business environment, an enterprise information portal is literally a "digital dashboard" that allows employees, suppliers, and customers to interact with an enterprise. The EIP accepts and delivers information, ranging from formal publications to dynamic business process data, anywhere the Internet can reach – with or without wires! The resulting requirements for portal servers are quite demanding, as this chapter reveals.

To meet the needs of today's interactive e-business portals, a portal server must do many things. It combines the functions of an application server, workflow manager, content manager, end-to-end publishing system, and database – either as a single product or a set of interconnected ones. But however they are implemented, the requirements are the same.

19.1 | Portal server requirements

The requirements for interactive e-business portals can be divided into three categories: performance, content distribution, and business process integration.

19.1.1 *Performance*

Performance, for a portal server, means reliability, availability, and scalability. An application server is required that can provide sophisticated load distribution and communication capabilities that allow an enterprise to scale its portal in multiple directions. It must be possible for administrators to add hardware to stress points as they expand the reach of the portal to new users and data sources.

19.1.2 *Content distribution*

It is no longer feasible to require that a portal user have access to a powerful PC and a large monitor. The reach of the EIP has extended to network PCs, thin clients, and mobile devices – including phones and personal digital assistants (PDA).

Content sources are also expanding. They now include ERP and MRP systems, legacy business applications, Internet sites, syndicated information sources, and information services integrated within the portal. To cope with the increasing variety of content, the server must offer a quickly extensible environment for adding new content sources.

A further requirement for content distribution is personalization. Users must be able to filter the content to satisfy personal profiles, and at the same time be able to specify a rendition style that best suits their personal needs and the capabilities of the delivery device.

19.1.3 *Business process integration*

The portal server must allow an enterprise to define complex business flows in a modular and flexible way. These modules can be thought of as *integration agents* because their individual small actions can have the combined effect of implementing a large and complex process.

For example, Figure 19-1 shows the workflow for an expense report that is submitted to the portal as an XML document. The first integration agent validates the report against the company expense report schema. The next agent interrogates the amount and, depending on the dollar value, either sends the report directly to the accounting department for processing, or else routes it to the manager's inbox for review and approval.

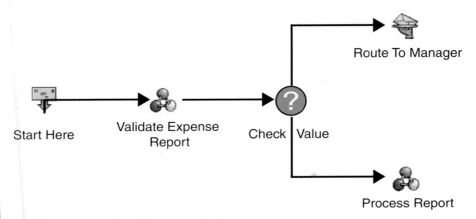

Figure 19-1   Expense report flow

19.2 | Architecture of an e-business portal server

To understand the workings of portal servers and discuss their requirements, it is helpful to have an architectural model in mind as a frame of reference. Figure 19-2 depicts the architecture of an XML-based portal server at a level where the components relate directly to the requirements categories we have been discussing.[1]

There are three major components, and XML plays a significant role in each of them:

- The *XML Application Server (XAS)* addresses performance issues by providing the necessary reliability and scaling. All data is packaged in XML "envelopes", thereby creating a messaging architecture that is easily connected to other systems, both internal and external.
- *Content Delivery Services* (CDS) brokers end-user requests for information and generates the appropriate response. Because the XML representation separates the abstract data from any

---

1. Important abbreviations are explained in this chapter; the others are in Chapter 67, "The XML Handbook Acronym Guide", on page 1120.

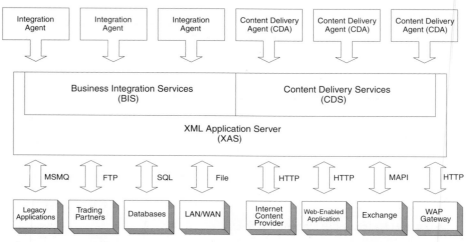

Figure 19-2   Portal server architecture

     specific presentation format, the data can easily be reformatted for multiple delivery devices.

■ *Business Integration Services* (BIS) automates work processes within the portal. A sophisticated rules engine can interrogate the XML envelopes in order to make routing decisions.

We will examine each of these components in detail in the following sections. Bear in mind that we are discussing an architecture, not a specific implementation. Although we use a single integrated product to illustrate the functionality, it would also be possible to satisfy the requirements by using several intercommunicating dedicated products.

19.2.1   *XML application server*

The XML application server provides load balancing and a messaging architecture.

19.2.1.1   Portal clusters

The load balancer distributes work among sets of portal servers known as *portal clusters*. Each cluster has a *cluster server*, which stores information about the portal cluster's configuration. That information is stored persistently in a relational database, which provides backup and replication capabilities.

The cluster environment provides fail-over capabilities that ensure that the portal is always available. When a message is sent to a load-balanced server, the XAS awaits a response from it. If that machine does not respond in a timely manner, the application server may re-submit the request to the next available portal server, or enter a failure event into the auditing system. The administrator can set a threshold for failures, which will determine the number of negative responses a given machine can have prior to becoming deactivated within the cluster.

19.2.1.2   Messaging architecture

XML messages are the interface between the portal server and external systems. All communications with the XAS, whether business objects (e.g. documents) or remote procedure calls (e.g. search requests), are encapsulated in XML envelopes.

19.2.1.2.1   *Messaging protocols*

The application server abstracts the notion of envelopes through the definition of *message types*. Message types provide the routing and metadata information necessary to transmit data between an application and the portal by means of a *message protocol*. Although there are several industry initiatives for message protocols, the XAS is not limited to just one because it abstracts the message types.

There are two directions a message might take, depending on the message type. Presentation requests coming from a browser or Wireless Application Protocol (WAP) gateway are routed to the *Content Delivery Services* component. Business objects, such as documents and business interactions, are routed to the *Business Integration Services* component.

19.2.1.2.2 *Receivers and senders*

Receivers and senders are modules that provide access to the portal. They are shown at the bottom of Figure 19-2.

Receivers listen for new messages coming into the portal. Senders transmit messages to external applications. The modular design allows the XAS to provide support for any data communications protocols, including HTTP, MSMQ, SMTP, COM, FTP, and directory polling.

This flexible support for data communications protocols allows the portal server to interoperate with enterprise application integration (EAI) tools. The portal server is thereby able to leverage corporate experience and expenditures on existing EAI applications.

19.2.1.3   Load balancing

As messages flow into the portal, a message processor communicates with the load balancer to distribute the processing across the known load-balanced servers within the cluster.

Once a load-balanced server is selected, XAS instantiates a new transaction to process the message. Depending on the success or failure of the transaction, XAS will log one or more events into the auditing component. The auditing component provides system monitoring and health status for all portal services.

19.2.1.4   Rules engine

The XAS dispatcher routes messages to the appropriate services, such as integration agents. It has a sophisticated rules engine that interrogates the Document Object Model (DOM) of the XML envelope.

Rules are test conditions that are evaluated to determine the route a message will take through the portal. The rules include XML Path Language (XPath) expressions that address values in the DOM.

For example, the rule in Example 19-1 might be used at the `Check value` decision point in Figure 19-1 to route the expense report. It compares the `value` attribute of the `total` element of an `expense-report` document to "500.00".

Example 19-1. Rule containing an XPath expression

```
%/expense_report/total/@value% > 500.00
```

19.2.2 *Content delivery services*

The *Content Delivery Services* component controls the delivery of data to an end user. It allows for personalization of the rendered information, the portal desktop, and individual content sources.

19.2.2.1   Rendition

CDS exploits the fact that XML allows abstract information content to be separate from formatting style, so data can be rendered in the needed form on delivery.

This separation enables the portal to service requests coming in from Web servers or Wireless Access Protocol gateway servers. CDS dynamically associates an XSLT stylesheet with each XML document, based on the type of device on which it will be presented (e.g. Web browser, cellular phone, personal digital assistant). It then generates HTML or Wireless Markup Language (WML), as appropriate.

The rendering engine is controlled by rules that establish a one-to-many relationship of XSLT stylesheets to XML schemas. When a user requests a document, the rendering engine uses the rules to select a stylesheet, apply that stylesheet to the XML document, and deliver the result. The rules that select the stylesheet can be based on the user's name and/or role within the portal (explained later), as well as the type of requesting device.

In fact, rendition rules can also specify selection criteria based on the content of the document. For example, a rule might test for the payment method of an order, represented by the content of the `payment.method` element. The rules could apply different style sheets to the document depending on whether the payment method is Visa, Mastercard, or American Express.

19.2.2.2   Personalization

The essence of a portal is the personalized aggregation and delivery of information from multiple sources. The delivery point is the desktop, which is populated with information by means of *content delivery agents (CDA)*.

19.2.2.3   Personalized desktop

Figure 19-3 shows an example of a portal desktop that our portal server might generate. The tabs at the upper left allow different pages to be selected.

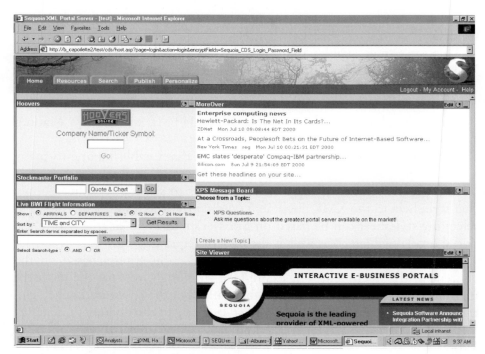

Figure 19-3   A generated portal desktop

The portal desktop is controlled by a template, which specifies the content and layout. Customization of the template occurs at two levels: roles and individual personalization.

19.2.2.3.1 *Roles*

The types of pages and CDAs available to a user are controlled by assigning each user to one or more "roles". A role corresponds conceptually to a mode of use of the portal, such as engineer, manager, administrator, etc.

In system terms, a role is a collection of pages, CDAs, and a default theme (i.e. a color scheme and background). As users log into the portal, their roles are used to generate the original desktop.

19.2.2.3.2 *Individual personalization*

The rightmost tab in Figure 19-3 allows the desktop to be personalized. With it the user can change the layout of any page. Content source windows can be moved around, added, and hidden. In addition, the user can select from a set of pre-configured themes that control the color and background images of the desktop.

19.2.2.4 Content delivery agents (CDA)

The portal administrator can associate content delivery agents with pages. A CDA is a program or script that creates a window for communicating with a data source. These include:

- Internet content providers (e.g. *Hoovers*, *CNBC*, etc.).
- Application programs (e.g. *Exchange*, *Lotus Notes*).
- Internal integration agents (see 19.2.3.2, "Integration agents", on page 338).

A CDA can provide a personalization option to elicit property settings for the data source, such as news categories, mail servers, or stock symbols. The CDA tailors the content delivered based on the user's current preferences.

19.2.3 *Business integration services*

The *Business Integration Services* component enables the administrator to automate business processes within the portal. The dispatcher controls the path through which a message flows.

19.2.3.1   Dispatcher

Message paths could be simple, routing a message to a single integration agent or content repository. However, they could also follow complex alternative routes among integration agents and decision points that must be resolved by use of the rules engine.

In BIS, unlike XAS, the rules can test not just the XML envelope, but the contained business object itself. If the object is an XML document, its content can be tested to determine the path.

A flow design tool enables the portal administrator to define routes graphically, using icons for integration agents and decision points, as in Figure 19-1. Icons for subflows allow the reuse of common business processes.

19.2.3.2   Integration agents

Integration agents can provide the following functions:

taxonomy
>   This agent provides a mechanism for organizing relevant information into a hierarchical view.

content management
>   The content management agent provides persistent local storage of information, including configuration management features.

smart summary
>   This agent provides summary views of data aggregated within the portal.

transformation
>   The transformation agent uses XSLT to map data from one schema to another.

data entry
>   This agent maps HTML form designs to XML schema definitions in order to generate XML documents from the completed forms.

indexing

    The indexing agent creates both XML-based contextual indices and full-text indices of information flowing through the portal.

scripting

    The scripting agent provides a mechanism for extending the functionality of the portal through scripts written in a variety of languages.

19.2.4 *Administration and configuration*

The sheer number of components and configuration options available within a portal server can be daunting even to contemplate, let alone to deal with in a production environment. The interface provided by a server implementation is therefore as important a consideration as the functionality.

RxML: Your prescription for healthcare

- Health portal system
- Dynamic patient summary
- Information aggregation
- Supply chain automation

Contributing expert: Bryan Caporlette

Chapter

20

When it comes to electronic information processing, the U.S. medical system is "terminally" ill, so to speak. Systems rarely share data, even in the same medical organization, and there is little chance that your doctor can usefully access all your records for a diagnosis. This chapter prescribes a cure.

I magine you're feeling under the weather, so you make an office visit to your primary care physician.

Dr. Caps enters the examination room with a portable device instead of a clipboard. From that device he can access a patient summary record that contains your complete medical history, follow-up visits, current medications, and your favorite pharmacy. This information has been pooled together from various sources in the ABC Medical Center to create a single integrated logical view.

After an initial evaluation, Dr. Caps orders a throat culture to check for streptococcus bacteria. A laboratory order request, in the form of an XML document, is transmitted to the microbiology department. A culture is obtained by the nurse and sent to the lab. The culture results will be sent directly to the doctor's electronic in-basket, where he can evaluate them to determine the appropriate course of action.

Until determination of the culture result, he prescribes Keflex for coverage. He chooses Keflex, rather than amoxicillin, because the patient summary indicates that in a previous "encounter" (office visit, etc.) you reported an adverse reaction to amoxicillin.

The prescription is sent electronically to your local pharmacy, where it will be awaiting your arrival as you head home for some much needed rest. Following your departure, the billing department will automatically generate an XML invoice that is electronically submitted to Blue Triangle, your healthcare provider.

That all-important patient summary is made possible for Dr. Caps through a collection of electronically stored medical information, aggregated and distributed through a *health portal system*, as shown in Figure 20-1. It enables you, as a patient, to receive the best service, and clinicians to make the most informed decisions regarding your care.

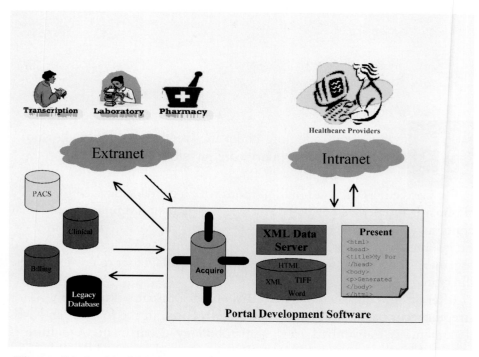

Figure 20-1   Health portal system

20.1 | Doing as well as can be expected – Not!

As you have probably noticed, real-world experiences with the healthcare industry do not resemble the integrated environment we've portrayed. Let's say you were born in upstate New York, went to school in Ohio, and now live in Silicon Valley. More likely than not, you have had to receive medical attention at each of these locations.

Most of us have been asked repeatedly to fill out the same forms, with our demographic and medical histories. The onus has been on us to remember our doctors' names, dates of injury and illness, arcane names of medications we are taking, and allergies that have been discovered over a lifetime. This information has been stored multiple times, in multiple systems, in multiple geographic locations.

Unless you have been fortunate enough to have the same doctor your whole life, your physicians probably haven't had all the information necessary to render the best diagnosis. Stories of duplicate laboratory tests, negative reactions to unknown medical allergies, and misdiagnosis due to missing or incorrect information abound within the industry.

There are many reasons the care we receive falls short of our expectations. Organizations have to deal with a copious amount of information. However, providing access to this information to the correct person at the correct time is often impossible.

The typical healthcare organization information system deploys between 30 and 70 applications. These applications are spread across multiple functional departments, hardware platforms, and geographical locations, which impedes effective use of their information. Other barriers include security considerations and the cost of software licenses.

20.2 | The prescription: a health portal system

Fortunately, there is a cure for this condition. Health portal systems like the one used by Dr. Caps in our example can exist. They are just examples of Enterprise Information Portals, which organizations can build using portal servers, like those we describe in Chapter 19, "Portal servers for e-business", on page 328.

A *health portal system* provides a single point of access for all your medical information. Clinicians log into the portal, after which they have sophisticated search and navigation capabilities to access a comprehensive library of information.

These capabilities enable the clinician to locate your patient summary record quickly. The patient summary is an aggregate view of your complete medical history, made up of information components extracted from the numerous systems deployed by the health enterprise. Figure 20-2 depicts what Dr. Caps saw in our example.

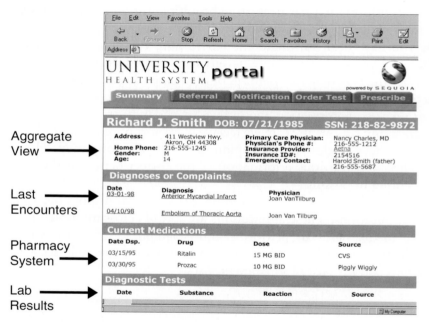

Figure 20-2   Rendition of patient summary

In addition to those internal systems, the portal provides access to medical libraries and external systems, such as laboratory results and pharmaceutical ordering systems. Its all done by the portal system's acquisition component and its connectors.

20.3 | Connectivity counts

The acquisition component of the portal software in Figure 20-1 uses senders and receivers to communicate with connectors that tap into various disparate systems. The connectors communicate with software applications, extract data from them, and package that data in XML messages that are passed on to the XML data server.

The connectors are a flexible bunch. One might be communicating directly with a radiology system, capturing the images and routing them into the portal. Another connector could be listening through a TCP/IP port for health industry standard (HL7) messages being transmitted from the "admit, discharge, transfer" application.

Yet another connector might poll an FTP directory that has been set up for our transcription service company to submit operative reports and other transcribed documents. As the documents are sent into the directory, the connector grabs them and converts the information into XML.

This functionality doesn't just happen. The portal administrator must train the system to perform the transformations by defining connectors. Systems typically provide a graphical user interface (GUI) that enables easy mapping of source data elements into their target XML documents. Once defined, the connectors are deployed across the enterprise to begin collecting the data needed by Dr. Caps.

But these connectors are not just one-way data pumps. The administrator can also enable connectors to dynamically query data stored in an electronic medical records (EMR) application. When Dr. Caps needs to find out if you have had streptococcus recently, the data server can formulate a search request. This request is serviced in real-time by the connector, communicating to the EMR application through an ODBC interface. Perhaps he will recommend a vitamin C supplement to your diet.

Figure 20-3 illustrates the portal's acquisition component and its connectors, which are labeled *Accessor* in the diagram.

20.4 | Aggregation adds value

As information flows into the portal's XML data server, it must be organized in a way that facilitates easy, intuitive access by Dr. Caps.

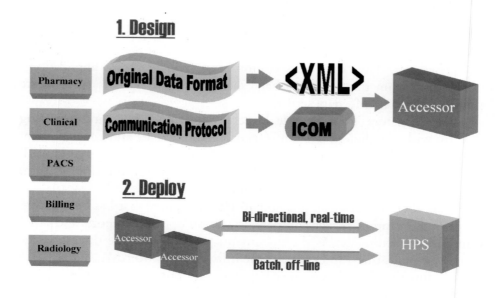

Figure 20-3   Acquisition component and its connectors ("Accessors")

Information overload could become a problem, if information is not properly presented to the physician. The obvious first step is to provide a categorization facility to help organize the data into folders. XML provides the ability to define element types such as patient name, encounter date, and attending physician that can be used to place documents into a particular folder.

However, the unique capability of a true enterprise information portal is that it can aggregate data from disparate sources to create a comprehensive view of your overall health. This is where XML really plays a significant role.

Imagine trying to assimilate information from a proprietary ASCII format, the results of an SQL query, and an operative report in some word processor format. But, if the connectors are doing their transformation job properly and sending only XML into the portal, a new breed of aggregate XML objects can be built dynamically from these sources.

The aggregate XML object in this case is a patient summary. The template that causes it to be created is shown in Figure 20-4. The template is an XML document with no data. The empty elements act as queries that retrieve the data of the same element types in other documents – the "data sources".

Actual patient summaries are constructed by filling in copies of the template with data extracted dynamically from the data sources as they enter the system. The patient summary becomes the universal access point for all information, with hyperlinks into the original data source documents supplementing the summary where appropriate.

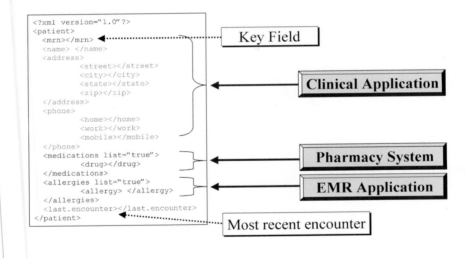

Figure 20-4   Template for patient summary

20.5 | Personalization assures usability

Not everyone needs to see, or should see, all the information flowing into the system. The portal can deliver personalized renditions of the XML information to the clinicians by using XSLT stylesheets. These provide very granular personalization, applying transformation rules at the element level.

The portal applies XSLT on the server-side, where it can employ a powerful rules engine to associate multiple stylesheets with the same document. Users can define profiles that choose their preferred stylesheet.

Personalization doesn't only apply to the presentation. Access and document routing can be controlled through XML documents so that physicians can automatically be sent a "today's appointments" report listing the day's schedule.

The portal can also limit access to patient records to their own doctors. For example, the access rule in Example 20-1 ensures that only Dr. Caps has access to the lab report in Example 20-2, where he is identified as the attending physician. The `%doctor_name%` variable accesses the user's login identity.

Example 20-1. Access rule for lab reports

```
Access Rule: Grant Read where
    Lab.report\attending.physician$eq$%doctor_name%
```

Example 20-2. Lab report

```
<lab.report>
<patient>
<name>John Smith</name>
<mrn>ID939393</mrn>
</patient>
<attending.physician>Dr. Caps</attending.physician>
<result>
<test>
<name>Throat culture</name>
</test>
</result>
</lab.report>
```

20.6 | Linking up the supply chain

Healthcare enterprises struggle constantly with managing all their external suppliers. The typical organization must deal on a daily basis with laboratories, physicians, transcription services houses, and most importantly, the benefit providers (Blue Triangle in your case).

The portal's ability to automate the relationship with provider organizations is one of the key benefits to the healthcare facility. The billing department will extract XML information from the portal to create an electronic billing invoice, passing it through an XML-enabled transaction server for transmittal over a secure extranet connection to Blue Triangle. Blue Triangle, in processing the invoice, verifies your benefits eligibility with Healtheon prior to transmitting a payment voucher back to ABC Medical Center.

Internet banking services will also impact the payment system. Soon you might be able to authorize electronic payment of your co-pay amount directly from your checking account.

20.7 | Conclusion

XML-powered health portals with dynamic patient summaries transform the healthcare experience. Patients receive better, faster healthcare service while clinicians gain greater access to information that enables them to make the best decisions.

Healthcare organizations also realize significant benefits. Their service reputation improves even while they cut costs because doctors don't order the same tests multiple times. In addition, automated billing lowers costs further while improving cash flow.

Publishing

- Extranet delivery of high-quality printing
- Hands-on WYSIWYG editing and formatting
- Using XSL Formatting Objects (XSL-FO)
- Beyond XSL: The real DSSSL

Part Seven

Publish or perish!

For decades that has been the mandate for academics seeking an assured career path. Today it is the mandate for enterprises of all kinds that are hostage to documentation requirements. If the manuals, reports, and marketing materials aren't ready, it is the products and business opportunities that will perish – not the career of some assistant professor.

And publishing today doesn't mean just a uniform static message on the corpses of dead trees: It means websites, CD-ROMs, multimedia, wireless, personalized delivery, and – yes – paper as well.

In this part we'll see how a leading financial management firm uses XML to meet the demands of this new publishing environment. Then we'll look closely at the three major approaches, each with its special strengths: the flexibility and expressiveness of hands-on WYSIWYG, the hands-off efficiency of XSL-FO, and the automated power of DSSSL.

Personalized financial publishing

- Frank Russell Company
- Business and technical requirements identification
- Structure-driven style

Sponsor: Synth-Bank LLC, http://www.synthbank.com

Contributing experts: Bryan Bell of Synth-Bank LLC and Randy Kelley of Frank Russell Company

Chapter

21

This chapter is the chronicle of an extraordinary project: demanding requirements, ambitious goals, leading-edge technology, business school management techniques, and – did we mention "mission-critical"? – a trillion dollars riding on the outcome. And XML figures in it as well.

Frank Russell Company is the investment management and asset consulting firm that is known for its *Russell 3000®* market index, the hallmark by which the performance of many investment advisors and mutual funds is judged. Russell provides investment solutions for institutions and individuals, guiding the investment of more than $1 trillion for clients in more than 25 countries.

21.1 | Background

During the eighties, Russell pioneered the use of high quality color presentations and "high touch" relationship management with its clients. Emblematic of this style were the beautifully printed portfolio performance reports known as the "client books".

Recently, Russell's investment management division experienced explosive growth, marketing private mutual fund products to the institutional marketplace, and retail funds through a group of selected distribution partners. This growth threatened Russell's ability to maintain its customer relationship style. It needed a way to address the increasing production volume demands for client books without sacrificing quality or profit margins.

The company engaged Synth-Bank LLC® to develop and implement a strategy for automating the process. A team of Synth-Bank and Russell employees was formed.

Russell had traditionally viewed its printed client books as products. The project team, however, realized that the real product was Russell's content, and that the book itself was merely one possible rendition.

Russell had been using the "print, then distribute" metaphor for decades. But as the newer digital technologies and communication processes were taking hold, and the World Wide Web's popularity became undeniable, the team began an effort to evangelize, design, produce and deliver a new metaphor: "distribute, then print".

Along with this shift in metaphors come real quality control issues, especially revolving around color printing. Not only were the traditional problems of re-purposing content for different media (i.e. for paper, CD-ROM, electronic, fax, and email) an issue, but also an entirely new set of workflow and editing issues was recognized with respect to the reuse of component objects from within the created documents.

Also, the trend to customizing the content product – moving from generic content to a specialized product for an individual information consumer, a "market of one" – was extremely interesting to Russell.

This chapter chronicles both the team's journey and the Russell solution that is currently in production.

21.2 | Project strategy considerations

Russell has steadily been increasing its own awareness that it truly is a large publishing concern, producing millions of pages of color and black and white output for its clients every year. And as a major financial intellectual property publisher, it is also realizing that printing and electronic delivery systems play a very strategic role in its continued growth and success.

There were five principle strategic considerations for the conduct of the project:

- Proceeding from a theoretical abstraction to practical applications.

- Phasing deliverables with measurable return on investment.
- Continuing research in parallel with focused development projects.
- Alignment with overall corporate strategies.
- Executive sponsorship.

21.2.1 *Proceeding from a theoretical abstraction to practical applications*

The project team, though capable of grasping both the short- and long-term objectives for the enterprise, required a methodology to manage scope creep. It chose to divide the tasks into two clear groups:

- the theoretical research and related effort towards general solutions; and
- day-to-day development.

The team was always able to have discussions from the abstract down to the practical by mapping them onto the architecture and life cycle models. When new technologies or vendor products came onto the radar, it was able to discuss them in the context of both the theory and practical project impact using a systematic method.

21.2.2 *Phasing deliverables with measurable return on investment*

This concept may sound similar to the concept of milestones, but is really quite different. This method assumes that there is *no* other project beyond the goals of this one.

It also assumes that this project must justify its own return on investment and bear management review based on its own merits.

Another key element is the openness of each phase's architecture, so that later phases can be bolted on seamlessly with very little trauma to users or developers.

21.2.3 *Continuing research in parallel with focused development projects*

Scope creep is an ever-present danger in technology. Change is a constant. Managing new inputs from press, rumors, research, and outside influence is a constant pressure on fixed milestones and deliverables.

The project team chose discretion as the better part of valor by separating the tasks of research and development into two distinct activities. The development tasks have clearly documented milestones, schedules, and budgets, with methodology in place to monitor their success weekly.

The research tasks are managed more loosely, with overall topics of interest. They use annual funding, rather than project-based funding, and measure deliverables by the published output from the team.

The team believes that this separation keeps developers on the hook for cleaner deliverables and return on investment, while still allowing a response to the crucial happenings that are a day-to-day part of the technology world.

21.2.4 *Alignment with overall corporate strategies*

Any technology project can be fraught with risk. Any technology project can solve a specific technical application and add value if properly executed. Russell's experience was that the real grand slam winner projects are the ones that support the overall mission, culture, vision, and business objectives of an enterprise.

In theory every part of an enterprise is supposed to be working on things that contribute to the goals of the entire enterprise. Straying too far from this principle increases risk and confuses observers, whereas following this principle makes a project's justification much easier to defend and publicize.

21.2.5 *Executive sponsorship*

For several reasons, this is the most powerful thing you can do to enhance a project's chance for success:

- Executives are generally seasoned professionals who have earned a place of authority by knowing how to exploit strengths and manage around weaknesses.
- Executives are generally the best funded portion of an enterprise.
- Executives generally have a clear understanding of the long-term objectives of the enterprise.
- Executives generally have a feeling for the short-term pressures on operations.

These executive qualities enhance a group's ability to make sure their work is done with the support and point-of-view of the senior management and shareholders.

21.3 | Identifying the needs

Russell began to realize the extremely high importance of publishing to the company when it found out the cost. A study determined that almost 1/3 of every expense dollar worldwide was attributable to documents and their production, printing and distribution.

21.3.1 *Business requirements*

The question then became: "How to distribute financial services publications better to a geographically diverse audience, while maintaining premium typographical quality, data integrity, security and compliance?"

Compliance
Russell operates in a heavily regulated environment. There is a legal requirement to reproduce documents related to a customer from many years in the past.

Premium typographic quality
Russell customers typically evaluate large amounts of financial information in a limited time. Russell adds tremendous value for

their customers by simplifying and clarifying these numbers through the use of text, graphics, charts, and color.

Data integrity

It is extremely important that the document received by a customer is identical to the one that was sent to it.

Security

Because of the confidential nature of financial information, it is imperative that only the appropriate people can view these files.

21.3.2 *Technical requirements*

There were significant technical requirements to be met in addition to the business requirements.

Scalability

At Russell, a *Quarterly Investment Review* (QIR) runs from 20-125 pages, averaging around 50 pages. There are hundreds of clients who each get a customized QIR each quarter. Multiple writing, editing, assembly, and compliance steps are required throughout the process.

Low licensing impact for reader software

The problem with end-user licensing of software is that it penalizes a business for the success of a document.

Ease of use

The team felt ease of use to be the single most important factor in the true success of a product.

Cross-platform

Russell cannot control the platforms that its customers use. It has to provide its information in an easily accessible form on virtually every platform available.

Multilingual capability

Russell has offices in London, New York, Winston-Salem, Paris, Hong Kong, Toronto, Tokyo, Sydney, and Auckland. Russell has clients in 25 countries.

21.4 | Create an abstract architecture

The Synth-Bank/Russell team set off to learn about the state of the art in publishing systems, SGML, PDF, and document delivery systems.

Russell had been a pioneer of Postscript assembly and color graphics in the financial services industry. Now the team desired to modernize Russell's publication capabilities to support lower than page granularity and the "distribute then print" metaphor. The team felt that this type of system could meet Russell's business objectives.

The team, working with consultants, created a "Request For Information and Statement of Direction" for a system to purchase (Figure 21-1).

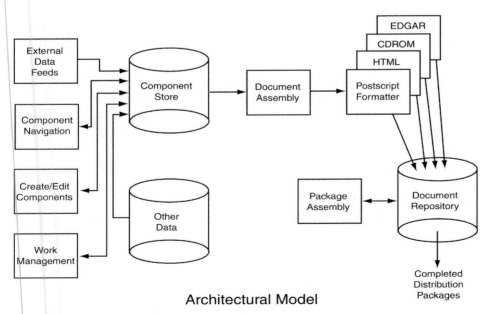

Architectural Model

Figure 21-1   Architectural model of desired system.

The team also performed research on document life cycles and included the life cycle requirements shown in Figure 21-2.

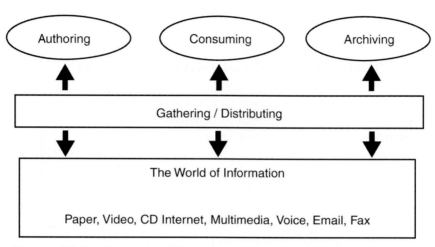

Figure 21-2   Document life cycle requirements.

Russell searched the SGML community for a publishing solution to meet its requirements and found no single commercial product in the marketplace. It then asked the big question: "Why isn't there one already"? The team felt that there were many companies and institutions with document problems similar to, if not more complex than, Russell's.

So the team spent several more months analyzing vendor capabilities and mapping them onto the life cycle graphic until it finally found what it felt was a possible reason. Namely, that the creating, consuming, and archiving stages of a document's life require different system capabilities and orientations: component management, document management, and records management, respectively (Figure 21-3).

Armed with this insight, the team developed the knowledge management model shown in Figure 21-4.

Russell's management and the Synth-Bank team then decided to build and integrate a solution out of *commercially available off-the-shelf (COTS)* products. The team decided to break the deliverables into different phases that would be integrated upon completion.

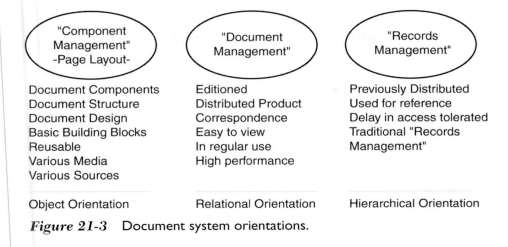

Figure 21-3   Document system orientations.

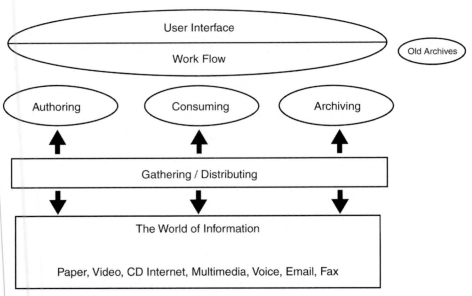

Figure 21-4   Knowledge Management Model

21.5 | Implement applications

The team's initial choice for an application was the *Quarterly Investment Review*. The QIR is representative of many of Russell's publications because it consists of a combination of generic, proprietary, customer-specific, and reusable components.

21.5.1 *Real-world design issues*

In order to apply the theoretical architecture to specific application designs for the QIR publications, the team had to come to grips with real-world issues of internetworking and document representation (file format) standards, to name a few.

21.5.1.1   Internetworking

The WWW family of technologies was chosen for its popularity. Its open-standard nature met the team's basic technical requirements for global electronic delivery, easy access, cheap per-seat licensing costs, cross-platform availability, and security.

The extranet model best served Russell's clients in this application. That is, WWW technologies connected, via public and/or private networks, to a restricted website.

21.5.1.2   Document representation

Synth-Bank firmly believes that document representation is the key to an organization's success with knowledge management. In the *SGML Buyers Guide* (1998), the authors clearly express this point: *"Don't let the software you buy determine the representation. Let the representation you need determine the software you buy"*.

In Russell's case, they needed to choose document representations for all three stages of the document life cycle.

During the creation stage, documents are most useful in an abstract unrendered representation, in which the data can easily be reused and reprocessed. During the consumption and archiving stages, however, the document must be in a rendered form so that it can be presented and displayed quickly and consistently.

21.5.1.2.1 *Abstract document representation*

At the time the work began, SGML was the only document representation that preserved the abstract data and had the "industrial strength" for Russell's requirements. So Russell used it.

XML, as a streamlined subset of SGML, is by definition, not as feature-rich. However, like its parent it preserves the abstraction, and it proved sufficient for Russell's purposes when they eventually converted to it.

21.5.1.2.2 *Rendered document representation*

Portable Document Format (PDF) was chosen for the rendered document representation. The archiving requirement, that it must be readable for a minimum of ten years time, was the dominant deciding criterion.

Large document collections have been faced with this need for some time; for example, those of the Library of Congress and Department of Defense in the U.S. At Russell and many other enterprises, the final formatted image of a document must be retrievable to meet business needs for compliance and reference. Russell's strong desire to use electronic documents to meet its goals was dependent upon a satisfactory decision in this single topic.

Synth-Bank first considered using SGML to meet Russell's archiving requirements. It has successfully been used for simple partial renditions (e.g., HTML), but fully rendered final-form and graphics are outside its design objectives. Although it is undeniably the best representation for long-term preservation of text, that is not what Russell meant by archiving. To be compliant, from Russell's archive it must be possible to retrieve exactly what the client printed originally.

The team made the choice to use PDF because it met the rendered image requirement for both text and graphics, was widely used across many platforms, had a publicly specified format, and supported a large set of the world's languages. It was also attracted to PDF's usability for email distribution and on-screen display.

PDF supports full text search, linking, and page by page loading. It has a development kit available, a compressed file size, interactive forms, cheap seats, and also prints extremely well.

21.5.2   *Phased implementation plan*

The work involved some parallel processing, with secondary teams doing research and advanced studies on upcoming phases. The implementation teams, however, focused on the deliverables.

One team was assigned to create archiving requirements for the corporation. Another team worked on object databases and SGML abstractions.

A third team worked on graphical design. Its goal was to constrain the number of presentation layouts in order to optimize for batch processing. Finally, a fourth team had the task of tracking and understanding key standards like SGML, XML, HyTime, and various related W3C activities.

21.5.2.1   Phase I: Records management business study

The technical work on this phase was deferred. The main candidate for an archiving product was in the middle of an acquisition, which created an unacceptable business risk.

However, Russell did conduct a two-year study on document archiving requirements for its Investment Management Business. Once the business case for records management was made, Russell hired a full-time professional archivist to champion the deployment of the technology.

21.5.2.2   Phase II: Document management of PDF files

Russell's corporate Information Technology department had previously deployed a document management system. The project team used it in the interests of corporate harmony, and worked with its vendor's R&D department on the beta version of an application to make documents available over the Web.

This product allows you to build a query on a Web-based form (Figure 21-5), which can be tailored to meet application requirements.

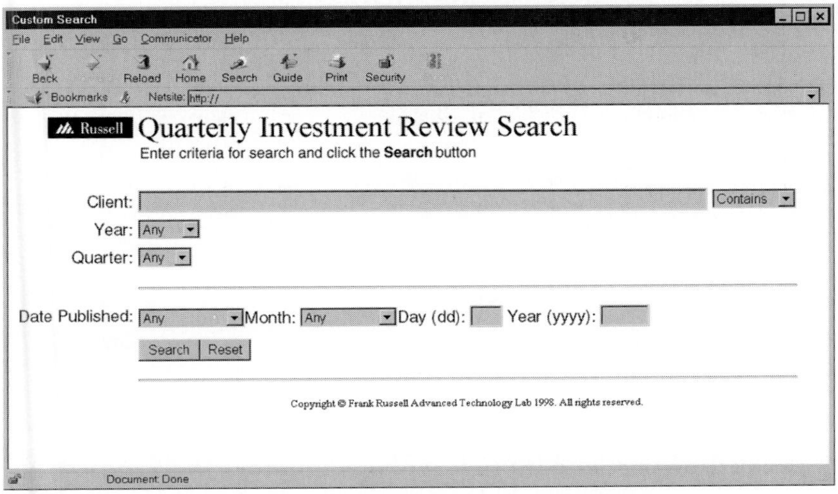

Figure 21-5 Document management search screen.

The query results are delivered as an HTML frame (Figure 21-6), the form of which can also be customized. Russell's users found that it made the interface to the product's library services, particularly document check-out, much more appealing than it had been.

21.5.2.3   Phase III: Document assembly and formatting

The objective of this phase was to create structured documents in SGML that could be auto-assembled, and to implement auto-check-in to the document management system.

As the assembly and formatting phase of the project began, the team focused on the issues of: How much structure is needed?, What are the quality levels required for the publication in its final form? What should the user interface experience be like for editing sections, book assembly and releasing books to the document management system?

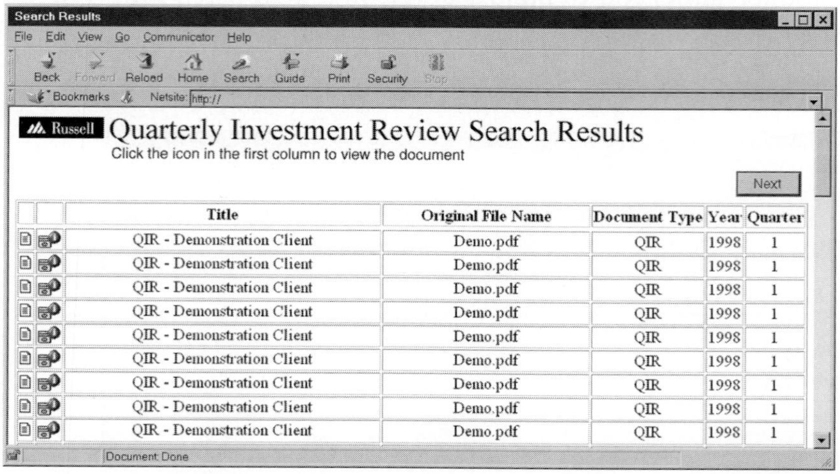

Figure 21-6   Document management search results.

Russell decided to purchase a product that supported integrated structured editing, layout, and typographic control.

The users for this phase are a small group of document editors who compile and author the QIR documents for clients at Russell. Their typical quarterly work cycle involves revising the previous quarter's document files, graphics, and tables, and launching a new composite book for each client. New document pages are created approximately 10% of the time.

The users are trained in popular word processors, spreadsheet, and graphics packages, but have no experience in SGML. They are accustomed to setting the indents, font style, size of a page, and common typography settings. They are often under the spotlight to make a production deadline in hours and therefore must be able to make edits quickly with minimal amount of new steps. They are only interested in software that makes their life easier.

The team quickly found that the system must make the SGML transparent to the user, that the layout must be WYSIWYG, and that the application should assist in the creation of a consistent layout throughout the book.

21.5.2.3.1 *How structure was used*

The approach taken was to replace the use of paragraph style codes with meaningful SGML element-type names. The document was then formatted in real time, based on the element types, thereby giving the users their customary WYSIWYG effect.

A welcome side-effect was that the list of element-type choices was much smaller than the full list of paragraph styles typically presented by a WYSIWYG editor, because of the context enforced by the DTD. In addition, the product has a guided creation feature, which automatically inserts required elements. It allowed us to lay out a typical page easily, and still allowed deviations by making choices permitted by the DTD.

One area of improvement to the overall professionalism of the book was in the consistency of format and layout. In the old system, each page was laid out individually and it often deviated slightly as editing continued over several quarters of revisions.

The new system, however, used a series of matched templates created by a professional typographer, and it used structure to drive the formatting of the text. The resultant books were consistent, and compliant with corporate guidelines. This achievement was a significant win since "document police" (people trying to enforce style quality control issues from a corporate perspective) are not often welcome.

21.5.2.3.2 *Document editing*

With all of these facilities available, the team found that it needed to simplify the application menus. Doing so would limit access to designer pallets and provide users with a simpler interface to this complex and powerful tool.

Simplifying was done by using the application's custom user interface feature. It required no programming, although some developer expertise is required.

Training the users on the new system consisted of five sessions of one day in length, including hands on lab sessions. The editing tool took 50% of the training time, with the remaining time being spread on a general introduction, graphics, book building, and lab sessions. The users quickly grasped the system's capabilities and found it to be a huge improvement over the previous system.

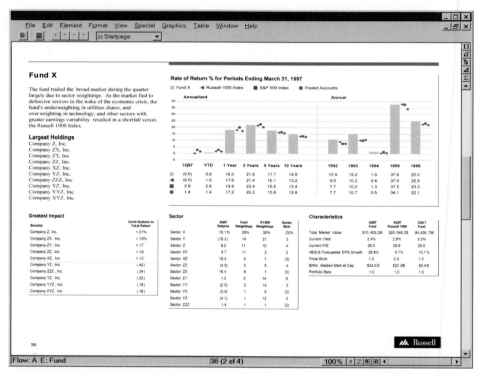

Figure 21-7   Fund page example in editing system.

21.5.2.3.3 *How much structure is needed?*

Once the decision was made to use a structured representation of its publications, the challenge became to decide how much structure was appropriate and for what reasons. The team approached this from two viewpoints: long-term and short-term.

The long-term objectives of using structure were to add value to the intellectual property and aid with reuse, navigation, automation and archiving.

The short-term goals were to enforce consistency in the typography, assure better quality control, and facilitate the aggregation of disparate content sources into single publications with a high degree of automation. Other short-term goals were to facilitate document assembly with automation, and to improve the user's experience.

21.5.2.3.4 *Final-form quality requirements*

Russell's output quality requirements are extremely high (Figure 21-7). When it looked at the commercially available database-driven publishing systems and dynamic Web page assemblers, none were capable of presenting publications as well as Russell's legacy systems. Also, although the Web publishing systems were great for producing pages from the current state of the database, they were not capable of satisfying Russell's compliance requirements.

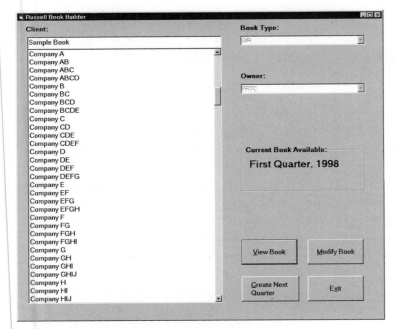

Figure 21-8   Russell BookBuilder (1 of 2)

21.5.2.3.5 *Book assembly*

The team wanted to make the user experience during book building as straightforward as possible by presenting only immediately relevant infor-

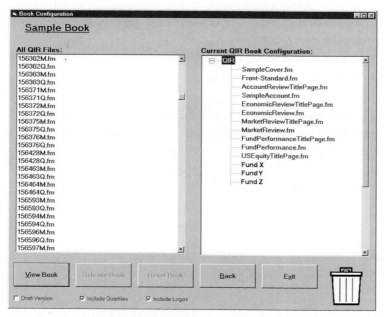

Figure 21-9   Russell BookBuilder (2 of 2)

mation. It built a simple windowing scheme, based on a customer database, that presented the bookbuilding experience on two screens (Figure 21-8 and Figure 21-9).

Along with the customer name and the component bill of materials list selections, the book building interface also gathers the metadata required for check-in to the document management system and stores it for later use. This may seem trivial, but it completely removes the user pain from the document management check-in process.

21.5.2.3.6 *Releasing books to the document management system*

Final preparation of a book for review and release is invoked by a single custom menu item, `Publish`, on the `File` menu. The `Publish` command creates a PostScript file of the book, which is then distilled into a PDF file (Figure 21-10). During this process, the PDF file is updated with the document management system check-in metadata that was gathered during the book building.

The `Publish` command eliminates a large number of print and configuration item choices for the user and controls the way PDF files are created. This plug-in also automatically generates bookmark hyperlinks for the PDF table of contents from the SGML structural element hierarchy.

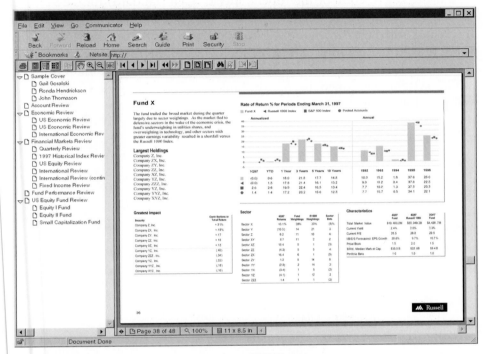

Figure 21-10   Fund page example in PDF book.

21.5.2.4   Phase IV: XML and the future

In 1995 Synth-Bank began a pure research project for Russell into the notion of "Knowledge Management Systems". These are automated systems that would be the next logical extension for publishing, collaborative creation, and electronic delivery.

Because of the importance of the Internet in such systems, XML seemed better for the purpose than full SGML. The SGML to XML conversion took one developer three days.

21.6 | Conclusion

In the past, internetworking of systems was complex. Now, with the World Wide Web and TCP/IP, internetworking is routine and affordable. The next frontier is content interoperability.

And the key to content interoperability is open standards for data representation. Not the proprietary data formats used by most popular word processing and publishing tools, but true open standards like XML. The power and future of information technologies is determined by the degree of vendor and platform independence that they offer for the long term.

The system developed by Synth-Bank for Frank Russell Company is well-positioned for that future.

WYSIWYG XML editing and formatting

- Stand-alone vs. hands-on formatting
- Editing in the context of rendition
- Concurrent abstract and rendered views
- Structure-based formatting
- Benefits of the hands-on approach
- Software on CD-ROM

Sponsor: Adobe Systems Incorporated,
http://www.adobe.com/products/framemaker

Contributing expert: Max Dunn of Silicon Publishing

Chapter
22

Why edit *or* format when you can edit *and* format at the same time? That's the premise behind WYSIWYG XML tools. They provide a word processor user experience, while still preserving the abstract XML document. That means that what you see doesn't have to be all you get!

When SGML – and later XML – came on the scene, they offered an alternative to WYSIWYG word-processing systems. XML enables authors to avoid a cluttered middle ground between abstraction and rendition, allowing content to be maintained independently of the rendering systems used for publication.

Throwing away the word processor and working with documents in their abstract state – without worrying about how they will be rendered – can be a liberating experience. But there are times when it is most effective to edit such abstract document content in the context of an intended rendition.

There are high-end graphic-arts quality publishing systems available that offer that ability. In these systems, WYSIWYG XML editing does not mean a return to the early dark days of the word processor. Rather, benefits of word processing – such as being able to see your rendition as you type – can be obtained while maintaining the benefits of separating abstraction from rendition.

In this chapter we will discuss the characteristics and benefits of WYSI-WYG XML. We'll use *Adobe® FrameMaker®* to illustrate.

22.1 | Stand-alone vs. hands-on formatting

Figure 22-1 illustrates the typical information flow when formatting an XML document. An XML source document is transformed with a stylesheet or template (which may or may not be an XML document) into a rendition (which also may or may not be an XML document). Both the source and the stylesheet are based on the document type, which is expressed as a DTD or other form of schema definition.

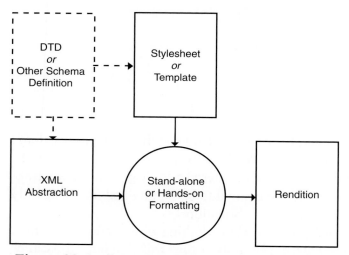

Figure 22-1   Formatting an XML abstraction into a rendition

A distinction between two types of formatting can be made, based on when the generation of the rendition occurs:

stand-alone formatting
> The rendition is generated outside of the editing environment (for example, as a batch process).

hands-on formatting
> The rendition is generated in real time within the editing environment, facilitating WYSIWYG editing.

22.2 | Editing in the context of rendition

WYSIWYG XML tools let you edit the source XML abstraction using hands-on formatting, within a user interface that looks like a particular rendition. As it is possible to generate many different renditions from a single source, there are several possibilities for the "what you get" of WYSIWYG XML editing: a PDF, a Web page, a rendition designed for presentation on a particular device, etc.

In Figure 22-2, the user is editing an XML document as it would be formatted for print or PDF delivery.

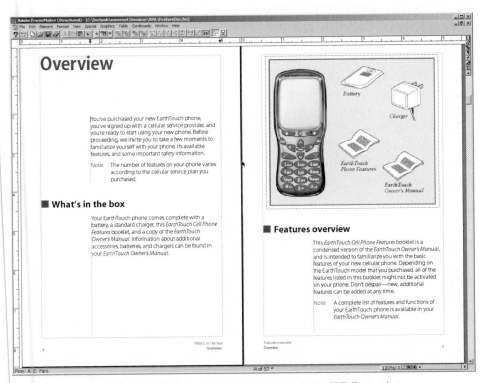

Figure 22-2   Editing XML in the context of a print/PDF rendition

Such an environment allows authors a constant view of the way the document will look when rendered. In the print/PDF paradigm, this means, for example, that authors can see whether the text they've just written will flow across pages. Seeing how a document paginates can be important for estimating the size of print output. Moreover, page numbers can be useful reference points when collaborating with others on a document.

22.3 | Concurrent rendition and abstraction

Editing within the context of a particular rendition offers one set of benefits. There are other benefits associated with editing the source XML solely in terms of its abstract structure, without reference to a rendition.

For this reason, WYSIWYG XML tools typically provide concurrent modes of editing. For example, *FrameMaker* includes a "structure view", shown in the lower right portion of Figure 22-3. With it you can navigate and manipulate the structure of the XML source and see your work immediately reflected in the concurrent "document view" on the left.

Icons representing XML tags can be toggled on or off in the document view (they are on in the figure). The icons provide an indication of the markup of the XML source, while the view still shows the characteristics of the rendition.

22.4 | Structure-based formatting

Despite the illusion created by real-time hands-on formatting, the source XML doesn't miraculously format itself into a rendition. Whether formatting is stand-alone or hands-on, the information flow shown in Figure 22-1 still occurs. That means a stylesheet must exist that specifies – based on the DTD of the abstract XML document – how the content should be rendered.

In *FrameMaker*, the stylesheet function is provided by an *Element Definition Document (EDD)*, shown in Figure 22-4. The EDD contains rules for applying paragraph and character formatting styles to structural elements, and also the structural rules themselves (from the DTD). In terms of Figure

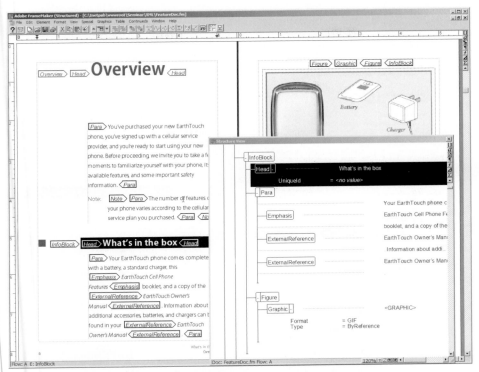

Figure 22-3 Editing in concurrent structure and document views

22-1, it is as though the stylesheet contained the DTD.

An EDD can be derived from a DTD and synchronized with it. For that reason, it isn't necessary to maintain multiple copies of the DTD even if multiple renditions – and therefore multiple EDDs – are defined for the same document type.

Style rules can be conditional. In Figure 22-4, for example, the EDD specifies different paragraph styles for Para elements, depending on the structural context in which an element occurs in the XML source.

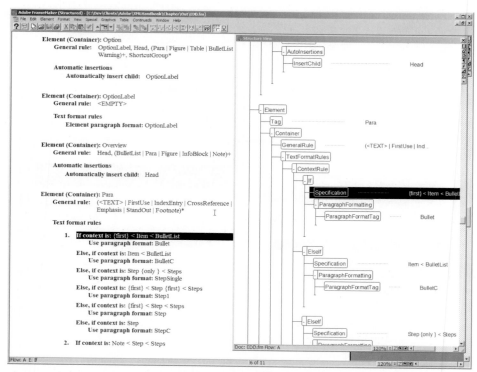

Figure 22-4   Specifying formatting based on structural context

22.5 | When should hands-on formatting be used?

When does it make sense to use hands-on formatting as opposed to stand-alone formatting? It really depends on the needs of a given author or publishing group. Whether hands-on formatting is appropriate depends on the extent to which some or all of the following conditions are present:

- One form of intended rendition outweighs any others in importance: for example, PDF pages for printing and website distribution.
- Complex formatting that benefits from close human attention is essential to the rendered output: for example, when printed

documents require tight control over pagination and/or graphic arts quality output.

■ Editing workflows and/or document types are well-suited to a word-processing editing paradigm.

22.6 | Benefits of the hands-on approach

When conditions are present that recommend the hands-on approach, WYSIWYG XML offers several benefits: less exposure to markup, instant proofing, and increased author control.

22.6.1 *Markup behind the scenes*

One benefit of hands-on formatting is that authors spend less time working directly with markup. Although the content is still abstract, its structure can often be recognized by the formatting of the rendition, with no need to access the markup.

The instant transformation of structural context to formatting can help authors proof the structural integrity of the abstraction ("was that the right tag?"). Such a visual interface can be especially appealing to users who are not used to working with XML. Some participants in an editing workflow (copy editors, for example) may be able to avoid markup altogether.

22.6.2 *Real-time proofing*

In stand-alone formatting, the generation of a *proof* (a draft rendition) is a distinct process, independent of editing the XML abstraction. Hands-on formatting, on the other hand, provides a constant view of the rendition, updated as authors work. That enables authors to avoid surprises at the time of publication. Such real-time proofing can identify errors in both the content of the XML source and in the formatting rules that determine how it is rendered.

22.6.3 *Decentralized editing and publishing*

In a collaborative editing environment, stand-alone processing is often performed as a server-side process. While this arrangement can help provide centralized control over publishing, it also potentially limits the frequency with which authors can generate draft renditions.

WYSIWYG XML tools can typically generate a final (*camera-ready*) form of the rendition that was used during editing. *FrameMaker*, for example, can print directly to a local printer or directly save Adobe PDF files, as shown in Figure 22-5.

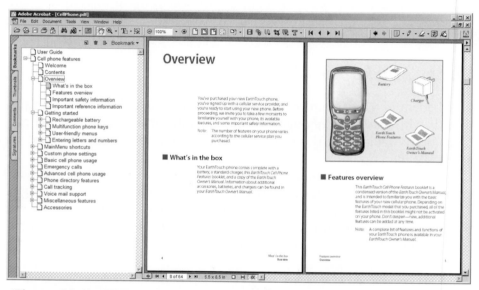

Figure 22-5   PDF rendition generated by *FrameMaker*

This ability to create the literal final rendition on demand gives authors complete control of the publishing process (for some forms of rendition, at any rate) without dependence on a centralized system.

22.7 | Conclusion

Markup languages were originally considered a "cure" for WYSIWYG. By capturing document content as an unrendered abstraction, SGML and XML allowed the content to be reused and reformatted for many different purposes.

Today, WYSIWYG editing and hands-on formatting need no longer be a barrier to the creation and preservation of reusable abstractions. Modern WYSIWYG XML tools allow XML editing with simultaneous access to a real-time rendition.

Tip   *You can experience hands-on WYSIWYG XML for yourself. A trial version of the full Adobe FrameMaker product is included on the CD accompanying this book.*

Using XSL-FO formatting objects

Tool Discussion

▪ Capabilities of XSL-FO

▪ Implementing XSL-FO

▪ XSL-FO case study

Sponsor: Antenna House, Inc., http://www.antennahouse.com
Contributing expert: Keiko Hiraide

For centuries, humanity has accessed information with proven page-oriented navigational tools and sophisticated formatting. Just printing Web pages won't do this job for your data — you need the power of XSL formatting objects!

S amuel Wesley said it best, back in 1700:

Style is the dress of thought.

In other words, if you want to communicate your data well, you need to dress it in a style that will be accepted and understood by your intended audience.

For centuries, the needed styles have been achieved by means of sophisticated formatting and page-oriented navigational tools. The popular Web-based presentation technologies, such as HTML and CSS, can't do this job. But the alternatives, until recently, have all been proprietary.

Now the W3C's *Extensible Stylesheet Language* Recommendation offers a standard XML vocabulary for describing almost any print-like style. It is called *XSL formatting objects (XSL-FO)*.

In other parts of this book we've seen examples of XPath and XSLT. Both of these languages were once exclusively part of XSL, so we know the power of XSL to transform a document. XSL-FO is the rest of the XSL standard. It lets you style the rendition of your data with meticulous control, so you can accommodate the cultural expectations of diverse readers and the constraints of their environments.

23.1 | What can we do with XSL?

The W3C XSL Recommendation defines objects for specifying page layouts, such as paragraph, table, list, etc. They are called *formatting objects* and you can think of them as roughly corresponding to elements of a page-oriented rendered document. Specifications such as page sizes, font family names, font sizes, and line heights are defined as properties of the formatting objects.[1]

The formatting objects and their properties allow layout to be specified with the precision associated with high-quality graphic-arts printing technologies. For example:

page layouts

A page is divided into 5 regions: the body, and regions above, below, and to either side of the body. The size of each region can be specified.

columns

The body region can be divided into columns. It is possible to define spans across all the columns.

layout sequences

It is possible to alternate different page layouts on odd and even pages, blank forced pages, and the first, middle or last page in a page sequence.

line properties

Line property settings include indention, justification, line height, and spacing between blocks.

breaks and keeps

Page breaks and column breaks can be forced by break-before and break-after settings. Keeps can be used to prevent page and column breaks.

---

1. There is a more detailed introduction in Chapter 61, "XSL formatting objects (XSL-FO)", on page 990.

markers

Markers can be placed in text and the marked text can be retrieved into the static content of headers and footers; for example, in a directory headers could reference markers in the first and last entries on the page.

floats

Content can be floated out of line as footnotes, side-floats (at the sides of the page body), or top floats.

page numbers

Pages can be numbered automatically. Page number citations can be flowed anywhere in the content to make reference to other pages in the formatted result.

links

Link objects can be rendered in several ways; for example, as printed cross-references or as traversable hyperlinks in PDF or other e-book files.

XSL has facilities that are particularly useful when rendering different languages. They are discussed in 23.3.3, "Globalization support", on page 390.

23.2 | Implementing XSL-FO

Figure 23-1 shows the typical information flow when formatting with XSL. There are two separate steps:

1. An XSLT processor uses an XSLT stylesheet to transform the abstract XML source into an XSL-FO document.
2. An XSL formatting engine interprets the XSL-FO document and creates a rendition for a particular medium or device – commonly PDF.

XSL-FO formatting engines are available for all common computing platforms, often with multiple interfaces. For example, Antenna House provides its *XSL Formatter* on Windows, Solaris®, and Linux. The product

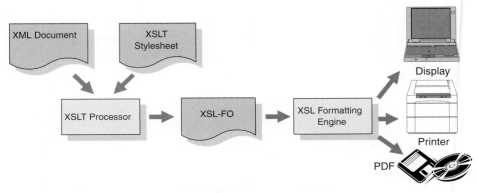

Figure 23-1   Formatting XML documents with XSL-FO

interfaces include COM, .NET, JAVA, command line, and C/C++. In Windows, users may preview the rendition using a graphical user interface. The product is also available for use on a server.

23.3 | Benefits of XSL

XSL offers several advantages: a standardized page-oriented stylesheet language, the ability to support high-volume stand-alone formatting, and features for global language support.

23.3.1 *Standardized page-oriented stylesheet language*

Formatting software requires a stylesheet to lay out the XML elements because an XML abstraction has no layout information of its own. Most page-oriented typesetting programs use proprietary styling interfaces and languages for this purpose.

Graphic-arts quality composition tends to be complicated, so stylesheet development tends to be time-consuming and expensive. As a result, users get locked into their composition programs because of the cost of developing new stylesheets for another program.

XSL, because it is a standardized language, offers the possibility of migration without the need to abandon or redevelop existing stylesheets.

23.3.2 *High-volume stand-alone formatting*

XSL differs from most proprietary graphic-arts quality formatting solutions in that it is completely automatable, requiring no human involvement once the stylesheets are created. That makes it practical for implementation on a server, as shown in Figure 23-2. Multiple clients can request, for example, that the XSL formatting engine render their documents and return them in PDF for display on the client computer (or PDA!) using *Acrobat Reader*.

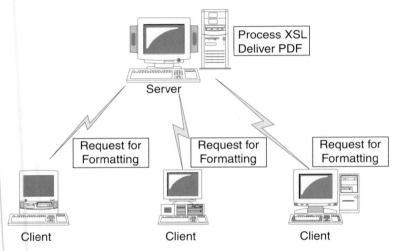

Figure 23-2   XSL formatting engine running as a server

XSL can also be valuable in corporate data reporting, particularly when a report must be customized dynamically and rendered individually for each recipient.

There are stand-alone systems that solve this problem by rendering XML as PDF, using dedicated form software. However, if the length of any item in a report is variable, or if an item can repeat an arbitrary number of times, typical forms software can't handle it. Moreover, forms software can only process forms, while XSL can format other documents as well.

23.3.3 *Globalization support*

Manufacturers often seek to expand their markets beyond the linguistic borders of their products' origin. Doing so requires *localization* of documentation, such as instruction, operation, maintenance, and service manuals. Traditionally, translation and printing of localized manuals took place only after the originals were produced.

As products face shorter life cycles and increased competition, localization delays have become unacceptable. They are seen as impediments to realizing a product's full revenue potential.

The need for localization to proceed in parallel with product development is now well-recognized. Fortunately, XML and XSL have characteristics that make it possible for a manufacturer to generate manuals from a single location for worldwide needs, in multiple languages, with minimum additional effort.

23.3.3.1   Component management

XML document types can be designed with very fine granularity of the element structure. That allows very small components of the document to be managed individually, and multiple translations of them can be kept. At publication time, desired components for a given language can be assembled, along with any graphics, and submitted to an XSL processor for rendition as a single publication.

We discuss component management in detail in Part 5, "Content Management", on page 266.

23.3.3.2   Unicode

XML and XSL use the Unicode character set, which has a number of benefits for globalization:

- Any language can be represented in XML.
- Multiple languages can be represented in the same document.
- Unicode text can be formatted by XSL without any character code conversion.

For example, the Antenna House *XSL Formatter* can process XML text containing English, Japanese, Traditional Chinese, Simplified Chinese, Korean, Arabic, Hebrew, Thai, and Western and Eastern European languages. It also allows users to generate PDF output that contains these languages.

Figure 23-3 shows a page rendered by *XSL Formatter* with English and Arabic text.

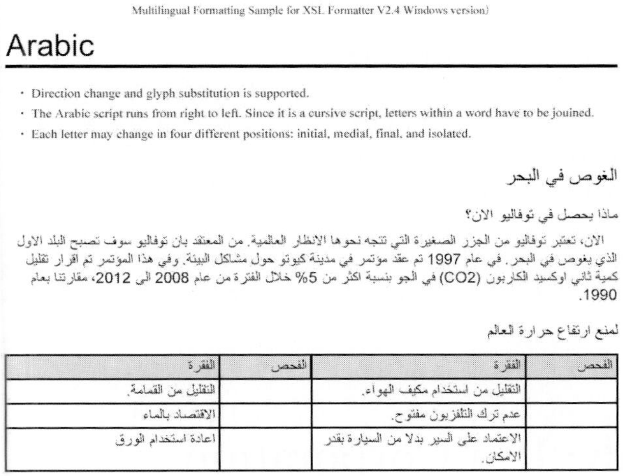

Multilingual Formatting Sample for XSL Formatter V2.4 Windows version)

Arabic

- Direction change and glyph substitution is supported.
- The Arabic script runs from right to left. Since it is a cursive script, letters within a word have to be jouined.
- Each letter may change in four different positions: initial, medial, final, and isolated.

الغوص في البحر

ماذا يحصل في توفاليو الان؟

الان، تعتبر توفاليو من الجزر الصغيرة التي تتجه نحوها الانظار العالمية. من المعتقد بان توفاليو سوف تصبح البلد الاول الذي يغوص في البحر. في عام 1997 تم عقد مؤتمر في مدينة كيوتو حول مشاكل البيئة. وفي هذا المؤتمر تم اقرار تقليل كمية ثاني اوكسيد الكاربون (CO2) في الجو بنسبة اكثر من 5% خلال الفترة من عام 2008 الى 2012، مقارنتا بعام 1990.

لمنع ارتفاع حرارة العالم

الفحص	الفقرة	الفحص	الفقرة
	التقليل من استخدام مكيف الهواء.		التقليل من القمامة.
	عدم ترك التلفزيون مفتوح.		الاقتصاد بالماء
	الاعتماد على السير بدلا من السيارة بقدر الامكان.		اعادة استخدام الورق

Figure 23-3 Multilingual page with English and Arabic text

23.3.3.3 Writing-mode

XSL offers a setting called *writing-mode* to specify the direction in which characters and lines progress. This facility is needed for languages that are written vertically (such as Japanese and Chinese), and languages that are written from right to left (such as Hebrew and Arabic).

The writing-mode setting also controls the progression direction of columns in a table or in a multi-column page.

23.3.3.4   Unicode BIDI

Specifying the writing direction of characters in a bidirectional multilingual text string is a more complex task. Such situations occur when a document intermixes characters that progress from left to right (such as Latin alphabets or Japanese characters) with those that progress from right to left (such as Arabic or Hebrew alphabets). XSL employs *Unicode BIDI*, the Unicode Standard algorithm for the display ordering of bidirectional text, so there is no need to deal with any of this in an XSL stylesheet.

23.3.3.5   Language-specific stylesheets

XSL formatting objects and their properties provide precise control over the layout and style of renditions. It is therefore possible to create stylesheets that conform to the accepted typesetting rules of virtually any language and culture.

   As a result, when the components of a localized document are assembled, an appropriate stylesheet for that language can be used to render the document.

23.4 | Case study: JSR Corporation

JSR Corporation was established in 1957 as Japan Synthetic Rubber Co., Ltd. It now has over 4,000 employees worldwide, engaged in the manufacture of electronic materials, synthetic rubber, latex, thermoplastic elastomers, and resin.

23.4.1   *Material Safety Data Sheet (MSDS)*

As a manufacturer of hazardous chemicals, JSR is required to prepare and deliver a *Material Safety Data Sheet (MSDS)* for its products (and for the components of its blended or mixed products). The purpose of the MSDS is to describe the proper procedures for handling or working with a particular substance. The MSDS is intended for use by emergency personnel as well as people who work with the substance routinely.

   JSR includes material like the following in an MSDS:

- Information about the manufacturer of the substance.
- What's contained in the substance?
- Physical and chemical nature of the substance.
- Potential hazards of the substance.
- How to cope with emergencies such as ingestion of the substance, skin or eye contact, fires, or spills.
- Procedures for handling, storing, disposing, and carrying.
- Applicable regulations and reference materials.

All together, an MSDS consists of 16 items, each item potentially having sub-items and sub-sub-items. The content consists of text and tables, and the length of items is variable.When rendered, an MSDS is a document of 4 to 8 pages, depending on the substance.

23.4.2 *Operation*

An MSDS system was developed for JSR Corporation by JNT SYSTEM Co., Ltd.

The MSDS content data for each product is prepared separately and stored in a database. When a sales staff member requests an MSDS for a customer, the product MSDS data is merged with information about the customer and system and an MSDS is assembled. Although there is basically just one format for an MSDS, there are some variations that are controlled by the XSLT transform during assembly.

The assembled MSDS is then previewed by the sales staff, using a Web browser. After review and approval, the MSDS is formatted on the server by *XSL Formatter* and delivered to a printer.

23.5 | Conclusion

XSL-FO changes the ground rules for the delivery of business data. There is no longer a need to limit formatting to the simple, Web-oriented capabilities of HTML or CSS. Instead, graphic-arts quality XSL-FO formatting engines can operate as standalone servers, dynamically rendering XML documents at high speed with the full capabilities of page-oriented navigation and sophisticated formatting.

Beyond XSL: The real DSSSL at work

- ▌ Unique capabilities of DSSSL
- ▌ Inside a DSSSL stylesheet
- ▌ Implementation of DSSSL
- ▌ Software on CD-ROM

Sponsor: NEXT SOLUTION CO., LTD.,
http://www.nextsolution.co.jp/English

Contributing expert: Takashige Noguchi

XML is blessed with a variety of formatting
methods, both interactive and stand-alone. But if
your formatting literally uses every trick in the book –
and some only found in magazines, brochures, forms,
and newsletters – and if you don't have time to tweak
10,000 documents by hand – then you may need the
original markup language formatting standard:
DSSSL!

W e have seen that XSL is a powerful style language, capable of
meeting many stylistic and navigational requirements that
HTML and CSS cannot satisfy. Although XSL-FO was partly
based on CSS, the real power of XSL comes from its amazing ancestor
DSSSL, the *Document Style Semantics and Specification Language*.

DSSSL is an International Standard (ISO/IEC 10179) that was developed over an 8-year period from 1988-1996. XSL is based on DSSSL and is
compatible with its fundamental design principles and processing model.
But DSSSL has some unique capabilities, as we shall see.

24.1 | DSSSL can do things that XSL cannot

Composing documents for paginated display is considered an art form in
most cultures. The process is so complex it is often considered unimple-
mentable by an automated rule-driven composition system. Indeed, most
successful high-end composition programs are designed to be interactive, so

that users can do by direct manipulation what might be difficult or impossible to express in stylesheet rules.[1]

DSSSL, however, was designed to express the full richness of high-quality graphic-arts formatting. The best way to see the implications of that ambitious design objective is to look at some of the things that DSSSL can do that XSL cannot.

Note   As the illustrations tend to be large, and the explanations short, you may have to turn the page at times to keep them in sync. We try to avoid exercise ourselves, but this effort is worth it. Your ideas about the best way to display your data will never be the same again!

24.1.1 *Multiple column layouts on a page*

The XSL page model allows a page body to be divided into columns. However, the number of columns cannot be changed within a page. DSSSL, however, does not have this restriction, so layouts like that in Figure 24-1 are possible.

24.1.2 *Mixed region sizes and flow ordering*

In XSL, the document content can flow into only one region of a page, usually the *body region*. There are many applications where such a simple page model is adequate[2], but there are many others where it is not.

Publications such as marketing brochures or company magazines may benefit from DSSSL's ability for a page to have multiple regions, each of which can be a different size if desired. They can even be arranged as mirror-images on facing pages, as shown in Figure 24-2 and Figure 24-3.

---

1. The TeX formatting language, though capable of high quality and not interactive, isn't necessarily rule-driven. It allows direct manipulation to be accomplished non-interactively by inserting formatting commands into the source document.
2. Books like this, for example!

Figure 24-1   Page layout with 4 columns and 3 columns simultaneously

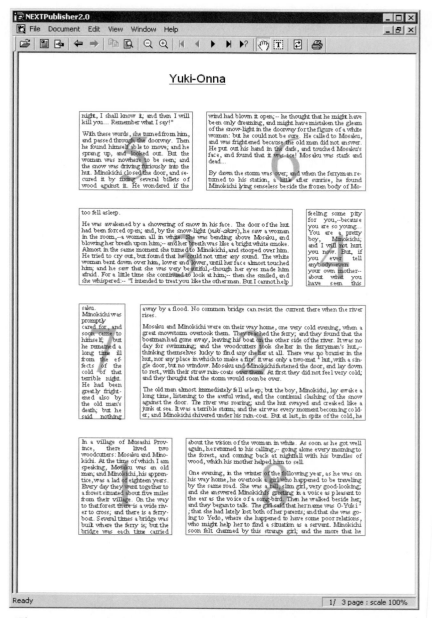

Figure 24-2   Left page of two-page layout with mixed region sizes

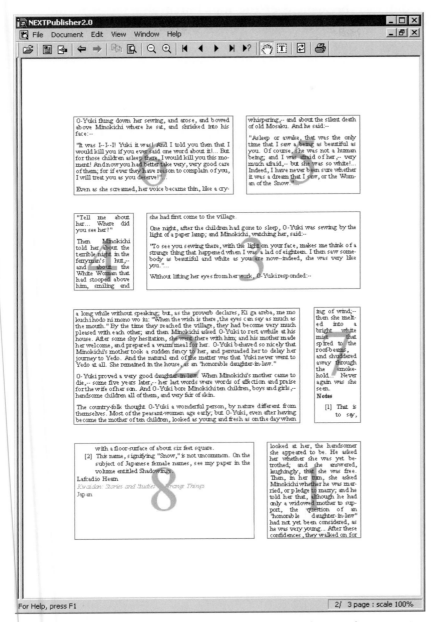

Figure 24-3   Right page of two-page layout with mixed region sizes

This layout may be a bit over the top, but it also serves to illustrate another unique capability of DSSSL: the order in which content flows into the different body regions can be controlled by the stylesheet.

For our convenience, the flow order is indicated in the illustrations by the overprinted numerals (which were also generated by the stylesheet).

Note   *In fact, it should be noted that all of the examples in Figure 24-1 through Figure 24-6 were generated under the control of DSSSL stylesheets by an automated formatter (NEXTPublisher from NEXT SOLUTION CO., LTD.). There was no human intervention in the process.*

24.1.3 *Partial-page column spans*

In advertising and magazine layouts (among others), it may be necessary for a headline or graphic to span several columns, but not necessarily the full width of the page, as shown in Figure 24-4. DSSSL supports this capability, which is not available in XSL. XSL allows spans of a single column or the full page, but not partial-page spans.

24.1.4 *Parallel content flows*

DSSSL has the ability to support multiple concurrent content flows, and to direct each one into a different body region of a page sequence.

Figure 24-5 illustrates a page with four body regions. Each region contains an independent content flow. For our convenience, the flows are identified with overprinted numbers.

Figure 24-6 illustrates the next page in the page sequence. It has the identical region layout. The four body regions contain the continuations of the four stories in the correspondingly-numbered flows of the previous page.

Figure 24-4   Graphic spanning two columns of four-column page

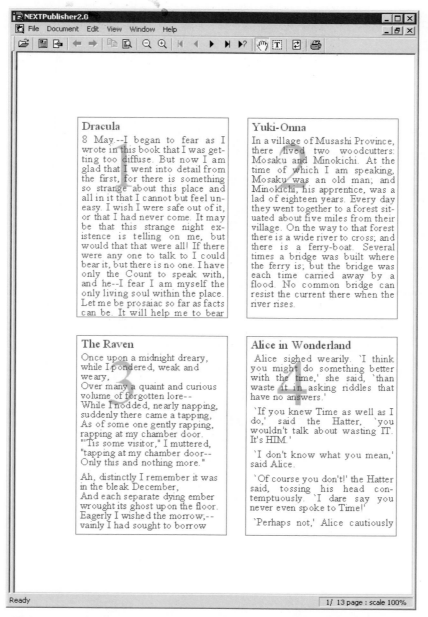

Figure 24-5   First page of layout with four stories flowing into four regions

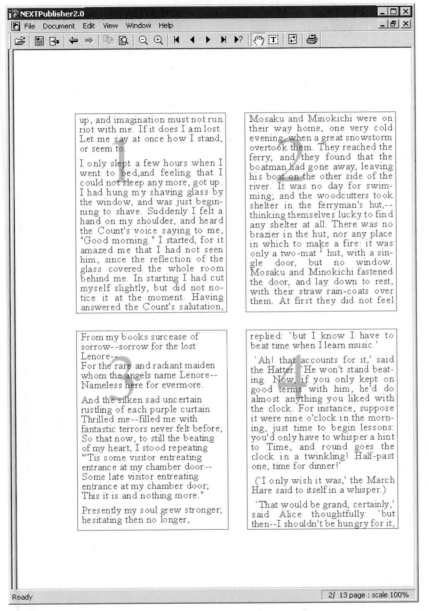

Figure 24-6   Second page of layout with four stories flowing into four regions

24.1.5 *Content-driven body region specification*

There are two methods of specifying the size of a body region:

layout-driven
> The margins are specified and what is left of the page is the body region (body region = paper size - margins).

content-driven
> The body region is specified and what is left of the page is the margins (margins = paper size - body region).

For typical alphabetic languages, there is no practical difference between the two; they are just different ways of arriving at the same result. However, a subtle problem arises when Chinese, Japanese, and Korean languages (*CJK languages*) are used.

These languages specify their character widths in *em spaces* – a unit of width that is equal to a character's height. For them, content-driven specification is the most reliable way to ensure that the size of a region is an exact multiple of ems and lines; for example, 30 characters wide and 40 lines high.

When layout-driven specification is used, the resulting body region might not be an exact number of em squares. This is not a problem for alphabetic languages, as their character glyph widths are variable and can be adjusted by the formatter. However, it can cause formatting misalignments for CJK languages.

XSL supports only layout-driven specification, but DSSSL supports content-driven specification as well.

24.1.6 *Japanese formatting features*

DSSSL supports several formatting conventions that are required for Japanese text, as shown in Figure 24-7. They are:

multiline inline text
> Multiple lines of text are inserted within a text line.

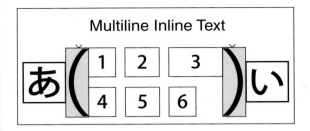

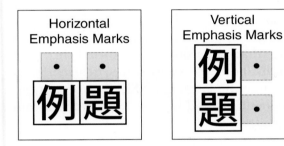

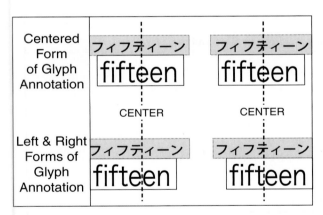

Figure 24-7 Japanese formatting techniques supported by DSSSL

emphasis marks

Marks are displayed above horizontal text or alongside vertical text.

glyph annotation
> Annotations are displayed below text. They can be centered on the annotated text, or aligned left or right.

24.2 | Inside a DSSSL stylesheet

As a child of DSSSL, XSL learned a lot from its parent. Both standards have the same basic components: a language and classes of formatting objects. DSSSL calls them an *expression language* and *flow objects*. The DSSSL objects work similarly enough to those of XSL-FO (although they differ in their properties and other details) that we needn't discuss them here. [3]

The DSSSL expression language, however, is a variant of Scheme, which is a full-blown procedural programming language. XSLT, in contrast, is a declarative language. Many programmers find it easier to accomplish complex tasks with a procedural language.

For comparison, consider a style rule for a paragraph in a 10pt font. Here it is in XSLT:

Example 24-1. XSLT rule for paragraph in 10pt font
```
<xsl:template match="p">
  <fo:block font-size="10pt">
    <xsl:apply-templates/>
  </fo:block>
</xsl:template>
```

Here is the same rule in DSSSL:

Example 24-2. DSSSL rule for paragraph in 10pt font
```
(element p
  (make paragraph
    font-size:10pt
  )
)
```

---

3. For an XSL-FO refresher, see Chapter 61, "XSL formatting objects (XSL-FO)", on page 990.

Those examples, of course, aren't very complex. A better example is the automatic generation of a table of contents from the `title` subelements of `chapter` and `section` elements. The rendered result is shown in Figure 24-8 and the DSSSL stylesheet that produced it is in Figure 24-9. The stylesheet figure is annotated to explain some of the code.

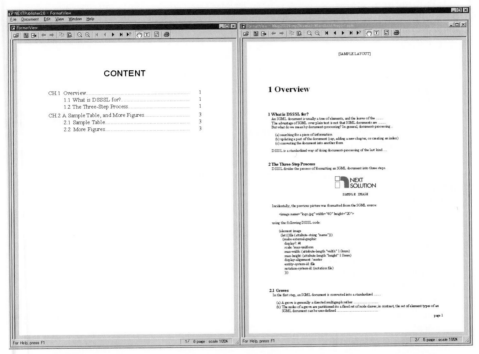

Figure 24-8   Table of contents generated from chapter and section titles

Tools are available to generate DSSSL stylesheets automatically, using a graphical user interface. For example, Figure 24-10 shows the design of the table of contents chapter entries using NEXT SOLUTION CO., LTD.'s *NEXTStylus*.

```
(mode contents_mode (default (empty-sosofo))
(element (chapter title)
 (make paragraph
   font-size: 16.0pt                                          Specify chapter style
   line-spacing: 24.0pt        ← space between lines
   quadding: 'justify          ← alignment of line
   last-line-quadding: 'justify ← alignment of last line
   start-indent: 10.0mm
   end-indent: 10.0mm
   first-line-start-indent: 0.0mm
   (make line-field        Specify the number before chapter title to be like "Ch.1", "Ch.2" ...
    (literal
     "CH."                          ↓ specify format of number ( "1"→"1,2,3"  "I"→"I, II,III" )
     (format-number-string "chapter" "1")
     " "                         ↑
    ))                          (Increment number for each chapter element)
   (process-children)  ←Obtain PCDATA [chapter title]
   (make leader  ← Create dot leader
      (literal "."))
   (current-node-page-number-sosofo) ))  ← Obtain current page number
(element (section title)
 (make paragraph
   font-size: 16.0pt
   line-spacing: 20.0pt
   quadding: 'justify
   last-line-quadding: 'justify
   start-indent: 25.0mm
   end-indent: 10.0mm
   first-line-start-indent: 0.0mm
   (make line-field                          Specify the number as "1.1", "1.2" ...
    (literal
     (format-number-string "chapter" "1")
     "."
     (format-number-string "section" "1")
     " "
    ))
   (process-children)
   (make leader
      (literal "."))
   (current-node-page-number-sosofo)
))
)
```

Figure 24-9   DSSSL stylesheet for Figure 24-8 (annotated)

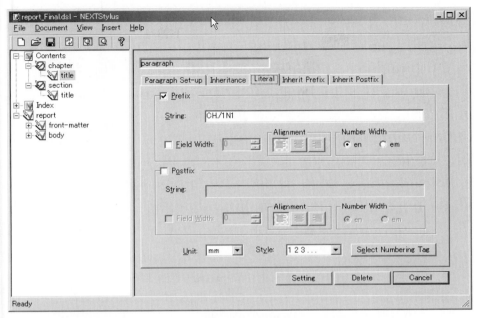

Figure 24-10   Designing a DSSSL stylesheet with a GUI tool

24.3 | Implementation of DSSSL

As DSSSL processors are automated and stylesheet-driven, they can be deployed as servers. A typical system flow is shown in Figure 24-11.

1. Clients select XML documents to be formatted and send them to the server. Each document contains the location of the DTD and stylesheet to use.
2. The server receives orders from many clients and manages them in the input queue.
3. As each XML document reaches the head of the queue it is formatted in *DSSSLprint* under control of the designated stylesheet.
4. The rendered result is created in the notation (PDF, XML or PostScript,®) specified by the client.

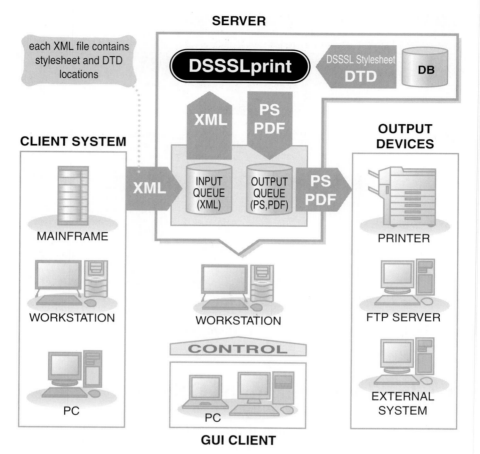

Figure 24-11   DSSSL system flow

5. Rendered documents are managed in the output queue until the user's chosen output device is available.
6. Rendered documents are sent to the designated printer for printing and/or an FTP server or external system for storage and future use.

In addition to a stand-alone processor for server use, a vendor may offer a GUI interface to facilitate human management of what still remains an automated process. For example, NEXT SOLUTION CO., LTD. offers *NEXTPublisher*, which wraps the functionality of *DSSSLprint* in a GUI.

The GUI lets you select an XML document and stylesheet and view the formatted result on the monitor. By right-clicking in the rendered text you can cause the corresponding source document to be displayed. There is also a history feature that lets you repeat the processing of previously rendered documents.

24.4 | Conclusion

DSSSL is easily the most powerful of the stylesheet standards for XML. Its layout capabilities and expression language make it capable of tasks beyond what XSL can do, particularly for the CJK languages.

Tip   You can experience the power of DSSSL with a trial version of NEXTPublisher on the CD-ROM. The examples of things that only DSSSL can do are included, so you can verify them yourself!

Desktop XML

- Microsoft Office XML capabilities
- Application integration on the desktop
- Flexible data capture with adaptive forms

Part Eight

For some 300 million users, the last word in word processing isn't "processing"... it's *Word*!

And now that ubiquitous product and its Microsoft Office suite-mates have received a massive infusion of XML – not just under the covers, but right out where solution developers and even users can see and work with it.

The impact on the XML world will be profound. Millions of desktop computers with Office Professional will become – with the help of some VBA or Visual Studio code – XML editors, rich clients for Web services, and portals for business integration.

In this part we'll tour the XML facilities of Office in the context of two application scenarios. Then we'll look at a new, totally XML-based product that breaks down the barrier between document processing and data processing.

XML in office applications

Tool Discussion

- Information capture and reuse
- End-user data connection
- Data-driven application enhancement

Sponsor: Microsoft, http://www.microsoft.com

Contributing experts: Microsoft staff and Priscilla Walmsley

Chapter

25

Attention information workers! Tired of cutting and pasting from Excel to Word? Angry that your brilliant reports can't be found outside your group? Concerned that your spreadsheet analyses may not be using the latest data? Worried about hair loss? Well, we can't help you with the last item, unless you've been tearing your hair out because of the first three! But we've got a cure for those: Add generalized, "all schemas welcome", XML to your office apps!

ML software for machine-to-machine functions is virtually standard equipment for all platforms. But until September 2003, XML on the desktop was present in a generally useful way only in specialized products. Common productivity tools like office suites supported only specific XML document types, when they supported XML at all.

Microsoft Office Professional Edition 2003 changed that situation forever, by accepting custom schemas as first-class citizens. As a result, millions of desktop computers were transformed from mere word processors into rich clients for Web services, editors for XML content management systems, and portals for XML-based application integration.

This chapter is a partial overview of the XML features of Office. (Covering it all would take a separate book.[1]) We discuss the major XML-enabled Office products – Word, Excel, Access, FrontPage, and the newly introduced InfoPath – but they are only the supporting cast.[2] The real stars are

---

1. The one we recommend is *XML in Office 2003: Information Sharing with Desktop XML* by Charles F. Goldfarb and Priscilla Walmsley, published in this series.

415

the enablers of that dramatic transformation of the desktop; that is, the advances XML brings to:

- information capture and reuse;
- end-user data connection; and
- data-driven application enhancement.

25.1 | Information capture and reuse

For all the valuable abstract data that is managed in database systems, there is even more that is hidden in rendered word processing documents. That fact represents an enormous intellectual property loss for enterprises, of course, but it also represents a nuisance and a time-waster for the information workers who work with those documents.

Consider the articles written for a company's websites and newsletters. Every one is likely to contain a title, author, and date within it, but more often than not that information has to be retyped, or individually copied and pasted, to get it into a catalog entry. That's because there is no reliable way for a computer to recognize those data items in order to extract them.

25.1.1 *Word processing*

In contrast, look at Figure 25-1, which shows an article being edited in Microsoft Word.

The article is actually an XML document that conforms to a schema of the user's choosing, in this case `article`. The user has opted to display icons that represent the start- and end-tags. Note that there are distinct elements for the `title`, `author`, and `date`.

Solution developers can use the XML elements to check and normalize information as it is entered, whether or not the tag icons are displayed. An application, for example, could notify the user if the text entered for a `date` element isn't really a valid date. Or it could automatically supply the current year if none was entered.

---

2. Visio also has XML facilities, as we saw in 4.8.4.2, "Diagramming", on page 100.

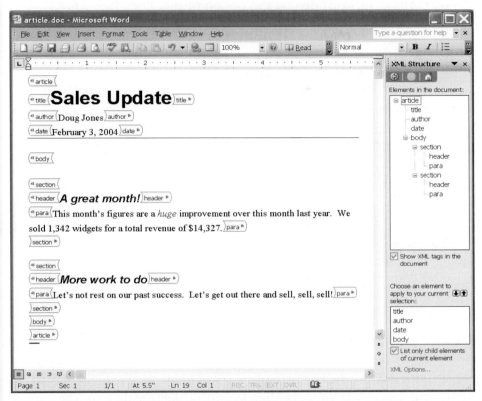

Figure 25-1 Word document showing optional tag icons and task pane with XML structure

The right-hand pane is called the *task pane*; it can be used for various purposes. In the figure, the top of the task pane shows the XML structure of the document. At the bottom is a list of the types of element that are valid at the current point in the document, according to the `article` schema.

The document is also a normal Word document, so Word's formatting features can be used in the usual way.

There are three ways to save this document as XML:

WordML

WordML is Word's native XML file format. It preserves the Word document just as the DOC format would, including formatting and hyperlinks. However, it doesn't include any of the `article`

markup, so we won't discuss this option further here. (See 4.8.1.1, "Microsoft Word", on page 94 for more on WordML.)

custom XML

The document can be saved as an XML document conforming to a custom schema; in this case, `article`. A custom schema would normally be defined by an enterprise, or by a committee set up by an industry to which the enterprise belongs. For that reason, it would be designed to preserve the abstract data needed for the user's applications. For example, the `title`, `author`, and `date` can easily be identified by software and extracted for use in a catalog of articles.

mixed XML

The saved document could contain both WordML and the `article` markup, since the two are in different namespaces. This option preserves the formatting applied by the user, while still preserving the abstract data and distinguishing it from the rendition information.

In our example, the article is the entire Word document, but that isn't a requirement. It is possible to intersperse short XML documents within a larger Word document. For example, a travel guide might include multiple XML structures that describe hotels, with subelements for the name, address, number of rooms, rates, etc.

Using XML with Word documents enables companies to capture more of the intellectual property that is created informally by individuals and work groups, and that typically remains inaccessible to enterprise information systems. As XML, that property becomes a portable asset that can be reused as needed.

25.1.2 *Forms*

For many purposes, a data entry form is more suitable for information capture than a typically larger and less constrained word processing document. InfoPath lets you design and use forms that are really XML documents that conform to your own custom schemas.[3]

Figure 25-2 shows the layout of an order form in InfoPath's design mode. The structure of the `order` schema is shown in the task pane on the right, from which element types can be dragged onto the form.

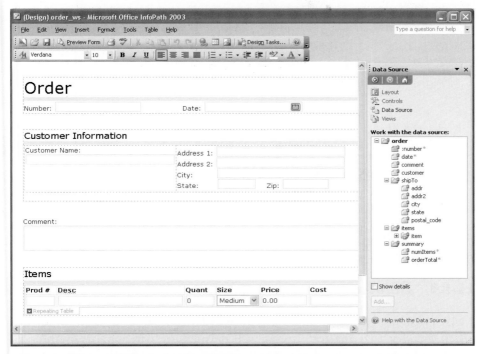

Figure 25-2   InfoPath design interface with data source in task pane

Note that there is only one `item` line in the form design. Because the `order` schema allows `item` elements to be repeated, a user entering data will be able to add `item` lines as needed. Had `customer` elements been repeatable, the form would expand to allow insertion of the group of customer information fields.

Unlike Word, InfoPath generates an XSLT stylesheet to control the rendering of the form, so there is no "InfoPathML". The formatting can even be based on the data entered in the form. For example, the dialog box in

3. InfoPath is available in the Office Professional Enterprise Edition and individually.

Figure 25-3 specifies that negative prices should be shown in a different color.

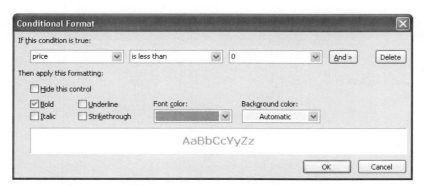

Figure 25-3   InfoPath conditional formatting dialog

InfoPath is described in detail in Chapter 26, "Flexible data capture with structured forms", on page 428.

25.1.3 *Relational data*

XML elements, whether captured in Word or Excel or InfoPath (or any other way, for that matter), are as well-defined and predictable as the columns and tables of a database. XML documents of all kinds are therefore a source of information as rich as any other operational data store. Companies can aggregate, parse, search, manage, and reuse the data in documents in the same way they do the transactional data that is typically captured for relational databases.

They can also import the document data into a database and use it in conjunction with data from other sources. In addition, they can export DBMS data as XML documents.

Figure 25-4, for example, shows the options Access offers when exporting data as XML. You can specify which tables and records to export and how to sort and/or transform them.

Figure 25-5 shows the options for exporting a schema as XML. You can choose whether or not to export the schema, and whether it should be

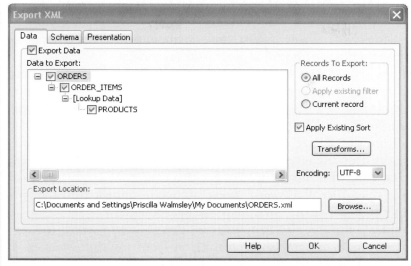

Figure 25-4   Access dialog for exporting data as XML

exported within the data document or as an independent schema document.

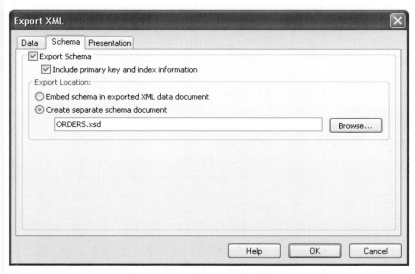

Figure 25-5   Access dialog for exporting schema as XML

25.2 | End-user data connection

Including custom XML elements in Office documents presents companies with new opportunities for business process integration.

For example, an end-user can connect directly to enterprise systems and data sources using a Web services interface. The products do the heavy lifting: natively, in the case of InfoPath, and via VBA or an external extension, in the case of Word and Excel.

The data from the Web service can be cached by the product, which can then disconnect from the server. The user still maintains the ability to work with that data, even while disconnected. For this reason, Microsoft refers to Word, InfoPath, and Excel as *smart clients*.[4] Once reconnected to the corporate server, the smart client can update the data sources.

The individual end-user also benefits from this ability to search for specific information and to aggregate information from multiple sources. It eliminates such time-consuming, error-prone tasks as:

- opening and closing files to find information;
- cutting and pasting information between documents; and
- searching for labels to combine data in like fields.

25.2.1 *Spreadsheets*

Consider how a smart client can assist in the creation and processing of expense reports.

Prior to leaving on a trip, during which she won't have access to the corporate network, Ellen opens the Excel worksheet shown in Figure 25-6. Its cells are mapped to the element types of the expenseReport schema, as shown in the task pane.

Each mapped element type corresponds to an area of the worksheet, either a single cell or a column of cells. The mapping allows XML data to be imported into, and exported from, the appropriate areas of the worksheet.

---

4. What Microsoft calls a "smart client" is essentially what the industry calls a "rich client". Perhaps Microsoft believes that if you're smart, you ought to be rich. Our readers – smart by definition – should agree!

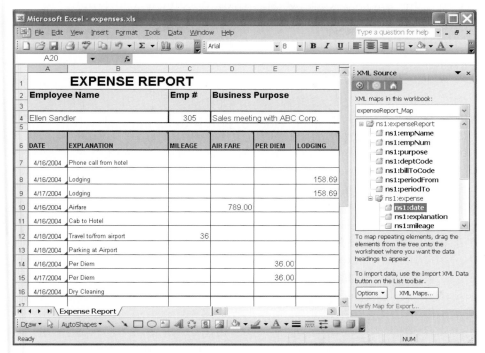

Figure 25-6   Excel worksheet and task pane with XML source map

Ellen enters her employee number and the business purpose of her trip. The other cells that are visible in the example are populated automatically from the enterprise data store.

- Her name comes from the human resources records, based on the employee number that she entered.
- The lodging and airfare amounts come from the bookings made by the travel department.
- The per diem is based on the location in the hotel booking.
- The mileage is the calculated distance between the airport and Ellen's home address, also taken from the human resources records.

Ellen adds more items to the worksheet during the trip, even without the network connection. When she returns, she completes the report and

exports the mapped cells as an XML document conforming to the
`expenseReport` schema.

25.2.2 *Web pages*

Ellen next wants to submit her report for management approval. It needs
five levels of sign-off, so she decides to post it to an internal website where
all the managers can read it.[5]

Figure 25-7 shows how FrontPage is used to design a Web page based on
an XML document. Elements can be dragged from the `expenseReport`
structure in the task pane onto the main page, and styles and other formatting options can be used to present the data.

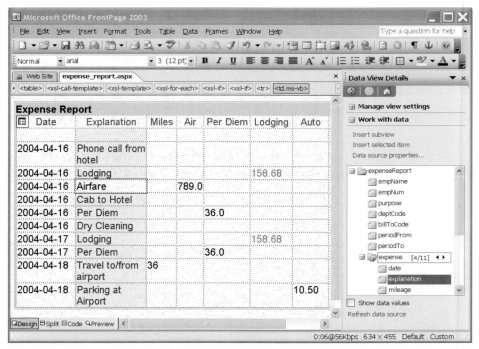

Figure 25-7   FrontPage website view with data view details in task pane

5. Yes, in most organizations five levels of management would be, ahem, over
the top!

Any XML document could be used as the data source, as could databases and Web services. Sorting, grouping, filtering, and conditional formatting of the data are supported.

FrontPage generates an XSLT stylesheet from the WYSIWYG display.

After Ellen's expense report is approved, the XML document is sent to the accounting department's system, which deposits the reimbursement in her bank account.

25.3 | Data-driven application enhancement

There are ways to enhance Ellen's experience with her expense report. Raising the per diem would undoubtedly provide the most satisfaction, but we have to stick to improvements enabled by mapping XML to the spreadsheet.

Solution developers have several ways to take advantage of the document knowledge that XML gives them: custom renditions, smart tags, and smart documents.

25.3.1 *Custom renditions*

The classic technique for data-driven application enhancement dates back to the dawn of markup languages, when GML first separated abstract data from presentation. It is to render the same data in different ways for different tasks or users.

In our scenario, for example, a report to the accounting department might contain only the summary totals from Ellen's spreadsheet, while her management gets to see every detail.

25.3.2 *Smart tags*

Office has a facility called *smart tags* that allows actions to be associated with words and phrases in a document. The "tags" don't have to be delimited, as XML tags are. Instead, they are defined by a program or by a lookup table that contains character strings (or regular expressions) and their associated actions. The product recognizes the matching strings in the document.

Usually, an icon is displayed when the cursor is over a smart tag. When the user clicks on it, the associated list of actions pops up.

It is also possible to define smart tags so that an action will take place automatically when the tag is recognized. For example, recognition of the employee number in Ellen's worksheet invoked an action to send the Web service request for her employee name, which was entered into the appropriate worksheet cell.

25.3.3 *Smart documents*

The ultimate data-driven application enhancement is to respond intelligently to user input, offering context-sensitive actions and guidance, suggesting content, and providing supporting data or links to related information.

The XML facilities we've looked at so far can be used in combination to approach that goal. Add a customized task pane and even more can be done. You have what in Office-speak is called a *smart document solution*.

For example, as a user moves the cursor to different elements in a document, the task pane could display help details, related data, tools to work with the document, or related graphics. Ellen could click in a lodging cell and see the hotel contact information displayed in the task pane. She could then click on the hotel's email address and send a quick note advising the hotel of her arrival time.

Analysis   John Donne reminded us that "no man is an island". Thanks to XML in Office, no desktop is either!

Flexible data capture with adaptive forms

Tool Discussion

■ Limitations of traditional forms

■ Flexible but rigorous form editing

■ Standards-based form processing

Sponsor: Microsoft, http://www.microsoft.com

Contributing expert: Michael Hoffman

> Want rugged off-road capability? Buy a Jeep.
> Want comfort and ease of handling? Buy a car. Want
> them both in the same package? Join the millions who
> own a hybrid SUV! And if you need the strict
> guidance and validation of a forms package, with the
> editing flexibility of a word processor – here's a hybrid
> to drive your data capture system!

Long ago, before computers – and maybe even right now at your plumber – business was transacted with printed forms: sales receipts, invoices, statements, etc. Today, even in the highest of high-tech companies, forms still record business transactions, but now they are also harvested for the data they contain. In fact, some forms exist *solely* to harvest data – as you know if you've ever registered at a website!

Why have forms survived the march of time and technology?

Perhaps because a well-designed form helps you get the data entry right. It provides a separate space for each piece of information, with the appropriate granularity (e.g. one address field, or separate fields for street, city, and state). It can constrain the length of each field (perhaps with a box for each character), or limit data values to items checked off from a printed list.

26.1 | Limitations of traditional forms

But these strengths of traditional forms – guided entry and constrained data values – can be weaknesses as well.

If a purchase order has five repeating rows for items and you want to buy six, you'll need a second purchase order – or at the very least a supplemental page.

And electronic forms are no better: Typical forms completion software lacks the flexibility to add that sixth line item on demand.

Forms created with a word processor may allow a user to add and remove content freely, but they provide little guidance for entering complete and valid information. Fields defined in the document normally have minimal validation of data values and datatypes unless supplementary scripts are developed.

Moreover, despite the illusion of formal structure that a form's layout creates, the data is free-form. "Address" is just a label, and not really a grouping of "Street", "City", and "State" fields.

Developers have addressed the need to couple flexible editing with rigorously-controlled data entry by creating custom applications. But these can be expensive to develop, difficult to modify, and may entail end-user training. Moreover, it may be difficult to reuse the gathered data for other business processes.

This last point can be fatal in a world where XML data sharing is the glue that holds commerce together. The real need is for an XML-based "flexible but rigorous" forms solution: one that supports any schema and that can be used with Web services and most applications and data repositories.

26.2 | Design challenges

To understand how such a solution differs from conventional forms packages or custom applications, we'll examine one in detail. *Microsoft® Office InfoPath™ 2003* is a hybrid tool that is intended to provide a word processing user experience while filling out forms under strict guidance. The experience is different enough from conventional forms completion that Microsoft calls it *forms editing*.

Three design challenges had to be met:

intuitive structure editing
The form being edited is a valid XML document. However, the user interface (*UI*) must allow users to edit the XML structure without dealing with XML syntax.

easily-used form views

The XML form conforms to a custom schema that normally is designed for efficient data interchange and repository loading. However, form designers must be able to organize the views presented to users for easy editing, regardless of the XML form's own organization.

standards-based product development

Data capture and sharing is the reason for the product, and sharing – whether by software interworking or data exchange – requires standards. Therefore, a design constraint was to maximize the potential for information sharing by using standards for everything: data, stylesheets, APIs, protocols – really everything![1]

26.2.1 *Intuitive structure editing*

An XML document has a tree structure in which elements are either *subtrees*, which contain other elements – possibly intermixed with data – or *leaves*, which are usually strings of data.

There is no problem with handling single leaves; they are invariably rendered as *fields* in a form – the places where the user enters and edits data. An electronic form design typically provides a *UI control* for each field: a text box for typing character strings, a calendar control for entering dates, and so on.

But subtrees are trickier. To show them in forms, *InfoPath* uses a *section* – a grouping of UI controls. Sections can also contain other sections, just as subtrees can contain other subtrees. And just as a schema allows elements to be optional and/or repeatable, sections (and individual fields) can be optional and/or repeatable as well.

In Figure 26-1, the broken line frames a `customer` section that the user has selected. At the bottom of the section, a `Click here` button allows the insertion of an optional `actions` subsection. The reason the UI control is optional is that the schema for `customer` makes `actions` an optional subelement. In Example 26-1 you can see that `actions` can occur either 0 or 1 time.

---

1. In case you missed it, we discussed APIs and protocols in Chapter 6, "Secrets of the XML programmers", on page 126.

Example 26-1. Schema excerpt for `customer`

```
<xsd:complexType name="customerType">
  <xsd:sequence>
     <xsd:element ref="customerName"/>
     <xsd:element ref="companyInfo"/>
     <xsd:element ref="items"/>
     <xsd:element ref="customerTotals"/>
     <xsd:element ref="notes"/>
     <xsd:element ref="actions" minOccurs="0" maxOccurs="1"/>
```

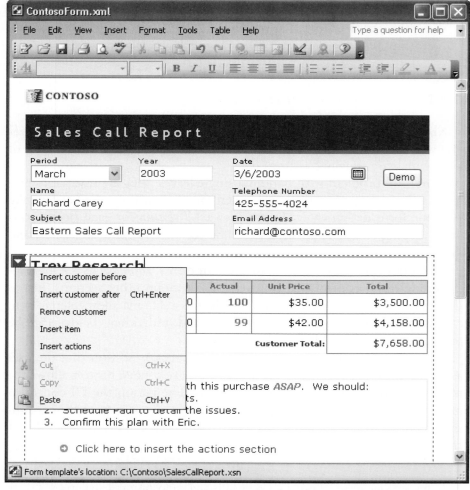

Figure 26-1   Editing interface with context menu for `customer` section

Figure 26-1 also shows the context menu for the selected section. It enables the user to insert and remove `customer` sections, indicating that the sections are *repeating sections* and that the schema makes the corresponding `customer` element type repeatable.

The menu also allows insertion of an `item` row in the table of purchased items. A *repeating table* is another way for a form to render certain repeatable subtrees. Their elements must all be leaves whose UI controls can fit on a single line. There is a context menu for the table rows as well.

The `customer` menu item `Insert  actions` is the equivalent of the `Click here` button.

Although the user interface is flexible and intuitive, editing is nevertheless guided by the schema. The schema ultimately determines whether `Insert` and `Remove` commands appear on a context menu, for example.

26.2.2 *Easily-used form views*

InfoPath exploits XML's ability to preserve abstract data separately from its rendition. That gives forms designers great flexibility in presenting views of a form to end users.

For example, Example 26-1 shows that the content of a `customer` must start with a `customerName`, which is immediately followed by `companyInfo`. However, there is no `companyInfo` shown in the form view in Figure 26-1. That data is most likely supplied automatically from a database so there is no need for the end user to see it.

XSLT also contributes to presentation flexibility. When a view is designed, the product generates a stylesheet that produces an XHTML rendition of the form. A different stylesheet is generated for each view.

The stylesheets also perform a function that may be unique to *InfoPath*. They maintain a mapping from the UI controls to the elements and data that populate them. When a user edits a field in a view, the data is actually placed in the corresponding element of the abstract XML form document.

Example 26-2 illustrates how mapping works. It is a greatly simplified excerpt from the stylesheet for Figure 26-1, showing the template rule for `customer`.[2]

The attribute `xd:xctname` is the name of a UI control, while `xd:binding` is the name of an element type to which it is mapped. This vocabulary is supplied by *InfoPath*.[3]

Example 26-2. Stylesheet excerpt for customer (simplified)

```
<xsl:template match="customer">
  <div xd:xctname="RepeatingSection">
    <span xd:xctname="PlainText" contentEditable="true"
          xd:binding="customerName">
      <xsl:value-of select="customerName"/>
    </span>
    <table>
      <tbody xd:xctname="RepeatingTable">
        <xsl:for-each select="items/item">
          ...a row for each purchased item goes here...
        </xsl:for-each>
      </tbody>
      <tbody>
        <tr>
          <td>Customer Total:</td>
          <td><span xd:xctname="PlainText" xd:disableEditing="yes"
                    xd:binding="customerTotals/total">
            <xsl:value-of select="customerTotals/total"/>
          </span></td>
        </tr>
      </tbody>
    </table>
    <span xd:xctname="RichText" contentEditable="true"
          xd:binding="notes">
      <xsl:copy-of select="notes/node()"/>
    </span>
    ...optional actions section goes here...
  </div>
</xsl:template>
```

The stylesheet shows that there is a RepeatingSection control for each customer. It begins with an editable PlainText control that is mapped to customerName.

Next is an XHTML table that begins with a RepeatingTable control for the purchased items and ends with a PlainText control for the total. That control is not editable because the value is calculated from the items.

---

2. Everything in the example was taken verbatim, and in the same order, from the actual XSLT stylesheet. However, virtually all style-oriented attributes and elements were omitted for clarity, along with other things that aren't relevant to mapping.

3. The product had the code-name *XDocs* during development, hence the xd namespace prefix.

After the XHTML table is a `RichText` control for `notes`, followed by the optional `actions` section that we discussed earlier.

As it happens, this view presents the UI controls in the same order as their mapped elements occur in the XML form, but this is not a requirement. For example, the UI control for `total` could have been presented before the line items instead of after.

26.2.3 *Standards-based product design*

The following list identifies the principal standards on which *InfoPath* relies. They are categorized by the product function for which they are most relevant, although some are used for other functions as well.

document representation
  XML, Namespaces

parsing, validation, and editing
  XML Schema, DOM, JavaScript

mapping from views to elements
  XSLT, XPath

rendition
  XHTML, CSS

Web services
  SOAP, WSDL, UDDI

The product uses and generates the same standard XML, XSLT, and XSDL files that are used by other XML-aware business processes. It employs MSXML and the Microsoft SOAP Toolkit to support these standards.

InfoPath also provides integrated support for the loosely-coupled model of Web services, in which data is sent between computers as entire XML documents. This coarse-grained, asynchronous communication model employs the document/literal SOAP style, rather than the Remote Procedure Call (RPC) style.[4]

26.3 | Form design

We can understand form design better if we first look at its end-product, the form template. Then we'll examine the actual process of designing a form.

26.3.1 *Form template*

A *form template* is the set of files that tells *InfoPath* how to process XML documents that conform to a particular schema. The files could be the sole occupants of a folder, or they could be packaged as a cabinet archive (using the extension XSN rather than the usual CAB).

Example 26-3 shows the cabinet listing for the form template of the *Sales Call Report* application we've been discussing. The files are described below.

Example 26-3. Cabinet listing of *Sales Call Report* form template

```
Cabinet salesCallReport.xsn

03-31-2003    5:17:22p A---       21,008  manifest.xsf
03-31-2003    5:12:32p A---        5,789  schema.xsd
03-31-2003    5:12:32p A---        8,532  common.xsd
03-31-2003    5:12:32p A---       46,060  SalesCall.xsl
03-31-2003    5:12:32p A---       30,740  SummaryView.xsl
03-31-2003    5:12:32p A---        5,730  agg.xsl
03-31-2003    5:12:32p A---        1,181  mso405382.gif
03-31-2003    5:12:32p A---        1,181  mso445072.gif
03-31-2003    5:15:28p A---       11,788  script.js
03-31-2003    5:12:32p A---       15,938  common.js
03-31-2003    5:12:54p A---          604  internal.js
03-31-2003    5:17:22p A---        2,101  template.xml
03-31-2003    5:12:32p A---        1,535  sampledata.xml
                     13 Files     152,187 bytes
```

`manifest.xsf`

An XML directory of the form template. It identifies the files and contains supplementary information (beyond the stylesheets) for

---

4. The industry debate over SOAP style is discussed in 6.4.4, "Slippery SOAP", on page 139.

rendering views, validating input, and supporting structural changes during editing.

`*.xsd`
> The all-important schema definition, plus a common library of schema components. The schema defines a document type named `salesReport`.

`*.xsl`
> One XSLT stylesheet for each view, plus one for special functions.

`*.gif`
> Graphics files for decorating the views.

`*.js`
> Scripts written by the designer or provided by the product.

`template.xml`
> An empty `salesReport` form.

`sampledata.xml`
> A `salesReport` form with initial placeholder data.

26.3.2 *Designing a form*

The user interface for designing a form is shown in Figure 26-2. A view of `sampledata.xml` is in the main pane on the left and `schema.xsd` is the data source in the task pane.

Let's see how to get to that point!

26.3.2.1 Start with a schema

You, as the designer, would choose `Data Source` for the task pane and take one of the following steps:

- Select an existing schema definition as the data source. It is loaded into the task pane and shown as a tree.

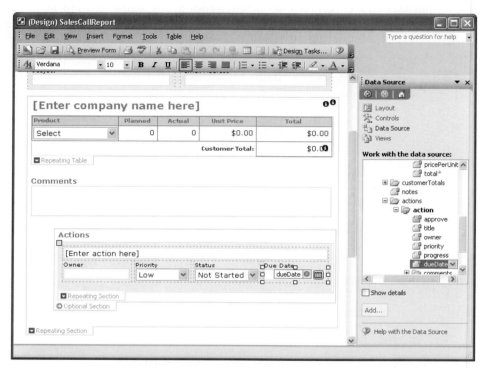

Figure 26-2   User interface for designing a form

- Alternatively, select a Web service (perhaps by using UDDI). *InfoPath* reads the service's WSDL file and identifies the XML schema to load.
- You could also load any well-formed XML document into the main pane and the product will generate a schema for it.
- You could even start out without a schema and one will be generated from the view you design (in the next step).

26.3.2.2   Design a view

With Layout in the task pane, use the design tools to select and position some UI controls, set their properties, add images, and so on. How much you do at this point depends on whether you have a schema loaded, or whether it will be generated from the design.

This step iterates with the next one, so if you have a schema, you can let the product help you with the design.

26.3.2.3   Map the element types

With Data Source back in the task pane, map element types by dragging them from the schema tree to the view design. You can either drop one on an existing control or allow *InfoPath* to propose a suitable control based on dataype (e.g., a calendar control for xsd:date).

You can go back and forth with the previous step to rearrange and beautify the controls.

26.3.2.4   Save the form template

You can either save the files in a dedicated folder or as an XSN cabinet archive, as described in 26.3.1, "Form template", on page 436. In either case, the form template is now ready for the end user to begin editing forms.

26.4 | Form editing

Figure 26-3 illustrates the flow of information during form editing. There are four steps that *InfoPath* takes, described in the following sections.

26.4.1 *Open a form and construct a DOM*

There are several ways that an end-user could choose a form to edit:

- The user could open a form that was previously saved by *InfoPath*. Such forms contain a reference to the form template, as you can see in the third line of Example 26-4.
- Alternatively, the user could create a new form. In this case, the user tells the product which form template to use.

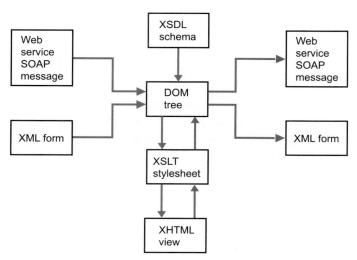

Figure 26-3   Form editing information flow

- Another choice is to select a Web service (perhaps by using UDDI). The product opens the body of the SOAP message that you receive.

The form is parsed and a DOM tree is constructed in memory. Recall from 6.3, "APIs", on page 131 that the nodes of the DOM tree structure are XML constructs of the conceptual document, such as elements and attributes. *InfoPath* communicates with the parser through the DOM API, which provides an interface for accessing and manipulating the tree.

26.4.2 *Present a view to the user*

An XSLT stylesheet with CSS style properties controls a transformation of the DOM tree, producing an XHTML rendition of the form in memory. The rendition is presented to the user as a form view (like that shown in Figure 26-1).

This step is repeated whenever the DOM is revised (in the next step).

26.4.3   *Revise the DOM*

The user edits the DOM with the UI controls presented in the form view: entering data, adding a repeating or optional element, selecting an option, entering rich text, etc. When the user selects a rich text field, for example, an XHTML editor is opened. The XHTML content created is added to the DOM as a subtree.

All edits are validated against the schema to ensure that the revised datatypes and values are valid. If not, a validation dialog box opens and the changes are not applied to the DOM tree. If the changes are valid, the DOM tree is updated.

The product determines which portion of the view is affected by the update. It then reprocesses only the part of the stylesheet that is necessary to refresh the affected area of the view.

26.4.4   *Close the form*

The revised DOM is converted to an XML document string (like that in Example 26-4). The form can be saved locally or transmitted elsewhere. For example, it could be transmitted in the body of a SOAP Web service message.

Analysis   Traditional form completion software constrained the user as much as it constrained the data. InfoPath demonstrates that open XML standards can allow flexible editing while still providing structure-directed data gathering. We think it represents a major step toward eliminating the artificial distinction between document processing and data processing.

Example 26-4. Saved *Sales Call Report* form

```xml
<?xml version="1.0" encoding="UTF-8"?>
<?mso-infoPathSolution solutionVersion="1.0.0.399"
  PIVersion="1.0.0.0" href="file:///C:\SalesCallReport.xsn"
  productVersion="11.0.4920" ?>
<?mso-application progid="InfoPath.Document"?>
<salesReport
  xmlns:my="http://schemas.contoso.com/sales/2003-02-08T17:08:27"
  xmlns:xhtml="http://www.w3.org/1999/xhtml" xml:lang="en-us">
<subject>Eastern Sales Call Report</subject><period>March</period>
<year>2003</year>
<date xmlns:xsi="http://www.w3.org/2001/XMLSchema-instance"
  >2003-03-06</date>
<salesPerson><name><prefix></prefix><givenName></givenName>
 <middleName></middleName><familyName></familyName><suffix></suffix>
    <singleName>Richard Carey</singleName></name>
  <address>empty elements omitted to fit on page</address>
  <identificationNumber></identificationNumber>
  <emailAddressPrimary>richard@contoso.com</emailAddressPrimary>
  <emailAddressSecondary></emailAddressSecondary>
  <telephoneNumberWork>425-555-4024</telephoneNumberWork>
  ...empty elements omitted to fit on page...
</salesPerson>
<customers>
  <customer><customerName>Trey Research</customerName>
    <companyInfo>empty elements omitted to fit on page</companyInfo>
    <items>
      <item><description>Pentosel</description>
        <unitsPlanned>100</unitsPlanned><unitsSold>100</unitsSold>
        <pricePerUnit>35</pricePerUnit><total>3500</total></item>
      <item><description>Ciprophen</description>
        <unitsPlanned>100</unitsPlanned><unitsSold>99</unitsSold>
        <pricePerUnit>42</pricePerUnit><total>4158</total></item>
    </items>
    <customerTotals><unitsSold>0</unitsSold><total>7658</total>
    </customerTotals>
    <notes>
<div xmlns="http://www.w3.org/1999/xhtml">Trey wants tomove ahead
with this purchase<strong><em>ASAP</em></strong>.We should:</div>
<ol style="MARGIN-TOP: 0px; MARGIN-BOTTOM: 0px" type="1"
    xmlns="http://www.w3.org/1999/xhtml">
<li>Identify and check with the primarycontacts.</li>
<li>Confirm this plan with Eric.</li></ol>
    </notes>
  </customer>
</customers>
<periodTotals><unitsSold>0</unitsSold><total>7658</total>
</periodTotals><notes></notes>
</salesReport>
```

Databases

- The XML data model
- XPath and databases
- Native XML databases
- XML in relational database management systems

Part Nine

Documents are humanity's database!

The very word "document" means "to make a record of", with no restrictions on the size or complexity of the record, whether stored on a cave wall or in a bound book. But computers, as you may have observed, aren't human. They like their records to be predictable and manageable for efficient processing, something that wasn't true of documents until markup languages came along.

So computer scientists developed their own *data models* for predictable and manageable records. In fact they developed several – *relational* and *object-oriented* being two – and they've been fighting ever since over which is best. Which hasn't stopped them from building powerful database management systems (DBMS) on which virtually every enterprise depends!

In this part we explore the impact of the XML data model on the DBMS world. We look at native XML databases, including a system based on XPath, and at the way that traditional DBMSs have adapted to XML.

XML and databases

Application Discussion

- What is a database?

- Database management system (DBMS)

- XML DBMS requirements

- Designing an XML database

- Native XML DBMS (XDBMS)

Contributing expert: Michael Kay

> Look inside XML portals and content management systems and you'll find XML databases. They may be native XML, an XML layer built on a relational platform – or something else. They vary in their query languages, indexing structures, and many other ways. In short, there's a large database of information you need to learn about them. This chapter will get you started.

I f you've been with us all the way, you've gotten a good idea of the sheer breadth of XML's MOM-to-POP usage spectrum.[1] As you go from one end of the spectrum to the other, one of the characteristics that changes is the need for permanent storage of XML documents.

27.1 | Who stores XML documents?

At the people-oriented publishing (POP) end, permanent storage is an unquestioned requirement. The management of long-lived reusable content is at the heart of these applications. As we have seen, XML content management systems are available to satisfy those requirements.

But in the machine-oriented messaging (MOM) world, XML is chiefly used as a transient medium, for sending messages from one application to

---

1. In fact, you might want to read about it again in the light of your newly-acquired knowledge. You can do so in Chapter 3, "The XML usage spectrum", on page 54.

another. The message documents might be exchanged in an infrastructure for enterprise application integration, or represent e-commerce transactions between customers and suppliers.

However, as MOM users have gained experience with XML, they have also begun to see it as a vehicle for long-term data storage. There are three main reasons:

■ The XML notation is not locked into any particular vendor, platform, or software product.

■ XML documents provide a more flexible representation than relational tables for complex business process data and its related publication-like data (invoices, spreadsheets, etc.).

■ An application might require the data to be in XML anyway. If it is received as XML or needs to be delivered in XML, it makes sense to store it as XML as well.

In fact, wherever XML is used for transient messages, there is often a need for those messages to be archived to provide a traceable record of the transactions that took place. There is then a very strong argument for storing the XML message in exactly the form it was transmitted.

27.2 | What is a database?

The term "database" has become somewhat degraded in popular usage, to mean almost any collection of data. We'll try to be more precise: a *database (DB)* is a collection of information managed as an asset for the benefit of a community of users.

You may have heard of – or participated in – the debates among fervent adherents to a particular database *data model*: relational, object-oriented, object-relational, etc., and lately, XML. But the definition applies to all of them; let's examine its two key ideas:

managed

This means there are policies in place defining what information is to be held, and for how long; defining who has access to it, and how its quality and integrity is to be maintained. And there are operational procedures in place to ensure that these policies are implemented.

community of users

Information is retained to meet the requirements of recognized user roles. Different users will have different requirements and the exact information needs will not always be known in advance. This leads to a requirement for ad-hoc query and reporting facilities, multiple views, and of course online concurrent access.

27.2.1 *Database management systems (DBMS)*

Databases don't exist in a vacuum. In order for them to be managed for a community of users, they must exist in a *database management system (DBMS)*.[2] A DBMS provides services such as caching, space management, locking, backup and restore, transactions, and logging.

All databases, regardless of their data model persuasion, benefit from these services, so it is sensible for XML DBMSs, which are relatively new, to take advantage of existing code in these areas. One approach is for a vendor to create a native XML DBMS that utilizes many of the same internal components as the vendor's longer-established relational DBMS.

Some companies have simply built an XML DBMS as a layer on top of an existing relational or object-oriented platform. Doing so gives the vendor a head start in bringing the product to market. It also benefits users by providing management services that are more likely to be robust, mature, and stable.

27.2.2 *Alternatives to a DBMS*

Documents have been around far longer than databases, so there are clearly other ways to store and retrieve them.

---

2. There is a confusing tendency to use the word "database" for both those things, although usually the context makes the meaning clear. But in this chapter, at least, we'll try to be scrupulous about minding our DBs and DBMSs.

27.2.2.1   Integral storage systems

A content management system or XML DBMS typically maintains XML documents in *dispersed storage*; that is, the documents are parsed and their data content, attribute values, and other components are stored in separate records and fields.

An alternative is *integral storage*, which normally keeps the unparsed document intact and stores it as a BLOB in a database or as a file in the operating system file store.[3]

Integral files are typically supplemented with an index database that allows searches based on metadata, such as descriptors, creation and modification dates, authorship, access rights, etc. But if the file store is unmanaged, users can access the files directly and change them. As a result, it can be difficult to maintain the integrity of the index and its consistency with the document files.

There are several products that overcome this problem. They support integral storage by providing managed access and specialized query facilities, either in OS file store or in dedicated repositories.

27.2.2.2   Full-text search systems

Another approach to XML document storage and retrieval is the full-text search system. These products focus on searching for documents based on their textual content. If you've used a Web search engine, you have some idea of how they work.

These products may offer management services. Some are even XML-aware and can take advantage of structural knowledge gained from the DTD or schema. It is in the nature of the queries they support that they differ from a mainstream DBMS.

With a relational database, you ask questions such as "How many tons of tomatoes were exported by Uruguay in 1987?". With a typical *full-text search*, however, you would ask "Find me documents that talk about exports of tomatoes from Uruguay, listed in order of likely relevance".

Chances are that some of the documents you find will talk about exports *to* Uruguay, and one of them might mention that tomatoes were thrown at

---

3. A *BLOB* is a "binary large object". XML, of course, is character-based and not binary, but BLOBs were invented for graphics and only later became a catch-all for anything that isn't relational. Now there are CLOBs as well.

the leader of the Uruguay trade delegation when he threatened to boycott the export of cotton socks (Figure 27-1).

Figure 27-1   Is this what you were searching for?

For information that is weakly structured and already rendered, which is the usual case with HTML Web pages, that may be all that is possible. But a key benefit of XML is its ability to represent as much structure and abstract semantics as the document creator wishes.

If your data is an archive of XML e-commerce transaction messages, you can do better than finding all the messages that mention cucumbers and Peru. You can ask what the total shipments of cucumbers to Peru were, in each of the last five years, broken down by country of origin. Full-text search is not designed to support that kind of query.

27.3 | XML DBMS requirements

A DBMS must offer more than the generic services we've discussed if it is to support XML. An XML DBMS has requirements that a typical relational DBMS does not. These stem primarily from differences in:

- data models,
- applications,
- update policies, and
- schema management.

27.3.1 Data models

In the relational model, data is organized into tables with rows and columns. A row is a data record, made up of data element cells, one per column of the table. All the cells in a given column have identical properties (datatype, semantics, etc.). The definition of those properties is the metadata of the table, its *schema*.

In XML, as we have seen, data can be organized in more complex and less rigid ways. An XML document's schema is its document type, expressed as a DTD or in another schema language. Unlike the relational model, however, there can be more metadata than just the schema; individual elements can have metadata, represented by attributes. There is also relationship metadata, represented by the hierarchical structure.

These differences result in unique requirements for several aspects of an XML DBMS.

27.3.1.1   Query language

The query language used to retrieve information needs to be closely aligned with the data model. So too must the indexing structures used to support efficient queries, and the query optimization strategies used to take advantage of these indexing structures.

The W3C is developing such a language, which is discussed in 59.5.2, "XML Query Language (XQuery)", on page 955. It is based on XPath 2.0, and some DBMS products have developed indexing structures and optimization algorithms to handle it.

27.3.1.2 Validation and integrity

The specification of validation processes and integrity constraints must be aligned with XSDL schema definitions and DTDs.

27.3.1.3 External relationships

XML has a well-defined data model for what happens inside a document, but there is no similar standard specifying how the documents within an XML database are related to each other. Most XML DBMSs will have some kind of concept of a document type, related to DTDs or schema definitions, and some kind of concept of a document collection or folder. However, the way in which document types and document folders are related to each other, and to URIs or unique document names, can vary from one product to another.

Many sorts of models are possible, for example:

- hyperlinking models in which documents refer to each other by URI;
- hierarchic structures, like file stores, in which documents are organized into named folders within folders; or
- structures like the WebDAV model, in which documents are not only arranged in a hierarchy, but also have external properties (metadata); the latter can be used to retrieve them, as an adjunct to content-based retrieval.

27.3.2 *Applications*

In Chapter 66, "Public XML vocabularies", on page 1090, we list over 300 XML vocabularies in 77 categories. By the time you read this there will be even more. One DBMS vendor, based on the experience of its users, has attempted to classify this overwhelming diversity of XML applications as follows:

document management applications
Storage and retrieval of business documents, such as records of safety inspections, job applications, or insurance quotations.

archival applications
Long term storage of operational information. XML is preferred because the operational data is in the form of XML messages, and the audit value is maximized if it is kept unchanged. Also, an accepted vendor-independent standard representation like XML is safest for data whose lifetime is likely to exceed that of any particular DBMS product.

complex data applications
Databases of information whose structure is too complex to store conveniently as rows and columns in a relational database. Examples are geographical information, biochemical information, engineering project plans, and medical records.

publishing applications
information intended primarily for human consumption, but organized to keep the information content separate from considerations of how it is displayed. Content management for the Web is of course part of this story, but many of the most interesting DBMSs are those concerned primarily with print publishing, and especially with information designed to be reused in different media.

27.3.3 *Update policies*

XML users require support for multiple update policies. Some examples:

- Data once in the system can never be updated or deleted; it can only be superseded by later versions.
- Users check out a document, work on it for a while, then return the revised document to the database.

- Users can append data to individual documents, such as a patient's medical history, but the previous content of the document must be immutable.

27.3.4 *Schema management*

Document schemas normally evolve with time. For example, a new employee appraisal form might be introduced that asks a different set of questions, perhaps mandated by changes in employment laws.

But whereas a typical relational DB might be restructured to conform to the new schema, it is often a requirement that existing documents should be unaffected by a schema change. They should be held in their original form, using the schema that was current at the time they were created.

Queries that span different generations of the document type can be difficult to formulate, and even more difficult to execute efficiently.

27.4 | XML DBMSs and the Internet

One way in which an XML DBMS differs from previous generations of DBMS technology is that it is typically designed for the Internet.[4]

This is more than a marketing claim. Many details of the product architecture are affected, including:

- the communications protocols by which applications talk to the DBMS server;
- the use of URIs as globally unique identifiers;
- the way that users are authenticated and authorized;
- the way that user sessions are managed and time-outs are handled;
- the design of user interfaces that reduce expensive and time-consuming interactions between client and server; and

---

4. XML DBMS adherents say that hierarchic and network DBMSs were designed for the mainframe, relational DBMSs were designed for client-server, object DBMSs for distributed computing, and XML DBMSs for the Internet. Of course, they are careful to whom they say it!

■ the support of open standards at every level of the system, because universal interworking is the goal of the Internet.

In fact, the requirements of running an Internet-based round-the-clock electronic commerce service have more in common with mainframe applications, such as airline reservation systems, than with the typical departmental applications of the client-server era. XML DBMS products are even offered for IBM mainframe operating systems!

27.5 | Designing an XML database

XML database design follows the traditional three-stage design process: conceptual modeling, logical design, and physical design.

27.5.1 *Conceptual modeling*

Conceptual modeling consists of analyzing the objects, properties and relationships that exist in the domain of interest.

Techniques such as the *Unified Modeling Language (UML)* are used. Just as with non-XML databases, you can start either by studying the way things are now – for example, the paper documents that are in use – or by creating a model of the way you want things to be in the future.

Perhaps because of the difference in applications, the models used for XML DBs are more closely related to business processes. Many of the objects that appear in the object model relate to dynamic entities, such as purchases or promotions or orders, rather than the traditional permanent entities, such as products and customers and employees.

27.5.2 *Logical design*

Logical design is the task of translating the conceptual model into the terms of the data model.

For XML, that means a DTD or schema, and designing one is still a craft. There aren't any standard recipes, like the use of normalization in the relational database world.

Newcomers are sometimes bewildered by the amount of choice available. Should I use elements or attributes? Should I represent relationships by nesting, or by ID/IDREF links, or by URI hyperlinks? The right answer usually comes naturally with experience.

The golden rule is to take advantage of the flexibility that XML gives you: don't try to structure the data in rows and columns because that's the only way you've been able to do it in the past. One good approach is to imagine the information on paper as a form or report, and then work back from the structure of the paper document to the abstract structure of the XML document.

Which raises a key question for logical design: what *is* a document?

The answer may be obvious for POP applications, or when dealing with data for which there is an associated form of manageable size (invoices, incident reports, etc.). But if your information is a rail timetable, the "right" level for a document is somewhere between the national timetable and the timetable for a single train.

The choice of what to represent as a single document is important. It will have a significant bearing on the usability of the database, as well as its performance characteristics.

27.5.3 *Physical design*

Physical design consists of deciding what data will be held where, how it will be organized, and what indexes are needed.

For an XML database, as with any other database, the task demands intimate knowledge of the implementation details of a specific product. Key factors are:

- the allocation and partitioning of space to hold different classes of document,
- the choice of storage and indexing options, and
- the design of a database loading strategy.

Database loading involves setting up the indexes and access structures to support efficient queries. For a database of several gigabytes, it can require a lot of time and storage space.

The indexing structures provided by an XML DBMS are highly specialized. and new structures are still being invented. Their techniques are often closely-guarded secrets – either because they are very clever, or because the vendor would like you to think they are. Here are some examples:

structure index

It records the elements that are present in the document, and their nesting, but not the data content. When a query references a particular element type, a structure index quickly eliminates from the search all documents that don't use this element type, or that don't use it in the right context.

value index

It indexes the values – that is, the data – of selected elements or attribute values in much the same way as a conventional index in a relational database. This is useful for queries that require a specific value to be present; for example, finding all the transactions processed on a particular date.

word-level index

It indexes individual words or phrases in the document data content, in the manner of a full-text search product. This is useful for queries that look for documents that mention particular words. This sort of indexing is typically the most expensive.

As always, the more indexes you choose to build, the faster your queries will run, but the longer it will take to load new documents or update existing documents, and the more space will be taken up on disk. Space on disk, of course, is cheap: but the bigger the database, the less of it will fit in cache, and the longer it will take to do operations such as backup.

27.6 | Native XML DBMS (XDBMS)

Some XML DBMS products are promoted as *native XML databases*. The term is used to distinguish a DBMS that uses XML as its data model, meaning that its primary storage structures and indexing techniques are designed specifically to support XML.

In contrast, a relational DBMS (RDBMS) might store an XML document as a BLOB, while a *universal DBMS* would provide XML storage, indexing and query as one of several plug-in modules for various data representations.

Native XML DBMS vendors argue that, because it is designed to do one job well, a native XML DBMS (XDBMS) is inherently superior to a DBMS that was designed for a different job and subsequently adapted to support XML.

Other DBMS vendors argue back![5]

27.7 | Conclusion

XML DBMSs are still in their infancy, and the understanding of their requirements is still evolving. But XML is, after all, SGML, and SGML DBMSs have been in use for many years. They provide experience on the performance trade-offs between fast document loading, fast retrieval, and economical use of space.

Object-oriented DBMSs are another source of knowledge in relevant areas, such as management of long transactions, version control, and efficient storage of fine-grained complex data structures. All this knowledge is finding its way into new generations of XML DBMS products.

---

5. As we'll see in subsequent chapters.

XPath-based XML DBMS

Tool Discussion

- Dispersed storage vs. integral storage

- Component-level access vs. document-level

- Variable information views

- Access and other controls

Contributing expert: Chris Brandin

> Most information is complex; it rarely comes in neat arrays. We try to make it look regular because it's so easy to address a cell in a relational table – a row number and a column number and you're there. Easy addressing makes for efficient processing, which is why we spend so much time and money fitting round information pegs into those square holes. But there is another path to finding information in databases, one that can free data from its cells!

I n some sense there is a fundamental conflict between XML and databases. XML derives a lot of its power from its *flexibility*: elements are easily added and deleted, even for valid documents. Schemas and other metadata are easily changed.

Databases, though, derive their power from their *predictability*: their rigid predefined structures and indexes make it easy to address data and optimize performance.

For a native XML DBMS (XDBMS), XPath offers the possibility of getting the best of both worlds: flexible data and metadata, plus efficient addressing. However, you need to make the right decisions regarding document storage and access.

28.1 | Document storage and access

The storage and access issues for XML are not as simplistic as a choice between "document-centric" and "data-centric". In fact, as we'll see shortly, those terms are ambiguous. There can be a big difference between how a document is stored and how it is accessed. Let's look at what is really going on.

28.1.1 *Storage approaches*

Unlike relational data, which exists as such only within a relational DBMS (RDBMS), XML data exists independently in the form of documents. Content management systems and DBMSs use a variety of techniques for storing XML documents, but they boil down to combinations and variations of just two approaches: dispersed and integral.

Dispersed storage
> *Dispersed storage* typically involves parsing the document and storing the parsed data content, attribute values, and other components in multiple fields of a database. Both relational and object DBMSs have been used successfully for this purpose, as well as hybrid object-relational. Indexes and maps are used to maintain the relationship between the element structure of the document and the underlying database schema. A variation of this approach stores the components as unparsed text.

Integral storage
> *Integral storage* effectively keeps the unparsed document intact and stores it in a single field of a database or as a file in a file system. The document is parsed, however, in order to build indexes that facilitate searching the document base and locating individual components within their documents.

Proponents of integral storage claim that dispersed storage does not scale well. They say that adding documents makes the database structure grow in complexity – not just in size – which slows performance.

28.1.2 *Access and retrieval*

In any document management system, documents can be addressed, and therefore retrieved, by properties of the document as a whole. Such properties typically include a unique document identifier (e.g. a catalog number or ISBN) or a location (e.g. a file identifier or URL).

In a component-based CMS, as we have seen, addressing and access are possible at the level of individual elements or other components.

However, even when documents are stored and accessed as whole objects, addressing the document need not be based solely on properties of the whole document. Most systems allow searches on the text of a document, for example. Plain text and word processing documents can be searched in this way (although spurious hits can occur if the system doesn't understand – and exclude – the word processing markup).

When a document is represented in XML, an XML-aware system can support addressing of properties of the whole document or any part of it. The XPath specification provides a standardized notation for expressing those properties. It is very powerful, as we shall see, as it is the basis for *XSL Transformations*, extended linking, and other sophisticated accessing of XML documents.

28.1.3 *Words to watch out for: document-centric and data-centric*

XML products and applications are sometimes characterized as *component-centric* or *data-centric*, in contrast to *document-centric*. Several possible meanings could be intended:

- distributed storage in contrast to integral storage,
- component-level access as opposed to whole-document access, or
- both of the above.[1]

We avoid these terms in this book because it is so important to distinguish clearly between storage and granularity of access. A system that uses integral storage can still offer component-level access, just as a distributed storage system can provide access to complete documents.

---

1. Data-centric vs. document-centric is also used in a totally different context: data that fits the relational model easily vs. everything else. This usage is particularly confusing because all XML documents contain data; see 7.11.2, "Data-centric vs. document-centric", on page 152.

In fact, there is a novel form of integral storage DBMS that provides full access to components with no need to create a physical schema. It is based on XPath, so before we look at it, you may want a quick introduction to XPath, which you can find in Chapter 58, "XPath Primer", on page 916.

28.2 | XPath and databases

XPath's ability to address an XML document at any level of granularity has interesting implications for a DBMS. It allows capabilities that have been difficult or impossible for a conventional relational DBMS.

To illustrate, let's look at examples of using an XPath-based DBMS for the basic DBMS processes: storing, retrieving, and controlling information.

28.2.1 *Storing information*

The first step in using a DBMS, of course, is getting information into it. Traditionally, this has been a big deal. With an RDBMS, for example, a logical schema of data elements must be established that organizes them into rows and columns. Search criteria and indexing parameters have to be designed as well. Only after all this has been completed can data be posted.

It is possible to create an XPath-based DBMS in which none of this is necessary: you simply start posting XML documents. There is no need to post schema definitions or DTDs (although it is always desirable to check validity before posting a document).

The benefit of having to do, well... nothing... to be able to start storing information is obvious; but it begs an interesting question: If you have not defined any structure or indexing parameters, how will you know how to access any of the information?

That is where XPath comes into play.

An XPath-based XDBMS locates information by matching patterns in queries – XPath expressions – with the structural patterns of the stored documents.[2]

---

2. At least one patent exists for a technique to convert patterns to numbers, with the result that comparisons require the same amount of time regardless of the length of the pattern or the size of the database.

This approach is equivalent to always indexing everything, so no decision about what to index has to be made. This means you can decide how to access information when you use it, instead of when you store it.

28.2.2   *Retrieving information*

Information represented in XML is organized into documents. Each document is presumably a convenient set of information for some purpose.

However, a complete document is rarely the right level of granularity for all purposes. For some tasks, a user may want a single fragment of information – a component of the document – or fragments of information from multiple documents.

XML lends itself well to these requirements because of its recursive element structure. Conceptually, a document is just an element that contains all the other elements and their data. Any element can be extracted from a document and made a document in its own right. The top-level element is called the "document element"; the subelements, data, and attributes are its components.

Some CMSs and DBMSs require you to define the accessible components when establishing a database. In an XPath-based XDBMS, however, you can make that decision dynamically, whenever you search for information.

To demonstrate this point, we will look at three different searches of the same database. The searches return:

- All documents of a type
- A single selected document
- Components from multiple documents

The database is treated as a single large document whose document type is ND. The documents stored in the database are actually its children, but we'll speak of them as documents nevertheless.

Now for the three searches!

28.2.2.1   Dumping the database

Let's say that there are 100GB of documents in the database and among them are a number of music CD catalog listings. To dump the contents of the music CD listings we enter the XPath expression seen in Example 28-1.

Example 28-1. Retrieving all documents of a type

```
/ND/CD
```

Note that the first element type name in the expression is that of the database document, ND. Although we *talk* about CD as "the document", we have to be quite precise with XPath.

The results are shown in Example 28-2. The CD documents in the result set are returned as components of a single Query-Results document.[3]

Example 28-2. Results of Example 28-1

```
<Query-Results>
<CD>
  <TITLE>Empire Burlesque</TITLE>
  <ARTIST>Bob Dylan</ARTIST>
  <COUNTRY>USA</COUNTRY>
  <COMPANY>Columbia</COMPANY>
  <PRICE>10.90</PRICE>
  <YEAR>1985</YEAR>
</CD>
<CD>
  <TITLE>Hide your heart</TITLE>
  <ARTIST>Bonnie Tylor</ARTIST>
  <COUNTRY>UK</COUNTRY>
  <COMPANY>CBS Records</COMPANY>
  <PRICE>9.90</PRICE>
  <YEAR>1988</YEAR>
</CD>
<CD>
  <TITLE>Dolly's Greatest Hits</TITLE>
      . . .
</Query-Results>
```

---

3. If you are getting the idea that everything in this native XML DBMS is a document, you are correct. The same is true for other data models: a relational result set, for example, is usually returned as a table.

28.2.2.2   Finding a CD by its title

Example 28-1 is an example of a single query that returns several complete documents. To return a single document based on a unique selection parameter, the XPath expression seen in Example 28-3 is used.

Example 28-3. Selecting a single document

```
/ND/CD[TITLE="Dolly's Greatest Hits"]
```

The predicate addresses only CD elements with a TITLE subelement whose value is "Dolly's Greatest Hits".[4]

The results are shown in Example 28-4. As you would expect, there is only one CD returned.

Example 28-4. Results of Example 28-3

```
<Query-Results>
<CD>
  <TITLE>Dolly's Greatest Hits</TITLE>
  <ARTIST>Dolly Parton</ARTIST>
  <COUNTRY>USA</COUNTRY>
  <COMPANY>RCA</COMPANY>
  <PRICE>9.90</PRICE>
  <YEAR>1982</YEAR>
</CD>
</Query-Results>
```

28.2.2.3   Selecting some of the artists

Now for something completely different: a query whose result is neither defined nor constrained by documents, and which uses a complex predicate to boot.

The XPath statement shown in Example 28-5 requests the artist name for any CD whose title contains "night only" and costs $9.90, or was produced in the UK in 1990 and costs $10.20.

The results are shown in Example 28-6.

---

4. In an RDBMS, TITLE might be defined as a "key" and an index of titles created to optimize searches. In this XDBMS, that isn't necessary.

Example 28-5. Retrieving fragments from multiple documents

```
/ND/CD[(TITLE=*"night only"* AND PRICE="9.90")
      OR (COUNTRY="UK" AND YEAR="1990" AND PRICE="10.20")]/ARTIST
```

Example 28-6. Results of Example 28-5

```
<Query-Results>
  <ARTIST>Bee Gees</ARTIST>
  <ARTIST>Gary More</ARTIST>
</Query-Results>
```

In conventional database terms we've accessed the same XML information according to two different views. The first two queries produced coarse-grained document-level results; the third produced fine-grained component-level results.

But because of the native XML database organization, there really aren't two different views. Neither CD nor AUTHOR is really a document; they are both components of ND. There is really only a single XML view, capable of emulating an unlimited number of conventional database views. You could think of this as a *variable view* capability.

28.2.3 *Modifying information*

For the next two examples we will use contact lists, as seen in Example 28-7, to illustrate two things: modifying part of a document, and adding elements to selected documents.

28.2.3.1 Changing an address

To change a document, we need to access it, just as if we were searching. However, we need to provide the system with more than the XPath expression; we must supply the replacement information as well. An application program, built on the XDBMS, would normally provide an interface for entering both these things.

Example 28-8 shows the XPath expression. It locates the Address of the Contact with the last name "Aardvark".

The revised Address is shown in Example 28-9.

Example 28-7. A contact list

```
<ContactList>
  <Contact>
    <Name>
      <Last>Aardvark</Last>
      <First>Jerry</First>
    </Name>
    <Address>
      <Number>818</Number>
      <Street>Main Street</Street>
      <City>Colorado Springs</City>
      <State>CO</State>
      <ZIPcode>80907</ZIPcode>
    </Address>
    <PhoneNumber>
      <AreaCode>719</AreaCode>
      <Number>555-3403</Number>
    </PhoneNumber>
  </Contact>
  ...
</ContactList>
```

Example 28-8. Locating Mr. Aardvark's Address

```
/ND/ContactList/Contact[Name/Last="Aardvark"]/Address
```

Example 28-9. Mr. Aardvark's new Address

```
<Address>
  <Number>2024</Number>
  <Street>West Street</Street>
  <City>Green Bay</City>
  <State>WI</State>
  <ZIPcode>54304</ZIPcode>
</Address>
```

This common type of operation demonstrates a benefit of component-level access. It avoids the need to download and re-post the entire ContactList just to change one address.

28.2.3.2 Adding some ZIP+4 codes

Let's say that some of our contacts are in an area where we can speed up postal delivery by heeding the US Postal Service's admonition to add a

4-digit extension to the ZIP postal code.[5] In XML terms, we want to insert a new `ZIPExtension` element after specific `ZIPcode` elements.

The XPath expression is in Example 28-10. It locates all 80907 ZIP codes.

Example 28-10. Locating ZIP codes to which extensions will be added

```
/ND/ContactList/Contact/Address/ZIPcode[.="80907"]
```

The `ZIPExtension` element we are adding is shown in Example 28-11. It follows the `ZIPcode` element within the parent `Address` element.

Example 28-11. Adding an empty `ZIPExtension`

```
<ZIPExtension></ZIPExtension>
```

The new element is empty because we have added it to many `Address` elements. Over time, as those addresses are revised, ZIP+4 data will be inserted into the content of the `ZIPExtension` elements.

This kind of operation illustrates the flexibility of the XML data model. The validity of the documents can be preserved by a simple change to the DTD: adding an optional `ZIPExtension` element type to the content model of `Address`.

In contrast, the relational model would require adding a new column, which would cause the new data field to be added to all addresses, not just those with a `ZIPcode` of 80907. For a typical RDBMS, that would require reorganizing the database.

28.2.4 *Controlling information*

XPath can be used for controlling information as well as accessing and modifying it. By "controlling" we refer to functions such as access control, asynchronous triggers, and referential integrity checks. To show how this works we will use an access control example.

---

5. Not to be confused with the ZIP archival file format!

Look again at the CD catalog listing in Example 28-4. Suppose we want certain users to see only CDs from the United States, but not see the prices of RCA CDs.

In other words, for these users – let's call them the "US-only" group – we want the results from the query in Example 28-3 to look like Example 28-12.

Example 28-12. Access-controlled results of Example 28-3

```
<Query-Results>
<CD>
  <TITLE>Dolly's Greatest Hits</TITLE>
  <ARTIST>Dolly Parton</ARTIST>
  <COUNTRY>USA</COUNTRY>
  <COMPANY>RCA</COMPANY>
  <YEAR>1982</YEAR>
</CD>
</Query-Results>
```

We accomplish the access control by means of the document shown in Example 28-13. It filters all queries made by any user who is a member of the "US-only" group.

Example 28-13. Access control document for "US-only" users

```
<AC user="US-only" type="All">
  <CD>
    <show>COUNTRY="USA"</show>
    <PRICE>
      <hide>/ND/CD[COMPANY="RCA"]</hide>
    </PRICE>
  </CD>
</AC>
```

The AC, show, and hide elements are the control information; the other elements are from the documents being controlled. The show and hide elements determine whether the content of the elements in which they occur will be shown or hidden. They each contain an XPath expression that, if true, will cause the showing or hiding to occur.

This approach makes it possible to implement very flexible access control rules. In Example 28-13 we hid a fragment of information based on the contents of a different field, according to rules assigned to an arbitrary group of users. Write, modify, and delete permissions can be handled similarly.

Control documents can be set up for processes as well as for human users. In this way, if you've added data elements to support new applications, you can hide the new elements from legacy programs that don't expect them.

Control functions are implemented with the same pattern-matching technology as searches. When a document is accessed that satisfies XPath expressions in the user's control document, a behavior is invoked that causes the control module to do something. In our example, the behavior caused the search results to be filtered.

Storing XML in a relational DBMS

Tool Discussion

- Choosing a DBMS
- RDBMS requirements for XML
- Storing XML hierarchies in tables
- Storing XML documents as CLOBs

Contributing experts: Martin Herbach and Paul Brown

Chapter

29

Some say that using XML as a data model "ignores the years of investment in relational database technology". Others say that Galileo heard the same argument applied to Copernican mapmaking technology! But if your world revolves around MOM applications more than POP, you'll want to see how XML documents can be handled by a non-XML DBMS.

ML documents are currently stored in DBMSs with both XML and non-XML data models, so choosing between them is not a cut-and-dried decision.

29.1 | Choosing a DBMS

Like many high-tech issues, choosing a DBMS depends on a mix of technical, practical, and quasi-theological criteria, such as:

- Do you use XML primarily for messages in business transactions, or for publications intended for human consumption?
- Are your documents stable, or in a constant state of revision?
- How large are they? Do you work with pieces or with the whole thing at once?
- How many documents are there? How many users?
- What are your passionate beliefs about the "rightness" of keeping XML documents in their official standardized representation?

- What are your passionate beliefs about the value of keeping XML documents together with all your other information in a managed, centralized data store?
- How much does your management care about your passionate beliefs?
- Do you need to ask combined XML/SQL queries, like: "show me all XML documents that have passed through the system this month for my five largest customers?"
- Do the products you are evaluating work well with your existing systems? Do they work at all?
- Can your staff cope with the complexity of the proposed solution? How will their passionate beliefs affect their efficiency?
- What is the cost of the solution?

In previous chapters we've looked at native XML databases. But since XML is widely used to interchange data to and from relational and object-relational databases, we'll now look at the way a relational DBMS handles XML.

29.2 | RDBMS requirements for XML

In earlier parts of this book we examined at length the role of XML in business integration and e-commerce. A key aspect is XML's use as an interchange representation, as shown in Figure 29-1.

The need for a DBMS to receive and send XML is obvious; that is the essence of using XML as an interchange representation. However, the reasons for storing the XML messages are worth reviewing:

- XML documents that convey information about orders and other business transactions become legal documents that must be retained as a "statement of record," meaning that the original source document may need to be examined at some future date.
- There may be elements of the XML exchange messages for which no corresponding place exists in the enterprise data schema.

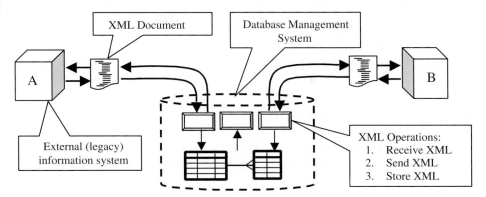

Figure 29-1   XML in machine-oriented messaging (MOM) applications

- Early adopters of XML-based integration may be using non-standardized messages without DTDs or mappings to relational schemas.
- Storing XML messages allows them to be included with operational data in the search domain for SQL queries.
- A single store for XML documents and operational data permits uniform administration and recovery.

RDBMS vendors are addressing these requirements with products having the following capabilities:

acting as receiver
Translating data from XML documents into relational tables.

acting as sender
Translating data from relational formats into appropriate XML message documents.

storing and manipulating XML documents
Preserving XML data in close to native form, at least on a temporary basis, while allowing it to be combined with relational data sources.

In the remainder of this chapter we'll look at two strategies for storing XML: storing XML hierarchies in tables and storing XML as a CLOB.

29.3 | Storing XML hierarchies in tables

Before we discuss XML specifically, lets look at the general techniques for modeling hierarchies in a relational database.

29.3.1 *Trees in general*

The hierarchy, or tree, is a common pattern in computer programming. We've seen many examples so far in this book. Mathematically, it is a special type of graph.

29.3.1.1   A little graph theory

A *graph* is formally defined as a set of nodes, a set of edges, and a set of relationships between nodes along edges.

Additional rules can be superimposed on this basic definition that restrict the construction of the graph. Impose enough rules, and you arrive at the kind of graph we call a hierarchy.

Why bother with the formalism? Well, it turns out that graph theory is a very well studied field. Over the years, techniques have been developed for working with graphs and they have found their way into commercial products. For example, Informix's approach to modeling hierarchies borrows from this body of knowledge.

29.3.1.2   The Node datatype

Extensible databases allow developers to augment their data models by introducing new datatypes into the SQL query language. We can model hierarchies by introducing a datatype whose value represents the position of a node within a hierarchy, and a set of methods for computing common hierarchical operations on that datatype.

These would include queries like:

- Is A under B in the hierarchy?
- Is C a sibling of D?

29.3.2 *Modeling a DTD*

A graph that models a tree is sometimes called a *holarchy*. An XML DTD can be represented by a holarchy. Example 29-1 shows the DTD for a business card.

Example 29-1. Business card DTD

```
<!ELEMENT business_card (name, title, address, contact)>
<!ELEMENT     name          (surname, given, other?)>
<!ELEMENT        surname    #PCDATA>
<!ELEMENT        given      #PCDATA>
<!ELEMENT        other      #PCDATA>

<!ELEMENT     title         #PCDATA>

<!ELEMENT     address       (street, city, state, zip)>
<!ELEMENT        street     #PCDATA>
<!ELEMENT        city       #PCDATA>
<!ELEMENT        state      #PCDATA>
<!ELEMENT        zip        #PCDATA>

<!ELEMENT     contact       (phone*)>
<!ELEMENT        phone      #PCDATA>
```

29.3.2.1   Creating a holarchy

Figure 29-2 shows the holarchy for the business card DTD.

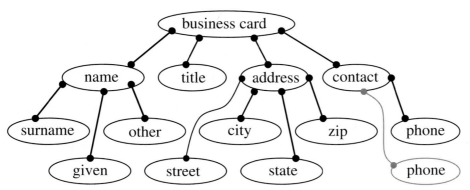

Figure 29-2   DTD in Example 29-1 depicted as a holarchy

Each node of the holarchy can be labeled with its position relative to the other nodes in the same holarchy. By implementing a new datatype to model these holarchy labels, it becomes possible to represent DTDs using relational constructs and to "shred" an XML document into a tabular form that is more amenable to queries.

We'll call this "node position" datatype Node.[1] It consists of a sequence of integers. When displaying a Node value it is customary to separate the integers with periods.

For example, the holarchy for the business card DTD introduced in Table 29-1 would be enumerated as in Figure 29-3.

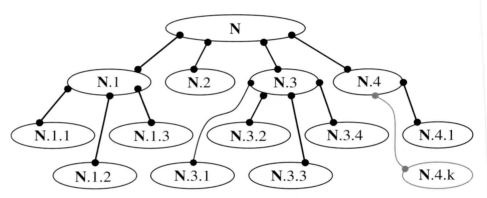

Figure 29-3   Figure 29-2 enumerated with Node values

The document type is the root of the holarchy, designated "N". (It will become an integer momentarily!) The position of each node within the holarchy is represented by the sequence of integers following the root.

29.3.2.2   Generating a relational table

Using an enumerated holarchy, a DTD can automatically be transformed into a relational table. The table for the business_card DTD is shown in Example 29-1. Of course, in practice a system would have multiple DTDs,

---

1. It has other uses besides DTDs. Holarchies are useful in any application with hierarchies, such as manufacturing management or chains of command.

so the "N" would be replaced by an integer that uniquely identifies the DTD.

Table 29-1   Relational table for DTD in Example 29-1

Node Id	Element Type	Datatype	Cardinality
N	business_card	Root Node	1
N.1	name	Structural Element	1
N.2	title	#PCDATA	1
N.3	address	Structural Element	1
N.4	contact	Structural Element	1..k
N.1.1	surname	#PCDATA	1
N.1.2	given_name	#PCDATA	1
N.1.3	other	#PCDATA	0..1
N.3.1	street	#PCDATA	1
N.3.2	city	#PCDATA	1
N.3.3	state	#PCDATA	1
N.3.4	zip	#PCDATA	1
N.4.1	phone	#PCDATA	1

29.3.3 *Modeling a document instance*

Example 29-2 is an excerpt from an XML document received from an Internet employment service. It is a list of candidates looking for work, in the form of business_card elements.

   After the document is parsed with a standard XML parser, it can be transformed into the relational table shown in Table 29-2.

Example 29-2. Two business_card elements

```
...
<business_card>
  <name>
    <surname>Brown</surname>
    <given>Paul</given>
    <other>G</other>
  </name>
  <title>Chief Plumber</title>
  <address>
    <street>20th Floor, 300 Lakeside</street>
    <city>OAKLAND</city>
    <state>CA</state><zip>94612</zip>
  </address>
  <contact>
    <phone>510 628 3999</phone>
  </contact>
</business_card>
<business_card>
  <name>
    <surname>Immanuel</surname>
    <given>Kant</given>
  </name>
  <title>Chief Philosopher</title>
  <address>
    <street>Ground Floor, 20 Leibenstrasse</street>
    <city>Konigsberg</city>
    <state>PRUSSIA</state><zip>12-A</zip>
  </address>
  <contact>
    <phone>4 343 2854 34</phone>
    <phone>4 343 2385 33</phone>
  </contact>
</business_card>
...
```

Table 29-2 shows how the Node type can be used to "shred" and store an XML document so that it can be retrieved and updated efficiently using SQL. Restoring the document to its original form is also straightforward. To understand why, we need to examine the Node values in more detail.

29.3.3.1   Understanding Node values

You can tell a lot about the relationships among nodes by examining their Node position values. For example:

Table 29-2   Relational table for document in Example 29-2

Doc_Node	DTD_Node	Value
. . .	. . .	. . .
M.K.1.1	N.1.1	Brown
M.K.1.2	N.1.2	Paul
M.K.1.3	N.1.3	G
M.K.2	N.2	Chief Plumber
M.K.3.1	N.3.1	20th Floor...
M.K.3.2	N.3.2	OAKLAND
M.K.3.3	N.3.3	CA
M.K.3.4	N.3.4	94612
M.K.4.1	N.4.1	510 628 3999
M.(K+1).4.1	N.1.1	Immanuel
M.(K+1).1.2	N.1.2	Kant
M.(K+1).2	N.2	Chief Philosopher
M.(K+1).3.1	N.3.1	Ground Floor...
M.(K+1).3.2	N.3.2	Königsberg
M.(K+1).3.3	N.3.3	PRUSSIA
M.(K+1).3.4	N.3.4	12-A
M.(K+1).4.1	N.4.1	4 343 2854 34
M.(K+1).4.2	N.4.2	4 343 2385 33
. . .	. . .	. . .

- If the first integer of two Node values is the same, but the remaining integers are different, the nodes occupy different positions in the same holarchy. For example, the values "70123.1.4" and "70123.1.5" tell us that both nodes come from the XML document or DTD numbered "70123".
- You can also tell that those two nodes are siblings; they share the parent that has Node position "70123.1.4".
- A third node, with Node value "70123.1.4.1", is underneath "70123.1.4"; correspondingly, the node at "70123.1.4" is above "70123.1.4.1".

29.3.3.2   Creating a B-tree index

Comparing Node positions is important in queries that, for example, find the number of distinct cities in the entire document, or the phone number of a person identified by his or her surname. A database designer would typically want to create a B-tree index of the Node column to optimize such queries.[2]

DBMSs differ in their approach to indexing user-defined datatypes. Many require the developer of a new type to create a user-defined function that converts an instance of the type into one of the SQL built-in types. However, it is unclear how that could work for the Node type.

A workable approach to indexing support is to embed a compare method that the B-Tree and data sorting algorithms use. The method supports >, <, and = operators, as shown in Example 29-3.

Note the last two lines of the example. They restrict the query to rows underneath the root node identified as "103". Because the DBMS was able to create a B-Tree index of the Node type, it can perform this "hierarchical" operation as it would a normal table operation.

---

2. A *B-tree index* is an index that has been optimized using the B-tree algorithm, which favors rapid search in preference to quick revision.

Example 29-3. SQL Query using Node **type**

```
REM     How many people listed in XML Document #103
REM     are from "Oakland"?

SELECT COUNT (DISTINCT Root_Value (T.Doc_Node))
  FROM Shred_XML_Table T, XML_DTD_Table D1
 WHERE T.DTD_Node       = D.Node Id
   AND D.Element_Type   = "city"
   AND T.Value          = "OAKLAND"
   AND (
          T.Doc_Node > "103"
   AND    T.Doc_Node < Node_Incr("103")
       )
;
```

29.4 | Storing XML documents as CLOBs

Perhaps the most common approach to managing XML in a relational or object-relational DBMS involves storing entire XML documents as binary or character large objects (BLOBs or CLOBs). Text indexing techniques are employed to speed up access to the document's contents. SQL can then be used to manipulate the XML documents.

This technique was widely used for other text before XML came on the scene, and still is. Some examples are product information, employee resumes, etc.

Example 29-4 contains SQL statements for the following functions:

- Create a table to hold XML documents.
- Insert a new document into the table.
- Build an index over the entire set of XML documents stored in the table.
- Query for documents with a VEGE_TYPE element containing "potato".

On the surface, the CLOB strategy might seem inferior to component-level access because the entire document is retrieved at once, preventing others from working on it. Even if a system did allow concurrent access

Example 29-4. SQL statements using text indexing to manage XML documents

```
CREATE TABLE XML_Docs (
       id         SERIAL      PRIMARY KEY,
       supplier VARCHAR(32) NOT NULL,
       xml_doc   CLOB        NOT NULL
);
INSERT INTO XML_Docs (supplier, xml_doc)
       VALUES (
           'ABC Inc',
           FileToClob('d:\xml\order_abcinc.xml','server'
       )
);
CREATE INDEX idx1 ON XML_Docs (xml_doc vts_clob_ops) USING vts
;
SELECT supplier FROM XML_docs
 WHERE vts_contains(xml_doc, '(potato) <IN> VEGE_TYPE')
;
```

to the complete document, there would be a danger of concurrent update as well.

A DBMS can address this problem by providing *transactional guarantees* for large object storage. Multiple users can read and update different regions of a single large object, and the DBMS' underlying disk storage algorithms will ensure the integrity of their actions.

29.5 | Conclusion

In order to support XML messaging, a DBMS must do more than be able to convert data to and from XML. Increasingly, there is also a need to store the messages in native form as XML documents.

XML, SQL, and XPath: Getting it all together

- Combining relational and text storage
- XPath in SQL statements
- SQL in XML documents
- Functional and text indexing

Contributing expert: Claire Dessaux and Mike Lehmann

Chapter

30

The world runs on relational DBMSs. Then again, as we showed in the Preface to this book, it also runs on markup languages, a necessity for documenting things as complex as RDBMSs. When titans meet they can easily clash, but this chapter shows a better way. There can be many paths to successful database management – but one has to begin with "X"!

Databases and XML documents are both ways to represent data, but they do so differently. In a DBMS, the metadata is kept in proprietary form; in XML, it is interspersed with the data in the form of tags, and may also be included in a DTD or schema definition. RDBMS data is stored in tables; XML data is organized in hierarchies.

The primary languages for accessing data in these two representations – SQL and XPath – reflect these differences. In an RDBMS environment in which XML has become an essential part, it makes sense to be able to use both languages, separately and together.

In this chapter, we'll show examples of doing just that for the key processes of a DBMS:

writing XML into a database
> Parsing an XML document and storing its components in a database, without losing the metadata that describes the properties of the components and the relationship among them.

reading XML from a database
> Exporting database objects and representing them as XML documents.

Indexing and searching
Building indexes to optimize searches for XML data.

Let's begin by looking at the schema and sample data that will be used in all the examples.

30.1 | An insurance claim example

Figure 30-1 depicts part of an insurance schema in a relational database. It shows the table for an insurance `Claim`, together with tables referenced from it.

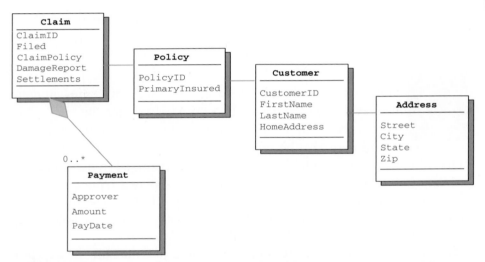

Figure 30-1   `Claim` portion of insurance schema in a relational database

An instance of a `Claim` can be represented as the XML document shown in Example 30-1, which preserves the data relationships and metadata set up by the database schema.

Field (column) names appear as element type names; some table names do as well: `Claim` because it is the root and `Payment` because there could be more than one of them.

Example 30-1. XML representation of a `Claim` instance

```
<Claim>
  <ClaimID>123456</ClaimID>
  <Filed>1999-01-01 12:00:00.0</Filed>
  <ClaimPolicy>
    <PolicyID>8895</PolicyID>
    <PrimaryInsured>
      <CustomerID>1044</CustomerID>
      <FirstName>John</FirstName>
      <LastName>Doe</LastName>
      <HomeAddress>
        <Street>123 Cherry Lane</Street>
        <City>San Francisco</City>
        <State>CA</State>
        <Zip>94100</Zip>
      </HomeAddress>
    </PrimaryInsured>
  </ClaimPolicy>
  <DamageReport>
    The driver lost control of the vehicle. This
    was because of <Cause>faulty brakes</Cause>.
  </DamageReport>
  <Settlements>
    <Payment id="0">
      <Approver>JCox</Approver>
      <Amount>7600</Amount>
      <PayDate>1999-03-01 09:00:00.0</PayDate>
    </Payment>
  </Settlements>
</Claim>
```

The hierarchy reflects the relationships among the tables. In the database, for example, `ClaimPolicy` is a *foreign key* that points to the `Policy` table. In the XML document, it appears as an element whose content is the fields of the `Policy` table. There are several others like this, shown by the nesting levels of the document.

The `DamageReport` field, although it contains XML markup, is different. We'll explain it in one of the examples.

This equivalence between the database and XML representations of data it important. It means, among other things, that XPath can be used to address the database!

There are potentially profound implications to this, such as direct hyperlinking between relational databases and Web pages. A DBMS could provide two SQL types for the purpose: one for linking within a database, and one for linking to and from the Web.

30.2 | Writing XML into a database

In previous chapters we've seen examples of the two basic strategies for storing XML documents: integral storage with markup intact, and distributed storage across a set of tables. Integral storage preserves the unparsed text[1] while distributed storage normally parses the document and discards the markup.

However, it is also possible to store some elements as text while storing others as relational data.

30.2.1 *Combining relational data and XML text storage*

You can store as relational fields those elements whose data content conforms to a primitive datatype, while storing those with mixed content (character data with interspersed subelements) intact. Example 30-2 shows how to store our insurance claim; the mixed content elements are given an SQL type called XMLtype.

30.2.2 *Generating SQL* INSERT *statements*

Creating an SQL INSERT statement for every record you need to add is laborious. You can use SQL in combination with XPath to reduce the work, by creating a stylesheet to act as a program generator.

Example 30-3 shows the fragment of an XSLT stylesheet that would generate values for the Payment table.

The fragment would be iterated over all the Payment elements within all the Claim elements.

Note that the stylesheet does not load the database by itself. It merely generates the necessary SQL statements.

---

1. Markup plus data characters, remember!

Example 30-2. Document storage using XMLType

```
REM     Create the Claim table

CREATE table Claim (
        ClaimID        number(3),
        Filed          date,
        ClaimPolicy    sys.XMLType,
        DamageReport   sys.XMLType,
        Settlements    sys.XMLType
);

REM     Insert a claim

INSERT INTO Claim VALUES (
        123456,
        sysdate(),
        sys.XMLType.createxml('
          <ClaimPolicy>
            ...details omitted for brevity...
          </ClaimPolicy>
        ')
        sys.XMLType.createxml('
          <DamageReport>
            The driver lost control of the vehicle. This
            was because of <Cause>faulty brakes</Cause>.
          </DamageReport>
        '),
        sys.XMLType.createxml('
          <Settlements>
            <Payment id="0">
              <Approver>JCox</Approver>
              <Amount>7600</Amount>
              <PayDate>1999-03-01 09:00:00.0</PayDate>
            </Payment>
          </Settlements>
        ')
);
```

Example 30-3. Generating SQL with XSLT

```
INSERT INTO Payment VALUES ('
  '<xsl:value-of select="Claim/Settlements/Payment/Approver"/>',
  <xsl:value-of select="Claim/Settlements/Payment/Amount"/>,
  <xsl:value-of select="Claim/Settlements/Payment/Paydate"/>
);
```

30.2.3 *XML SQL decomposition*

As an alternative method of storing XML, RDBMS vendors may offer a facility for *decomposing* (aka *shredding*) an XML document, as shown in Figure 30-2.

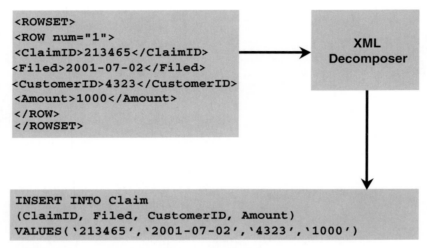

```
<ROWSET>
<ROW num="1">
<ClaimID>213465</ClaimID>
<Filed>2001-07-02</Filed>
<CustomerID>4323</CustomerID>
<Amount>1000</Amount>
</ROW>
</ROWSET>
```

XML Decomposer

```
INSERT INTO Claim
(ClaimID, Filed, CustomerID, Amount)
VALUES('213465','2001-07-02','4323','1000')
```

Figure 30-2   Decomposing an XML document

An XML document can be decomposed into any database table or view. Element type names are mapped to column (field) names in the table. Elements with data content only are mapped to scalar columns, and elements containing sub-elements are mapped to object types. Lists of elements are mapped to collections.

30.3 | Reading XML from a database

An RDBMS may offer several techniques for exporting database objects as XML. We'll look at two of them: embedded SQL in XML documents and built-in XML generation functions.

30.3.1 *Embedded SQL in XML documents*

One approach is to create an XML vocabulary for embedding SQL statements in XML documents.

Example 30-4 is an example. It contains a query that looks for Doe's insurance claims. As there is only one such claim in the database, the document in Example 30-1 is generated.

Example 30-4. Embedded SQL that generates Doe's claims

```
<?xml-stylesheet type="text/xsl" href="claim.xsl"?>
<query connection="xmldemo">
  SELECT VALUE(c) as Claim
  FROM    insurance_claim_view c
  WHERE   c.ClaimPolicy.PrimaryInsured.LastName = 'Doe'
</query>
```

The document in Example 30-4 is processed in several steps:

1. It is parsed by an XML parser.
2. XSLT instructions, such as those in the associated "claim.xsl" stylesheet, are passed to an XSLT processor.
3. The attributes and data content of the query element are processed by the DBMS.

30.3.2 *Built-in XML generation functions*

Some possible built-in functions are:

- Generate XML documents from the results of SQL queries.
- Generate XML documents by converting instances of other types.
- Generate XML documents of arbitrary complexity by aggregating (concatenating) multiple XML documents.

Example 30-5 uses a function to generate a document from the same query results as Example 30-4.

Example 30-5. Built-in function that generates Doe's claims

```
qryCtx := dbms_xmlgen.getContextHandle('
   SELECT VALUE(c) as Claim
   FROM   insurance_claim_view c
   WHERE  c.ClaimPolicy.PrimaryInsured.LastName = 'Doe'
');
result := dbms_xmlgen.getXMLClob(qryCtx);
```

30.4 | Indexing and searching

Database designers spend considerable effort on indexing, in order to optimize the performance of searches. XML, because of its different data model and mixed content, presents unique challenges in this area.

Let's examine two methods by which a DBMS can support indexing and searching for XML: functional indexes and textual indexes.

30.4.1 *Functional indexes*

A *functional index* is created by executing a function on a column (i.e., on all the elements of the same type) and indexing the result.

For example, it may be desirable to speed up searches for particular causes in damage reports, like that shown in Example 30-6.

Example 30-6. Search for specific Cause content

```
SELECT Filed
FROM   Claim c
WHERE  c.DamageReport.extract(
         '/DamageReport/Cause/text()'
       ).getStringVal() = 'faulty brakes'
```

A functional index can be created by using XPath to extract the data of all Cause elements, as shown in Example 30-7.

Example 30-7. Create functional index for `Cause`

```
CREATE INDEX cause_index ON Claim (
       DamageReport.extract(
          '/DamageReport/Cause/text()'
       ).getStringVal()
);
```

30.4.2 *Text indexes*

A *text index* is created from the words in a document or some portion of it. Searches on text can be used in combination with standard SQL query predicates, as shown in Example 30-8.

Example 30-8. Search for text in `Cause` content

```
SELECT ClaimID
FROM   Claim c
WHERE  c.Filed > '04-01-2001'
  AND    CONTAINS(
           DamageReport,
           '"faulty brakes" INPATH (/DamageReport/Cause)'
         )
       >0
;
```

The SQL statement searches for all damage reports filed after April 1, 2001, that have a `Cause` containing the phrase "faulty brakes". It uses the `CONTAINS` function in conjunction with the XPath query operator, `INPATH`, to accomplish this.

Note the distinction between searching on the value of a field and searching for text within a field. The search in Example 30-6 is satisfied only if "faulty brakes" is the *complete* data of the `Cause` element. In Example 30-8, though, the search is satisfied if "faulty brakes" occurs *anywhere* in the data.

30.5 | Conclusion

RDBMSs are the leading infrastructure for application support because of their flexibility and broad applicability. RDBMS users have adopted XML for largely the same reasons. Facilities like those we have discussed let them do so without changing existing systems or databases.

And their developers don't have to abandon proven tools while learning the new possibilities of the XML data model. They can use both SQL and XPath, independently and in combination.

Content Acquisition

- Syndicating content with Web services
- Acquiring reusable renditions
- Managing changes in acquired content

Part Ten

Content is king!

Yes, we said that before, but now we can tell the whole truth.

Actually, content is a royal family. There is the content of published documents, intended for people to read, and the content of machine-oriented transactions, which is a by-product of business processes. Ideally, we want the published content to be stored as unrendered abstractions, represented in XML, just as we want the transactional content to be in sharable enterprise databases.

But much of the time, the publications are *legacy documents* – either rendered or not XML (or both!) – and the transactions are *legacy data*, usable only by the application that created it.

Some content comes from a source by subscription, on a recurring basis. This is called *syndication* and we'll see how it can be managed by a Web service.

The sheer volume of legacy content may preclude its conversion to its most useful form, as XML abstractions. We'll examine how renditions can be reused without the conversion.

Finally, we explore how to tell when new content is really new or – better yet – how to limit content acquisition to genuine updates.

Syndicating content with Web services

Application Discussion

- ▌ The new role of syndication
- ▌ Managed content interchange
- ▌ ICE: A syndication Web service
- ▌ Step-by-step establishment of a syndication

Sponsor: ICE Authoring Group; an IDEAlliance working group, http://www.icestandard.org, http://www.idealliance.org

Contributing experts: Jay Brodsky, Marco Carrer, Dianne Kennedy, Daniel Koger, Richard Martin, and Laird Popkin

> The information economy feeds on *feeds* –
> automated recurring content flows: technical and
> marketing information from business partners,
> product manuals from your company's divisions, and
> publications from traditional media sources.
> Automating and managing the syndication of content
> feeds used to be time-consuming and expensive, but
> now there's a cool Web service for it!

ou may not realize it, but syndication is part of your business even if you have nothing to do with the media industry. To see why, let's have a brief history lesson.

31.1 | Beyond the newswire

Syndication – historically, the delivery of content to multiple subscribers simultaneously – began in the earliest days of the newspaper business. It was automated by the telegraph, with reporters and local newspapers transmitting articles to big city newspapers.

Syndication drove the growth of a media industry that is now dominated by giant content providers – the *syndicators*. They deliver everything from news articles to television programs, and they deliver them to a legion of newspapers, networks, and TV stations – the *subscribers*.

That original form of syndication – the newswire – is perhaps the oldest example of an automated supply chain. Unlike the EDI supply chain, however, which delivers only data about commercial transactions, the newswire delivers the actual goods – the news articles.

Now the Internet is redefining and expanding the concept of syndication. Today, *syndication* means *managed content interchange*, and it goes far beyond the newswire, or even the media industry.

31.2 | Managed content interchange

As business integration becomes pervasive, ordinary enterprises need to syndicate and subscribe to such content as supplier catalogs and maintenance manuals – even customer profiles and transaction records!

31.2.1 *Some syndication scenarios*

Let's look at some examples.

governmental and regulatory agencies
Governmental and regulatory agencies could syndicate regulatory information and forms to the public and other agencies. Syndication would be cheaper than mailing hard copy and would improve the timeliness of government information.

media companies
Media companies have high-value, frequently changing content. Licensing this information to intranets and portals could provide a new revenue stream for media companies.

purchasing departments
Your purchasing department could syndicate your specifications, drawings, and project reports to your vendors. Doing so can ensure that everyone has up-to-date project information.

product vendors
A product or service vendor could distribute product specifications, user manuals, and support information to its customers. Syndication could eliminate concerns over outdated or missing documentation while keeping the vendor visible to its customers.

31.2.2 *Business requirements*

The purpose of syndication is automated delivery of recurring content to subscribing business partners. Accomplishing it can be problematic, as adding a new partner requires time-consuming, customized, error-prone, manual processes. The syndicator must negotiate business requirements with each new subscriber, such as delivery times and frequency, notification, reporting, and monitoring. For example:

flexible delivery
> To operate properly and scale across a wide range of relationships, content syndication must support several delivery techniques. Some subscribers can accept delivery of content at any time, others only at specified times – for instance, off-peak hours. Some subscribers may want to initiate each content delivery (*pull content*); others will be set up for the syndicator to *push content* to them on its own initiative.

delivery guarantees
> Some content items, such as press releases, are withheld until a certain date and should not be accessible until that date. Also, most content has a shelf life and should be subject to expiration.

time value
> Some content has a time value for delivery. For example, investors need a guarantee that their stock transactions will be delivered promptly.

31.3 | ICE: A cool and solid solution!

These requirements, plus other needs of Internet-based content interchange, are addressed by the *Information and Content Exchange (ICE)* protocol. It is an XML-based protocol for specifying the business rules and processes needed for reliable content syndication.

ICE was originally developed by a consortium of more than 80 software developers, technology suppliers, content owners, and publishers. The current version is a SOAP-based Web service.[1]

31.3.1 *Tool capabilities*

The ICE protocol defines a model for the ongoing management of syndication relationships, including the roles and responsibilities of syndicators and subscribers. Here are some key capabilities that implementations can offer:

- Syndicators can describe business rules, such as usage constraints and intellectual property rights.
- Syndicators can create and manage catalogs of subscription offers. These can be accessed by content type, source, and other criteria.
- ICE uses XML to represent the messages that syndicators and subscribers exchange. The message structure keeps the content payload independent of the protocol itself, so virtually any data can be exchanged – from text to streaming video.
- Subscribers can specify a variety of push and pull delivery modes, as well as delivery times and frequency.
- Subscribers can specify content update parameters, such as incremental or full updates.
- Implementations can allow content to be obtained from, and delivered to, a variety of content repository types. These include databases, content management systems, file directories, Web servers, and Internet appliances.

31.3.2 *Message structure*

The ICE protocol is used for the delivery of content and the management of subscriptions. Its messages therefore contain information about those two processes, plus information about the messaging process itself. Figure 31-1 shows where the XML elements of an ICE message are positioned within the SOAP envelope that carries the message.

Let's take a closer look at each of the three processes: message, delivery, and subscribe.

---

1. This chapter discusses only the full compliance level of ICE 2.0. There is also a level with minimal function that does not use SOAP.

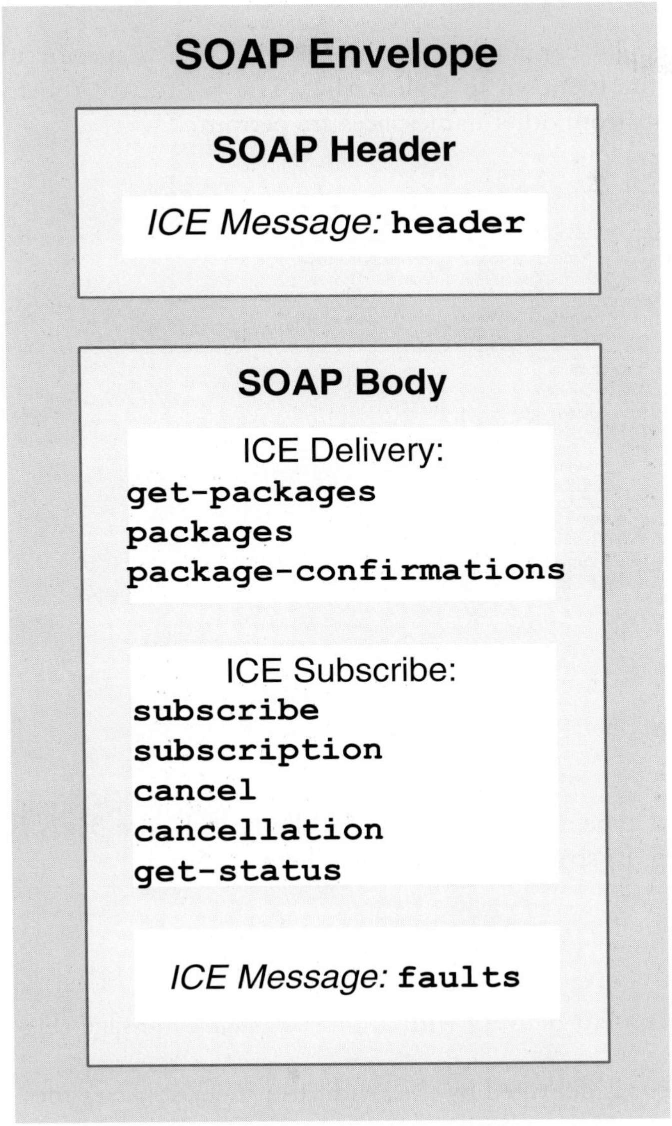

SOAP Envelope

SOAP Header

ICE Message: `header`

SOAP Body

ICE Delivery:
`get-packages`
`packages`
`package-confirmations`

ICE Subscribe:
`subscribe`
`subscription`
`cancel`
`cancellation`
`get-status`

ICE Message: `faults`

Figure 31-1   ICE elements in the SOAP envelope

31.3.2.1   Message

A message `header` element contains header information that is specific to syndication. Its structure is shown in Figure 31-2. The `#wildCard` tokens indicate where elements from other namespaces are permitted.

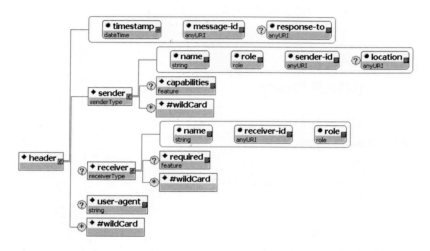

Figure 31-2   Message `header` **element type**

The `faults` element type, shown in the SOAP body in Figure 31-1, is used for error-handling. Its structure is not shown here.

31.3.2.2   Delivery

A subscriber requests content delivery with a `get-packages` message (Figure 31-3).

The requested content is delivered by the syndicator in a `packages` message. As the `#wildCard` tokens indicate, there is no restriction on the payload representation. A `package` could either contain the actual content, in an `item` element, or point to it, with an `item-ref` element.

The subscriber can confirm receipt with a `package-confirmations` message.

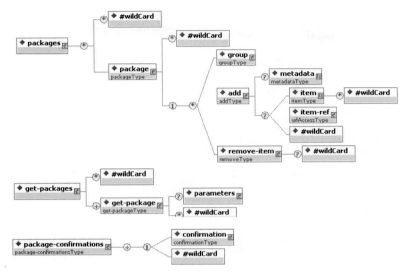

Figure 31-3   Delivery element types

31.3.2.3   Subscribe

A `subscribe` message contains an `offer` for a subscription (Figure 31-4). Its elements identify the offer uniquely, describe it, and establish conditions.

An `offer` must contain a `delivery-policy` that in turn contains at least one `delivery-rule` (Figure 31-5) specifying how and when content will be delivered.

Other element types (Figure 31-6) allow a subscriber to `cancel` a subscription and a syndicator to confirm the `cancellation`. There is also an element type that lets a subscriber `get-status` of a subscription.

31.4 | A simple syndication transaction

Let's look at a simple transaction between a syndicator and a subscriber in a familiar industry. It follows the steps illustrated in Figure 31-7.

The syndicator, the Best Code Company, is a software developer. It will set up and deliver a subscription for its press releases. The subscriber is Tech

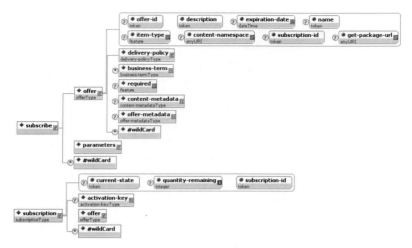

Figure 31-4   Subscription creation element types

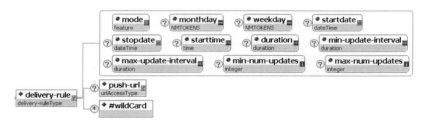

Figure 31-5   Subscription `delivery-rule` element type

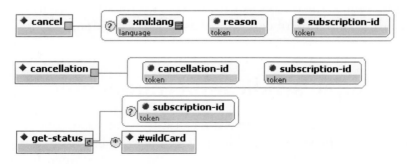

Figure 31-6   Subscription cancellation and status element types

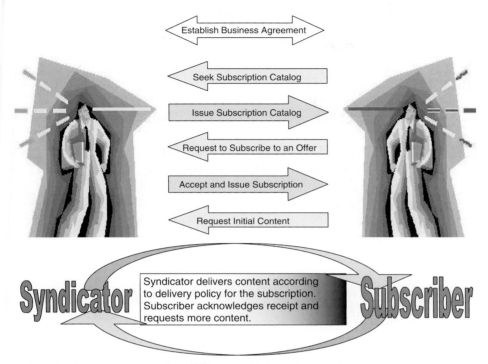

Figure 31-7   Steps to establishing a subscription

News, a trade paper that discovered it could save money by printing press releases instead of hiring reporters!

31.4.1   *Syndicator and subscriber set up a business agreement*

Syndication relationships begin with a business agreement. Best Code and Tech News agree on such terms as payment issues, usage rights, and subscription lifetime. The business agreement negotiation happens *without* ICE and can involve person-to-person discussion, legal review, and contracts.

Once the business agreement is in place, ICE comes into play as Best Code and Tech News start exchanging ICE messages to establish a subscription and begin content delivery.

31.4.2 *Subscriber seeks catalog of subscription offers*

Tech News can use three techniques obtain a catalog of subscriptions offered by Best Code:

- Visit the Best Code website and view or download a package of its offers.
- Use the UDDI Web services discovery mechanism. (We discuss UDDI in 40.2, "UDDI", on page 635.)
- Request a package of subscription offers from Best Code by using an ICE `get-packages` message (Figure 31-3). By convention, a package with `subscription-id="1"` (Figure 31-4) refers to a catalog of subscription offers.

31.4.3 *Syndicator issues catalog with just a single offer*

Regardless of how Tech News acquires the catalog, it will contain the same information: Best Code has just a single subscription offer – for its press releases. The `delivery-rule` (Figure 31-5) descendant of the `offer` (Figure 31-4) has a delivery `mode="pull"`. Tech News will have to pull this content from Best Code's server, rather than it being pushed to Tech News automatically.

31.4.4 *Subscriber sends a request to subscribe to the offer*

Tech News thinks the press releases are exciting stuff and promptly asks to sign up for the subscription offer. It agrees to pull the content from Best Code's server. In a `delivery-rule` (Figure 31-5) it specifies a `min-update-interval` that would allow it to pull new content at 5-minute intervals.

31.4.5 *Syndicator accepts request and issues subscription*

Best Code indicates that a subscription has been established by enclosing the agreed-upon `offer` within a `subscription` message (Figure 31-4). Best Code gives Tech News a `subscription-id` for the subscription and also confirms the delivery method and pull time interval.

31.4.6 *Subscriber requests initial subscription content*

Now that the subscription is established, Tech News is ready to receive content. It sends a `get-packages` message (Figure 31-3) to ask for subscription content. The message indicates that this is the initial request for this subscription, which alerts Best Code to download the full content.

31.4.7 *Syndication is established*

Best Code delivers the content of its subscription, consisting of a `package` (Figure 31-3) with two press releases. The first release is within the message – the content of an `item`. The second release, however, is not actually in the message. Instead, its URL is specified by an `item-ref`.

The `package` has other important information that gives Tech News permission to edit the content and changes the state of the subscription. The next time Tech News requests content, it will receive only content added or changed since this delivery, instead of receiving the entire content load all over again.

Tip   There is a copy of the ICE spec and other ICE information on the CD-ROM that accompanies this book.

Acquiring reusable renditions

■ Faithful rendition

■ Enriched content

■ Contextual metadata

Contributing expert: Jim Nichols

Chapter

32

One reason for XML's popularity in content management is its ability to preserve abstractions. However, there are situations in which it is important to preserve renditions, but still do all the things with them that a content system can do. Now there are XML-based technologies that allow you to acquire faithful renditions, analyze and enrich them, and manage and manipulate them at the component level. All it takes is the right metadata and the right schema!

Before SGML and XML became popular there was little or no *content management* in the sense we've been discussing it in this book. That is, there was no ability to manage fine-grained structured abstractions at the component level and assemble and render customized documents on demand.

There were *document management systems (DMS)*, which provided repository functions for whole documents. Their watchword was *print fidelity* – being able to reproduce the exact original printed page from the stored document. There was good reason to promote a capability that many needed, particularly in regulated industries, but it was also pretty much the only thing those systems could do with the data.

But those two extremes leave something lacking: a middle ground that allows component-level access to renditions, with metadata to support document assembly and reuse. And, of course, the sometimes vital ability to reproduce the original rendition with full fidelity.

The technology exists today to address that middle ground, but two key design questions must be resolved:

- How do you harvest the right metadata?
- How do you construct a suitable document type schema?

XML plays a role in the answers to both of them. Let's look at the meta-data first.

32.1 | Metadata for reusable renditions

To gather the needed metadata, we first have to find it!

In a typical enterprise, it can occur anywhere along the MOM-to-POP usage spectrum we discussed in Chapter 3, "The XML usage spectrum", on page 54.

32.1.1 *Machine-oriented messaging (MOM)*

MOM information is typically business process data, created and managed within applications. These can include legacy applications and such mainstream systems as enterprise resource planning (ERP) and customer relationship management (CRM).

The vast majority of MOM communication is from one program to another. However, a business often communicates MOM information to people – employees and partners – to support decision-making or to respond to queries. For example, a company might provide a customer with the "current stock levels", or the "contact address" of a particular employee.

MOM information, because it is created by a program, is explicitly marked and has known semantics. As a result, it is easy to harvest as both content and metadata.

32.1.2 *People-oriented publishing (POP)*

POP information could as well exist in paper form as electronic. It is typically created, received, and archived over time by employees, often without central management.

As with MOM information, a business communicates POP information to internal and external audiences to drive decision-making and in response to queries. Examples include:

- a salesperson giving a prospect a sales proposal,

■ a customer receiving technical support notes for a product, and

■ an employee receiving a health benefits summary during an open enrollment period.

POP information, because it is created by people, is not so rigorous in form or content as MOM information. As a result, much of its metadata is implied, rather than explicitly marked, and different harvesting techniques must be used.

32.1.3 *Content and context*

MOM and POP information both consist of content and metadata in their own right. In addition, the context in which the information is used provides further metadata, generated by the processes that operate on the information.

It is even possible for MOM applications to provide contextual metadata for POP information, as when a word processing document is circulated by email.

To make the most effective use of information assets, metadata must be harvested from both the content and the context.

32.1.3.1 Content metadata

Content metadata includes *structural properties*, which can be derived from the formatting and punctuation. These include elements like headings, paragraphs, and sentences.

Content also has *subject properties*, which must be derived by linguistic and semantic analysis of the data. The analysis can yield keywords, concepts, linguistic properties, and relationships with other content.

The analysis of subject properties also contributes to recognition of structural properties. For example, several contiguous paragraphs on the same topic could be recognized as subelements of a parent "section" element.

Content metadata is what allows information to be divided into components for reuse. It tends to be static, unless the content itself changes.

32.1.3.2   Contextual metadata

Contextual metadata is generated in the course of processing information. It includes properties generated when a document is created and when it is converted to XML. However, unlike content metadata, contextual metadata is dynamic. Each time a document is processed, more metadata is generated.

Contextual metadata can add significant value to a document.

Consider a customer receiving a compilation of technical support notes for various service requests. Each note could contain the identifying number and status of the corresponding service request, obtained from the technical support CRM system.

The customer not only receives the requested technical information, but is also likely to be satisfied that his service request is being looked after efficiently.

32.2 | A schema for reusable renditions

Of course we will use XML to store the content and its associated metadata. To meet our requirements for component-level management of enriched renditions, the document type schema will need to provide for three kinds of information:

faithful rendition

A perfect rendition of the original content in a form that allows it to be presented on a variety of devices.

enriched content

The original content, enriched with XML markup containing structural and subject metadata.

contextual metadata

Metadata inherent in processes that have acted on the content (e.g., "date created" from a word processor; "customers who have received it" from email).

32.2.1 *Faithful rendition*

There are industries in which faithful rendition is crucial, typically those subject to government regulation. One is the pharmaceutical industry.

Consider a new drug application to the US Food and Drug Administration. During the review process, it is quite common for the agency to inquire about particular information contained within the application. If the sponsor and reviewer aren't viewing the information in the exact same format and layout, serious communication difficulties could arise.

This issue is considered so vital that the US regulations governing the process mandate that all paper and electronic copies of applications be identical.

To achieve the required fidelity, a system should begin by using the original software that created the document to produce a rendition that is then converted into XML. Given the astounding variety of document and data object formats in the world, this is a non-trivial task.

For example, the specs for one system indicate support for 145 formats! The system converts them into an XML-based faithful rendition by utilizing two W3C standards: Scalable Vector Graphics (SVG) and XSL formatting objects (XSL-FO).

32.2.1.1 Scalable Vector Graphics (SVG)

We've previously discussed the difference between *raster graphics*, which are rendered arrays of points, and *vector graphics*, which describe pictures with geometric formulas.

Figure 32-1 shows how a page containing a simple drawing would be represented using a raster notation.

In contrast, SVG is a sophisticated notation that supports vector graphics, text, and even embedded raster images for photographs and the like, all in full color. And all in XML, which is a first for a notation with that kind of graphics expressive ability.

Example 32-1 shows the page in Figure 32-1 as it might be represented in an XML-based vector notation like SVG.[1]

---

1. The example uses simplified element type names and coordinates, not the actual SVG notation. However, it conveys the idea accurately.

```
00000000010000000000000000000000000000000000
00000000010000000000000000000000000000000000
00000000010000000000000000000000000000000000
00000000010000000000000000000000000000000000
00000000010000000011100000000001111111000000
00000000010000000100010000000001000001000000
00000000010000001000001000000001000001000000
00000000010000001000001000000001000001000000
00000000010000001000001000000001000001000000
00000000010000000100010000000001000001000000
00000000010000000011100000000001111111000000
00000000010000000000000000000000000000000000
00000000010000000000000000000000000000000000
00000000010000000000000000000000000000000000
00000000010000000000000000000000000000000000
```

Figure 32-1   Raster representation of a page

Example 32-1. XML-based vector representation of the page in Figure 32-1

```
<Page>
  <HSize>44</HSize>
  <VSize>15</VSize>
  <Line>
    <StartX>9</StartX>
    <StartY>1</StartY>
    <EndX>9</EndX>
    <EndY>15</EndY>
  </Line>
  <Circle>
    <CentreX>19</CentreX>
    <CentreY>8</CentreY>
    <Radius>4</Radius>
  </Circle>
  <Box>
    <TopLeftX>31</TopLeftX>
    <TopLeftY>5</TopLeftY>
    <BottomRightX>38</BottomRightX>
    <BottomRightY>11</BottomRightY>
  </Box>
</Page>
```

SVG is an approved W3C Recommendation with strong support and many implementations. It has sufficient expressive power to retain the fidelity of the original rendition for both print and electronic presentation. (We discuss SVG in 4.3, "Graphics and multimedia", on page 76.)

32.2.1.2   XSL-FO

SVG is designed to represent a picture accurately and therefore works well for a single page. To handle content that may comprise multiple pages, a system could employ the XSL-FO standard, which allows document level description of content pages.

A document is described using XSL-FO and each page within the document is described using SVG.

We discuss XSL-FO in more detail in Chapter 61, "XSL formatting objects (XSL-FO)", on page 990.

32.2.2   *Enriched content*

The content of a rendition contains data and implies metadata as well. Deriving the metadata and making it explicit enhances the content. There are several techniques for doing this, including analysis of the formatting and the subject matter.

32.2.2.1   Formatting analysis

Formatting is analyzed by examining the same visual cues used by a human reader. For example:

- Headings provide the reader with a visual cue to the start of a section in a document. We recognize these headings because they may be underlined, in bold type, in a different font size, or set apart by spacing.
- Paragraphs are recognized by indentions or gaps in the flow of text.
- Sentences are recognized through punctuation.
- Positioning allows us to recognize that a graphic is associated with a particular paragraph.

32.2.2.2   Linguistic and semantic analysis

Analysis of linguistics and semantics requires software that has more intimate knowledge of the content than the software for analyzing formatting. As there is an unbounded variety of content, an effective system must allow user-supplied components to participate in the analysis.

One objective of performing linguistic and semantic analysis on a rendition is the detection of information flow, both around objects on the page and across pages. Among other things, the analysis indicates whether objects are related.

32.2.2.3   Representing enriched content

The values of metadata properties recognized by content analysis are frequently data of the content itself. The purpose of the analysis is to make that data's role as metadata explicit by tagging it.

Often, the position of the tags and data is critical to its meaning. For example, hierarchical structure in XML is indicated by the nesting of tagged elements. Similarly, the position of a tagged index term is critical because the page it is on is part of the metadata.

These facts mean that the representation of enriched rendered content must allow for the intermixing of two kinds of markup vocabulary:

basic formatting objects
These include paragraphs, headings, and graphics, with relationships among them and style properties such as fonts and color. A system could, for example, use XHTML for this purpose.

custom vocabularies for linguistic and semantic metadata
The W3C Recommendation *Modularization of XHTML* allows custom vocabularies to be intermixed in XHTML text. Alternatively, the custom vocabularies can be used exclusively and XSLT stylesheets can be used to generate output for particular output devices. The faithful rendition would still be available when needed.

32.2.3 *Contextual metadata*

Contextual metadata is inherent in the processing of information. It can be harvested at all stages of processing.

To start with, the same technology that enables a system to convert scores of document and data representations to an XML faithful rendition can also gather contextual metadata. For example, a system could harvest metadata from a *Word* document that uses heading styles, or that has property values for title, subject, author, and category.

Metadata can also be obtained through interfaces to content management systems, databases, mail systems, and other processes. These can typically be added by users in the same way as analysis components.

Every use of a document presents another opportunity to harvest metadata. Consider a pharmaceutical company that uses a mail system to communicate between doctors and its medical informatics group. Each message can yield metadata on how the document has been used, along with feedback from the doctors regarding the usefulness of the content. The metadata can improve the responses to doctor inquiries.

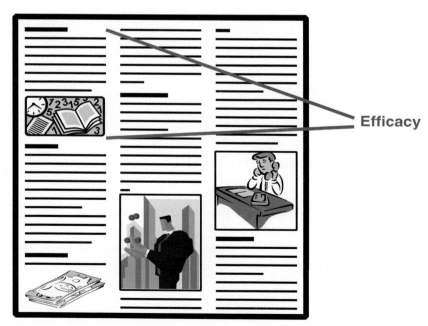

Efficacy

Figure 32-2   A pharmaceutical sales proposal

32.3 | A reusable rendition example

Figure 32-2 depicts a successful presentation made by a pharmaceutical company to a managed care organization. It resulted in the drug being added to the formulary and a percentage increase in the number of prescriptions written.

An XML representation of the enriched content is shown in Figure 32-3. It uses a custom vocabulary to express the structural metadata gathered by the content analysis.

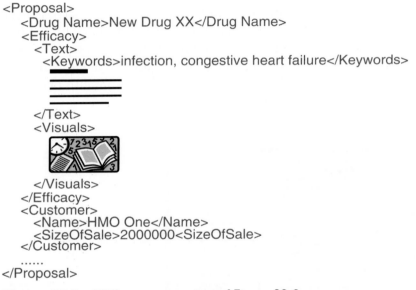

```
<Proposal>
    <Drug Name>New Drug XX</Drug Name>
    <Efficacy>
        <Text>
            <Keywords>infection, congestive heart failure</Keywords>

        </Text>
        <Visuals>

        </Visuals>
    </Efficacy>
    <Customer>
        <Name>HMO One</Name>
        <SizeOfSale>2000000<SizeOfSale>
    </Customer>
    ......
</Proposal>
```

Figure 32-3   XML representation of Figure 32-2

Note the Keywords element, which was added as a result of semantic analysis and is part of the enriched content.

The Customer element, however, is an example of contextual metadata, acquired from a sales tracking system.

Managing change in XML content

Tool Discussion

- Capabilities of XML change management
- Identifying changes
- Recording and reporting changes
- XML delta document
- Implementing XML change management

Sponsor: DeltaXML, http://www.deltaxml.com

Contributing experts: Martin Bryan and Robin La Fontaine

What's the difference? In any context, that's never been an easy question to answer. And where XML content is concerned, the answers are even tougher to come by: Did the data change? The structure? Did the markup change? Did it matter? You'll find some answers in this chapter.

D eadlines are deadlier than ever!

The insatiable information demands of 24/7 Web publishing means there is little time available to check changes to published data. Yet, whether the data comes from humans, computer programs or database reporting systems, the changes made during production must be identified and validated.

Managing changes reliably is tough enough with plain text. There are two problems to solve:

1. Identify when a change has occurred.
2. Make a record of the change and report it.

But, increasingly, your data is likely to be in XML, which presents a whole new set of problems. Now the data might change, or the structure, or both. A change in the markup might be significant, or it might not.

Fortunately, XML isn't just part of the problem. It is part of the solution as well.

33.1 | Change management with XML

Change management for – and with – XML can simplify and speed up production cycles. But it can do much more than that. By analyzing a stream of XML data, comparing it with the original, and recording the changes in XML, we have a new kind of XML document – the *delta file*.

Let's look at some things it can do.

33.1.1 *Document editing*

Delta files can be used to coordinate changes made on multiple systems by automatically merging the changes into the original XML file. To allow review of the changes, the delta files can be converted to HTML for viewing in a browser. Color and text characteristics can be used to highlight changes so that reviewers can see exactly what has been added, modified or deleted.

Tip   This technique applies to SVG graphics files as well, as SVG is an XML notation. And because it is SVG, the changes can be animated so they can't be missed. The CD-ROM includes an example that you can view with your browser.

33.1.2 *Data translation*

Delta files can assist in the management of multilingual websites and similar large document collections. Although the initial translation of a site's source material may be straightforward, problems can occur when the site is updated without a suitable change management system.

In order to update translations efficiently, you need to know the exact changes that have been made to the original text so you can translate only the changed parts of the files. A delta file, at a suitable level of granularity, can help. You can translate it and then merge the changes with the original translation.

Final touch-up of the translation can be made manually. Create a delta file of the updated translation compared to the original translation, then transform it to an HTML visualization of the changes.

33.1.3 *Database management*

File differencing techniques can allow remote users to update a database that is represented as an XML file.[1] For example:

- By exchanging only changed data in XML delta files, database repopulation costs can be reduced.
- Clients can merge delta files with their replicated local copies of the master database to keep the copies up-to-date.
- A differencing engine that knows XML can enforce integrity by controlling the granularity of changes. Where it is not permitted to modify part of an object, such as a single element in a structure, the engine can ensure that the whole set of interdependent elements is updated at the same time.

33.1.4 *Web services*

Exchanging XML delta files, rather than retransmitting large amounts of data, can reduce bandwidth requirements of Web services. A small change at one end of the pipeline can be sent to the other end as a delta file, encapsulated within a SOAP envelope.

Syndication services in particular could improve efficiency by delivering only changes instead of an entire revised document.

Security could be increased by splitting sensitive data into separate streams and transmitting one stream and a delta file.

33.2 | Identifying changes

What constitutes a change to an XML file, and what doesn't?

---

1. Or which appears that way! See 55.6.2, "Synthetic infosets", on page 892.

Comparing XML files requires the ability to identify the following types of changes:

- Data changes in the content of elements.
- Data changes in the values of attributes.
- Structural changes: The addition and deletion of elements and attributes.
- The reordering of elements.

Let's look at some of the issues of change identification.

33.2.1 *Irrelevant markup differences*

XML offers several ways to represent the same conceptual information – a document's *information set (infoset)*. XML documents should therefore be compared by their infosets, not by the character strings that represent them.

33.2.1.1   Whitespace and namespaces

Consider the files shown in Example 33-1 and Example 33-2. They are identical as far as XML is concerned, although a string-based differencing engine would identify changes. For example:

- Whitespace has been added to indent subelements and place them on separate lines.
- The attributes of `record` have been reordered.
- In Example 33-2 a namespace prefix is defined and used for all elements, whereas Example 33-1 uses that same namespace by default (without a prefix).

None of these changes affects the information sets of the two XML documents.

Example 33-1. No whitespace or namespaces

```
<record xmlns="http://www.myco.com/records" id="b123">
<name>Michael Brown</name><born>1984-03-08</born><sex>M</sex>
</record>
```

Example 33-2. With whitespace and namespaces

```
<staff:record id="b123" xmlns:staff="http://www.myco.com/records">
  <staff:name>Michael Brown</staff:name>
  <staff:born>1984-03-08</staff:born>
  <staff:sex>M</staff:sex>
</staff:record>
```

33.2.1.2 Canonicalization

One way to minimize irrelevant markup differences is to convert documents to a uniform representation (*canonical form*) before comparing them.

The W3C *Canonical XML* Recommendation specifies a method for canonicalizing XML documents:

- The document is encoded in UTF-8.
- Line breaks are normalized to #xA on input, before parsing.
- Attribute values are normalized, as if by a validating parser.
- Character references and parsed entity references are replaced.
- CDATA sections are replaced with their character content.
- The XML declaration and document type declaration (DTD) are removed.
- Empty elements are converted to pairs of contiguous start- and end-tags.
- Whitespace outside of the document element and within start- and end-tags is normalized.
- All whitespace in character content is retained (except for characters removed during line break normalization).
- Attribute value delimiters are set to quotation marks (double quotes).
- Special characters in attribute values and character content are replaced by character references.
- Superfluous namespace declarations are removed from each element.
- Specifications for default attributes are added to each element.
- Lexicographic order is imposed on the namespace declarations and attributes of each element.

Although this canonical form makes it easier to identify the first point at which the character strings differ, that is not enough to let programs identify all changes made to the structure or data.

33.2.2 *Structural differences*

Identifying structural differences and assessing their significance requires differencing software that knows XML.

Let's look at some reasons why.

33.2.2.1   New element types

Consider Example 33-3 and Example 33-4.

An XML-aware differencing engine should be able to identify when an element type is newly-introduced, like the `employee-no` elements in Example 33-4. It should also recognize that the remainder of the elements in each `record` are unchanged from the source document (although the order of the `record` elements has changed).

Example 33-3. Original records

```
<record id="b123">
  <name>Michael Brown</name>
  <born>1984-03-08</born>
  <sex>M</sex>
</record>
<record id="b124">
  <name>Gillian Bryan</name>
  <born>1951-03-06</born>
  <sex>F</sex>
</record>
```

33.2.2.2   Reordering of repeatable elements

An XML-aware differencing engine could allow users to indicate whether or not the order of repeatable elements is significant. The distinction could affect a comparison.

For example, if the order is significant then there is a significant mismatch between Example 33-3 and Example 33-4. But if order is not signif-

Example 33-4. Updated records

```
<record id="b124">
  <employee-no>BR12</employee-no>
  <name>Gillian Bryan</name>
  <born>1951-03-06</born>
  <sex>F</sex>
</record>
<record id="b123">
  <employee-no>BR24</employee-no>
  <name>Michael Brown</name>
  <born>1984-03-08</born>
  <sex>M</sex>
</record>
```

icant, the only change is the addition of the two new `employee-no` elements.

33.2.2.3   Structural change without data change

Identifying the minimal set of actual changes to an XML file is non-trivial because it involves look-ahead. When you find a change in the sequence of elements you need to search the rest of the data stream to identify a possible re-synchronization point. This may not occur at an element boundary, as Example 33-5 and Example 33-6 show:

Example 33-5. No nested element

```
<html>
<body>
<p>This paragraph has special text</p>
</body>
</html>
```

Example 33-6. Element nested within data content

```
<html>
<body>
<p>This paragraph has <em>special</em> text</p>
</body>
</html>
```

The data content of the two paragraph elements in these XML files is identical, but the structure of the files is different. The differencing engine has to determine whether or not the change of emphasis for one word in the text in any way changes the contents of the containing element.

Example 33-7 shows a delta file produced by the *DeltaXML* suite from Monsell EDM Ltd. The file differentiates words in the unchanged paragraph text from words that were changed, regardless of whether the changes are structural or just textual.[2]

Example 33-7. Delta file comparing Example 33-6 with Example 33-5

```
<html
 xmlns:deltaxml="http://www.deltaxml.com/ns/well-formed-delta-v1"
 deltaxml:delta="WFmodify">
<body deltaxml:delta="WFmodify">
 <p deltaxml:delta="WFmodify">
  This paragraph has
  <deltaxml:exchange>
   <deltaxml:old>special</deltaxml:old>
   <deltaxml:new>
    <em deltaxml:delta="add">special</em>
   </deltaxml:new>
  </deltaxml:exchange>
  text
 </p>
</body>
</html>
```

33.2.3 *Clarifying changes with keys*

As we'll see shortly, there is a class of differencing problems that occur when elements cannot be identified uniquely. That is to say, when the elements in some group (such as all the elements in a document) cannot be distinguished from one another conveniently and with complete accuracy.

The necessary distinguishing information is called a *key*. Keys can be derived from any combination of attributes, content, and/or position that is unique to an element.

Element-type names like p aren't *element names* and cannot serve as keys. The name p, for example, identifies *every* paragraph, not just one.

2. We look at the delta file in more detail in 33.3.2.2, "Full description", on page 539.

XML IDs are element names, but not all elements have them. When they do, the IDs can be used as *keys*.

When *keys* are required to be in an XML document, they are normally represented as attributes. They can be generated by an XSLT transform or other program.

Now we can consider the problems that keys help to solve.

33.2.3.1   Distinguishing changes from insertions

Without keys, the change from Example 33-8 to Example 33-9 would be visualized as shown in Figure 33-1.

Example 33-8. Original without keys

```
<p>This paragraph will be deleted.
A new one will be added after the next paragraph.</p>
<p>This paragraph will be modified.</p>
```

Example 33-9. Revision without keys

```
<p>This paragraph will be modified, like this.</p>
<p>This paragraph was added in version 2.</p>
```

This paragraph will be ~~deleted.~~
~~A new one will be added after the next paragraph.~~modified, like this.

This paragraph ~~will be modified.~~was added in version 2.

Figure 33-1   Visualization of change from Example 33-8 to Example 33-9 (without keys)

By adding keys to each paragraph, unchanged paragraphs can be matched correctly, thereby allowing changes to be reported accurately.

In Example 33-10 and Example 33-11, an XSLT transform has added unique ID attributes to the paragraphs of Example 33-8 and Example 33-9.

The IDs are based on the order of the paragraphs in the document. For the original paragraphs, they are in the form O1, O2 and so on, while for paragraphs added by the revision, R is used instead of O.

Example 33-10. Original using keys

```
<p id="O1">This paragraph will be deleted.
A new one will be added after the next paragraph.</p>
<p id="O2">This paragraph will be modified.</p>
```

Example 33-11. Changes using keys

```
<p id="O2">This paragraph will be modified, like this.</p>
<p id="R1">This paragraph was added in version 2.</p>
```

The visualization of the change is shown in Figure 33-2.

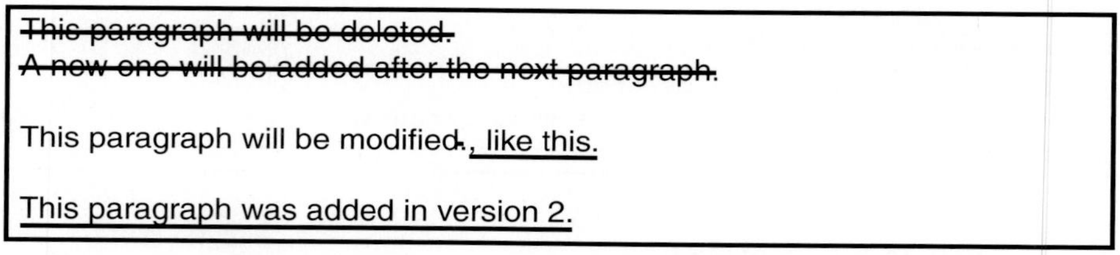

Figure 33-2   Visualization of change from Example 33-10 to Example 33-11 (with keys)

33.2.3.2   Distinguishing real changes from reordering

Differencing engines cannot normally distinguish between elements that have simply been reordered and those that have actually been changed. But when each element has a unique key, it is possible to tell when the same elements are in an updated file, but in a different order. (Whether the reordering is considered a change, of course, is for the user to decide.)

Keys also allow a differencing engine to identify when an element is replaced by an identical duplicate.

33.3 | Recording and reporting changes

Differencing engines typically record the location of a change and the text that is to be used in that position.

33.3.1 *Recording a change location*

33.3.1.1   Number pair

A simple differencing tool might record two numbers for a location:

1. the number of the character or line where a change has been identified, and
2. a number representing either the length of the original data or the point at which it ends.

These two numbers can then be associated with the data that is to replace the original data.

These numbers are adequate for internal recording, so that changes can be displayed on screen for as long as the numbers are retained in memory. They are not suitable for long-term storage of information because interpretation of the numbers depends on the software that created them.

33.3.1.2   XPath expression

An alternative approach is to use a standardized addressing notation like XPath to record the locations of changes. However, this method could fail if one of a set of successive changes modifies the element structure,

For example, the word `special` in Example 33-5 is located by a reference to a substring in an element:

```
xhtml/body/p[(substring(text(),19,7)]/
```

whereas for the revised file in Example 33-6 a reference to the same word takes the form:

```
xhtml/body/p[1]/em
```

33.3.2 *Recording the changed text*

Recording a change by its location and replacement text makes it difficult to verify whether the change is correct, or to audit the change at a later date. Let's look at some other ways to record changes.

33.3.2.1   Editing instructions

One way to represent changes is to record the editing instructions for causing the changes.

For example, the proposed *XML Update Language (XUpdate)* defines an
XML vocabulary for recording insertions, additions and removals of elements. It uses XPath expressions to identify the points in the source document at which changes occur. The changes are represented by element types
named `insert-before`, `insert-after`, `append`, `update`, `remove`,
`rename`, `variable`, `value-of` and `if`.

Example 33-14 shows how XUpdate can represent the changes from
Example 33-12 to Example 33-13.

Example 33-12. Original file

```
<directory>
  <firm>Change Management, Inc.</firm>
  <president>Strings R. Enuff</president>
  <date>2003</date>
</directory>
```

Example 33-13. Revised file

```
<directory>
  <firm>Change Management, Inc.</firm>
  <ceo>U. Need Structure</ceo>
  <date>2003</date>
</directory>
```

Example 33-14. XUpdate representation of changes from Example 33-12 to Example
33-13

```
<xupdate:modifications version="1.0"
  xmlns:xupdate="http://www.xmldb.org/xupdate">
  <xupdate:remove select="/directory/firm[1]/president" />
  <xupdate:insert-after select="/directory/firm[1]" >
    <xupdate:element name="ceo">U. Need Structure</xupdate:element>
  </xupdate:insert-after>
</xupdate:modifications>
```

33.3.2.2   Full description

The delta file produced by *DeltaXML* takes a more comprehensive approach. It records both the original text and the replacement text at the actual point of replacement.

33.3.2.2.1 *Structure and data content changes*

For example, for the source file in Example 33-12 and the revised version in Example 33-13, the delta file would contain the pair of exchanged elements, as shown in Example 33-15.

Example 33-15. Delta file representation of changes from Example 33-12 to Example 33-13

```
<directory deltaxml:delta="WFmodify"
  xmlns:deltaxml="http://www.deltaxml.com/ns/well-formed-delta-v1">
  <firm deltaxml:delta="unchanged" />
  <deltaxml:exchange>
    <deltaxml:old>
     <president deltaxml:delta="delete">Strings R. Enuff</president>
    </deltaxml:old>
    <deltaxml:new>
     <ceo deltaxml:delta="add">U. Need Structure</ceo>
    </deltaxml:new>
  </deltaxml:exchange>
  <date deltaxml:delta="unchanged" />
</directory>
```

DeltaXML can generate a *contextual delta file* that also includes all of the unchanged elements, as shown in Example 33-16.

With XSLT, a contextual delta file can be transformed to HTML or a print format for a display that includes both the original text and the changes. Figure 33-3 is a visualization of the changes recorded in Example 33-16.

33.3.2.2.2 *Attribute changes*

A delta file records changes to attributes as shown in Example 33-17.

If a new attribute is added then only the `deltaxml:new-attributes` attribute is required. If an attribute is removed then only the `deltaxml:old-attributes` attribute is required.

Example 33-16. Contextual form of the delta file in Example 33-15

```
<directory deltaxml:delta="WFmodify"
  xmlns:deltaxml="http://www.deltaxml.com/ns/well-formed-delta-v1">
  <firm deltaxml:delta="unchanged">Change Management, Inc.</firm>
  <deltaxml:exchange>
    <deltaxml:old>
     <president deltaxml:delta="delete">Strings R. Enuff</president>
    </deltaxml:old>
    <deltaxml:new>
     <ceo deltaxml:delta="add">U. Need Structure</ceo>
    </deltaxml:new>
  </deltaxml:exchange>
 <date deltaxml:delta="unchanged">2003</date>
</directory>
```

Company: *Change Management, Inc.*
~~**President:** Strings R. Enuff~~ **CEO:** U. Need Structure
Date: 2003

Figure 33-3   Visualization of changes recorded in Example 33-16

Example 33-17. Delta file representation of changed attribute specification

```
<date deltaxml:delta="WFmodify"
      deltaxml:old-attributes="datatype='integer'"
      deltaxml:new-attributes="datatype='date'">
```

33.3.2.2.3 *Data content changes*

Changes to *parsed character data (PCDATA)* are recorded as shown in
Example 33-18.

Example 33-18. Delta file representation of changed parsed character data

```
<p xmlns:deltaxml="http://www.deltaxml.com/ns/well-formed-delta-v1"
 deltaxml:delta="WFmodify">
 The text
 <deltaxml:PCDATAmodify>
  <deltaxml:PCDATAold>originally shown in</deltaxml:PCDATAold>
  <deltaxml:PCDATAnew>displayed using</deltaxml:PCDATAnew>
 </deltaxml:PCDATAmodify>
 a fixed width font is now bold.
</p>
```

33.3.2.2.4 *Namespace changes*

A *DeltaXML* delta file also records namespace changes. The differencing engine recognizes that a namespace prefix is only a shorthand for the URI that identifies the namespace in the namespace declaration. When comparing two files, namespace prefixes are replaced by their corresponding URIs. Unqualified names within the scope of a default namespace are assigned default namespace URIs.

33.3.2.3 File size

The simple examples we've seen may suggest that delta files are larger than the source files. But in a typical application this is unlikely to be true (except, of course, when the contextual form of the delta file is generated).

Normally, only a small proportion of a file is updated. For the remainder, unchanged text is recognized by sequences like the following:

- a start-tag for the highest unchanged element in the hierarchy,
- some parsed character data or elements, and
- an end-tag.

In the delta file, the sequence is replaced by an empty-element tag with a single attribute, like this:

```
<date deltaxml:delta="unchanged" />
```

Regardless of the element type, the attribute specification is always the same 27 characters:

```
deltaxml:delta="unchanged"
```

As long as the replaced sequence exceeds 27 characters, the length of even an uncompressed delta file will be reduced. And if the file is compressed, all instances of the 27-character string will become single tokens, each typically occupying four or five bytes.[3]

---

3. We discuss compression techniques for XML in Chapter 48, "Compression techniques for XML", on page 730.

33.4 | Implementing XML change management

Differencing engines range from the familiar string-oriented Unix `diff` utility, to software that understands the subtleties of XML change identification and creates useful XML delta files. Product packaging also varies, from Web-based services, to stand-alone utilities, to code libraries.

DeltaXML, for example, is distributed as a Java API that allows calls to the differencing engine to be integrated with calls to XML parsers and XSLT processors. Pipelines like those in Figure 33-4 can be created, with pre- and post-comparison processing by XSLT or other programs. Both 2- and 3-way merges and multithreading are supported.

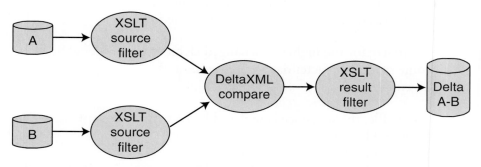

Figure 33-4   Pipeline created with *DeltaXML*

33.5 | Conclusion

Using XML to record changes to XML files enhances the ways in which change data can be used. At the same time, it simplifies the change management process by allowing it to be integrated with other data management operations. As the XML delta files can be stored in your data repository, they can become a permanent, auditable record of the updates to your XML documents.

Now when you're asked "What's the difference?" you'll have a precise answer – and a lot of options for communicating it!

Semantic Web

- Extended linking
- Topic maps tutorial
- RDF and its applications

Part Eleven

The W3C vision of the Semantic Web is one where data is defined and linked so that machines can do more than display it to people; they can share it among themselves to automate tasks and integrate applications. In other words, the very things we've been discussing in this book.

This part focuses on the weak "link" in the vision!

Hyperlink anchors today use physical addresses (URIs). Although the links themselves represent topical (semantic) associations, there is no hint of the *reason* why things might be linked. And although search engines operate in topical space, they are totally undisciplined and routinely return thousands of irrelevant pages.

XML can be used today to cure these problems. Extended linking supports meaningful relationships. RDF metadata allows rich descriptions of Web resources. And topic maps can chart the Web's information space so you can use topical querying and addressing and never get lost.

Extended linking

Introductory Discussion

- Extended linking defined
- XLink applications
- XPointers
- Strong link typing

Sponsor: Coolheads Consulting, `http://www.coolheads.com`

Contributing experts: Steven R. Newcomb and Victoria T. Newcomb

Chapter

34

Extended linking and strong link typing will let the Web traverse to locations where it has never been. Those concepts are explained simply and clearly in this chapter.

F uture generations of Web browsers and editors will reduce the effort required to keep our personal affairs organized and our corporate memories up to the minute. The productivity of many kinds of work will be enhanced, and in many ways. It's all going to happen basically because of two simple enhancements to the Web paradigm.

The W3C's *XML Linking Language (XLink)* Recommendation for extended linking proposes to give all of us the ability to annotate documents, and to share those annotations with others, even when we cannot alter the documents we are annotating. In other words, we won't have to change a document in order to supply it with our own annotations – annotations that a browser can make appear as though they were written right into the annotated document.

34.1 | The shop notes application

As an example, consider a technician's set of online maintenance manuals. These are electronic books that the technician is not (and should not be) authorized to change. With HTML hyperlinks, the technician cannot write a note in a manual that can take future readers of that manual, including himself, to his annotations. Nor can the technician's annotations be displayed in their proper context – the parts of the manual that they are about.

34.1.1 *What is extended linking?*

By using *extended linking*, when the technician makes an annotation, he does so purely by editing his own document; no change is made to the read-only manual document that he is annotating.

The big difference between extended linking and HTML linking is this. With an HTML link (or *simple link*), traversal can only begin at the place where the link is; traversal cannot begin at the other end. With an *extended link*, however, you can click on any of the link's anchors, and traverse to any other anchor, regardless of where the link happens to be.

Tip   Extended linking allows the starting anchor of a link to be different from the link itself. Instead of HTML's "A" tagged element that is linked to one other element, you can have (say) an "L" tag that links two or more other elements to one another.

A simple link (top of Figure 34-1) is always embedded (*inline*) in (for example) the InstallLog text from which it provides traversal; the link cannot be traversed by starting at the target anchor (for example, the Installation procedure document).

An extended link (bottom of Figure 34-1) can appear in a separate document, and provide traversal between the corresponding parts of two other documents: for example, the technician's shop notes document ("TechLog") and the read-only installation manual. Because the location of this particular link is not the same as any of its anchors, it is said to be *out-of-line* (not embedded).

In our example, an annotation takes the form of just such an extended link element.

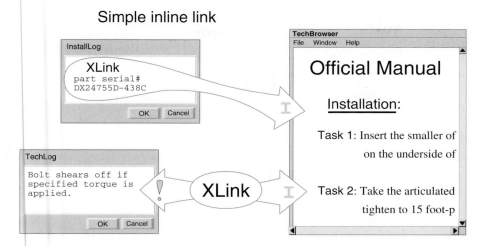

Simple inline link

Extended, out-of-line link

Figure 34-1   Simple vs. extended linking.

34.1.2   *Displaying extended links*

One way to realize the benefits of extended links is to display an icon at each anchor that indicates something about the other anchor. (The mechanism that supports this is discussed in greater detail under "Strong link typing", below.)

For example, as shown in Figure 34-2, a reader of the installation manual on the right will know that, if he clicks on the exclamation point displayed near Task 2, he will see a shop note about that task. If he clicks on the pound sign, he will be shown the serial number of a part that was installed according to the procedure, recorded in an "InstallLog" document.

Similarly, a reader of the annotation in the shop notes document ("TechLog") will know that clicking on the "I" icon will bring him to the installation instruction that the annotation discusses.

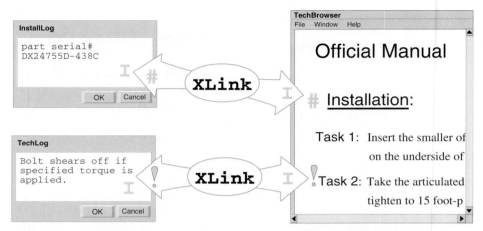

Figure 34-2   The exclamation point icon near Task 2 indicates that a shop note is available.

34.1.3   *Notes survive to new versions of manuals*

The technician's annotations – his "shop notes" – accumulate over time, and they represent a valuable asset that must be maintained. If the technician were to write shop notes inside each manual, when a new version of a manual is received it would be a chore to copy annotations from the old manual to the new manual.

With extended linking, however, the annotations are not in the old version; they are in a separate document. Therefore, the shop notes don't disappear when an annotated manual is replaced by a newer version.

That is because each link is equipped with "pointers" – pieces of information that can tell a browser where (for example) clickable icons should be rendered that indicate the availability of an annotation. Each such "XPointer" (as it is called) can point at anything in any XML document.

In our technician's shop, when a manual is replaced by a new version, the XPointers keep on working, even with the new manual, so the new manual is instantly and automatically equipped with the old manual's annotations.

In most cases, the XPointers don't have to be changed, because they continue to point at the right things, even in the new manual. If, because of differences between the old and new versions of the manual, some XPointers in the shop notes don't still point at the right things (or perhaps have nothing to point at any more), there are techniques that can be used to detect such situations.

Moreover, XPointers and extended links enhance the potential for achieving high levels of quality and consistency, even when there are voluminous shop notes that annotate many manuals.

34.1.4 *Vendors can use the notes*

Some shop notes may also have value to the vendors of the manuals they annotate; they may beneficially influence subsequent versions of the manual. An editor of the manual can load (i.e., make his browser aware of) all the shop notes of many repair shops; this has the effect of populating the manual with icons representing the annotations of all the shops. The most common trouble spots in the manual will be made obvious by the crowds of annotation icons that they appear to have accumulated (Figure 34-3).

The fact that the shop notes take the form of interchangeable XML documents that use standardized extended links makes the task of sharing internal shop notes with manual vendors as easy as sending them any other kind of file. There is no need to extract them from some other resource, or to format them in such a way that they can be understood by their recipients. They are ready to work just as they are, in the tradition of SGML, HyTime, HTML, and now XML.

34.2 | Other applications of extended linking

The above "shop notes" example is just a sample of the kinds of enhancements that extended linking will bring to our interactions with information resources. Some of the broader implications are a bit more startling.

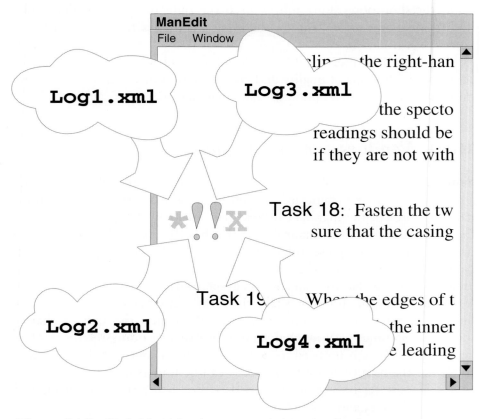

Figure 34-3   Task 18 evidently prompted three kinds of annotations in four different shop logs.

34.2.1 *Public resource communities of interest*

For example, many web sites today contain HTML links to public resources. One is the U.S. Government's online service for translating any U.S. postal code into its corresponding Congressional district and the name of its current incumbent Representative:

```
http://www.house.gov/zip/ZIP2Rep.html
```

However, if those HTML links were to become XLink extended links, an XLink-enabled browser could render this U.S. government Web page in such a way as to add to it a catalog of the activists and lobbying organizations who refer readers of their websites to this particular U.S. government resource. The "marketplace of ideas" represented by the aggregate of such organizations is thus revealed in a new and interesting way.

34.2.2 *Guidance documents*

Another startling possibility is the association of browser-controlling metadata with any and all Web resources.

In this scenario, a document of annotations (or a set of such documents) can be a user's companion during excursions on the Web. These annotations might make suggestions to users as to where to find more recent material, or they might even take control of the browser's link traversal ability in order to protect children from disturbing material.

While the latter XLink-enabled possibility may sound inimical to the freedom of speech, in fact it enhances liberty. It provides a new public medium for free speech: documents that censor the Web and/or otherwise provide guidance to Web travelers in the form of annotations that appear only in their designated contexts.

Of course, no adult is required to use any such guidance document, just as no one is required to read any particular book, but it's easy to predict that many will pay for the privilege of using many kinds of such "guidance documents".

More importantly, everyone will have the tools to write such guidance documents, so the technical ability to provide guidance (and, yes, even to provide censorship services) will be widely distributed, rather than being dangerously concentrated in a few generalized rating services. The creation and maintenance of guidance documents may well become a thriving cottage industry. Anyone can be a critic.

In the case of electronic commerce, it's easy to imagine that vendors will attempt to provide guidance documents designed to annotate the online sales catalogs of their competitors. In response, some providers of online sales catalogs will take steps to render the pointers in these kinds of guidance documents invalid and unmaintainable.

Regardless of all this, the overall impact on electronic commerce will certainly be positive; increasing the meaningful interconnectedness of the Web will help more people find exactly what they're looking for.

And it may turn out to be a mistake, in many cases, for catalog owners to attempt to render the pointers used to annotate their catalogs invalid, because similar pointers could be used, for example, by impartial consumer testing organizations to attach "best buy" recommendations to certain products. The guidance documents of consumer testing organizations will probably be quite popular, and well worth the cost of using them.

34.2.3 *Computer-augmented memory*

Extended linking has the potential to make radical improvements in our ability to keep track of what we are doing. Someday, we can expect to automatically annotate each piece of information we work with in such a way that, in effect, it refers future readers to the work we did with respect to it.

In other words, practically everything we do can be usefully seen as an annotation of one or more other pieces of work. If everything we do is, in some sense, an annotation of one or more other things, everything we do can all be found far more easily, starting from any piece of work anywhere in the "chain" (or, more likely, "tree" or "graph") of relevant information.

This is because extended linking allows all links to be bidirectional. (Or, rather, "n-directional", to account for extended links with more than two ends.) All of the connections among our affairs can then be tracked more or less automatically, so that each of us can enjoy a radical reduction in filing, cross-indexing, and other organizational chores, and with vastly increased ability to find what we're looking for quickly and easily.

Obviously, this same idea is even more significant in the realm of corporate memory. Even with today's behemoth enterprise integration technologies, it's still too hard to figure out what has happened, who is doing what, how various plans and projects are going to integrate, and where the relevant paperwork can be found.

Going a step further, there is an International Standard (ISO/IEC 13250) that seeks to exploit extended linking in such a way as to create living, easily explored and maintained "topic maps" of sets of information resources (see Chapter 35, "Topic maps: Knowledge navigation aids", on page 560). This goal sounds almost insanely ambitious, but extended linking, in combination with strong link typing (see below), should make it practical and achievable.

The topic maps paradigm elegantly solves consistency and usability problems faced by people who must collaborate in developing indexes and glossaries, or who must merge multiple indexes into master indexes. When applied to the Web, topic maps are analogous to the Global Positioning System provided by earth-orbiting satellites, allowing Web users to determine their current locations in a multidimensional "topic space".

34.2.4 *Intellectual property management*

The advent of extended linking also offers interesting new possibilities for the management and exploitation of intellectual property.

For example, metadata regarding the licensing policies of owners of Web resources could be associated with those resources by means of extended links. Such metadata could be changed when the resources are sold or licensed, without requiring any changes to the assets themselves.

This method greatly reduces the likelihood of inadvertent damage to the assets, and greatly increases the ease with which ownership and/or management policies can change. There is already an official, internationally-ratified ISO standard for using extended linking for exactly this purpose.

Such activity policies, and the means by which they are associated with online assets, could well become a source of private law that will strongly influence the development of intelligent agents.

34.3 | Strong link typing

With the XLink extended link facility, there is no limit to the number of links that can be traversed from a single point in a single document. Many different documents can contain links to the very same anchor, with the result that, theoretically, at least, an unlimited number of traversals are possible, starting from a single point. In addition, there are no limits on the kinds of annotations that can be made, nor on the purposes to which such annotations may be put.

Therefore, it makes sense to provide some easy way to sort the annotations (i.e., the links) into categories. For example, some kinds of annotations will be made in order to provide "metadata" about the document, and these will often take effect in some way other than by rendering an icon on the display screen. Some kinds of annotations are interesting only for specialized purposes.

34.3.1   *Hiding the installation log*

Going back to our earlier example, the technician can create an annotation that indicates the serial number of a new part that he installed in accordance with a particular maintenance procedure. The fact that such an annotation is available would be of interest only to someone who was auditing the installation of parts; it probably wouldn't appear even to the technician, despite the fact that it was he who created the annotation.

The technician's installation log annotation can be hidden from most people because it is "strongly typed": it has been clearly and unambiguously labeled as to its intended meaning and purpose, so all browsers can see what kind of link it is. In effect, the link says, "I am a Part-Installation-Log-Entry". People who aren't interested in part installation records can arrange for their browsers to hide them.

34.3.2   *Why do we need strong link typing?*

People may still choose to be made aware of other kinds of annotations made by our technician. For example, other technicians may wish to read our technician's accounts of any special situations that he has experienced when attempting to follow a particular instruction, or about successful and unsuccessful experiments with substitute parts.

The notion of "strong link typing" is virtually absent from HTML links. Basically, in HTML, the browser software knows where the user can go, but not why the author of the document being browsed thought the user might like to go there. The human reader can usually divine something from the context about the material that will be shown if the "anchor" hyperlink is traversed, but the browser itself is basically unable to help the user decide whether to click or not to click, so it can't hide any available traversals.

To be able to hide the availability of unwanted kinds of links can save a lot of time and effort. So the W3C XLink Recommendation also provides for the addition of strong typing features, not only to extended links, but also to the "simple" links that closely resemble the familiar HTML anchor (<a>) element. Thus, browsers can start supporting strong link typing promptly, even before they can handle extended linking.

34.3.3 *Anchor role identification*

The notion of strong link typing includes the notion of "anchor role" designation.

For example, the simple link at the top of Figure 34-1 characterizes its target anchor as an installation instruction; in the diagram, this is indicated by the "I" icon in the arrowhead. Similarly, the extended link at the bottom of Figure 34-1 characterizes one of its anchors as a shop note (the exclamation point) and the other anchor as an installation instruction (another "I" arrowhead).

Thus, a link can do more than just identify itself by saying, for example, "I am a Part Installation Log Entry". It can also specify which of its anchors fulfill which roles in the relationship it expresses.

For example, our Part Installation Log Entry link can say, in effect, "I signify that part [pointer to entry in parts catalog or inventory record] was installed in [pointer to information that identifies the unit being maintained] in accordance with maintenance directive [XPointer to instruction in manual]".

In other words, the log entry link is a three-ended link whose anchor roles might be named "replacement-part" (indicated with a "#" icon), "maintained-unit" ("@" icon), and "maintenance-directive" ("I" icon) (Figure 34-4).

The fact that an anchor plays some specific role in a relationship often determines whether the relationship is interesting or even relevant in a given application context.

34.4 | Conclusion

It is easy to see that the impact of extended linking will be significant, and that technical workers and electronic commerce will be early beneficiaries. Extended linking will enhance the helpfulness and usefulness of the Web

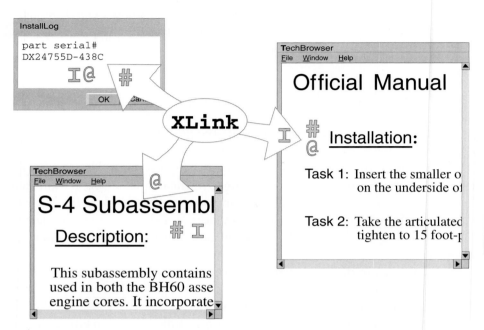

Figure 34-4 Link with two traversal possibilities at each anchor, distinguishable because of anchor role identification.

environment. The burden of many kinds of paperwork will be very substantially mitigated.

On the horizon, there appears to be serious potential for significant improvements in the availability of all kinds of knowledge, due to the possibility of creating and interchanging topic maps. Intellectual property management, and the Web-based utilization of intellectual property, will become easier and more orderly.

All of these benefits, and probably many more, emanate from two very simple enhancements of the Web paradigm in the XLink and XPointers Recommendations of the World Wide Web Consortium:

- Allowing the starting anchor of a link to be different from the link itself; and

■ Strong link typing, in which links plainly exhibit the kind of relationship they represent, and the roles their anchors play in that relationship.

Tip   For more on XLink, see Chapter 65, "XML Linking Language (XLink)", on page 1068. XPointer is covered in Chapter 64, "XML Pointer Language (XPointer)", on page 1052. The text of the XLink and XPointer specs are on the CD-ROM.

Topic maps: Knowledge navigation aids

Introductory Discussion

- Topic maps in a nutshell
- Indexes, glossaries, and thesauri
- Topic map applications
- Tools for topic maps
- Free software on CD-ROM

Sponsor: Ontopia, http://www.ontopia.net

Contributing experts: Hans Holger Rath and Steve Pepper, of the ISO topic map standards group (ISO/IEC JTC1/SC34/WG3)

Chapter
35

Here's another reason we need the Semantic Web. True story: Charles was searching an online shopping site for a CD by the doo-wop greats, the Flamingos. Because of his interest, he was also offered a pink neon bird sculpture. That site needs topic maps! This chapter explains why, and might lead you to think that yours does too.

Ever want to fire your Web search engine for bringing you thousands of useless pages? Or to navigate from one Web page to another on the same subject when there is no link between them? Then you want topic maps.

When you ask your Web browser to search for "Mozart", that composer is the "topic" of your search and you hope to find Web pages that are in some way devoted to it. The browser might actually find such pages, but they will probably be lost among the thousands of pages in which "Mozart" is simply a word that occurs in passing and in no way the main topic of the page.

Similarly, when you look up "Mozart" in the index of a book, you hope to find the pages whose topic is Mozart.

So topics are a familiar concept, one that we work with all the time. What then are topic maps and why do we need them?

Well, suppose you want to find out about operas composed by German composers that were influenced by Mozart. There is no way to formulate such a query in a Web search engine. You can try to use a set of relevant keywords such as "opera + Germany + composer + Mozart", but you are guaranteed to get an enormous number of useless hits. You are also guaranteed to miss some of the most interesting pages. More importantly, even if the search were extremely accurate, you would still have to wade through all the resulting documents simply to find the names of the works you are interested in.

How much easier if you could simply query your index for all *operas* "written by" *composers* associated with *Germany* ("born in" or "lived in") and with *Mozart* ("influenced by")!

The key difference between the two approaches is that the former simply uses a full text index built from the raw content of a set of information resources. The latter, however, utilizes an index that encapsulates the structure of the underlying knowledge.

The latter solution is actually an example of a *topic map*; that is, a structured network of hyperlinks above an information pool. Each node in the network represents a named topic (e.g. Germany, Mozart, Wagner). The links connecting the nodes express the associations between the nodes (e.g. written by, lived in, influenced by).

From this it should be clear that indexes are actually very simple forms of topic maps. So, too, are glossaries and thesauri. This chapter will explain the basic concepts of topic maps, how they relate to the kinds of navigational aids we are already familiar with, what additional benefits they provide, and how to create and use them. We'll also look at some applications and consider requirements for topic map tools.

35.1 | Topic maps in a nutshell

A topic map models a domain of knowledge in terms of:

- the topics of that domain,
- their interrelationships (or "associations"), and
- occurrences of relevant information resources. [1]

We'll explain those concepts in this section, along with a few more:

- topic types,
- association types,

1. The map can be interchanged as an XML document conforming to the XML Topic Maps (XTM) Specification or as an SGML document conforming to the International Standard ISO/IEC 13250.

- occurrence types,
- identity, and
- scope

35.1.1   *Topic and topic type*

In the context of an encyclopedia, a *topic* might represent a subject such as "Germany", "Bavaria", "Munich", the king "Ludwig II", or the opera "Lohengrin" by the composer "Richard Wagner": anything that might have an entry (or indeed a mention) in the encyclopedia.

The subject represented by a topic can be any "thing" whatsoever – a person, an entity, a concept, really *anything*, regardless of whether it exists or has any other specific characteristics, about which anything whatsoever may be asserted by any means whatsoever. Exactly what one chooses to regard as topics in any particular application will vary according to the needs of the application, the nature of the information, and the uses to which the topic map will be put.

A topic can have a number of characteristics. First of all, it can have a *name* – or more than one. The standard provides an element form for *topic name* which consists of at least one *base name*, and optional *display* and *sort* names.

A topic also has a *topic type* – or perhaps multiple topic types. Thus, Germany would be a topic of type "country", Bavaria a topic of type "state", Munich and Würzburg topics of type "city", Ludwig II a topic of type "king", etc. In other words, topic types express typical *class-instance* relationships or the *is a* relation (see Figure 35-1).

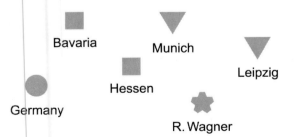

Figure 35-1   Topic names and types (represented by different symbols)

Topic types are themselves defined as topics. In order to use them for typing, you have to explicitly declare "country", "state", "city", etc. as topics in your topic map, and this then allows you to say more about them using the topic map model itself.

35.1.2 *Topic occurrence and occurrence type*

A topic can have one or more *occurrences*. An occurrence of a topic is a link to an information resource (or more than one) that is deemed to be somehow relevant to the subject that the topic represents. It could be an article about the topic in an encyclopedia, a picture or video depicting the topic, a simple mention of the topic in the context of something else, a commentary on the topic, or any of a host of other forms in which an information resource might have some relevance to a given subject.

Such resources are generally outside the topic map document itself, and they are "pointed at" using whatever addressing mechanisms the system supports, typically XPointer or HyTime.

Occurrences may be of any number of different types (we gave the examples of "article", "illustration", "mention" and "commentary" above). Such distinctions are supported in the standard by the concept of the *occurrence type* (see Figure 35-2). As with topic types, each occurrence type is formally considered to be a topic, although the actual occurrences are not.

35.1.3 *Indexes and glossaries*

As described so far, topics and occurrences provide a model for explicitly stating which subjects a pool of information pertains to and how. That is basically what an index also does.

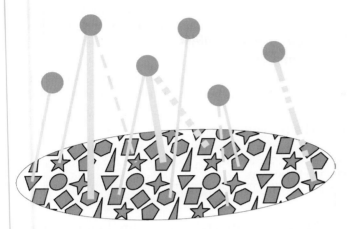

Figure 35-2   Occurrences of topics in an information pool and their various occurrence types (represented by different line types).

In Example 35-1, the index terms are topics and the page numbers are locators for their occurrences.

Example 35-1. An index is a simple form of topic map.

Germany 17, 77
Mozart 72
Wagner 49
Würzburg 22

But topic maps offer more. Through the concept of occurrence types, they generalize and extend the conventions used to distinguish different kinds of references from one another.

In Example 35-2 the use of different typefaces indicates that the occurrences on pages 17 and 77 are of different types (perhaps a *main description* and a *mention*).

Example 35-2. An index with occurrence types

Germany **17**, 77

Some books contain more than one index (index of names, index of places, etc.). *Topic types* provide the same facility, but extend it in several directions to enable the creation of multiple, dynamic, user-controlled indexes organized as taxonomic hierarchies.

Glossaries, too, can be implemented using just the bare bones of the topic map standard that has been described so far. Like an index, a glossary is also a set of topics and their occurrences, ordered by topic name. Here, though, the occurrence type is "definition".

Example 35-3. A glossary is a topic map.

Federal Republic of Germany: see *Germany*.

...

Germany: Federal republic in the northern part of central Europe, population (1998) approx. 82 million.

...

Würzburg: City in Bavaria, Germany on the river Main, 90 km south-east of Frankfurt. 128.000 inhabitants (1998).

Note that "Federal Republic of Germany" does not have a definition. It is just another name for the topic that also has the name "Germany", and in this map there can be only one definition per topic.

The definitions in Example 35-3 are instances of just one kind of occurrence — those whose type is "definition". With a topic map it is easy to create and maintain much more complex glossaries than this; for example, ones that use multiple kinds of definitions (perhaps suited to different kinds of users).

35.1.4 *Association and association type*

Topic maps don't stop here, however. They go far beyond just providing a mechanism for creating more robust and powerful indexes and glossaries. The key to their true potential lies in their ability to model *relationships* between topics, and for this the topic map standard provides a construct called a *association*.

An association is an assertion of a relationship between two or more topics. Examples might be as follows:

- Munich *is in* Bavaria.
- Bavaria *is in* Germany.
- Wagner was *born in* Leipzig.
- Lohengrin was *composed by* Wagner.
- Wagner was *influenced by* Mozart.

Just as topics can be grouped according to type (country, state, city, etc.) and occurrences likewise (definition, article, illustration, commentary, etc.), so too can associations between topics be grouped according to their type. The *association types* of the five relationships in the list above are "is in", "born in", "composed by" and "influenced by" (see Figure 35-3). Association types are themselves topics (e.g. "is in"), although associations (e.g. "Bavaria *is in* Germany") are not.[2]

35.1.4.1 Association role

Each topic that participates in an association has a corresponding *association role* which states the role played by that topic in the association. In the case of the relationship "Wagner was born in Leipzig" those roles might be "person" and "birthplace"; for "Lohengrin was written by Wagner" they might be "opera" and "composer".

Like topic types, individual association roles must be declared as topics in order to be used.

35.1.4.2 Association topology

In the topic map model, associations do not have a direction; that is, they are not one-way (or "unilateral"). The "born in" relationship between Wagner and Leipzig implies what might be called a "fostered" relationship between the city and the composer ("Leipzig fostered Wagner"), and the "composed by" relationship between Lohengrin and Wagner is also a "composed" relationship between the composer and his opera ("Wagner composed Lohengrin").

---

2. However, associations can become topics when required through a process called *reification*, which allows statements to be made about statements (e.g., "Wagner was influenced by Mozart *according to Ernest Newman*").

Sometimes associations are *symmetrical*, in the sense that the nature of the relationship is the same whichever way you look at it. For example, the corollary of "Wagner was a friend of Ludwig II" would be that "Ludwig II was a friend of Wagner". Sometimes the association roles in such symmetrical relationships are the same (as in this case: "friend" and "friend"), sometimes they are different (as in the case of the "husband" and "wife" roles in a "married to" relationship).

Other association types, such as those that express supertype/subtype and some part/whole relationships, are *transitive*: If we say that Munich is in Bavaria, and that Bavaria is in Germany, we have implicitly asserted that Munich is in Germany and any topic map search engine should be able to draw the necessary conclusions without the need for making the assertion explicitly. Much of the real power of topic maps results from using transitive relations between topics, types, and roles for querying the map.

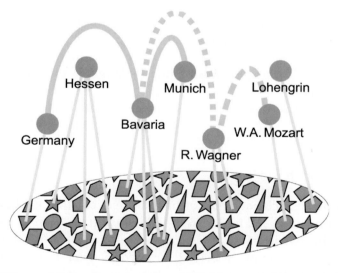

Figure 35-3   Associations of various types between topics (represented by different line types)

35.1.5 *Thesauri and semantic networks*

The concept of typed associations extends the power of topic maps to the modeling of thesauri and other networks of information and knowledge.

A *thesaurus* is a network of interrelated terms (along with their definitions, examples, or whatever) within a particular domain. There exist various standards for thesauri that predefine relationship types, such as "broader term", "narrower term", "used for", and "related term", all of which correspond directly to association types in a topic map. Other thesaurus constructs, such as "source", "definition", and "scope note" would be modeled as occurrence types in a topic map.

One advantage of applying the topic map model to thesauri is that it becomes possible to create hierarchies of association types that extend the thesaurus schema without deviating from accepted standards (for example, by subclassing "used for" as "synonymous for", "abbreviation for", and "acronym for"). Further advantages would be gained from using the facilities for scoping, filtering and merging described in the next three sections.

"Semantic networks", "associative networks" and "knowledge" (or "conceptual") "maps" are terms used within the fields of semantics and artificial intelligence to describe various models for representing knowledge structures within a computer. Many of these already correspond closely to the topic/association model. Adding the topic/occurrence axis provides a means for "bridging the gap" between these fields and the field of information management, thereby establishing a basis for true knowledge management.

35.1.6 *Scope*

When I refer to "Paris", you know immediately that I am talking about the capital city of France. Or do you? How do you know that I'm not talking about the town of the same name in Texas or the hero of Troy? Presumably because you are assuming a *scope* set by some form of context, whether it be a particular subject area under discussion or a generally accepted default.

The concept of scope is important for avoiding ambiguities like this and for increasing the precision with which assertions can be made. In topic maps, any assignment of a characteristic to a topic, be it a name, an occurrence or a role in an association, is considered to be valid within certain limits, which may or may not be specified explicitly. The limit of validity of such an assignment is called its *scope*; scope is defined in terms of *themes*, and themes are modeled as topics.

So, in topic maps where the scope is defined by the themes "France", "USA", and "Greek mythology", the name "Paris" could be used unambiguously. Similarly the association expressing the assertion that "Leipzig *is in* East Germany" could be qualified by giving it the scope "1949-90".

35.1.7 *Subject identity*

Sometimes the same subject is represented by more than one topic. This can be the case when two topic maps are merged. In such a situation it is necessary to have some way of establishing the identity between seemingly disparate topics.

This can be done in either of two ways:

■ Explicitly, by specifying the same *subject identity* for the two topics; or
■ Implicitly, through the *topic naming constraint*, which states that any topics that have the same name in the same scope refer to the same subject.

The ability to merge topic maps opens up the possibility of *federating knowledge*. Topic maps can even be used to federate knowledge expressed according to different ontologies.

35.2 | Applications of topic maps

We will consider two applications. They both involve publishing, but topic maps have broad applicability in other areas as well.

35.2.1 *Reference work publishing*

In the age of digital information all commercial publishers face major new challenges, but perhaps none more so than publishers of reference works, especially encyclopedias and dictionaries. Not only has the advent of the

World Wide Web finally forced all such publishers to think seriously about moving into electronic publishing; it has also turned out to be perhaps their biggest and most threatening competitor.

The reason for this, of course, is that the raw material from which reference works are fashioned consists for the most part of "hard facts" that cannot be owned. The knowledge that Wagner was born in Leipzig or that the population of Germany is about 82 million cannot be copyrighted. Almost every piece of information to be found in any modern, commercial encyclopedia can be found somewhere on the Internet for free. So how is a reference work publisher to compete?

35.2.1.1   Adding value

Paradoxically, the answer lies in the fact that most users today do not need more information – if anything, they need less, because they are already drowning in enormous quantities of it. At the very least, they need the ability to be able to find their way to relevant information as quickly as possible and to be able to filter out the "noise" created by all the information for which they have no use. They also need to be able to trust the information they receive, to know that it is reliable and up-to-date. Thus, two of the most important "value-adds" that commercial publishers can provide are

- tools and methods for finding the required information in a timely manner; and
- the confidence that the information so found can be trusted.

Topic maps can greatly assist the discovery of relevant information. In addition, the topic paradigm turns out to provide an *organizing principle* for many kinds of information that helps ensure its timeliness and accuracy.

35.2.1.2   A typical topic map

Encyclopedia articles are – at a very abstract level – about persons, geographical objects, history, culture, and science. These are the main *topic types*. Existing classification systems list further subclasses of these topic types, such as:

- historic person (monarch [emperor, king, queen], politician, [president, chancellor], explorer), artists (writer [novelist, poet], painter, sculptor, composer, musician), scientists (mathematician, physicist, chemist, biologist, physician);
- country, state, landscape, city/town, river, mountain, island.

The *occurrence types* point to the resources of an encyclopedia publisher. Typical data assets are articles, definitions, mentions of the topic in an article, pictures/images, audio, and video clips.

Even more interesting (because of the value added to the publication) are the *association types* that are used to structure the mass of cross-references normally found in such works. Common examples are:

- ruled over, conquered;
- painted, composed, wrote, played, discovered, invented;
- parent of, child of;
- located in, larger than;
- took place, before, after;
- discovered by, conquered by, founded by, invented by.

Some of these are simply different names for the same association type viewed from different perspectives (e.g. conquered/conquered by, parent of/child of). Others exhibit the important property of transitivity (e.g. located in, larger than).

It is a good idea to identify transitive relationships like these because the topic map engine can use this information to generate more intelligent answers to the queries of the user.

An encyclopedia that is based on and governed by a comprehensive topic map has a number of unique advantages:

- Navigation is much easier and much more consistent.
- The user interface (indeed, multiple user interfaces) can be generated automatically from the topic map.
- New information resources are easily integrated.
- Multiple viewpoints of the same subject matter can be represented.
- The map itself becomes an asset in its own right, independent of the information resources it covers.

35.2.2 *Technical documentation*

Technical documentation for a complex product could consist of thousands of pages, or megabytes of textual data. Corporate publishers have to manage and publish the documentation for different product versions and product variants. More ambitious corporate publishers add reader-related information to the publications ("skill level" is the typical example) or publish different views of the same material ("Overview", "Reference Manual", "Questions and Answers", etc.).

Versions, variants, and views require a more complex organization of the text than the sequential ordering of a printed book. XML alone cannot meet these requirements; publishers must also change the information management paradigm.

35.2.2.1 Text modules

Modularization of the text is the first step towards an appropriate solution. The existing chapter-section-subject structure of book-oriented technical documentation is split up into hundreds or thousands of separate text modules (information objects). The modules consist of "self-contained" text about a given subject (e.g. "Installation"). Hyperlinks connect the modules.

Hierarchical subject codes – assigned as metadata – allow quick access when querying the database containing the modules.

These two characteristics (self-contained text, hierarchical subject codes) indicate a class of technical documentation that is an ideal candidate for a topic map application.

35.2.2.2 A typical topic map

The identification of *topic types* can be based on the subject code classification. If this is not available, the technical design of the product or semantic markup in the documentation will give the necessary hints. In software documentation for example, the topic types might consist of "program block", "command group", "command", "macro", "parameter", "error", etc.

The *occurrence types* would relate to existing modularized material. Data modules, functional diagrams, tables, screen shots, error messages, and syntax examples are among the possibilities.

Finally, *association types* can be derived from knowledge of the relationships between the topic types already identified: "command group A *consists of* commands X, Y, and Z", "command X *has parameters* P and Q", etc.

35.3 | Tool support for topic maps

Possibilities for tool support exist at each phase of the topic map life cycle.

35.3.1 *Topic map design*

The design of topic maps is an incremental process. The definition of the various types and roles and sub-/super-classes of them should be done under the control of a topic map design tool. Doing so will help ensure the consistency of the map.

Outside the scope of the topic map standard, but nevertheless very useful, are constraining conditions that can drive consistency checks. They make it possible to check whether transitive associations are used correctly, whether the types of topics in an association correspond to the respective association roles, etc.

Another part of the topic map design is the generation of all the topics, associations, and occurrences. In a large application these can be numbered in the thousands or even millions. The design tool has to offer an easy access to all these objects of the map.

As in a content management system, user access rights play an important role in a topic map design tool. Permission for creating, changing, and deleting parts of the map could be assigned to different user groups with different responsibilities, and the system has to take care that these rules are enforced.

35.3.2 *Creation and maintenance*

The boundary between the design and the creation of a topic map is fluid. Only the initial design will distinguish the declaration of types and roles on the one hand, and the topics, associations, and occurrences on the other.

During the maintenance of the map these will be done concurrently – maybe by different user groups.

The editors (designer, author) of the topic map need a visualization tool besides the consistency checker. The visualization tool produces a rendition of the map that is similar to the one the end-users will see. The querying possibilities should also be similar.

The initial creation of the map out of an existing information pool can probably be supported by an automatic rule-based process. This process can be compared to the conversion of word processor files to XML. Both add explicit structure to apparently "flat" data.

A conversion for topic maps takes as its input information objects in which the topics and associations exist only implicitly, and produces a linked and structured knowledge base as output.

35.3.3 *Exchange of topic maps*

The publication of topic maps will be done electronically, since paper-based presentations of any but the simplest of topic maps are to all intents and purposes impossible. The topic map document architecture defined in the standard is the interface between topic map design and creation tools, and the topic map browser – the rendition and navigation tool of the end-user.

Note that this interchange standard does not address application-specific semantics such as the "association topology" properties described earlier. Work is currently underway in the ISO and the topic map community to address this requirement through a "Topic Map Constraint Language".

35.3.4 *Navigating a map*

There are two ways to navigate a topic map: by traversing the links or by directly addressing the nodes through queries.

Traversal of a large link network – possibly consisting of millions of nodes and links – requires an easy-to-use and easy-to-understand user interface. Very sophisticated colorful graphical user interfaces with nodes and edges that move in accordance with physical laws (like magnetism or gravity) might be eye-catchers.

However, a familiar interface like a Web search engine might prove to be practical. Figure 35-4, for example, shows the *Ontopia Omnigator*, which is built on top of the *Ontopia Topic Map Engine*. It provides a browser-like interface for navigating via associations from topic to topic and also from topics to occurrences.

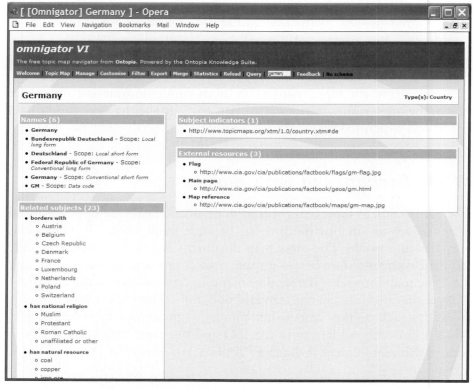

Figure 35-4   The *Ontopia Omnigator*

Querying a topic map requires a query language covering the concepts of the topic map standard and desirable application-specific semantics (associations, transitivity). The user needs additional support when defining a query – the information available in the map can be offered to the user by the query interface, e.g. in a menu-like style.

There should also be the possibility to "build-in" the knowledge that, say, the (virtual) topic type "clarinetist" is in fact a synthesis of all topics of type "person" that are connected via a "player of" association with the topic "clarinet". This will allow the user to work in a very intuitive manner and ensure very precise query results.

35.4 | Adoption

Topic map capabilities are starting to appear in products for content management, source code control, product data management, and groupware, among others.

Topic maps also complement the Resource Description Framework (RDF).[3] RDF makes it possible to assign metadata to information resources in the World Wide Web. Topic maps can utilize this metadata to automatically build a navigational layer – "conceptual map" – of the resource domain.

And as we have seen, topic maps have also been designed to be merged easily, and to mediate between different ontologies. All of these facts underscore the importance of topic maps to the Semantic Web.

35.5 | Conclusion

The ability to apply multiple topic maps to arbitrary information pools has enormous potential for the World Wide Web. Website owners and independent third parties can develop and apply topic maps to collections of websites, thereby providing an overall information context for them.

Instead of relying solely on physical addresses, which have no information context, a surfer could check his location in an applicable topic map to

---

3. Discussed in Chapter 36, "RDF: Metadata description for Web resources", on page 580.

see where he is in an information space. In other words, topic maps can act as the global positioning system (GPS) for the World Wide Web.

Tip   *Try out topic maps for yourself with the free copy of Omnigator on the CD-ROM. There are eight sample topic maps and you can create your own as well.*

RDF: Metadata description for Web resources

Introductory Discussion

- Resource Description Framework (RDF)
- Resources and resource identifiers
- RDF schemas
- Harvesting metadata
- Metadata queries

Contributing experts: Dr. Janne Saarela and Dr. Martyn Horner

Chapter

36

To paraphrase Will Rogers: "I never metadata I didn't like!" The problem is that we don't meet with enough of it. The Web floods us with information, but not enough metadata to organize that information and make it navigable. RDF is another technology that offers the promise of a Semantic Web, and powerful information routing for the enterprise as well.

The World Wide Web has made it possible to spread information further and in greater quantities than ever before. So much so that most of us are drowning in it!

36.1 | What is metadata?

Finding what you need on the Web is becoming harder and harder. Tools like search engines, which are everyone's key to the Web, must become ever more ingenious to sort out the good from the bad, the harmful, and the simply irrelevant.

The solution depends on metadata.

36.1.1 *Indexes are metadata*

Search engines traditionally deal directly with information. They find it by looking through the text of Web pages. This is like browsing in a library, going from shelf to shelf and book to book, when the fast way to the book you need is through the library index.

Making such indexes for the Web and keeping them current is the job of the Web's librarians. Modern search engines are investing more and more computing power for this purpose. An index is a form of *metadata*: "data about data" or "information about information".

In a library, the book you want – or on the Web, the content you want – is a *resource* that your work (or recreation!) requires. To find that resource, you must first know some metadata about it, and knowledge about resources is what RDF is all about.

36.1.2   *Properties are metadata*

RDF stands for *Resource Description Framework*. A description of a thing is actually a description of its characteristics, or *properties*, another form of metadata. RDF is a method of recording such descriptions.

The basic unit of RDF is the *statement*. It makes a single connection between a resource and the value of one of that resource's properties. A book, for example, can have such properties as:

- author,
- publisher,
- page count,
- publication date,
- books that it refers to,
- books that refer to it, and so on.

Each of these properties has a name – "author", "publisher", etc. – that is, in some sense, universal. The RDF statement associates a resource through a property to the resource's value of that property; that value is particular to the resource. In other words, RDF brings together the universal – property names – and the particular – property values of resources.

The property value may be a literal character string or a number. However, it might also be something else in the information landscape – perhaps a book, a Web page or a person – in which case that, too, is a resource to which connections can be made.

The association of resources with other resources constructs a "web" of metadata potentially as rich and detailed as the World Wide Web that it describes. Because information has no worth if it can't be found, the metadata adds value to its underlying information and therefore has value in its own right.

36.2 | RDF data model

RDF is normally represented in XML, but XML itself only provides semantics for generic characteristics of all structured information, such as:

- the identification of data elements of named types, but not the meaning of the types;
- hierarchical relationships among the elements; and
- the existence of named properties (attributes) of elements, but not their meaning.

RDF, like other XML applications, provides additional meaning. In this case, the *RDF data model.*

36.2.1 *Resources*

The core concept of RDF is the recognition of a resource. The simplistic way to think of a resource is as a URI, but there are subtleties lurking behind that simplification.

As we try to locate useful items in our information universe, we necessarily assume that they will stay still long enough to be located. We think of the target of our search as a physical item – a document, a person, an institution, even a piece of text or a number – and we believe that it is constant, at least until we locate it.

Of course, this is a false belief.

People change even as you try to find them: they grow older and perhaps wiser. Documents can be updated even when they have the good manners to stay in the same place. Equally, they can stay unchanged (and maintain their usefulness to you) even though they are moved around physically on a computer's disk.

The important mental step to take here is to think of your search target not as the item itself, but as a *resource*: something that contains the *relevant essence* of the item. In other words, the aspects of the item that you need to rely on for your present purposes.

So locating a person as an email address might be quite sufficient for business purposes, even though your correspondent's appearance and geographical location might have changed. If the "person" is an institution, it might even have changed its entire physical identity.

However, those kinds of change don't matter. The resource for your purpose is the relevant essence of the person; in this case, the email address.

Conceiving of resources in this way allows references to them to survive many changes over time and space.

36.2.2 *Resource identifiers*

In the real data universe of the World Wide Web, resources are identified by URIs.

A URI doesn't actually say where a resource is to be found, but gives a (supposedly reliable) procedure for locating it. Location should be possible over a practically useful stretch of time and from a reasonable range of equipment. The access procedures of the Web – DNS name servers, routers, proxies, etc. – work to guarantee that the URI will provide access to the indicated resource.

The concept of URI is therefore tightly bound to the concept of resource. However, the concept of resource, as we have seen, is less tightly bound to a physical item than one might have thought.

Now that we understand what a resource is, we can use the term more precisely. A resource, as identified by a URI, is both unique and universal. We therefore apply the term not only to items being connected by an RDF statement, but also for the property names and other fixed points in the RDF data model.

For example, we will shortly refer to some property names taken from a vocabulary called "Dublin Core". The "creator" property from this vocabulary would formally be referred to by its full resource identification: `http://purl.org/dc/elements/1.1/creator`.

36.2.3 *Triples*

An element of RDF is called a `triple`. It connects a resource – the "subject" – via a universal property name – the "predicate" – to a particular property value – the "object".

subject
> This can be any resource.

predicate
> This resource is a member of a relatively restricted set of resources.

object
> This is either another resource or a literal character string or number.

These three elements of a triple – subject, predicate and object – form a *statement*.[1] Resources can participate in multiple statements, as shown in Figure 36-1.

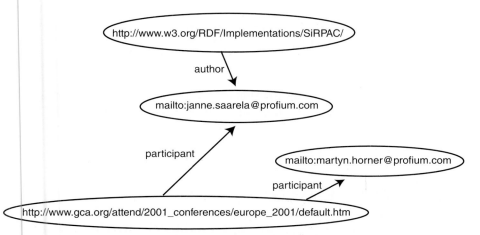

Figure 36-1   Graphical representation of three RDF statements

---

1. The term is an accurate English grammar metaphor for an RDF triple.

36.3 | RDF schemas

RDF offers the facility of constructing type systems called *RDF schemas*.

The RDF type system follows the object-oriented modeling paradigm, utilizing classes and properties. Membership in a class implies the sharing of common characteristics of the class.

Properties, however, are not bound to classes: any property can be exhibited by any type of object.

RDF schemas provide a formal means to describe the semantics of properties. The semantics are expressed in one or more natural languages. Applications can make use of this information to prompt users who are unfamiliar with a property.

In the same way that XML DTDs and schemas can be used to validate XML documents, RDF schemas can be used to validate RDF data model instances. However, just as with XML, validation is an option; applications can choose to deal only with the data.

We've discussed several metadata vocabulary initiatives in this book. Some of them have bindings to RDF schemas, for example:

Dublin Core, `www.dublincore.org`
> Dublin Core defines bibliographic metadata, such as "creator", "date", and "format". Bindings of its properties exist for markup languages like HTML, as well as for RDF.

PRISM, `www.prismstandard.org`
> PRISM defines metadata for the syndication and post-processing of media industry content. Its properties include "event", "industry", "location", "expiration time", and "has alternative".

36.4 | Putting RDF to work

RDF, like WebDAV and topic maps, is a technology widely promoted for its potential to contribute to the Semantic Web. Fortunately, as with those other technologies, we can start with a more tractable domain!

At the enterprise level, RDF can be applied with a single vocabulary, designed to suit the activity. A quality-controlled process can be put in place for creating RDF metadata models. And because there is a known target audience, firm criteria can be established for functionality and performance.

Let's take a high level look at the stages in utilizing RDF.

36.4.1 *Harvesting metadata*

An RDF application begins by storing the input information stream, at the same time harvesting metadata from it. The metadata could occur in several forms, both implicit and explicit:

annotated

Some XML documents are annotated with metadata in the form of additional elements and attributes. This markup might have been inserted with an XML editor during editing, or applied with a suitable tool during conversion to XML.

derived

Metadata that isn't explicitly marked can be derived from the data content using tools that can be attached to the input process. These *metadata enrichment* programs use various levels of machine intelligence and heuristics to extract metadata from plain text.

intrinsic

In between the previous two there are representations, such as SOAP and ICE, where metadata must be present as an integral part of the delivery mechanism. Unlike derived metadata, parsing is straightforward and unambiguous. And unlike annotated metadata, it has to be there or the information couldn't have been delivered in the first place!

The product can compensate for a degree of irregularity in the input stream. It also maps between vocabularies and can derive metadata from the stream itself, such as "source", "dates", "ownership", etc.

The result of this stage is a managed pool of content and a web of metadata to describe it.

36.4.2 *Querying*

Metadata, as we have seen, represents information about information. Therefore, to find answers to questions about the information, you must first ask (slightly different) questions about the information about the information.

These questions can become even more complex than that sentence!

Generally, though, it is easier to ask about metadata than about data, since the vocabulary is controlled and specific to the enterprise.

For example, you could ask regarding a financial news feed:

> Find any mention of Nokia's activities in Helsinki during the years 1995 to 2001 and compare the reports from Reuters and United Press International; I only read English.

If you had no metadata repository, but only the text in a huge collection of files, you would have to devise some pretty clever search algorithms. They would need to look for:

- the names "Nokia" and "Helsinki" (and only in context: no use looking for activities in the little Finnish town of Nokia, since Nokia the corporation has long since moved to Espoo!);
- numbers that look like the specified dates (all of them, in all formats);
- the copyrighted texts from the news agencies; and
- something to ensure that the text is in English.

Imagine what a Web search engine would do with this problem!

Figure 36-2 illustrates a browser-based graphical interface to assist in formulating queries like this one.

Queries can be simple ("documents by author Smith") or complex, involving comparisons and correspondences and levels of sub-queries. The visual form of the query is converted into an internal form for execution, or into XML for interchange.

Figure 36-2   An RDF-based query editor

36.4.3 *Routing*

The value of RDF metadata is not just in *finding* information in a large information base. It also allows us to *evaluate* that large body of information by executing queries on a much smaller sample.

That in turn provides an automatic means of determining what to do with the content – send it by email, transmit it to a PDA, publish it on paper, broadcast it via TV – and what sort of embellishments one can add – styles, annotations, branding.

Think of it as "semantic-based routing". Formatting and delivery can be controlled according to the semantic metadata.

Topic Map Applications

- Enhancing gathered intelligence
- Topic map interfaces and constraints
- Application integration with topic maps

Part Twelve

Topic maps might seem like an arcane technology, but you've been using topic map applications forever.

A back-of-the-book index is a simple topic map. It is an alphabetical list of – well, topics! The page numbers serve as pointers to occurrences of the topics within the book.

A thesaurus is a more complex topic map application. Its topics are ideas, organized in a hierarchy. Lists of words and phrases are the occurrences of the topics.

In this part we'll show you much more interesting topic maps. One helps a military intelligence agency find precise answers to questions about its millions of documents.

Another shows that topic maps aren't limited to static information bases. You can use them to manage workflow and integrate your applications!

Improving intelligence for Intelligence

Case Study

- Maritime Intelligence Organization
- Topic map application
- Automatically generated user interfaces
- Schema constraints for topic maps

Sponsor: Innodata Isogen, http://www.innodata-isogen.com
Contributing expert: Jennifer M. Brock

Chapter

37

For the Maritime Intelligence Organization, full text searches of intelligence documents yielded too much text and not enough intelligence. Skilled analysts combed search results for insights and relationships – which just wound up in more documents. To provide precise answers for specific questions, topic maps were the intelligent choice!

T he Maritime Intelligence Organization (MaritInt) is the chief provider of maritime intelligence for a large community of government intelligence services and their clients. Like most things military, MaritInt's information base is vast, not just in shear size, but in its breadth and historical scope.[1]

The organization is currently moving from a traditional publishing model, in which comprehensive publications on a subject are shipped in hard copy. The goal is to provide intelligence on demand, tailored to a specific user's immediate needs.

The first step toward that goal was to provide indexing and search tools that allowed customers to search MaritInt's huge plain text database to choose the documents they needed. That left unresolved the problem of assimilating the information to find important relationships in it.

There are analysts who create such reports, of course, with professional assessments of the raw information. However, their work is part of the same document base as the raw data itself. Any relationships they observed

---

1. MaritInt is a fictitious name for a real intelligence organization that, true to the tenets of its trade, wishes to keep its identity secret!

among the raw data items were not queryable as such; they just became more text to be searched with keywords.

37.1 | Full text was a partial solution

The system exhibited problems with both of the classic measures of successful information retrieval: recall and precision.

recall
> Some intelligence was not making it to the consumers. Its full text did not contain the words that described it best. A classic example of this problem is in researching early legal decisions that apply to automobile accidents: those cases concerned horses and wagons, so the word "automobile" never appears in them.

precision
> The information that does reach the consumers requires manually sifting through the results, hit after hit, like a search of the World Wide Web. There is no context to the search, so the reason why a search term appears in the result may have no bearing on the reason for the search. In the legal research for "automobile", for example, a case may have concerned automobile theft, rather than an accident.

Skilled searchers could improve their results by clever use of multiple keywords and Boolean logic, but too much intelligence was still not being found in a timely manner, if indeed it was found at all. In some industries, those failings would be considered annoying, but in the intelligence community they could be fatal!

37.2 | The topic map solution

MaritInt needed to provide its consumers with an efficient way to find precise answers to specific questions. They engaged Innodata Isogen, Inc. to help them explore the feasibility of a new system based on topic maps. We introduced that subject in detail in Chapter 35, "Topic maps: Knowledge navigation aids", on page 560, but we'll cover the basics again in context as we look at the solution.

37.2.1 *Topics and topic types*

The organization has collected data on thousands of topics related to its mission. To keep our discussion simple, we'll reduce the number just slightly – to twenty! Our list of topics is shown in Figure 37-1.

Country	Germany	Russia
Time Frame	Cold War	WWII
Craft	Aircraft	Aircraft A
Watercraft	Destroyer	Destroyer A
Battleship	Battleship A	Battleship B
What	When	Where
Manufactured	Purchased	

Figure 37-1   List of topics

One thing that should be clear from the list is that a topic can be anything! Ours range from countries to crafts to concepts, and from types of topics to specific instances of those types.

The visualization in Figure 37-2 shows the *topic types* Country and Time Frame. They are connected to their topics by broken lines.

Figure 37-2   Two topic types and their topics

Topic types are also topics and can have types of their own, as visualized in Figure 37-3. Once again, types are connected to their topics by broken lines, but another type of relationship is also shown. The solid lines represent the supertype/subtype relationship. That means that `Battleship A`, for example, is not only a `Battleship`, but also a `Watercraft` and a `Craft`.

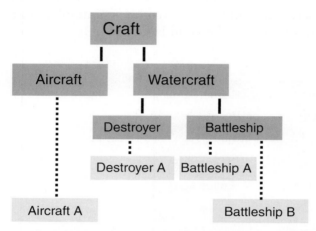

Figure 37-3   A hierarchy of topic types and topics

The figure could as well represent part of a hierarchical thesaurus, or a multiple-level entry in an index. And in fact, those familiar navigation aids are actually simple topic maps. But where a printed index has page numbers to point to the topic *occurrences* within the book, a topic map browser has links into the underlying information base.

That's important, since any one of MaritInt's topics could have thousands of occurrences! Even more important, topic maps can have multiple *occurrence types*, so that occurrences in raw data, for example, can be distinguished from occurrences in a situation analysis.

A hierarchy of topic types provides some context that is lacking in a Web-style full text search, but more was needed to satisfy the requirements. MaritInt's users needed precise answers to questions like:

What information is available about watercraft that was manufactured by Germany in WWII and sold to Russia during the cold war?

You're not likely to find the answer to that by Googling, no matter how lucky you feel! But topic maps can provide it, by using a construct called associations.

37.2.2 *Associations*

A topic *association* is a relationship between two or more topics. Two associations are visualized in Figure 37-4. The left one asserts that Battleship A was manufactured in Germany during WWII. The right one asserts that Battleship A was sold to Russia during the cold war.

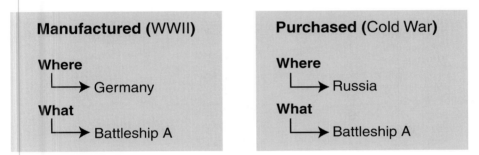

Figure 37-4   Visualization of two associations

Example 37-1 shows how the two associations might be represented in an XML topic map.

The first association is an instance of the *association type* Manufactured, while the second is an instance of Purchased. Both types of association have three *members* – the associated topics.

An association type defines the *roles* that the members play in an association. For both of these association types, the roles are when, what, and where.[2] In the Manufactured example, Battleship A is *what* was manufactured, Germany is *where*, and WWII is *when*.

With these associations, plus the taxonomy in Figure 37-3, there was enough information to answer MaritInt's question. The associations

---

2. Just like topic types, association types and roles are also topics, which is why they are referenced with the same syntax as the actual members.

Example 37-1. Associations represented in an XML topic map

```
<association>
  <instanceOf>
    <topicRef xlink:href="#Manufactured"/>
  </instanceOf>
  <member>
    <roleSpec>
      <topicRef xlink:href="#When"/>
    </roleSpec>
    <topicRef xlink:href="#WWII"/>
  </member>
  <member>
    <roleSpec>
      <topicRef xlink:href="#Where"/>
    </roleSpec>
    <topicRef xlink:href="#Germany"/>
  </member>
  <member>
    <roleSpec>
      <topicRef xlink:href="#What"/>
    </roleSpec>
    <topicRef xlink:href="#Battleship_A"/>
  </member>
</association>
<association>
  <instanceOf>
    <topicRef xlink:href="#Purchased"/>
  </instanceOf>
  <member>
    <roleSpec>
      <topicRef xlink:href="#When"/>
    </roleSpec>
    <topicRef xlink:href="#Cold_War"/>
  </member>
  <member>
    <roleSpec>
      <topicRef xlink:href="#Where"/>
    </roleSpec>
    <topicRef xlink:href="#Russia"/>
  </member>
  <member>
    <roleSpec>
      <topicRef xlink:href="#What"/>
    </roleSpec>
    <topicRef xlink:href="#Battleship_A"/>
  </member>
</association>
```

revealed that Battleship A was manufactured in Germany during WWII and sold to Russia during the cold war. The taxonomy indicated that Battleship A is a watercraft. A topic map engine tied it all together and provided the required precise answer.

37.2.2.1   Creating associations

Associations were the key to solving MaritInt's problem, but they presented a problem of their own – how to create them.

Tools exist for automatic creation of topic maps from a corpus of information, but some amount of human creation of association types and instances is invariably required. Fortunately, there are also tools that can help with the human's task.

Figure 37-5 shows a user interface for creating an instance of the `Manufactured` association type. The tool generated it from the topic map, which includes the definition of the association type. The tool can therefore display the member role names. Each is next to the list box in which the user will select the topic to play that role in the association.

The role names provide essential hints, as you can see by the drop-down list! Every topic in the map is listed, because there is no way for the tool to know which ones are appropriate for each role. It is up to the human to remember which (or consult a list).

This situation presents a significant obstacle, since the time of the trained analysts who are capable of creating associations is valuable. Moreover, in a large topic map (there are actually several thousand more than twenty topics in our case, remember), an interface without constraints on the member topics would be unworkable.

37.2.2.2   Constraining associations

A DTD or schema constrains the occurrence of element types and data within a document. In a similar way, *topic map constraints* can specify which topics are permitted to play a member role in an association.

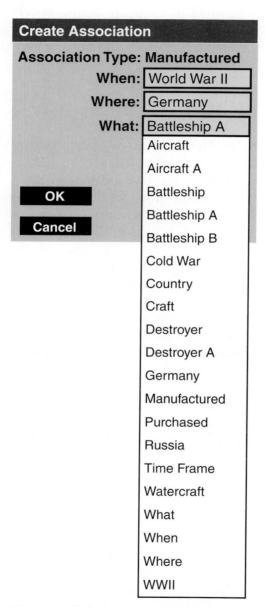

Figure 37-5   User interface for creating an unconstrained association

Example 37-2 shows the constraints on our two associations.[3] We constrained the topic type of each of the member roles in both association types. That means, for example, that a topic that plays the When role must be an instance of Craft.

Example 37-2. Constraints on associations

```
<Constraints>
  <AssociationType              name = "Manufactured">
    <member role="When"   TopicType = "Time Frame"/>
    <member role="Where"  TopicType = "Country"/>
    <member role="What"   TopicType = "Craft"/>
  </AssociationType>
  <AssociationType              name = "Purchased">
    <member role="When"   TopicType = "Time Frame"/>
    <member role="Where"  TopicType = "Country"/>
    <member role="What"   TopicType = "Craft"/>
  </AssociationType>
</Constraints>
```

Figure 37-6 shows the improved interface that results.

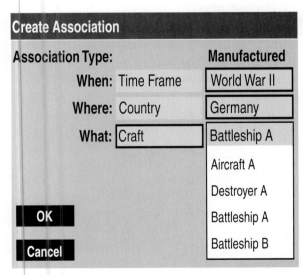

Figure 37-6 User interface for creating a constrained association

3. As the *Topic Map Constraint Language (TMCL)* is still being standardized, and vendors are typically implementing their own in the interim, we created a simple XML vocabulary for use in this example.

There is a new column between the role names and member topics. It contains the topic types to which the member roles must belong. In the case of `What`, it means that the drop-down list contains only the four topics that are instances of `Craft`.

Note that `Craft` itself is in a list box (as indicated by the heavy border). That is because it has subtypes. In the event that the user finds the list of instances too long, he can select a subtype (or sub-subtype, etc.) of `Craft` from Figure 37-7, which would result in a shorter list.

Figure 37-7 shows an example. The user knows that the craft that was manufactured was `Battleship A`, so to get the shortest list in the right column he selects `Battleship` instead of `Craft`. In the real world, that might reduce a list from a thousand topics to fifty. However, in our example there would be only two topics in the drop-down list: `Battleship A` and `Battleship B`.

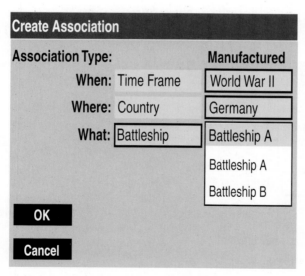

Figure 37-7   Selecting from a subtype

37.3 | Lessons learned

The topic map solution easily met MaritInt's technical requirements. However, deployment revealed problems with any system's most sensitive components – its users!

Topic maps are relatively new, so there was little familiarity with the technology or the terminology used to describe it. Unfamiliarity is often a breeding ground for doubt, suspicion, and resistance to acceptance.

For example, MaritInt wanted its topic maps to preserve new kinds of information that the analysts were not accustomed to capturing. Because of this added dimension – and the change in the analysts' work – the perception arose that the new system was more costly than the old. Even after it was demonstrated that the topic map system was more cost-effective – because the full-text system couldn't meet requirements – the false perception still held.

The lessons learned for solving this problem, like the problem itself, depend on people:

- Caution all the experts to show patience in answering any questions that come up about topic maps.
- Provide topic map education for the project team immediately preceding the project start, so it will still be fresh.
- Train the users of the finished system only after system acceptance, so that the system won't change after the training.

It can also help to be flexible in your development methodology, to temper science with humanity when necessary.

For example, as we saw in the last few examples, software can generate user interfaces directly from a topic map. But generic interfaces like those are rarely intuitive for people who are not topic map experts. As a result, the users resist the change even more.

MaritInt concluded it was worth the effort to develop custom interfaces for the specific topic maps that it used. The interfaces were favorably received by the analysts and the maps were more easily understood and maintained.

These are all sensible – even obvious – lessons for any project. But they are worth emphasizing for a disruptive technology like topic maps, because resistance to newness is likely to be greater than usual.

Application integration using topic maps

Application Discussion

- Distributed objects
- Workflow topic maps
- Application integration architecture

Contributing expert: Suriya Narayanan

Chapter 38

It's midnight ... do you know where your applications are? There was a time when the answer was "wrapped in a rubber band in my desk drawer", but that time is gone forever. Today's Web applications are composed of a multitude of cooperating components. You might not even know *what* they are, let alone where they are. Unless, of course, you've got a topic map!

L ong, long ago, in a data processing center far, far away, applications were implemented as monolithic programs. Today, with the evolution of the Web and the driving forces behind it, distributed object computing has become the prevailing architecture for developing applications.

38.1 | Distributed objects

Just about any application can be modeled and developed as a collection of objects in a network, collaborating to accomplish what the application is expected to accomplish. The network where the applications run can span the globe or be limited to a single computer's internal bus.

An object has an *interface* that exposes its *methods* – operations performed on the object. Objects can invoke one another's methods while collaborating, in order to perform the application functionality.

Even a legacy application that was developed back in that ancient data processing center can participate. It can be *wrapped*, using an appropriate *object wrapper*, to provide an object-oriented interface and object-oriented access to its functionality.

38.1.1 *Navigating the object ocean*

What if we treated the operations on the distributed objects as topics in a topic map?[1] More precisely, we want to treat the methods defined in the classes as topics, and the methods on specific instances of the classes – the objects – as the corresponding topic occurrences.

Recall that associations are relationships between topics. The fact that the topic "method A" is calling the topic "method B" is an *association* between the two topics. The *association roles* that the topics – the methods – play in that association would be `caller` and `callee`.

38.1.2 *Mapping control flow*

What happens when you navigate a topic map that represents the methods of distributed objects? As the *control flow* – the logic – of the application is captured in the topic map, the application executes as those methods are called during the navigation.

This is an important notion.

Programmers have customarily included the control flow in the code. After all, this is a good part of what programming is all about and is actually fun to do! Is it even feasible, let alone desirable, to move control flow out of the code in this way?

The answer lies in the granularity of the objects and methods that we choose to model in the topic map.

At the micro, physical data structure level, encapsulating the control flow in the code is unavoidable. Although in principle even this control flow could be represented in a topic map, that map would be too large, too focused on the physical aspects, and too detailed to serve any useful purpose.

---

1. If you aren't certain of what that means, take a few moments to read the tutorial in Chapter 35, "Topic maps: Knowledge navigation aids", on page 560.

However, if the objects and methods being modeled as a topic map are at a sufficiently high level – representing abstractions of real-life business objects – then the topic map of the object interactions is immediately meaningful. Such topic maps are useful for integration because they model the workflow of the business.

38.1.3 *Workflow*

Workflow is a discipline for modeling real-life systems as a sequence of tasks, with the ability to make some branching decisions along the way.

For example the processing of a sales order in a business can be modeled as a workflow. A workflow could also describe how a patient is handled when visiting the physician's office. You can see a workflow illustrated in Figure 38-1; we'll discuss it in detail later on.

A well-designed workflow is *loosely-coupled*, meaning that the components that implement the individual tasks know nothing about one another's internals or data formats, only about their formally-defined interfaces. In contrast, traditional applications (including the components themselves) are termed *tightly-coupled* because their internal objects do have intimate knowledge of one another.

38.1.3.1 Topic maps and workflow

As we have seen, a topic map can model interactions of meaningful high-level business objects. As those interactions represent the workflow of the business, we are effectively modeling business workflow with topic maps.

Given tools to define and manage distributed object topic maps, and a runtime platform for map navigation, topic maps could become vehicles for application integration without heavy-duty programming.

38.1.3.2 Content and workflow

Business objects return business data, which has formally-defined semantics and a known format. It is the same sort of data found in relational databases and spreadsheets.

Enterprises also have large amounts of free-form creative data, such as reports, plans, procedures, and similar documents. Chapter 35, "Topic maps: Knowledge navigation aids", on page 560 explained how to navigate within such content using topic maps.

Suppose that in addition to business objects, a workflow were to include distributed objects that generated free-form content from a topic map. That content topic map would be distinct from the distributed object topic map, although as both are topic maps they could be stored and managed in the same topic map database, using the same access mechanisms.

However, the distributed object topic map could model the operations of the content-generation objects together with the operations on the application business objects. Doing so would facilitate tighter integration of free-form content with business process data.

Let's look at an architecture that could support such workflows.

38.2 | Architecture for application integration

Figure 38-1 illustrates an architecture for application integration by means of topic maps. It is based on an actual implementation of a topic-based integration platform.

The architecture provides for application business objects and content generation objects. Their behavior is controlled by topic maps of their interactions and topic maps of the content.

The primary components of the architecture are the three managers: the context manager, the semantic manager, and the service manager. These components essentially act as brokers, by connecting a client browser service request to an appropriate server component.

38.2.1 *Context manager*

The context manager is responsible for managing the session and maintaining its state. As the user navigates the information space described by the topic map, the context manager maintains the state across the navigations and makes session-level data available to the other components.

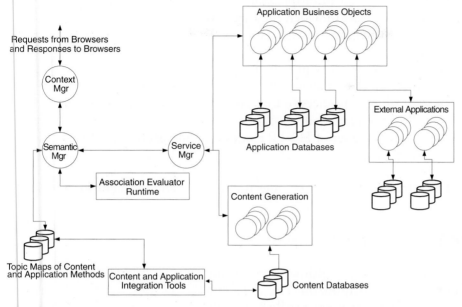

Figure 38-1   Application integration architecture using topic maps

38.2.2   *Semantic manager*

The semantic manager has the most to do of all the managers. Its role is to navigate the topic maps that model the interactions of the application business objects. The semantic manager also manages the topic maps database.

38.2.2.1   Topic maps

The semantic manager understands workflows that are represented as topicmap XML documents, like the one shown in Example 38-1.

38.2.2.2   Association evaluators

The semantic manager evaluates the associations defined in the topic maps by running *association evaluators (AEs)* that are included in the association definitions. AEs can be implemented as snippets of Java code that have access to the context in which they are running.

The runtime context for AEs consists of:

- the user's security principal,
- the state data managed by the context manager,
- the object instances of the classes that are defined as topics in the topic map, and
- the specific set of HTTP request parameters that the browser sent.

The semantic manager provides the runtime environment for the AEs.

38.2.3 *Service manager*

The service manager's primary responsibility is to bridge the connections among the application objects, the content generation objects, and the external systems. It is essentially a specialized directory service for locating those things.

The service manager isn't fundamental to the architecture, but it helps draw the line between those software components that are responsible for the integration and those that need to be integrated.

38.3 | A simple workflow example

Let's look at a simple example of a workflow topic map.

Suppose you decide to take your spouse out on a surprise date to dinner, followed by a show or a movie. This "system" can be modeled using the workflow in Figure 38-2.

The topic map representing this workflow model is in Example 38-1. It begins with a bit of housekeeping in which it defines the "types" of things that occur in the map, then topics for the complete workflow (SurpriseDate) and for the exit from it (GoHome).

The map then defines the HaveDinner, EnjoyTheShow and EnjoyTheMovie topics.

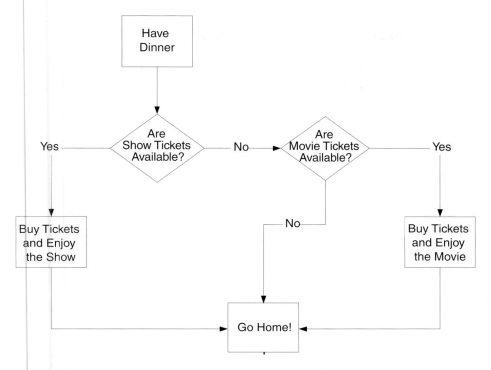

Figure 38-2   Simple workflow for a surprise date

These topics represent class-methods of objects, not their specific instances. The instances will not be determined until a runtime instantiation of the workflow is made. Associations representing paths through the workflow are defined. They associate the topics that represent the workflow steps.

Example 38-2 shows a topic map representing such a runtime instantiation. Again, housekeeping topics occur, as do the class-method topics `HaveDinner`, `EnjoyTheShow` and `EnjoyTheMovie`. This time, however, the latter three topics have occurrences, which are references to object-methods.

The workflow instance topic map inherits from the workflow definition topic map the associations that define the flow of control.

Example 38-1. Simple workflow definition topic map

```
<topicmap>
<!-- "Types" for categorizing topics and associations -->
<topic id="class-method"/> <!-- For topics -->
<topic id="control-flow"/> <!-- For control flow -->
<topic id="caller"/>  <!-- Calling object in association -->
<topic id="callee"/>  <!-- Called object in association -->
<topic id="AE"/>      <!-- Association evaluator -->
<!-- Topics -->
<topic id="SurpriseDate" types="class-method">
  <topname><basename>SurpriseDate</basename></topname>
</topic>
<topic id="GoHome" types="class-method">
  <topname><basename>GoHome</basename></topname>
</topic>
<topic id="HaveDinner" types="class-method">
  <topname><basename>HaveDinner</basename></topname>
</topic>
<topic id="EnjoyTheShow" types="class-method">
  <topname><basename>EnjoyTheShow</basename></topname>
</topic>
<topic id="EnjoyTheMovie" types="class-method">
  <topname><basename>EnjoyTheMovie</basename></topname>
</topic>
<!-- Associations -->
<assoc type="control-flow">
  <assocrl type="caller" href="SurpriseDate"/>
  <assocrl type="callee" href="EnjoyTheShow"/>
  <assocrl type="AE"     href="AreShowTicketsAvailable()"/>
</assoc>
<assoc type="control-flow">
  <assocrl type="caller" href="SurpriseDate"/>
  <assocrl type="callee" href="EnjoyTheMovie"/>
  <assocrl type="AE"     href="AreMovieTicketsAvailable(Cabaret)"/>
</assoc>
<assoc type="control-flow">
  <assocrl type="caller" href="SurpriseDate"/>
  <assocrl type="callee" href="GoHome"/>
  <assocrl type="AE"     href="Always()"/>
</assoc>
</topicmap>
```

38.4 | A compound workflow example

Real life workflows are more complex than the simple workflow defined above. But the complexity usually derives from the repetition of simple

Example 38-2. Simple workflow instance topic map

```
<topicmap>
<!-- "Types" for categorizing topics -->
<topic id="class-method"/> <!-- For topics -->
<!-- Topics and occurrences -->
<topic id="SurpriseDate" types="class-method">
  <topname><basename>SurpriseDate</basename></topname>
  <occurs type="object-method" href="OurDate"/>
</topic>
<topic id="HaveDinner" types="class-method">
  <topname><basename>HaveDinner</basename></topname>
  <occurs type="object-method" href="BonesSteakHouse"/>
</topic>
<topic id="EnjoyTheShow" types="class-method">
  <topname><basename>EnjoyTheShow</basename></topname>
  <occurs type="object-method" href="Ragtime"/>
</topic>
<topic id="EnjoyTheMovie" types="class-method">
  <topname><basename>EnjoyTheMovie</basename></topname>
  <occurs type="object-method" href="Cabaret"/>
</topic>
<topic id="GoHome" types="class-method">
  <topname><basename>GoHome</basename></topname>
  <occurs type="object-method" href="OurHome"/>
</topic>
</topicmap>
```

workflows in various combinations. In other words, the supposedly complex workflow is actually a compound one, consisting of a hierarchy of simple workflows with relatively straightforward logic relating them.

Topic maps lend themselves well to representing compound workflows because they are easily combined. Any of the topics in a topic map can be a topic map in its own right.

Suppose we complicate the SurpriseDate workflow in Figure 38-2. Let's say that the kids need to be taken care of before the surprise date with your spouse can begin.

The new workflow, shown in Figure 38-3, is conceptually more complex, but actually simpler than Figure 38-2 in practice, as it is built on top of the SurpriseDate workflow. Its topic map is shown in Example 38-3.

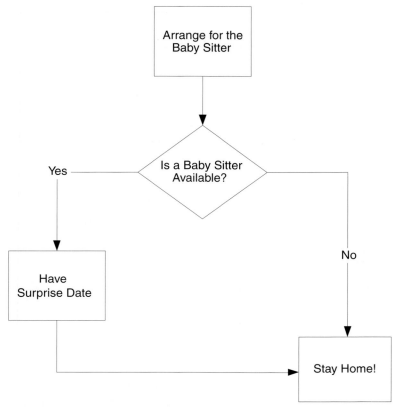

Figure 38-3   Compound workflow

38.5 | Conclusion

We have seen many examples in this book of using XML for data sharing among disparate applications. XML workflow topic maps offer an elegant technique for coordinating the execution of those applications. Industries, such as healthcare, where there is currently a serious lack of effective integration among systems, could especially benefit from topic-based integration.

Example 38-3. Compound workflow topic map

```
<topicmap>
<!-- "Types" for categorizing topics and associations -->
<topic id="class-method"/> <!-- For topics -->
<topic id="control-flow"/> <!-- For control flow -->
<topic id="caller"/>  <!-- Calling object in association -->
<topic id="callee"/>  <!-- Called object in association -->
<topic id="AE" />     <!-- Association evaluator -->
<!-- Topics -->
<topic id="KidlessDate" types="class-method">
  <topname><basename>KidlessDate</basename></topname>
</topic>
<topic id="GoHome" types="class-method">
  <topname><basename>GoHome</basename></topname>
</topic>
<topic id="ArrangeBabySitter" types="class-method">
  <topname><basename>ArrangeBabySitter</basename></topname>
</topic>
<topic id="SurpriseDate" types="class-method">
  <topname><basename>SurpriseDate</basename></topname>
</topic>
<!-- Associations -->
<assoc type="control-flow">
  <assocrl type="caller" href="KidlessDate"/>
  <assocrl type="callee" href="ArrangeBabySitter"/>
  <assocrl type="AE"     href="IsBabySitterAvailable()"/>
</assoc>
  <assocrl type="caller" href="KidlessDate"/>
  <assocrl type="callee" href="SurpriseDate"/>
  <assocrl type="AE"     href="DoesWorkflowExist()"/>
</assoc>
<assoc type="control-flow">
  <assocrl type="caller" href="KidlessDate"/>
  <assocrl type="callee" href="GoHome"/>
  <assocrl type="AE"     href="Always()"/>
</assoc>
</topicmap>
```

Web Services

- The vision and the reality
- Applications and technologies
- Deploy your own Web service!

Part Thirteen

The hype about Web services has been voluminous and relentless.

One reader of this book even asked whether we would be changing the focus from XML to Web services. Our reply was that you wouldn't notice the difference! And that's regardless of what you think Web services is. (Besides thinking that it's ungrammatical!)

Some think it is business integration on steroids: companies finding one another automatically and purchasing services without human intervention.

Some think it is universal content processing: user access to any data from any computing device at any location.

And programmers, who have to do the work, think about the reality: some improved technologies for distributed computing.

But all of these thoughts involve XML. Web services is *XML* Web services, the culmination of everything you've been reading. In this part, we'll look at both the vision and the reality.

The Web services vision

Introductory Discussion

- Next-generation Internet
- Web-based services using XML
- Integrated user experience

Sponsor: Microsoft Corporation, http://msdn.microsoft.com/xml

Contributing experts: Microsoft staff

Chapter

39

Some say Web services is revolutionary; others that it is merely an incremental change to distributed processing. But enhancing a technology sufficiently can lead to a point at which amazing new applications are possible. If Web services really is a revolution, it may be the first in history to be led by the parties in power!

Picture an online world where constellations of PCs, servers, smart devices and Internet-based services can collaborate seamlessly. Businesses will be able to share data, integrate their processes, and join forces to offer customized, comprehensive solutions to their customers. And the information you or your business need will be available wherever you are – whatever computing device, platform or application you are using.

Today, all we *can* do is picture it.

39.1 | Can we get there from here?

In many respects, today's Internet still mirrors the old mainframe world. It's a server-centric computing model, with the browser playing the role of dumb terminal. Much of the information your business needs is locked up in centralized databases, served up a page at a time to individual users.

Worse, Web pages are simply a "picture" of the data, not the data itself, forcing many developers back to "screen scraping" to acquire information.

And integrating that underlying data with your business' existing systems – never mind those of your partners – is a costly and frustrating challenge.

Compounding this frustration is the fact that today's standalone applications and Web sites create islands of functionality and data. You have to navigate manually between Web sites, devices and applications, logging in each time and rarely being able to carry data with you. You have to keep constant track of which particular application or device or Web site gives you which level of access to which particular data. Tasks that ought to be simple – such as arranging a meeting with colleagues from partner companies and automatically updating every attendee's calendar – are a nightmare. Productivity is one of the main casualties.

Solving such problems is the key challenge for the next generation of the Internet. A revolution is needed.

39.2 | A revolution is upon us – again!

Fortunately, one is easily found.

Revolutions are a way of life in the computer industry. Only 20 years ago, the world was still in the mainframe era. Few people had access to or used computers. When they did, it was only through the company IT department. The PC, the graphical user interface, and the introduction of the Internet changed all that. They democratized computing for hundreds of millions of people and transformed the computer into a mass-market product.

Since then, standards such as HTML and HTTP have exponentially increased people's use of the Internet. These base protocols for viewing content on the Web (and the associated software for browsing this content) grew Web usage to what it is today – a key activity in the daily lives of business employees and consumers.

And it is HTML's sibling, XML, that is enabling the revolution that will make the next generation of the Internet possible. As we have seen throughout this book, XML enables developers to describe data being exchanged among PCs, smart devices, applications and Web sites. Because XML separates the underlying abstract data from the way that data is rendered and displayed, the data itself can easily be organized, programmed, edited and exchanged.

XML is a lingua franca for the Internet age. Just as the Web revolution-ized the way users talk to applications, XML can transform the way applica-tions talk to one another.

39.3 | Web services

As developers become more familiar with XML, they are moving beyond simply using it for data. With the help of XML-based technologies such as SOAP, WSDL, and UDDI,[1] they are creating a new type of software, called *Web services*, that uses XML to provide Web-based services.

The vocabulary here has some subtle distinctions:

- *Web-based services* are services of any kind delivered over the Web.
- *Web services technologies* are WSDL and two XML-based protocols: SOAP and UDDI.
- *Web services* are Web-based services implemented with Web services technologies.

Web services programs are configurable and reusable, much like compo-nent software, and they are accessible anywhere via the Internet. Programs using this model can coordinate multiple Web sites, draw on information and services from each of them, and combine and deliver the result in cus-tomized form to any device.

Because Web services breaks down the distinctions between the Internet, standalone applications and types of computing devices, businesses can col-laborate on integrated and customized solutions.

For example:

- A company offering an online electronic-payment service can expose it to partners, so they can deliver it as part of their own offerings regardless of the platform they are using.

---

1. SOAP is described in 5.4, "Web services", on page 116; WSDL and UDDI were introduced there and are described in more detail in Chapter 40, "Web services technologies", on page 626.

- An airline can link its online reservation system to that of a car-rental partner, so travelers can book a car at the same time they book a flight.
- An online auction company can notify bidders when they are outbid or have won an auction, or could partner with other firms to offer alternative shipping, fulfillment or payment options.

39.3.1 *Basic principles*

This new Internet-based integration methodology has four basic principles.

Internet connection
The first principle is that systems connect through the Internet – a safe assumption given the high availability and low-cost connectivity it provides.

Service discovery
Second, there needs to be a simple way to find services on the Internet with which businesses can work. UDDI and WSDL fulfill that function. Traditional means are usable as well, such as word of mouth or printed directories. However, UDDI and WSDL, by formalizing the process, help to automate it.

Common data representation
Third, a common language is needed to ensure that information can be shared with others. XML is the ingredient that makes this possible. XML provides a common data representation so that your business partners and customers won't need to use a particular programming language, application, or operating system to interact with your systems.

Common communication protocol
The final principle is that there must be a common protocol for actually conducting business; for example, to call the service, book the appointment, order the part, or deliver the information. SOAP is this protocol. It enables systems to talk to one another and make requests.

These four principles embody flexible technologies that can bind disparate systems with different programming languages, thereby unifying personal computing, enterprise computing, and the Web.

39.3.2 *Expected benefits*

Web services should provide several benefits for businesses. It is hard to describe them without some hype, but that's the nature of revolutions.

- Easier integration

  Your software will more easily integrate with other pieces of software – from the desktop to the mainframe – both within your enterprise and at external sites. These integration capabilities will enable you to forge closer ties with business partners and pursue development of joint business processes.

- Faster application development

  As the impact of Web services grows, developers will deliver more and more software and services, including legacy applications, that operate within the Web services programming model. If there is existing code that can help on a project, you can find and integrate it through Web services instead of reinventing it.

- Easier personalization

  Data can be accessed from common data sources rather than collected and maintained on an application-by-application basis. You can simply request common data as needed and transform it dynamically to deliver individualized results.

39.4 | Implementing the vision

As you might expect, a vision with this much excitement – not to mention economic potential – is shared by more than one computer company. In fact, because the Web services technologies are industry-backed open specifications, virtually every major software and hardware vendor is building implementation tools.

And in principle, they should all interoperate. After all, integration is the reason for building them in the first place!

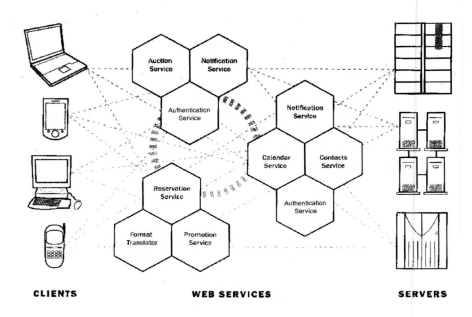

Figure 39-1   Combining Web services to create "user experiences"

One of the aims of applications built with Web services – and certainly one of the claims – is that the end user experience will be something very different from today's.

Because Web services link applications, services, and devices together in connected solutions, the claim goes, software arrives as part of an integrated and simplified experience. Users will be able to act on information any time, any place, from any smart device.

The concept is illustrated in Figure 39-1.

Analysis   Web services is a very far-reaching and ambitious vision, with implications for all Web users and, if the goals are achieved, for much of the economy as well. All of the major software and hardware vendors are promoting Web services, and Microsoft has made it central to its plans for the future. Reliability, security and privacy of the services will obviously be of paramount importance. Regardless, from a purely technical standpoint it is fascinating to see plans for such a wide array of services based on XML and XML-based protocols.

Web services technologies

Application Discussion

- Service discovery
- Web Services Description Language (WSDL)
- Universal Description, Discovery, and Integration

Chapter

40

Computer programs are brittle. It is easier for
applications to talk to people than to other
applications. That's why Web services specifications
are less mature than pure Web specifications.
Although the grand vision of Web services may take
years to arrive, the same could have been (and was!)
said of XML itself when the First Edition of this book
was published. Just so you won't miss the leading
edge, here's how the Web services technologies work.

There are three major Web services technologies: SOAP, WS-
DL, and UDDI. In 6.4, "Protocols", on page 135 we covered
SOAP in some detail and briefly introduced the others. Now
we'll take a closer look at the other two. Unlike SOAP, whose object-ori-
entation was pretty much limited to its erstwhile name, WSDL and UDDI
are imbued with the object-oriented model.[1]

40.1 | Web Services Description Language

If I agree to provide you with some XML documents, we will also agree on
the document type. That agreement is usually recorded formally in a DTD
or schema definition. The definition is like a recipe: It lists the ingredients
of a dish – in this case, the data elements of the documents that I'm serving.

---

1. If you are a developer, you are probably similarly imbued. Other readers
   may want to review 6.1, "Object-oriented", on page 127.

If I agree to provide you information through an XML-based protocol, you'll want to know the offerings I have available and how to request each one. For this you'll need a description of my service, which I can express formally using the Web Services Description Language (WSDL). The service description is like a menu from a take-out restaurant: It tells you in great detail what is available and your options for getting it.

Figure 40-1 shows the components of WSDL in the form of a stack. Ignore the details for now; just focus on the middle column.

40.1.1 *Starting at the top: service*

WSDL is a layered specification. Each layer depends upon the layer directly below it. There is a certain elegance to layered designs. When you are working with them, you can concentrate on one layer at a time. Using this technique, let's explore WSDL by working from the top down with an application example.[2]

Logically enough for a language that describes Web services, the top concept is the *service*. In our case, it is a global meteorological service offered to subscriber corporations. It might, in turn, get its information from other Web services run by national meteorological departments.

40.1.2 *Dividing up work: port*

A service could offer multiple functions, called *operations*. To balance the resources for supporting them, the service could span multiple physical computer systems. Access to particular groups of operations is provided by *ports*. Each port could exist on a different machine or multiple ports could be on the same machine. That is totally up to the Web service creator.

Each port has a name. Perhaps one port would serve the temperatures, another the humidity and a third the barometric pressure. It would all depend on what was most convenient for the person constructing the service. Let's call our ports `temperature`, `humidity` and `pressure`. They might have Web addresses such as:

---

2. A sample WSDL document from a different example is shown in 41.4, "Describing our service with WSDL", on page 646.

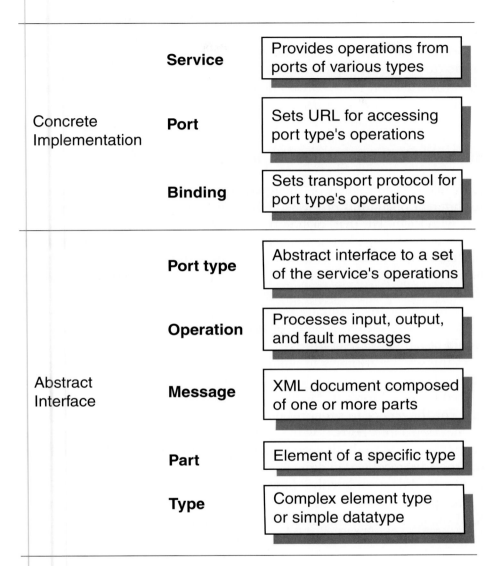

Figure 40-1   The WSDL stack

- ■ http://temperature.weatherworld.com/
- ■ http://humidity.weatherworld.com/ and
- ■ http://pressure.weatherworld.com

We could have put two ports on the same machine if that was convenient.

Because ports are URL-specific, it makes no sense for this part of a Web service to be defined in an industry standard, as you might define an industry standard DTD or schema. The other parts of a WSDL definition are more reusable than the ports.

40.1.3 *Choosing a transport protocol: binding*

Now that we know where on the Internet to go for the ports that give access to different operations of the service, we need to know how to communicate with them. For that, each port must specify a *binding*.

Recall from 6.4, "Protocols", on page 135 that protocols tend to build on one another. A binding is basically a way of defining a new protocol based on an existing one. In this case, the existing protocol is the *transport protocol* that is used to transport the messages from place to place. It makes sense to build on top of an existing transport protocol because otherwise you would have to specify the exact order of the bits travelling down the wire. That would be a total waste of time!

In this case we are going to build our new meteorological protocol on top of SOAP. We could also specify a binding based on the HTTP protocol that is used by Web browsers. However, each port may support only one binding. For the service to support both transport protocols, we would have to define separate ports, with names like `temperature_soap`, and `temperature_http`. Both ports would support the same operation; only the transport protocol would differ.

The WSDL spec describes how to use WSDL with SOAP and HTTP. Third parties could define how to use WSDL with (for example) XML-RPC or the popular mail protocol SMTP. Any existing transport protocol could be used, but somebody, somewhere would have to write a document explaining how WSDL and the protocol fit together.

The binding does more than just choose the transport protocol. It also specifies some details about how to use the transport protocol for each operation. These details depend upon which transport protocol you have chosen. For instance if you choose SOAP, you get to choose options that are available in the SOAP specification and generally tweak the layout of the SOAP messages that are sent across the network.

40.1.4 *Getting abstract: port type*

Each binding is associated not only with a transport protocol but also with a *port type*, which is a set of operations provided by the service. All the operations of a service are grouped into one or more port types. In our example, we've created three port types with one operation each, `temperature`, `humidity` and `pressure`.

This is the layer at which we start to lift off from the very concrete into the land of the abstract. The bindings and ports were concrete in that they defined how the information would be laid out in terms of SOAP messages (or HTTP messages) and where on the Internet the messages would physically go.

Port types are abstract. They do not say what exactly should go on the wire nor where that information should go. Rather they define in the abstract what sort of things can be said. That means, for example, that an industry group could define a single port type for handling temperatures and then specify a variety of bindings for it.

Doing so would allow some Web services to handle temperatures using SOAP (the most popular Web services protocol), some to use XML-RPC (the older protocol), and some to use HTTP (the protocol for the existing Web). Service providers could compete based on which concrete bindings they provide for the same abstract port types.

40.1.5 *Defining behavior: operation*

Each port type has a name and a set of *operations*. Any Web service that claims to support the port type must have concrete bindings for each of the operations. Just as a DTD or schema requires many XML documents to have the same element structure, all ports of the same type must support the same operations.

Operations are defined in terms of input, output, and faults.

Imagine a real-world service for delivering pizza. To place an order, you must give the pizzeria a list of toppings, an address and a credit card number. In WSDL terms these are the *input* to the process.

Hopefully you will eventually get a pizza. This is called the *output*. If something goes wrong, you can expect a phone call along the lines of "we could not find your house" or "we could not process your credit card." These error messages are called *faults*.

40.1.6   *The information unit: message*

In our meteorological example, the output certainly is not a pizza and a fault is not a phone call. Web services deal in information represented as XML. The unit of information sent back and forth between programs is an XML document called a *message*. Operations define their input, output and faults in terms of messages.

The operation `query_temperature` would have as its input a geographical location. Users are probably interested in the temperature where they live! We would therefore define a message type for asking about the temperature at a particular point on the globe. It might also allow the user to specify whether the result should be in celsius or fahrenheit. The output would be another XML message, containing the temperature represented as an integer.

We might send fault messages for requesting an unsupported location (e.g. Antarctica) and for requesting an unsupported temperature unit (e.g. Kelvin).

Let us say we called our output message type `temperature_report`. The interesting thing about this element type is that it could be useful in a totally different operation, wherein a remote weather station reports the temperature to our server. For that operation, it would be an input message rather than an output.

In other words, the remote station would contact us and send a `temperature_report` message as input. Later, an end-user could request the neighborhood temperature and we would send another `temperature_report` message, this time as output.

40.1.7   *Composing messages: part and type*

Each message has one or more components, called *parts*. Every part is an element, either one whose content is a datatype defined in the *XML Schema* specification, or one that conforms to a defined complex element type.

For instance the input to our `query_temperature` operation would need a latitude and longitude. Each of these could be a part with data content conforming to the *XML Schema* integer datatype.

Alternatively, we could define a single complex `position` element type with subelements or attributes for the latitude and longitude. We would then refer to that one element type in our message part definition.

It is possible to define new element types by embedding their definitions right in the Web service description, or else by referring to external schema definitions. You can define types that are very simple, such as credit card number, or very complex, such as purchase order.

Creating definitions in WSDL is easiest with the *XML Schema* definition language (XSDL), but other schema languages can be used as well.

40.1.8 *Summary of WSDL*

Here is a summary of the WSDL hierarchy shown in Figure 40-1, working from the top down. Now the details we encouraged you to skip the first time should be meaningful.

service
> A Web service performs operations.[3] These are grouped into one or more sets, called "port types". Each port type is accessed from one or more ports.

ports
> A port establishes a binding between a port type and a Web address for accessing the port type's operations. There could be several ports of the same type, each bound to a different transport protocol. The addresses of a service's ports could point to the same or different machines.

bindings
> Bindings are the links between the physical implementation of a Web service and the abstract interface. Each binding specifies how a particular transport protocol is used for the operations of a given port type.

port types
> The operations provided by a Web service are grouped into one or more port types. Port types define the abstract interface to a Web service.

---

3. If you think of a Web service as an object, the operations are its methods.

operations

An operation could consume a particular input and/or produce a particular output. If errors occur, it could also produce faults. Inputs, outputs, and faults are types of messages.

messages

Messages are XML documents. They are made up of parts.

parts

A part is an element of a specific type.

types

Part types can be complex element types (with subelements and/or attributes) or simple datatypes. They are typically defined in XSDL.

The layers obviously go from most complex ("a complete Web service") to simplest ("a single element"). They also go from concrete implementation ("send these bits, to this URL, on this machine, using this transport") to abstract interface ("the types of things we are talking about are temperatures and air pressures").

Most importantly, the layers go from most specific to most reusable. Compare the definition "Sal's Pizza on the corner of Main Street and First Avenue" with the generic term "pizzeria". The first is very specific because it includes a concrete location. Web services also have one or more concrete locations because they are provided by the ports.

It is the lower layers that are reusable and might be defined by an industry consortium rather than a specific company. There is not necessarily anything company-specific about bindings, operations, messages or element types. In many circumstances it would make sense to share these and have multiple competing implementations.

But it would never make sense to share ports themselves. It is no more possible to "compete" by sharing a port than it would be to open two pizzerias at the same address!

40.2 | UDDI

Now we know how to check the temperature or order a pizza. But from whom? What if you wanted to find a weather information service or pizzeria? You might know in the abstract what sort of service (bindings, operations, etc.) you want, but you wouldn't necessarily know how to find all of the relevant service providers.

40.2.1 *Finding a service provider*

Universal Description, Discovery, and Integration (UDDI) is a set of OASIS specifications for the Web services world's equivalent of phone books. When you want to find a service in your town, you pick up the **Universal** yellow pages business **Description** listings and scan through them to **Discover** one that meets your requirements. Then you might **Integrate** the listing with your wallet by using the "scissors" protocol!

UDDI is based on SOAP and WSDL. Service providers use it to let Web services consumers know that their services exist, just as yellow pages help off-line consumers to know that businesses exist.

UDDI is different from existing business directories because of its integration with Web services. For instance, a UDDI business registry is actually a Web service itself, so programmers can contact it and ask it questions through SOAP. UDDI and SOAP are also integrated in a more important way. The UDDI registry can report which Web services are available from a particular business.

In theory a computer could connect to a UDDI registry, use SOAP to search it for a Web service implementing a "real-time currency conversion" operation, connect to that service and do the conversion without human intervention.

The information available through UDDI is typically described as falling into one of three categories, based on the telephone book metaphor:

white pages
These describe an organization's name, address and contact information.

yellow pages
> Yellow pages categorize businesses by industrial category and geographical location.

green pages
> The so-called green pages are technical descriptions of how to interact with each organization's services.

40.2.2   *UDDI data structures*

A UDDI *registry* is a database of *business entities, business services, binding templates* and *tModels*. These are known as the UDDI *data structures*.

40.2.2.1   Business entities

Business entities are records of corporations or departments. They contain names, contacts, descriptions and other identifying information.

A business entity is uniquely identified by a `businessKey`, which is a long random-looking string of numbers and letters known as a *Universally Unique ID (UUID)*.

40.2.2.2   Business services

Business services are records of the services provided by a business entity. These can be true Web services. However, they can just as easily be traditional offline services, such as phone lines, or non-automated services, such as email.

Each service has a UUID called a `serviceKey`. It also has other identifying information, such as a name and a description. Most importantly, each service refers to one or more `bindingTemplates`.

40.2.2.3   Binding templates

Binding templates specify how to contact the company and consume the service. The most important subelement of the binding template is the access point, which tells how to communicate with the service.

Valid types of access point are:

- `mailto` for email,
- `http` for Web browsers or SOAP,
- `https` for secure HTTP,
- `ftp` for File Transfer Protocol,
- `fax` for fax machine, and
- `phone` for telephone.

40.2.2.4   tModels

tModels[4] are typically used as assertions that a service meets a certain specification. As UDDI is designed to be extremely general, the structure of tModels will vary widely.

tModels can be used to refer to almost any kind of service description. The description can be as technically precise as a WSDL definition or as informal as a prose document.

For Web services, of course, the formal tModels are the useful ones. Other businesses, however, simply cannot be described in that way. What is the input and the output of a dentist? Is biting his finger a fault?

40.2.3   *Will it work?*

The original emphasis in UDDI was on a single public registry for service discovery, now dubbed a *Universal Business Registry (UBR).*[5]

In the Fourth Edition of this book we cautioned:

> Some wonder whether there is even a good reason to think that service discovery will be any different in the Web services world. Perhaps businesses will continue to find one another through advertisements in magazines, introductions through social networks, and other traditional means. Business does require a certain level of trust after all!

---

4. The word tModel does not really stand for anything.
5. A UBR actually exists; it is operated jointly by IBM, Microsoft, NTT Com, and SAP.

The UDDI developers appear to have wondered the same thing. UDDI 3.0 recognizes that most of today's Web services are intended for use either internally or among existing trusted trading partners. Accordingly, it provides for multiple registries – private and shared, as well as public – and for their technical interoperability.

40.3 | Implementation

It is important to keep in mind that no matter how related they may seem, Web services technologies and Web-based delivery of services are two different things. This is particularly confusing right now because the industry is moving on both fronts at once, which causes people to think that they are the same thing.

Obviously there are already services on the Web that are not based on the new Web services technologies. *HotMail* and *Kazaa* are two examples.

Similarly, Web services technologies have nothing technically to do with subscription-based content syndication services, although some of those services are being built *using* Web services technologies.

40.4 | Conclusion

Although the specifications are under active development, much of the promise of Web services remains a dream of the future, not a here-and-now reality. Retain a degree of skepticism.

On the other hand, you can understand why this prospect has so excited the executives of every major software company.

Computers already talk to each other, with and without human supervision. The complexity of this communication will only increase in the future. Just as XML helps you manage the complexities of data representation, the new XML-based Web services technologies will help you with the complexities of computer communication.[6]

---

6. And remember that in one sense at least, Web services is a proven concept: Churches in L.A. have been holding them for years!

Deploying a Web service

Application Discussion

- From legacy application to Web service
- Describing a service with WSDL
- Registering a service with UDDI
- Software on CD-ROM

Sponsor: IBM Corporation,
http://www.ibm.com/developerworks/webservices/start

Contributing expert: Doug Tidwell

Chapter

41

We've seen the grand vision for Web services and looked at the technology that could make that vision a reality. In this chapter we'll get down to the details and see just how easily you can deploy a Web service – even if it's the first program you ever wrote!

W eb services as a grand vision of dynamically interoperating software uniting business partners who've never met isn't quite here yet. However, the need for independent programs to cooperate has been around for quite a while. As software, Web services is just the latest means of accomplishing that task.

We'll show you how you can deploy a Web service with technology that's available today.

41.1 | Who does what to whom?

In the Web services world, there are three basic operations, commonly known as *publish*, *find*, and *bind*.

publishing
The process a Web service uses to advertise itself.

find
The operation by which an application finds a Web service.

bind
> The act of attaching to the Web service and using its methods.

These operations involve three parties: *service providers*, *service requestors*, and *service brokers*.

service provider
> An application that publishes and provides a service over a network.

service requestors
> Applications that hope to find a particular service and bind to it.

service broker
> A business that brings service providers and requestors together by operating a registry of services.

To publish a Web service, the provider adds a description of that service to the registry. To find a Web service, the requestor describes a service and the broker returns information about the Web services that match the request. Once the requestor has selected a particular service, the requestor contacts the provider and e-business ensues.

41.2 | A dull but familiar example

Let's look at a sample program. We'll take an underwhelming piece of code and deploy it as a Web service. The point of this example is to demonstrate that virtually any program can be a Web service, which means even the legacy applications that keep your business running.
Example 41-1 shows our sample application. [1]

---

1. The code in Example 41-1 is a slightly modified version of the "Hello, World" application made famous by Brian Kernighan and Dennis Ritchie, everyone's first program. This version is placed in the public domain with the proviso that it may not be used to develop weapons of mass destruction. No animals were harmed during the development, debugging, deploying, or deploring of this application.

Example 41-1. Source code for a less-than-exciting Web service

```
public class HelloWorld
{
  String message = "Hello, World!";

  public String getMessage()
  {
    return message;
  }

  public void setMessage(String m)
  {
    message = m;
  }
}
```

The application provides two methods, `getMessage` and `setMessage`. The `getMessage` method simply returns the current message, whatever it might be, while `setMessage` allows an application to change the message.

Note that nowhere in the code is there even a hint of modern technologies such as SOAP, XML, or networking. Despite this lack of sophistication, we can still deploy this program as a Web service.

41.3 | Making our code a Web service

Deployment of our example is done with the Apache SOAP toolkit, available at `xml.apache.org`. To deploy the service, we simply give it a name, define the Java class that implements the service, the names of the methods, and other details as needed. All this is done through a Web form on the SOAP administration console, depicted in Figure 41-1.

We give our Web service an ID, define the methods that it supports (for various reasons, we might not want to support all of a class's public methods in our Web service), and a few other details.

How does a client application invoke this Web service after we've deployed it? Example 41-2 shows a fragment of the Java code needed to invoke our service.[2]

---

2. For simplicity's sake, Example 41-2 omits some of the details, such as defining the encoding used for our data, and setting up a vector of parameters for our method.

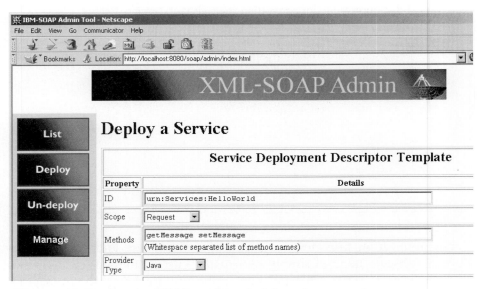

Figure 41-1   Apache SOAP toolkit administration console

Example 41-2. Client application for our Web service

```
URL url = new URL("http://localhost:8080/soap/servlet/rpcrouter");
String urn = "urn:Services:HelloWorld";
Call call = new Call();
call.setTargetObjectURI("urn:Services:HelloWorld");
call.setMethodName("getMessage");
. . .
Response response = call.invoke(url, "");
```

This code also uses the Apache SOAP toolkit, which defines the `Call` and `Response` objects that are used to invoke the service. The application creates the `Call` object, fills in the data for the method call (the method name, the parameters, etc.), then calls the `Call.invoke` method.

Example 41-3 is a SOAP message that requests invocation of the `getMessage` method.

Note the line beginning `<hw1:getMessage`. That element tells the SOAP router how to map the information in the XML message document to a particular Java class. The name of the invoked method is the XML element type name, `getMessage`.

Example 41-3. Request for the `getMessage` method

```
<?xml version='1.0' encoding='UTF-8'?>
<SOAP-ENV:Envelope
xmlns:SOAP-ENV="http://schemas.xmlsoap.org/soap/envelope/"
xmlns:xsi="http://www.w3.org/1999/XMLSchema-instance"
xmlns:xsd="http://www.w3.org/1999/XMLSchema">
<SOAP-ENV:Body>
<hw1:getMessage xmlns:hw1="urn:Services:HelloWorld"
SOAP-ENV:encodingStyle="http://schemas.xmlsoap.org/soap/encoding/">
</hw1:getMessage>
</SOAP-ENV:Body>
</SOAP-ENV:Envelope>
```

Example 41-4 is the XML document that carries the response. It is in the return subelement of the `getMessageResponse` element.

Example 41-4. Response to the request in Example 41-3

```
<?xml version='1.0' encoding='UTF-8'?>
<SOAP-ENV:Envelope
xmlns:SOAP-ENV="http://schemas.xmlsoap.org/soap/envelope/"
xmlns:xsi="http://www.w3.org/1999/XMLSchema-instance"
xmlns:xsd="http://www.w3.org/1999/XMLSchema">
<SOAP-ENV:Body>
<hw1:getMessageResponse xmlns:hw1="urn:Services:HelloWorld"
SOAP-ENV:encodingStyle="http://schemas.xmlsoap.org/soap/encoding/">
<return xsi:type="xsd:string">Hello, World!</return>
</hw1:getMessageResponse>
</SOAP-ENV:Body>
</SOAP-ENV:Envelope>
```

As we have seen, the entire remote method call is done using XML. An XML document describes the method to be invoked and carries the parameters for that method. The SOAP router returns an XML document containing the results of the method call. Notice also that the results of the method call are described with an *XML Schema* data type: string in this example.

Web services has enabled us to deploy a completely unremarkable piece of code as a Web service. Any application that can access the SOAP router can invoke the methods of our Web service. That means that legacy applications can become Web services with little or no modification.

Be aware that SOAP is designed to be completely neutral with regard to operating system, programming language, and object model. SOAP defines the interfaces we'll use, but we don't have to worry about the platform that's running the Web service, or the language used to write it. We're simply building an XML document and sending it to a particular URL, then receiving another XML document in response. XML's role as the universal representation for structured data makes this possible.

Notice, however, that all of the important information here (such as the URL of the SOAP router, the ID of the service, and the name of the method) is fixed. Our client application can use our Web service remotely, but it can't use any other Web service. With a way to find that information at runtime, we could set the values of those strings and invoke any method of any SOAP service on any server. That's where WSDL comes in.

41.4 | Describing our service with WSDL

If Web services are to be discovered at runtime, we need a standard way of describing them. A service provider who publishes information about a Web service must do so using a standard XML vocabulary. Service request-ors searching for it had better describe their needs with the very same vocabulary. WSDL is designed to be that vocabulary.

Example 41-5 shows the WSDL document that describes our *Hello World* service.

Everything a client would need to invoke the methods of our Web service is there. You can see most of the elements that we discussed in 40.1, "Web Services Description Language", on page 627. The interface elements are shown first (`message` and `portType`), then their implementation (`binding` and `service`).

We won't go into all of the details, but note the following:

`urn:Services:HelloWorld`
> This is the ID of the service. It occurs several times in the document.

`name` **attribute of** `operation`
> The values of these attributes (there are two occurrences) are the names of the methods.

Example 41-5. Our Web service described in WSDL

```
<definitions name="HelloWorldDefinitions"
  targetNamespace="http://www.HelloWorld.com/wrapperedService"
  xmlns="http://schemas.xmlsoap.org/wsdl/"
  xmlns:tns="http://www.HelloWorld.com/wrapperedService"
  xmlns:soap="http://schemas.xmlsoap.org/wsdl/soap/"
  xmlns:xsd="http://www.w3.org/1999/XMLSchema">
<message name="InsetMessageRequest">
  <part name="meth1_inType1" type="xsd:string"/></message>
<message name="IngetMessageRequest"/>
<message name="OutgetMessageResponse">
  <part name="meth2_outType" type="xsd:string"/></message>
<portType name="HelloWorldPortType">
  <operation name="setMessage">
    <input message="tns:InsetMessageRequest"/></operation>
  <operation name="getMessage">
    <input message="tns:IngetMessageRequest"/>
    <output message="tns:OutgetMessageResponse"/></operation>
</portType>
<binding name="HelloWorldBinding" type="tns:HelloWorldPortType">
  <soap:binding style="rpc"
    transport="http://schemas.xmlsoap.org/soap/http"/>
  <operation name="setMessage">
    <soap:operation soapAction="urn:Services:HelloWorld"/>
    <input><soap:body
      encodingStyle="http://schemas.xmlsoap.org/soap/encoding/"
      namespace="urn:Services:HelloWorld" use="encoded"/>
    </input>
  </operation>
  <operation name="getMessage">
    <soap:operation soapAction="urn:Services:HelloWorld"/>
    <input><soap:body
      encodingStyle="http://schemas.xmlsoap.org/soap/encoding/"
      namespace="urn:Services:HelloWorld" use="encoded"/>
    </input>
    <output><soap:body
      encodingStyle="http://schemas.xmlsoap.org/soap/encoding/"
      namespace="urn:Services:HelloWorld" use="encoded"/>
    </output>
  </operation>
</binding>
<service name="HelloWorld">
  <documentation>Class HelloWorld as service</documentation>
  <port binding="tns:HelloWorldBinding" name="HelloWorldPort">
    <soap:address
      location="http://localhost:8080/soap/servlet/rpcrouter"/>
  </port>
</service>
</definitions>
```

part **subelements of** message
> Attributes of these elements specify the number and type of each argument passed to or returned from the methods.

location **attribute of** address
> This element is in the SOAP namespace. The attribute value is the URL of a SOAP router, which serves as the Web address for our service.

An XML application can parse the information here, connect to the SOAP router, and supply the needed details such as method names, arguments, etc.

One nice feature of WSDL is that tools are currently available to generate most of it for us. Example 41-5 was generated by IBM's *XML and Web Services Development Environment.*[3] The tool can, among other things, examine a JavaBean and generate a WSDL document from it. It can also generate bean skeletons from a WSDL. This allows you to benefit from Java's strong, static type checking and simplify your Web services calling code.[4]

A standard way to describe Web services is all well and good, but we also have to put the descriptions where service providers and service requestors can find them. That's what UDDI is designed to do.

41.5 | Using a UDDI registry

The UDDI spec defines how registries of Web services should work. There are four kinds of information defined in a UDDI registry, with a separate XML element type for each:

businessEntity
> Information about businesses

---

3. The tool can be found on the CD-ROM accompanying this book.
4. Of course, generating WSDL in this way doesn't provide the flexibility of late binding and loose coupling that we've been describing, but it does get you started quickly. It's like converting a rendered document to XML by putting tags around the style codes; you lose the power of an abstraction that can be reused in a variety of ways

businessService
Information about services

bindingTemplate
Information about individual templates or methods

tModel
Information about the specifications or standards implemented by a given service (which we'll discuss in a minute).

All of the data structures and APIs in the UDDI specification are representable in XML.

Example 41-6 shows a businessEntity element that describes our company.

Example 41-6. The XML representation of a UDDI BusinessEntity object

```
<businessEntity businessKey="">
  <name>DougCo Manufacturing</name>
  <description xml:lang="en">
    Sample business created to exercise a UDDI registry
  </description>
  <contacts>
    <contact>
      <personName>Doug Tidwell</personName>
      <phone useType="voice">1-919-555-5583</phone>
      <phone useType="fax">1-919-555-2389</phone>
      <email>dtidwell@us.ibm.com</email>
      <address>
        <addressLine>1234 Main Street</addressLine>
        <addressLine>Anytown, TX  73958</addressLine>
      </address>
    </contact>
  </contacts>
</businessEntity>
```

We could use this document to define a new BusinessEntity object in the registry. The businessKey attribute is empty; that tells the registry to assign a unique identifier to our object.

When a service requestor finds a business that implements the *Hello World* service, it receives the service provider's businessKey. It might then use the businessKey to request service details by sending the XML document in Example 41-7 to the registry.

Example 41-7. Request for *Hello World* service details

```
<find_service generic='1.0' xmlns='urn:uddi-org:api'
    businessKey='00038F2D-EC27-95A6-BA21-2399DEA396E7'>
    <name>Hello World service</name>
</find_service>
```

In response to the query in Example 41-7, the registry would return an XML document with a serviceList element that describes the services in more detail. We can then use the information from that element for further queries, drilling down through the information in the registry until we find the exact service we are looking for. Example 41-8 shows what a bindingTemplate for a specific service might look like.

Example 41-8. Binding template for a *Hello World* service

```
<bindingTemplate bindingKey="28BC2890-28CC-380C-3131-8FFCA08A7309"
                 serviceKey="821B38A9-38AC-8103-8CA2-03829A38CC28">
  <description xml:lang="en">
    Hello World interface, provides get and set support
  </description>
  <accessPoint URLType="http">
    http://localhost:8080/uddi/servlet/uddi/
  </accessPoint>
  <tModelInstanceDetails>
    <tModelInstanceInfo
        tModelKey="uuid:83C9AFB0-DD83-280A-381C-FF829A9380CB">
      <description xml:lang="en">
        Hello World interface
      </description>
    </tModelInstanceInfo>
  </tModelInstanceDetails>
</bindingTemplate>
```

The information in Example 41-8 tells us the access point for the service. However, it doesn't contain detailed information about the APIs that the service provides. That's where the TModel concept comes in.

The set of potential Web services is so vast and varied that UDDI doesn't attempt to provide a vocabulary for describing them all. Instead, The TModel element type was created as a way to reference other specifications. This TModel could reference the WSDL description in Example 41-5, for example.

In other words, if there is an externally-defined specification for the *Hello World* service, we can use UDDI queries to find the unique identifier for the *reference* to that spec. We can then use that identifier (the `tModelKey`) to find all service providers that support that same specification. When we find one, we can use the SOAP messages we discussed earlier to invoke the methods defined in the spec.

41.6 | What's next?

The technologies we've reviewed so far are an important step on the way to dynamic applications that are built from a variety of services discovered at runtime. There are a number of things yet to come, however, such as:

service provider ratings
You might find twenty providers that implement the *Hello World* service; how have other users rated those twenty providers?

micropayments
Although no one is likely to pay for a *Hello World* service, there are lots of other Web services that might charge for what they provide. If a stock quote service charges one-quarter of a cent for each quotation, for example, its cost per transaction would be squarely in the micropayment range.

contract terms
If our application decides to use a given Web service, there may be times when we need legally binding agreements for our use of the service. What happens if the service provides incorrect information? What happens if the service is unavailable? How much will each invocation of the service cost? It would be extremely useful if these terms could be negotiated automatically by agents.

41.7 | Conclusion

Although the sample program we've used in this chapter doesn't do anything useful, it does demonstrate how to use Web services standards and software to deploy even unsophisticated code over a network. The enabling technology behind all of this is XML.

Analysis   Whether publishing or searching for a service, describing the service's methods and parameters, or interacting with the service itself, everything in Web services involves an XML document. As Web services grows in importance, XML will become the backbone of the Web of the future.

Rich Clients

- Service-Oriented Architecture (SOA)
- Rich client vs. server-centric
- Player technology
- XML business application player

Part Fourteen

No, this part is not about a lawyer's dearest wish! It's about a trend that is emerging in the three-tier application model.

Classically, the middle-tier server did all the work of data aggregation and most of the processing. Although the server in theory could send the aggregated XML to the client for processing, in practice it wound up sending HTML pages for presentation to the user.

Things had to be that way because, even with XML, there was still some chaos with non-standard connectors and scripts that the middle-tier had to deal with. Then Web services came along and suddenly everything was standardized and the chaos turned to calm.

Well, not quite, but enough so that a Web-services enabled client can now do some data aggregation on its own, and application processing as well. Moreover, it can cache the data so the application can run even without a network connection.

This part will show you how to convert an existing application to this new *rich client* model. It will also show you a way to make rich clients portable, and to build them without code!

Converting to rich client Web services

Application Discussion

- Service-oriented architecture (SOA)
- Server-based vs. rich client
- Object model analysis
- Step-by-step conversion plan

Sponsor: Intel Corporation, http://www.intel.com/ids

Contributing expert: Sandip H. Mandera

42

> We've seen how easy it is to make a Web service out of "Hello World". But if your server-based application has something more interesting to say – and gets an overwhelming number of messages in reply – you may want to reduce its burden by changing to a rich client application. That raises the burning question: Can you get there from here? This chapter will lead the way!

T here's more than one way to build an application, and redesigning one after it's been deployed can be a challenge. But if you are seeking the easy interoperability of Web services, and the load sharing and client-side independence of a rich client application, we can show you how to reach your goal.

First, it helps to consider why we want Web services in the first place.

42.1 | Service-oriented architecture (SOA)

Web services allow independently-written programs to share data and be used together to accomplish a business objective. The programs must have interfaces that conceal their implementation details (operating system, programming language, etc.). They can then simply operate as *services* that respond to requests, take actions, and return information.

A system that is designed on these lines is said to have a *Service-oriented architecture (SOA)*. The unstated implication of SOA is that all services are technically capable of being used by any program (although there may be non-technical impediments, such as the need to pay!).

Web services is not the first SOA, but thanks to XML it is arguably the first that really works. That's because there is universal acceptance of WSDL, the language for describing the interfaces, and SOAP, the protocol for the messages that carry the data. Figure 42-1 illustrates a service-oriented architecture.

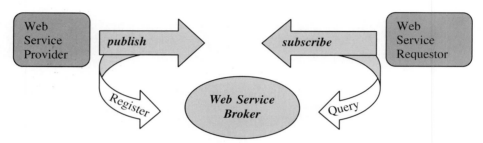

Figure 42-1   Components of a service-oriented architecture

42.2 | Web services

There are several approaches to Web services design, although two methods are the most common: server-centric and rich client.

42.2.1 *Server-centric design*

A *server-centric application* is designed so that almost all business logic and data processing happens on the server. The high-performance desktop computer functions simply as a query and display device. Figure 42-2 shows a server-centric Web service.

The downside to this design is that the high-performance desktop computer is not being utilized in an optimal manner. Most of the load is being supported by the infrastructure on the server side. As the demand on the servers increases, you may have to increase the server capacity even though the desktop machines have capacity to spare.

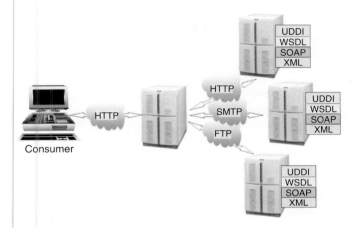

Figure 42-2   Server-centric Web service

42.2.2 *Rich client design*

Figure 42-3 shows a *rich client Web services* design. It has two principal advantages:

disconnected operation
> You can use a rich client application even when the client computer is not connected to the Internet. The application and its data will be synchronized with the server when the Internet connection again becomes available.

improved resource balancing
> There is true loose coupling, which permits the computation and data processing to be distributed among the personal computers and the servers. This efficiency translates into cost savings and – by minimizing the load on the network and server – better response time for the client.

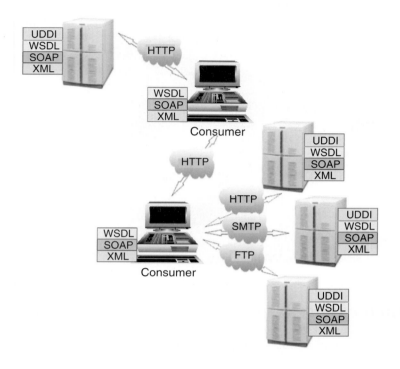

Figure 42-3   Rich client Web services design

42.3 | Steps to rich client conversion

Let's take a hypothetical existing application and follow the steps to make it a rich client Web service. But before we can convert the application, we need to learn what it does now and what the new version must do.

42.3.1 *Application requirements*

Travel Software, Inc. (TSI) creates commercial off-the-shelf software for air and car rental reservation services. The product is aimed at small-to-medium travel agencies.

TSI regularly works with several business partners to integrate TSI's software with other types of travel reservation – hotel reservations, cruise packages, and so forth. For this they must write connectors between their travel reservation engine and those of their partners. Their engine is designed as a three-tier application with only browse-and-query capability on the client side.

Every time TSI changes the interfaces of its reservation engine, it must again engage its business partners to ensure that the interworking hasn't failed. The testing and rework are time consuming and often result in product release delays.

TSI's architecture team would like to redesign the reservation engine to expose its functions as Web services. They expect that would make it easier to interwork with their partners' software, and to add other vendors as well. The team would also like the revised engine to be a rich client application.

42.3.2 *Implementing the conversion*

Figure 42-4 shows TSI's original object model in a *Unified Modeling Language (UML)* class diagram. The objective is to transform it so that some modules and interfaces can be exposed as Web services.

First, we identify collaboration between classes and packages that exemplify unique behavior. Such packages are good candidates for exposure.

Then we convert the application to a rich client design.

Let's look at the process step-by-step.

42.3.3 *Step 1: Identify and classify*

To identify packages that exemplify unique behavior, examine the object model and categorize the classes as follows:

1. Business process
2. Persistence/DB
3. Utilities
4. User interface

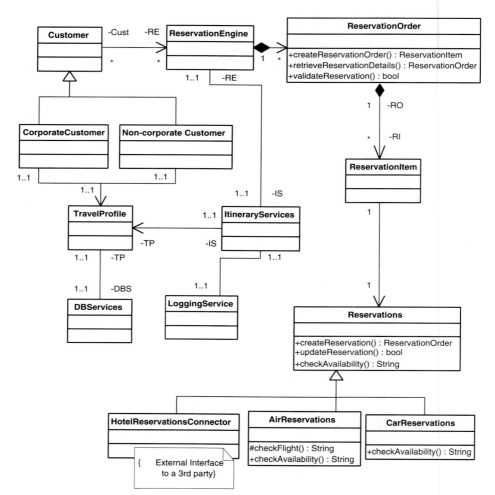

Figure 42-4 Original class diagram

42.3.4 *Step 2: Simplify the inheritance hierarchy*

Next, simplify classes in the inheritance hierarchy that do not add function.

If a subclass serves only for specialization, it can be folded into its super-class. In Figure 42-5 the following classes are marked in gray to indicate that they can be simplified in this way:

- CorporateCustomer
- Non-corporateCustomer
- HotelReservationsConnector
- AirReservations
- CarReservations

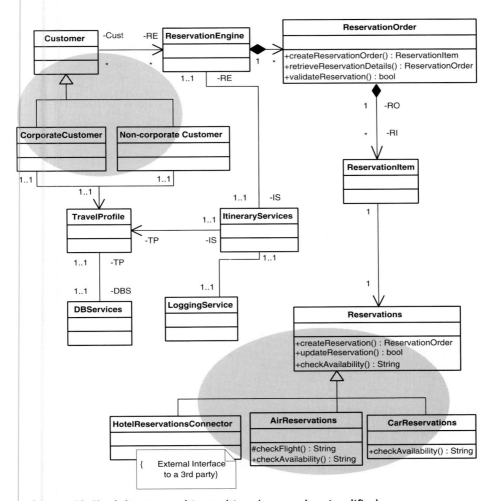

Figure 42-5 Inheritance hierarchies that can be simplified

The result of simplifying the inheritance hierarchy is shown in Figure 42-6.

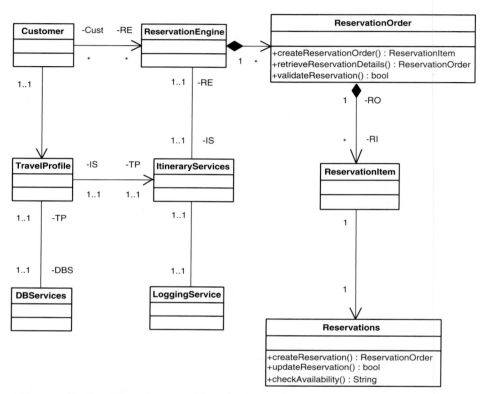

Figure 42-6   Class diagram after applying Step 2

42.3.5   *Step 3: Ignore persistence/DB and simplify utilities*

The next step is to isolate and ignore any persistence or database connectivity classes as these won't need to be redesigned.

If there are utility classes, simplify any inheritance and association links, as was done in Step 2.

In Figure 42-6, DBServices is a database connectivity class and can be ignored. LoggingService is a utility class and should be collapsed into the ItineraryServices class. The result is shown in Figure 42-7.

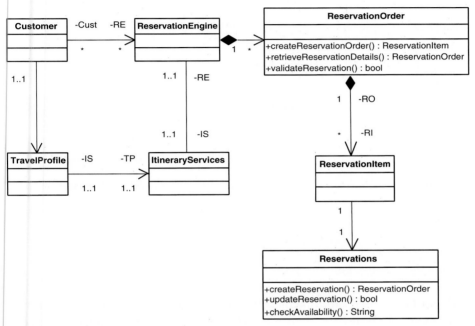

Figure 42-7   Simplified class diagram

42.3.6   *Step 4: Identify related interactions*

Next, analyze Figure 42-7 to identify related interactions among classes. The objective is to create a *component diagram*, as shown in Figure 42-8.

A component diagram allows software architects and designers to recognize interfaces and accomplish two tasks:

■ expose function as Web services; and
■ identify function that could be distributed among clients and servers.

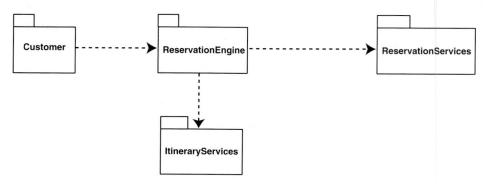

Figure 42-8   Component diagram

42.3.6.1   Expose function as Web services

After analyzing Figure 42-8, the TSI architects exposed the following components as Web services:

- ReservationEngine
- ItineraryServices
- ReservationServices

A more gradual approach could have been taken by using simple XML-based APIs at first, then migrating to Web services in a later release.

42.3.6.2   Distribute function between rich client and server

To take advantage of rich client architecture, the TSI architects made the following decisions.

- They felt that travel agents may want to keep customer profiles on their desktop computers. It therefore made sense to have the Customer component on the client side.
- They also decided to distribute the ItineraryServices component on the client side. That would allow travel agents to query third-party air, car, and hotel reservation Web services when preparing itineraries.

42.4 | Conclusion

Web services appears to have solved the problems that plagued earlier service-oriented architectures, thanks to its use of XML.

When utilized in rich client applications, the combination benefits both server and client. The server has less to do because the client is doing more. But in compensation, the client can run its application without a network connection and can also utilize other available Web services.

Portable rich client applications

Tool Discussion

- Player technology
- XML business application player
- Application layer
- Rich client XML applications
- Software on CD-ROM

Sponsor: ObjectBuilders, Inc., http://www.objectbuilders.com
Contributing expert: Robert L. Schmitter

43

What if business applications were like MP3s? Does that mean the recording industry would sue you for running an inventory report? Not likely, but it might mean that your applications would be portable, platform-neutral, and easily created without programming. If that sounds like music to your ears, here's your chance to be a player in the next generation of XML application development. (Or if not exactly to *be* a player, at least to *use* one!)

M P3s have enormous appeal – even when you have to pay for them!

- They are portable. You can take your music to your car and your handheld player, as well as your desktop PC and the DVD player in your hi-fi system. MP3s have no platform dependencies.
- The players are generic. Any MP3 works with any player.
- You can create them easily, without programming. Lots of tools are available to generate MP3s from your CD collection.

Wouldn't it be nice if business applications were like MP3s?

43.1 | Player technology

MP3s are an example of *player technology*, in which descriptive documents (i.e. not program code) direct the behavior of a generic (i.e. not application-specific) engine called a *player*. The power of the player can vary from a specialized function with limited interaction, such as a media player, to something with more general application capability, such as a Web browser.

Ideally, the documents can be created with a WYSIWYG *assembly tool*, avoiding the need for traditional programming. Media player documents, such as MP3s, are invariably created this way, while Web browser documents are mixed. Plenty of assembly tools can create HTML for simple presentations, but you need to resort to scripting if you want more powerful application functions.

Other well-known examples of player technology are Adobe® *Acrobat*®, used primarily for electronic replication of high-quality print renditions, and Macromedia® *Flash*™, used primarily for interactive multimedia presentations. Both use proprietary document types: PDF and SWF, respectively.

The widely-used player technologies have either a limited application domain, are dependent on proprietary document representations, or both. Let's consider an *XML business application player (XBAP)*, one that could implement mission-critical business applications and that would represent its documents in XML. First we'll look at a requirements scenario, then at the way such a scenario would be implemented without an XBAP. Finally, we'll look at how an actual XBAP – the *LiveXML*™ *Suite* from Object-Builders, Inc. – would approach the job.

And now we'll meet Joe, whose business life – you might say – is *part* madness!

43.2 | Joe's Custom Computers

Buying things through the Internet works well when you are ordering a single item. You just surf the Web, find the best deal, pay for it securely, and track the package to its destination. But when Joe, a high-end custom computer builder, is trying to compete with companies like Dell, he needs more power.

Assume Joe is selling and filling three customer orders for four different computers, each with 25 different parts. Some parts are used in more than one machine and some vendors supply more than one part, so collectively the 100 parts are sourced from 60 vendors.

To obtain the parts, Joe has to purchase and track them at 60 separate vendor sites. Moreover, for project management and customer communication, he also has to correlate and track the 100 parts according to the computer in which they will be used. These are labor-intensive processes for Joe.

Before the Internet, Joe's distributor would have performed these functions. He would have accepted a consolidated order from Joe for all the parts for a specific computer. When parts were shipped to Joe, the distributor would include a consolidated invoice that showed the status of each item ordered.

In the absence of a distributor to integrate the vendors, Joe needs an Integrated e-commerce application, like the one shown in Figure 43-1.

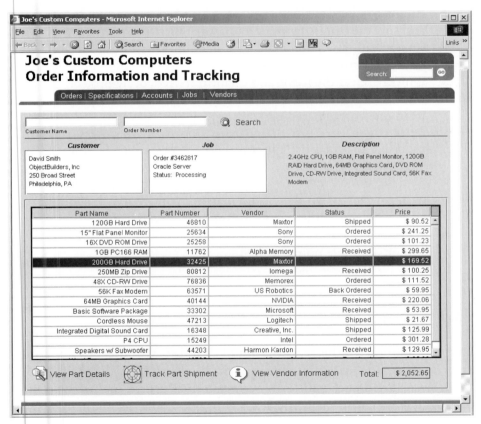

Figure 43-1 Integrated e-commerce application

Joe would first use the application in the proposal stage of a project, to show the customer the computer's technical specification. It is likely that Joe would not be connected to the Internet at that time. It is also possible that the customer would want to make changes to the proposal.

The vendors, of course, would offer their product and ordering information via XML Web services. The application would integrate these services.

Consider some of the requirements the application would have to meet:

- A means for dynamically discovering and selecting among available or preferred vendors and storing the selections in a local profile.
- Ability to query all vendors at once for products and to display and sort the results by price and availability.
- Quick drill-down for detailed product information and related vendor information.
- Quickly select the items and quantities needed, by project.
- Place the individual vendor orders and track them by project from one consolidated parts inventory.

Joe would like to access the application on several client platforms:

- A stand-alone client that can support browsing and order creation even when there is no network connection. It should be available on both a desktop computer and a PDA.
- A browser client, also available on both a desktop and a PDA, and on a mobile phone as well.

43.3 | The conventional solution

A typical solution for this scenario would be to use XML data sources and a lot of custom code, on either the server or the client. Over the years, preferences have shifted back and forth between server-centric and client-centric design. Server-centric currently leads, but Joe could use either, or even intermix them.

43.3.1 *Server-centric design*

A *server-centric design* uses Web servers and application servers to serve static and dynamic content to a browser on a desktop or other platform. The most common arrangement uses platform-specific code on the server and some or all of HTML, XML, and scripts for the client.

One benefit of server-centric design is that both the application and the content can be centrally maintained and updated. Another is that the content is portable across delivery platforms.

Some problems that arise are poor performance, minimal user interface capability, and inability of the application to operate when disconnected from the network.

43.3.2 *Client-centric design*

A *client-centric design* uses client-side applets, stand-alone executables, or browser plug-ins to communicate with data servers and application servers. The benefit of this approach is a rich, interactive client that can work when both connected and disconnected from the Internet.

On the negative side, client-centric design requires custom code and a download for each application. Moreover, the code may be tied to a specific platform.

43.3.3 *Common challenges*

Both design approaches – server-centric and client-centric – share some common challenges:

- Creating a rich-client look-and-feel over a thin Internet pipe.
- Deploying to multiple platforms simultaneously: browser-based, PDA, TV, disconnected clients, etc.
- Reducing latency, bottlenecks and congestion.
- Integration of disparate systems, multiple data sources, multiple XML vocabularies, and Web services.
- Typical development concerns of extensibility, maintainability, reuse, and (possibly) dynamic extensibility.

43.3.4 *Combined approach*

Table 43-1 shows the strengths of each of the two design approaches. It also indicates the benefits if the two could be combined.

Table 43-1   Comparison of design approaches

Strengths	Server-centric	Client-centric	Com-bined
Centrally maintained application and content	X	-	X
Content portable across platforms	X	-	X
High performance	-	X	X
Rich interactive presentation	-	X	X
Works offline	-	X	X

The combined approach enhances the standard three-tiered application architecture. It changes the presentation layer, which is on the client, to a complete three-tiered application of its own. Think of it as an *application layer*. Figure 43-2 shows this transformation.

By creating data and business-logic layers on the client, those portions of an application can be implemented on either client or server, or both simultaneously.

A conventional client-centric or *rich client* solution is actually using an application layer to some degree. However, the need for custom code prevents achieving the full benefits of this approach.

Now let's look at an XBAP solution, which is capable of making full use of the application layer.

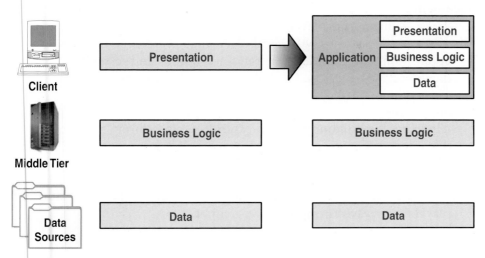

Figure 43-2   Application layer

43.4 | The XBAP solution

It's a shame that Joe will need to develop his own application, since he probably owns one that might have done the job.

Personal finance products like *Microsoft Money*® and *Quicken*® are actually integrated e-commerce applications. They provide a consolidated interface to multiple financial institutions for viewing and managing transactions such as credit card charges, investments, check writing, and bill paying.

If computer part vendors could be substituted for financial firms, purchases for investments, and so forth, Joe might be able to use these programs. But as the programs are custom coded, those substitutions can't be made.

Player technology, however, could have allowed the substitutions. Let's see why by taking a closer look at the workings of an XBAP. We'll use a real product to illustrate – the ObjectBuilders, Inc. *LiveXML Suite*.

Recall the three components of player technology:

documents

These control the player. For example, *LiveXML's Application XML (APX)* is an XML vocabulary that represents a business application. It provides for the integration and assembly of databases, Web services, GUI objects, logic components, etc.

assembly tools

These are for building the application (i.e., for editing the player documents). Ours is called *LiveIntegrator*.™

generic players

These read the player documents and execute the application. The players themselves are application-neutral.

43.4.1 *Application development without coding*

LiveIntegrator uses the familiar *visual programming* paradigm in which the developer selects objects from a palette and positions them in a window. Object types include familiar GUI controls, such as buttons, panes, list boxes, etc.

An object has properties and associated events. Typical visual programming systems require you to write code to handle the events.

For example, to open a new window when the user clicks on a button, you might code a `Clicked()` method like this:

Example 43-1. Custom code for mouse click

```
Clicked()
{
NewWindow.OpenWindow
return
}
```

The properties of the object can usually be inspected and modified directly, including size, position, font, icons, etc. (There was a time when those had to be coded too!)

LiveIntegrator has eliminated programming for events by defining additional properties for the variables that might show up in the method code. For example, a button has the properties `Action` and `Target`, which you can set with the property inspector:

Example 43-2. Property settings

Action: OpenWindow
Target: NewWindow

The code for the `Clicked()` method is now generic and built-in. It looks like the following:

Example 43-3. Generic code for mouse click

```
Clicked()
{
Target.Action
return
}
```

Figure 43-3 shows an application being assembled in *LiveIntegrator*. The application window is at the lower left. At its right is the *Inspector Window*, in which property values can be examined and modified.

At the top is the *Documents Window*, which has several functions. It allows the management of documents and the selection of palettes from which window and object types can be chosen.

43.4.2 *Deploying an application*

Both browser and client platforms use generic executables, applets, components and plug-ins to render and operate the APX, XHTML, and other XML vocabularies.

The application-specific APX documents are either downloaded from a software provider or served by the vendor's servers. The workload balance between server and client is defined by the first APX document loaded. It can differ among concurrent clients, so that a PDA client, for example,

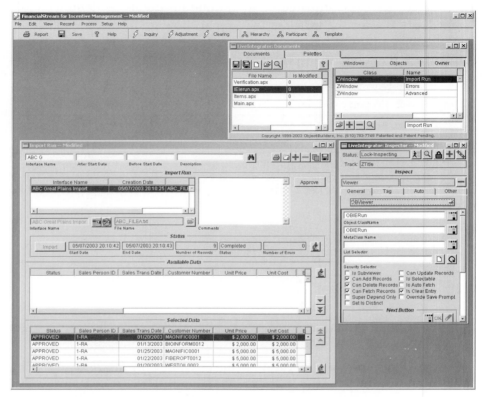

Figure 43-3   Application being assembled in *LiveIntegrator*

might do less of the work than a rich client on the desktop would do. XSLT stylesheets can be used to manage differences among deployment strategies.

In effect, an application *player*, using an application *layer* design, can share middle-tier integration responsibilities between the client and the server.

Tip   Try XML player technology for yourself! There's a full-blown application on the CD-ROM, along with explanations and annotated copies of the XML application documents.

Schemas

- Schema design
- Schema development
- Vocabulary development

Part Fifteen

Nature abhors a schema-less database equally as much as she abhors a vacuum. Create a data table in a spreadsheet and the program immediately searches for field names, and supplies them even if you haven't.

Although XML will let you create a document without an explicit formally-written expression of the document type schema, the benefits of having one are enormous. These chapters will provide insight into schemas, whether you write them using XML DTD declarations or another schema definition language.

We start with a hands-on introduction to schema design, focusing on concepts rather than syntax.

We then consider vocabularies – sets of named element types and attributes – as they are the building blocks of schemas. Since the vocabulary determines the information that will be available at your portal and for use by your applications, you ultimately have to develop your own. We show you how to get started.

Building a schema for a product catalog

Friendly Tutorial

- Schema design considerations
- Step-by-step schema design
- DTD declarations and schema notations
- Datatypes

Contributing expert: Lee Buck

Chapter

44

The better your schema, the better your data! In the case of product catalogs, you could add: And the better your business! In this chapter we will walk you through the analysis and design of a schema for an online product catalog.

T he online catalog is in many respects the heart of electronic commerce. With XML, it can provide a standard and platform-independent way of exchanging information between resellers, manufacturers and customers.

Such exchanges can be thought of as information flows between the various organizations. We'll look at one such flow between manufacturers and the folks at a fictitious website called www.we-sell-everything.com.

We'll use a schema to define what information may exist in the flow, where it may appear and how it should be used. This schema establishes a vocabulary by which we can exchange information and a contract that ensures that the information conforms to our expectations. It must reflect the requirements of our product catalog application.

44.1 | Online catalog requirements

Online catalogs have no bounds. Electronic catalogs provide resellers and manufacturers the opportunity to personalize the customer's experience. Rather than merely publishing a conventional print based catalog on the

Internet, our catalog example will use XML to build part of the framework for a catalog application. This application will build upon existing information resources to provide enriched content interaction and access.

Because XML objects are processable both as documents and as data, the catalog can include not only blocks of descriptive text but also database information. The two will allow our site to provide the user with flexible presentation of the information as well as powerful comparison facilities. This content may be in the form of character text and audio and video files.

The components of our online catalog will enable personalized product pricing for prospects and customers. By including promotional codes and rebate information, the reseller and manufacturer gain added pricing flexibility. Additionally, the catalog will link complementary products to create dynamic solution offerings.

By creating an online catalog, results of customer buying habits can be determined quickly. Using the appropriate approach for schema design, changes to the catalog can be deployed quickly, further enhancing results.

44.2 | Design considerations

Schema design involves a number of issues.

Validation

XML DTDs provide a strong foundation for ensuring that all the necessary pieces of information are present at the right places in a document (i.e. required elements are included, inappropriate ones are not, attributes are supplied when required, etc.). DTDs can also offer some help in constraining the value of a particular attribute or data content of an element. (See 44.3, "Datatypes", on page 686.) The *XML Schema* definition language (XSDL) is a more comprehensive language that also offers these facilities.[1]

Modularity

Modular schemas are one of the best means to build a flexible and reusable schema repository. A modular approach to schema

---

1. And lots of other facilities as well. See the advanced tutorial in Chapter 63, "XML Schema (XSDL)", on page 1030.

creation delivers application flexibility and component reuse. Libraries of modular schemas can facilitate e-commerce in heterogeneous environments. Taking a modular approach to schema design is an important goal for our little project. In our case it will mean pulling out the notion of an address and placing it into a budding corporate standards schema which will contain such often repeated element types.

Relationship modeling

Schemas provide several facilities to model the relationships between pieces of information. One is the structure of the document: the context in which an element appears. Another is ID/IDREF relationships. These permit all kinds of relationships to be modeled independently of the structure of the document. In our example we'll use these two facilities to model the relationships involved.

Collaboration

Collaborative design efforts help ensure that schemas reflect diverse corporate needs. Schemas will be shared between organizations to help ensure successful e-commerce applications. Resellers and manufacturers will want to collaborate on schemas to establish mutually agreeable rules for data interchange.

Elements vs. attributes

Many pieces of information which we want to model could be represented either as elements or as attributes. While each has its own strengths and limitations, the choice between them is often a matter of style. In our case we'll tend to use attributes for atomic data with a corresponding datatype and use elements for organizing concepts and for representing structures of data items.

Iterative design and schema flexibility

Schemas are living documents that must change as business requirements change. When such change occurs, two sets of compatibility issues arise: a) can existing XML documents be validated against the new schema and b) can existing processes handle documents conforming to the new schema? Careful design can maximize the potential for answering "yes" to both. For our example, we'll design the `promotion` element type to accommodate new kinds of promotions in the future.

44.3 | Datatypes

A *datatype* is a category of information, usually the kind that comes in small pieces and is used to build bigger ones. The examples in Table 44-1 will convey the idea better than any formal definition. They are a subset of those defined in the W3C Datatypes spec (Chapter 62, "Datatypes", on page 1000).

Table 44-1   Common datatypes

string	decimal	IDREFS
boolean	float	date
anyURI	integer	time

It is good for a schema to be able to identify and enforce the use of datatypes because it strengthens the contract between the producer and the consumer of an XML document. In e-commerce applications such as our catalog, we need to assure the integrity of the information to the maximum extent possible at the earliest moment. We'll want to specify datatypes for the attribute values in our schema.

44.4 | The design

Our catalog is to come from one or more manufacturers. It needs to contain information about each manufacturer, the products available and any special promotions available for the products.

44.4.1 *The catalog*

We'll model a catalog as the root element of the document. It contains a repeatable sequence of elements which provide information about each of the concepts: manufacturer, product, and promotion. Our model is as shown in Figure 44-1.

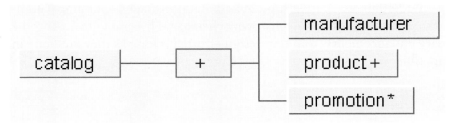

Figure 44-1   `catalog` **content model** `(manufacturer, product+, promotion*)+`

A catalog element will need various bits of housekeeping information like its effective date and its expiration date. More robust implementations might well contain routing information, authentication and other bells and whistles but we'll keep it simple. We'll model the dates as attributes as shown in Table 44-2:

Table 44-2   `catalog` **attributes**

Attribute Name	Element Type	Datatype
date.expires	catalog	date
date.issued	catalog	date

44.4.2 *Manufacturer*

A manufacturer element will contain name and address information, as shown in Figure 44-2. The former we'll model as an ID attribute type since we need it to uniquely identify a particular manufacturer (see Table 44-3).

The address information provides a simple example of a powerful concept in schema design: modularization. It enables us to build an inventory of reusable chunks that can be referenced from multiple schemas. The address model shown is rather limited and inappropriate to our global audience. By separating it out into its own schema, we'll be able to isolate the necessary enhancements from our design efforts (as long as they are done in a compatible way).

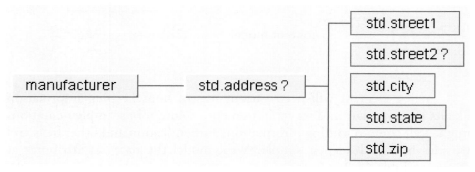

Figure 44-2   manufacturer **content model** (std.address?) **and** std.address **content model** (std.street1, std.street2?, std.city, std.state, std.zip)

Table 44-3   manufacturer **attributes**

Attribute Name	Element Type	Datatype
name	manufacturer	ID

44.4.3 *Product*

The product element type provides basics like name, SKU (essentially its bar-code), and SRP (standard retail price). These we'll model as attributes. Importantly, we'll model SKU as an ID attribute so we can refer to it later from within a promotion. We can then also use SKUs in a complements attribute to refer to other products that are complementary to this product (i.e. taken as a whole they comprise a complete solution). We want to be able to include a picture or other such media about the product so we'll define a media attribute that locates such media.

We'll also include a mixed element type for a product description that permits portions of the description to be marked as a feature or a benefit (see Figure 44-3 and Table 44-4). This simple refinement of the description enables a much richer set of presentation possibilities on our website. More advanced designs would include a much richer set of potential markup here, providing maximum flexibility to our website designers to present the information in various ways.

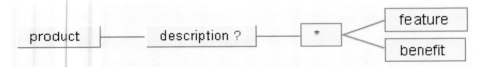

Figure 44-3   product **content model** (description?) **and** description **content model** (feature | benefit)*

44.4.4 *Promotion*

Finally we have the promotion element type. A promotion element may contain information about two different types of price reduction: bundle, which provides for a lower price for a particular product when one or more other products are purchased at the same time, and discount, which provides volume-based pricing (see Figure 44-4 and Table 44-5). In the future, as shown in Figure 44-4, rebate could be added without affecting existing documents.

Table 44-4   `product` attributes

Attribute Name	Element Type	Datatype
complements	product	IDREFS
media	product	ENTITY
product.name	product	string
sku	product	ID
srp	product	currency

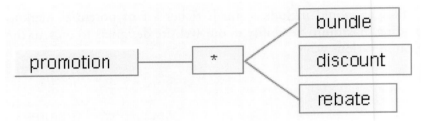

Figure 44-4   `promotion` content model after adding `rebate (bundle |`
`discount | rebate)*`

44.4.5 *The big picture*

We did it. Taken as a whole our schema's structure looks like Figure 44-5.
   A sample document that conforms to the schema looks like Example
44-1.

44.5 | Schema definition languages

We designed our schema at a conceptual level, using tables and a visualization of the schema definition. Software, however, requires a character string

Table 44-5   Attributes of `promotion` subelements

Attribute Name	Element Type	Datatype
other.skus	bundle	IDREFS
sku	bundle	ID
price	bundle	currency
sku	discount	ID
min.qty	discount	integer
pct.off	discount	float

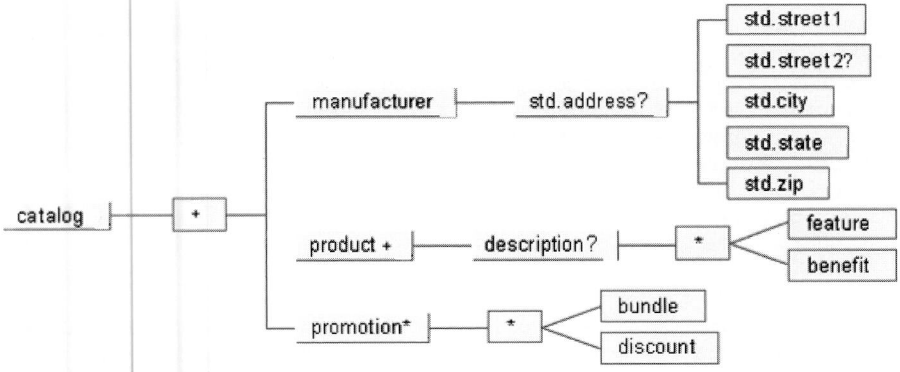

Figure 44-5   Document type structure

representation of the schema definition. We show several examples in this section.

44.5.1   *DTD declarations*

In Example 44-2 we can take a look at part of the schema, expressed as DTD declarations. Notice the use of `dt4dtd:a` fixed attributes to specify the datatype for various attributes.

Example 44-1. Sample `catalog` document instance

```
<catalog date.issued = "2001-05-31" date.expires = "2001-06-30">
<manufacturer name = "Stuff-o-rama">
   <std.address>
      <std.street1>127 Walking Way</std.street1>
      <std.city>Chapel Hill</std.city>
      <std.state>NC</std.state>
      <std.zip>27514</std.zip>
   </std.address>
</manufacturer>

<product sku = "12-3783-23" product.name = "foozle" srp = "29.99">
<description>
The foozle is the finest in plastic oven-ware.
Its <feature>patented melt-away containment
</feature>means that <benefit>you'll never have
to wash another dish.</benefit>
</description>
</product>

<product sku = "12-2412-23" product.name = "singey" srp = "19.99">
<description>
The singey aluminum oven mitts are ideal for
accessories for any kitchen. Available in three
sizes with convenient <feature>teflon
coating</feature> to <benefit>ensure a steady
grip.</benefit>
</description>
</product>

<promotion>
   <bundle sku="12-2412-23" price="14.99" other.skus="12-3783-23"/>
   <discount sku = "12-2412-23" min.qty = "10" pct.off = "10" />
   <discount sku = "12-2412-23" min.qty = "20" pct.off = "15" />
   <discount sku = "12-2412-23" min.qty = "50" pct.off = "20" />
</promotion>
</catalog>
```

A single `a-dtype` names the datatypes for all of an element type's attributes that need them. In order to link each datatype name with its attribute, the `a-dtype` value is a list of pairs, each attribute name being followed by its datatype name.[2]

---

2. `dt4dtd:a` is explained in 62.6.3, "XML DTDs", on page 1028. The CD-ROM contains open source software that lets programmers support `dt4dtd:a` with both the DOM and SAX interfaces.

Example 44-2. Schema excerpt expressed as DTD declarations

```
<!ELEMENT catalog   (manufacturer , product+ , promotion* )>
<!ATTLIST catalog   date.issued  CDATA     #IMPLIED
                    date.expires CDATA     #IMPLIED
                    dt4dtd:a     NMTOKENS  #FIXED 'date.issued date
                                                  date.expires date'>
<!ELEMENT manufacturer  (std.address? )>
<!ATTLIST manufacturer  name     ID        #IMPLIED >
<!ELEMENT product (description? )>
<!ATTLIST product sku           ID         #REQUIRED
                  product.name  CDATA      #IMPLIED
                  srp           CDATA      #REQUIRED
                  complements   IDREFS     #IMPLIED
                  media         ENTITY     #IMPLIED
                  dt4dtd:a      NMTOKENS   #FIXED 'srp currency'>
<!ELEMENT promotion  (bundle | discount )*>
<!ELEMENT bundle    EMPTY>
<!ATTLIST bundle    price        CDATA     #REQUIRED
                    complements  IDREFS    #REQUIRED
                    sku          ID        #REQUIRED
                    dt4dtd:a     NMTOKENS  #FIXED 'price currency'>
<!ELEMENT discount EMPTY>
<!ATTLIST discount min.qty       CDATA     '1'
                   pct.off       CDATA     #REQUIRED
                   sku           ID        #REQUIRED
                   dt4dtd:a      NMTOKENS  #FIXED 'min.qty integer
                                                  pct.off float'>
```

44.5.2 *XML Schema definition language (XSDL)*

Example 44-3 shows the XSDL version of most of the element types defined in Example 44-2. The XSDL definition is an XML document. Note that the datatype is specified individually for each attribute definition, using the type attribute.

44.6 | Conclusion

Our catalog schema provides the foundation for building an e-commerce website. By formulating and expressing our information flows using schemas we are assured that we can connect with our business partners no mat-

Example 44-3. Schema excerpt expressed in XSDL

```
<xsd:element name="catalog">
<xsd:complexType>
 <xsd:sequence>
  <xsd:element ref="manufacturer"/>
  <xsd:element ref="product" minOccurs="1" maxOccurs="unbounded"/>
  <xsd:element ref="promotion" minOccurs="0" maxOccurs="unbounded"/>
 </xsd:sequence>
 <xsd:attribute name="date.issued" type="xsd:date"/>
 <xsd:attribute name="date.expires" type="xsd:date"/>
</xsd:complexType>
</xsd:element>
<xsd:element name="manufacturer">
<xsd:complexType>
 <xsd:sequence>
  <xsd:element ref="std.address" minOccurs="0" maxOccurs="1"/>
 </xsd:sequence>
 <xsd:attribute name="name" type="xsd:ID"/>
</xsd:complexType>
</xsd:element>
<xsd:element name="product">
<xsd:complexType>
 <xsd:sequence>
  <xsd:element ref="description" minOccurs="0" maxOccurs="1"/>
 </xsd:sequence>
 <xsd:attribute name="sku" type="xsd:ID" use="required"/>
 <xsd:attribute name="product.name" type="xsd:string"/>
 <xsd:attribute name="srp" type="currency" use="required"/>
 <xsd:attribute name="complements" type="xsd:IDREFS"/>
 <xsd:attribute name="media" type="xsd:ENTITY"/>
</xsd:complexType>
</xsd:element>
<xsd:element name="promotion">
<xsd:complexType>
 <xsd:choice minOccurs="0" maxOccurs="unbounded">
  <xsd:element ref="bundle"/>
  <xsd:element ref="discount"/>
 </xsd:choice>
</xsd:complexType>
</xsd:element>
```

ter what type of technical infrastructure they may have. We can maximize the business impact of the information and respond quickly to new opportunities as they emerge.

Building your e-commerce vocabulary

Application Discussion

■ Creating a schema

■ Capturing business semantics

■ Reuse for e-commerce

Contributing expert: Priscilla Walmsley, author of *Definitive XML Schema*

Chapter

45

Your computers may walk the walk, but can they talk the talk? In today's e-commerce, just as in human discourse, vocabulary is vital. Your computer and those of your business partners might speak the same language – XML, of course – but do they attach the same meaning to the words? Let this chapter be your guide to straight talk!

The people in your company have a vocabulary that they use when talking about your business. Words like *part*, *adjustment*, and *transaction* have a specific meaning when used in the context of your organization, and they're not just meaningful to people.

45.1 | Why do you need an e-commerce vocabulary?

Your specialized company vocabulary might have developed initially as purely human discourse, but information systems have since influenced it and made it more structured and precise. While developing those systems, users, programmers, and data analysts have painstakingly documented the terms and data elements used in your business. They have described what the words mean, how they relate to one another, what type of data they represent, and how to determine that data's validity.

Now e-commerce challenges us to share data with external business partners, customers, and suppliers. That means all parties must be using the same words to ensure that they understand each other. In XML terms, they must agree on schemas that define those words: the corporate e-commerce vocabulary.

45.2 | Where do schemas come from?

Sorry to say, the stork doesn't bring them. You either have to build them or borrow them.

45.2.1 *Building a new schema*

In some cases, your organization will have the luxury of defining the schemas that are to be used for data interchange with your trading partners. This may be the case if you are a large organization with many small trading partners.

We call this a luxury because there are lots of ways to model data. It is certainly convenient if you have the opportunity to use a vocabulary and data structure that closely match your own.

Consider two possible variations in something as elemental as telephone contact information, for example.

1. One way to model the phone number would be to allow for two specific phone numbers: day and evening. Many systems are currently designed this way.
2. Other systems may be designed to allow an unlimited number of phone numbers, with a description for each (e.g. "home", "mobile", "office", "pager", etc.).

To complicate things further, a different vocabulary might be used in each of these models. One may use the term "business phone" to represent what the other system calls "office number". Neither of these approaches is necessarily better, just different.

Being the creator of the schema reduces the amount of work required to convert your existing data structures to XML documents. For example, if you used the second model in your database and you had to use someone else's schema that was based on the first model, you would need to search through your data for each "home" phone number and convert it to "evening". Although this task may seem trivial taken alone, hundreds of these minor conversions require time to analyze and process.

Another benefit of owning the vocabulary is that the people in your organization will understand it intuitively and find it easier to assess the impact of a change. Also, if you eventually open up your schema to competing companies, they will have the extra task of converting their vocabulary to match yours.

45.2.2 *Borrowing an existing schema*

In many cases, you will not be creating the schemas you will use for interchange with other parties. Instead, you will be using schemas defined by an industry standards group, trading partner, or vendor. In this case, it may seem that capturing your own corporate vocabulary is less important, since a vocabulary is already provided for you. This is a fallacy.

It is essential to understand the interface between your own systems and the data you share with your trading partners. You won't be revising your internal systems to conform to the interchange schemas. Rather, you will be converting data back and forth between your internal systems and the external ones, and all the schemas will be subject to change over time.

Developing your internal vocabulary for e-commerce allows you to split the problem into two independent parts:

1. Capturing your existing data and metadata in its original format and translating it to XML using a vocabulary you understand; and
2. Translating the semantic meanings from one XML schema to another.

45.3 | Capturing existing business semantics

You may recall that we said earlier that, while developing your systems,

... users, programmers, and data analysts have painstakingly documented the terms and data elements used in your business. They have described what the words mean, how they relate to one another, what type of data they represent, and how to determine that data's validity.

That's the good news!

The bad news is that your corporate vocabulary is probably not neatly documented in a single place, but rather embedded in legacy systems on various platforms. These legacy systems are often cryptic, but they contain the key to understanding the data that will be exchanged.

A vast resource of information about your business processes exists embedded in your legacy systems and models. The reason for building an e-commerce vocabulary is to expose this system information, or metadata, and thereby allow it to be used easily in e-commerce applications.

Fortunately, there's more good news: Business semantics gathering tools can scan existing systems and models and unify them in a common, tree-structured XML-based model. Let's see how that is done.

45.3.1 *Relational databases*

A large percentage of the data that is to be used in e-commerce applications currently resides in relational databases. These databases were designed by database administrators and developers who understood the business logic behind the data.

The catalogs of relational databases precisely describe the data they contain. From an ODBC data source, a semantics gathering too should be able to extract relational database information, including table layouts, table and column descriptions, datatypes, and primary and foreign keys.

45.3.2 *Electronic data interchange (EDI)*

The EDI standard dictionaries provide a semantically rich model for e-commerce. If your organization is using EDI, chances are many of your existing processes use the EDI vocabulary, or at least understand it.

Much of the semantics of the EDI standards can be leveraged for use in XML-based e-commerce systems. For example, EDI defines thousands of atomic data elements in detail, including lengthy lists of valid values for each one. There is no need to throw this information away and start from scratch.

Example 45-1 shows how XML can represent EDI semantics.

Example 45-1. Excerpt from a schema definition of an ANSI X12 EDI data element

```
<simpleType name="element-482">
<annotation>
  <documentation>Payment Action Code</documentation>
</annotation>
<restriction base="string">
  <maxLength value="2" />
  <enumeration value="AJ">
    <annotation>
      <documentation>Adjustment</documentation>
    </annotation>
  </enumeration>
  <enumeration value="ER">
    <annotation>
      <documentation>Evaluated Receipts Settlement</documentation>
    </annotation>
  </enumeration>
  <enumeration value="FL">
    <annotation><documentation>Final</documentation></annotation>
  </enumeration>
  <enumeration value="NS">
    <annotation>
      <documentation>Not Specified</documentation>
    </annotation>
  </enumeration>
  <enumeration value="PA">
    <annotation>
      <documentation>Payment in Advance</documentation>
    </annotation>
  </enumeration>
  <enumeration value="PO">
    <annotation>
      <documentation>Payment on Account</documentation>
    </annotation>
  </enumeration>
  <enumeration value="PP">
    <annotation>
      <documentation>Partial Payment</documentation>
    </annotation>
  </enumeration>
</restriction>
</simpleType>
```

45.3.3 *Program data structures*

Large mainframe files contain most of the production data that is not stored in relational databases. Programmers have written complex *copybooks* to represent this data, including names and datatypes of the elements in these files, and valid values in some cases. A gathering tool should be able to parse a copybook and match it to a corresponding XML tree structure.

45.3.4 *Logical models*

Your company may have logical models of your business systems and processes. These models have additional descriptive information to supplement your corporate e-commerce vocabulary.

For example, a database administrator may have created an entity-relationship model of a database for an accounting system. The model contains detailed information about each column in the database, including use cases, examples, and valid values. A business semantics gathering tool should incorporate such models into your e-commerce vocabulary.

45.3.5 *Repositories*

Some organizations have already put a lot of effort into capturing and managing their corporate metadata. These organizations have built metadata repositories, which centrally store system information such as database layouts, copybook structures, and logical models. The tool should leverage these efforts by extracting metadata from commercially available repository products.

45.3.6 *Customized sources*

Many organizations have metadata stored in proprietary or less-common formats. For example, some systems may be documented in customized HTML files. A business semantics gathering tool should be extensible to handle these situations; for example, by means of scripts or plug-in modules that understand unsupported data formats.

45.4 | Reuse for e-commerce

After capturing the existing semantic business definitions, the next step is to make them useful for e-commerce systems.

45.4.1 *Editing and refining*

Because descriptive data is often incomplete, or is merged from many sources, some manual refinement might be required. It is helpful if your semantics gathering tool allows editing of the descriptive information in the new XML data definitions.

45.4.2 *Schema generation*

After the descriptive information has been refined, users can generate DTDs and schema definitions that incorporate the new vocabulary. These DTDs might represent only fragments of complete document types.

For example, a schema generated from a relational table may contain customer header information only. This is desirable, since schemas are more likely to be used and reused if they are modular. An XML document could contain data from many different subject areas (e.g. customer information, sales data, and product information), and several XML documents might use the same customer information.

45.4.3 *Managing the vocabulary*

Capturing your existing vocabulary and preparing it for e-commerce is an important initiative. However, the bulk of the effort is wasted if that vocabulary languishes in text files somewhere and is never reused.

It is important to provide access to the corporate e-commerce vocabulary so that it can be understood and reused freely. There are schema repositories that allow you to store and manage the definitions centrally.

Voice

- VoiceXML
- Voice in a mobile environment
- Adding telephony to websites

Part Sixteen

One of the prized souvenirs of markup language pioneers is a coffee mug that states "SGML spoken here". The joke, of course, is that SGML, like modern Latin, is strictly a written language.

Linda Goldfarb used to embroider that statement onto bibs for SGML community newborns. The joke there was that any sounds uttered by the bib wearer were as likely to be SGML as any other language.

The SGML community's latest newborn – we refer now to XML – still can't speak for itself. But increasingly it is becoming the means of controlling what is spoken. XML-based languages like VoiceXML, coupled with advances in speech recognition and synthesis, are making the Web a spoken medium. In this part you'll learn how to voice-enable your website, and how XML can be a vehicle for voice control – or voice control for a vehicle!

VoiceXML in a mobile environment

Case Study

■ Introduction to the VoiceXML language

■ Architecture of a VoiceXML application

■ A moving case study

Sponsor: IBM Corporation, www.ibm.com/alphaWorks

Contributing experts: Chuck Lam, Ying Lee, Lucas Ryan and Daniel Jue

> Keyboards and mice are hardly a natural way to communicate, as anyone with carpal tunnel syndrome can tell you! What people are really good at is talking, and computers finally have the hardware that lets them understand and talk back. Now XML is making it easier to program that hardware, driving new applications and giving a whole new meaning to the term "mobile environment".

V endors would like us to become dependent on ubiquitous computing and information services. They want us to manage emails, check stock quotes, and do other tasks at any time, anywhere.

But early adopters are finding that miniature screens, micro keyboards, and stylus scribbles are not the ideal interface. They are impediments to widespread utilization of ubiquitous services.

Fortunately, improvements in speech recognition and automated text-to-speech technologies are finally making voice interfaces feasible. The challenge now is making them easy to develop.

In this area, as in so many others, XML is coming to the rescue, here in the form of *Voice Extensible Markup Language (VoiceXML)*. VoiceXML is an XML-based markup language for developing voice applications. It was defined by the *VoiceXML Forum* (`http://www.voicexml.org`), an industry consortium of over 300 companies, and is being standardized by the W3C.

46.1 | Why VoiceXML?

VoiceXML is attractive to developers for many reasons. Some of the major ones are:

- It abstracts away the complexity of speech processing from application developers. The application developer does not need to know anything about the signal processing techniques to make speech work.
- It is based on the client-server architecture of the Internet, and its component architecture is similar to many existing Web technologies.
- A VoiceXML application can share the back-end infrastructure of a graphical Web application, particularly if the back-end data layer is based on XML.
- VoiceXML allows portable applications that can scale from small-footprint speech processing systems like IBM's *Embedded ViaVoice* to full-blown speech servers, such as IBM's *Websphere Voice Server*.
- Numerous VoiceXML outsourcers (*voice portals*) will host the speech processing system and telephony equipment for application developers.

Today the most popular voice applications are *interactive voice response services (IVR)* using the telephone. These include voice dialing, information retrieval such as voice-mail management, and transactions such as stock trading.

These are popular initial applications because:

- their limited vocabulary is well suited for highly accurate speech recognition, and
- the expensive hardware (speech recognizer, text-to-speech generator, etc.) can be centralized and amortized among many users.

46.2 | Components of a VoiceXML application

Figure 46-1 illustrates a typical VoiceXML application architecture. Its main components are:

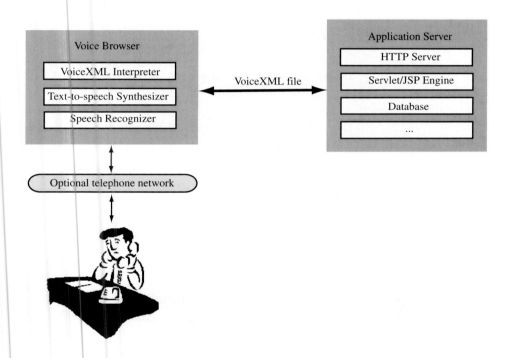

Figure 46-1   A typical VoiceXML application architecture

application server
It hosts the application logic and serves the appropriate VoiceXML files.

VoiceXML file
Like an HTML file, a VoiceXML file specifies what to present and the allowable inputs from the user.

Voice browser

It is analogous to an HTML browser. It renders the speech and converts the user's voice input into a machine-understandable form. The browser and end user might require a telephone network to communicate.

Let's look at each of these components in more detail.

46.2.1 *VoiceXML file*

A VoiceXML file is an XML document conforming to the VoiceXML DTD. A partial example is shown in Example 46-1.

The top-level element types, such as `form`, are called *dialogs*. They are composed of `field` elements, which specify audible prompts and the `grammar` of user inputs that can validly respond to the prompts.[1]

46.2.2 *Application server*

The back-end database and application logic are exactly the same as for a graphical Web application. They can be developed using familiar technologies such as a Java servlet/JSP engine, a Web server using the HTTP or HTTPS protocol, and a conventional DBMS.

The presentation layer, however, now renders the output as a VoiceXML file instead of HTML. If the application content is already in XML, the change to the presentation layer may be as simple as specifying a different XSLT stylesheet.

---

1. The notation for grammars is not defined by the VoiceXML spec, which considers them comparable to graphic formats; vendors define their own. The content of the `grammar` element in this example is character data. The strings that look like `option` tags are not actually XML.

46.2.3 *Voice browser*

The Voice browser does the heavy-duty work of speech processing and interpretation of VoiceXML files. It thereby frees application developers from the complexity of speech recognition and text-to-speech processing.

The user interacts with the browser in much the same way as with an HTML browser, except now the user "views" the content verbally instead of visually. Some voice browsers even support the navigation concepts of HTML browsers, such as bookmarks, "go back", and "go forward".

There are even full-duplex voice browsers that allow a user to *barge in*. That is, the user can issue a command or a response before the browser has finished speaking. In older half-duplex systems, the user must wait for the prompts to complete before speaking. The barge-in feature allows experienced users of an application to navigate rapidly, while still allowing novices to be guided by prompts.

46.3 | A VoiceXML case study

We've previously discussed the vital role XML plays in automotive documentation. You could, if you were as inclined to bad puns as we are, call it a "driving force", a technology that accelerates in the parsing lane, etc.

But VoiceXML is leading us to even greater transports of inspired wordplay, and to some inspired technology as well. We'll[2] now look at an application that adds a new component to the concept of a mobile environment – self-propulsion!

46.3.1 *The IBM alphaWorks TechMobile*

The automobile is a natural environment for voice technology. A driver should keep eyes on the road and hands on the wheel, so exclusive dependency on a graphical user interface isn't feasible.

To demonstrate how its technologies can work in this setting, in 2000 IBM alphaWorks created the *TechMobile*, shown in Figure 46-2.

---

2. Please admire our restraint: we might have said "wheel"!

Figure 46-2   The *TechMobile*

46.3.2 *Features*

The voice controller inside the *TechMobile* utilizes IBM's *ViaVoice* for speech recognition and text-to-speech processing. It supports the following functions:

- Check email.
- Control the car's MP3 player.
- Lock and unlock the car doors.
- Flash the headlights.
- Control the air conditioning system, including fans.
- Raise and lower the windows.

And just for fun, one can activate a voice-controlled number-guessing game by saying "I'm bored."

The same functions are also accessible through an onboard touch-sensitive screen that acts as an HTML browser interface. Because of modular architecture and VoiceXML's hiding of the underlying speech processing, much of the application logic is shared by the HTML interface and the VoiceXML interface.

46.3.3 *Architecture overview*

The architecture of voice applications for a car differs from that of voice applications for phones in several aspects. One is that a phone is a "thin" client, whereas a car is a "thick" client. That is, phones are more constrained in terms of physical size, power consumption, and price, which in turn affects the available computational power, memory size, etc.

Because of these constraints, the voice browser in a telephony application typically acts as a proxy and resides separately from the phone client itself. In a car environment, however, the voice browser can be installed internally.

Moreover, as most functions of the application server are for controlling the car itself, it makes sense to design the system so that all components are inside the car. Doing so limits the use of wide area wireless networks (which can be unreliable) to functions like email that inherently require them.

VoiceXML makes such a distributed architecture possible without painful trade-offs. The voice browser and all application logic for controlling the car, including the server, are inside the car; in effect, they form an intranet.

External application services, such as email, are hosted remotely from the car. VoiceXML has a linking feature that enables both internal and external services to be presented to the user as a seamless whole.

46.3.4 *How the system works*

Example 46-1 is an edited skeleton of the actual VoiceXML text used in the *TechMobile*. It is activated when entering the car.

The first `form` element, named "Introduction", greets the driver with the words:

> Welcome to IBM alphaWorks *TechMobile*. You can control different functions by voice command.

The `goto` element then directs the browser to the next `form`, called "ChooseFunction", which begins by defining a `grammar` of valid user inputs.

The `grammar` also indicates whether any inputs are considered synonymous by the application. For example, the inputs "mail" and "email" both

Example 46-1. A VoiceXML application

```
<?xml version="1.0"?>
<vxml version="1.0">
<form id="Introduction">
  <block>
    <audio>Welcome to I.B.M alphaWorks TechMobile.</audio>
    <pause>200</pause>
    <audio>
      You can control different functions by voice command.
    </audio>
    <pause>200</pause>
    <goto next="#ChooseFunction"/>
  </block>
</form>
<form id="ChooseFunction">
  <field name="function">
    <grammar><![CDATA[
      [
        [mail email]                             {<option "EMAIL">}
        [music mp3]                              {<option "MUSIC">}
        [door doors]                             {<option "DOORS">}
        [headlights headlight light lights] {<option "HEADLIGHTS">}
      ]
    ]]></grammar>
    <prompt>
      <audio>
        Please choose a function. Doors, MP3, headlights, or email.
      </audio>
      <pause>2000</pause>
    </prompt>
    <filled>
      <result name="DOORS">
        <audio>You selected doors.</audio>
        <goto next="#ControlDoor"/>
      </result>
      <result name="EMAIL">
        <audio>You selected email.</audio>
        <goto next="http://email.server.net/servlet/CheckEmail"/>
      </result>
      ...
```

select the same option, "EMAIL". Similarly, both "music" and "mp3" select the "MUSIC" option.

The "ChooseFunction" form next prompts the user to:

Please choose a function: doors, MP3, headlights, or email.

As the voice browser supports the barge-in feature, the user can respond with a selection before hearing the complete prompt.

The `filled` element contains a `result` for each selectable function. The `result` confirms the user's choice audibly (`audio`) and directs the browser to `goto` the associated `form`.

For internal functions, the `form` can be in the same VoiceXML file, as is the case for "ControlDoor". For external services, like "EMAIL", the location of the `form` is specified by a URI.

46.3.5 *Conclusion*

Cars and computers have been talking back to us for a long time. Now they are starting to listen to, and understand, us as well. Although the hardware and software for low-level voice control are complex, VoiceXML can hide that complexity from the application developer.

As a result, voice-based interfaces are becoming more prevalent. And, as the *TechMobile* demonstrates, even if they can't yet drive towards a brilliant future by themselves, they can at least make sure the doors are safely locked for the journey!

 Tip   IBM alphaWorks has provided a suite of free software for you on the CD-ROM.

Adding telephony to your website

- Human/machine dialog
- Interactive voice systems
- Telephony application development
- Building a customer notification system

Contributing expert: Lee Anne Phillips

Chapter

47

> Can we talk? Well, if one of us is human and the other a computer, probably not. At least not in any meaningful way. But recent advances in voice recognition and synthesis, telephony switches, and XML-based languages are leading us toward true dialog – and a new definition of what it means to have XML call out to you!

P ersonalized dialog – directed at ourselves alone – is the most engaging form of verbal communication. Voice-enabled computers, however, typically just parrot monologs. Now new technology, based on XML, is letting computers take the first steps toward true dialog. The dialog is conducted by telephone, and one of the parties can be your website.

47.1 | The need for human/machine dialog

There is a growing dependency on self-service in most of our day-to-day business transactions. From supermarkets to gas stations, from parking meters to banking at the automated teller machine, the only interaction with human beings most of us have while shopping is with the clerk at the checkout stand.

In fact, in many stores it's difficult even to find a human being not actively involved in taking money from customers. This is commerce pared down to its bare essentials, with every resource being dedicated to supplying goods for a price, and as little as possible spent on ancillary activities.

But we often need advice or information along with our purchase, or want a service instead of goods. The new self-service paradigm often precludes any such interaction without waiting in a long queue.

And if that queue is for telephone support, it is punctuated at best by cheery messages describing the approximate wait time, and at worst by inane insistence on offering unwanted automated service instead.

But phone calls don't have to be this one-sided.

47.2 | Interactive voice systems

While we're still some years away from talking freely to our computers with the expectation of a coherent reply, the conversation has become far less one-sided. Advances in automated speech recognition and speech synthesis make it at least possible to give a simple order, with a reasonable expectation of a simple action or report being generated in response.

We're seeing this happen in several areas, including:

interactive voice response (IVR)
Auto-attendant, telesales, telephone banking, call center integration, self-help menus and fax-back services, teleconferencing, and automatic callback.

Web by telephone
Calendars and contacts, FAQs and support content, weather, travel directions, stock quotes, personalized news, directories, and listings.

personal communications
Follow-me/find-me, Internet call waiting, intelligent call forwarding, email by phone, reply by phone, voicemail replacement, and unified messaging.

instant notification

Travel information, consumer and business auctions, stock trades and price changes, important email, network equipment failure, meetings and appointments, and instant messaging.

47.3 | Telephony application development

One of the inhibitors to better computer telephony has been the cost and difficulty of implementation.

Until recently, the total number of qualified telephony application developers in the world numbered in the thousands. Developing an application and tying it to corporate data was an arduous and expensive process, typically involving:

- Proprietary hardware with dedicated telephone interface cards.
- Proprietary APIs requiring knowledge of telephony.
- Programming without visual program design tools.
- Platforms that did not include interfaces to provisioning or billing services.
- Direct interaction with multiple regional telephone companies and knowledge of local rules.

The situation today is changing for the better:

- Open XML-based standards, such as VoiceXML, are being developed for voice and telephony, hiding much of the technical complexity from developers.
- Web telephony service providers lease bandwidth and ports, eliminating the need to purchase proprietary hardware or deal with telephone companies.
- Visual design tools are available for telephony application development, such as that shown in Figure 47-1.

Let's see how a telephony application can be developed for your website using these new facilities.

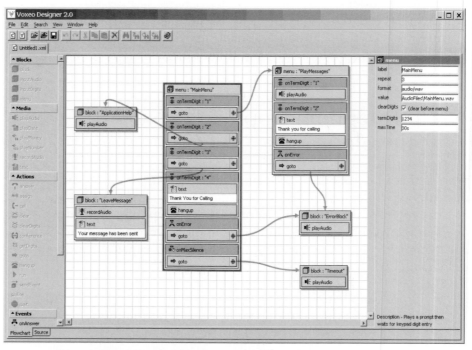

Figure 47-1   Telephony application design tool

47.4 | Case study: customer notification system

We'll construct a simple client-notification application for an imaginary company, the Underland Stagecoach Company. The application's sole function will be to notify a passenger when a planned trip has been canceled. Callers leave a telephone number and, if the trip is canceled, the system calls to deliver the unfortunate news.

47.4.1 *Background and strategy*

Underland is an industry leader in terms of automation and online bookings and now wants to extend that leadership into new areas. The company's existing website offers a typical online reservation and trip planning interface. It works well for travelers with access to a computer.

The telephone notification system was planned to be the first step in a process integrating the entire customer relationship management system with a full-fledged XML-based ERP system. All parts of all company databases would then be accessible by means of industry-standard query formats.

Since the existing database was working effectively, the initial stages of the project did not address the data infrastructure. Nor did it touch the design of the existing corporate website, shown schematically in Figure 47-2.

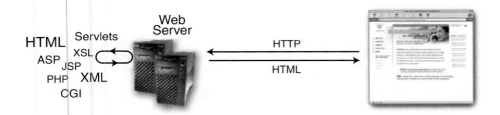

Figure 47-2   Website with traditional visual interface

Instead, an additional interface was added to provide telephone access to the same information, as depicted in Figure 47-3.

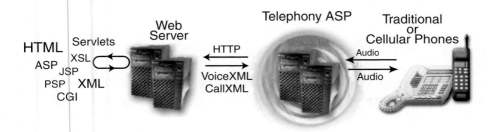

Figure 47-3   Website in Figure 47-2 extended for telephony

47.4.2   *Designing for telephonic interaction*

The website's existing HTML page for client notification has a total of forty navigation choices, including ten choices that duplicate a client-side image map as text, to accommodate visually disabled clients.

Telephone interfaces cannot support such rich navigation options without extremely careful design; it's usually better to simplify. In this case, the telephonic equivalent was pared down to a single choice: to request the notification service.

Navigating the entire site from one phone number was determined to be too confusing for practical use. Instead, a group of toll-free numbers was reserved for the most common interactions, allowing very shallow menu trees to be used in all parts of the site. This solution was reasonable because telephone numbers are inexpensive.

People don't remember what they heard and said very well, so telephone interfaces can't carry much context with them. A visual site can display an entire page of data that the user can glance at to refresh his memory; a voice browser can only read that data aloud.

As people can stand just so much reminding, confirmation and reminder phrases were made:

- short and to the point, to avoid boring listeners; and
- interruptible, so a user could skip what he didn't want to hear.

47.4.3   *How the application works*

Let's look at some key steps in the application to see how they work.

47.4.3.1   Database access

Callers are tentatively identified by the *Caller ID* passed in from the phone network. A database lookup is performed on the incoming phone number to load an initial caller information set.

As the database access was already part of the website, acquiring the needed information for the voice interface was just a matter of selecting it.

47.4.3.2   Verifying the notification number

The opening dialog brands the service and asks whether the *Caller ID* phone number received is the correct number for notification. If so, the user is thanked and notification proceeds. If not, the user is prompted for the notification number, that number is verified, and only then does the notification proceed.

A future enhancement will allow Underland's system to deal with several alternative numbers at which the user might be found ("follow-me/find-me").

47.4.3.3   Developing a spoken grammar

People talk in ways characteristic of their neighborhoods and cultural heritage. Trying to enforce a stilted vocabulary frustrates users, so they attempt to bypass the system in order to talk to a "real person" who can understand them.

As the cost drivers for this project depend on minimizing such bypass attempts, the user interaction has to be natural and flexible. Extensive grammars must be provided covering the most common ways in which people can say the responses sought by the system. Fortunately, most of these grammars are pre-written.

Example 47-1 shows a grammar for a simple yes or no response, as used in this application.

Note the large number of variations available for these two words. Even more are possible, like:

- "right-o" and "not on your life"
- military "affirmative" and "negative", or
- utterances that a computer has trouble understanding, like the difference between "uh, uh" and "uh huh".

More like these could easily be added, but doing so isn't usually necessary as long as the original set of variations is sufficiently broad. Users will typically learn and use an appropriate vocabulary within the limits of their natural speech, since we do that in everyday life when talking to a child, a young adult, a peer, or a person in authority.

Example 47-1. Yes/no grammar for a VoiceXML application

```
LIB_YES_NO [
  [ yes
    yeah
    yup
    sure
    okay
    correct
    right
    ( ?( ?yes that's ) [ right correct ] )
    ( ?yes it is )
    ( you got it )
    ( yes i do )
    ( yes i would )
    ( yes it is correct )
  ] {return("yes")}
  [ no
    nope
    incorrect
    wrong
    ( no way )
    ( no it isn't )
    ( ?no [ it's that's ] not [ correct right ] )
    ( ?no it isn't )
    ( ?no it is not )
    ( ?no it's not )
    ( no i don't )
    ( no i do not )
    ( no i wouldn't )
  ] {return("no")}
```

47.4.3.4   Handling keyed input

For some parts of a dialog, it is natural for the user to employ the telephone keypad. Grammars can be defined for keyed input in much the same way as for spoken input. These are called *DTMF grammars*, after the name of the signalling standard used in touch-tone phones.

Example 47-2 shows a portion of the application that uses a DTMF grammar.

The `field` listens for a keyed phone number and prompts the user if none is entered, or if it doesn't match the grammar. Once the system recognizes a valid phone number, it proceeds (in the `filled` element) to direct the browser to a `form` that will confirm the number.

Example 47-2. Keypad input and recognition

```
<form id="GetNewPhone">
  <field name="newnumber">
    <grammar src="dtmf_phonenumber.gram#MAINMENU"/>
    <prompt>
      <audio src="audio/enter_phone.wav"/>
    </prompt>
    <!-- If silence then tell user that we didn't  -->
    <!-- hear any input. Reprompt the user.        -->
    <noinput>
      <audio src="audio/no_hear_pressed.wav"/>
      <reprompt/>
    </noinput>
    <!-- If the user's key input isn't matched by the grammar -->
    <!-- we need to tell the user we didn't understand,        -->
    <!-- then reprompt the user to enter the number again.    -->
    <nomatch>
      <audio src="audio/figure_out_pressed.wav"/>
      <reprompt/>
    </nomatch>
    <!-- Give the user a little help. -->
    <help>
      <audio src="audio/please_enter_number.wav"/>
      <reprompt/>
    </help>
    <filled>
      <assign name="selectedphone" expr="newnumber"/>
      <goto next="#ConfirmPhone"/>
    </filled>
  </field>
</form>
```

47.4.3.5   Delivering the goods

The last step in the application is to make a telephone call. As VoiceXML has no direct call-handling capabilities, the Underland used the CallXML language.

Example 47-3 shows the CallXML code that makes the outbound call.

Note the onanswer element. The user is greeted with a recording (playAudio), but his name, which was obtained from the database access, is rendered as text-to-speech (text).

As the number of human names is impossibly large, it was necessary to use machine synthesis rather than access a recorded vocabulary of names. In other places, where there was a smaller number of possible announcement candidates, a more natural sound was achieved by recording them all.

Example 47-3. Initiate call, detect answer, announce

```
<callxml>
<block label="UserCallBack">
  <!-- Wait before calling user back. -->
  <wait value="$outbound_wait"/>
  <!-- Make outbound call to user. -->
  <call value="$numtocall" callerID="$callerid"
        maxtime="30s"/>
  <!-- Wait until the call is answered. -->
  <onanswer>
    <!-- Greet the user. -->
    <playAudio format="audio/wav"
               value="audio/cxml_hello_passenger.wav"/>
    <!-- Synthesize the user's name. -->
    <text>$randomName.</text>
    <!-- Give user the bad news and say goodbye. -->
    <playAudio format="audio/wav" value="audio/cxml_bad_news.wav"/>
    <playAudio format="audio/wav" value="audio/cxml_goodbye.wav"/>
    <!-- Done delivering bad news, so hang up. -->
    <hangup/>
  </onanswer>
</block>
...
</callxml>
```

47.4.4 *Deploying the application*

Based on projections made by polling users on its website, Underland fore-saw an ROI great enough to justify the system. However, this conservative approach ignored the possibility of luring computer-challenged customers into the expanded system by promoting the new service through conventional media.

Initial provisioning and deployment of the application took about five minutes, using the facilities of one of the online telephony service providers.

Going into production required two additional days, as Underland and the service provider had to sign a service level agreement. The agreement guaranteed the bandwidth that would be available and the number of calls that would be handled simultaneously.

Infrastructure

- Programming technology
- XML file compression
- XML and security
- XML in low-level system functions

Part Seventeen

So far in this book, any mention of "infrastructure" was in the context of XML being a vital part of the infrastructure provided by information distribution and electronic business applications.

In the following chapters, however, we dig down a lot further and see the role that XML plays in the infrastructure that supports those very applications.

We've seen throughout the book how products support XML for content management and data integration, and in this part we'll see how programming technology supports many of those products.

First we'll look at how file compression – increasingly important in these days of growing network loads and low-speed wireless access – can be enhanced by taking advantage of the predictability of XML documents.

Then we'll examine the many issues involved in supporting secure transactions and Web services on a fundamentally insecure Internet.

Finally, we'll get a glimpse into a future where XML is ubiquitous, even finding its way into low-level system functions and specialized hardware.

Compression techniques for XML

Application Discussion

- Generic compression
- XML-aware compression
- Schema-specific compression

Contributing expert: Bill Sebastian

Chapter

48

XML has had a great impact on messaging, and an even greater one on the length of the messages! Short XML messages can be more tag than data, even as much as double or triple. Fortunately, diet plans are available for your overweight documents. We'll show you how they work in this chapter.

onsider the stock market quotation in Example 48-1 on page 734. It is 582 bytes in length, but only 281 bytes of that is data. In other words, using XML has more than doubled the size of this message, with a corresponding increase in storage and transmission costs. Worse yet, because increased transmission time means decreased response time, customer satisfaction is reduced.

The cure for this problem is called *data compression*.[1] There are various techniques and a range of possible results. Let's see how our example can be reduced to 407 bytes, or even to an amazing 29 bytes – a 95 percent reduction!

---

1. In this phrase, "data" refers to the full text of the document, not just the data characters. In fact, it is the markup that is usually compressed the most.

48.1 | Data compression techniques

Data compression is the encoding[2] of text so that the same information can be stored in a smaller number of bytes. The text can therefore be transmitted faster and stored in less space. After the compressed ("coded") file has been received or retrieved, it is decoded to restore the original text.

Figure 48-1 shows how an encoder and decoder can be placed on either side of the transmission network. For example, the encoder could be embedded in a server and the decoder could be invoked by a Web browser or embedded in a client applet.

Figure 48-1   Using compression to accelerate file transmission

There are several approaches to compression that can be taken for XML documents:

generic compression
The many implementations of the ubiquitous "zip" format are examples of *universal coders,* so-called because they neither know nor care whether they are processing a shopping list or a photograph of Mars. Zip coding reduced Example 48-1 by 30 percent. Although zip's flexibility makes it useful for many applications, its performance can be improved on substantially by programs that know more about the text to be compressed.

XML-aware compression
Data compression systems work by preparing models that predict text. More knowledge of a file improves the models and provides better predictions. Better predictions in turn result in greater compression. Knowing the rules of XML can provide such an

---

2. Data compression is an important technology with its own accepted terminology. In this chapter we use "code" and its derivatives in the data compression sense, not in the XML sense of "character encoding".

improvement, although knowing the particular document type can provide even more.

schema-specific compression
> This approach employs maximum knowledge of the file. It reduced our example from 582 bytes to 29. Let's take a closer look at the technology involved.

48.2 | Schema-specific compression

These compression systems utilize two types of knowledge that are available for most XML applications:

- Knowledge of the document type properties, such as structure, obtained from the schema definition or DTD.
- Statistical knowledge of the text that the document type knowledge makes it possible to obtain.

48.2.1 *Document type knowledge*

XML provides a general method for marking up data. Any file that follows the general markup rules is a well-formed XML document. However, XML applications impose additional constraints that are defined by a DTD or schema definition. These constraints usually include specifying the elements that will occur in a document and the order they are likely to appear.

For example, a schema definition or DTD for Example 48-1 might tell a compression system that the first element was going to be a QReply whose content would begin with an ID sub-element.

Structural knowledge allows the XML markup to be encoded (i.e., compressed) efficiently. For example, if an element type requires two subelements (A, B), the decoder can reconstruct the tags even if the element type names are missing from the encoded file. As it knows exactly where the start- and end-tags of the two elements will be located, it can determine from the DTD what strings to write at those places.

Example 48-1. Reply to stock quote request

```
<QReply>
  <ID>0</ID>
  <SYM>QCOM</SYM>
  <EX>O</EX>
  <LAST>+61.75</LAST>
  <VOL>+13490800</VOL>
  <BID>+61.84</BID>
  <ASK>+61.85</ASK>
  <BIDVOL>+25</BIDVOL>
  <ASKVOL>+5</ASKVOL>
  <BIDTIC>U</BIDTIC>
  <CUR>USD</CUR>
  <EXID>NMS</EXID>
  <HI>+61.85</HI>
  <LO>+55.75</LO>
  <NETCHG>+4.39</NETCHG>
  <OPEN>+56.72</OPEN>
  <PERCHG>+7.65</PERCHG>
  <PQ></PQ>
  <UPC71></UPC71>
  <NEWHI>n/a</NEWHI>
  <NEWLO>n/a</NEWLO>
  <CURYLD>+0.00</CURYLD>
  <DIV>+0.00</DIV>
  <DIVPDT>30 DEC 1999</DIVPDT>
  <EPS>+0.09</EPS>
  <EXDIVDT>31 DEC 1999</EXDIVDT>
  <PE>+644.49</PE>
  <YRHI>+120.0000</YRHI>
  <YRLO>+42.7500</YRLO>
  <TIME>20:01</TIME>
  <DATE>01 MAY 2001</DATE>
</QReply>
```

Similarly, for an element type whose content requires one of two subelements (A|B) with no attributes, we only need to store a binary decision in the encoded file as to which of the two was present.

The sample file in Example 48-1 lends itself exceptionally well to this kind of treatment, as it consists of a mandatory sequence of elements with no attributes. Removing the tags can reduce the encoded size from 582 bytes back nearly to the original (pre-XML) 281 bytes. The next problem is how to get the 281 bytes of uncompressed data down to just 29 bytes of encoded data.

48.2.2 *Data knowledge*

Once we've used a schema to identify each element of an XML document, we can look at a representative sampling of documents to develop models of the content of those elements.

48.2.2.1 Statistical analysis

For example, statistical analysis of sample stock quotes as shown in Example 48-1 might reveal that most companies on the NYSE price their stocks in "USD", or that share prices over 200.00 only occur in the dreams of the shareholders.

In addition to analyzing individual elements, we can also look at relationships among them and, for example, discover that the asking price usually is greater than the bid price. With this type of information we can create compression models that reduce the number of bytes needed to encode the data.

48.2.2.2 An example: the ASK element

To see how statistical analysis works, let's look at the operations used to process the ASK element. Its data content is the string +61.85.

The compression system recognizes the datatype as a fixed decimal with a 2-digit fraction. It converts the character text to the binary value "6185". From this, it subtracts the previously encoded BID value of "6184", which exploits the relationship between these items that was observed when analyzing the sample files. Subtraction produces the remainder "1", which occurs about 25% of the time for this pair of elements in the sample documents.

Now we can encode the remainder, using what compression scientists call an *entropy coder*. The encoding of a value that occurs 25% of the time will use about two bits. As the original data +61.85 used up 48 bits (six bytes), these two bits represent a compression ratio of 24:1. So on this particular entry, we did much better than the 10:1 average needed to reduce the original 281 bytes of data to 29 bytes.

These examples illustrate the algorithms that allow schema-specific XML compression to obtain compression gains 15 times greater than zip on this test set.

48.2.3 *Schema model file (SMF)*

Real-time communication applications require extremely fast encoding. In these cases, reading and interpreting a complicated schema definition or analyzing sample documents in real time is obviously impractical. Instead, that information is captured once, in advance, in a *schema model file (SMF)*.

An SMF is generated by an automated offline routine that reads a schema definition or DTD and creates parsing models that allow the real-time encoders to operate at the highest speed.

An SMF can also include encoding models developed by statistical analysis, as we just described. Such models are especially helpful for achieving maximum compression performance with smaller files.

Each SMF supports a specific schema. To compress an XML file, the real-time encoder needs to have access to the SMF that supports the schema to which the file conforms, as shown in Figure 48-2.

Figure 48-2   Using a schema model file

The same SMF is provided to both the encoder and the decoder. Those programs can support any number of schemas, as long as they have the appropriate SMFs.

48.2.4 *Database query responses*

For some XML applications, the text that needs to be compressed consists of responses to queries for information contained in a large database. While the database as a whole may conform to a schema, the query responses may consist of arbitrary elements arranged in an order that does not follow the schema definition.

For this reason the SMF incorporates access to the Document Object Model (DOM) of the database, which enables access to arbitrary elements. As long as those elements conform to their type definitions, schema-specific compression is possible.

48.3 | Choosing a compression technique

Schema-specific XML compression provides the ultimate in compression performance. It also has drawbacks, including more complicated maintenance and higher cost. For some applications, the performance benefits will justify the drawbacks. For others, application developers may want to explore some of the alternatives.

48.3.1 *No compression*

The easiest solution is to send the text in its original form. This is feasible when storage sizes and transmission times are not significant concerns. It may be the only option if the application does not allow the installation of decoders on the client side.

48.3.2 *Generic compression*

The next easiest solution is to use a universal coder, like zip. Such coders usually work by building a table of strings that are repeated frequently in the document. The occurrences of the strings are then replaced with short pointers to the appropriate table entry.

Zip can be quite effective on XML documents, in some cases achieving compression ratios as high as 10:1. The first step in evaluating compression options for an application is usually to try zip and see if it provides an adequate solution. It is a relatively fast coder as well and free implementations are available.

Other universal coders may provide better compression than zip, but may be slower or cost money.

48.3.3 *XML-aware compression*

Generic compression systems have been developed for XML documents. Some are wrappers around the standard zip algorithm, allowing it to be used more easily and effectively in XML applications. Others utilize XML's tags to isolate data into homogeneous blocks and improve on compression of both tags and data.

These coders are easier to set up and maintain than schema-specific coders because there is no need to deal with individual schemas or DTDs.

48.3.4 *Homespun schema-specific remedies*

Developers who know little about compression might look at their XML files, see all the repeated tags, and then cleverly write routines that replace the tags with codes referenced in a schema-specific table. Except for very small files, this approach is rarely an improvement over zip.

48.3.5 *Schema-specific compression*

This approach has the potential to perform extremely well, as we have seen. However, the very schema knowledge that makes superior performance possible necessarily introduces some costs.

schema changes
Schema model files must be changed or added when a schema is changed or newly supported. However, if an SMF isn't available, the coding automatically falls back to a generic algorithm.

file footprint
SMF files use space proportional to the number of schemas supported and their complexity, typically from 20KB to 600KB. The size of the compression engine itself is static, usually around 200KB.

installation

Installation may require statistical analysis or other custom work in order to achieve the best possible compression results.

These costs tend to scale with the benefits, and should easily be justified for the right kind of documents. For short tags interspersed in lots of data, there is little improvement over generic compression. But for documents with many small elements and no attributes, such as those created by tagging the items of a financial database, the technology offers the highest possible compression performance.

48.4 | Conclusion

Although XML makes the use and interchange of data easier and more flexible, it can substantially increase the number of bytes that must be transmitted and stored. Several compression techniques can reduce that number, resulting in faster transfer times and more economical use of storage resources. The highest compression is achievable by techniques that employ knowledge of XML, especially knowledge of specific schemas and a sampling of their conforming documents.

XML security

Introductory Discussion

- Identity management
- Signatures
- Biometrics
- Encryption
- Digital rights management

Chapter

49

High on the list of favorite oxymorons – right up with software quality and hip-hop music – is Internet security. Fortunately, XML is showing that this need no longer be so. Whether you want to secure your XML documents, or use XML to secure other things, this chapter will introduce you to the available techniques.

I f you've got a Web site or a Web service, you need to protect your data and scrutinize everyone who asks for it. You need to ask: Who are you? Can you prove it? Are you entitled to what you request?

In other words, you need to know about:

- Confidentiality: protection against eavesdropping and theft
- Identity: knowing with whom you are dealing
- Access control: verifying a requestor's rights

XML can help with all of these.

49.1 | Confidentiality

For information in computers, confidentiality invariably involves encryption – plus a way to keep the password secure.

49.1.1 *Encryption*

You may have created a ZIP archive with a tool that gives you the option of protecting the archive with a password. If you send such a password-protected archive to a friend, he'll be prompted for the password in order to open the archive. Without the password, the archive is indecipherable.

And with that carefully chosen adjective, we oh so subtly shift the discussion to cryptography. In cryptographic terms, that password is a *key* with which the sending system encrypts the ZIP archive. Since the sender and recipient both use the same key, the process is called *symmetric cryptography* – the fastest kind.

XML Encryption is a W3C Recommendation that specifies a process for encrypting data and representing the result in XML. The data may be arbitrary data, an XML document, an XML element (including tags), or the content of an XML element (without the element's start- and end-tags). It may be encrypted by any means (not just symmetric), and the key may be encrypted as well. The encrypted data is represented by an `EncryptedData` element and is either contained in one of that element's children or is referenced by it.

The problem with symmetric cryptography is communicating the key. How can you do that securely? You could encrypt it, but then you would need to transmit the key to the original key, and so on.

And what if the key is stolen?

49.1.2 *Biometrics*

One way to make it hard to steal the key is to store it behind some kind of password. But then the password could be stolen! This is a fundamental problem with passwords. There are a variety of ways to discover them, from looking at Post-It notes under the keyboard to sophisticated hacking techniques.

A more secure system is to use physical properties of a human being as a password. We have all seen movies where people use thumb prints or retina scans to open doors or unlock computers. This kind of device is becoming more common in real life and is known as *biometrics*.

Popular forms of biometrics include fingerprint imaging, hand geometry measurement, facial recognition, iris recognition, retinal scanning and voice authentication.[1] The *XML Common Biometric Framework (XCBF)* is an

OASIS XML vocabulary for storing and transferring biometric data. It can transmit all sorts of biometric measurements, and can be extended to support new ones that do not exist yet.

49.1.3 *Public key infrastructure*

A non-physical solution to the problem of key theft is called *public key cryptography*, which is *asymmetric cryptography*. Instead of a single *symmetric key*, shared by both parties, there is a mathematically-related pair of keys. You keep your own *private key* and you distribute a related *public key* to your friends so they can send you encrypted email. They encrypt their messages to you by using your public key, but you decrypt them using your private key.[2]

A system for deploying public key cryptography is called a *public key infrastructure (PKI)*. It requires a means of managing public keys. The *certificates* that are the cause of so many mysterious messages from your Web browser are actually descriptions of public keys, digitally signed by a *Certification Authority (CA)*.

Public keys can be transmitted in a variety of ways: email, on Web sites, through secret decoder rings, you name it! The W3C is working on an XML-based specification for distributing public keys and building registries for them. It is called the *XML Key Management Specification (XKMS)*.

XKMS has two parts:

XKRSS

The *XML Key Registration Service Specification (XKRSS)* is for registration and management of public keys. For example, it can generate a key pair for you, associate your name with the public key so others can find it, and securely send you your private key in case you lose it.

---

1. More esoteric ones include gait and body odor.
2. At least that's the way it seems, but because symmetric cryptography is so much faster, the sender's software actually encrypts the message with a randomly-generated symmetric key. It then encrypts the symmetric key with your public key so your software can decrypt it with your private key, and then use the decrypted symmetric key to decrypt the message. Whew!

XKISS

The romantically named *XML Key Information Service Specification (XKISS)* defines a service that verifies XML signatures – which oh so subtly leads us to our next topic!

49.2 | Identity management

One of the most basic security questions is "Who goes there?" – the question of user *identification*. Closely related is the requirement that the person prove to be who he claims to be – the question of *authentication*.

49.2.1 *Signatures*

For documents, the classic means of identification is the signature. The signed name provides identification and the uniqueness of handwriting provides a (less-than-perfect!) means of authentication.

Just as in the written world, the digital signature is intended to identify and authenticate the author of a machine-readable document. The authentication is provided by public key encryption – but operating in reverse! A digital signature is encrypted with the signer's private key and decrypted with the public key.

XML Signature is a W3C specification for representing digital signatures in XML. With XML Signature, it is possible to attach signatures to any object, whether it be XML or binary, standardized or proprietary.

When you sign a printed contract, your signature goes on the last or only piece of paper of the contract (and perhaps you also initial every page). That way, the signature cannot be shifted to a different contract from the one you signed originally. This procedure maintains the *integrity* of the signed contract.

Similarly, an XML signature is generated in a way that binds it to a single object. The receiver can check that the object has not changed by looking at a summary (*hash*) of it embedded in the signature. The digital signature acts as a *seal*, but without the messy hot wax!

The receiver can also, of course, use the sender's public key to check that the signature was generated by his private key. If both tests are successful, then the recipient has got exactly the message that was signed and knows exactly who sent it.

Just as with printed signatures, digital signatures serve as a basis for *non-repudiation*. In other words, they prove that you endorsed the signed content. If you claim that you did not agree to a (digital) contract that has your (digital) signature, you had better have proof that your (private) key was stolen!

49.2.2 *Authentication*

OASIS is developing a framework for XML authentication called the *Security Assertions Markup Language (SAML)*. SAML is very general but is chiefly used as a method for Web sites and Web services to exchange authentication information.

As a Web user you would allow the sites to exchange information about you so that logging into one site would automatically log you into another. This would remove the requirement to remember dozens of passwords and to type your name and address into multiple Web sites. This objective is called *single sign-on*.

A consortium called the Liberty Alliance has contributed its authentication specification for use in SAML. Microsoft has a competing specification, called *.NET Passport* which it claims provides authentication services for 200 million users.

49.3 | Access control

Once an XML message arrives, it can be decrypted and authenticated. But if the message asks for something, you must still decide whether the requestor is allowed to invoke the desired operation or see the requested information. That's called *access control*.

You may also need to decide whether the requestor can share that information with anyone else – a sort of access control once-removed!

49.3.1   *XACML*

OASIS has developed a standard for access control known as the *Extensible Access Control Markup Language (XACML)*. It defines an XML language for expressing access control policy: who can use which resources under what restrictions. The spec also defines XML representations for access requests and the responses to them.

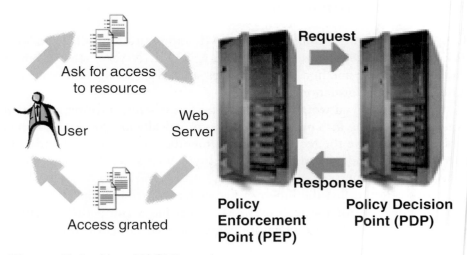

Figure 49-1   How XACML works

Figure 49-1 illustrates the principle of XACML access control.

1. A user (who looks relatively human here but might in fact be a program) asks to do something to a Web page (or a program, a data file, or some other resource).
2. The Web server (or file system, etc.) that protects the resource must find out whether it can do what the user asks. In XACML terms, it acts as a *Policy Enforcement Point (PEP)*.
3. The PEP creates an XACML `request` document that identifies the user, the resource, and the action requested. It may also include properties of the user (e.g. department, job title, etc.) and other information.

4. The `request` is sent to a server that acts as a *Policy Decision Point (PDP)*. The PDP retrieves relevant XACML policy documents from its database, compares them to the `request`, and decides whether or not to grant access. Policies can refer to other policies, so that a departmental policy could incorporate provisions of an enterprise policy.

5. The PDP returns an XACML `response` document to the PEP, which then allows or denies access accordingly.

Standardizing access control and operating it independently of applications and resource types reduces both development and administrative costs. It also permits a consistency of enforcement that would not be obtainable any other way.

49.3.2 *Digital rights management*

It is relatively easy to maintain control over access to data until the moment you share the data with someone else. Have you ever told someone a secret prefaced with "I shouldn't tell you this, so please do not tell anyone else." You have a pretty good idea how effective that security technique is! If you have a true secret, the only secure mechanism is not to share it with anyone.

Unfortunately, this solution is not sufficient for owners of copyrighted content who wish to distribute their content and yet maintain control over further distribution. Their business depends upon disclosing the information, but they also want to have control over further disclosures (e.g. preventing college students from sharing music with ten thousand of their best friends).

There is no easy answer to the complex technical and legal problems that arise when content creators try to keep control of asset distribution in a digital world. However, one part of the equation may be the variously-called *(Digital) Rights (Expression) Languages* (where the parenthesized words are optional). A company named *ContentGuard* is successfully promoting the standardization of the *Extensible rights Markup Language (XrML)*, which uses XML as its syntax.

The principal behind XrML, as indeed behind all digital rights management, is that information and the rights to it should be sealed in the same file. In the case of XrML, that would include rights to view, copy, print, save, forward, and/or modify, among others.

Any applicable conditions pertaining to the exercise of the rights would also be sealed in the file. For example, the right to play content might be subject to such conditions as a fixed time limit and/or a specific user.

Legal thinkers have noted that digital "rights" is something of a misnomer. These languages actually express permissions granted to consumers by content producers. In some cases they actually curtail activities protected by traditional fair-use rights, such as making a backup copy or a printed rendition of content.

Rights management is a hot issue. The technical, social and legal ramifications are very complicated and there are billions of dollars involved. Most of the solutions (including XrML) involve taking control away from consumers and giving it to content producers. This is bound to be controversial.

49.4 | Conclusion

As the Internet continues to expand its role as a business and entertainment communication infrastructure, security will become even more important. As we have seen, there are many aspects to this complex problem, and many different (often competing) standards are being developed.

In order for Web services, in particular, to achieve widespread acceptance, there needs to be complete trust among the parties to a transaction. To that end, OASIS is standardizing the *WS-Security* specification. It defines SOAP extensions that apply security standards to SOAP messages: XML digital signatures to sign a message, SAML to authenticate its sender, XML Encryption to encrypt parts of the message, and so forth.

Thanks to XML, we are heading towards a future where the acronym for "Internet Security" won't have to be "InSecure"!

New directions for XML applications

Application Discussion

- Performance analysis
- XML does television
- Load balancing and routing

Sponsor: Intel Corporation, http://www.intel.com/ids

Contributing experts: Walter Shands, Murali Rajappa, John Abjanic, and Randy E Hall

XML is going where no markup language has gone before. Thanks to a company that really knows about bits and bytes, XML is now in low-level, performance-oriented applications. You can even find it on television – or at least in the computer that provisions your television!

I n the 35-year history of markup languages, we have seen several major trends in application emphasis:

- The first wave, using GML and SGML, was large-scale industrial publishing on paper.
- The second wave, using HTML, was (and is) online information presentation.
- The third wave, using XML, is electronic business and application integration.

And now XML is starting to make inroads in performance-oriented areas that were never before open to an "inefficient" text-based interchange representation. Let's see how Intel Corporation is leading XML into the 21st century.

50.1 | Performance analysis

For a long time a debate raged – and in some quarters is still raging – about the wisdom of using XML for messaging in distributed systems. Despite the many obvious benefits of platform neutrality, human readability, self-description, standardized support, and the rapid deployment and inexpensive maintenance that goes with such characteristics, there is always the last resort of the nay-sayers – resources. After all, the anti-XML argument goes, with an overhead of 300% in a message like `<price>10.00</price>`, XML is clearly an unacceptable drag on performance.

So there is a delicious irony in the fact that one of Intel's envelope-stretching XML applications is ... (fanfare) ... performance analysis!

50.1.1 *Remote data collection*

The company's *VTune* performance analyzer helps developers identify program hot spots and provides advice on how to remedy them. To do that, it needs to collect and present data from distributed machines running on *Microsoft Windows* or *Linux* operating systems. Windows supports remote data collection via Distributed Component Object Model (DCOM), but DCOM is not available on the Linux operating system

50.1.2 *A clean solution ... with SOAP!*

The solution lay in the use of XML requests formatted according to the Simple Object Access Protocol (SOAP). The SOAP specification defines rules for representing both messaging data and remote method invocation requests within a document.

Each request consists of a mandatory header, optional application-specific data conforming to the HTTP Extension Framework, and an envelope. Schema definitions provide support for multiple namespaces and ensure that datatype fidelity is maintained across process and server boundaries.

The remote data collection process in *VTune* works as shown in Figure 50-1:

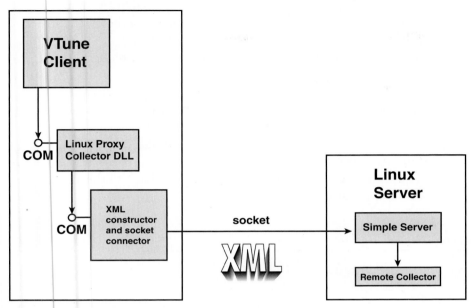

Figure 50-1   Remote data collection in *VTune*

Example 50-1. SOAP request

```
POST ... HTTP/1.1
Host: ###.###.###.###
Content-Type: text/xml
Content-Length: ###
SOAPMethodName: urn:SamplingCollector:IVTCollector#DoStart
<Envelope>
  <Body>
    <m:DoStart xmlns:m='urn:SamplingCollector:IVTCollector'>
    </m:DoStart>
  </Body>
</Envelope>
```

1. The *VTune* client, which runs on the *Microsoft Windows* platform, makes a Component Object Model (COM) call to a remote collection proxy object.
2. The remote collection proxy collector opens a socket connection to the *Linux* machine.

3. The remote collection proxy collector formats a SOAP request containing a collector name, interface name, method name to execute, and parameter data (Example 50-1).

4. The remote collection proxy collector sends the request to the *Linux* machine.

5. A stub collector on the *Linux* machine either invokes an executable or makes a method call to a sample collector implemented in a C programming language driver.

6. The stub collector collects data and constructs a SOAP response (Example 50-2).

7. The stub collector sends the XML response back to the *VTune* client application.

Example 50-2. SOAP response

```
200 OK
Content-Type: text/xml
Content-Length: ###
<Envelope>
  <Body>
    <m:DoStartResponse
      xmlns:m='urn:SamplingCollector:IVTCollector'>
      <result>OK</result>
    </m:DoStart>
  </Body>
</Envelope>
```

The current SOAP specification is focused on requests and responses over HTTP. XML, however, can be layered on top of other protocols – including SMTP and WAP – making remote data collection possible from cellular phones and other hand-held devices. The SOAP capabilities in the *VTune* performance analyzer support remote data collection on non-*Windows* machines in a way that could permit adding protocols in the future.

50.2 | Coming soon to a television near you ...

XML-TV?

Not exactly, but XML provides such a clean and predictable way to exchange data between disparate systems that it's a natural for an application where no errors can be tolerated. For this reason XML is being deployed in the distribution of digital television (DTV) programming, for consumers to view via DTV-enabled PCs, digital TV sets, and set-top boxes.

Such programming, for example, enables viewers to check an electronic program guide, send electronic greeting cards, take interactive quizzes, watch movie trailers, check sports statistics, and more – all on demand.

50.2.1 *Distribution system design*

In one set-top box system, the content served includes regular television channels, interactive programming in which the user becomes an active participant, and Web-based media.

Service providers are organized in a hub configuration, wherein a primary network operations center (PNOC) supports multiple franchised network operations centers (FNOCs) located in different cities. The PNOC broadcasts content that is cached locally and redistributed by the FNOCs. This approach conserves PNOC/FNOC bandwidth and reduces content delivery latency when serving Web pages.

Subscriber data for specific services resides at both the PNOC and FNOC sites, with the PNOC owning the master record. To ensure that customers receive the services they request, the PNOC subscription center's information must be replicated to the FNOC.

Because the PNOC and FNOC most likely have different subscriber database implementations, the data must be exchanged in a format that disparate systems can easily understand. In the current implementation, the PNOC's master subscriber database is implemented using Oracle database products running on Microsoft *Windows NT* servers. At the FNOC, *Linux* servers host databases for local data storage of customer subscription data.

50.2.2 *Adding a subscriber*

A document type definition is used to describe the subscriber data to be exchanged. In this case, the DTD acts as a contract between the PNOC and the FNOC so the data elements from the customer document, shown in Example 50-3, are correctly mapped to database columns in tables.

Example 50-3. New account request

```
<Action RefNo="999999999999" Actiontype="Add Record">
  <IP_Address>192.168.2.7</IP_Address>
  <MAC_Address>00:D0.B7:1C:B7:5D</MAC_Address>
  <FNOC_ID>FNOC1</FNOC_ID>
  <Hostname>fnoc1.cn.now.com</Hostname>
  <LoginId>carmen</LoginId>
  <Password>password</Password>
  <ActiveService><Service>modem</Service></ActiveService>
</Action>
```

The process for adding a new subscriber is illustrated in Figure 50-2. It is described as follows:

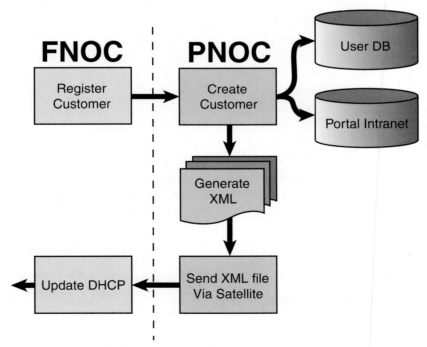

Figure 50-2   Adding a subscriber

1. The FNOC sends a new account request to the PNOC.
2. Subscriber information is inserted into the PNOC customer database.
3. The PNOC customer database generates an XML document containing subscriber information.
4. The system transmits the XML subscriber record document via satellite to the FNOC.
5. The FNOC receives the data and inserts it into its local database.
6. The FNOC configures the subscriber's set-top box for the requested services.

Subscriber updates and deletions are handled in a similar fashion.

As this example makes clear, XML can be used to represent data exchanged between components of a multi-vendor and multi-platform system. With XML, best-of-breed products can be packaged in new and innovative ways to provide services that otherwise would require porting all pieces to a common operating system.

50.3 | Performance enhancement

Remember the raging debate about the wisdom of using XML in distributed systems because it is supposedly such a drain on performance?

Well, here is another delicious irony: Intel is using XML in specialized networking hardware to ... (fanfare) ... enhance performance!

50.3.1 *Load balancing and routing*

One way to guarantee that network transactions are processed in a reliable and expedient manner is to build an infrastructure of high-end servers that can support unpredictable traffic loads. In industries where demand is volatile or difficult to predict, this option could prove to be expensive and could limit the ability to respond to the rapid pace of change.

A more economical and flexible alternative is to offload certain capabilities from the main application processing servers onto specialized devices. A single such "accelerator" or "director" can serve multiple application servers and improve their performance by several means.

The devices operate in domains that system designers call *load balancing* and *routing*. Let's look at what they do.

50.3.1.1   Offload routine tasks

An accelerator can perform such routine tasks as decoding an encrypted message before forwarding it to an application server for fulfillment. It can also encrypt the reply before sending it to the client.

50.3.1.2   Route requests for best response time

On busy websites, several application servers perform the same task. A network device can enhance client response times by routing each request to the server that can fulfill it most quickly. The device typically needs to know (or calculate) the speed of each server and the number of messages enqueued on it.

50.3.1.3   Route requests based on message content

This technique is used for websites that perform multiple services and use different application servers for each. It requires a device that acts like a bank receptionist who decides whether to send you to the loan officer or the new account representative. The device looks at the incoming message to make the routing decision.

For example, URI references can be analyzed to distinguish content requested by clients performing online transactions, from content typically requested by casual surfers. In this way, users performing online transactions can be given higher priority access to server resources (and better response times) than other users.

The choice of server for fulfillment of a request is determined by a table that associates pattern-matching expressions with server names. Possible expression types might include:

■   Filetype expressions, such as `*.asp` or `*/order.htm`

- Path expressions, such as `/home/*` or `/home/images/*` or `/home/images/a*`
- Unique file expressions, such as `/index.html`
- Wildcard expressions, such as `*`
- Negations of the other expression types, such as `!*.gif` or `!*/index.html`

50.3.2 *XML content matching*

The phenomenal growth in the use of XML for e-commerce and other applications suggests that a richer source of information might be available for routing: the data and metadata in XML messages.

One of the first devices to use that richer source was the now discontinued Intel *NetStructure 7280 XML Director*. It incorporates a rules-based XML engine that can identify and classify incoming XML requests based on data within the XML object.

Once classified, the device can then transparently prioritize and direct the "most important" XML transactions, according to predefined business rules. Those could be transactions from key trading partners, those with a high dollar value, or perhaps those that are considered time-sensitive.

50.3.2.1 How the rules-based engine works

How can the *XML Director* route XML transactions to application servers based on business parameters such as "all orders over $50,000 *and* from the Western region"?

Rules, in the form of expressions using a subset of the XPath abbreviated syntax, are associated with specific servers. If a message satisfies a rule, it is routed to the associated server.

One application of the rules engine is to identify the XML framework, if any, used by a message, such as *BizTalk* or *RosettaNet* (see 5.1.3, "Frameworks and libraries", on page 106). The message can then be directed to the appropriate back-end server for processing.

50.3.2.2   An XML-based routing scenario

For example, Figure 50-3 illustrates an implementation that uses three groups of servers:

- Set 1 for high-value transactions of the *RosettaNet* framework.
- Set 2 for high-value transactions of the *BizTalk* framework.
- Set 3 for medium and low-value transactions of both *RosettaNet* and *BizTalk* frameworks, plus regular HTTP traffic that may at times contain XML messages.

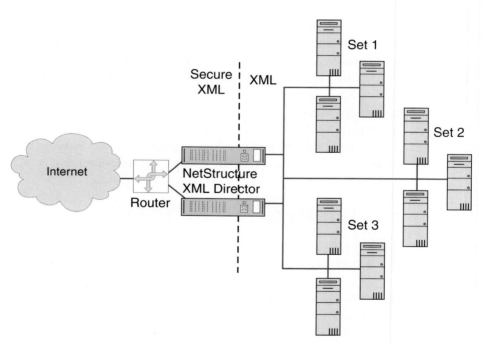

Figure 50-3   *NetStructure 7280 XML Director* configuration

All three server sets can handle any transaction; the dedication to specific frameworks is strictly to increase performance for the high-value transactions.

The *XML Director* can be configured so that if the traffic volume becomes too great for Set 1, either of the other sets can temporarily be enlisted.

50.3.3 *Other XML Director capabilities*

As Figure 50-3 shows, the *XML Director* is installed inline between the router and the XML servers. No changes to the existing XML implementation are needed.

The product enables businesses to offload Secure Sockets Layer (SSL) encryption and decryption processing from the server, offering up to 150 times faster processing for secure transactions. The decryption is a prerequisite for inspecting the data packets for their XML tags; it reduces server workloads as a by-product. The device can handle up to 1200 new SSL connections per second.

The *XML Director* can also use URI reference analysis, port number, and virtual IP address as routing criteria.

The device is capable of detecting failing or overloaded XML servers and resubmitting the requests to another server for processing. High availability is supported via a serial cable connection to a backup *XML Director*; if the primary device goes offline, the backup will automatically pick up the load.

Analysis The dominant use of XML today is for e-business, squarely at the MOM end of the application spectrum. Most of the original thinking about XML, however, has appeared to be at the POP end, where ideas like extended linking and topic maps promise to revolutionize our whole approach to information. So it may have come as a surprise to see that originality is occurring in the mundane, message moving arena as well. Intel's XML applications defy conventional notions of the "appropriate" places to use markup technology.

XML Core Tutorials

- The core of Extensible Markup Language
- Basic XML markup
- Document type definitions
- Namespaces
- Full specs on CD-ROM

Part Eighteen

This part continues the XML tutorial that we began in Part One. If you haven't read Part One in its entirety, please go back and do so, as we introduced some critically important ideas there.

In this part, you'll learn the most important details of the Extensible Markup Language. At the end you'll be able to read most of the markup of both DTDs and document instances, and you'll understand namespaces as well.

The part is intended to be read in order. However, as you read these chapters you'll notice that here and there we've included excerpts from the W3C XML specification. The tutorials are written so that *you can skip the spec excerpts*. They are not required for continuity; they are there so that the hard-core techies among you can get down with the deepest details.

But they need a little tutorial of their own to be read, which is why we have Chapter 57, "Reading the XML specification". Dig into that when – and if – you decide to read the spec excerpts, or to tackle the full spec itself, which is on the CD-ROM.

XML basics

Friendly Tutorial

- Syntactic details
- The prolog and the document instance
- XML declaration
- Elements and attributes

X ML's central concepts are quite simple, and this chapter out-
lines the most important of them. Essentially, it gives you what
you need to know to actually create XML documents. In subsequent chapters you will learn how to combine them, share text between
them, format them, and validate them.

Before looking at actual XML markup (don't worry, we'll get there soon!)
we should consider some *syntactic* constructs that will recur throughout our
discussion of XML documents. By *syntax* we mean the combination of
characters that make up an XML document. This is analogous to the distinction between sounds of words and the things that they mean. Essentially, we are talking about where you can put angle brackets, quote marks,
ampersands, and other characters and where you cannot! Later we will talk
about what they mean when you put them together.

After that, we will discusses the components that make up an XML document instance[1]. We will look at the distinction between the prolog (information XML processors need to know about your document) and the
instance (the representation of the actual document itself).

---

1. Roughly, what the XML spec calls the "root element".

51.1 | Syntactic details

XML documents are composed of characters from the *Unicode* character set. Any such sequence of characters is called a *string*. The characters in this book can be thought of as one long (but interesting) string of text. Each chapter is also a string. So is each word. XML documents are similarly made up of strings within strings.

Natural languages such as English have a particular *syntax*. The syntax allows you to combine words into grammatical sentences. XML also has syntax. It describes how you combine strings into well-formed XML documents. We will describe the basics of XML's syntax in this section.

51.1.1 *Grammars*

Natural language syntax is described with a *grammar*. XML's syntax is also. Some readers will want to dig in and learn the complete, intricate details of XML's syntax. We will provide grammar rules for them as we go along. These come right out of the XML specification. If you want to learn how to read them, you should skip ahead to Chapter 57, "Reading the XML specification", on page 904. After you have read it, you can come back and understand the rules as we present them. We advise most readers to read the chapters without worrying about the grammar rules, and then only use them when you need to answer a particular question about XML syntax.

You can recognize grammar rules taken from the specification by their form. They will look like Spec Excerpt 51-1.

Spec Excerpt (XML) 51-1. An example of a grammar rule

```
xhb ::= 'a' 'good' 'read'
```

We will not specifically introduce these rules, because we do not want to interrupt the flow of the text. They will just pop up in the appropriate place to describe the syntax of something.

51.1.2 *Case-sensitivity*

XML is *case-sensitive*. That means that if the XML specification says to insert the word "ELEMENT", it means that you should insert "ELE-MENT" and not "element" or "Element" or "ElEmEnT".

For many people, particularly English speaking people, case-insensitive matching is easier than remembering the case of particular constructs. For instance, if a document type has an element type named img English speakers will often forget and insert IMG. They confuse the two because they are not accustomed to considering case to be significant. This is also why some people new to the Internet tend to TYPE IN ALL UPPER CASE. Most vocabularies of SGML, including HTML, are designed to be case-insensitive. Designers of these vocabularies argue that this eliminates case as a source of errors.

Others argue that the whole concept of case-insensitivity is a throwback to keypunches and other early text-entry devices. They also point out that case-sensitivity is a very complicated concept in an international character set like Unicode for a variety of reasons.

For instance, the rules for case conversion of certain accented characters are different in Quebec from what they are in France. There are also some languages for which the concept of upper-case and lower-case does not exist at all. There is no simple, universal rule for case-insensitive matching. In the end, internationalization won out in XML's design.

So mind your "p's" and "q's" and "P's" and "Q's". Our authoritative laboratory testing by people in white coats indicates that exactly 74.5% of all XML errors are related to case-sensitivity mistakes. Of course XML is also spelling-sensitive and typo-sensitive, so watch out for these and other by-products of human fallibility.

Note that although XML is case-sensitive it is not case-prejudiced. Anywhere that you have the freedom to create your own names or text, you can choose to use upper- or lower-case text, as you prefer. So although you must type XML's keywords exactly as they are described, your own strings can mix and match upper- and lower-case characters however you like.

For instance, when you create your own document types you will be able to choose element-type names. A particular name could be all upper-case (SECTION), all lower-case (section) or mixed-case (SeCtION). But because XML is case-sensitive, all occurrences of a particular element-type name would have to use the same case. It is good practice to create a simple convention such as all lower-case or all upper-case so that you do not have to depend on your memory. Unfortunately there is not a single dominant convention in the XML world. One popular convention is all lower-case with dashes. Another one uses upper-case for the start OfEveryWord. A variation of that uses upper-case for only the secondAndSubsequentWords.

51.1.3 *Markup and data*

The constructs such as tags, entity references, and declarations are called *markup*. These are the parts of your document that are supposed to be understood by the XML processor. The parts that are between the markup constitute the *character data*. The XML processor does not concern itself with character data. Whereas it rips markup apart and analyzes it, the processor merely passes the character data on to the application.

Recall that the processor is the part of the program dedicated to separating the document into its constituent parts. The application is the "rest" of the program. In a word processor, the application is the part that lets you edit the document; in a spreadsheet it is the part that lets you crunch the numbers.

We haven't explained all of the parts of markup yet, but they are easy to recognize. All of them start with less-than (<) or ampersand (&) characters. Everything else is character data.

Spec Excerpt (XML) 51-2. Markup

Markup takes the form of start-tags, end-tags, empty-element tags, entity references, character references, comments, CDATA section delimiters, document type declarations, and processing instructions.

Spec Excerpt (XML) 51-3. Grammar for character data

```
[14]  CharData ::= [^<&]* - ([^<&]* ']]>' [^<&]*)
```

Spec Excerpt (XML) 51-4. Grammar for character range

```
[2]  Char ::= #x9 |  #xA |  #xD |  [#x20-#xD7FF]
                  |  [#xE000-#xFFFD] |  [#x10000-#x10FFFF]
```

51.1.4 *White space*

There is a set of characters called *white space* characters that XML processors treat differently in XML markup. They are the "invisible" characters: space (Unicode/ASCII 32), tab (Unicode/ASCII 9), carriage return (Unicode/ASCII 13) and line feed (Unicode/ASCII 10). These correspond roughly to the spacebar, tab, and Enter keys on your keyboard.

When the XML specification says that white space is allowed at a particular point, you may put as many of these characters as you want in any combination. Just as you might put two lines between paragraphs in a word processor to make a printed document readable, you may put two carriage returns in certain places in an XML document to make your source file more readable and maintainable. When the document is processed, those characters will be ignored.

In other places, white space will be significant. For instance you would not want the processor to strip out the spaces between the words in your document! Thatwouldmakeithardtoread. So white space outside of markup is always preserved in XML and white space within markup may be preserved, ignored, and sometimes combined in weird, and wonderful ways. We will describe the combination rules as we go along.

Spec Excerpt (XML) 51-5. White space

[white space] consists of one or more space (#x20) characters, carriage returns, line feeds, or tabs.

Spec Excerpt (XML) 51-6. Grammar for white space

```
[3]  S  ::=  (#x20  |  #x9  |  #xD  |  #xA)+
```

51.1.5 *Names and name tokens*

When you use XML you will often have to give things names. You will name logical structures with element-type names, reusable data with entity names, particular elements with IDs, and so forth. XML names have certain common features. They are not nearly as flexible as character data.

Letters or underscores can be used anywhere in a name. There are thousands of characters that XML version 1.0 considers a "letter" because it includes characters from every language including ideographic ones like Japanese Kanji. XML version 1.1 is even more liberal: it treats a character as a "letter" unless it is from a small list designated as punctuation.[2] Characters that can be used anywhere in a name are known in XML terms as *name start* characters. They are called this because they may be used at the start of names as well as in later positions.

This implies that there must be characters that can go in a name but cannot be the first character. You may include digits, hyphens and full-stop (.) characters in a name, but you may not start the name with one of them. These are known as *name characters*. Other characters, like various white space and Western punctuation characters, cannot be part of a name at all. Examples of these non-name characters include the tilde (~), caret (^) and space ( ).

You cannot make names that begin with the string "xml" or some case-insensitive variant like "XML" or "XmL".

There is another related syntactic construct called a *name token*. Name tokens are just like names except that they *may* start with digits, hyphens, full-stop characters, and the string XML. In other words, name tokens do not treat the start of the token as being special.

Spec Excerpt (XML) 51-7. Name tokens

An Nmtoken (name token) is any mixture of name characters.

It follows from these rules that every name is also a name token, but Example 51-1 shows some name tokens that are not names.

Example 51-1. Name tokens

```
.1.a.name.token.but.not.a.name
2-a-name-token.but-not.a-name
XML-valid-name-token
```

Like almost everything else in XML, names and name tokens are matched case-sensitively. Names and name tokens may not contain white

---

2. The two versions differ only in some character set details, which is why XML 1.1 hasn't been mentioned before. We mention it a lot in Chapter 56, "XML version 1.1", on page 896.

space, punctuation or other "funny" characters other than those listed above. The remaining "ordinary" characters (including letters from non-Latin alphabets) are called *name characters* because they may occur anywhere in a name.

Spec Excerpt (XML) 51-8. Names

A Name [begins] with a letter or one of a few punctuation characters, and [continues] with letters, digits, hyphens, underscores, colons, or full stops, together known as name characters. Names beginning with the string "xml", [matched case-insensitively] are reserved for standardization in this or future versions of this specification.

Spec Excerpt (XML) 51-9. XML 1.0 grammar for names and name tokens

```
[4] NameChar ::= Letter | Digit | '.' | '-' | '_' | ':' |
                 CombiningChar | Extender
[5] Name ::= (Letter | '_' | ':') (NameChar)*
[6] Names ::= Name (S Name)*
[7] Nmtoken ::= (NameChar)+
[8] Nmtokens ::= Nmtoken (S Nmtoken)*
```

51.1.6 *Literal strings*

The data (text other than markup) can contain almost any characters. Obviously, in the main text of your document you need to be able to use punctuation and white space characters! But sometimes you also need these characters *within* markup. For instance, an element might represent a hyperlink and need to contain a URL. The URL would have to go in markup, where characters other than the name characters are not usually allowed.

Literal strings allow users to use funny (non-name) characters within markup, but only in contexts in which it makes sense to specify values that might require those characters. For instance, to specify the URL in the hyperlink, we would need the slash character. Example 51-2 is an example of such an element.

Example 51-2. Literal string in attribute value

```
<REFERENCE URL="http://www.documents.com/document.xml">...
</REFERENCE>
```

The string that defines the URL is the literal string. This one starts and ends with double quote characters. Literal strings are always surrounded by either single or double quotes. The quotes are not part of the string.

Spec Excerpt (XML) 51-10. Literal data

Literal data is any quoted string not containing the quotation mark used as a delimiter for that string. Literals are used for specifying the content of internal entities, the values of attributes, and external identifiers.

You may use either single (') or double (") quotes to mark (*delimit*) the beginning and end of these strings in your XML document. Whichever type of quote the string starts with, it must end with. The other type may be used within the literal and has no special meaning there. Typically you will use double quotes when you want to put an actual single-quote character in the literal and single quotes when you want to embed an actual double quote. When you do not need to embed either, you can take your pick. For example, see Example 51-3.

Example 51-3. Quotes within quotes

```
"This is a double quoted literal."
'This is a single quoted literal.'
"'tis another double quoted literal."
'"And this is single quoted" said the self-referential example.'
```

The ability to have quotes within quotes is quite useful when dealing with human speech or programming language text as in Example 51-4.

Example 51-4. Quoted language

```
"To be or not to be"
'"To be or not to be", quoth Hamlet.'
"'BE!', said Jean-Louis Gassee."
'$B = "TRUE";'
```

Note that there *are* ways of including a double quote character inside of a double-quoted literal. This is important because a single literal might (rarely) need both types of quotes. We'll talk about the most important of these mechanisms in 51.7.1, "Predefined entities", on page 785.

51.2 | Prolog vs. instance

Most document representations start with a header that contains information about the actual document and how to interpret its representation. This is followed by the representation of the real document.

For instance, HTML has a HEAD element that can contain the TITLE and META elements. After the HEAD element comes the BODY. This is where the representation of the actual document resides. Similarly, email messages have "header lines" that describe who the message came from, to whom it is addressed, how it is encoded, and other things.

An XML document is similarly broken up into two main parts: a *prolog* and a *document instance*. The prolog provides information about the interpretation of the document instance, such as the version of XML and the document type to which it conforms. The document instance follows the prolog. It contains the actual document data organized as a hierarchy of elements.

Spec Excerpt (XML) 51-11. Grammar for entire document

```
[1] document ::= prolog element Misc*
```

51.3 | The logical structure

The actual content of an XML document goes in the document instance. It is called this because if it has a document type definition, it is an *instance* of a *class* of documents defined by the DTD. Just as a particular person is an instance of the class of "people", a particular memo is an instance of the class of "memo documents". The formal definition of "memo document" is in the memo DTD (or schema definition, if that means of expressing the document type was employed).

Here is an example of a small XML document.

Example 51-5. Small XML document

```
<?xml version="1.0"?>
<!DOCTYPE memo SYSTEM "memo.dtd">
<memo>
<from>
   <name>Paul Prescod</name>
   <email>papresco@prescod.com</email>
</from>
<to>
   <name>Charles Goldfarb</name>
   <email>charles@sgmlsource.com</email>
</to>
<subject>Another Memo Example</subject>
<body>
<paragraph>Charles, I wanted to suggest that we
<emphasis>not</emphasis> use the typical memo example in
our book. Memos tend to be used anywhere a small, simple
document type is needed, but they are just
<emphasis>so</emphasis> boring!
</paragraph>
</body>
</memo>
```

Because a computer cannot understand the data of the document, it looks primarily at the *tags*, the markup between the less-than and greater-than symbols. The tags delimit the beginning and end of various elements. The computer thinks of the elements as a sort of tree. It is the XML processor's (aka parser's) job to separate the markup from the character data and hand both to the application.

Figure 51-1 shows a graphical view of the logical structure of the document. The memo element is called either the *document element* or the *root element*.

The document element (memo) represents the document as a whole. Every other element represents a component of the document. The from and to elements are meant to indicate the source and target of the memo. The name elements represent people's names. Continuing in this way, the logical structure of the document is apparent from the element-type names.

Experts refer to an element's real-world meaning as its *semantics*. In a particular vocabulary, the semantics of a P element might be "paragraph" and in another it might mean "pence".

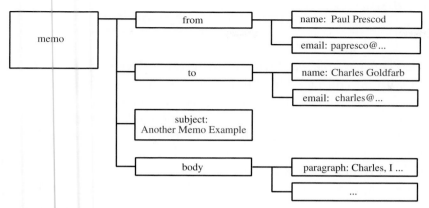

Figure 51-1   The memo XML document viewed as a tree

If you find yourself reading or writing markup and asking: "But what does that *mean*?" or "What does that look like?" then you are asking about semantics.

Computers do not yet know anything about semantics. They do not know an HTTP protocol from a supermodel. Vocabulary designers must describe semantics to authors some other way. For instance, they could send email, write a book or make a major motion picture (well, maybe some day).

What the computer does care about is how an element is supposed to look when it is formatted, or how it is to behave if it is interactive, or what to do with the data once it is extracted. These are specified in *stylesheets* and computer programs. There is a project to help computers to understand semantics. This is called the Semantic Web project and is a long-term goal of the World Wide Web Consortium.

51.4 | Elements

XML elements break down into two categories. Most have content, which is to say they contain characters, elements or both, and some do not. Those that do not are called *empty elements*. Elements within other elements are called *subelements*.

Example 51-6 is an example of an element with content.

Example 51-6. Simple element

```
<title>This is the title</title>
```

Most elements have *content*. Elements with content begin with a start-tag and finish with an end-tag. The "stuff" between the two is the element's content. In Example 51-6, "This is the title" is the content.

XML start-tags consist of the less-than (<) symbol ("left angle bracket"), the name of the element's type, (sometimes termed a *generic identifier* or *GI*), and a greater-than (>) symbol ("right angle bracket"). Start-tags can also include attributes. We will look at those later in the chapter. The start-tag in Example 51-6 is <title> and its element-type name is "title".

Spec Excerpt (XML) 51-12. Grammar for start-tags

```
[40] STag ::= '<' Name (S Attribute)* S? '>'
```

XML end-tags consist of the string "</", the same generic identifier (or *GI*) as in the start-tag, and a greater-than (>) symbol. The end-tag in Example 51-6 is </title>.

You must always repeat the generic identifier in the end-tag. This helps you to keep track of which end-tags line up with which start-tags. If you ever forget one or the other, the processor will know immediately, and will alert you that the document is not well-formed. The downside of this redundancy is that it requires more typing. Some people like belts and some prefer suspenders. The XML Working Group likes belts *and* suspenders.

Spec Excerpt (XML) 51-13. Grammar for end-tags

```
[42] ETag ::= '</' Name S? '>'
```

Note that less-than symbols in content are always interpreted as beginning a tag. If the characters following them would not constitute a tag, then the document is not well-formed.

Caution   Many people use the word "tag" imprecisely. Sometimes they mean "element-type name", sometimes "element type", sometimes even "element", and sometimes they actually mean "tag". This leads to confusion. In XML, tags always start with less-than symbols and end with greater-than symbols. Nothing else is a tag. DTDs and schemas do not define tags, they define element types.

It is possible for an element to have no content at all. Such an element is called an *empty element*. One way to denote an empty element is to merely leave out the content. But as a shortcut, empty elements may also have a different syntax. Because there is no content to delimit, they may consist of a single empty-element tag. That looks like this: `<MyEmptyElementTag/>`.

The slash at the end indicates that this is an empty-element tag, so there is no content or end-tag coming up. The slash is meant to be reminiscent of the slash in the end-tag of an element with both tags. This is just a shortcut syntax. XML processors do not treat empty-element tags differently from elements that merely have no content between the start- and end-tag.

Spec Excerpt (XML) 51-14. Grammar for empty-element tags

```
[44] EmptyElemTag ::= '<' Name (S Attribute)* S? '/>'
```

Usually empty elements have *attributes*. Occasionally an empty element without attributes will be used to flag a particular location in a document. Example 51-7 is an example of an empty element with an attribute.

Example 51-7. Empty element with attribute

```
<EMPTY-ELEMENT ATTR="ATTVAL"/>
```

Remember what the slash at the end means! You will see it often and it is easy to miss when there are attributes like this. The slash indicates that this is an empty element so that the processor need not look for a matching end-tag.

In summary, elements are either empty or have content. Elements with content are represented by a start-tag, the content, and an end-tag. Empty elements can either have a start-tag and end-tag with nothing in between, or a single empty-element tag. An element's type is always identified by the generic identifiers in its tags.

The reason we distinguish element types from generic identifiers is because the term "generic identifier" refers to the syntax of the XML document – the characters that represent the actual document. The term "element type" refers to a property of a component of the actual document.[3]

Spec Excerpt (XML) 51-15. Grammar for elements

```
[39] element ::= EmptyElemTag | STag content ETag
[43] content ::= (element | CharData | Reference |
                  CDSect | PI | Comment)*
```

51.5 | Attributes

In addition to content, elements may have *attributes*. Attributes are a way of attaching characteristics or properties to elements of a document. Attributes have *names*, just as real-world properties do. They also have *values*. For instance, two possible attributes of people are their "shoe size" and "IQ" (the attributes' names), and two possible values are "12" and "12" (respectively).

In a DTD or schema definition, each attribute is defined for a specific element type and is allowed to exhibit a certain type of value. Multiple element types could provide attributes with the same name and it is sometimes convenient to think of them as the "same attribute" even though they technically are not.

Attributes have semantics also. They always *mean* something. For example, an attribute named height might be provided for person elements

---

3. The grammar in Spec Excerpt 51-15 is from the first edition of the XML Recommendation. It is clearer than the the second edition version, which was revised to deal with an obscure interaction with another production.

(allowed occurrence), exhibit values that are numbers (allowed values), and represent the person's height in centimeters (semantics).

Here is how attributes of person elements might look:

Example 51-8. Elements with attributes

```
<person height="165cm">Dale Wick</person>
<person height="165cm" weight="165lb">Bill Bunn</person>
```

As you can see, the attribute name does not go in quotes, but the attribute value does.

Spec Excerpt (XML) 51-16. Grammar for Attributes

```
[41] Attribute ::= Name Eq AttValue
[25] Eq ::= S? '=' S?
```

Like other literals (see 51.1.6, "Literal strings", on page 771 for a refresher), attribute values can be surrounded by either single (') or double (") quotes. When you use one type of quote, the other can be used within that attribute value. As we discussed earlier, this makes it convenient to create attribute values that have the quote characters within them. This is shown in Example 51-9.

Example 51-9. Attribute values can have quotes in them

```
<PERSON HEIGHT='80"'> ... </PERSON>
<PERSON QUOTE="'To be or not to be'">...</PERSON>
```

A DTD or schema constrains an attribute's allowed occurrence and values. One possibility is to require an attribute to be specified for all elements. For example, a military document might require SECTION elements to have a security attribute with the value unclassified, classified, or secret. Example 51-10 demonstrates.

Example 51-10. Security attribute declaration

```
<!ATTLIST SECTION
          SECURITY (unclassified | classified | secret) #REQUIRED >
```

The attribute would need to be specified for each `section` element as shown in Example 51-11.

Example 51-11. Security attribute specification

```
<SECTION SECURITY="unclassified">...</SECTION>
```

It would be a validity error to create a `section` element without a `security` attribute.

Usually empty elements have attributes. Sometimes an element with subelements can be modeled just as well with an empty element and attributes. Example 51-12 shows two ways of modeling a `person` element in an email message.

Example 51-12. Alternative person element

```
<FROM><NAME>Paul Prescod</NAME>
      <EMAIL>"papresco@prescod.net"</EMAIL>
</FROM>
vs.
<FROM NAME="Paul Prescod" EMAIL="papresco@prescod.net"/>
```

Yet another way to do it would be to let the person's name be data content as shown in Example 51-13.

Example 51-13. Another alternative person element

```
<FROM><PERSON EMAIL="papresco@prescod.net">Paul Prescod
      </PERSON>
</FROM>
```

As you can see, there can be many different ways to represent the same construct. There is no one right way to do so. In the case of `person`, the last version shown is the most typical because the character data of a document generally represents what you would expect to see in a "print-out".

But that is not a hard and fast rule (after all, renditions vary widely). Because there are so many ways to represent the same thing, it is advisable to use a DTD or schema. Its constraints can maintain consistency across a range of documents, or even within a single large document. There may be many ways to represent a particular concept, but once you choose one, let the DTD (or schema) help you stick to it.

Spec Excerpt (XML) 51-17. Grammar for attribute values

```
[10] AttValue ::= '"' ([^<&"] | Reference)* '"'
               |  "'" ([^<&'] | Reference)* "'"
```

51.6 | The prolog

XML documents may start with a prolog that describes the XML version ("1.0" or "1.1", for now), document type, and other characteristics of the document.

The prolog is made up of an *XML declaration* and a *document type declaration*, both optional. Though an author may include either, neither, or both, it is best to try to maximize the amount of prolog information provided. This will make later processing more reliable.

The XML declaration must precede the document type declaration if both are provided. Also, comments, processing instructions, and white space can be mixed in among the two declarations. The prolog ends when the first start-tag begins.

Example 51-14 is a sample prolog as a warm-up.

Example 51-14. A simple prolog

```
<?xml version="1.0"?>
<!DOCTYPE book SYSTEM "http://www.oasis-open.org/.../docbookx.dtd">
```

This prolog says that the document conforms to XML version 1.0 and declares adherence to a particular document type, book.

Spec Excerpt (XML) 51-18. Grammar for prologs

```
[22] prolog ::= XMLDecl? Misc* (doctypedecl Misc*)?
[27] Misc ::= Comment | PI | S
```

51.6.1 *XML declaration*

The XML declaration is fairly simple. It has several parts and they fit together one after another.

A minimal XML declaration looks like this:

Example 51-15. Minimal XML declaration

```
<?xml version="1.0"?>
```

Example 51-16 is a more expansive one, using all of its parts.

Example 51-16. More expansive XML declaration

```
<?xml version="1.0" encoding="UTF-8" standalone="yes"?>
```

There is one important thing to note in the last example. It looks like a start-tag with three attributes, but it is *not*. The different parts of the XML declaration just happen to look like attributes. Well, not quite "just happen": it could have had a completely different syntax, but that would have been harder to memorize. So the parts were chosen to look like attributes to reduce the complexity of the language. One important difference between XML declaration parts and attributes is that the parts are strictly ordered whereas attributes can be specified in any order.

Spec Excerpt (XML) 51-19. Grammar for XML declarations

```
[23] XMLDecl ::= '<?xml' VersionInfo EncodingDecl? SDDecl? S? '?>'
```

51.6.1.1 Version info

The *version info* part of the XML declaration declares the version of XML that is in use. It is required in all XML declarations, although the XML declaration itself is optional. At the time of writing, the only permitted version strings are "1.0" and "1.1". If you leave out the entire XML declaration (thereby leaving out the version) then your document is presumed to be an XML 1.0 (not 1.1) document.

The XML version information is part of a general trend towards information representations that are *self-identifying*. This means that you can look at an XML document and (if it has the declaration) know immediately both that it is XML and what version of XML it uses. As more and more document representations become self-identifying, we will be able to stop relying on error-prone identification schemes like file extensions.

Spec Excerpt (XML) 51-20. Version information

```
[24] VersionInfo ::= S 'version' Eq
                    ("'" VersionNum "'" | '"' VersionNum '"')
[25] Eq ::= S? '=' S?
[26] VersionNum ::= ([a-zA-Z0-9_.:] | '-')+
```

51.6.1.2   Encoding declaration

An XML declaration may also include an *encoding declaration*. It describes what character encoding is used. This is another aspect of being self-identifying. If your documents are encoded in the traditional 7-bit-ASCII used on most operating systems and with most text editors, then you do not need to worry about the encoding-declaration. 7-bit-ASCII is a subset of a Unicode encoding called *UTF-8* which XML processors can automatically detect and use. If you use 7-bit ASCII and need to encode a character outside of 7-bit-ASCII, such as the trademark sign or a non-English character, you can do so most easily by using a numeric character reference, as described in 55.2, "Character references", on page 880.

It normally not a problem to type non-ASCII characters directly into an XML document, using a Unicode-aware text editor, as these editors generally create UTF-8 documents directly. You need only use the encoding declaration if you are using some national or regional encoding like Russia's KOI8-R, Western Europe's ISO-8859-1 or Japan's Shift-JIS. If you want to use one of these encodings you should put the encoding name in the encoding declaration as shown in Example 51-17.

Spec Excerpt (XML) 51-21. Grammar for encoding declarations

```
[80]EncodingDecl ::= S 'encoding'
                   Eq ('"' EncName '"' | "'" EncName "'" )
[81]EncName ::= [A-Za-z] ([A-Za-z0-9._] |'-')*
```

Example 51-17. Encoding declaration

```
<?xml version="1.0" encoding="KOI8-R"?>
```

51.6.1.3   Standalone document declaration

An XML declaration can include a *standalone document declaration*. It declares what components of the document type definition are necessary for complete processing of the document. This rarely used, arguably useless declaration is described in 55.5, "Standalone document declaration", on page 887.

51.6.2   *Document type declaration*

After the XML declaration (if present) and before the first element, there may be a *document type declaration* which declares the document type that is in use in the document. A "book" document type, for example, might be made up of chapters, while a letter document type could be made up of element types such as ADDRESS, SALUTATION, SIGNATURE, and so forth.

The document type declaration is at the heart of the concept of *validity*, which makes applications based on XML robust and reliable. It includes the markup declarations that express the *document type definition (DTD)*.

The DTD is a formalization of the intuitive idea of a document type. The DTD lists the element types available and can put constraints on the occurrence and content of elements and other details of the document structure. This makes an information system more robust by forcing the documents that are part of it to be consistent.

A schema definition can also be used for this purpose, but other means must be used to associate it with documents. There are several schema languages; we discuss the official W3C one in Chapter 63, "XML Schema (XSDL)", on page 1030.

51.7 | Markup miscellany

This section contains information on some additional markup constructs. They are not as important or as widely used as elements, attributes and the XML declaration, but they are still vital parts of a markup expert's toolbox.

51.7.1 *Predefined entities*

Sometimes when you are creating an XML document, you want to protect certain characters from markup interpretation. Imagine, for example, that you are writing a user's guide to HTML. You would need a way to include an example of markup. Your first attempt might be to create an `example` element and do something like this Example 51-18.

Example 51-18. An invalid approach to HTML examples in XML

```
<p>HTML documents must start with a DOCTYPE, etc. etc. This
is an example of a small HTML document:
<sample>

  <!DOCTYPE HTML PUBLIC "-//W3C//DTD HTML 3.2 Final//EN">
  <HTML>
  A document's title
  <H1>A document's title</H1>
  </HTML>

</sample>
```

This will not work, however, because the angle brackets that are supposed to represent HTML markup will be interpreted as if they belonged to the XML document you are creating, not the mythical HTML document in the example. Your XML processor will complain that it is not appropriate to have an HTML DOCTYPE declaration in the middle of an XML document! There are two solutions to this problem: predefined entities and CDATA sections.

Predefined entities are XML markup that authors use to represent characters that would otherwise be interpreted as having a special meaning, such as a start-tag or an entity reference. There are five *predefined* ("built-in") entities in XML. These were included precisely to deal with this problem. They are listed in Table 51-1.

Table 51-1   Predefined entities

Entity reference	Character
&amp;	&
&lt;	<
&gt;	>
&apos;	'
&quot;	"

Why these specific five characters? See Spec Excerpt 51-22 and Spec Excerpt 51-23 for the answer.

Spec Excerpt (XML) 51-22. Predefined entities

The ampersand character (&) and the left angle bracket (<) may appear in their literal form only when used as markup delimiters, or within a comment, a processing instruction, or a CDATA section. [...] If they are needed elsewhere, they must be escaped using either numeric character references or the strings "&" and "<" respectively.

Spec Excerpt (XML) 51-23. Attribute values

To allow attribute values to contain both single and double quotes, the apostrophe or single-quote character (') may be represented as "'", and the double-quote character (") as """.

An entity for the right angle bracket is provided primarily for symmetry. It is also sometimes useful to avoid putting a special string called *CDEnd* (discussed in 51.7.2, "CDATA sections", on page 787) into your document. But you do not have to use this entity in most cases.

We can use references to the predefined entities to insert these characters, instead of typing them directly. Then they will not be interpreted as markup. Example 51-19 demonstrates this.

Example 51-19. Writing about HTML in XML

```
<p>HTML documents must start with a DOCTYPE, etc. etc. This
is an example of a small HTML document:
<sample>
   &lt;!DOCTYPE HTML PUBLIC "-//W3C//DTD HTML 3.2 Final//EN">
   &lt;HTML>
   &lt;HEAD>
   &lt;TITLE>A document's title
   &lt;/TITLE>
   &lt;/HEAD>
   &lt;/HTML>
</sample>
```

When your XML processor parses the document, it will replace the entity references with actual characters. It will not interpret the characters it inserts as markup, but as "plain old data characters" (character data).

51.7.2 CDATA sections

While predefined entities are convenient, human beings are not as good at decoding them as computers are. Your readers will get the translated version, so they will be fine. But as the author, you may spend hours staring at character entity references while you are editing your XML document in a text editor (if you choose not to use a graphical XML editor). You may also spend hours replacing special characters with character entity references. This can get annoying.[4]

Another construct, called a *CDATA section*, allows you to ask the processor not to interpret a chunk of text as containing markup: "Hands off! This isn't meant to be interpreted." CDATA stands for "character data". You can mark a section as being character data using this special syntax as shown in Example 51-20.

Example 51-20. CDATA section

```
<![CDATA[ content  ]]>
```

---

4. This is especially nasty when you are writing an XML book, where examples tend to contain many angle brackets.

Example 51-21 and Example 51-22 are other examples.

Example 51-21. Writing about HTML in a CDATA section

```
<![CDATA[
<HTML>
This is an example from HTML for Dumbbells!
<p>It may be a pain to write a book about HTML in HTML,
but it is easy in XML!
</HTML>
]]>
```

Example 51-22. Java code in a CDATA section

```
<![CDATA[
if( foo.getContentLength() < 0  && input = foo.getInputStream() )
    open = true;
]]>
```

As you can see, it does not usually matter what you put in CDATA sections because their content is not scanned for markup. There is one obvious exception (and one not-so-obvious corollary). The string that ends the CDATA section,]]> (known as *CDEnd*), cannot be used inside the section. Use Example 51-23 as a cautionary tale.

Example 51-23. Illegal CDATA usage

```
<![CDATA[
 Javascript code: if( a[c[5]]> 7 ) then...
]]>
```

The first occurrence of CDEnd (]]>) in the middle of the Javascript expression will terminate the section. You simply cannot use a CDATA section for content that includes CDEnd. You must end the section and insert the character as in Example 51-24.

Example 51-24. Legal CDATA usage

```
<![CDATA[
 Javascript code: if( a[c[5]]]]>><![CDATA[ 7 ) then...
]]>
```

This is quite painful and can cause a problem for embedding programming languages. But even in those languages, CDEnd is probably a fairly rare character string, so you should just keep an eye out for it.

The non-obvious corollary is:

Caution   CDEnd (]]>) should only be used to close CDATA sections. It must not occur anywhere else in an XML document.

This is an absolute requirement, not just a recommendation. Because of it you can easily check that you have closed CDATA sections correctly by comparing the number of CDEnd strings to the number of sections. If you do not close a CDATA section correctly, some of your document's markup may be interpreted as character data. Since (]]>) is not something that typical documents contain, this restriction is rarely a problem.

With all of these warnings, CDATA sections may sound tricky to use, but they really aren't. This book, for example, has several hundred. Mistakes involving CDATA sections are usually quite blatant, because either markup will show up in your rendered document, or data characters will be interpreted as markup and probably trigger an error message.

Predefined entities and CDATA sections only relate to the interpretation of the markup, not to the properties of the real document that the markup represents.

Spec Excerpt (XML) 51-24. Grammar for CDATA sections

```
[18] CDSect  ::= CDStart CData CDEnd
[19] CDStart ::= '<![CDATA['
[20] CData   ::= (Char* - (Char* ']]>' Char*))
[21] CDEnd   ::= ']]>'
```

51.7.3 *Comments*

Sometimes it is useful to embed information about a document or its markup in a manner that will be ignored by computer processes and renditions of the document. For example, you might insert a note to yourself to clean up the wording of a section, a note to a co-author explaining the reason for a particular section of the document, or a note in a DTD describing the semantics of a particular element. This information can be hidden from the application in a *comment*. Comments should never be displayed in a browser, indexed in a search engine, or otherwise processed as part of the data of the actual document.

Example 51-25. A comment

```
<!-- This section is really good! Let's not change it. -->
```

Comments consist of the characters "<!--" followed by almost anything and ended by "-->". The "almost anything" in the middle cannot contain the characters "--". This is a little bit inconvenient, because people often use those two characters as a sort of dash, to separate thoughts. This is another point to be careful of, lest you get bitten.

Comments can go just about anywhere in the instance or the prolog. However, they cannot go within declarations, tags, or other comments. Example 51-26 is a document using some comments in several correct places.

Example 51-26. Comments all over the place

```
<?xml version="1.0"?>
<!-- 1.0 is the XML version! -->
<!-- Now on to the doctype -->
<!DOCTYPE SAMPLE [
  <!-- This is a comment in the
  doctype declaration internal subset! -->
  <!ELEMENT SAMPLE (#PCDATA)>
  <!-- This is a very simple DTD. -->
]> <!-- Here comes the "root" or "document" element. -->
<SAMPLE>This is some character data.
<!-- That was some character data. -->
</SAMPLE>
<!-- That's all folks -->
```

Markup is not recognized in comments. You can put less-than and ampersand symbols in them, but they will not be recognized as the start of elements or entity references.

Comments are a good place to describe the semantics of element types and attributes. So you might use a comment to tell other DTD maintainers and authors that an element type with a cryptic name like p is actually intended to model paragraphs and not (for example) British currency. Comments are not just about being helpful to other people. After all, even expert document type designers have a limited and imperfect memory. Some day even you will wonder exactly what it was you meant by a particular element-type name. The DTD comments will help. The job that you are saving might be your own!

Spec Excerpt (XML) 51-25. Grammar for comments

```
[15]   Comment ::= '<!--'((Char - '-')|('-'(Char - '-')))*'-->'
```

51.8 | Summary

An XML document is composed of a prolog and a document instance. The prolog is optional, and provides information about how the document is structured both physically (where its parts are) and logically (how its elements fit together). Elements and attributes describe the logical structure. As we will see, *entities* describe the physical structure. To use a rough analogy, the entities are like a robot's body parts, the elements are his thoughts, and stylesheets and software provide his behavior.

Creating a document type definition

- Document type declaration
- Element type declarations
- Attribute list declarations

Chapter

52

C reating your own document type definition or schema definition is like creating your own markup language. If you have
ever chafed at the limitations of a language with a fixed set of
element types, such as HTML or TEI, then you will embrace the opportunity to create your own language.[1] DTDs are XML's built-in mark-
up-language definition language.

Another way of expressing your ideas formally is by creating a schema
definition using XSDL, which we discuss in Chapter 63, "XML Schema
(XSDL)", on page 1030, or one of the other new schema languages.
Schema definitions allow even more power (and complexity!) than DTDs,
so they are also important to learn.

We feel that it is important for serious XML users to understand both.
Because schema definitions employ DTD concepts, learning one will help
you learn the other. Indeed, *XML Schema* datatypes, covered in Chapter 62,
"Datatypes", on page 1000, can even be used in conjunction with DTDs.

We should note again that it is possible to keep a document type definition completely in your head rather than writing the declarations for a
DTD or schema. Sometimes DTD designers do that while they are testing

---

1. With its own set of limitations!

out ideas. Usually, though, you actually commit your ideas to declarations so that a validating processor can help you to keep your documents consistent.

Note also that, for the present, we are maintaining the distinction, discussed in 7.4, "Document type, DTD, and markup declarations", on page 147, between a document type, the XML markup rules for it (DTD), and the markup declarations that declare the DTD. Those *DTD declarations* are connected to the big kahuna of markup declarations – the *document type declaration*.

52.1 | Document type declaration

A document type declaration for a particular document might say "This document is a concert poster." The document type definition for the document would say "A concert poster must have the following features." As an analogy: in the world of art, you can *declare* yourself a practitioner of a particular movement, or you can *define* the movement by writing its manifesto.

The XML spec uses the abbreviation DTD to refer to document type definitions because we speak of them much more often than document type declarations. The DTD defines the allowed element types, attributes and entities and can express some constraints on their combination.

A document that conforms to its DTD is said to be *valid*. Just as an English sentence can be ungrammatical, a document can fail to conform to its DTD and thus be *invalid*. That does not necessarily mean, however, that it ceases to be an XML document. The word valid does not have its usual meaning here. An artist can fail to uphold the principles of an artistic movement without ceasing to be an artist, and an XML document can violate its DTD and yet remain a well-formed XML document.

As the document type declaration is optional, a well-formed XML document can choose not to declare conformance to any DTD at all. It cannot then be a valid document, because it cannot be checked for conformance to a DTD. It is not invalid, because it does not violate the constraints of a DTD.

XML has no good word for these merely well-formed documents. Some people call them "well-formed", but that is insufficiently precise. If the document were not well-formed, it would not be XML (by definition). Saying that a document is well-formed does not tell us anything about its conformance to a DTD at all.

For this reason, we prefer the terms used by the ISO for full-SGML: *type-valid*, meaning "valid with respect to a document type", and *non-type-valid*, the converse.

Example 52-1 is an XML document containing a document type declaration and document type definition for mailing labels, followed by an instance of the document type: a single label.

Example 52-1. XML document with document type declaration

```
<!DOCTYPE label[
    <!ELEMENT label (name, street, city, state, country, code)>
    <!ELEMENT name (#PCDATA)>
    <!ELEMENT street (#PCDATA)>
    <!ELEMENT city (#PCDATA)>
    <!ELEMENT state (#PCDATA)>
    <!ELEMENT country (#PCDATA)>
    <!ELEMENT code (#PCDATA)>
]><label>
<name>Rock N. Robyn</name>
<street>Jay Bird Street</street>
<city>Baltimore</city>
<state>MD</state>
<country>USA</country>
<code>43214</code>
</label>
```

The document type declaration starts on the first line and ends with "`]>`". The DTD declarations are the lines starting with "`<!ELEMENT`". Those are *element type declarations*. You can also declare attributes, entities and notations for a DTD. The element type declarations that contain `#PCDATA` (parsed character data) allow textual data content.

Recall from 2.4, "Entities: The physical structure", on page 38 that an XML document can be broken up into separate objects for storage, called "entities".[2] The document type declaration occurs in the first (or only) entity to be parsed, called the "document entity".

In Example 52-1, all of the DTD declarations that define the label DTD reside within the document entity. However, the DTD could have been partially or completely defined somewhere else. In that case, the document

---

2. Loosely, an entity is like a file.

type declaration would contain a reference to another entity containing those declarations.

A document type declaration with only external DTD declarations looks like Example 52-2.

Example 52-2. Document type declaration with external DTD declarations

```
<?xml version="1.0"?>
<!DOCTYPE label SYSTEM "http://www.sgmlsource.com/dtds/label.dtd">
<label>
...
</label>
```

They keyword SYSTEM is described more completely in 54.9.1, "System identifiers", on page 864. For now, we will just say that it tells the processor to fetch some resource containing the external information. In this case, the external information is made up of the declarations that define the label DTD. They should be exactly the ones we had in the original label document. The big difference is that now they can be reused in hundreds, thousands, or even millions of label documents. Our simple DTD could be the basis for the largest junk mailing in history!

All document type declarations start with the string "<!DOCTYPE". Next they have the name of an element type that is defined in the DTD. The root element in the instance (described in 51.4, "Elements", on page 775) must be of the type declared in the document type declaration. If any of the DTD declarations are stored externally, the third part of the document type declaration must be either "SYSTEM" or "PUBLIC". We will cover "PUBLIC" later. If it is "SYSTEM", the final part must be a "URI" pointing to the external declarations. A URI is, for all practical purposes, a URL. URIs are discussed in 64.2, "Uniform Resource Identifiers", on page 1054.

Spec Excerpt (XML) 52-1. DOCTYPE declaration

```
[28] doctypedecl ::= '<!DOCTYPE' S Name (S ExternalID)? S? ('['
                      (markupdecl | PEReference | S)* ']' S?)? '>'
[75] ExternalID  ::= 'SYSTEM' S SystemLiteral
                     | 'PUBLIC' S PubidLiteral S SystemLiteral

[29] markupdecl  ::= elementdecl | AttlistDecl | EntityDecl
                     | NotationDecl | PI | Comment
```

52.2 | Internal and external subset

In Example 52-1, the DTD declarations were completely *internal*. They were inside of the document type declaration. In Example 52-2, they were completely external. In many cases, there will be a mix of the two. This section will review these options and show how most XML document type declarations combine an internal part, called the *internal subset* and an external part, called the *external subset*.

From now on, as we'll almost always be writing about DTD declarations, we'll refer to them as "the DTD". We'll resort to the finer distinctions only when necessary for clarity.

We will start with an example of a DTD in Example 52-3.

Example 52-3. Garage sale announcement DTD.

```
<!ELEMENT GARAGESALE (DATE, TIME, PLACE, NOTES)>
<!ELEMENT DATE (#PCDATA)>
<!ELEMENT TIME (#PCDATA)>
<!ELEMENT PLACE (#PCDATA)>
<!ELEMENT NOTES (#PCDATA)>
```

These markup declarations would make up an ultra-simple DTD for garage sale announcements.[3] As you may have deduced, it declares five element types. We will get to the syntax of the declarations soon. First we will look at how they would be used. These could reside in a separate file called garage.dtd (for instance) and then every document that wanted to conform to them would declare its conformance using a document type declaration. This is shown in Example 52-4.

Instead of a complete URL, we have just referred to the DTD's file name. Actually, this is still a URL. It is a *relative URL*. That means that in a standard Web server setup, the XML document entity and its DTD entity reside in the same directory. You could also refer to a full URL as we do in Example 52-5.

The relative URL is more convenient while you are testing because you do not need to have a full server installed. You can just put the two entities

---

3. A garage sale is where North Americans spend their hard-earned money on other people's junk, which they will eventually sell at their own garage sales.

Example 52-4. Conforming garage sale document.

```
<!DOCTYPE GARAGESALE SYSTEM "garage.dtd">
<GARAGESALE>
<DATE>February 29, 1998</DATE>
<TIME>7:30 AM</TIME>
<PLACE>249 Cedarbrae</PLACE>
<NOTES>Lots of high-quality junk for sale!</NOTES>
</GARAGESALE>
```

Example 52-5. Specifying a full URL

```
<!DOCTYPE GARAGESALE SYSTEM
            "http://www.tradestuff.com/stuff.dtd">
<GARAGESALE>
...
</GARAGESALE>
```

in the same directory on your hard drive. But your DTD and your instance can get even more cozy than sharing a directory. You can hoist your DTD into the same entity as the instance as in Example 52-6.

Example 52-6. Bringing a DTD into the same entity as the instance

```
<!DOCTYPE GARAGESALE
[
<!ELEMENT GARAGESALE (DATE, TIME, PLACE, NOTES)>
<!ELEMENT DATE (#PCDATA)>
<!ELEMENT TIME (#PCDATA)>
<!ELEMENT PLACE (#PCDATA)>
<!ELEMENT NOTES (#PCDATA)>
]>
<GARAGESALE>
...
</GARAGESALE>
```

The section between the square brackets is called the *internal subset* of the document type declaration. For testing, this is very convenient! You can edit the instance and the DTD without moving between entities. Since entities usually correspond to files, this means that instead of moving between two files, you need only edit one.

Although this is convenient, it is not great for reuse. The DTD is not available anywhere but in this file. Other documents cannot conform to this DTD without copying the declarations into their internal subset.

Often you will combine both approaches. Some of the DTD declarations can go in an external entity where it can be reused, and some of it can go in the same entity as the instance. Often graphic entities (see 54.2.1.3, "Unparsed entities", on page 851) would be declared in the internal subset because they are specific to a document. On the other hand, element type declarations would usually be in the *external subset*, the external part of the document type declaration. Example 52-7 demonstrates.

Example 52-7. Reference to an external subset

```
<!DOCTYPE GARAGESALE SYSTEM "garage.dtd"[
<!ENTITY LOGO SYSTEM "logo.gif">
]><GARAGESALE> ... </GARAGESALE>
```

The declarations in the internal subset are processed before those in the external subset. This gives document authors the opportunity to override[4] some kinds of declarations in the shared portion of the DTD.

Note that the content of both the internal subset and the external subset makes up the DTD. garage.dtd may have a dtd extension but that is just a convention we chose to emphasize that the file contains DTD declarations. It is *not* necessarily the full set of them. The full set of DTD declarations is the combination of the declarations in the internal and external subsets.

Caution   Many people believe that the file containing the external subset is "the DTD". Until it is referenced from a document type declaration and combined with an internal subset (even an empty one) it is just a file that happens to have markup declarations in it. It is good practice, however, when an external subset is used, to restrict the internal subset to declarations that apply only to the individual document, such as entity declarations for graphics.

It is often very convenient to point to a particular file and refer to it as "the DTD" for a given document type. As long as the concepts are straight in your mind, it does seem a trifle simpler than saying "the file that contains

---

4. Actually, preempt.

the markup declarations that I intend to reference as the external subset of the document type declaration for all documents of this type".

52.3 | Element type declarations

Elements are the foundation of XML markup. Every element in a valid XML document must conform to an element type declared in the DTD. Documents with elements that do not conform could be well-formed, but not valid. Example 52-8 is an example of an element type declaration.

Example 52-8. Element type declaration.

```
<!ELEMENT memo (to, from, body )>
```

Element type declarations must start with the string "`<!ELEMENT`", followed by the name (or *generic identifier* of the element type being declared. Finally they must have a *content specification*. The content specification above states that elements of this type must contain a `to` element followed by a `from` element followed in turn by a `body` element.

Spec Excerpt (XML) 52-2. Element type declaration

```
<!ELEMENT' S Name S contentspec S? '>'
```

Element-type names are XML *names*. That means there are certain restrictions on the characters allowed in them. These are described in 51.1.5, "Names and name tokens", on page 769. Each element type declaration must use a different name because a particular element type cannot be declared more than once.

Caution   *Unique element type declaration. Unlike attributes and entities, element types can be declared only once.*

52.4 | Element type content specification

Every element type has certain allowed content. For instance a document type definition might allow a chapter to have a title in its content, but would probably not allow a footnote to have a chapter in its content (though XML itself would not prohibit that!).

There are four kinds of content specification. These are described in Table 52-1.

Table 52-1 Content specification types

Content specification type	Allowed content
EMPTY content	May not have content. They are typically used for their attributes.
ANY content	May have any content at all.
Mixed content	May have character data or a mix of character data and subelements specified in mixed content specification.
Element content	May have only subelements specified in element content specification

52.4.1 *Empty content*

Sometimes we want an element type that can never have any content. We would give it a content specification of EMPTY. For instance an image element type like HTML's img would include a graphic from somewhere else. It would do this through an attribute and would not need any subelements or character data content. A cross-reference element type might not need content because the text for the reference might be generated from the target. A reference to an element type with the title "More about XML" might become "See *More about XML* on page 14".

You can declare an element type to have empty content by using the EMPTY keyword as the content specification. See Example 52-9.

Example 52-9. Empty element type

```
<!ELEMENT MY-EMPTY-ELEMENT EMPTY>
```

52.4.2 *ANY content*

Occasionally, you want an element type to be able to hold any element or character data. You can do this if you give it a content spec of ANY as in Example 52-10.

Example 52-10. Element type with ANY content

```
<!ELEMENT LOOSEY-GOOSEY ANY>
```

This is rarely done. Typically we introduce element type declarations to express the structure of our document types. An element type that has an ANY content specification is completely unstructured. It can contain any combination of character data and subelements. Still, ANY content element types are occasionally useful, especially while a DTD is being developed. If you are developing a DTD for existing documents, then you could declare each element type to have ANY content to get the document to validate. Then you could try to figure out more precise content specifications for each element type, one at a time.

52.4.3 *Mixed content*

Element types with *mixed content* are allowed to hold either character data alone or character data with child elements interspersed. A paragraph is a good example of a typical mixed content element. It might have character data with some mixed in emphasis and quotation subelements. The simplest mixed content specifications allow data only and start with a left parenthesis character (( ), followed by the string #PCDATA and a final close parenthesis ( )). Example 52-11 demonstrates.

Example 52-11. Data-only mixed content

```
<!ELEMENT emph (#PCDATA)>
<!ELEMENT foreign-language ( #PCDATA ) >
```

You may put white space between the parenthesis and the string #PCDATA if you like. The declarations above create element types that cannot contain subelements. Subelements that are detected will be reported as validity errors.

In other words, these elements do not really have "mixed" content in the usual sense. Like the word "valid", XML has a particular meaning for the word that is not very intuitive. Any content specification that contains #PCDATA is called mixed, whether subelements are allowed or not.

We can easily extend the DTD to allow a mix of elements and character data. This is shown in Example 52-12.

Example 52-12. Allow a mix of character data and elements

```
<!ELEMENT paragraph (#PCDATA|emph)*>
<!ELEMENT abstract (#PCDATA|emph|quot)*>
<!ELEMENT title ( #PCDATA | foreign-language | emph )* >
```

Note the trailing asterisk. It is required in content specifications that allow a mix of character data and elements. The reason it is there will be made clear when we study content models. Note also that we can put white space before and after the vertical bar (|) characters.

These declarations create element types that allow a mix of character data and subelements. The element types listed after the vertical bars (|), are the allowed subelements. Example 52-13 would be a valid title if we combine the declarations in Example 52-12 with those in Example 52-11.

Example 52-13. Sample data

```
<title>this is a <foreign-language>tres gros</foreign-language>
       title for an <emph>XML</emph> book</title>
```

The title has character data ("This is a"), a foreign-language subelement, some more character data ("title for an"), an emph subelement and some final character data "book". We could have reordered the emph and foreign-language elements and the character data however we wanted.

We could also have introduced as many (or as few) `emph` and `foreign-language` elements as we needed.

52.5 | Content models

The final kind of content specification is a "children" specification. This type of specification says that elements of the type can contain only child elements in its content. You declare an element type as having *element content* by specifying a content model that has only element-type names, instead of a mixed content specification or one of the keywords described above.

A content model is a pattern that you set up to declare what subelement types are allowed and in what order they are allowed. A simple model for a `memo` might say that it must contain a `from` followed by a `to` followed by a `subject` followed by a `paragraph`. A more complex model for a `question-and-answer` might require `question` and `answer` elements to alternate.

A model for a `chapter` might require a single `title` element, one or two `author` elements and one or more `paragraphs`. When a document is validated, the processor would check that the element's content matches the model.

A simple content model could have a single subelement type as in Example 52-14.

Example 52-14. A single subelement

```
<!ELEMENT WARNING (PARAGRAPH)>
```

This says that a `WARNING` must have a single `PARAGRAPH` within it. As with mixed content specifications, you may place white space before or after the parentheses. We could also say that a `WARNING` must have a `TITLE` and then a `PARAGRAPH` within it as in Example 52-15.

Example 52-15. Two subelements

```
<!ELEMENT WARNING (TITLE, PARAGRAPH)>
```

The comma (,) between the TITLE and PARAGRAPH GIs indicates that the TITLE must precede the PARAGRAPH in the WARNING element. This is called a *sequence*. Sequences can be as long as you like (Example 52-16).

Example 52-16. Longer sequence

```
<!ELEMENT MEMO (FROM, TO, SUBJECT, BODY)>
```

You may put white space before or after the comma (,) between two parts of the sequence.

Sometimes you want to have a choice rather than a sequence. For instance Example 52-17 shows a declaration for an element type that allows a FIGURE to contain either a GRAPHIC element (inserting an external graphic) or a CODE element (inserting some computer code).

Example 52-17. Allowing choice

```
<!ELEMENT FIGURE (GRAPHIC|CODE)>
```

The vertical bar character (|) indicates that the author can choose between the element types. We say that this is a *choice group*. You can put white space before or after the vertical bar. You may have as many choices as you want:

Example 52-18. Multiple Choices

```
<!ELEMENT FIGURE (CODE|TABLE | FLOW-CHART| SCREEN-SHOT)>
```

You may also combine choices and sequences using parenthesis. When you wrap parenthesis around a choice or sequence, it becomes a *content particle*. Individual GIs are also content particles. You can use any content particle where ever you would use a GI in a content model:

Example 52-19. Content particles

```
<!ELEMENT FIGURE (CAPTION, (CODE|TABLE|FLOW-CHART|SCREEN-SHOT) )>
<!ELEMENT CREATED ((AUTHOR | CO-AUTHORS), DATE )>
```

The content model for FIGURE is thus made up of a sequence of two content particles. The first content particle is a single element-type name. The second is a choice of several element-type names. You can break down the content model for CREATED in the same way.

You can make some fairly complex models this way. But when you write a DTD for a book, you do not know in advance how many chapters the book will have, nor how many paragraphs each chapter will contain. You need a way of saying that the part of the content specification that allows captions is *repeatable* – that you can match it many times.

Sometimes you will also want to make an element optional. For instance, some figures may not have captions. You may want to say that part of the specification for figures is optional.

XML allows you to specify that a content particle is optional or repeatable using an *occurrence indicator*. Table 52-2 shows the three occurrence indicators.

Table 52-2   Occurrence indicators

Indicator	Content particle is...
?	Optional (0 or 1 time).
*	Optional and repeatable (0 or more times)
+	Required and repeatable (1 or more times)

Occurrence indicators directly follow a GI, sequence or choice. The occurrence indicator cannot be preceded by white space.

Example 52-20 illustrates how we can make captions optional on figures:

Example 52-20. Captions are optional.

```
<!ELEMENT FIGURE (CAPTION?, (CODE|TABLE|FLOW-CHART|SCREEN-SHOT))>
```

We can allow footnotes to have multiple paragraphs:

Example 52-21. Footnotes have multiple paragraphs

```
<!ELEMENT FOOTNOTE (P+)>
```

Because we used the "+" indicator, footnotes must have at least one paragraph. We could also have expressed this in another way:

Example 52-22. Multiple paragraphs: the sequel

```
<!ELEMENT FOOTNOTE (P, P*)>
```

This would require a leading paragraph and then 0 or more paragraphs following. That would achieve the same effect as requiring 1 or more paragraphs. The "+" operator is just a little more convenient than repeating the preceding content particle.

We can combine occurrence indicators with sequences or choices:

Example 52-23. Occurrence indicators and sequences

```
<!ELEMENT QUESTION-AND-ANSWER (INTRODUCTION,
                               (QUESTION, ANSWER)+,
                               COPYRIGHT?)>
```

It is also possible to make all of the element types in a content model optional:

Example 52-24. Optional content

```
<!ELEMENT IMAGE (CAPTION?)>
```

This allows the IMAGE element to be empty sometimes and not other times. The question mark indicates that CAPTION is optional. Most likely these IMAGE elements would link to an external graphic through an attribute. The author would only provide content if he wanted to provide a caption.

In the document instance, empty IMAGE elements look identical to how they would look if IMAGE had been declared to be always empty. There is no way to tell from the document instance whether they were declared as empty or are merely empty in a particular case.

52.5.1 *Mixed content models*

We have already talked about mixed content but we should look at it a little more in light of our new understanding of content models. They say that a little knowledge can be a dangerous thing. It's true! Now that you know about content models, you can interpret the syntax for mixed content a little bit better.

Example 52-25. Mixed content again

```
<!ELEMENT abstract (#PCDATA|emph|quot)*>
```

Take a look at Example 52-25 We can see now that this model is similar to element-only content models. What it really says is that you can have a mix of as many parsed characters and elements (emph and quot, in this example) as you like.

First you could select to add some data characters (choosing the #PCDATA branch of the choice group) and then the asterisk would allow you to select from the group again. You could select a quot and then select again and so forth. In this manner you would build up a list of character data, emph elements and quot elements.

Here is where this knowledge becomes a little dangerous. You might think that you could use #PCDATA however and wherever you want in a content model. That is not true. You must use it in the exact pattern we have shown you. The #PCDATA must be the first token in the group. The group must always be a choice, never a sequence. The other components must be element-type names, never parenthesized groups. The symbol at the end must always be an asterisk (*). It can never be a plus (+). You can only omit the asterisk if the mixed content model allows character data but no elements, as in Example 52-26.

It is somewhat confusing to call the model in Example 52-26 "mixed" because it only allows character data. Nevertheless, that is the correct terminology. If it helps, you can remember that it is always possible to mix char-

Example 52-26. Mixed content with no elements

```
<!ELEMENT abstract (#PCDATA)>
```

acter data with character references, entity references, processing instructions and other kinds of markup. Really, the only markup that is prohibited in an element like that is subelement markup.

52.6 | Attributes

Attributes allow an author to attach extra information to the elements in a document. For instance a code element for computer code might have a lang attribute declaring the language that the code is in. On the other hand, you could also use a lang subelement for the same purpose. It is the DTD designer's responsibility to choose a way and embody that in the DTD. Attributes have strengths and weaknesses that differentiate them from subelements so you can usually make the decision without too much difficulty.

The largest difference between elements and attributes is that attributes cannot contain elements and there is no such thing as a "sub-attribute". Attributes are always either text strings with no explicit structure (at least as far as XML is concerned) or simple lists of strings. That means that a chapter should not be an attribute of a book element, because there would be no place to put the titles and paragraphs of the chapter. You will typically use attributes for small, simple, unstructured "extra" information.

Another important difference between elements and attributes is that each of an element's attributes may be specified only once, and they may be specified in any order. This is often convenient because memorizing the order of things can be difficult. Elements, on the other hand, must occur in the order specified and may occur as many times as the DTD allows. Thus you must use elements for things that must be repeated, or must follow a certain pattern or order that you want the XML parser to enforce.

These technical concerns are often enough to make the decision for you. But if everything else is equal, there are some usability considerations that can help. One rule of thumb that some people use (with neither perfect success nor constant abject failure) is that elements usually represent data that is the natural content that should appear in every print-out or other rendition, Most formatting systems print out elements by default and do not print out attributes unless you specifically ask for them. Attributes represent data that is of secondary importance and is often information about the information (*metadata*).

Also, attribute names usually represent properties of objects, but element-type names usually represent parts of objects. So given a `person` element, subelements might represent parts of the body and attributes might represent properties like weight, height, and accumulated karma points.

We would advise you not to spend too much of your life trying to figure out exactly what qualifies as a part and what qualifies as a property. Experience shows that the question "what is a property?" ranks with "what is the good life?" and "what is art?". The technical concerns are usually a good indicator of the philosophical category in any event.

52.6.1 *Attribute-list declarations*

Attributes are declared for specific element types. You declare attributes for a particular element type using an *attribute-list declaration*. You will often see an attribute-list declaration right beside an element type declaration:

Example 52-27. My first ATTLIST

```
<!ELEMENT PERSON (#PCDATA)>
<!ATTLIST PERSON EMAIL CDATA #REQUIRED>
```

Attribute declarations start with the string "`<!ATTLIST`". Immediately after the white space comes an element type's generic identifier. After that comes the attribute's *name*, its *type* and its *default*. In the example above, the attribute is named `EMAIL` and is valid on `PERSON` elements. Its value must be *character data* and it is required – there is no default and the author must supply a value for the attribute on every `PERSON` element.

Spec Excerpt (XML) 52-3. Attribute-list declarations

```
[52]   AttlistDecl ::=   '<!ATTLIST' S Name AttDef* S? '>'
[53]   AttDef ::=   S Name S AttType S DefaultDecl
```

You can declare many attributes in a single attribute-list declaration.[5]

Example 52-28. Declaring multiple attributes

```
<!ATTLIST PERSON EMAIL CDATA #REQUIRED
                 PHONE CDATA #REQUIRED
                 FAX CDATA #REQUIRED>
```

You can also have multiple attribute-list declarations for a single element type:

Example 52-29. Multiple declarations for one element type

```
<!ATTLIST PERSON HONORIFIC CDATA #REQUIRED>
<!ATTLIST PERSON POSITION CDATA #REQUIRED
                 ORGANIZATION CDATA #REQUIRED>
```

This is equivalent to putting the declarations altogether into a single attribute-list declaration.

It is even possible to have multiple declarations for the same attribute of the same element type. When this occurs, the first declaration of the attribute is binding and the rest are ignored. This is analogous to the situation with entity declarations.

Note that two different element types can have attributes with the same name without there being a conflict. Despite the fact that these attributes have the same name, they are in fact different attributes. For instance a SHIRT element could have an attribute SIZE that exhibits values SMALL, MEDIUM and LARGE and a PANTS element in the same DTD could have an attribute also named SIZE that is a measurement in inches:

Example 52-30. Two size attributes

```
      <!-- These are -->
<!ATTLIST SHIRT SIZE (SMALL|MEDIUM|LARGE) #REQUIRED>

      <!-- two different attributes -->
<!ATTLIST PANTS SIZE NMTOKEN #REQUIRED>
```

---

5. That's why it is called a list!

It is not good practice to allow attributes with the same name to have different semantics or allowed values in the same document. That can be quite confusing for authors.

52.6.2 *Attribute defaults*

Attributes can have *default values*. If the author does not specify an attribute value then the processor supplies the default value if it exists. A DTD designer can also choose not to supply a default.

52.6.2.1   Default values

Specifying a default is simple. You merely include the default after the type or list of allowed values in the attribute list declaration:

Example 52-31. Default values

```
<!ATTLIST SHIRT SIZE (SMALL|MEDIUM|LARGE) MEDIUM>
<!ATTLIST SHOES SIZE NMTOKEN "13">
```

Any value that meets the constraints of the attribute list declaration is legal as a default value. You could not, however, use "***" as a default value for an attribute with declared type NMTOKEN any more than you could do so in a start-tag in the document instance.

52.6.2.2   Impliable attributes

Sometimes you want to allow the user to omit a value for a particular attribute without forcing a particular default. For instance you could have an element SHIRT which has a SIZE attribute with a declared type of NMTOKEN. But some shirts are "one size fits all". They do not have a size. You want the author to be able to leave this value out and you want the processing system to *imply* that the shirt is "one size fits all". You can do this with an *impliable* attribute:

Example 52-32. Impliable attribute

```
<!ATTLIST SHIRT SIZE NMTOKEN #IMPLIED>
```

The string "#IMPLIED" gives any processing program the right to insert whatever value it feels is appropriate. This may seem like a lot of freedom to give a programmer, but typically implied attributes are simply ignored. In the case of our SHIRT, there is no need to worry about "one size fits all" shirts because anybody can wear them. Authors should only depend upon the implied value when they do not care or where there is a well-defined convention of what the lack of a value "really" means. This is again a case of semantics and would be communicated to the author through some other document, DTD comment or other communication mechanism.

It is easy for an author to not specify a value for an attribute that is not required: just do not mention the attribute. Note that specifying an attribute value that is an empty string is *not* the same as not specifying an attribute value:

Example 52-33. Empty versus non-existent

```
<SHIRT>          <!-- This conforms to the declaration above. -->
<SHIRT SIZE=""> <!-- This does *not* conform to the declaration. -->
```

52.6.2.3   Required attributes

The opposite situation to providing a default is where a document type designer wants to force the author to choose a value. If a value for an attribute is important and cannot reliably be defaulted, the designer can require authors to specify it with a *required* attribute default:

Example 52-34. Required attribute

```
<!ATTLIST IMAGE URL CDATA #REQUIRED>
```

In this case, the DTD designer has made the URL attribute required on all IMAGE elements. This makes sense because without a URL to locate the image file, the image element is useless.

52.6.2.4   Fixed attributes

It may be surprising, but there are even times when it is useful to supply an attribute value that cannot be overridden at all. This is rare, but worth knowing about. Imagine, for instance, that an Internet directory provider decides to write a robot[6] that will build a table of contents for websites automatically. It does so by extracting the first-, second-, and third-level section titles of every document indexed by the directory.

The difficulty is that different DTDs will have different element-type names for titles. HTML-like DTDs use H1 for the first level, H2 for the second, etc. Other DTDs might use HEAD1, HEAD2, and HEAD3, or CHAPTER, SECTION, and SUBSECTION.

Even if the robot knows about these DTDs, what about all of the others? There are potentially as many DTDs in existence as there are XML documents! It is not feasible to write a robot that can understand every document type.

The vendor needs to achieve some form of standardization. But it cannot force everyone to conform to the same DTD: that is exactly what XML is supposed to avoid! Instead, it can ask all document creators to label the elements that perform the *role of* section titles. They could do this with an attribute, such as TITLE-LEVEL. The robot can then use the content of those elements to generate its index.

Each DTD designer thinks through the list of element types to add the attribute to. They specify what their element types mean in terms of the indexing system understood by the robot. They don't want authors changing the value on an element by element basis. They can prevent this with *fixed* attributes:

Example 52-35. Fixed attributes

```
<!ATTLIST CHAPTER     TITLE-LEVEL CDATA #FIXED "FIRST">
<!ATTLIST SECTION     TITLE-LEVEL CDATA #FIXED "SECOND">
<!ATTLIST SUBSECTION TITLE-LEVEL CDATA #FIXED "THIRD">
```

6. A *robot* is an automatic Web information gatherer.

Now all of the appropriate elements are marked with the attribute. No matter what else is in the DTD, the robot can find what it is looking for.

52.6.3 *Attribute types*

An important feature of attributes is that attributes have *types* that can enforce certain *lexical* and *semantic* constraints. *Lexical* constraints are constraints like "this attribute must contain only numerals". Semantic constraints are along the lines of "this attribute must contain the name of a declared entity". These constraints tend to be very useful in making robust DTDs and document processing systems.

However, it is vital to remember that *the value of an attribute is not necessarily the exact character string that you enter between the quotation marks.* That string first goes through a process called *attribute-value normalization* on its way to becoming the attribute value. Since attribute types apply to the *normalized value*, we had better digress for a moment to master normalization.

52.6.3.1   Attribute value normalization

XML processors normalize attribute values to make authors' lives simpler. If it were not for normalization, you would have to be very careful where you put white space in an attribute value. For instance if you broke an attribute value across a line:

Example 52-36. Normalization

```
<GRAPHIC ALTERNATE-TEXT="This is a picture of a penguin
    doing the ritual mating dance">
```

You might do this merely because the text is too long for a single line in a text editor.

This sort of thing is normalized by the XML processor. The rules for this are a little intricate, but most times they will just do what you want them to. Let's look at them.

All XML attribute values are entered as quoted strings. They start and end with either single-quotes (') or double-quotes ("). If you want to embed a single-quote character into an attribute value delimited by single quotes or a double-quote character into an attribute value delimited by double quotes, then you must use an entity reference as described in 51.7.1, "Predefined entities", on page 785.

The first thing the XML parser does to prepare for normalization is to strip off the surrounding quotes.

Then, character references are replaced by the characters that they reference. As we discussed earlier, character references allow you to easily insert "funny" characters.

Next, general entity references are replaced. This is important to note. While it is true that entity references are not allowed in markup, unnormalized attribute values are *text* – a mixture of markup and data. After normalization, only the data remains.[7].

If the expansion for an entity reference has another entity reference within it, that is expanded also, and so on and so forth. This would be rare in an entity used in an attribute value. After all, attribute values are usually very short and simple. An entity reference in an attribute value cannot be to an external entity.

Newline characters in attribute values are replaced by spaces. *If* the attribute is known to be one of the tokenized types[8] (see below), then the parser must further remove leading and trailing spaces. So `"    token    "` becomes `"token"`. It also collapses multiple spaces between tokens into a single space, so that `"space    between"` would become `"space between"`.

Caution   The distinction between unnormalized attribute value text and normalized attribute value data trips up even the experts. Remember, when reading about attribute types, that they apply to the normalized data, not the unnormalized text.

---

7. Philosophically, attribute values are metadata, but it is an article of faith in the XML world that metadata is data.
8. If, in other words, attribute-list declarations were provided and the processor is either a validating processor or a non-validating processor that decides to read them.

52.6.3.2   CDATA and name token attributes

The simplest type of attribute is a *CDATA* attribute. The CDATA stands for "character data". The declaration for such an attribute looks like this:

Example 52-37. CDATA Attributes

```
<!DOCTYPE ARTICLE[
<!ELEMENT ARTICLE>
<!ATTLIST ARTICLE DATE CDATA #REQUIRED>
...
]>
<ARTICLE DATE="January 15, 1999">
...
</ARTICLE>
```

Character data attribute values can be any string of characters. Basically anything else is legal in this type of attribute value.

Name token (NMTOKEN) attributes are somewhat like CDATA attributes. The biggest difference is that they are restricted in the characters that name tokens allow. Name tokens were described in 51.1.5, "Names and name tokens", on page 769. To refresh your memory, they are strings made up of letters, numbers and a select group of special characters: period (.), dash (-), underscore (_) and colon (:).

Example 52-38. Name token attribute type

```
<!DOCTYPE PARTS-LIST[
...
<!ATTLIST PART DATE NMTOKEN #REQUIRED>
...
]>
<PARTS-LIST>
...
<PART DATE="1998-05-04">...</PART>

</PARTS-LIST>
]>
```

An empty string is not a valid name token, whereas it would be a valid CDATA attribute value.

Name tokens can be used to allow an attribute to contain numbers that need special characters. They allow the dash, which can be used as a minus sign, the period, which can be a decimal point, and numbers. These are useful for fractional and negative numbers. You can also use alphabetic characters to specify units.

Name tokens can also be used for naming things. This is similar to how you might use variable names in a programming language. For instance, if you used XML to describe the structure of a database, you might use name tokens to name and refer to fields and tables. The restrictions on the name token attribute type would prevent most of the characters that would be illegal in field and table names (spaces, most forms of punctuation, etc.). If there is a reason that all fields or record names must be unique, then you would instead use the *ID* attribute type discussed in 52.6.3.4, "ID and IDREF attributes", on page 819.

If it is appropriate to have more than one name token, then you can use the NMTOKENS attribute type which stands for "name tokens". For instance Example 52-39 shows how you might declare a DTD representing a database.

Example 52-39. Name tokens attribute type

```
<!DOCTYPE DATABASE [
...
<!ELEMENT TABLE EMPTY>
<!ATTLIST TABLE NAME NMTOKEN #REQUIRED
                FIELDS NMTOKENS #REQUIRED>
...
]>
<DATABASE>
...
<TABLE NAME="SECURITY" FIELDS="USERID PASSWORD DEPARTMENT">
...
</DATABASE>
```

One other difference between CDATA attributes and NMTOKEN attributes is in their *normalization*. This was discussed in 52.6.3.1, "Attribute value normalization", on page 815.

52.6.3.3   Enumerated and notation attributes

Sometimes as a DTD designer you want to create an attribute that can only exhibit one of a short list of values: "small/medium/large", "fast/slow"; "north/south/east/west". *Enumerated attribute types* allow this. In a sense, they provide a choice or menu of options.

The syntax is reminiscent of choice lists in element type declarations:

Example 52-40. Choice lists

```
<!ATTLIST OPTIONS CHOICE (OPTION1|OPTION2|OPTION3) #REQUIRED>
```

You may provide as many choices as you like. Each choice is an XML *name token* and must meet the syntactic requirements of name tokens described in 51.1.5, "Names and name tokens", on page 769.

There is another related attribute type called a *notation* attribute. This attribute allows the author to declare that the element's content conforms to a declared notation. Here is an example involving several ways of representing dates:

Example 52-41. Different date representations

```
<!ATTLIST DATE TYPE NOTATION (EUDATE|USDATE|ISODATE) #REQUIRED>
```

In a valid document, each notation allowed must also be declared with a notation declaration.

52.6.3.4   ID and IDREF attributes

Sometimes it is important to be able to give a name to a particular occurrence of an element type. For instance, to make a simple hypertext link or cross-reference from one element to another, you can name a particular section or figure. Later, you can refer to it by its name. The target element is labeled with an *ID* attribute. The other element refers to it with an *IDREF* attribute. This is shown in Example 52-42.

The stylesheet would instruct browsers and formatters to replace the cross-reference element with the name of the section. This would probably be italicized and hyperlinked or labeled with a page number if appropriate.

Example 52-42. ID and IDREF used for cross-referencing

```
<!DOCTYPE BOOK [
...
<!ELEMENT SECTION (TITLE, P*)>
<!ATTLIST SECTION MY-ID ID #IMPLIED>
<!ELEMENT CROSS-REFERENCE EMPTY>
<!ATTLIST CROSS-REFERENCE TARGET IDREF #REQUIRED>
...
]>
<BOOK>
...
<SECTION MY-ID="Why.XML.Rocks"><TITLE>Features of XML</TITLE>
...
</SECTION>


...
If you want to recall why XML is so great, please see
the section titled <CROSS-REFERENCE TARGET="Why.XML.Rocks"/>.
...
</BOOK>
```

Note that we made the section's MY-ID optional. Some sections will not need to be the target of a cross-reference, hypertext link or other reference and will not need to be uniquely identified. The TARGET attribute on CROSS-REFERENCE is required. It does not make sense to have a cross-reference that does not actually refer to another element.

IDs are XML names, with all of the constraints described in 51.1.5, "Names and name tokens", on page 769. Every element can have at most one ID, and thus only one attribute per element type be an ID attribute. All IDs specified in an XML document must be unique. A document with two ID attributes whose values are the same is invalid. Thus "chapter" would not be a good name for an ID, because it would make sense to use it in many places. "introduction.chapter" would be a logical ID because it would uniquely identify a particular chapter.

IDREF attributes must refer to an element in the document. You may have as many IDREFs referring to a single element as you need. It is also possible to declare an attribute that can potentially exhibit more than one IDREF by declaring it to be of type IDREFS:

Example 52-43. IDREFS attribute

```
<!ATTLIST RELATED-CHAPTERS TARGETS IDREFS #REQUIRED>
```

Now the TARGETS attribute may have one or more IDREFs as its value. There is no way to use XML to require that an attribute take two or more, or three or more, (etc.) IDREFs. You will recall that we could do that sort of thing using content models in element type declarations. There is no such thing as a content model for attributes. You could model this same situation by declaring RELATED-CHAPTERS to have content of one or more or two or more (etc.) CHAPTER-REF elements that each have a single IDREF attribute (named TARGET in Example 52-44).

Example 52-44. IDREF attributes

```
<!DOCTYPE BOOK[
...
<!ELEMENT RELATED-CHAPTERS (CHAPTER-REF+)>
<!ELEMENT CHAPTER-REF EMPTY>
<!ATTLIST CHAPTER-REF TARGET IDREF #REQUIRED>
...
]>
<BOOK>
...
<RELATED-CHAPTERS>
<CHAPTER-REF TARGET="introduction.to.xml"/>
<CHAPTER-REF TARGET="xml.rocks"/>
</RELATED-CHAPTERS>
...
</BOOK>
```

As you can see, element type declarations have the benefit of having content models, which can define complex structures, and attributes have the benefit of attribute types, which can enforce lexical and semantic constraints. You can combine these strengths to make intricate structures when this is appropriate.

52.6.3.5   ENTITY attributes

External unparsed entities are XML's way of referring to objects (files, CGI script output, etc.) on the Web that should not be parsed according to XML's rules. Anything from HTML documents to pictures to word processor files fall into this category. It is possible to refer to unparsed entities using an attribute with declared type *ENTITY*. This is typically done either to hyperlink to, reference or include an external object. This is shown in Example 52-45.

Example 52-45. Entity attribute type

```
<!DOCTYPE BOOK[
<!ATTLIST BOOK-REF TARGET ENTITY #REQUIRED>
...
<!ENTITY another-book SYSTEM
        "http://www.buyOurBooks.com/TheOtherBook.html" NDATA HTML>
...
]><BOOK>
...
<BOOK-REF TARGET="another-book">
...
</BOOK>
```

You can also declare an attribute to be of type *ENTITIES*, in which case its value may be the name of more than one entity. It is up to the application or stylesheet to determine whether a reference to the entity should be treated as a hot link, embed link or some other kind of link. The processor merely informs the application of the existence and notation of the entity. You can find information on unparsed entities and notations in Chapter 54, "Entities: Breaking up is easy to do", on page 842 and 52.7, "Notation Declarations", on page 823.

52.6.3.6   Summary of attribute types

There are two *enumerated* attribute types: *enumeration* attributes and NOTATION attributes.

Seven attribute types are known as *tokenized* types because each value represents either a single token (ID, IDREF, ENTITY, NMTOKEN) or a list of tokens (IDREFS, ENTITIES, and NMTOKENS).

The final type is the CDATA string type which is the least constrained and can hold any combination of XML characters as long as "special characters" (the quote characters and ampersand) are properly entered. Table 52-3 summarizes.

Table 52-3   Summary of attribute types

Type	Lexical constraint	Semantic constraint
CDATA	None	None
Enumeration	Name Token	Must be in the declared list.
NOTATION	Name	Must be in the declared list and a declared notation name.
ID	Name	Must be unique in document.
IDREF	Name	Must be some element's ID.
IDREFS	Names	Must each be some element's ID.
ENTITY	Name	Must be an unparsed entity's name.
ENTITIES	Names	Must each be unparsed entity's name.
NMTOKEN	Name Token	None
NMTOKENS	Name Tokens	None

52.7 | Notation Declarations

Notations are referred to in various parts of an XML document, for describing the data content notation of different things. A data content notation is the definition of how the bits and bytes of class of object should be interpreted. According to this definition, XML is a data content notation, because it defines how the bits and bytes of XML documents should be interpreted. Your favorite word processor also has a data content notation. The notation declaration gives an internal name to an existing notation so that it can be referred to in attribute list declarations, unparsed entity declarations, and processing instructions.

The most obvious place that an XML document would want to describe the notation of a data object is in a reference to some other resource on the web. It could be an embedded graphic, an MPEG movie that is the target of a hyperlink, or anything else. The XML facility for linking to these data resources is the entity declaration, and as we discussed earlier, they are referred to as *unparsed entities*. Part of the declaration of an unparsed entity is the name of a declared notation that provides some form of pointer to the external definition of the notation. The external definition could be a public or system identifier for documentation on the notation, some formal specification or a helper application that can handle objects represented in the notation.

Example 52-46. Notations for unparsed entities

```
<!NOTATION HTML SYSTEM "http://www.w3.org/Markup">
<!NOTATION GIF SYSTEM "gifmagic.exe">
```

Another place that notations arise are in the notation attribute type. You use this attribute type when you want to express the notation for the data content of an XML element. For instance, if you had a date element that used ISO or EU date formats, you could declare notations for each format:

Example 52-47. Notations for data content

```
<!NOTATION ISODATE SYSTEM "http://www.iso.ch/date_specification">
<!NOTATION EUDATE SYSTEM "http://www.eu.eu/date_specification">
<!ELEMENT TODAY (#PCDATA)>
<!ATTLIST TODAY DATE-FORMAT NOTATION (ISODATE|EUDATE) #REQUIRED>
```

Now the DATE-FORMAT attribute would be restricted to those two values, and would thus signal to the application that the content of the TODAY element conforms to one or the other.

Note   *You can specify datatypes more precisely for data content and attribute values by using the facilities described in Chapter 62, "Datatypes", on page 1000.*

Finally, notations can be used to give XML names to the targets for processing instructions. This is not strictly required by XML, but it is a good practice because it provides a sort of documentation for the PI and could even be used by an application to invoke the target.

This seems like a good way to close this chapter. DTDs are about improving the permanence, longevity, and wide reuse of your data, and the predictability and reliability of its processing. If you use them wisely, they will save you time and money.

Tip Learning the syntax of markup declarations so that you can write DTDs is important, but learning how to choose the right element types and attributes for a job is a subtle process that requires a book of its own. We suggest David Megginson's Structuring XML Documents, also in this series (ISBN 0-13-642299-3).

Namespaces

- Unique names
- URI-based namespaces
- Namespaces and DTDs

Chapter

53

The *Namespaces in XML* specification is an extension to XML that answers the burning question: Are we talking about the same subject?

Using namespaces it is possible to create elements with the generic identifier para in two different documents, with two different document types (or no explicitly-declared document types at all) and write software and queries that recognize that both represent a paragraph. This might not seem like much of a feat, but consider that in a third document an element with that element-type name might represent a paramedic (consider an employment record from the television show "ER"), a paranormal encounter (in a document from the FBI's "X-Files") or a paralegal (court records).

Even a fully spelled-out word can be ambiguous. A list can be a list of items or the angle of list (tilt) of a seagoing vessel. Besides, if two different people invented two different document types, they might use the words "list" and "para" to mean the same basic thing but their underlying model of paragraphs and lists might be different. One might expect elements of type "list" to be ordered. The other might want to allow lists to have a header.

Everyone in the world is allowed to invent document types, so we need to be clear about the origin of our element types. If you have a document database containing both ship records and technical manuals, a database-wide query needs to be able to figure out which `list` is which – even if the documents do not have DTDs or associated schemas.

Despite the general agreement on the need for this sort of *disambiguation*, we should mention that the XML namespaces concept is not universally embraced as the best solution. In fact XML namespaces are downright controversial.

Nevertheless, namespaces are already in widespread use. Many World Wide Web Consortium specifications already build upon the namespace mechanism and will do so in the future. Primary among these are the *XML Schema* definition language (XSDL), Extensible Stylesheet Language (XSL), and SOAP.

Let's see how namespaces work, then we'll take a closer look at the controversy.

53.1 | Problem statement

Namespaces are easiest to understand if we work in the realm of well-formed documents without DTDs. We will address the relationship to DTDs later on.

You may be familiar with email programs that can recognize and visually highlight URLs and email addresses. This works nicely in the program, but when the email is saved to disk or forwarded to a less intelligent email program, that highlighting is lost. It might be better if the program could actually introduce markup representing the highlighting. That way other applications could get the benefit of the email program's analysis and recognition. We could use `web` and `email` element types to capture this information.

Our system would work fine for a while, but the time would come when people would want to send XML documents (remember, well-formed but DTD-less XML documents) through email. We might want to allow our system to continue to work on these documents. The problem is that it is a bad idea for us to presume that any element with an element-type name of `web` or `email` was meant to refer to our element types.

Perhaps an XML document will come through the email with a `web` element that is meant to represent spider webs or knowledge webs. Perhaps the `web` elements really do represent URLs, but they use an attribute to hold the address instead of content. Then we have the same meaning but a different internal structure.

What we need to do is clearly separate our names from other people's names. We need to have different so-called *namespaces*. We do this in the real world all of the time.

What would you do if you needed to refer to a particular John Smith without confusing him with any other John Smith. You qualify the name: "John Smith from London." That sets up a namespace that separates Londoners from everyone else.

If that isn't sufficient then you further qualify the namespace: "John Smith from East London". That makes a namespace that separates Easterners from everyone else. You could narrow it down even more: "John Smith from Adelaide Street in East London." The trick is qualifying names in order to separate them from other names. The separate groups of names are known as "namespaces."

53.2 | The namespaces solution

Given that what we want to do is qualify names, the most obvious idea is to have a prefix that does the qualification. `myEmailProgram:web` or `myEmailProgram:email`. This seems to work at first, but eventually two people will make program names that clash. In fact, there will be a strong tendency to use three-letter acronyms. There are only so many of these acronyms!

In the real world people constantly choose names that other people also choose. Even city names can clash: consider how many there are named "Springfield"! If people are allowed to choose names without any central authority then they will eventually choose names that clash.

The World Wide Web Consortium could set up a registry of these acronyms and names. But that would require a great deal of effort both in setting up the registry and in registering individual namespaces.

A better mechanism would be to use a registry that already exists. One such registry is the domain name registry. We could use prefixes like: `mycompany.com:email`. We would call "mycompany.com" the *namespace* and "email" a particular name in that namespace.

This solution is getting much closer but it still is not as democratic as we would like. One problem is that domain names require an annual registration fee. What if an ordinary America Online (AOL) user wants to develop a namespace? Does he have to register a domain name?

Every AOL user has a little bit of space to put files and assign a URL such as `http://www.aol.com/EmailAppGuy`. If we could use that as the basis for a namespace identifier, then we would open up the namespace-creating process to a larger number of people.

This idea also works for organizations other than Internet Service Providers. Consider a big company like General Electric. Various parts of the company may develop XML namespaces. The company probably already has a mechanism for delegating Web URIs (typically "http:" URLs). It makes sense to reuse that mechanism for XML namespaces.

There is a more future-thinking reason why URIs are better than domain names. As part of the Semantic Web project, it will be possible to associate metadata with things that are addressed by URIs. If namespaces are associated with URIs, it will be possible to associate metadata with them.

Example 53-1 shows what URI-based namespace prefixes might look like.

Example 53-1. Mythical (illegal!) URI-based namespace prefix

```
<http://www.aol.com/EmailAppGuy:email>email@machine.com
</http://www.aol.com/EmailAppGuy:email>
```

There are two problems with these prefixes. First, they are not legal XML names because of all of the funny characters such as slashes and dots. Second, they are ugly and incredibly verbose. We need a way to set up a local abbreviation. The *Namespaces in XML* specification defines the mechanism for setting up such abbreviations.

53.2.1 *Namespace prefixes*

The *Namespaces in XML* specification defines a rule that attributes that start with the prefix `xmlns:` should be interpreted as prefix-defining attributes. The name immediately following the prefix is a local abbreviation for the namespace.

The attribute value is a URI. You can use any URI (typically a URL) that you would normally have control over. Throughout the element exhibiting that attribute, the prefix stands for the namespace identifier. Example 53-2 demonstrates.

Example 53-2. Using XML namespaces

```
<eag:email xmlns:eag="http://www.aol.com/EmailAppGuy">
  email@machine.com
</eag:email>
```

The actual prefix you use is not relevant. It is just a stand-in for the URI. So, for example, when creating an XSL stylesheet you do not need to use the `xsl:` prefix for names defined in the XSL spec. Doing otherwise might be confusing, but it is totally legal.

Note that the details of the URI are not relevant either. It does not matter whether there is a document at that location or whether the client machine is Internet-connected. There is no need to connect to the Internet to check the contents of the document at that address.

The data (or lack of data) at the other end of the URI is absolutely irrelevant to the namespaces design. Its only goal is to have a long, globally unique string to use in comparisons.

That's an important point! Namespaces work with broken URIs because namespaces only disambiguate names, they don't define names. The URIs therefore don't have to address the definitions of the names in the namespace (although they may).

The only requirement is that you really do control the URI that you use. It is your responsibility to guarantee that nobody else (your spouse?) will accidently but legitimately use the same URI and mean something different by it. It is also good practice to put a date (at least a year) in your URIs. Then, if you lose control of the URI or domain over the course of time, you can still be sure that nobody will use it as a namespace.

Note   In Namespaces in XML 1.1 you can use something called an Internationalized Resource Identifier (IRI) for a namespace identifier. These are identical to URIs except that they allow non-ASCII characters, so existing URIs can still be used. We will talk more about URIs and IRIs in 64.2, "Uniform Resource Identifiers", on page 1054.

53.2.2 *Scoping*

The prefix scheme is still pretty verbose, but it is some improvement. It looks better when you realize that namespace declarations are *scoped* by their declaring elements. That means that they apply to the element, its children, and the children's children and so forth unless some child has a declaration that specifically overrides the first declaration. Example 53-3 shows a document that uses a namespace associated with the `myns` prefix many times despite declaring it only once.

Example 53-3. Using an ancestor's namespace

```
<myns:a xmlns:myns="http://www.someurl.com/2002">
    <myns:b>
    </myns:b>
    <myns:c>
        <myns:d>
        </myns:d>
    </myns:c>
</myns:a>
```

Therefore you could declare namespaces in the document (root) element and have them apply throughout the entire document! Example 53-4 demonstrates.[1]

Although it is seldom necessary, it is also possible to redefine namespaces that were previously declared in an "outer scope". The inner declaration is effective on the declaring element, its attributes and all of its sub-elements (unless it is overridden also). Example 53-5 demonstrates four different `myns:p` elements with no relationship to each other (from the point of view of the XML namespaces specification). Each contains an `myns:q` element which is in the namespace of whichever `myns:p` contains it.

The ability to override namespaces is most useful in some data-transfer applications, where machines automatically combine portions of different documents. Perhaps to support such applications, XML 1.1 added the ability to "undeclare" a namespace by associating its namespace prefix with the empty string. Within the element that undeclares the namespace, the prefix is now disabled, as if it had never been defined.

---

1. Note that `.con` is the new high-level domain for Internet scams.

Example 53-4. XML namespace scope

```
<html:html
    xmlns:eag="http://www.aol.com/EmailAppGuy"
    xmlns:html="http://www.w3.org/TR/WD-HTML40"
    xmlns:math="http://www.w3.org/TR/REC-MathML/">
  <html:title>George Soros Personal Wealth Page</html:title>
  <html:h2>Counting My Cash</html:h2>
  <html:p>As you know, my cash rivals the gross national
  product of some small countries. Consider the following
  equation:
  <math:reln>
    <math:eq/>
    <math:ci>wealth</math:ci>
    <math:ci>gnp</math:ci>
  </math:reln>
  If you have any ideas of how I could spend
  this money. Please contact
  <eag:email>georges@aol.con</eag:email>.
  </html:p>

</html:html>
```

Example 53-5. Overriding namespace scopes

```
<myns:p xmlns:myns="http://www.someurl.com/2000">
  <myns:q>First namespace.</myns:q>
  <myns:p xmlns:myns="http://www.anotherurl.com/2001">
      <myns:q>Second namespace.</myns:q>
      <myns:p xmlns:myns="http://www.someotherurl.com/2002">
          <myns:q>Third namespace.</myns:q>
      </myns:p>
  </myns:p>
  <myns:p xmlns:myns="http://www.yetanother.com/2003">
      <myns:q>Fourth namespace.</myns:q>
  </myns:p>
</myns:p>
```

But if you don't absolutely need such facilities, it is much simpler to use unique prefixes for different namespaces and to declare namespaces on the root element. Declaring namespaces once at the top reduces the namespace clutter thoughout the document.

53.2.3 *Default namespace*

We can minimize namespace clutter even more by removing some of the prefixes. There is a special namespace called the *default namespace*. This namespace is defined without a prefix, so element-type names in the scope of the definition that have no prefix are considered to be in this namespace.[2] If you expect to use many elements from a particular namespace, you can make it the default namespace for the appropriate scope. In fact, you can even have a document in which the namespaces correspond cleanly to the elements and there are no prefixes at all, as Example 53-6 demonstrates.

Example 53-6. Two default namespaces: HTML and MathML

```
<html
    xmlns="http://www.w3.org/TR/WD-HTML40">
 <title>George Soros Personal Wealth Page</title>
 <h2>Counting My Cash</h2>
 <p>As you know, my cash rivals the gross national
 product of some small countries. Consider the following
 equation:
 <reln xmlns="http://www.w3.org/TR/REC-MathML/">
   <eq/>
   <ci>wealth</ci>
   <ci>gnp</ci>
 </reln>
 If you have any ideas of how I could spend
 this money.</p>
</html>
```

Note that the default namespace is HTML both before and after the `reln` element. Within the `reln` element the default namespace is MathML. As you can see, we can eliminate many of the prefixes but still keep the relationship between the element-type names and the namespaces.

We can also establish a scope in which names without prefixes have no namespace, by using an empty string instead of a URI. In Example 53-7, `notes` and `todo` are not in the MathML namespace.

---

2. You can think of the default namespace as having a null prefix, if that helps any.

Example 53-7. A scope for local names

```
<reln xmlns="http://www.w3.org/TR/REC-MathML/">
  <eq/>
  <ci>wealth</ci>
  <ci>gnp</ci>
  <notes xmlns="">
    <todo>check the math</todo>
  </notes>
</reln>
```

53.2.4 *Attribute names*

Attribute names can also come from a namespace, which is indicated in the usual way by prefixing them with a namespace prefix. For instance, the XML Linking Language (XLink) uses the namespace mechanism to allow XLink attributes to appear on elements that themselves come from some other namespace. Example 53-8 shows such attributes.

Example 53-8. Attributes in XLink namespace

```
<myLink xmlns:xlink="http://www.w3.org/1999/xlink"
  xlink:type="simple">
. . .
</myLink>
```

It does not matter what the namespace of the element type is. The XLink attributes are in the XLink namespace even when they are exhibited by an element type that is not in the XLink namespace.

In fact, even attributes without prefixes are not in the same namespace that their element type is in. Nor are they in the default namespace. Attributes without prefixes are in no namespace at all.[3]

---

3. From the syntactic standpoint of the *Namespaces* spec, that is. All names have to be in *some* namespace or they couldn't function as names. An unprefixed attribute is in a (non-syntactic) namespace that is *defined* by its element type, which, as we said, is not the same as the namespace that its element type itself is *in*. The href attribute of html:img, for example, is in the (non-syntactic) html:img namespace, while its element type, img, is in the (syntactic) html namespace.

From a processing standpoint, the lack of a namespace doesn't matter. The attribute name can still be specified in a stylesheet pattern or utilized by the template for the element type's template rule.

In other words, an `html:img` element could have an `href` attribute and that attribute could be processed properly even though it is not formally part of the `html` namespace. Any application that knows how to handle `html:img` will know what to do with an `href` attribute.[4]

From a data modeling standpoint, unprefixed attributes are normal. They are defined by the semantics of their specific element types. In contrast, prefixed attributes have semantics that apply to the class of all element types. XLink is a good example because, in principle, any element can be linked.

53.3 | Namespaces and DTDs

You read about DTDs and type-validation in Chapter 52, "Creating a document type definition", on page 792 and might have wondered why that chapter had no mention of namespaces. That's because namespaces were invented after DTDs.[5] Therefore, type-validation does not behave as you would expect it to behave had it been designed with namespaces in mind.

In fact, the base XML language has no inherent knowledge of namespaces. There is no special part of an element-type name or attribute name called the prefix. The name is all one string that, when name spaces are used, just happens to have a colon in it. The colon could just as easily be an underscore, dot or happy face character from the XML point of view. It is not a special character.

You might think, from learning about namespaces, that it would be possible to have two different `list` element types in the same DTD. However, you can only do that if you give them different prefixes. But in DTDs, prefixes must be *hard-wired onto the names*. They are not namespace prefixes and you cannot depend on the default namespace: a DTD is permitted only one element type declaration for the element type `list`.

---

4. That's because, as we saw in the last footnote, `href` is in the `html:img` namespace.
5. About 30 years after, but who's counting.

Declaring my:list and your:list would be fine. These are seen as no more the same than my_list and your_list or my.list and your.list. But once you define the element types this way, you cannot default them or change the prefix. A validating parser would not recognize list as a synonym for my:list. These are no more related than list and my_list or foo and bar.

Therefore, when you create a DTD that uses namespaces, you must declare every prefix:name combination individually, exactly as you would if the : were just another name character (which it is!).

Example 53-9 illustrates declarations for two different email element types. The prefixes disambiguate them, but not in the same way that namespace prefixes would. As far as an XML validator is concerned, these are two nine-letter element-type names that differ in their first three letters.

Example 53-9. Disambiguating two email element types

```
<!ELEMENT eag:email ...>
<!ATTLIST eag:email
    xmlns:eag CDATA #FIXED "http://www.aol.com/EmailAppGuy">
<!ELEMENT cmp:email ...>
<!ATTLIST cmp:email
    xmlns:cmp CDATA #FIXED "http://www.compuserve.com/email">
```

Note that the xmlns attributes are fixed. That is because the prefixes are hard-wired to the names; they can't be changed in a valid document instance regardless of what the *Namespaces* spec says. If authors try to act otherwise, the document will become invalid.

Defining each namespace attribute with a fixed value protects against such mistakes. The parser will issue an error message if an author tries to specify a different namespace value in the document instance.

Fixing namespace attributes enforces markup practices that make a document both type-valid and namespace compatible. It is the sensible thing to do.[6]

A DTD can also simulate scoping and default namespaces, as shown in Example 53-10.

---

6. In fact, it makes so much sense that it probably should have been a requirement of the *Namespaces* spec. The XML implementation in *Internet Explorer 5* enforces it as though it were.

Example 53-10. Scoping and default namespaces in a DTD

```
<!ELEMENT music ...>
<!ATTLIST music
    xmlns CDATA #FIXED "http://www.ihc.org/smdl">
<!ELEMENT math ...>
<!ATTLIST math
    xmlns CDATA #FIXED "http://www.w3.org/TR/REC-MathML/">
```

However, remember that the declared names in a valid document are the *only* names. Example 53-10 works only when the subelement types of `music` and `math` have different names from one another.

One final example to drive home the point: In Example 53-11, the first namespace prefix has no effect. The two element-type names are different in a valid document, even though they are the same according to the *Namespaces* spec.

Example 53-11. `rap:music` isn't `music`

```
<!ELEMENT music ...>
<!ATTLIST music
    xmlns CDATA #FIXED "http://www.rude-noises.go">
<!ELEMENT rap:music ...>
<!ATTLIST rap:music
    xmlns:rap CDATA #FIXED "http://www.rude-noises.go">
```

Remember: The rule is that colons and namespace declarations are not relevant or special to a DTD validator. Always define fixed values for your namespace attributes and your documents should be able to get the best of both worlds.

53.4 | Are namespaces a good thing?

We said in the introduction to this chapter that namespaces are controversial. We've seen how namespace prefixes cause clutter and how redefining them causes confusion. Why then were they considered so vital that they were rushed to Recommendation status almost as soon as XML was approved?

And why does the spec allow all that flexibility in their use?

As the application parts of this book show, the predominant use for XML on the Web is data integration. In those applications, a middle-tier server may aggregate XML fragments from many sources into a single well-formed (but not valid) document and send it to a client for processing.

Because only computers ever see those documents, prefix clutter doesn't matter. It adds to the overhead somewhat, but it could also aid in debugging.

And reusing prefixes for different namespaces doesn't matter in those applications either, since the software must base its processing strategy on the full URI, rather than the short nickname. Namespace-aware applications and specifications such as XPath and XML Schema work on the full namespace name, not the short prefix.

Furthermore, there are cases where namespace prefixes cause less clutter than alternative approaches might have. In XSL specifications, for example, the prefixes disambiguate the markup that controls the XSL processing from the markup of the generated text in the templates.

But more than that, namespaces provide a mechanism for universal vocabularies of element type names that can be used in all document types. Namespaces provide a way to define element types so that their names are unique throughout the world. As long as everyone adheres to the namespaces convention there can be no confusion about whether element types with identical names belong to one vocabulary or another.

Additional XML Tutorials

- The rest of Extensible Markup Language
- Entities
- Advanced features
- XML version 1.1
- How to read the spec
- Full spec on CD-ROM

Part Nineteen

This part builds on Part 18, "XML Core Tutorials". It covers entities and other features that are less fundamental than those already covered.

There is also a tutorial on XML 1.1, which introduced changes in the way that XML uses the Unicode character set.

Again we've included appropriate excerpts from the W3C XML specification and again you can freely skip them. For those who want it all, though, the mini-tutorial for reading the spec excerpts is also in this part.

Entities: Breaking up is easy to do

- Parameter and general
- Internal and external
- Parsed and unparsed
- XML Inclusions (XInclude)

Chapter

54

X ML allows flexible organization of document text. The XML constructs that provide this flexibility are called *entities*. They allow a document to be broken up into multiple storage objects and are important tools for reusing and maintaining text. Entities are used in many publishing-oriented applications of XML but are much less common in machine to machine applications.

> *Note* You can use entities with schemas. In that case your "DTD" would consist solely of declarations needed for the entities.

54.1 | Overview

In simple cases, an entity is like an abbreviation in that it is used as a short form for some text. We call the "abbreviation" the *entity name* and the long form the *entity content*. That content could be as short as a character or as long as a chapter. For instance, in an XML document, the entity dtd could have the phrase "document type definition" as its content. Using a reference to that entity is like using the word DTD as an abbreviation for that phrase – the parser replaces the reference with the content.

You create the entity with an *entity declaration*. Example 54-1 is an entity declaration for an abbreviation.

Example 54-1. Entity used as an abbreviation

```
<!ENTITY dtd "document type definition">
]>
```

Like other markup declarations, entity declarations occur in the document type declaration section of the document prolog (Example 54-2

Note   You can use entities with schemas. In that case your "DTD" would consist solely of declarations needed for the entities.

Example 54-2. Entity declarations occur in the document type declaration

```
<!DOCTYPE mydoc ...[
  <!ENTITY dtd "document type definition">
  ... other markup declarations ...
]>
```

Entities can be much more than just abbreviations. There are several different kinds of entities with different uses. We will first introduce the different variants in this overview and then come back and describe them more precisely in the rest of the chapter. We approach the topic in this way because we cannot discuss the various types of entity entirely linearly. Our first pass will acquaint you with the major types and the second one will tie them together and provide the information you need to actually use them.

Another way to think of an entity is as a box with a label. The label is the entity's name. The content of the box is some sort of text or data. The entity declaration creates the box and sticks on a label with the name. Sometimes the box holds XML text that is going to be *parsed* (interpreted according to the rules of the XML notation), and sometimes it holds data, which should not be.

54.1.1 *Parsed entities*

If the content of an entity is XML text that the processor should parse, the XML spec calls it a *parsed entity*.

If the content of an entity is data that is not to be parsed, the XML spec calls it an *unparsed entity*.

The abbreviation in Example 54-1 is a parsed entity. Parsed entities, being XML text, can also contain markup. Example 54-3 is a declaration for a parsed entity with some markup in it.

Example 54-3. Parsed entity with markup

```
<!ENTITY dtd "<term>document type definition</term>">
```

54.1.2 *External entities*

The processor can also fetch content from somewhere on the Web and put that into the box. This is an *external* entity. For instance, it could fetch a chapter of a book and put it into an entity. This would allow you to reuse the chapter between books. Another benefit is that you could edit the chapter separately with a sufficiently intelligent editor. This would be very useful if you were working on a team project and wanted different people to work on different parts of a document at once. Example 54-4 demonstrates.

Example 54-4. External entity declaration

```
<!ENTITY intro-chapter SYSTEM "http://www.megacorp.com/intro.xml">
```

Entities also allow you to edit very large documents without running out of memory. Depending on your software and needs, either each volume or even each article in an encyclopedia could be an entity.

54.1.3 *Entity references*

An author or DTD designer refers to an entity through an *entity reference*. The XML processor replaces the reference by the content, as if it were an abbreviation and the content was the expanded phrase. This process is called *inclusion*. After the operation we say either that the entity reference has been *replaced* by the entity content or that the entity content has been *included*. Which you would use depends on whether you are talking from the point of view of the entity reference or the entity content. The content of parsed entities is called their *replacement text*.

Example 54-5 is an example of a parsed entity declaration and its associated reference.

Example 54-5. Entity Declaration

```
<!DOCTYPE MAGAZINE[
...
<!ENTITY title "Hacker Life">
...
]>
<MAGAZINE>
<TITLE>&title;</TITLE>
...
<P>Welcome to the introductory issue of &title;. &title; is
geared to today's modern hacker.</P>
...
</MAGAZINE>
```

Anywhere in the document instance that the entity reference "`&title;`" appears, it is *replaced* by the text "Hacker Life". It is just as valid to say that "Hacker Life" is *included* at each point where the reference occurs. The ampersand character starts all general entity references and the semicolon ends them. The text between is an entity name.

Spec Excerpt (XML) 54-1. General entity reference

```
[68]   EntityRef ::=   '&' Name ';'
```

54.1.4 *Parameter entities*

We have looked at entities that can be used in the creation of XML documents. Others can only be used to create XML DTDs. The ones we have been using all along are called *general* entities. They are called general entities because they can generally be used anywhere in a document. The ones that we use to create DTDs are called *parameter* entities because their use involves the parameters of markup declarations.

We would use parameter entities for most of the same reasons that we use general entities. We want document type definitions to share declarations for element types, attributes and notations, just as we want documents to share chapters and abbreviations. For instance many DTDs in an organization might share the same definition for a paragraph element type named *para*. The declaration for that element type could be bundled up with other common DTD components and used in document type definitions for memos, letters and reports. Each DTD would include the element type declaration by means of a parameter entity reference.

54.1.5 *Unparsed entities*

Unparsed entities are for holding data such as images or molecular models in some data object notation. The application does not expect the processor to parse that information because it is not XML text.

Although it is an oversimplification, it may be helpful in your mind to remember that unparsed entities are often used for pictures and parsed entities are usually used for character text. You would include a picture through an unparsed entity, since picture representations do not (usually!) conform to the XML specification. Of course there are many kinds of non-XML data other than graphics, but if you can at least remember that unparsed entities are used for graphics then you will remember the rest also. Example 54-6 demonstrates.

Example 54-6. Unparsed entity declaration

```
<!ENTITY picture SYSTEM "http://www.home.org/mycat.gif" NDATA GIF>
```

We use unparsed entities through an ENTITY attribute. A processor does not expand an ENTITY attribute, but it tells the application that the use occurred. The application can then do something with it. For instance, if the application is a Web browser, and the entity contains a graphic, it could display the graphic. We cover ENTITY attributes are covered in 52.6.3.5, "ENTITY attributes", on page 821.

54.1.6 *How entities are used*

There are many interesting things that you can do with entities. Here are some examples:

- You could store every chapter of a book in a separate file and link them together as entities.
- You could "factor out" often-reused text, such as a product name, into an entity so that it is consistently spelled and displayed throughout the document.
- You could update the product name entity to reflect a new version. The change would be instantly visible anywhere the entity was used.
- You could create an entity that would represent "legal boilerplate" text (such as a software license) and reuse that entity in many different documents.
- You could integrate pictures and multimedia objects into your document.
- You could develop "document type definition components" that could be used in many document type definitions. These would allow you to reuse the declarations for common element types (such as paragraph and emphasis) across several document types.

54.2 | Classification of entities

Because XML entities can do so many things, there are five different varieties of them. Think of each entity as having three properties that define its type. This is analogous to the way that a person could be tall or short and at the same time male or female and blonde or brunette.

XML entities can be:

- *internal* or *external,*
- *parsed* or *unparsed,* and
- *general* or *parameter.*

However, as only external general entities can be unparsed, there are just five types:

- (External) unparsed (general) entities
- External parsed general entities
- Internal (parsed) general entities
- External (parsed) parameter entities
- Internal (parsed) parameter entities

There is no single word for a short, blond, male, and there is similarly no single word for an internal, parsed, parameter entity. But we can – and do – shorten things by eliminating redundant words (which are parenthesized in the above list).

In the following sections we look at each of the five types of entity in greater depth.

Note   *In a section on, for instance, internal parsed general entities, we may describe a constraint or feature of all general entities. When we do so, we will use the word "general entity" instead of "internal general entity". This convention will allow us to avoid repeating text that is common among entity types.*

54.2.1 *General entities*

General entities are either parsed (internal or external), in which case they are accessed by means of an entity reference, or unparsed, in which case they are accessed by an ENTITY attribute.

54.2.1.1   Internal general entities

Internal general entities are the simplest type of entity. They are essentially abbreviations defined completely in the document type declaration section of the XML document.

All internal general entities are parsed entities. This means that the XML processor parses them like any other XML text.

The content for an internal general entity is specified by a string literal after the entity's name. The string literal may contain markup, including references to other entities. An example is in Example 54-7.

Example 54-7. Internal general entity

```
<?xml version="1.0"?>
<!DOCTYPE SAMPLE SYSTEM "sample.dtd"[
    <!ENTITY fullxml "Extensible Markup Language">
]>
<SAMPLE>
    &fullxml;
</SAMPLE>
```

Internal general entities can be referenced anywhere in the content of an element or attribute value, including an attribute default value (in the DTD). They can also be referenced in the content of another general entity. Because they are general entities, they cannot be used to hold markup declarations for expansion in the DTD. They can only hold the content of elements or attributes. Because of this, Example 54-8 is not well-formed. The only contexts in which general entity references can occur in a DTD are entity replacement values and attribute default values.

Example 54-8. Prohibited general entity reference in DTD

```
<?xml version="1.0"?>
<!DOCTYPE SAMPLE[
  <!ENTITY general-entity "<!ELEMENT SAMPLE (#PCDATA)>">
  &general-entity;
]>
```

The grammar rules for internal general entities are described in Spec Excerpt 54-2.

Spec Excerpt (XML) 54-2. Internal general entities

```
[70]  EntityDecl ::=  GEDecl | PEDecl
[71]  GEDecl ::=  '<!ENTITY' S Name S EntityDef S? '>'
[73]  EntityDef ::=  EntityValue | (ExternalID NDataDecl?)
[9]   EntityValue ::=  '"' ([^%&"] | PEReference | Reference)* '"'
                   |  "'" ([^%&'] | PEReference | Reference)* "'"
```

54.2.1.2 External parsed general entities

Every XML entity is either internal or external. The content of internal entities occurs right in the entity declarations. External entities get their content from somewhere else in the system. It might be another file on the hard disk, a Web page or an object in a database. Wherever it is, it is located through an *external identifier*. Usually this is just the word SYSTEM followed by a URI (which in XML 1.1 can be "internationalized"; see 64.2, "Uniform Resource Identifiers", on page 1054).

Example 54-9 declares an external parsed general entity.

Example 54-9. External parsed general entity

```
<!ENTITY ent SYSTEM "http://www.house.gov/Constitution.xml">
```

It is the keyword SYSTEM that tells the processor that the next thing in the declaration is a URI. The processor gets the entity's content from that URI. The combination of SYSTEM and the URI is called an external identifier because it identifies an external resource to the processor. There is another kind of external identifier called a PUBLIC identifier. It is denoted by the keyword PUBLIC. External identifiers are described in 54.9, "External identifiers", on page 863.

External parsed general entities can be referenced in the same places as internal general entities, except not in the value of an attribute.

54.2.1.3 Unparsed entities

Every XML entity is either an *unparsed* entity or a *parsed* entity. Unparsed entities are external entities that the XML processor does not have to parse. For example a graphic, sound, movie or other multimedia object would be included through an unparsed entity. You can imagine the number of error messages you would get if an XML processor tried to interpret a graphic as if it were made up of XML text!

It is occasionally useful to refer to an XML document through an unparsed entity, as if it were in some unparsable representation. You might embed a complete letter document in a magazine document in this way. Rather than extending the magazine DTD to include letter elements, you would refer to it as an unparsed entity. Conceptually, it would be handled in the same way a picture of the letter would be handled. If you refer to it as an unparsed entity, the XML processor that handles the magazine does not care that the letter is actually XML.

All unparsed entities are external entities because there is no way to express non-XML information in XML entities. They are also all general entities because it is forbidden (and senseless) to embed data in XML DTDs. Hence, the term "unparsed entity" implies the terms "general" and "external".

Syntactically, declarations of unparsed entities are differentiated from those of other external entities by the keyword NDATA followed by a *notation* name.

Spec Excerpt (XML) 54-3. Non-XML data declaration

```
NDataDecl ::=  S 'NDATA' S Name
```

The name at the end is the name of a declared notation. Notation declarations are described in 52.7, "Notation Declarations", on page 823. The processor passes this to the application as a hint about how the application should approach the entity.

If the application knows how to deal with that sort of entity (for instance if it is a common graphics notation) then it could do so directly. A browser might embed a rendition of the entity. It might also make a hyperlink to the entity. If it needs to download or install some other handler such as a Java program or Active-X control, then it could do so. If it needs to ask the user what to do it could do that also. The XML specification does not say what it must do. XML only expects processors to tell applications what the declared notation is and the applications must figure out the rest.

In the case that the entity is an XML document, the application might decide to process it, create a rendition of it, and then embed it. Alternatively, it might decide to make a hyperlink to it.

54.2.2 *Internal and external parameter entities*

XML entities are classified according to whether they can be used in the DTD or in the document instance. Entities that can only be used in the

DTD are called *parameter* entities. For instance, you might want to wrap up a few declarations for mathematical formulae element types and reuse the declarations from DTD to DTD.

The other entities can be used more generally (throughout the entire document instance), and are called *general* entities. Authors can use general entities as abbreviations, for sharing data among documents, including pictures, and many similar tasks.

There is an important reason why the two types are differentiated. When authors create documents, they want to be able to choose entity names without worrying about accidently choosing a name that was already used by the DTD designer. If there were no distinction between entities specific to the DTD and general to the document instance, according to XML's rules, the first declaration would win. That means that either the author would accidently take the place of ("clobber") a declaration that was meant to be used in the DTD, and thus trigger a cryptic error message, or the DTD designer's entity would clobber the entity that was meant to go in the document instance, and a seemingly random string of DTD-text would appear in the middle of the document! XML prevents this by having two different types of entities with distinct syntaxes for declaration and use.

54.2.2.1 Internal parameter entities

Parameter entities are distinguished from general entity declarations by a single percent symbol in their declaration, and by a different syntax in their use. Example 54-10 is an example of an internal parameter entity declaration and use.

Example 54-10. Internal parameter entity

```
<!DOCTYPE SAMPLE[
    <!-- parameter entity declaration -->
<!ENTITY % sample-entity "<!ELEMENT SAMPLE (#PCDATA)>">
    <!-- parameter entity use -->
%sample-entity;
]>
<SAMPLE>
</SAMPLE>
```

This entity is declared with a syntax similar to that of general entities, but it has a percent sign between the string `<!ENTITY` and the entity's name. This is what differentiates parameter entity declarations from general entity declarations. If you want a general entity you just leave the percent character out.

The entity contains a complete element type declaration. It is referenced on the line after it is declared. Parameter entity references start with the percent-sign and end with the semicolon. The parser replaces the entity reference with the entity's content. In Example 54-10, the processor replaces the reference with the element type declaration "`<!ELEMENT    SAMPLE (#PCDATA)>`". It then parses and interprets the element type declaration as if it had occurred there originally. The element type *is* declared and so the example is valid.

Spec Excerpt (XML) 54-4. Parameter Entity Declaration

```
[72]   PEDecl  ::=   '<!ENTITY' S '%' S Name S PEDef S? '>'
[74]   PEDef ::=   EntityValue | ExternalID
[75]   ExternalID ::=   'SYSTEM' S SystemLiteral
              | 'PUBLIC' S PubidLiteral S SystemLiteral
[69]   PEReference ::=   '%' Name ';'
```

Parameter entities cannot be referenced in the document instance. In fact, the percent character is not special in the document instance, so if you try to reference a parameter entity in the instance, you will just get the entity reference text in your data, like "%this;".

54.2.3 *External parameter entities*

Parameter entities can be external, just as general entities can be. An example of an external parameter entity is in Example 54-11.

The entity name suggests that the entity contains declarations for external unparsed entities. Collecting external entity declarations into an external parameter entity is a useful technique for managing them. In this example, access to all of the external graphics entities can easily be suppressed by removing the parameter entity reference `%graphics-decls;`.

Example 54-11. External parameter entity

```
<!DOCTYPE SAMPLE[
    <!-- parameter entity declaration -->
<!ENTITY % graphics-decls SYSTEM "graphics-entity-declarations.ent">
    <!-- parameter entity use -->
%graphics-decls;
]>
<SAMPLE>
</SAMPLE>
```

54.3 | Declaration details

54.3.1 *Entity names*

Caution   Like other names in XML, entity names are case-sensitive: &charles; refers to a different entity from &Charles;.

It is good that XML entity names are case-sensitive because they are often used to name letters. Case is a convenient way of distinguishing the upper-case version of a letter from the lower-case one. "Sigma" would represent the upper-case version of the Greek letter, and "sigma" would be the lower-case version of it. It would be possible to use some other convention to differentiate the upper- and lower-case versions, such as prefixes. That would give us "uc-Sigma" and "lc-Sigma".

54.3.2 *Multiple declarations*

Entities may be declared more than once (Example 54-12), but only the first declaration is *binding*. All subsequent ones are ignored as if they did not exist.

Example 54-12. Contradicting entity declarations

```
<!ENTITY abc "abcdefghijklmnopqrst"> <!-- This is binding. -->
<!ENTITY abc "ABCDEFGHIJKLMNOPQRST"> <!-- This is ignored. -->
<!ENTITY abc "AbCdEfGhIjKlMnOpQrSt"> <!-- So is this.        -->
```

Declarations in the internal DTD subset are processed before those in the external subset, as described in Chapter 52, "Creating a document type definition", on page 792. In practice, document authors can override parameter entities in the external subset of the DTD by declaring entities of the same name in the internal subset.

54.4 | Resolution of entity references

Entities can only be referenced after they have been declared. General entities may appear to be referenced before they are declared but that is a mere trick of the light.

Example 54-13. General entity usage

```
<!ENTITY user "This entity uses &usee;.">
<!ENTITY usee "<em>another entity</em>">
```

Example 54-13 is legal because the entity replacement for &usee; does not take place until the point where the user entity is *referenced*.

With one exception (described below), general entities can only be expanded in the document instance. So the fact that user refers to usee is recorded, but the replacement is not immediately done. Later, in the document instance, the author will refer to the user entity using the general entity reference, &user;. At that point, the inclusion of its replacement text will trigger the expansion of the &usee; entity reference and the inclusion of its replacement text.

The exception is general entity references in default attribute values. These must be expanded immediately – in the DTD so that they can be checked for validity. These general entities must have been declared before they are used. Whether this exception is important or not depends on how much you use general entities in default attribute values.

Note that the text of a general entity can contain references to other general entities that are declared after it, while the text of a parameter entity cannot reference later-declared parameter entities. That is because parameter entity references are resolved when an entity declaration containing them is *parsed* (i.e., at declaration time). In contrast, general entity references are not resolved until the entity whose declaration contains them is *referenced*, which usually occurs in the document instance, after all DTD declarations have been processed. Referencing can also occur in a default value of an attribute declaration, after all relevant general entity declarations have been processed.

54.5 | The document entity

There is one special entity, called the *document entity* which is not declared, does not have a name and cannot be referenced. The document entity is the entity in which the processor started the current parse. Imagine you download a Web document called `catalog.xml`. Before a browser can display it, it must start to parse it, which makes it the document entity. It may include other entities, but because parsing started with `catalog.xml`, those others are not the document entity. They are just ordinary external entities.

If you click on a link and go to another XML Web page, then the processor must parse that page before it can display it. That page is the document entity for the new parse. In other words, even the simplest XML document has at least one entity: the document entity. The processor starts parsing the document in the document entity and it also must finish there.[1]

The document entity is also the entity in which the XML declaration and document type declaration can occur.

---

1. To put it mystically: it is the alpha and the omega of entities.

You may think it is strange for us to call this an entity when it is not declared as such, but if we were talking about files, it would probably not surprise you. It is common in many computer languages to have files that include other files. Even word processors allow this. We will often use the word entity to refer to a concept analogous to what you would think of as a file, although entities are more flexible. Entities are just "bundles of information". They could reside in databases, zip files, or be created on the fly by a computer program.

54.6 | Use care with external parsed entities

XML processors are allowed, but not required, to validate an XML document when they parse it. The XML specification allows a processor that is not validating a document to completely ignore declarations of external parsed entities (both parameter and general). There is no way to control this behavior with the standalone document declaration or any other XML markup.[2]

Unfortunately this is very inconvenient for authors, because it means that external parsed entities are essentially unreliable in systems that you do not completely control (e.g. the Internet vs. an intranet).

 Caution   Use external parsed entities only with parsers that you know will resolve them!

---

2. The XML working group thought pages might download faster if a browser could display external parsed entity references unresolved, as hypertext links that the user could click on to receive. But a document creator who wants that behavior could get it by using an `href` attribute, so it was unnecessary to deprive him of the ability to insist on entity resolution. Worse yet, in the process they made external entity references unpredictable for all non-validating parsing, not just for Web browsers.

54.7 | Markup may not span entity boundaries

Parsed entities may contain markup as well as character data, but elements and other markup must not span entity boundaries. This means that a particular element may not start in one entity and end in another. If you think of entities as boxes, then an element cannot be half in one box and half in another. Example 54-14 is an example of illegal entity use:

Example 54-14. Elements spanning entity boundaries.

```
<!DOCTYPE SAMPLE[
    <!ENTITY start "<title>This is a">
    <!ENTITY finish "title</title>">
]>

&start;&finish;
```

This document is not well-formed. When the entity references are replaced with their text, they create a title element. This element spans the entities.

Other markup cannot span entities either. Declarations, comments, processing instructions and entity references must all finish in the entity in which they started. This applies to the document entity as much as any other. Markup strings and elements may not start in the document entity and finish in an included entity. This is a subtle but important rule. Documents which fail to conform are not well-formed.

In Example 54-15, entities are used in ways that are illegal. They are all illegal because they start markup without finishing it or finish it without starting it.

The entities in Example 54-16 can be used legally or illegally. They do not necessarily represent the start or end of elements or markup, because they do not contain the strings that are used to start a tag (<), comment (<!--), general entity reference (&) or other markup. Entity content is interpreted as markup if the replacement text would be interpreted as markup in the same context. In other words, the processor expands the entity and then looks for markup. If the markup it finds spans entity boundaries, then it is illegal.

Example 54-15. Illegal entities

```
<!DOCTYPE TEST[
    <!ENTITY illegal1 "This will soon be <em>illegal">
    <!ENTITY illegal2 "This will too <em">
    <!ENTITY illegal3 "This will also </em>">
    <!ENTITY illegal4 "And so will <!-- this">
    <!ENTITY illegal5 "And this &too;">
    <!-- note that none of these are illegal yet. -->
...
]><TEST>
<!-- These references are all illegal -->
&illegal1; <!-- Start-tag in entity with no end-tag there. -->
&illegal2; <!-- Start of tag in entity -->
&illegal3; <!-- End-tag in entity with no start-tag there. -->
&illegal4; <!-- Comment start but no end in entity. -->
&illegal5; <!-- Entity reference starts in entity. -->
</TEST>
```

Example 54-16. Sometimes legal entities

```
<?xml version="1.0"?>
<!DOCTYPE TEST[
<!ELEMENT TEST (#PCDATA)>
<!ENTITY maybelegal1 "em>"> <!-- May not be part of tag -->
<!ENTITY maybelegal2 "-->"> <!-- May not be comment delimiter -->
<!ENTITY maybelegal3 "ph>"> <!-- May not be part of tag -->
]>
<TEST>
&maybelegal1; <!-- Legal: Interpreted as character data -->
&maybelegal2; <!-- Legal: Interpreted as character data -->
&maybelegal3; <!-- Legal: Interpreted as character data -->

<&maybelegal1; <!-- Illegal: Markup (tag) spans entities -->
<!-- &maybelegal2; Ignored: entity ref ignored in comment -->
<em&maybelegal3;    <!-- Illegal: Markup (tag) spans entities -->
</TEST>
```

In this case, it is not the declared entities themselves that are causing the problem, but the fact that elements, entities and markup started in the document entity must end there, just as in any other entity. The context of an entity reference is very important. That is what decides whether it is legal or illegal.

This is true even of entities that hold *complete* tags, elements, comments, processing instructions, character references, or entity references. References to those entities are legal anywhere their replacement text would be

legal. The same applies to *validity* (conformance to a document type definition). Example 54-17 is well-formed, but not valid, because the fully
expanded document would not be valid. Validity is covered in Chapter 52,
"Creating a document type definition", on page 792.

Example 54-17. Well-formed but not valid

```
<?xml version="1.0"?>
<!DOCTYPE TEST[
  <!ELEMENT EVENT (TIME, DESCRIPTION)>
  <!ELEMENT TIME (#PCDATA)>
  <!ELEMENT DESCRIPTION (#PCDATA)>
  <!ENTITY accident "<ERROR>Error</ERROR>">
]>
<EVENT>&accident;</EVENT>
```

The document in the example is well-formed. Both the EVENT and ERROR
elements start and end in the same entity. It meets all of the other rules
required for it to be well-formed. But it is not valid, because accident's
replacement text consists of an ERROR element which is not valid where the
entity is referenced. (in the EVENT element).

Conceptually, validation occurs after all entities have been parsed.

Spec Excerpt (XML) 54-5. General entity definition

```
[70]   EntityDecl ::=  GEDecl | PEDecl
[71]   GEDecl ::=  '<!ENTITY' S Name S EntityDef S? '>'
[73]   EntityDef ::=  EntityValue | (ExternalID NDataDecl?)
[72]   PEDecl ::=  '<!ENTITY' S '%' S Name S PEDef S? '>'
[74]   PEDef ::=  EntityValue | ExternalID
```

54.8 | Restrictions on parameter entity references

Neither general entities nor parameter entities may span markup boundaries, but parameter entities have other restrictions on them. There are specific places where parameter entity references are allowed.

54.8.1 *Internal subset*

Within the internal subset, the rules are simple: parameter entities can only be expanded in places where full markup declarations are allowed. For them to be legal in these contexts they must always contain one or more markup declarations.

Example 54-18. Multiple markup declarations in one parameter entity

```
<!ENTITY % several-declarations
                "<!ELEMENT FOO (#PCDATA)>
                 <!ELEMENT BAR (#PCDATA)>
                 <!ELEMENT BAZ (#PCDATA)>">
%several-declarations;
```

Because of the way XML handles white space, the replacement text for the entity declaration in Example 54-18 is parsed as it would if the entity declaration had occurred on a single line. In this case we have defined the literal entity value over several lines to make the DTD more readable. When we refer to the parameter entity "several-declarations", the three element types are declared.

54.8.2 *External subset*

The rules for parameter entities in the external subset are much more complex. This is because parameter entities in the external subset are not restricted to complete markup declarations. They can also be parts of a markup declaration. XML restricts parameter entities in the internal subset to full declarations because the internal subset is supposed to be very easy to process quickly by browsers and other processors. The external subset allows more complex, powerful parameter entity references. For instance, in the external subset, Example 54-19 would be a legal series of declarations.

Example 54-19. Entities in the external subset

```
<!ENTITY % ent-name "the-entity">
<!ENTITY % ent-value "This is the entity">
<!ENTITY %ent-name; "%ent-value;">
```

Both the name and the replacement text of the final entity declaration are specified through parameter entity references. Their replacement texts become the entity's name and replacement text.

The tricky part is that there are only particular places that you can use parameter entity references in markup declarations. You might wonder, for instance, if you could replace the string "<!ENTITY" with a parameter entity reference. You might guess that this is impossible because XML does not allow a markup declaration to start in one entity and end in another. You would guess correctly. It would be harder to guess whether you could use an entity reference to fill in the string "ENTITY" which follows the "<!" It turns out that this is illegal as well.

To be safe, we would advise you to stick to using parameter entities only to hold full markup declarations and portions of another entity's replacement text until you are familiar with the text of the XML specification itself. The specification relies on knowledge of grammatical tokens to constrain the places that parameter entity replacement is allowed in the external subset. Those token boundaries are only described in the complete grammar.

54.9 | External identifiers

External identifiers refer to information outside the entity in which they occur. There are two types. System identifiers use URIs to refer to an object based on its location. Public identifiers use a publicly declared name to refer to information.

Spec Excerpt (XML) 54-6. External identifier

```
[75]  ExternalID ::=  'SYSTEM' S SystemLiteral
                    | 'PUBLIC' S PubidLiteral S SystemLiteral
```

54.9.1   *System identifiers*

The *SystemLiteral* that follows the keyword SYSTEM is just a URI. Example 54-20 is another example of that.

Example 54-20. System identifier

```
<!ENTITY ent SYSTEM "http://www.entities.com/ent.xml">
```

You can also use relative URIs to refer to entities on the same machine as the referring entity. A relative URI is one that does not contain a complete machine name and path. The machine name and part of the path are implied from the context. Example 54-21 demonstrates.

Example 54-21. Local external general entity

```
<!ENTITY local SYSTEM "local.xml">
```

If this were declared in a document at the URI `http://www.baz.org/`, then the processor would fetch the replacement text from `http://www.baz.org/local.xml`.

These URIs are relative to the location of the referring entity (such as an external parameter entity or the external subset of the DTD) and not necessarily to the document entity. If your document entity is on one machine, and it includes some markup declarations from another machine, relative URIs in the included declarations are interpreted as being on the second machine.

For example, your document might be at `http://www.myhome.com`. It might include a DTD component with a set of pictures of playing cards from `http://www.poker.com/cards.dtd`. If that DTD component had a URI, `4Heartss.gif`, it would be interpreted relative to the poker site, not yours.

54.9.2   *Public identifiers*

It is also possible to refer to a DTD component or any entity by a name, in addition to a URI. This name is called a "public identifier". If a few entities become widely used in XML circles then it would be inefficient for everyone to fetch the entities from the same servers. Instead, their software should come with those entities already installed (or else it should know the most efficient site from which to download them, perhaps from a corporate intranet). To enable these smarter lookup mechanisms, you would refer to those DTDs by public identifiers, as shown in Example 54-22.

Example 54-22. Referencing a DTD by public identifier

```
<!DOCTYPE MEMO PUBLIC "-//SGMLSOURCE//DTD MEMO//EN"
                "http://www.sgmlsource.com/dtds/memo.dtd">
<MEMO> </MEMO>
```

The public identifier is a unique name for the entity. It should be unique world-wide. Usually they contain corporate or personal names to make them more likely to be unique. If the software knows how to translate the public identifier into a URI, it will do so. If not, it will use the system identifier.

The translation from public identifier to URI is typically either hard-wired into a processor or controlled through files called "entity catalogs". Entity catalogs list public identifiers and describe their URIs, in the same way that phone books allow you to look up a name and find a number. Documentation for XML software should mention the format of the catalogs it supports, if any.

54.10 | XML Inclusions (XInclude)

In 2.4, "Entities: The physical structure", on page 38 we discussed some of the tradeoffs between XML entities and HTML-style `href` attributes for organizing large documents. The *XML Inclusions (XInclude)* specification takes yet another approach.

Caution   XInclude is still under development by the W3C at this writing and is subject to change. It is not part of the XML Recommendation and is included in this chapter only because it relates closely to entities.

XInclude is similar in concept to XML's general entities but has quite a different syntax and processing model. Where entities have a distinct syntax that is built into XML itself, XInclude uses an XML element type to represent an inclusion.

54.10.1   *The* xi:include *element type*

The xi:include element type comes from the namespace http://www.w3.org/2001/XInclude. It has three attributes, only one of which is required.

href
> href is a URI reference to the resource to include. It is required. After all, including that other resource is the whole point.

parse
> The parse attribute has two values. The default, xml, declares that the referenced resource should be parsed as XML in the normal way (that is, like a parsed entity), while text indicates it should be treated as character data and not parsed.

encoding
> The encoding attribute declares the Unicode encoding of the referenced resource when the parse value is text. Because XML documents declare their own encodings or can have them auto-detected, the encoding attribute is ignored when parse is

specified as XML. (Encoding is discussed in 51.6.1.2, "Encoding declaration", on page 783.)

Example 54-23 shows an XML document that includes an XML element. As xml is the default value for the parse attribute, we can omit it. We also omit the encoding attribute because it is only used when including plain text data.

Example 54-23. A simple xi:include element

```
<doc xmlns:xi="http://www.w3.org/2001/XInclude">
<xi:include href="element.xml"/>
</doc>
```

54.10.2 *Including plain text data*

In Example 54-25, an XML document includes boilerplate text from the plain text data file in Example 54-24 – twice!

Example 54-24. Contents of disclaimer.txt

```
We do not accept responsibility for anything.
```

Example 54-25. Including plain text data

```
<doc xmlns:xi="http://www.w3.org/2001/XInclude">
<p>Please read our disclaimer.</p>
<p><xi:include parse="text"
               href="http://.../disclaimer.txt"/></p>
<p>No. Really. Please read it. Crucial!</p>
<p><xi:include parse="text"
               href="http://.../disclaimer.txt"/></p>
</doc>
```

The result of the XInclude processing would look like Example 54-26.

54.10.3 *Inclusions with XPointer*

XPointer is a W3C Recommendation that allows a URI to address XML documents, fragments of documents, and multiple documents and frag-

Example 54-26. Result of XInclude processing of Example 54-25

```
<doc xmlns:xi="http://www.w3.org/2001/XInclude">
<p>Please read our disclaimer.</p>
<p>We do not accept responsibility for anything.</p>
<p>No. Really. Please read it. Crucial!</p>
<p>We do not accept responsibility for anything.</p>
</doc>
```

ments in many powerful ways. XInclude supports some of XPointer, so we'll show some examples of how they are used together here. (For a detailed explanation of XPointer, see Chapter 64, "XML Pointer Language (XPointer)", on page 1052.)

Example 54-27 is an XML document with two p elements. The elements have unique identifiers.

Example 54-27. Contents of `disclaimer.xml`

```
<disclaimers>
<p id="total">We disclaim everything.</p>
<p id="reasonable">We disclaim some things.</p>
</disclaimers>
</doc>
```

Example 54-28 includes one of the elements by specifying its unique identifier in the xpointer portion of the href URI.

Example 54-28. XInclude with XPointer

```
<doc xmlns:xi="http://www.w3.org/2001/XInclude">
<xi:include
    href="http://.../disclaimer.xml#xpointer(id('total'))"/>
</doc>
```

The result is shown in Example 54-29.

Example 54-29. Result of XInclude processing of Example 54-28

```
<doc xmlns:xi="http://www.w3.org/2001/XInclude">
<p id="total">We disclaim everything.</p>
</doc>
```

An XPointer can also point to more than one node. In that case, all of them are included. In Example 54-30, the XPointer selects all p elements, with the result shown in Example 54-31.[3]

Example 54-30. Including multiple elements

```
<doc xmlns:xi="http://www.w3.org/2001/XInclude">
<xi:include
    href="http://.../disclaimer.xml#xpointer(//p)"/>
</doc>
```

Example 54-31. Result of XInclude processing of Example 54-30

```
<doc xmlns:xi="http://www.w3.org/2001/XInclude">
<p id="total">We disclaim everything.</p>
<p id="reasonable">We disclaim some things.</p>
</doc>
```

54.10.4 *Nested inclusions*

It is possible for included content to have an xi:include element within it. An XInclude implementation should process these by including the documents they reference. If those documents also happen to contain xi:include elements then of course they are processed as well.

These nested inclusions continue until there are no more xi:include elements to resolve. It is illegal to set up situations where, for example, A.xml includes B.xml which includes C.xml which includes A.xml. The XInclude processor would continue resolving forever!

An xi:include element typically references another document, but there is nothing preventing it from referencing some part of the document in which it occurs. The XInclude processor would duplicate that content at the point of reference. Here too, one must be careful not to include the fragment of the document with the xi:include element in it, lest you cause an infinite loop.

---

3. The result makes no sense, of course, but it doesn't matter because no one ever reads disclaimers anyway.

54.10.5   *Handling missing resources*

There may be circumstances where the referenced resource is not available. Perhaps it was deleted, or is unavailable because of networking problems. XInclude allows the author to specify fallback content that should be used in such circumstances.

Example 54-32 tries to download an XML version of the disclaimer. If that fails, it tries to fall back on a plain text version. If that fails, it gives up and generates an error message.

Example 54-32. XInclude fallback

```
<doc xmlns:xi="http://www.w3.org/2001/XInclude">
<xi:include parse="xml"
            href="http://.../disclaimer.xml#xpointer(id('total'))"/>
  <xi:fallback><xi:include parse="text"
                           href="http://.../disclaimer.txt">
    <xi:fallback>Cannot find disclaimer!</xi:fallback>
  </xi:include></xi:fallback>
</xi:include>
</doc>
```

If the XInclude processor cannot find the XML or plain text versions, it will produce the result in Example 54-33.

Example 54-33. Result of fallback failure in Example 54-32

```
<doc xmlns:xi="http://www.w3.org/2001/XInclude">
Cannot find disclaimer!
</doc>
```

54.10.5.1   XInclude is unpredictable

The XInclude spec defines *inclusion* as a transformation that operates on an *information set*; that is, on the information items found by the XML parser as a result of parsing.[4] The result of this *inclusion transformation* is a different information set. (It is a "synthetic" one, which introduces a whole separate set of problems. See 55.6.2, "Synthetic infosets", on page 892.)

---

4. See 55.6, "XML Information Set (Infoset)", on page 890.

The XInclude spec deliberately does not say when the inclusion transformation should occur.

Spec Excerpt (XML) 54-7. Infoset creation intentionally unspecified

The specifics of how an infoset is created are intentionally unspecified, to allow for flexibility by implementations and to avoid defining a particular processing model for components of the XML architecture. Particulars of whether DTD or XML schema validation are performed, for example, are not constrained by this specification.

Some programmers might see this ambiguity as a good thing (flexibility!) because it leaves the software developer building the system in control. But it clearly flies in the face of the goal of XML: consistent interpretation of document markup across systems.[5]

If a schema validation error occurs because the inclusion transformation happened before the schema processing, is it the fault of the author, or of the processor that did the steps in an unexpected order?

Conversely, must an author add `xi:include` element declarations to all schemas in case schema processing occurs before the inclusion transform? If not, the schema validator will complain about them as an unknown element type.

XInclude has brought to the fore an issue that has been bubbling in the background of the XML world: How does one specify sequences of processes such as XSLT transformations, validations, and now inclusions? Arguably, inclusions should not be part of this discussion!

54.11 | Comparison of entities, XInclude, and href

This chapter has discussed several methods for incorporating resources in an XML document: entity references, entity attributes, and XInclude.

---

5. Note that "consistent interpretation of document markup" just means that all processors have the same unambiguous understanding of the author's intention. What they do about it isn't addressed by the XML spec.

Another way comes from HTML: an element with an attribute, frequently named `href`, whose value is a URI reference.

Table 54-1 compares these four methods. There is a table column for each of them and each row characterizes the traits of the method in one of seven categories.

Table 54-1   Entities, `href`, and XInclude compared

	Entity reference	`ENTITY` **attribute**	`href` **attribute**	**XInclude**
Infoset	Document	Optional independent	Optional independent	Transform
Validation	Well-defined	Well-defined	Well-defined	Undefined
Resource	Declared	Declared	Undeclared	Undeclared
Fallback	Not allowed	`ENTITIES` attribute	`IDREFS` attribute	`xi:fallback`
Structure	Physical	No effect	No effect	Conflated
Semantics	Transparent	Element-type	Element-type	`xi:include`
Data	PCDATA	Any	Any	Plain text

54.11.1 *Traits of resource access methods*

The traits reveal potential benefits and drawbacks of each method, depending on your requirements. Let's examine those tradeoffs in detail. In the following discussion, the characterization keywords from the table appear in bold.

54.11.1.1   Infoset

The access methods cause different infoset impacts for well-formed XML resources:

entity reference
> A resource accessed by an entity reference is incorporated transparently into the **document** infoset returned by the XML processor.

attribute methods
> In the case of a resource accessed by either attribute method, the resource does not affect the document infoset. However, the application could invoke an XML processor to create an **optional independent** infoset for the resource.

XInclude
> The inclusion is parsed and an infoset is created for it. A **transform** is applied to merge that infoset into the document infoset, thereby creating a synthetic infoset.

54.11.1.2   Validation

For all of the methods except XInclude, all infosets can be validated against DTDs or schemas and the expected behavior of processors is **well-defined**.

For XInclude, DTD and schema validation are possible for the unresolved infoset, but that would require the DTD or schema to allow for `xi:include` elements. Schema validation is also possible for the resolved infoset, but processor behavior is **undefined** and a document author cannot predict which infoset will be validated.

54.11.1.3   Resource

For the two methods that use entities, all resources required are **declared** in the prolog of the document. For the other two methods, resources are **undeclared**.

Declarations require more work, but they make it clear up-front exactly which resources may be needed for the document. They also enable indirect addressing, so that only entity names appear in the document instance. As a result, if resources are moved or replaced, only the entity declarations need to be changed.

54.11.1.4   Fallback

XInclude provides the `xi:fallback` element-type for specifying alternative resources if the requested one cannot be accessed.

For the attribute-based methods, there is no built-in fallback mechanism. However, it is common to handle the problem with a `fallback` attribute. The attribute value is a list of alternatives in priority order, either in the form of entity names (ENTITIES attribute) or of unique identifiers of elements with `href` attributes (IDREFS attribute).

Entity references require a specific resource, so fallbacks are **not allowed**.

54.11.1.5   Structure

With the two attribute-based methods, the referenced resources have **no effect** on the element structure.

The entity reference method treats entities as a separate **physical** structure. It uses a distinct syntax (&name;) to avoid confusion with the logical element structure.

XInclude, however, **conflates** the two by using an element as the reference to the resource.

54.11.1.6   Semantics

In XML, *semantics*, or meaning, is represented by the element-type and attribute names, as defined in a particular namespace. The attribute-based access methods can therefore apply the semantics of the **element-type** and attribute name to the relationship between the document and the resources; for example, hyperlink, cross-reference, source, previous version, etc.

There are no semantics for the `xi:include` element-type other than the mechanism of inclusion.

As the entity reference does not use element syntax, it is completely **transparent** and has no logical semantics at all.

54.11.1.7   Data

In 54.11.1.1, "Infoset", on page 873 we discussed the accessing of well-formed XML. In this section we look only at the accessing of data.

The two attribute-based methods can access any kind of data, including multimedia. It isn't parsed as XML and doesn't affect the document infoset.

The only data that an entity reference can access is `PCDATA` – text characters that are allowed in the mixed content of XML elements.[6]

When `parse="text"`, the resource accessed by an `xi:include` element is treated as plain text data. No XML markup is recognized in it and a character encoding can be specified for it.

54.12 | Conclusion

XML entities allow the separation of issues of logical structure from those of the physical storage of the document. This means that document type designers do not have to foresee every possible reasonable way of breaking up a document when they design the document type. This is good, because that sort of decision is best made by those who know their system resource limits, bandwidth limits, editor preferences, and so forth. The document type designer, in contrast, takes responsibility for deciding on a good structure for the document.

Other techniques of incorporating external resources into an XML document offer other benefits. The tradeoffs can be quite complex, as we've seen. Your own application requirements should indicate the ones to use.

---

6. Remember that in XML the term "mixed content" includes content that is only data.

Advanced features of XML

Friendly Tutorial

- Conditional sections
- Character references
- Processing instructions
- Standalone declaration
- XML Information Set (Infoset)

T he features in this chapter are advanced in the sense that only advanced users will get around to reading them. They do not require advanced degrees in computer science or rocket science to understand. They are just a little esoteric. Most XML users will get by without ever needing to use them.

However, one subject in this chapter – the XML Information Set (Infoset) – is different, although it isn't even part of the XML Recommendation. The Infoset W3C Recommendation defines the information that is represented by an XML document, and many think it should have been part of the XML spec itself. We discuss it in 55.6, "XML Information Set (Infoset)", on page 890.

55.1 | Conditional sections

Conditional sections can only occur in the external subset of the document type declaration, and in external entities referenced from the internal subset. The internal subset proper is supposed to be quick and easy to process. In contrast, the external subset is supposed to retain some of the full-SGML mechanisms that make complicated DTDs easier to maintain. One of these mechanisms is the conditional section, which allows you to turn on and off a series of markup declarations.

Like the internal and external subsets, conditional sections may contain one or more complete declarations, comments, processing instructions, or nested conditional sections, with optional white space between them.

A conditional section is turned on and off with a keyword. If the keyword is INCLUDE, then the section is processed just as if the conditional section markers did not exist. If the keyword is IGNORE, then the contents are ignored by the processor as if the declarations themselves did not exist, as in Example 55-1.

Example 55-1. Conditional sections

```
<![INCLUDE[
<!ELEMENT magazine (title, article+, comments* )>
]]>
<![IGNORE[
<!ELEMENT magazine (title, body)>
]]>
```

This is a useful way of turning on and off parts of a DTD during development.

The real power in the feature derives from parameter entity references. These are described in 54.2.2, "Internal and external parameter entities", on page 852.

If the keyword of the conditional section is a parameter entity reference, the processor replaces the parameter entity by its content before the processor decides whether to include or ignore the conditional section. That means that by changing the parameter entity in the internal subset, you can turn on and off a conditional marked section. In that way, two different documents could reference the same set of external markup declarations, but get slightly (or largely) different DTDs. For instance, we can modify the example above:

Example 55-2. Conditional sections and parameter entities

```
<![%editor[
 <!ELEMENT magazine (title, article+, comments* )>
 ]]>
 <![%author[
 <!ELEMENT magazine (title, body)>
]]>
```

Now editors will have a slightly different DTD from authors. When the parameter entities are set one way, the declaration without comments is chosen:

Example 55-3. Internal subset of a document type declaration

```
<!DOCTYPE MAGAZINE SYSTEM "magazine.dtd"[
    <!ENTITY % editor "IGNORE">
    <!ENTITY % author "INCLUDE">
]>
```

Authors do not have to worry about comments elements that they are not supposed to use anyway. When the document moves from the author to the editor, the parameter entity values can be swapped, and the expanded version of the DTD becomes available. Parameter entities can also be used to manage DTDs that go through versions chronologically, as an organization's needs change.

Conditional sections are also sometimes used to make "strict" and "loose" versions of DTDs. The loose DTD can be used for compatibility with old documents, or documents that are somehow out of your control, and the strict DTD can be used to try to encourage a more precise structure for future documents.

55.2 | Character references

It is not usually convenient to type in characters that are not available on the keyboard. With many text editors, it is not even possible to do so. XML allows you to insert such a character with a *character reference*. If, for instance, you wanted to insert a character from the "International Phonetic Alphabet", you could spend a long time looking for a combination of keyboard, operating system and text editor that would make that straightforward. Rather than buying special hardware or software, XML allows you to refer to the character by its *Unicode number*.

Here is an example:

Example 55-4. Decimal character reference

```
<P>Here is a reference to Unicode character 161: &#161;.</P>
```

Unicode is a character set. The character numbered 161 in Unicode happens to be the inverted exclamation mark. Alternatively, you could use the *hex* (hexadecimal) value of the character number to reference it:

Example 55-5. Hex character reference

```
<P>Here is a different reference to Unicode character 161: &#xA1;.
```

Hex is a numbering system often used by computer programmers that translates naturally into the binary codes that computers use. The *Unicode Standard book* uses hex, so those that have that book will probably prefer this type of character reference over the other (whether they are programmers or not).

Here are the specifics on character references from the XML spec:

Spec Excerpt (XML) 55-1. Character reference

```
CharRef ::=  '&#' [0-9]+ ';'
     | '&#x' [0-9a-fA-F]+ ';'
```

Spec Excerpt (XML) 55-2. Interpreting character references

If the character reference begins with "`&#x`", the digits and letters up to the terminating ; provide a hexadecimal representation of the character's code point in ISO/IEC 10646. If it begins just with "`&#`", the digits up to the terminating ; provide a decimal representation of the character's code point.

ISO/IEC 10646 is the Borg of character set standards. It seemingly includes every character from every other character set and leaves room for characters not yet created. Unicode is an independently developed industry-standard character set that is identifiable as a subset of ISO/IEC 10646. For XML purposes, there's no real need to distinguish them.

Note that character references are not entity references, though they look similar to them. Entities have names and values, but character references only have character numbers. In an XML document, all entities except the predefined ones must be declared. But a character reference does not require a declaration; it is just a really verbose way to type a character (but often the only way).

Because Unicode numbers are hard to remember, it is often useful to declare entities that stand in for them:

Example 55-6. Entity declaration for a Unicode character

```
<!ENTITY inverted-exclamation "&#161;">
```

Most likely this is how most XML users will refer to obscure characters. There will probably be popular character entity sets that can be included in a DTD through parameter entity references. This technique will free users from learning obscure character numbers and probably even from learning how to use character references.

55.3 | Processing instructions

XML comments are for those occasions where you need to say something to another human being without reference to the DTD, and without changing the way the document looks to readers or applications. Processing instructions are for those occasions where you need to say something to *a computer program* without reference to the DTD and without changing the way that the document is processed by other computer programs. This is only supposed to happen rarely.

Many people argued that the occasions would be so rare that XML should not have processing instructions at all. But as one of us said in *The SGML Handbook*: "In a perfect world, they would not be needed, but, as you may have noticed, the world is not perfect." It turns out that processing instruction use has changed over the years and is not as frowned upon as it was in the early days of SGML.

Processing instructions are intended to reintroduce software-specific markup. You might wonder why you would want to do that. Imagine that you are creating a complex document, and, like a good user of a generalized markup language, you are concentrating on the structure rather than the formatting. Close to the deadline you print the document using the proprietary formatting system that has been foisted on you by your boss. There are many of these systems, some of which are of fantastic quality and others which are not.

Your document looks reasonable, but you need a way to make the first letter of each paragraph large. However, reading the software's manual, you realize that the formatter does not have a feature that allows you to modify the style for the first letter of a word. The XML Purist in you might want to go out and buy a complete formatting system but the Pragmatist in you knows that would be impossible.

Thinking back to the bad-old days of "What You See is All You Get" word processors, you recall that all you really needed to do is to insert a code in the beginning of each paragraph to change the font for the first letter. This is not good "XML Style" because XML Purists do not insert formatting codes and they especially do not insert codes specific to a particular piece of software – that is not in the "spirit" of generalized markup. Still, in this case, with a deadline looming and stubborn software balking, a processing instruction may be your best bet. If the formatter has a "change font" command it may be accessible through a processing instruction:

Example 55-7. Processing instruction

```
<CHAPTER>The Bald and the Dutiful
<P><?DUMB-FORMATTER.FONT="16PT"?>N<?DUMB-FORMATTER.END-FONT?>ick
took Judy in his arms</P>
```

If you find yourself using many processing instructions to specify formatting you should try to figure out what is wrong with your system. Is your document's markup not rich enough? Is your formatting language not powerful enough? Are you not taking advantage of the tools and markup you have available to you? The danger in using processing instructions is that you can come to rely on them instead of more reusable structural markup. Then when you want to reuse your information in another context, the markup will not be robust enough to allow it.

Processing instructions start with a fixed string "<?". That is followed by a name and, after that, any characters except for the string that ends the PI, "?>".

Here are the relevant rules from the XML specification:

Spec Excerpt (XML) 55-3. Processing Instruction

```
[16]   PI ::=  '<?' PITarget (S (Char* - (Char* '?>' Char*)))? '?>'
[17]   PITarget ::=  Name - (('X' | 'x') ('M' | 'm') ('L' | 'l'))
```

This name at the beginning of the PI is called the *PI target*. This name should be standardized in the documentation for the tool or specification. After the PI target comes white space and then some totally proprietary command. This command is not processed in the traditional sense at all. Characters that would usually indicate markup are totally ignored. The command is passed directly to the application and it does what it wants to with it. The command ends when the processor hits the string "?>". There is absolutely no standard for the "stuff" in the middle. Markup is not recognized there. PIs could use attribute syntax for convenience, but they could also choose not to.

It is possible that more than one application could understand the same instructions. They might come from the same vendor or one vendor might agree to accept another vendor's commands. For instance in the early days of the Web, the popular NCSA (National Center for Supercomputing Activities) Web Server introduced special commands into HTML documents in the form of special HTML comments. Because the NCSA server was dominant in those days, many servers now support those commands.

Under XML we would most likely use processing instructions for the same task. The virtue of XML processing instructions in this case is that they are explicitly instructions to a computer program. In our opinion, one of the central tenets of generalized markup is that it is important to be *explicit* about what is going on in a document. Reusing markup constructs for something other than what they were intended for is not explicit.

For instance, since comments are meant to be instructions to users, an ambitious Web Server administrator might decide to write a small script that would strip them out to save download time and protect internal comments from being read by others. But if instructions to software (like the NCSA server commands) were hidden in comments, they would be stripped out as well. It would be better to use the supplied processing instruction facility, which was designed for the purpose.

Better still (from a purist's point of view) would be a robust XML-smart mechanism for accomplishing the task. For instance, one thing that the NCSA servers do is include the text of one HTML file into another. XML's entity mechanism (see Chapter 54, "Entities: Breaking up is easy to do", on page 842) can handle this, so you do not need processing instructions in that case.

If you want to insert the date into a document, then you could connect the external entity to a CGI[1] that returns the date. If you want to insert information from a database then you could have software that generates XML entities with the requested information.

Sometimes, though, the processing instruction solution may be the most expedient. This is especially the case if your application vendor has set it up that way. If your document is heavily dependent on a database or other program, then it is not very "application independent" in any case. If a document is inherently dependent on an application then you may decide that strictly adhering to generalized markup philosophy is just too much work. In the end you must choose between expediency and purity. Most people mix both.

Processing instructions are appropriate when you are specifying information about a document that is unrelated to the actual structure of the document. Consider, for instance, the problem of specifying which stylesheets go with which XML documents on a web site. Given enough money and time you could erect a database that kept track of them. If you already had your XML documents in a text database then this would probably be the most efficient mechanism. If you did not have a text database set up, then you could merely keep the information in a flat text file. But you would

---

1. CGI is the "Common Gateway Interface", a specification for making Web pages that are generated by the server when the user requests them, rather than in advance.

have to keep that external information up-to-date and write a program to retrieve it in order to do formatting. It would probably be easier to simply stick the information somewhere in the file where it is easy to find (such as at the beginning).

You could add a STYLESHEET element or attribute to each document, but that could cause three problems. First, it would violate the XML Purist principle that elements should represent document components and not formatting or other processing information. Second, if you are using DTDs with your documents then you must add the element or attribute to each DTD that you will be using. This would be a hassle.

The third reason to use processing instructions instead of elements is the most concrete: you may not be able to change those DTDs. After all, DTDs are often industry (or international!) standards. You cannot just go monkeying around with them even if you want to. Instead, you could put a processing instruction at the start of each document. Processing instructions are not associated with particular DTDs and they do not have to be declared. You just use them.

As we described in 60.9, "Referencing XSLT stylesheets", on page 983), XML provides a processing instruction for associating stylesheets:

Example 55-8. Stylesheet PI

```
<?xml-stylesheet
          href="http://www.sgmlsource.com/memo.xsl"
          type="text/xsl"?>
```

Note that the stylesheet processing instruction does not really add anything to the content or structure of the document. It says something about how to *process* the document. It says: "This document has an associated stylesheet and it is available at such and such a location." It is not always obvious what is abstract information and what is merely processing information. If your instruction must be embedded in documents of many types, or with DTDs that you cannot change, then processing instructions are typically your best bet.

The XML *encoding PI* is an example of another processing instruction. It says what character encoding the file uses. Again this information could be stored externally, such as in a database, a text file or somewhere else, but XML's designers decided (after weeks of heated discussion) that it would be most convenient to place it in the XML document itself rather than require it to be stored (and transmitted across the Internet) externally.

If you go back to 51.6.1, "XML declaration", on page 782 you will also notice that the XML declaration has the same prefix (<?) and suffix (?>) as processing instructions do. Formally speaking, the XML declaration is a special form of processing instruction. From an SGML processor's point of view, it is a processing instruction that controls the behavior of a particular class of software: XML processing software. Software that treats XML as just another kind of SGML will ignore it, as they do other types of processing instructions.

To summarize: PIs (processing instructions) were invented primarily for formatting hacks but based on our experience with SGML we know that they are more widely useful. There are already predefined processing instructions in the XML specification for some kinds of processing. Processing instructions will probably be used for other things in the future. Everything that can be accomplished with PIs would be accomplished by other means in a perfect world of pure generalized markup, but in the real world they are often convenient.

55.4 | Special attributes and newlines

There are two attribute names that the XML specification treats as special whenever it encounters them. If a document is to be valid then it must have declarations for these attributes but if it is well-formed but not valid then it may just use them undeclared, as it would any other attribute.

The attribute xml:lang is a convention for stating the language of the content of an element. This is language not in some esoteric computer sense but in the normal, human languages sense. The attribute's value is typically a language code like "en" for English and "fr" for French.

It is also common to follow the language code with a dash and a country code to indicate a more precise dialect. The country codes are the same ones used in Internet domain names: "uk", "us", "ca" etc. If you do serious internationalization work you should check the XML specification for the full details.

The attribute xml:space is a hint to an application about how it should handle whitespace in an element. For instance, an XML editor might use the attribute to know whether it is appropriate to collapse several spaces into a single one or to convert newline characters into spaces. The two valid values are `default` and `preserve`. Default means that an application should do whatever it usually does with whitespace – collapse, delete, preserve or anything. Preserve means that the application should not change the whitespace in any way.

Both of these attributes are *inherited*. That means that an attribute applies to the element and all descendants unless some descendant has a conflicting value for it. In that case the descendant's attribute value would be in effect for that element and *its* descendants, but the ancestral value would again be in effect after that element ends.

Regardless of the value of these attributes, XML processors must always convert end-of-line markers to a single Unix-style newline character. It does not matter what platform (e.g. Windows, Macintosh, Unix) the document is processed on nor what platform it was created on. The various end-of-line conventions are all converted automatically to the Unix convention before the application sees the data. This means that software programs can behave in exactly the same way on all platforms and documents.

55.5 | Standalone document declaration

We should start by saying that the standalone document declaration is only designed for a small class of problems, and these are not problems that most XML users will run into. We do not advise its use. Nevertheless, it is part of XML and we feel that you should understand it so that you can understand why it is seldom useful.

A DTD is typically broken into two parts, an external part that contains declarations that are typically shared among many documents, and an internal part that occurs within the document and contains declarations that only that document uses (see Chapter 52, "Creating a document type definition", on page 792). The external part includes all external parameter entities, including both the external subset of the document type declaration and any external entities referenced from the internal subset.

The DTD describes the structure of the document, but it can also control the interpretation of some of the markup and declare the existence of some other entities (such as graphics or other XML documents) that are required for proper processing. For instance, a graphic might only be used in a particular document, so the declaration that includes it (an *entity declaration*) would usually go in the internal subset rather than the external one.

Processors that validate a document need the entire DTD to do so. A document is not valid unless it conforms to both the internal and external parts of its DTD. But sometimes a system passes a document from program to program and it does not need to be validated at each stage. For instance, two participants in an electronic data interchange system might agree that the sender will validate the document once, instead of having both participants validate it.

Even though the receiving processor may not be interested in full validation, it may need to know if it understands the document in exactly the same way that the sender did. Some features of the DTD may influence this slightly. Documents with defaulted attributes would be interpreted differently if the attribute declarations are read rather than ignored. Entity declarations would allow the expansion of entity references. Attribute values can only be normalized according to their type when the attribute declarations are read. Some white space in content would also be removed if the DTD would not allow it to be interpreted as text.

If a process can reliably skip a part of the DTD dedicated exclusively to validation, then it would have less data to download and process and could let the application do its work (browsing, searching, etc.) more quickly. But it would be important for some "mission critical" applications to know if they are getting a slightly different understanding of the document than they would if they processed the entire DTD.

The *standalone document declaration* allows you to specify whether a processor needs to fetch the external part of the DTD in order to process the document "exactly right." The Standalone document declaration may take the values (case sensitive) of yes and no.

A value of yes says that the document is *standalone* and thus does not depend on the external part of the DTD for correct interpretation. A value of *no* means that it either depends on the external DTD part or it might, so the application should not trust that it can get the correct information without it. You could always use no as the value for this attribute, but in some cases applications will then download more data than they need to do their jobs. This translates into slower processing, more network usage and so forth.

Example 55-9 will tell the application that unless the processor fetched the pictures, the application might get a different understanding of the doc-

Example 55-9. A standalone document declaration that forces processing of the internal subset.

```
<?xml version="1.0" standalone="no"?>
<!DOCTYPE MEMO SYSTEM "http://www.sgmlsource.com/memo.dtd" [
<!ENTITY % pics SYSTEM "http://www.sgmlsource.com/pics.ent">
 %pics;
]>
<MEMO></MEMO>
```

ument than it would if it processed the whole document. For instance, the MEMO element might have defaulted attributes.

But if the value is *yes*, the receiving application may choose not to get the external part of the DTD. This implies that it will never know what was in it. Still, it needs to be able to trust the accuracy of the declaration. What if the security level for a document is set in an attribute and the default level is top-secret? It would be very bad if a careless author could obscure that with a misleading standalone document declaration. In the scenario we outlined, the sender has already validated the document. So the sender has enough information to check that the information is correct. The XML specification requires a validating processor to do this (see Spec Excerpt 55-4).

Spec Excerpt (XML) 55-4. Standalone document declaration

The standalone document declaration must have the value "no" if any external markup declarations contain declarations of:

- attributes with default values, if elements to which these attributes apply appear in the document without specifications of values for these attributes, or
- entities (other than amp, lt, gt, apos, quot), if references to those entities appear in the document, or
- attributes with values subject to normalization, where the attribute appears in the document with a value which will change as a result of normalization, or
- element types with element content, if white space occurs directly within any instance of those types.

The last one is very likely to happen. Often people use white space between tags to make the source XML document readable, but that can slightly change the interpretation of the document. Validating processors will tell applications that there are some contexts where character data is not legal, so the white space occurring in those places must be merely formatting white space (see 52.5, "Content models", on page 804). If an application that does not want to validate a document is to get exactly the same information out of the document, it must know whether there are any elements where white space should be interpreted just as source formatting. We say that this sort of white space is *insignificant*.

The standalone document declaration warns the application that this is the case so that mission critical applications may download the DTD just to get the right information out of the document, even when they are not interested in validating it.

The standalone document declaration is fairly obscure and it is doubtful if it will get much use outside of a few mission critical applications. Even there, however, it is safest to just get the external data and do a complete validation before trusting a document. You might find that it had been corrupted in transit.

55.6 | XML Information Set (Infoset)

Note   This section covers material that is not part of the XML recommendation itself, although many believe that it should be. It is included in this chapter because it covers fundamental aspects of XML of the same ilk as those covered in the XML Recommendation.

According to the W3C XML Recommendation, an XML document is a character string that is "well-formed" according to the Recommendation's requirements. But as we observed in 7.6, "Document, XML document, and instance", on page 148, before you can create an XML document, you need to have in mind the set of information that the document is intended to communicate. We called that information set the *conceptual document*.

The W3C has also taken notice of the fact that XML documents represent information! It has developed a Recommendation that defines an "abstract data set" called the *XML Information Set (Infoset)*.

Caution   In this book, we try to minimize confusion by referring to the information set of a given document as **an** infoset (uncapitalized) and to the data set defined by the W3C Recommendation as **the** Infoset (capitalized). Other sources aren't as punctilious.

55.6.1 *Information items*

The Infoset Recommendation contains definitions for the "important information" in an XML document. You can think of these *information items* as the conceptual document (somewhat augmented), or, in a programming-oriented way, as information returned by an XML processor after parsing.

Either way, the information items are directly useful to implementors of XML software and developers of XML-related specifications. They are also important to XML information owners, as they define what software will see as your document.

There is one information item for the document, one for the document type declaration, and one for each element, attribute, processing instruction, data character, and comment. There are also information items for each namespace, unparsed entity, notation, and unreplaced ("unexpanded") entity reference.

Each information item has properties. For example, among the properties of an element information item are the element's children (e.g. sub-elements, data characters) and its attributes.

Several items possess name properties. For elements, the name is called a `local part` because element-type names can be qualified by a namespace. Element information items also have properties for the namespace (if any) to which the element-type belongs and the prefix used as the namespace nickname. Attribute items also have a `local part` and these namespace-related properties.

Consider the document in Example 55-10. Its information set contains the following information items:

Example 55-10. Sample document for infoset gathering

```
<?xml version="1.0"?>
<msg:message doc:date="19990421"
          xmlns:doc="http://doc.example.org/namespaces/doc"
          xmlns:msg="http://message.example.org/"
>Phone home!</msg:message>
```

- A document information item.
- An element information item with `namespace name` "http://message.example.org/", `local part` "message", and `prefix` "msg".
- An attribute information item with the `namespace name` "http://doc.example.org/namespaces/doc", `local part` "date", `prefix` "doc", and `normalized value` "19990421".
- Three namespace information items for the namespaces "http://www.w3.org/XML/1998/namespace", "http://doc.example.org/namespaces/doc", and "http://message.example.org/".
- Two attribute information items for the namespace attributes.
- Eleven character information items for the character data.

The Information Set Recommendation is largely successful at distinguishing the conceptual information from the syntax used to represent it. The spec includes a long – and acknowledged incomplete – list of syntactic things that aren't part of a document's infoset; for example, the kind of quotation marks (single or double) used to quote attribute values.

XML-related specifications such as XPath, XQuery, and XML Schema have data models that are based upon the Infoset. Implementations of such specifications can be thought of as *infoset processors*, as they process the infosets of specific documents.

55.6.2 *Synthetic infosets*

If infoset processors can both act on and return infosets, why can't they share them directly as well?

For example, if you had a pipeline of ten XSLT transforms you might be able to improve performance substantially by passing an infoset from one to another instead of the normal *serialized* XML document character string that represents the very same information items. The Infoset Recommendation calls these generated result infosets *synthetic infosets*:

Spec Excerpt (infoset) 55-5. Synthetic infosets

This specification describes the information set resulting from parsing an XML document. Information sets may be constructed by other means, for example by use of an API such as the DOM or by transforming an existing information set.

As a synthetic infoset can be created by an API, one could address an entire relational database with an XPath expression. This is not done by serializing the database as an XML document before feeding it to an XSLT processor. Rather, it is done by treating the database as if it *were* an XML document. The synthesized infoset is the result of simulating the parsing of that notional XML document.

Unfortunately, there are a variety of APIs for synthesized infosets. The most popular are the DOM and SAX, but there are dozens of others. This means that synthetic infosets have much worse interoperability than serialized XML documents. The only reason to even consider them is for performance. Applying an XPath to a massive database that is pretending to be an XML document is usually much, much faster than serializing the whole database as XML.

API access to dynamic infosets has clear benefits, but some would like to go further and make infosets persistent. Rather than interchange XML documents, they argue that it would be more efficient to pass around optimized, compressed, binary infosets. That "efficiency" argument has repeatedly been raised – and successfully refuted! – since the dawn of markup languages.

We've already seen[2] the reasons why XML has largely replaced binary object interchange among systems. Binary infosets are just another kind of binary object, so there is no need to repeat all the arguments here.

---

2. In 6.1.2, "Inter-object communication", on page 128.

Those of us given to paranoia – which should include anyone who deals with the software industry – will find one reason sufficient: The easier an information interchange format is to read, the more likely that control of the information will reside with its owners, rather than with software vendors.

55.7 | Is that all there is?

We've pretty much covered all the details of XML, certainly all that are likely to see extensive use. There are some things we didn't touch on, such as restrictions that must be observed if you are using older SGML tools to process XML. As the generalized markup industry is retooling rapidly for XML, such restrictions will be short-lived and, we felt, did not warrant complicating our XML tutorial.

In any case, you are now well-prepared – or will be after reading Chapter 57, "Reading the XML specification", on page 904 – to tackle the XML spec yourself. You'll find it in the XML SPECtacular section of the CD-ROM that accompanies this book.

XML version 1.1

fter XML was published, there was a strong concensus that it should evolve very slowly if at all. Although its related speci-fications (XSLT, XML Schema, XPointer, etc.) may accumu-late and change quickly, XML itself is the foundation for the house. There are many tools and applications that use XSLT but not XML Schema or XPointer and others that use XML Schema but not XPointer or XSLT. In fact there are many that use just XML and no related specifications at all. Any change to XML necessarily affects tens of thousands of XML con-suming and creating programs.

Even so, the world changes around XML and many feel that XML must keep pace.

56.1 | What's the difference?

XML 1.1 is a new version of XML that makes various small changes to the way XML uses Unicode. Tempting as it might seem to make many deep changes to XML, there was a strong concensus that such a process might never end. For this reason, XML 1.1 was designed to deal only with Unicode issues.

XML 1.1 documents are differentiated from XML 1.0 documents by the version parameter of the XML declaration: `<?xml version="1.1"?>` Documents without XML declarations are presumed to be XML 1.0.

Processors should now support documents with either the XML 1.0 or XML 1.1 declarations using the appropriate set of rules. With the rare exceptions described in 56.5.2, "Prohibited control characters", on page 901, XML 1.0 documents can be made XML 1.1 documents just by changing their XML declarations.

If you are interested in details of Unicode, the rest of this chapter may be of interest. Otherwise, you might want to skip ahead. Unicode is a little like a bad tasting medicine. If you do not have a reason to learn about it, you may want to procrastinate until you do.

56.2 | Unicode

Although XML is the foundation for a family of standards it is itself built on the bedrock of the Unicode internationalized character set. Unicode is up to version 4.0 now and will probably continue to change: human language is always evolving as is our understanding of how to encode it best. For instance, Unicode 4.0 added ideographic telegraph symbols and Limbu, a Tibeto-Burman language spoken by about 280,626 people in eastern Nepal, Bhutan, and northern India

In some ways, XML was designed to anticipate changes to Unicode. Its design allows new characters to be used as character data more or less "automatically". So it is automatically possible to use (e.g.) Limbu characters as character data in XML documents. But it is not possible to use them in names of element types, attributes, etc.

It is a matter of some debate whether this is actually a big problem. On the one hand, it is hardly fair to the residents of eastern Nepal that their symbols cannot be used as XML element-type names.[1] On the other hand, even speakers of mainstream languages like French and Spanish tend to use

---

1. At the same time, a case could be made that they have bigger things to worry about than their element-type names.

standardized vocabularies defined in English: XHTML, DocBook, RSS, SOAP and so forth.

But people do in fact use element-type names from their natural languages when they are building systems that work within a single company. And later versions of Unicode are better even in their support of languages such as Japanese and Chinese with millions of computer users. According to some Japanese XML experts, the inclusion of the katakana middle dot character was reason enough for a new version of XML.

56.3 | Name characters

XML 1.1 allows many more Unicode characters to be used in names. Whereas XML 1.0 picked certain characters from Unicode to be name characters, XML 1.1 picks which characters (e.g. certain punctuation characters) to exclude. The difference is minor for those using Western languages and frankly will have no impact upon the majority of readers whatsoever. For those using Eastern languages it means that characters that would usually be interpreted as punctuation (e.g. katakana middle dot) can now be used in names. Western punctuation characters are still disallowed so that they can be used as separators in lists of XML names. For instance, the space character is used between an element-type name and attributes in a tag.

Spec Excerpt (XML) 56-1. XML 1.1 grammar for names and name tokens

```
[4] NameStartChar ::= ":" | [A-Z] | "_" | [a-z] |
       [#xC0-#x2FF] | [#x370-#x37D] | [#x37F-#x1FFF] |
       [#x200C-#x200D] | [#x2070-#x218F] | [#x2C00-#x2FEF] |
       [#x3001-#xD7FF] | [#xF900-#xEFFFF]

[4a] NameChar ::= NameStartChar | "-" | "." | [0-9] | #xB7 |
       [#x0300-#x036F] | [#x203F-#x2040]

[5] Name ::= NameStartChar NameChar*

[6] Names ::= Name (S Name)*

[7] Nmtoken ::= NameChar+
```

56.4 | Newline conventions

XML 1.0 supports the newline conventions used on Windows, Unix and the Macintosh, but not that used on mainframes. Mainframes use a character named "NEL" with Unicode number 133 (hex 0085) to split lines. XML 1.1 allows this in all of the same places that Windows, Unix and Macintosh newlines are used. For completeness XML 1.1 also allows character 8232 (hex 2028) which is yet another Unicode newline character called "Line Separator". There is always room for one more way to represent a break between lines!

56.5 | Control characters

XML 1.1 changes the treatment of control characters in several ways: It permits some to be entered directly that XML 1.0 prohibited, and vice versa.

56.5.1 *Permitted control characters*

XML 1.0 disallowed certain Unicode control characters from being represented in XML documents. For instance, there is a hangover from the teletype days called the "BEL" (bell) character that can (under some circumstances) cause the computer speaker to beep. There is also a "BS" character, which stands for backspace. [2]

These XML 1.0 restrictions made it difficult to add XML markup to data containing those characters. XML 1.1 allows these characters. You cannot type them directly on your keyboard in Unicode, but you can insert them using character references (see in 55.2, "Character references", on page 880. [3]

---

2. Native English speakers may be aware of the use of the "BS" initialism to refer to mistruths and obfuscations (Bad Statements?). These, unfortunately, are not prohibited by XML.
3. There is only one Unicode character that cannot be expressed in XML even with a character reference: character 0 (hex 0000). This is because the C and C++ programming languages reserve that character for their own nefarious purposes.

56.5.2 *Prohibited control characters*

XML 1.1 is stricter than XML 1.0 in one respect: some control characters that *were* directly allowed in XML 1.0 are now only allowed as character references. These are obscure characters between positions 127 and 159 (hex 007F and 009F). They have names like "SPA", "PLU", "PU1" and "PU2". It was never a good idea to put these characters directly in documents so few people did so except perhaps by accident. It was mostly by oversight that XML 1.0 allowed them but disallowed the other characters.

If you are converting a document from 1.0 to 1.1, you must convert any occurrences of the characters in this range to character references, with one exception: "NEL", the mainframe newline. Even as its peers are being demoted, "NEL" is promoted not just into the family of regular characters, nor even into the class of whitespace characters, but into the elite realm of the newline characters!

56.6 | Character normalization

XML 1.1 also specifies some rules for XML processors relating to so-called *character normalization*. Character normalization treats two physical characters like an "a" and an "accent grave" as a single character like the French "a with grave". These rules are outside the scope of this book, but can be found in any complete Unicode reference.

56.7 | Conclusion

Formally, XML 1.1 is a very small change to XML; the major change is philosophical. XML 1.1 takes an approach to Unicode that says "if we have no reason to exclude a character, we will not." This means that as Unicode grows, XML automatically inherits those new characters without the W3C publishing new versions of the XML Recommendation. This is good because changing XML even slightly was very controversial. If you consider the number of XML parsers and XML applications out there, you can see that the cost of upgrading XML is quite high. Because of this, the debate over XML 1.1 was long and bitter and no one is looking forward to another one!

Note   *XML 1.1 is almost but not quite a final standard at the time of writing. The chances of significant change are very slim but we felt it better to warn you on the off-chance that something we wrote is no longer accurate by the time you read this. We would hate for you to lose a barroom bet over the exact status of the "PU2" control character!*

Reading the XML specification

Tad Tougher Tutorial

- Grammars
- Rules
- Symbols

Chapter

57

The XML specification is a little tricky to read, but with some work you can get through it by reading and understanding the glossary and applying the concepts described so far in this book. One thing you'll need to know is how to interpret the *production rules* that make up XML's *grammar*. This chapter teaches how to read those rules.

When discussing a particular string, like a tag or declaration, we often want to discuss the parts of that string individually. We call each part of the string a *token*. Tokens can always be separated by white space as described above. Sometimes the white space between the tokens is required. For instance we can represent the months of the year as tokens:

Example 57-1. Tokens

```
JANUARY  FEBRUARY   MARCH     APRIL      MAY         JUNE
```

White space between tokens is *normalized* (combined) so that no matter how much white space you type, the processor treats it as if the tokens were separated by a single space. Thus the example above is equivalent to the following:

Example 57-2. Tokens after normalization

```
JANUARY FEBRUARY MARCH APRIL MAY JUNE
```

Whenever we discuss strings made up of tokens, you will know that you can use as much white space between tokens as you need and the XML processor will normalize it for you.

57.1 | A look at XML's grammar

There are two basic techniques that we could use to discuss XML's syntax precisely. The first is to describe syntactic constructs in long paragraphs of excruciatingly dull prose. The better approach is to develop a simple system for describing syntax. In computer language circles, such systems are called *grammars*. Grammars are more precise and compact. Although they are no less boring (as you may recall from primary school), you can skip them easily until you need to know some specific detail of XML's syntax.

As a bonus, once you know how to read a grammar, you can read the one in the XML specification and thus work your way up to the status of "language lawyer".[1] As XML advances, an ability to read the specification will help you to keep on top of its progress.

The danger in this approach is that you might confuse the grammar with XML markup itself. The grammar is just a definitional tool. It is not used in XML applications. You don't type it in when you create an XML document. You use it to figure out what you *can* type in. Before "the new curriculum", students were taught grammar in primary school. They would be taught parts of speech and how they could combine them. XML's grammar is the same. It will tell you what the parts of an XML document are, and how you can combine them.

Grammars are made up of production *rules* and *symbols*. Rules are simple: they say what is allowed in a particular place in an XML document.

---

1. You too can nitpick about tiny language details and thus prove your superiority over those who merely use XML rather than obsess over it.

Rules have a symbol on the left side, the string "::=" in the middle and a list of symbols on the right side:

Example 57-3. A Rule

```
people ::= 'Melissa' 'Tiffany' 'Joshua' 'Johan'
```

If this rule were part of the grammar for XML (which it is not!) it would say that in a particular place in an XML document you could type the names listed in the order listed.

The symbols on the right (the names, in the last example) define the set of allowed values for the construct described by the rule ("people"). An allowed value is said to *match*. Rules are like definitions in a dictionary. The left side says what is being defined and the right side says what its definition is. Just as words in a dictionary, are defined in terms of other words, symbols are defined in terms of other symbols. Rules in the XML grammar are preceded by a number. You can look the rule up by number. If an XML document does not follow all of the XML production rules, it is not *well-formed*.

57.2 | Constant strings

The most basic type of symbol we will deal with is a *constant string*. These are denoted by a series of characters in between single quote characters. Constant strings are matched case-sensitively (as we discussed earlier). Here are some examples:

Example 57-4. Matching constant strings

```
AlphabetStart ::= 'ABC'
Example1 ::= '<!DOCTYPE'
```

This would match (respectively) the strings

Example 57-5. Matches

```
ABC
<!DOCTYPE
```

When we are discussing a constant string that is an English word or abbreviation, we will refer to it as a *keyword*. In computer languages, a keyword is a word that is interpreted specially by the computer. So your mother's maiden name is not (likely) a keyword, but a word like #REQUIRED is.

Symbols in XML's grammar are separated by spaces, which means that you must match the first, and then the second, and so on in order.

Example 57-6. Representing sequence

```
AlphabetStartAndEnd ::= 'ABC' 'XYZ'
NumbersAndLetters ::= '123' 'QPZ'
```

These would match:

Example 57-7. Sequence matches

```
ABCXYZ
123QPZ
```

Note that a space character in the grammar does not equate to white space in the XML document. Wherever white space can occur we will use the symbol "S". That means that wherever the grammar specifies "S", you may put in as much white space as you need to make your XML source file maintainable.

Example 57-8. Whitespace

```
SpacedOutAlphabet ::= 'ABC' S 'XYZ'
```

matches:

Example 57-9. Matching whitespace

```
ABC XYZ
ABC     XYZ
ABC                   XYZ
```

This is the first example we have used where a single rule matches multiple strings. This is usually the case. Just as in English grammar there are many possible verbs and nouns, there are many possible strings that match the rule SpacedOutAlphabet, depending on how much white space you choose to make your XML source file maintainable.

Obviously XML would not be very useful if you could only insert predefined text and white space. After all, XML users usually like to choose the topic and content of their documents! So they need to have the option of inserting their own content: a *user defined string*. The simplest type of user defined string is *character data*. This is simply the text that isn't markup. You can put almost any character in character data. The exceptions are characters that would be confused with markup, such as less-than and ampersand symbols.

57.3 | Names

The XML specification uses the symbol "Name" to represent names. For example:

Example 57-10. Names

```
PersonNamedSmith :: = Name S 'Smith'
```

When we combine the name, the white space and the constant string, the rule matches strings like these:

Example 57-11. Matching names

```
Christina Smith
Allan      Smith
Michael     Smith
Black        Smith
Bla_ck        Smith
_Black         Smith
```

57.4 | Occurrence indicators

Sometimes a string is *optional*. We will indicate this by putting a question mark after the symbol that represents it in a rule:

Example 57-12. Optional strings

```
Description ::= 'Tall' S? 'dark'? S? 'handsome'? S? 'person'
Tall person
Tallperson
Tall handsomeperson
Tall dark person
Talldarkhandsomeperson
```

Notice that optionality does not affect the order of the tokens. For example, dark can never go before tall. We can also allow a part of a rule to be matched multiple times. If we want to allow a part to be matched one or more times, we can use the plus symbol and make it *repeatable*.

Example 57-13. Repeatable parts

```
VeryTall ::= 'A' S ('very' S)+ 'tall' S 'person.'
A very tall person.
A very very tall person.
A very very very tall person.
```

An asterisk is similar, but it allows a string to be matched zero or more times. In other words it is both repeatable and optional.

Example 57-14. Both repeatable and optional

```
VerySmall ::= 'A' S ('very' S)* 'small' S 'person.'
A small person.
A very small person.
A very very small person.
A very very very small person.
```

Symbols can be grouped with parentheses so that you could, for instance, make a whole series of symbols optional at once. This is different from making them each optional separately because you must either supply strings for all of them or none:

Example 57-15. Grouping with parentheses

```
Description2 ::= 'A' S ('tall' S 'dark' S 'handsome' S)? 'man.'
```

This rule matches these two strings (and no others):

Example 57-16. Matching groups

```
A tall dark handsome man.
A man.
```

We will sometimes have a choice of symbols to use. This is indicated by separating the alternatives by a vertical bar:

Example 57-17. Optional parts

```
Description3 ::= 'A' S ('short'|'tall') S
                     ('fair'|'tan'|'dark') S ('man'|'woman') '.'
A tall dark man.
A short fair woman.
A short tan man.
A tall dark woman.
```

Note that we broke a single long rule over two lines rather than having it run off of the end of the page. This does not in any way affect the meaning of the rule. Line breaks are just treated like space characters between the symbols.

We can combine all of these types of symbols. This allows us to make more complex rules.

Example 57-18. Combining types of symbols

```
Book ::= (('Fascinating'|'Intriguing') S ('XML'|'SGML') S 'Book')
              | ('Yet another HTML' S 'Book')
Fascinating XML Book
Yet another HTML Book
Intriguing SGML Book
```

So in this case, you should treat the first large parenthesized expression (saying good things about SGML and XML books) as one option, and the second (saying not as good things about HTML books) as another. Inside the first set, you can choose different adjectives and book types, but the ordering is fixed and there must be white space between each part.

57.5 | Combining rules

Finally, rules can refer to other rules. Where one rule refers to another, you just make a valid value for each part and then put the parts together like building blocks.

Example 57-19. Combining rules

```
FunnyDate ::= Month S Day ',' Year
Month ::= 'Jan'|'Feb'|'Mar'|'Apr'|'May'|'Jun'
             |'Jul'|'Aug'|'Sep'|'Oct'|'Nov'|'Dec'
Day ::= ('1'|'2'|'3')?
             ('1'|'2'|'3'|'4'|'5'|'6'|'7'|'8'|'9'|'0')
Year ::= '1998'|'1999'|'2000'|'2001'|'2002'
```

This would match strings such as:

Example 57-20. Matching strings

```
Jan 21,1998
May 35,2000
Sep 2,2002
```

As you can see, this is not quite a strict specification for dates, but it gets the overall form or *syntax* of them right.

57.6 | Conclusion

We've explained the bulk of what is needed to understand XML's production rules. There are a few more details that you can find in section 6 of the XML spec itself. It is included in the XML SPECtacular on the CD-ROM.

XPath Tutorials

- A stroll down XPath!
- XML Path Language primer
- Formal XPath tutorial
- Full spec on CD-ROM

Part Twenty

This part covers the XML Path Language (XPath), the primary means of addressing and querying XML documents. You'll need a pretty firm grasp of the material in Part 18, "XML Core Tutorials" before you tackle this subject.

To help you follow the XPath, we've included both a primer and a more formal tutorial.

XPath Primer

Friendly Tutorial

- Location paths
- Addressing multiple objects
- Children and descendants
- Attributes
- Predicates

X Path is a notation for addressing information within a document. That information could be:

- An "executive summary" of a longer document.
- A glossary of terms whose definitions are scattered throughout a manual.
- The specific sequence of steps, buried in a large reference work, needed to solve a particular problem.
- The customized subset of information that a particular customer subscribes to.
- All the sections and subsections of a book that were written by a particular author or revised since a specific date.
- For documents holding information from relational databases, all the typical queries made of relational databases: a particular patient's medical records, the address of the customer with the most orders, the inventory items with low stock levels, and so on.
- For documents that are containers for document collections, all the typical queries made in a library catalog or on a website:

articles about Abyssinian cats, essays on the proper study of mankind, etc.

A programmer working with an XML-aware programming or scripting language could write code to search the document for the information that meets the specified criteria. The purpose of XPath is to automate this searching so that a non-programming user can address the information just by writing an expression that contains the criteria.

58.1 | Location paths

In order to retrieve something, you need to know where to find it – in other words, its *address*.

An address doesn't have to be an absolute location; you can address things relatively ("two doors down from 29 Jones St."). It doesn't have to be an explicit location at all: you can address things by name ("Lance") or description ("world's greatest athlete").

You can address several things at once ("Monty and Westy"), even if you don't know exactly what they are or whether they even exist ("inexpensive French restaurant downtown").

All those forms of address can be used to locate things in XML documents, by means of an *XPath expression.*

The most important form of XPath expression is called a *location path.* If you use UNIX or Windows, you may already be familiar with location paths because they are used to address files by specifying the path from the file system's root to a specific subdirectory. For example, the path /home/bob/xml/samples identifies a particular one of the four samples subdirectories shown in Figure 58-1.

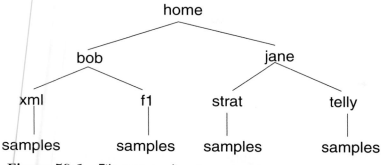

Figure 58-1   File system directory structure

58.2 | Addressing multiple objects

A location path is capable of addressing multiple objects. For example, the expression in Example 58-1 addresses all `caption` elements within `figure` elements that are within `chapter` elements within `book` elements.

Example 58-1. Location path

```
/book/chapter/figure/caption
```

In the book whose structure is shown in Figure 58-2, the expression in Example 58-1 would address the first two `caption` elements, because they are children of `figure` elements. It would not address the third, which is the child of an `example` element.

Example 58-2 shows the XML representation of the book.

58.3 | Children and descendants

The `/book/chapter/figure/caption` expression addresses two elements with no children other than data. The expression `/book/chapter/figure`,

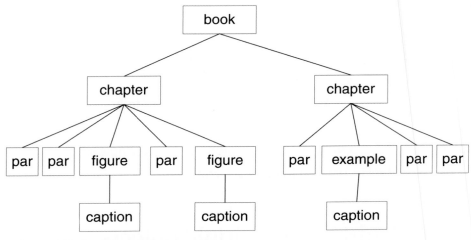

Figure 58-2   Document structure

Example 58-2. A short book in XML

```
<?xml version="1.0"?>
<book>
  <chapter>
    <par author="bd">First paragraph. <emph>Really.</emph></par>
    <par author="cg">Second paragraph.</par>
    <figure picfile="one.jpg">
      <caption>The first figure's caption</caption>
    </figure>
    <par>Third paragraph.</par>
    <figure picfile="two.jpg">
      <caption>The second figure's caption.</caption>
    </figure>
  </chapter>
  <chapter>
    <par author="pp">Chapter 2, first paragraph.</par>
    <example>
      <caption>The first example.</caption>
    </example>
    <par>Chapter 2, second paragraph.</par>
    <par author="bd">Chapter 2, third paragraph.</par>
  </chapter>
</book>
```

however, addresses the figure elements with their caption children, as shown in Example 58-3.

Example 58-3. Figure elements with their caption children

```
<figure picfile="one.jpg">
  <caption>The first figure's caption</caption>
</figure>
<figure picfile="two.jpg">
  <caption>The second figure's caption.</caption>
</figure>
```

The location path /book addresses the entire document.

In a location path, the slash character (/) means "child of." A double slash (//) means "descendant of," which is more flexible as it includes children, grandchildren, great-grandchildren, and so on. For example, /book//caption addresses any caption element descended from a book element. In the book shown in Figure 58-2 it would address the example element's caption from the book's second chapter along with the figure elements' two caption elements:

Example 58-4. Caption elements descended from the book element

```
<caption>The first figure's caption</caption>
<caption>The second figure's caption.</caption>
<caption>The first example.</caption>
```

58.4 | Attributes

An address in XML document navigation is not a storage address like a file system path, despite the similarity in syntax. An XPath expression locates objects by their position in a document's structure and other properties, such as the values of attributes.

A diagram like Figure 58-2 should not present an attribute's information as a child of the element exhibiting the attribute. To do so would be incorrect, because attributes are not siblings of subelements. For this reason, XPath uses /@ to show the element/attribute relationship.

For example, the expression in Example 58-5 addresses all the values of the `par` elements' `author` attributes.

Example 58-5. Expression with an attribute

```
/book//par/@author
```

Example 58-6. Objects addressed by Example 58-6

```
bd
cg
pp
bd
```

58.5 | Predicates

A *predicate* is an expression that changes the group of objects addressed by another expression that precedes it. A predicate expression is delimited by square brackets and is either true or false. If true, it adds to the objects addressed; if false, it removes objects.

For example, the expression in Example 58-7 addresses all chapters that have a `figure` element in them.

Example 58-7. Addressing chapters with a `figure` element

```
/book/chapter[figure]
```

The predicate expression `figure` is true for any `chapter` that contains a `figure`. If true, that `chapter` is included among the addressed objects. Note that the `figure` itself is not among the objects addressed (although it is contained within the addressed `chapter` object).

A predicate expression can be a comparison. For example, `.=` lets you address an element by comparing its content data to a specific character string. Example 58-8 uses this technique to address all the `par` elements that have "Second paragraph." as their content data.

Example 58-8. Addressing `par` elements with specific content data

```
/book//par[.="Second paragraph."]
```

Example 58-9. Objects addressed by Example 58-8

```
<par author="cg">Second paragraph.</par>
```

 Tip   An advanced tutorial on XPath can be found in Chapter 59, "XML Path Language (XPath)", on page 924.

XML Path Language (XPath)

Tad Tougher Tutorial

- XPath applications
- XPath data model
- Location expressions
- XPath 2.0
- XQuery

Contributing expert: G. Ken Holman of Crane Softwrights Ltd.,
http://www.CraneSoftwrights.com, author of *Definitive XSLT and XPath*

Chapter

59

All XML processing depends upon the idea of *addressing*. In order to do something with data you must be able to locate it. To start with, you need to be able to actually find the XML document on the Web. Once you have it, you need to be able to find the information that you need within the document.

The Web has a uniform solution for the first part. The XML document is called a *resource* and *Uniform Resource Identifiers* are the Web's way of addressing resources. The most popular form of Uniform Resource Identifier is the ubiquitous Uniform Resource Locator (URL).

The standard way to locate information *within* an XML document is through a language known as the *XML Path Language* or *XPath*. XPath can be used to refer to textual data, elements, attributes and other information in an XML document.

XPath is a sophisticated, complex language. We will cover its most commonly used features, most of which are available using an abbreviated form of its syntax.

59.1 | XPath applications

Over the last few years, XPath has become a basic building block of XML systems. Let's look at just a few of the applications of XPath.

59.1.1 *User scenarios*

Consider the process of stylesheet creation. A paragraph of text in one chapter may refer to another chapter through a cross-reference. During style application it makes sense to fetch the title of the referenced chapter and its chapter number. The stylesheet could then insert those pieces of information into the text of the cross-reference. For example, the marked-up phrase "`Please see <crossref refid="introduction.chapter">`" might be rendered as "Please see Chapter 1, Introduction." XPath can be used within XSLT to find the appropriate chapter, find its title and locate the text of the title.

Now consider an e-commerce application. It might receive a purchase order from another system. In order to do accounting it would need to know the prices of the purchased items. In XPath notation it would locate "`/po/item/price`", meaning all of the prices in all of the items in the current purchase order document.

Finally, imagine an ordinary Web surfer of the near future. He might be reading his favorite recipes Web page. Unbeknownst to him, the page is written in XML (this is the near future, after all!). As he scrolls through, he finds a recipe that he would really love to share with his brother-in-law. He clicks the right mouse button at the beginning of the recipe. One of the choices in the popup menu might be: "email this Web address."

The menu item would instruct the browser to email a string of characters, termed a *URI reference* to a particular email address. The URI reference would uniquely identify not just the Web page but also the particular `recipe` element. The first part of the string would be an ordinary URI, pointing to the Web page. The last part would be an *XPointer*. XPointers are a customization of XPath for use in URI references.

As you can see, XPath is a valuable tool in all sorts of XML processing. By the way, only the last of these examples is slightly science-fiction-ish. The use of XPath in the other contexts is quite common these days.

59.1.2   *Specifications built on XPath*

XPath was developed when the groups responsible for XSLT and XPointer realized that they had to provide many of the same addressing functions and could develop a shared solution.

These two World Wide Web Consortium specifications depend upon XPath today. XPointer uses XPath to build Web addresses (URI references) that reference parts of XML documents. URI references can address individual points and elements, as in our recipe example. They can also address lists of elements, attributes or characters.

The XSL Transformations language (XSLT) uses XPath for transformation and style application. As in our cross-reference example, XPath can be used to retrieve information from somewhere else in the document. XPath can also be used to declare that certain XSLT style rules apply to particular elements in the input document.

The *XML Schema* definition language (XSDL) also uses XPaths. It uses them to express so-called identity constraints. Using identity constraints you could require that every `employee` or `customer` element has a unique `person-id` sub-element. An XPath would be used to select the `employee` and `customer` elements and another XPath would select the contained `person-id` subelements. There is even a schema language that uses XPath to express *all* constraints. It is called *Schematron*.

XQuery is yet another W3C specification embedding XPath. XQuery is a full query language. We discuss it in 59.5.2, "XML Query Language (XQuery)", on page 955.

XPath's syntax was carefully chosen. XPath needs to fit easily into attribute values, browser URI fields and other places where XML's element-within-element syntax would be cumbersome. XSLT, XPointer, XSDL, Schematron and XQuery all use XPath within attribute values. Accordingly, XPath's syntax is very concise and does not depend on an XML parser.

XPath is designed to be extensible. W3C specifications and other XPath applications can create extensions specific to the application's problem domain. XPointer and XSLT already extend XPath.

59.1.2.1   An XLink example

Example 59-1 shows an anchor element with an `xlink:href` attribute. The attribute value contains a URI reference. The reference contains an XPointer (starting with the string `xpointer`). The characters within the parentheses are an XPath expression.

Example 59-1. XLink use of XPath

```
<A xlink:type="simple"
   xlink:href="info.xml#xpointer(id('smith')/info[@type='public'])">
   Mr. John Smith
</A>
```

59.1.2.2   An XSLT example

An example of the XSLT use of the same XPath expression is the `select` attribute of Example 59-2.

Example 59-2. XSLT selecting based on XPath

```
<xsl:apply-templates select="id('smith')/info[@type='public']"/>
```

This `select` attribute finds the element identified `smith` and identifies the `info` subelements with the attribute `type` having the value "public". It then processes each of those `info` elements with an XSLT *template rule*. The applicable rule is found by matching each element against an XSLT pattern in the template's match attribute. Example 59-3 demonstrates.

Example 59-3. XSLT use of XPath

```
<xsl:template match="info[@type='public']">
   ...
</xsl:template>
```

59.2 | The XPath data model

It is only possible to construct an address — any address — given a model. For instance the US postal system is composed of a model of states containing cities containing streets with house numbers. To some degree the model falls naturally out of the geography of the country but it is mostly artificial. State and city boundaries are not exactly visible from an airplane. We give new houses street numbers so that they can be addressed within the postal system's model.

Relational databases also have a model that revolves around tables, records, columns, foreign keys and so forth. This "relational model" is the basis for the SQL query language. Just as SQL depends on the relational model, XPath depends on a formal model of the logical structure and data in an XML document.

59.2.1 *Sources of the model*

You may wonder if XML really needs a formal model. It seems so simple: elements within elements, attributes of elements and so forth. It *is* simple but there are details that need to be standardized in order for addresses to behave in a reliable fashion. The tricky part is that there are many ways of representing what might seem to be the "same" information. We can represent a less-than symbol in at least four ways:

- a predefined entity reference: `&lt;`
- a CDATA section: `<![CDATA[<]]>`
- a decimal Unicode character reference: `&#60;`
- a hex Unicode character reference: `&#x3c;`

We could also reference a text entity that embeds a CDATA section and a text entity that embeds another text entity that embeds a character reference, etc. In a query you would not want to explicitly search for the less-than symbol in all of these variations. It would be easier to have a processor that could magically *normalize* them to a single model. Every XPath-based query engine needs to get exactly the same data model from any particular XML document.

The XML equivalent of the relational model is termed, depending on the context, either a *grove*, an *information set* or a *data model*.

59.2.1.1   Grove

The *grove* is the original SGML model from ISO and is important when you are working with International Standards like HyTime, Topic Maps and DSSSL.

59.2.1.2   XML Information Set (Infoset)

The *XML Information Set* W3C Recommendation defines the important information in an XML document, for use by other W3C specifications.[1] Whereas the grove is generalized and can work with both XML and non-XML data notations, the Information Set is specific to XML.

As XPath is a W3C specification and is only for addressing into XML documents, its data model is derived from the W3C XML Information Set.[2]

59.2.1.3   XPath data model

The XPath specification does not use the Information Set directly. The Information Set takes a more liberal view of what is "important" than XPath does. Therefore XPath has a concept of an *XPath data model*: an Information Set with some XPath-irrelevant parts filtered out.

For instance the Information Set says that it may be important to keep track of what entity each element resides within. The XPath developers chose not to care about that information and it is not, therefore, part of the XPath data model.

Although the XPath data model and the Infoset differ, XPath's data model is inherited to some extent or other by all of the specifications that build on it. This is especially true of the new XQuery specification.

---

1. The infoset is discussed in detail in 55.6, "XML Information Set (Infoset)", on page 890.
2. Perhaps one day a grove-based XPath might be invented. It might allow querying arbitrary information types based on topic metadata.

59.2.2 *Tree addressing*

The XPath data model views a document as a tree of nodes, or *node tree*. Most nodes correspond to document components, such as elements and attributes.

It is very common to think of XML documents as being either families (elements have child elements, parent elements and so forth) or trees (roots, branches and leaves). This is natural: trees and families are both hierarchical in nature, just as XML documents are. XPath uses both metaphors but tends to lean more heavily on the familial one.[3]

XPath uses genealogical taxonomy to describe the hierarchical makeup of an XML document, referring to children, descendants, parents and ancestors. The parent is the element that contains the element under discussion. The list of ancestors includes the parent, the parent's parent and so forth. A list of descendants includes children, children's children and so forth.

As there is no culture-independent way to talk about the first ancestor, XPath calls it the "root". The root is not an element. It is a logical construct that holds the document element and any comments and processing instructions that precede and follow it.[4]

Trees in computer science are very rarely (if ever) illustrated as a natural tree is drawn, with the root at the bottom and the branches and leaves growing upward. Far more typically, trees are depicted with the root at the top just as family trees are. This is probably due to the nature of our writing systems and the way we have learned to read.[5] Accordingly, this chapter refers to stepping "down" the tree towards the leaf-like ends and "up" the tree towards the root as the tree is depicted in Figure 59-1. One day we will genetically engineer trees to grow this way and nature will be in harmony with technology.

---

3. Politicians take note: in this case, family values win out over environmentalism!
4. In the full Information Set, the root is called the document information item and it also contains information about the document's DTD.
5. To do: rotate all tree diagrams for Japanese edition of *The XML Handbook*.

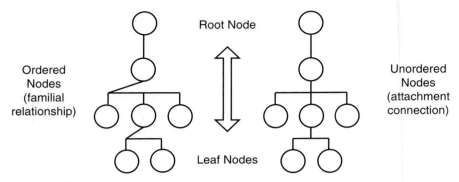

Figure 59-1   Vertical tree depictions

59.2.3   *Node tree construction*

A *node tree* is built by an XPath processor after parsing an XML document like that in Example 59-4.

Example 59-4. Sample document

```
<?xml version="1.0"?>
<!--start-->
<part-list><part-name nbr="A12">bolt</part-name>
<part-name nbr="B45">washer</part-name><warning type="ignore"/>
<!--end of list--><?cursor blinking?>
</part-list>
<!--end of file-->
```

In constructing the node tree, the boundaries and contents of "important" constructs are preserved, while other constructs are discarded. For example, entity references to both internal and external entities are expanded and character references are resolved. The boundaries of CDATA sections are discarded. Characters within the section are treated as character data.

The node tree constructed from the document in Example 59-4 is shown in Figure 59-2. In the following sections, we describe the components of node trees and how they are used in addressing. You may want to refer back to this diagram from time to time as we do so.

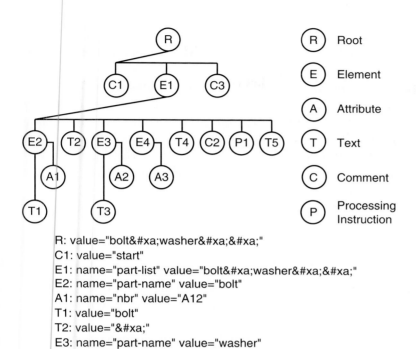

R: value="bolt
washer

"
C1: value="start"
E1: name="part-list" value="bolt
washer

"
E2: name="part-name" value="bolt"
A1: name="nbr" value="A12"
T1: value="bolt"
T2: value="
"
E3: name="part-name" value="washer"
A2: name="nbr" value="b45"
T3: value="washer"
E4: name="warning" value=""
A3: name="type" value="ignore"
T4: value="

C2: value="end of list"
P1: name="cursor" value="blinking"
T5: value="

C3: value="end of file"

Figure 59-2   Node tree for document in Example 59-4

59.2.4   *Node types*

The XPath data model describes seven types of nodes used to construct the node tree representing any XML document. We are interested primarily in the root, element, attribute and text node types, but will briefly discuss the others.

For each node type, XPath defines a way to compute a *string-value* (labeled "value" in Figure 59-2). Some node types also have a "name".

59.2.4.1 Root node

The top of the hierarchy that represents the XML document is the root node.

It is important to remember that in the XPath data model the root of the tree representing an XML document is *not the document (or root) element of the document*. A root *node* is different from a root *element*. The root node *contains* the root element.

The nodes that are children of the root node represent the document element and the comments and processing instructions found before and after the document element.

59.2.4.2 Element nodes

Every element in an XML document is represented in the node tree as an element node. Each element has a parent node. Usually an element's parent is another element but the document element has as its parent the root node.

Element nodes can have as their children other element nodes, text nodes, comment nodes and processing instruction nodes.

An element node also exhibits properties, such as its name, its attributes and information about its active namespaces.

Element nodes in documents with DTDs may have unique identifiers. These allow us to address element nodes by name. IDs are described in 52.6.3.4, "ID and IDREF attributes", on page 819.

The string-value of an element node is the concatenation of the string-values of all text node descendants of the element node in the document order. You can think of it as all of the data with none of the markup, organized into one long character string.

59.2.4.3 Text nodes

The XML Recommendation describes character data as all text that is not markup. In other words it is the textual data content of the document and it does not include data in attribute values, processing instructions and comments.

> *Caution*   The word "text" means something different in XPath from its meaning in the XML Recommendation (and the rest of this book!). We'll try to minimize the confusion by always saying "text node", even when the context is clear, reserving "text" as a noun for its normal meaning.

XPath does not care how a character was originally represented. The string "<>" in an XML document is simply "<>" from the data model's point of view. The same goes for "&60;&62;" and "<![CDATA[<>]]>". The characters represented by any of these will be grouped with the data characters that precede and follow them and called a "text node." The individual characters of the text node are not considered its children: they are just part of its value. Text nodes do not have any children.

Remember that whitespace is significant. A text node might contain nothing else. In Figure 59-2, for example, nodes T2, T4, and T5 contain line feed characters, represented by hexadecimal character references.[6]

59.2.4.4   Attribute nodes

If an element has attributes then these are represented as attribute nodes. These nodes are not considered children of the element node. They are more like friends that live in the guest house.

An attribute node exhibits name, string-value, and namespace URI properties. Defaulted attributes are reported as having the default values. The data model does not record whether they were explicitly specified or merely defaulted. No node is created for an unspecified attribute that had an #IMPLIED default value declared. Attribute nodes are also not created for attributes used as namespace declarations.

---

6. Character references are describe in 55.2, "Character references", on page 880.

elements that have (or do not have) particular attributes with particular values. Or we may be interested in the first or seventh element, or just the even-numbered ones.

We can express these constraints with qualifiers called *predicates*. Any step can be qualified. The location path in Example 59-5, for example,

Note that an XML processor is not required to read an external DTD unless it is validating the document. This means that detection of ID attributes and default attribute values is not mandatory.

59.2.4.5   Other node types

N̶...̶ ̶ ̶n̶o̶d̶e̶s̶ keep track of the set of namespace prefix/URI pairs that

selects the seventh paragraph from each section with a security attribute whose string-value is "public".

Example 59-5. Selecting the seventh para from each public section

```
/mydoc/section[@security="public"]/para[7]
```

59.3.1.3   Selection

Note that we use the word *select* carefully. We could say that the expression *returns* certain nodes but that might put a picture in your head of nodes being ripped out of the tree and handed to you: "Here are your nodes!"

Rather, what you get back is a set of locations – pointers to the nodes. Imagine the result of a location path as a set of arrows pointing into the node tree, saying: "Your nodes are here!"

59.3.1.4   Context

The context node keeps changing as we step down the path. As each step is evaluated, the result is a set of nodes – in XPath talk, a *node-set*. The node-set could have one or more nodes, or it could be empty.

The next step is then evaluated for each member of that node-set. That is, each member is used as the context node for one of the evaluations of the next step. The node-sets selected by each of those evaluations are combined (except for any duplicates) to produce the result node-set.

Consider what happens in Example 59-5.

1. The XPath processor first evaluates the "/". The root node becomes the initial context node.
2. Next it looks for every child of the context node with the name "mydoc". There will be only one member of that node-set because XML allows only a single root element. It becomes the context node for the next step, which is evaluated only once.
3. Next the processor looks for all of the section children in the context of the mydoc element that have the appropriate attribute value and returns their node-set. The next step will

be evaluated once for each selected `section` node, which is the context node for that evaluation.

4. We're almost done. The processor looks for the seventh `para` several times, once for each `section` in the node-set. It puts the selected `para` nodes together into the final node-set and returns a set of pointers to them: "Your nodes are here!".

The initial context does not always have to be the root node of the document. It depends on the environment or application. Whatever application (e.g. database or browser) or specification (e.g. XSLT or XPointer) is using XPath must specify the starting context.

In XSLT there is always a concept of the *current node*. That node is the context node for location paths that appear in XSLT transforms. In XPointer, the starting context is always the root node of the particular document, selected by its URI. In some sort of document database, we might be allowed to do a query across thousands of documents. The root node of each document would become the context node in turn. XPath itself does not have a concept of working with multiple documents but it can be used in a system that does.

In addition to the current node, an application could specify some other details of the context: it could supply some values for variables and functions that can be used in the XPath expression. It could also include namespace information that can be used to interpret prefixed names in a location path.

59.3.1.5 Axes

But wait. That's not all! Up to now we've always stepped down the tree, to a child element. But we can also step *up* the tree instead of down and step many levels instead of one.

We can step in directions that are neither up nor down but more like sideways. For example we can step from elements to attributes and from attributes to elements.

We can also step from an element directly to a child of a child of a child (a descendant).

These different ways of stepping are called *axes*.

For example, the *descendant axis* (abbreviated `//`) can potentially step down all the levels of the tree. The location path "`/mydoc//footnote`" would select all footnotes in the current document, no matter how many levels deep they occur.

The *parent axis* uses an abbreviated syntax (..) that is similar to that for going up a directory in a file system. For instance we could select all of the elements *containing* a footnote like this: "`/mydoc//footnote/..`".

The *attribute axis* (abbreviated "@") steps into the attribute nodes of an element.

The *namespace axis* is used for namespace information associated with an element node.

There are a number of less commonly used axes as well. You can find out more about them in the XPath specification.

59.3.1.6   Node tests

The attribute and namespace axes each have only one type of node, which is (necessarily!) its principal node type.

The other axes, however, have element as the principal node type but have comment, processing instruction, and text node types as well. We'll refer to such an axis as a *content axis* and its nodes as *content nodes*.

A step normally selects nodes of the principal type. In the case of content axes, a node test can be used to select another type. For example, the node test `text()` selects text nodes.

59.3.2   *Anatomy of a step*

We've now seen enough of the basics to take a formal look at the parts of a location step. There are three:

- An axis, which specifies the tree relationship between the context node and the nodes selected by the location step. Our examples so far have used the child axis.
- A node test, which specifies the node type of the nodes selected by the location step. The default type is element, unless the axis is one that can't have element nodes.
- Zero or more predicates, which use arbitrary expressions to further refine the set of nodes selected by the location step. The expressions are full-blown XPath expressions and can

include function calls and location paths. In Example 59-5 the first predicate is a location path and the second uses an abbreviation for the `position()` function.

In this tutorial, we've only been using abbreviated forms of the XPath syntax, in which common constructs can often be omitted or expressed more concisely. Example 59-6 shows the unabbreviated form of Example 59-5. Note the addition of explicit axis names (`child` and `attribute`) and the `position()` function call.

Example 59-6. Unabbreviated form of Example 59-5

```
/child::mydoc/child::section[attribute::security="public"]
            /child::para[position()=7]
```

In the remainder of the chapter, we'll take a closer look at each of the three parts: node tests, axes, and predicates.

59.3.2.1   Node tests

Some node tests are useful in all axes; others only in content axes.
Node tests for all axes are:

`*`

any node of the principal type; i.e., element, attribute, or namespace.[8]

`node()`

any node of any type

Node tests solely for content axes are:

`text()`

any text node

---

8. The asterisk *cannot* be used as a prefix (`"*ara"`) or suffix (`"ara*"`) as it is in some regular-expression languages.

```
comment()
```
> any comment node

```
processing-instruction()
```
> any processing-instruction node, regardless of its target name

```
processing-instruction(target-name)
```
> any processing-instruction node with the specified target name

Here are some examples of node tests used in a *content* axis:

```
processing-instruction(cursor)
```
> all nodes created from a processing instruction with the target name "cursor"

```
part-nbr
```
> all nodes created from an element with the element-type name `part-nbr`

```
text()
```
> all text nodes (contrast below)

```
text
```
> all nodes created from an element with the element-type name `text`

```
*
```
> all nodes created from elements, irrespective of the element-type name

```
node()
```
> all nodes created from elements (irrespective of the element-type name), contiguous character data, comments or processing instructions (irrespective of the target name)

59.3.2.2   Axes

The most important axes are described here.

59.3.2.2.1 *Child*

The default axis is the child axis. That means that if you ask for "/section/para" you are looking for a para in a section. If you ask merely for "para" you are looking for the para element children of the context node, whatever it is.

59.3.2.2.2 *Attribute*

When using the symbol "@" before either an XML name or the node test "*", one is referring to the attribute axis of the context node.

The attribute nodes are attached to an element node but the nodes are not ordered. There is no "first" or "third" attribute of an element.

Attribute nodes have a string-value that is the attribute value, and a name that is the attribute name.

Some examples of abbreviated references to attribute nodes attached to the context node are:

@type
   an attribute node whose name is "type"

@*

   all attributes of the context node, irrespective of the attribute name

59.3.2.2.3 *Descendant*

We can use the double-slash "//" abbreviation in a location path to refer to the descendant axis.[9] This axis includes not only children of the context node, but also all other nodes that are descendants of the context node.

This is a very powerful feature. We could combine this with the wildcard node test, for example, to select all elements in a document, other than the document element, no matter how deep they are: "/doc//*".

Some examples:

9. You may read in the XPath spec that the axis referred to by the abbreviation is actually the descendant-or-self axis. However, that is merely a technical device to enable the abbreviation to have the desired effect of referencing all descendants. The formal expansion of the abbreviation introduces another step, which would otherwise have caused children of the context node to be excluded. We refer to "//" as standing for the descendant axis because that's the way it acts.

```
/mydoc//part-nbr
```
> all element nodes with the element-type name `part-nbr` that are descendants of the `mydoc` document element; that is, all of the `part-nbr` elements in the document

```
/mydoc//@type
```
> all attribute nodes named `type` attached to any descendant element of the `mydoc` document element; i.e., all of the `type` attributes in the document

```
/mydoc//*
```
> all elements that are descendants of the `mydoc` document element; i.e., every element in the document except the `mydoc` element itself

```
/mydoc//comment()
```
> all comment nodes that are descendants of the `mydoc` document element

```
/mydoc//text()
```
> all of the text nodes that are descendants of the `mydoc` document element; i.e., all of the character data in the document!

We do not have to start descendant expressions with the document element. If we want to start somewhere farther into the document we can use "`//`" in any step anywhere in the location path.

We could also begin with "`//`". A location path that starts with "`//`" is interpreted as starting at the root and searching all descendants of it, including the document element.

59.3.2.2.4 *Self*

The self axis is unique in that it has only one node: the context node. This axis can solve an important problem.[10]

10.In fact, we suspect it was invented for that purpose only. It is another ingenious hack, like the one in the previous footnote, for enabling convenient abbreviations to be mapped onto a coherent normalized form.

For instance in an XSLT transformation we might want to search for all descendants of the current node. If we begin with "//" the address will start at the root. We need a way to refer specifically to the current node.

A convenient way to do this is with an abbreviation: a period (.) stands for the context node.[11]

So ".//footnote" would locate all footnote descendants of the context node.

59.3.2.2.5 *Parent*

The parent axis (..) of a content node selects its parent, as the axis name suggests. For a namespace or attribute node, however, it selects the node's attached element.

You could therefore search an entire document for a particular attribute and then find out what element it is attached to: "//@confidential/..". You could go on to find out about the element's parent (and the parent's parent, etc.): "//@confidential/../..".

59.3.2.2.6 *Ancestor*

There is also a way of searching for an ancestor by name, but it does not have an abbreviated syntax. For example, "ancestor::section" would look for the ancestor(s) of the context node that are named "section".

This location path locates the titles of sections that contain images: "//image/ancestor::section/title".

59.3.3 *Our story so far*

Here are some examples of location paths using features we have covered so far:

item
     item element nodes that are children of the context node

---

11. This "dot-convention" also comes from the file system metaphor. Unix and Windows use "." to mean the current directory.

`item/para`

para element nodes that are children of `item` element nodes that are children of the context node; in other words, those `para` grandchildren of the context node whose parent is an `item`

`//para`

para element nodes that are descendants of the root node; in other words, all the `para` element nodes in the entire document

`//item/para`

para element nodes that are children of all `item` element nodes in the entire document

`//ordered-list//para`

para element nodes that are descendants of all `ordered-list` element nodes in the entire document

`ordered-list//para/@security`

security attribute nodes attached to all `para` element nodes that are descendants of all `ordered-list` element nodes that are children of the context node

`*/@*`

attribute nodes attached to all element nodes that are children of the context node

`../@*`

attribute nodes attached to the parent or attached node of the context node

`.//para`

para element nodes that are descendants of the context node

```
.//comment()
```
comment nodes that are descendants of the context node

> *Tip*   The XPath specification includes numerous other examples of location paths. You can find it on the CD-ROM.

59.3.4 *Predicates*

It is often important to filter nodes out of a node-set. We might filter out nodes that lack a particular attribute or subelement. We might filter out all but the first node. This sort of filtering is done in XPath through *predicates*. A predicate is an expression that is applied to each node. If it evaluates as false, the tested node is filtered out.

We'll discuss some common types of predicate expressions, then look at some examples.

59.3.4.1   Expression types

59.3.4.1.1 *Node-sets*

A location path expression can be used as a predicate. It evaluates to `true` if it selects any nodes at all. It is false if it does not select any nodes. So Example 59-7 would select all paragraphs that have a footnote child.

Example 59-7. Using a location path as a predicate
```
//para[footnote]
```

Recall that the evaluation of a step in the path results in a node-set, each member of which is a context node for an evaluation of the next step.[12]

One by one, each member of the result node-set, which in this case is every paragraph in the document, would get a chance to be the context

---

12. In other words, Example 59-7 is really an abbreviation for "`//para[./footnote]`".

node. It would either be selected or filtered out, depending on whether it contained any footnotes. Every paragraph would get its bright shining moment in the sun when it could be ".".[13]

A number of predicates can be chained together. Only nodes that pass all of the filters are passed on to the next step in the location path. For example, "`//para[footnote][@important]`" selects all paragraphs with `important` attributes and `footnote` children.

Like other location paths, those in predicates can have multiple steps with their own predicates. Consider the complex one in Example 59-8. It looks for `sections` with `author` child elements with `qualifications` child elements that have both `professional` and `affordable` attributes.

Example 59-8. A complex location path predicate

```
section[author/qualifications[@professional][@affordable]]
```

59.3.4.1.2 *String-values*

Not all predicates are location path expressions. Sometimes you do not want to test for the existence of some node. You might instead want to test whether an attribute has some particular value. That is different from testing whether the attribute exists or not.

Testing an attribute's value is simple: "`@type='ordered'`" tests whether the context node has a `type` attribute with value "`ordered`".

In XPath, every node type has a string-value. The value of an element node that is the context node, for example, is the concatenation of the string-values from the expression: "`.//text()`". In other words, it is all of the character data content anywhere within the element and its descendants.

So we can test the data content of a section's `title` child element with "`section[title='Doo-wop']`" and both of the sections in Example 59-9 would match.

---

13. Unfortunately, the moment is brief and the price of failure is exclusion from the selection set.

Example 59-9. Matching sections

```
<section><title>Doo-wop</title>
...
</section>

<section><title>Doo-<emph>wop</emph></title>
...
</section>
```

59.3.4.1.3 *Context position*

There is more to the context in which an expression is evaluated than just the context node. Among the other things is the node's *context position*, which is returned by a function call: position()=number.

In practice, an abbreviation, consisting of the number alone, is invariably used. A number expression is evaluated as true if the number is the same as the context position.

Context position can be a tricky concept to grasp because it is, well, context-sensitive. However, it is easy to understand for the most common types of steps.

In a step down the child axis (a/b) the context position is the position of the child node in the parent node. So "doc/section[5]" is the fifth section in a doc. In a step down the descendant axis (a//b[5]) it still refers to the position of the child node in its *parent node*, not its numerical order in the list of matching nodes.

XPath also has a function called "last()". We can use it to generate the number for the last node in a context: "a//b[last()]". We can also combine that with some simple arithmetic to get the next-to-last node: "a//b[last()-1]".

59.3.4.2   Predicate examples

Here are some examples, using the predicate types that we've discussed:

item[3]
>   third item element child of the context node

item[@type]/para
>   para element children of item elements that exhibit a type attribute and are children of the context node

```
//list[@type='ordered']/item[1]/para[1]
```
first `para` element child of the first `item` element child of any `list` element that exhibits a `type` attribute with the string-value "ordered"

```
//ordered-list[item[@type]/para[2]]//para
```
`para` elements descended from any `ordered-list` element that has an `item` child that exhibits a `type` attribute and has at least two `para` element children (whew!)

This last example is illustrated in Figure 59-3.

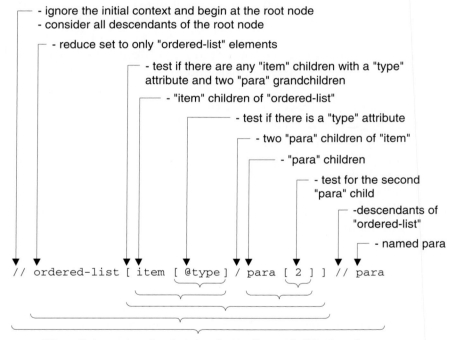

Figure 59-3   Evaluating multiple steps

The XPath spec includes numerous other examples of using predicates. XPath is a powerful expression language, including operators and functions that operate on node-sets, numbers, strings, and booleans.

59.4 | ID function

The most common high-level expression in XPath is the location path, which we have explored in some detail. And, as we have seen, a location path can also be used at lower levels – as a predicate expression, for example.

Another form of expression that returns a node-set is a function call to the id(string) function. The main use of the function is to select the element node whose ID is the same as the string. For example, "id('final')". selects the element node whose unique identifier is "final".

An ID function and a location path can be used in the same expression. One way is to create the union of the two, as in Example 59-10. The result node-set is the element whose ID is "final", plus all para elements descended from ordered-list elements.

Example 59-10. Union expression

```
id('final') | /ordered-list//para
```

Another way to combine the two is to use the ID function as the initial context node of a location path, to create a path expression like that in Example 59-11. It locates the title child of the element whose ID is "A12345".

Example 59-11. Path expression

```
id('A12345')/title
```

Instead of a literal string, the argument could be a node whose string-value would be used, as in "id(@IDREF)". This expression locates the element referenced by the IDREF attribute of the context node.

59.5 | XPath's future

At this writing, the W3C is developing a new version of XPath and an XPath-based query language called XQuery.

59.5.1 *XPath 2.0*

XPath 2.0 is a major upgrade to XPath 1.0. It is much more powerful but also much more complicated. This is what tends to happen to successful software technologies! XPath 2.0 is complicated enough that it will take quite a while to finish its standardization and even longer for various XPath implementations to catch up. You may wonder what you will get when this glorious future arises.

59.5.1.1   Datatypes

Where XPath 1.0 has only four datatypes (node-set, boolean, number and string), XPath 2.0 supports all of the types from *XML Schema*. That includes 19 built-in primitive types (such as dates and URIs) and 25 built-in types derived from numbers and strings. User-derived types are also supported.[14]

XPath 2.0 also adds the sort of features that programming languages with many types tend to have: ways of testing types, converting between types and declaring the types of things. There are dozens of new functions relating to these datatypes. In fact, there are dozens of functions relating to dates alone!

Strings also have a much richer set of associated functions in XPath 2.0. Among other things, they can now be matched against patterns written as regular expressions (discussed in 62.5.6, "The pattern facet", on page 1020). They can also be *tokenized*: broken into component parts that alternately match or fail to match such a pattern. Tokenization results in a *sequence* of strings.

---

14. We describe all of these in Chapter 62, "Datatypes", on page 1000.

59.5.1.2   Sequences

Sequences are another new feature of XPath 2.0. In XPath 1.0, if you want to keep track of multiple "things" it is easy – as long as the "things" are nodes. Otherwise, you are out of luck. XPath 1.0 has only one data structure for managing multiple things and it is the node-set. As the name implies it is only for nodes. In XPath, you can keep track of multiple things of any sort using a sequence.

Sequences have several advantages over node-sets. We'll review some of the major ones here.

59.5.1.2.1   *Set operations*

XPath 2.0 can treat a sequence as a mathematical set (remember high school?) to do intersection, union and difference operations. An intersection of two sequences returns all of the items that occurred in both of the sets. A union returns all of the items that were in either. And the except (difference) operator returns the items that were in one set but not the other.

59.5.1.2.2   *Ordering*

Sequences can be ordered and re-ordered in code. XPath 1.0 node-sets are always processed in an order defined by the notation that is using XPath (e.g. XSLT, XPointer or XQuery). The person creating the node-set has no influence over the order of processing of that node-set.

59.5.1.2.3   *Duplication*

Sequences also allow duplicates whereas node-sets automatically remove duplicates. Consider an XML document that reports occurrences of some event, perhaps solar flares. An XPath expression could select all of the day, year and month attributes of a set of elements to construct date values. Then it could sort them according to the order, or perhaps reverse order, of their chronology. If the flares could happen multiple times in a particular day then it would be useful to allow the same date to appear more than once.

59.5.1.3   Looping

In XPath 1.0, it is not even possible to construct the date values in the solar flare scenario; there is no way to apply a function to each node in a node-list. XSLT could do it but XPath alone could not.

XPath 2.0 is now a more powerful language in its own right. It has a new expression called `for` that can loop over multiple items and do something with each of them. Example 59-12 demonstrates.

Example 59-12. XPath 2.0 looping

```
for $x in //item return $x/@price * $x/@quantity * $x/@tax
```

This expression multiplies the `price`, `quantity` and `tax` attributes of each `item` element in the document. It does this by letting each item in turn become the *variable* `$x` and then processing it using the expression after the keyword `return`. The results are grouped together into a single sequence which is returned as the result of the expression. Other calculations could be done with the resulting sequence or it could be returned to the embedding language such as XSLT for further processing or output.

59.5.1.4   `if` expressions

An `if` expression can be used to return one thing if a particular circumstance holds and another thing otherwise, as Example 59-13 illustrates.

Example 59-13. XPath 2.0 `if` expression

```
if (@security = "eyes-only")
   then "disallowed"
else if (@security = "public-knowledge")
       then "allowed"
else "error"
```

As you can see, XPath 2.0 is adding the sorts of features usually found in programming languages. But XPath 2.0 also adds features that you will not find in most such languages. The new `some` and `every` keywords allow `if` expressions to be quite powerful. For instance you could select an `employee` element if `some` of its performance appraisal sub-elements have a `rating` attribute of "abysmal" or only if every appraisal sub-element was in that dire state.

Analysis   XPath 2.0 will have many features that XPath 1.0 does not. Only real-world use will determine whether those features are worth the price in complexity. Prominent XPath users and implementors are on both sides of the debate. In the meantime, XPath 1.0 works for the vast majority of situations and is a more appropriate focus for your energy. XPath 2.0 will be compatible or very close to compatible with XPath 1.0 through the use of an "XPath 1.0 compatibility mode".

59.5.2 *XML Query Language (XQuery)*

XPath 2.0 is being developed in conjunction with another specification, *XQuery*. Unlike XPath alone, which can only select nodes from a single source document, *XQuery* can actually return XML fragments synthesized from information in multiple XML documents.

59.5.2.1   FLWOR expressions

XQuery extends the direction taken by XPath 2.0's for expression with a group of five expressions, collectively called the *FLWOR expressions*. In acronymical order, the expression types are for, let, where, order by, and return.[15]

Example 59-14 employs them to retrieve the headcount and average salary of all departments with 10 or more employees, in descending order of average salary.

The for statement is used just as in XPath 2.0, but in conjunction with a let statement, which allows the creation of new variables. In this case, the let statement generates the list of all employees with a particular depart-

---

15. Pushing the limits of both the arboreal metaphor for documents and the spelling distortions of puns – and the patience of our readers – we could say that XML documents are trees and XQuery surrounds them with FLWORs.

Example 59-14. XQuery search returning newly-created elements

```
for $d in doc("depts.xml")//deptno
let $e := doc("emps.xml")//emp[deptno = $d]
where count($e) >= 10
order by avg($e/salary) descending
return
  <big-dept>
    {$d}
    <headcount>{count($e)}</headcount>
    <avgsal>{avg($e/salary)}</avgsal>
  </big-dept>
```

ment number. The where statement prunes departments that have fewer than ten individuals. The order by statement orders by average salary in descending order.

The return statement is also like that in XPath 2.0, but here it returns a newly created big-dept element for each selected department. Note that XPath 2.0 alone cannot create new XML like this. It can participate in the process only when it is embedded in XQuery or – as we'll discuss shortly – XSLT.

59.5.2.2   Environmental features

XQuery, as an embedding environment for XPath 2.0, is responsible for things like namespace declarations and function definitions.

59.5.2.2.1 *Declaring a namespace*

XQuery facilities for declaring a namespace are shown in Example 59-15.

Example 59-15. Declaring a namespace in XQuery

```
declare namespace foo = "http://example.org"

/foo:section/foo:p
```

Schemas can be associated with declared namespaces. Example 59-16 demonstrates.

Built-in schema support allows XQuery processors to perform some optimizations and error checks more easily than can be done with XSLT or with

Example 59-16. Declaring a schema in XQuery

```
import schema "http://www.example.org/ns/some_namespace"
            at "http://www.example.org/schemas/schema.xsd"
declare namespace myns = "http://www.example.org/ns/some_namespace"

/myns:chapter/myns:title
```

XPath alone. This notion of "static type checking" is a big part of the "database mindset" that permeates XQuery (and which we'll discuss shortly).

59.5.2.2.2 *Defining a function*

XQuery allows the definition of new functions. A query can be constructed of functions that call functions that call more functions. Such a query strongly resembles a program in a programming language.

Example 59-17 defines and uses a function that builds an XML document summarizing the number of individuals and payroll for all of the departments.

Example 59-17. XQuery function definition

```
define function summary($emps)
{
  for $d in distinct-values($emps/deptno)
  let $e := $emps[deptno = $d]
  return
    <dept>
      <deptno>{$d}</deptno>
      <headcount>{count($e)}</headcount>
      <payroll>{sum($e/salary)}</payroll>
    </dept>
}

summary(doc("acme_corp.xml")//employee[location = "Denver"])
```

Functions can call themselves to handle *recursive* elements, such as lists that contain lists that contain lists.

59.5.2.3   Will XQuery be useful?

As we will see in Chapter 60, "XSL Transformations (XSLT)", on page 962, it is possible to use XSLT for the sort of things that XQuery will be able to do. However, the two languages approach a problem differently.

XQuery uses a query approach: Find some information, fit it into this pattern and return it. XSLT, however, uses a transformational approach: Transform this source document into a new vocabulary.

Whereas XPath 1.0 and XSLT come from a document processing tradition, XQuery is designed with more of a database mindset. XQuery expressions look similar to the SQL expressions used to query relational databases.

This difference in traditions can make the relationship between XPath, XQuery and XSLT somewhat confusing. Some have argued that XQuery is redundant because it overlaps too strongly with XSLT. Advocates of XQuery argue that it makes query functionality available in a manner that is familiar to users and implementors of relational query languages. They also claim that XQuery allows those implementors to build on years of experience optimizing queries with a well-defined "query algebra". Others reply that this argument amounts to adopting the flat earth theory because it makes ocean navigation easier for users of street maps.[16]

Even people in the relational world have criticized XQuery for leaving out features that they have come to expect: insertions, updates and deletions. For example, as defined today, XQuery cannot tell an XML database to delete all elements with the attribute "old". It can define a transformation from the old database to a new database without those elements, but

---

16. We discuss the native-XML vs. relational database tradeoffs in depth in
    Part 9, "Databases", on page 444.

that is more like copying the good stuff than deleting the bad stuff. Future versions of XQuery should be able to accomplish these kinds of tasks.

Analysis   In the absence of insertion, update, and deletion facilities, XQuery's contribution to the XML world may seem underwhelming. It does a fair bit more than XPath 2.0, but many of its features have XSLT equivalents. On the other hand, XQuery could prove its worth, even in its limited 1.0 form, if it either makes XML querying much more accessible to average programmers or it greatly improves the performance of XML queries over large data sets. Time will tell.

59.6 | Conclusion

XPath is an extremely powerful language for addressing an XML document. Although it has depths that we could not address even in a "tad tougher" tutorial, we have covered all of the most common features.

XPath 1.0 is rapidly becoming as important in the XML world as SQL is in the relational world. XPath is already in use in the universally-used XSLT, and also in XPointer and XML Schema. XPath 2.0 and XQuery are on their way and may add to XPath's utility and acceptance. In short, XPath is already a central part of many XML systems and is on track to becoming ubiquitous.

Transform Tutorials

- Stylesheets for transforms and formatting
- XSL Transformations (XSLT)
- XSL formatting objects (XSL-FO)
- Full specs on CD-ROM

Part Twenty-one

This part covers the two parts of the XML Stylesheet Language from the World Wide Web Consortium.

A good (but not necessarily complete) understanding of Part 18, "XML Core Tutorials" is a prerequisite for XSLT and a similar understanding of XSLT is a prerequisite for XSL-FO.

XSL Transformations (XSLT)

Friendly Tutorial

- ▮ Template rules
- ▮ Patterns
- ▮ Templates
- ▮ Referencing stylesheets

Chapter

60

T he *Extensible Stylesheet Language Transformations* (*XSLT*) is a spin-off of the *Extensible Stylesheet Language (XSL)*, which applies formatting to XML documents in a standard way.[1]

We have seen XSLT used at a high level in the application chapters, now we'll look at the details of how it works. But be aware that the full details on XSLT could fill a book[2] and we don't cover them all here. The objective of this chapter is to provide a basic understanding for the way that XSLT stylesheets cause XML documents to be processed.

XSLT's processing model is very similar to that of many XML processing tools. Unlike general purpose programming languages, XML-aware tools can take care of some of the tedious parts of processing so that you can concentrate on your application needs. If you understand XSLT then you will be able to use other languages and systems much more effectively.

---

1. We discuss XSL in Chapter 61, "XSL formatting objects (XSL-FO)", on page 990.
2. The one we recommend is *Definitive XSLT and XPath* by Ken Holman, published in this series.

60.1 | Transforming vs. rendering

XSL is designed to apply style to an XML document by using XSLT to *transform* it into a rendition, represented by XSL formatting objects (XSL-FO). The XSL processor may then display the rendered document on a screen, print it, or convert it to some other rendition representation, such as PDF, PostScript, or even voice synthesis!

But "style" in the world of generalized markup encompasses every kind of processing. The transformation could be very powerful and complex, as XSLT can reorder, duplicate, suppress, sort, and add elements. There are many applications besides formatting where such transformations would be useful.

Consider an electronic commerce application where many companies must communicate. Each of their internal systems may use similar but different document types. To communicate they need to translate their various document types into a common one. An XSLT transformation provides a sophisticated but straightforward way to do so.

To summarize: name notwithstanding, XSLT is more than just a style language. While it can transform documents into XSL-FO renditions, it can also transform them into other XML abstractions, and into other rendered representations as well. In fact, XSLT is the Simon in this Simon and Garfunkel: it has become wildly popular to the extent that an XSLT processor ships with most operating systems. XSL-FO has also achieved success, but primarily in the high-volume publishing market.

60.2 | XSLT stylesheets

Most XSLT looks more or less like ordinary XML. Simple XSLT stylesheets are merely a specialized form of XML markup designed for specifying the transformation of other XML documents. You can think of XSLT as just another document type.

The XSLT language defines element types and attributes, constrains them to occurring in particular places, and describes what they should look like. However, because of its heavy use of XML namespaces it is not possible in general to use a validating parser to ensure that an XSL document conforms to the XSL specification.

A stylesheet that transforms a document into another XML document might have a root element that looks like Example 60-1.

Example 60-1. XSLT stylesheet using XML output elements

```
<xsl:stylesheet xmlns:xsl="http://www.w3.org/1999/XSL/Transform"
                version="1.0">
<xsl:output method="xml"/>
    <!-- template rules go here -->
</xsl:stylesheet>
```

The root element is `xsl:stylesheet`.[3] It must have a namespace declaration for XSLT. It makes sense to use the same declaration and `xsl:` prefix every time. You can also specify the output method to be used by the processor, choosing between XML, HTML and plain text.

The `xsl:stylesheet` element is usually filled with template rules. The template rules describe how to transform elements in the source document. Of course almost every element type could be processed differently from every other element type so there are many rules in an XSLT stylesheet. Particular elements could even be processed differently if they share a type but have different attributes or occur in a different context.

60.3 | Using HTML with XSLT

Many XSLT implementations allow transformations from XML into HTML. This is good for serving to today's mainstream browsers (6.x and up) and the legacy (3.x-5.x) browsers that most websites must still support.

It also takes advantage of many Web designers' knowledge of HTML. If you format a document using element types from HTML instead of from the formatting object vocabulary, the page will look to a browser as if it had been created in HTML directly. You can think of this process as a conversion from XML markup to HTML markup. Recent (5.0+) versions of Internet Explorer, Mozilla and Netscape can actually do this conversion right in the browser.

---

3. The spec also allows the root element to be called `xsl:transform`, presumably for the benefit of people with no style sense!

Because basic HTML is widely understood, we will use HTML element types in most of our examples. We will restrict our usage to only a few HTML types, namely:

- h1 and h2 element types for top-level and second-level headings,
- p element type for paragraphs
- body element type to contain the document's content; and the
- em element type to emphasize a series of characters.

A stylesheet that generates HTML elements might have a root element that looks like Example 60-2.

Example 60-2. XSLT stylesheet using HTML elements

```
<xsl:stylesheet xmlns:xsl="http://www.w3.org/1999/XSL/Transform"
                version="1.0">
<xsl:output method="html"/>
    <!-- template rules go here -->
</xsl:stylesheet>
```

There is a subtlety in how this transformation works. An XSLT stylesheet typically converts XML to XML. It is true that an XML document can look very much like an HTML document if it uses HTML element types, as we saw in 4.1.2, "Extensible HTML (XHTML)", on page 71.

However, XHTML is not quite what older browsers understand as HTML. Real HTML, for example, uses a different syntax for empty elements.

Fortunately, most XSLT processors can generate real HTML. The xsl:output instruction in Example 60-2 invokes this feature.

60.4 | Rules, patterns and templates

In the application sections of this book, we looked at applications that mapped parts of a source document into a result document. They did so to convert from a word processor file to XML, to create stylesheets, to convert from XML to a legacy data format, etc. Often, they used a graphical interface to allow the user to define the transformation and generate XSLT or some earlier or variant version of it, or proprietary equivalent.

In XSLT, the mapping construct is called a *template rule*. During XSLT processing every element, character, comment and processing instruction in an XML document is processed by some template rule. Some of them will be handled by template rules that the stylesheet writer created. Others are handled by *built-in* template rules that are hard-coded into every XSLT processor.

Template rules consist of two parts, the *pattern* and the *template*. Be careful with the terminology: a template is not a template rule. The pattern describes which source nodes (elements, textual data strings, comments or processing instructions) should be processed by the rule. The template describes the XML structure to generate when nodes are found that match the pattern.

In an XSLT stylesheet, a template rule is represented by an xsl:template element.[4] The pattern is the value of the xsl:template element's match attribute, and the template proper is the element's content.

Template rules are simple. You do not have to think about the order in which things will be processed, where data is stored or other housekeeping tasks that programming languages usually require you to look after. You just declare what you want the result to look like and the XSLT processor figures out how to make that happen. Because everything is done through declarations we say that XSL is a *declarative* language. One important benefit of declarative languages is that they are easy to *optimize*. Implementors can use various tricks and shortcuts in order to make them execute quickly.

60.5 | Creating a stylesheet

XSLT's processing model revolves around the idea of *patterns*. Patterns are XPath expressions designed to test nodes. Patterns allow the XSLT processor to choose which elements to apply which style rules to. XSLT's pattern language is basically XPath with a few extensions and restrictions. Patterns are used in the match attribute of template rules to specify which elements the rule applies to.

---

4. It would have been clearer had they called it an xsl:template-rule element, but they didn't.

XPath expressions are also used in XSLT template rules to select other elements (and other nodes) so that the stylesheet can process them also.

60.5.1 *Document-level template rule*

Consider a document whose root element-type is book and that can contain title, section and appendix element types. section and appendix elements can contain title, para and list subelements. Titles contain #PCDATA and no subelements. Paragraphs and list items contain emph and #PCDATA. Example 60-3 is a DTD that represents these constraints and Example 60-4 is an example document.

Example 60-3. DTD for book example

```
<!ELEMENT book (title, (section|appendix)+)>
<!ELEMENT section (title, (para|list)+)>
<!ELEMENT appendix (title, (para|list)+)>
<!ELEMENT title (#PCDATA)>
<!ELEMENT para (#PCDATA|emph)*>
<!ELEMENT emph (#PCDATA)>
<!ELEMENT list (item)+>
<!ELEMENT item (#PCDATA|emph)*>
```

Example 60-4. Book document instance

```
<book>
    <title>Chicken Soup for the Chicken's Soul</title>
    <section>
        <title>Introduction</title>
        <para>I've always wanted to write
            this book.</para>
    </section>
</book>
```

First the XSLT processor would examine the root element of the document. The XSLT processor would look for a rule that applied to books (a rule with a *match pattern* that matched a book). This sort of match pattern is very simple. Example 60-5 demonstrates.

We can choose any basic structure for the generated book. Example 60-6 shows a reasonable one.

Example 60-5. Simple match pattern

```
<xsl:template match="book">
  <!-- describe how books should be transformed -->
</xsl:template>
```

Example 60-6. Generated book structure

```
<xsl:template match="book">
  <body>
    <h1><!-- handle title --></h1>
    <!-- handle sections -->
    <hr/> <!-- HTML horizontal rule -->
    <h2>Appendices</h2>
    <!-- handle appendices -->
    <hr/>
    <p>Copyright 2004, the establishment.</p>
  </body>
</xsl:template>
```

The template in this template rule generates a body to hold the content of the document. The tags for the body element are usually omitted in HTML but we will want to add some attributes to the element later. The body is called a *literal result element.*

60.5.2 *Literal result elements*

The XSLT processor knows to treat body as a *literal result element* that is copied into the output because it is not an XSLT instruction (formally, it is not in the XSLT namespace). Elements in templates that are not part of the XSLT namespace are treated literally and copied into the output. You can see why these are called templates! They describe the form of the result document both by ordering content and by generating literal result elements. If the XSLT processor supports legacy HTML output, and the HTML output method is being used to serialize the result, then it will know to use legacy HTML conventions.

The h1, h2 and hr elements are also literal result elements that will create HTML headings and horizontal rules. As the stylesheet is represented in XML, the specification for the horizontal rule can use XML empty-element syntax. Finally the document has a literal result element and literal text representing the copyright. XSLT stylesheets can introduce this sort of *boiler-plate* text.

60.5.3   *Extracting data*

The template also has comments describing things we still have to handle: the document's title, its sections and the appendices.

We can get the data content from the `title` element with the `xsl:value-of` instruction. It has a `select` attribute which is a pattern. If this pattern names a simple element type then it will match a subelement of the *current* element.

In this case the current element is the `book` element as that is the element matched by the template rule. Example 60-7 shows what the data extraction would look like.

Example 60-7. Extracting data from a subelement

```
<h1><xsl:value-of select="title"/></h1>
```

60.5.4   *The* apply-templates *instruction*

The next step is to handle sections and appendices. We could do it in one of two ways. We could either create a new template rule for handling sections or we could handle sections directly in the `book` template rule.

The benefit of creating a new rule is that it can be used over and over again. Before we create the new rule we should ensure it will get invoked at the right point. We will use a new instruction, `xsl:apply-templates`. Example 60-8 shows this instruction.

Example 60-8. The `xsl:apply-templates` instruction

```
<xsl:apply-templates select="section"/>
```

The `xsl:apply-templates` instruction does two important things.

1.   It finds all nodes that match the `select` attribute pattern.

2. It processes each of these in turn. It does so by finding and applying the template rule that matches each node.

This important principle is at the heart of XSLT's processing model.

In this case, the *select* pattern in the `xsl:apply-templates` element selects all of the book's subelements of type `section`. The `xsl:apply-templates` instruction always searches out the rule that is appropriate for each of the selected nodes. In this case the `xsl:apply-templates` instruction will search out a rule that applies to sections. The expanded `book` template rule is in Example 60-9.

Example 60-9. Handling section elements

```
<xsl:template match="book">
  <body>
    <h1><xsl:value-of select="title"/></h1>
    <xsl:apply-templates select="section"/>
    <hr/>
    <h2>Appendices</h2>
    <xsl:apply-templates select="appendix"/>
    <p>Copyright 2004, the establishment</p>
  </body>
</xsl:template>
```

60.5.5 *Handling optional elements*

Our sample document does not have appendices but the stylesheet should support anything that the DTD or schema allows. Documents of this type created in the future may have appendices.

Our stylesheet generates the title element followed by section elements (in the order that they occurred in the document) followed by appendix elements (also in *document order*).

If our DTD allowed more than one title subelement in a book element then this stylesheet would generate them all. There is no way for a stylesheet to require that the document have a single title. These sorts of constraints are specified in the DTD.

Our DTD does permit documents to have no appendices. Our "Appendices" title and horizontal rule separating the appendices from the sections would look fairly silly in that case. XSLT provides an instruction called `xsl:if` that handles this situation. We can wrap it around the relevant parts as shown in Example 60-10.

Example 60-10. Using `xsl:if`

```
<xsl:if test="appendix">
  <hr/>
  <h2>Appendices</h2>
  <xsl:apply-templates select="appendix"/>
</xsl:if>
```

The `xsl:if` instruction goes within a template. We could drop it into our `book` template as a replacement for our current appendix handling.

The instruction also contains another template within it. The contained template is only instantiated (generated) if there is some element that matches the pattern exhibited by the `test` attribute – in this case, an `appendix` element.

As with the `select` attribute, the context is the current node. If there is no node that matches the pattern in the `test` attribute then the entire contained template will be skipped.

There is another instruction called `xsl:choose` that allows for multiple alternatives, including a default template for when none of the other alternatives match.

60.5.6 *Reordering the output*

If the DTD had allowed titles, sections and appendices to be mixed together our stylesheet would reorder them so that the title preceded the sections and the sections preceded the appendices.

This ability to reorder is very important. It allows us to use one structure in our abstract representation and another in our rendition. The abstract structure is optimized for editing, validating and processing convenience. The rendered structure is optimized for viewing and navigation.

Reordering is easy when you know exactly the order in which you want elements of various types to be processed. In the case of the body, for example: titles before sections before appendices. But within a section or appendix, reordering is somewhat trickier because we don't know the complete output order.

That is, we need to process titles before any of the paragraphs or lists, but we cannot disturb the relative order of the paragraphs and lists themselves. Those have to be generated in the document order.

We can solve this fairly easily. In XPath pattern syntax the vertical bar (|) character means "or". So we can make a rule like the one in Example 60-11.

Example 60-11. The section rule

```
<xsl:template match="section">
    <h2><xsl:value-of select="title"/></h2>
    <xsl:apply-templates select="para|list"/>
</xsl:template>
```

This rule forces titles (in our DTD there can be only one) to be handled first and paragraphs and lists to be processed in the order that they are found. The rules that are defined for paragraphs and lists will automatically be selected when those types of element appear. We'll create those rules next.

60.5.7 *Data content*

Next we can handle paragraphs. We want them each to generate a single HTML element. We also want them to generate their content to populate that element in the order that the content occurs, not in some order pre-defined by the template.

We need to process all of the paragraph's *subnodes*. That means that we cannot just handle emph subelements. We must also handle ordinary character data. Example 60-12 demonstrates this.

Example 60-12. Paragraph rule

```
<xsl:template match="para">
    <p><xsl:apply-templates select="node()"/>
    </p>
</xsl:template>
```

As you can see, the rule for paragraphs is very simple. The xsl:apply-templates instruction handles most of the work for us automatically. The select attribute matches all nodes: element nodes, text nodes, etc. If it encounters a text node it copies it to the result; that is a *default* rule built into XSLT. If it encounters a subelement, it processes it using the appropriate rule.

XSLT handles much of the complexity for us but we should still be clear: transformations will not always be this easy. These rules are so simple because our DTD is very much like HTML. The more alike the source and result DTDs the simpler the transformation will be. It is especially helpful to have a very loose or flexible result DTD. HTML is perfect in this regard.

60.5.8 *Handling inline elements*

The rule for `emph` follows the same basic organization as the `paragraph` rule. Mixed content (i.e. character-containing) elements often use this organization. The HTML element-type name is `em` (Example 60-13). Note that in this case we will use an abbreviated syntax for the `xsl:apply-templates` element: Because the `select` attribute defaults to `node()`, we can leave it out.

Example 60-13. Handling emphasis

```
<xsl:template match="emph">
    <em><xsl:apply-templates/></em>
</xsl:template>
```

List items also have mixed content, so we should look at the rules for lists and list items next. They are in Example 60-14.

Example 60-14. List and item rules

```
<xsl:template match="list">
    <ol>
       <xsl:apply-templates/>
    </ol>
</xsl:template>
<xsl:template match="item">
    <li><xsl:apply-templates/></li>
</xsl:template>
```

The rules in Example 60-13 and Example 60-14 work together. When a list is detected the literal result element is processed and an ol element is generated. It will contain a single li element for each item. Each li will in turn contain text nodes (handled by the default rule) and emph (handled by the emph rule).

60.5.9 *Sharing a template rule*

We still need a template rule for appendices. If we wrote out the rule for appendices we would find it to be identical to sections. We could just copy the sections rule but XSLT has a more elegant way. We can amend our rule for sections to say that the rule applies equally to sections *or* appendices. Example 60-15 demonstrates.

Example 60-15. The rule in Example 60-11 revised to handle appendices as well as sections

```
<xsl:template match="section|appendix">
    <h2><xsl:value-of select="title"/></h2>
    <xsl:apply-templates select="para|list"/>
</xsl:template>
```

60.5.10 *Final touches*

We now have a complete stylesheet but it is rather basic. We might as well add a background color to beautify it a bit. HTML allows this through the bgcolor attribute of the body element. We will not go into the details of the HTML color scheme but suffice to say that Example 60-16 gives our document a nice light purple background.

Example 60-16. Adding a background color

```
<xsl:template match="book">
  <body bgcolor="#FFDDFF">
    <!-- Handling of body content is unchanged -->
    ...
  </body>
</xsl:template>
```

There is also one more detail we must take care of. We said earlier that the more flexible a document type is the easier it is to transform to. Even though HTML is pretty flexible it does have one unbreakable rule. Every document must have a `title` element, but "title" means something different in the HTML vocabulary from what it does in our `book` DTD.

We've handled the `title` element from the source as a heading, but in HTML the title shows up in the window's title bar, in the bookmark list and in search engine result lists. We need the document's title to appear as both the HTML title and as an HTML heading element. Luckily XSLT allows us to duplicate data.

With these additions our stylesheet is complete! It is shown in Example 60-17.

As you can see, simple XSLT transformations can be quite simple – evidence of XSLT's good design. The important thing to keep in mind is that the basic XSLT processing model is based on template rules, patterns and templates. Flow of control between rules is handled by special instructions. In fact this processing model is ubiquitous in XML processing.

60.6 | Top-level instructions

XSLT also allows you to do more complex things. It supports all of XPath, sophisticated selections, stylesheet reuse and many other advanced features. We will introduce a few of these in this section.

`Top-level` instructions are those that go directly in the `xsl:stylesheet` element. They do not apply to any particular template rule but rather declare behaviors, variables and other things that affect the entire stylesheet. Except for `xsl:import` instructions, which we'll describe shortly, the order of top-level statements is not important.

60.6.1 Combining stylesheets

There are two ways to combine stylesheets: inclusion and import.

Example 60-17. Complete stylesheet

```
<?xml version="1.0"?>
<xsl:stylesheet xmlns:xsl="http://www.w3.org/1999/XSL/Transform"
                version="1.0">
<xsl:output method="html"/>

<xsl:template match="book">
  <body bgcolor="#FFDDFF">
    <title><xsl:value-of select="title"/></title>
    <h1><xsl:value-of select="title"/></h1>
    <xsl:apply-templates select="section"/>
    <hr/>
    <xsl:if test="appendix">
      <hr/>
      <h2>Appendices</h2>
      <xsl:apply-templates select="appendix"/>
    </xsl:if>
    <p>Copyright 2004, the establishment</p>
  </body>
</xsl:template>

<xsl:template match="para">
    <p><xsl:apply-templates/></p>
</xsl:template>

<xsl:template match="emph">
    <em><xsl:apply-templates/></em>
</xsl:template>

<xsl:template match="list">
    <ol>
       <xsl:apply-templates/>
    </ol>
</xsl:template>

<xsl:template match="item">
    <li><xsl:apply-templates/></li>
</xsl:template>

<xsl:template match="section|appendix">
    <xsl:apply-templates select="title"/>
    <xsl:apply-templates select="para|list"/>
</xsl:template>
</xsl:stylesheet>
```

60.6.1.1   Including other stylesheets

The `xsl:include` instruction includes another stylesheet. Stylesheets may not include themselves directly or indirectly. The instructions in an included stylesheet are treated exactly as if they had been typed directly in the including stylesheet. They are not second-class in any sense. Example 60-18 demonstrates the inclusion of other stylesheets through both absolute and relative URIs.

Example 60-18. Including another stylesheet

```
<xsl:include href="http://.../currency.xsl"/>
<xsl:include href="bonds.xsl"/>
```

60.6.1.2   Importing from other stylesheets

Importing is a little bit different from *including*. Just as in the real world, there are restrictions on imports! In the XSLT context that means imports are second-class. Imported rules only take effect when no rule in the main stylesheet matches. Also, import statements earlier in the document take precedence over later ones.

Import instructions *must* go at the top of a stylesheet, preceding any other top-level instructions and the `xsl:template` elements. A stylesheet must not directly or indirectly import itself. Example 60-19 demonstrates the importation of other stylesheets through both absolute and relative URIs.

Example 60-19. Importing another stylesheet

```
<xsl:import href="http://.../stocks.xsl"/>
<xsl:import href="credit-cards.xsl"/>
```

60.6.2   *Whitespace handling*

In machine-to-machine applications, whitespace nodes are usually irrelevant. Even in publishing applications, some whitespace is not important for processing. A blank line between two section elements is just intended to make the source XML easier to read. It is not intended to affect what is seen by the ultimate readers of the rendered document.

As we saw in Figure 59-2, whitespace nodes are ordinary text nodes that happen to have only whitespace (tab, space, newline) characters in them. Nodes T2, T4, and T5 in that figure are examples.

XSLT has a feature that allows you to strip out these whitespace-only nodes based on the elements in which they occur. The xsl:strip-space instruction strips space from elements of specified types in the source document. Example 60-20 shows how you would strip space from address and date elements.

Example 60-20. Stripping space

```
<xsl:strip-space elements="address date"/>
```

In some vocabularies, all element types are so-called *space-stripping*. You can accomplish this by using an asterisk in the xsl:strip-space instruction. (Example 60-21)

Example 60-21. Strip space from all elements

```
<xsl:strip-space elements="*"/>
```

If a vocabulary has only a few non-whitespace stripping elements (*whitespace-preserving elements*), you can selectively override the blanket stripping statement with the xsl:preserve-space instruction. By default, whitespace is preserved.

60.6.3 *Output descriptions*

The xsl:output instruction sets various options that control what the stylesheet should generate as output. The main attribute in the instruction is the method attribute, which typically takes a value like "xml", "html" or "text".

"xml" is appropriate for (surprise!) generating XML; it is the default. "html" uses html conventions for empty-elements, processing instructions and similar constructs. The "text" output is useful when you want to generate plain text without the XSLT processor representing delimiter characters such as less-than signs (<) as <, and so forth.

Other attributes can control whether the output is indented for "pretty printing", what character encoding to use, whether to add an XML declaration and/or document type declaration and other (even more obscure) output options. Most XSLT stylesheets will not need to change these options from their defaults.

But if you find that the output of your stylesheet is not quite what you would expect, then `xsl:output` may have the answer for you.

60.6.4 *Numeric formats*

The `xsl:decimal-format` instruction allows you to describe how decimal numbers will be printed by your stylesheet. For instance, you can use this to change the character that separates the decimals from the integral part of the number. You could set that option to period for North Americans and comma for Europeans.

Other options allow you to change the "grouping-separator" between the billions, millions and thousands and to choose characters or strings to represent "infinity", "minus", "percent", "per-mille" (per thousand), "the zero digit" and "Not a number". The latter is used for error handling.

60.6.5 *Attribute sets*

`xsl:attribute-set` allows you to define a reusable set of attributes. If you have several different types of images that must share certain attributes then it is more efficient to define those in an attribute set than to repeat them all in each template rule. Example 60-22 demonstrates the basic idea.

Example 60-22. Reusable set of attribute values

```
<xsl:attribute-set name="big-image">
    <xsl:attribute name="width">500px</xsl:attribute>
    <xsl:attribute name="height">500px</xsl:attribute>
</xsl:attribute-set>
<xsl:attribute-set name="small-image">
    <xsl:attribute name="width">100px</xsl:attribute>
    <xsl:attribute name="height">100px</xsl:attribute>
</xsl:attribute-set>

... in a template ...
<img xsl:use-attribute-sets="big-image">
```

60.6.6 *Namespace alias*

Just as `xsl:output` helps you to solve the problem of how to treat a less-than sign as an ordinary data character, `xsl:namespace-alias` helps you to treat a namespace prefixed literal result element as just a literal result element, even if the namespace happens to be XSLT! This sounds strange but it could happen if you were writing an XSLT stylesheet that generates an XSLT stylesheet. Needless to say, this is not a common situation so we will not dwell on it further.

60.6.7 *Keys*

Keys are a performance-enhancement concept borrowed from the database world. Their main use is to provide a (possibly) faster way to reference elements by the values of their attributes or subelements. You get to decide which attribute or element values form the key by declaring it, as shown in Example 60-23.

Example 60-23. Declaring a key

```
<xsl:key name="employees-by-ssn"
         match="employee"
         use="social-security"/>
```

   Keys don't let you do anything that can't be done with normal XPath addressing, which is why we're not explaining them in detail. Their major benefit is to allow the XSLT processor to build a lookup table to attempt to speed up keyed references. Whether the attempt succeeds depends on the number of keys, how often they are referenced, and the complexity of the XPath expressions they replace.
   Keys can also simplify a stylesheet by letting you use simple key names in place of possibly complex XPath expressions. Not all XSLT processors support keys.

60.7 | Variables and parameters

XSLT variables and parameters are closely related. A variable is a value that a stylesheet creator stores away for use in some other part of the stylesheet. A top-level variable is one defined outside of any template rule. The value is automatically available for use in any template. For instance a variable could hold the company name. The value that the variable holds could even be extracted from the input XML document. Example 60-24 demonstrates.

Example 60-24. Defining a variable

```
<xsl:variable name="company-name" select="/doc/creator/company"/>
```

Variables can be referred to in XPath expressions by preceding the variable name with a dollar-sign ($). Example 60-25 demonstrates.

Example 60-25. Referencing a variable

```
<xsl:value-of select="$company-name"/>
```

A parameter is just like a variable except that the value can be overridden. How it would be overridden depends on your XSLT implementation. Command-line XSLT transformation engines typically use command-line options. Graphical environments might use options in a graphical user interface. In other words, parameters are user options that change the stylesheet's behavior. They are declared and referenced just as variables are. Example 60-26 demonstrates.

Example 60-26. Defining a parameter

```
<xsl:param name="company-name" select="/doc/creator/company"/>
```

The select attribute of a parameter is used as a *default value*. If the user fails to supply a parameter, the default value is used when the stylesheet is processed.

It is also possible to define template rules that have parameters. In that case, the parameters are only available within that template. Template rule parameters are passed not from the user, but from other templates. For instance a template for a chapter might use a parameter to pass the chapter number to a template rule for a section. That way the section number could be derived from the chapter number (e.g. section number 5.4 within chapter 5).

60.8 | Extending XSLT

XSLT permits customized extensions (the "X" in "XSLT") to be supported by an XSLT processor.

The XSLT language has a mechanism that allows you to call into a component written in any programming language. You could refer to a *Java* class file, Python program, Perl script or an ActiveX control. You could even embed a small script from a scripting language such as *Javascript* or *Python*. The script can be defined right in your stylesheet!

60.9 | Referencing XSLT stylesheets

There is a W3C Recommendation that specifies how XML documents should refer to their stylesheets. Here is the relevant text:

Spec Excerpt (xml-ss) 60-1. The `xml-stylesheet` processing instruction

The `xml-stylesheet` processing instruction is allowed anywhere in the prolog of an XML document. The processing instruction can have pseudo-attributes `href` (required), `type` (required), `title` (optional), `media` (optional), `charset` (optional).

These are called *pseudo-attributes* because, although they use attribute syntax, they do not describe properties of an element. The only real syntactic difference between pseudo-attributes and attributes is that you must use pseudo-attributes in the order they are defined. You can use attributes in any order.

The most important pseudo-attributes for this processing instruction are `href`, which supplies a URI for the stylesheet, and `type`, which says whether the stylesheet is in XSLT, DSSSL, CSS, or some other stylesheet language.

Example 60-27 is a sample stylesheet processing instruction (PI).

Example 60-27. Stylesheet PI

```
<?xml-stylesheet href="http://www.xmlbooks.com/memo.xsl"
                 type="text/xsl"?>
```

You can provide multiple PIs to allow for different output media or stylesheet language support. You could, for example, have different stylesheets for print (with footnotes and page breaks), online (with clickable links), television (large text and easy scroll controls) and voice (read aloud using inflection to render emphasis). In such cases, you would want to specify a `media` pseudo-attribute and possibly a `title` that the browser might use when offering a list of stylesheet choices. Example 60-28 demonstrates this.

Example 60-28. Alternative stylesheets

```
<?xml-stylesheet rel=alternate
                 href="mystyle1.xsl"
                 title="Fancy"
                 media="print"
                 type="text/xsl"?>
<?xml-stylesheet
                 rel=alternate
                 href="mystyle2.css"
                 title="Simple"
                 media="online"
                 type="text/css"?>
<?xml-stylesheet
                 rel=alternate
                 href="mystyle2.aur"
                 title="Aural"
                 media="voice"
                 type="text/aural"?>
```

60.10 | XSLT 2.0

XSLT 2.0 is a new version of XSLT that is based on XPath 2.0.

XSLT 2.0 gains many new capabilities just by inheriting datatypes and sequence manipulation from XPath 2.0. We discuss those items in 59.5.1, "XPath 2.0", on page 952, which you may want to review before going forward. In this section we introduce some of the other new features of XSLT 2.0.

> *Caution*   Both XSLT 2.0 and XPath 2.0 are under development at the time of writing, so the details of what we discuss here – especially the syntax – are subject to change.

60.10.1 *Regular expressions*

XSLT 2.0 can build on XPath 2.0's regular expression features to allow the handling of non-XML notations within the data of XML documents.

For example, an XML document might have some elements that contain programming code. If it were important to process each program line individually, XSLT 2.0 could easily separate the element's content into a sequence of lines by using a regular expression that matches the line breaks.

In Example 60-29, the data that doesn't match the newline character is processed.

Example 60-29. Using a regular expression to process individual data lines

```
<xsl:analyze-string select="code" regex="\n">
<xsl:non-matching-substring>
 <!-- code to handle each line here -->
</xsl:non-matching-substring>
</xsl:analyze-string>
```

60.10.2 *Schema importation*

XSLT 2.0 has strong datatyping (unlike XSLT 1.0) because it is based on XPath 2.0. It can import a schema definition to find names of user-defined types. These can then be used for type-checks and declarations in XPath 2.0 and for variable and parameter declarations in XSLT itself.

Example 60-30 indicates the location of the schema definition and the namespace within it from which the declarations should be imported.

Example 60-30. Importing a schema definition

```
<xsl:import-schema
  namespace=http://www.example.org/ns/some_namespace"
  schema-location="http://www.example.org/schemas/schema.xsd"/>
```

60.10.3 *Temporary trees*

XSLT 1.0 has very weak features for making reusable templates that do more complex processing than just outputting XML text. For instance you might want to create a template that could take a list of floating point numbers as a parameter and return a list of calculated numbers. But the only thing that XSLT 1.0 can return is a so-called *result tree fragment*. These result tree fragments are fairly difficult to work with because they have no easily accessible internal structure. To the XSLT programmer, they are just character strings and it is inconvenient to use them for anything other than just outputting.

In XSLT 2.0, however, templates accept and return node trees. These generated node trees can be manipulated just as if they had come from the source XML document. This means that one XSLT template could create an arbitrarily complex structure of elements and attributes (perhaps even a complete document) and then pass it to another template. This helps to create more sophisticated transformations reliably, by building them from simpler ones.

60.10.4 *Multiple result documents*

XSLT 2.0 can create multiple output documents. Instead of a transformation generating a single file, it could generate a whole directory or even multiple directories. This function is commonly implemented in XSLT 1.0 processors through extensions to the standard.

Now there is a standard way to accomplish this common task. The results are streamed to a URI, so it is even conceivable that a single XSLT 2.0 stylesheet could populate an entire remote website or portion thereof using the FTP or WebDAV protocols.

In Example 60-31, the stylesheet creates separate HTML output documents for the table of contents and for each section of the source document.

Example 60-31. Multiple result documents

```
<xsl:template match="/">
  <xsl:result-document href="table-of-contents.html">
    <xsl:for-each select="/doc/section">
      ... make a link to each section in the TOC...
    </xsl:for-each>
    ...
  </xsl:result-document>
  <xsl:for-each select="/doc/section">
    <xsl:result-document href="{position()}.html">
      ... output a section as a new result document ...
    </xsl:result-document>
  </xsl:for-each>
</xsl:template>
```

60.10.5 *Function definition*

XSLT 2.0 allows programmers to define functions that can be called from within XPath expressions. For instance a stylesheet might convert a number into a roman numeral. Defining a function for that conversion makes it easier to perform the same conversion multiple times in a stylesheet and even to use it in multiple stylesheets. Example 60-32 demonstrates.

Example 60-32. Function definition in XSLT 2.0

```
<xsl:function name="num:roman" as="xs:string">
  <xsl:param name="value" as="xs:integer"/>
  <xsl:number value="$value" format="i"/>
</xsl:function>
```

60.10.6 *Backward compatibility*

XSLT 2.0 processors will have a backward compatibility mode to patch up the few small incompatibilities between 1.0 and 2.0. The compatibility mode is invoked when the processor sees an XSLT 1.0 version attribute.

Such *backward compatibility flags* are not appreciated by implementors, who are required to support both the new and old versions. Nevertheless, it is a pragmatic approach that saves users from having to install and use multiple XSLT processors.

60.11 | Conclusion

XSLT is not a general purpose language like Java or Python. It would be difficult to use it to calculate your taxes or do cryptography. You should think twice (nay, thrice!) before trying to build a video game in XSLT. It really excels at only one thing: translating between XML vocabularies. It does one thing and does it well.

There are, however, rare circumstances in which XSLT is not appropriate even for that one thing. XSLT is designed for situations where the XSLT processor can access the entire parsed document in memory as a tree. This requirement does not work well for very large documents, or even for medium-sized documents processed by computers without much memory. An implementation might require several kilobytes for a node whose XML source text might be just a few bytes.

Most developers consider the requirement of sufficient memory a small price to pay for the convenience of XSLT's easy navigation and native understanding of XML. That explains why XSLT has become ubiquitous – arguably the most popular way to process XML documents.

XSL formatting objects (XSL-FO)

Friendly Tutorial

- Extensible Stylesheet Language (XSL)

- Styling on steroids!

- Introductory example

T he *Extensible Stylesheet Language* (*XSL*) project was originally undertaken by the World Wide Web Consortium to develop
a recommendation for applying screen and pagination formatting to XML documents in a standard way. Over time a part of XSL called
the *XSL Transformations (XSLT)* evolved into an independently useful
language for transforming one XML document to another. It is now a separately published approved recommendation. We discuss it in Chapter
60, "XSL Transformations (XSLT)", on page 962.[1]

The remainder of the original XSL is also an approved recommendation.
It defines the semantics of formatting, in the form of a processing model
and catalog of *XSL formatting objects (XSL-FO)*, represented as XML elements. XSL supports both online (non-paginated) and print (paginated)
publishing.

Under the covers, XSL borrows from two other specifications: *DSSSL*
and *CSS*.

---

1. XSLT in turn gave birth to XPath, which is discussed in Chapter 59, "XML
   Path Language (XPath)", on page 924.

DSSSL

Document Style Semantics and Specification Language (DSSSL) is an International Standard. It provides the transformational template application paradigm that XSLT uses, as well as a complete set of pagination-oriented constructs expressed using flow objects. DSSSL inspired many of the flow-oriented formatting objects in XSL.

CSS

Cascading Style Sheets (CSS) is a W3C Recommendation that informs many Web formatting technologies, including HTML, SVG and SMIL. CSS provides many of the formatting-oriented objects and properties in XSL.

61.1 | Styling on steroids!

As we saw in Chapter 60, "XSL Transformations (XSLT)", on page 962, style is applied to XML documents by using XSLT to transform them into XSL formatting object documents. The XML *source* documents are usually marked up according to their abstract structure, with no markup (in theory at least) that is tailored for style application or any other particular kind of processing.

XSL and XSLT, therefore, form the "missing link" between the abstract data that is intended for computer processing and the formatted rendition required for comfortable reading in a paginated form. In technical terms, the document is transformed from an abstraction to a rendition.

Simple stylesheet languages such as CSS help documents to put on a little make-up. XSL and XSLT allow them to get a complete make-over.

XSLT can, among other things:

- move end-notes to the end of a document;
- duplicate the title of a chapter so that it appears not only in the chapter, but also in the page running head and in the table of contents;
- suppress a corporation's internal annotations and metadata;
- sort the names in a phone directory; and
- add boilerplate text such as a copyright or corporate logo.

In fact, XSLT does not so much apply a makeover as perform complete Cher-style plastic surgery!

An XSL implementation must support both the XSLT transformation to XSL-FO, plus the rendering of XSL-FO into PDF or some other page description or device stream. There are two distinct steps that could be run separately or marshalled by a single program:

1. XSLT transformation to an intermediate XSL-FO document.
2. Rendering of the XSL-FO document.

Note   **This division of labor, not to mention the division of the XSL Recommendation itself, raises the burning question: Is a stylesheet XSL or XSLT? Technically, it is both. However, in order to keep the process clear, in this book we use "XSLT" to characterize all stylesheets and "XSL" only for stylesheets whose output is XSL formatting objects.**

61.2 | A simple stylesheet example

A stylesheet that uses XSL formatting objects might have a root element that looks like Example 61-1.

Example 61-1. XSLT stylesheet using XSL formatting objects

```
<xsl:stylesheet xmlns:xsl="http://www.w3.org/1999/XSL/Transform"
                xmlns:fo="http://www.w3.org/1999/XSL/Format"
                version="1.0">
<xsl:output method="xml"/>
    <!-- template rules go here -->
</xsl:stylesheet>
```

Note that the output is XML. The only indication that we are using XSL-FO is the declaration of the fo namespace.

Let's start simply, with a style that says "Paragraphs should use a 12pt font" and "Titles should be 20 point and boldfaced." Example 61-2 adds two template rules to apply font styles to titles and paragraphs.

Example 61-2. Example 60-1 with two rules added

```
<?xml version="1.0"?>
<xsl:stylesheet xmlns:xsl="http://www.w3.org/1999/XSL/Transform"
                xmlns:fo="http://www.w3.org/1999/XSL/Format"
                version="1.0">
<xsl:output method="xml"/>

    <xsl:template match="PARA">
        <fo:block font-size="12pt">
            <xsl:apply-templates/>
        </fo:block>
    </xsl:template>

    <xsl:template match="TITLE">
        <fo:block font-size="20pt" font-weight="bold">
            <xsl:apply-templates/>
        </fo:block>
    </xsl:template>

</xsl:stylesheet>
```

The rules say that whenever the XSLT processor encounters a PARA or TITLE element in an XML document, it should create a fo:block element. Because the result uses the formatting object vocabulary, an XSL processor would immediately render the document. An XSLT processor, however, would create an XSL-FO document for subsequent rendering by an XSL formatting engine.

The renderer generates a block (fo:block) of text on the screen which is separated from the text above and below it. This makes sense. Visually a paragraph is just a text block set off from other text.

The fo:block element has an attribute called font-size. This attribute is also defined by the XSL specification and will be properly interpreted by the XSL processor.

Similarly, this stylesheet will look for TITLE elements and make them bold and 20pt.

Let's take a closer look at those formatting objects.

61.3 | Formatting objects

Imagine rendering an XML document with a word processor. You would have to use the constructs provided by the word processor, such as page layouts, paragraph styles, character styles, and so on. In XSL terms, those constructs are the formatting objects.

XSL stylesheets typically contain such objects as blocks, display graphics, leaders (for horizontal rules), and tables. A table formatting object might itself contain blocks.

Blocks would normally contain characters, and also inline objects. The latter apply formatting, like italics and bold, to sequences of characters.

Every formatting object has *properties*. For example, blocks may specify the space before and after the block, links may specify their destinations, characters may specify their font sizes, and pictures may specify their heights and widths.

The `fo:root` object is the root element and contains everything else. It is illustrated in Figure 61-1.

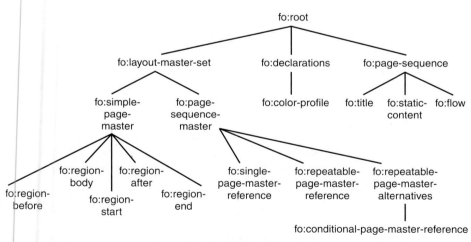

Figure 61-1 Formatting objects for pagination

Within the root you can have one or more `fo:page-sequence` elements, shown at the far right of the diagram. Each represents a sequence of pages whose content is a single `fo:flow` object that contains the block-level constructs for the page sequence.

61.4 | Going with the flow!

The main content of the document goes into the `fo:flow` objects, which flow from one page to another in the rendition. The length of a page sequence depends on the size of the content of its flow object and descendants.

There are many different types of block-level and inline-level object; we list just a few here to give the general idea.

`fo:block`

> The `fo:block` element type creates lines upon which text, graphics and other inline-level objects sit. It can be used for paragraphs, titles, block quotations and so forth. Blocks have a huge number of properties for changing the background color, background image, font size, padding (space around block), orphans (handling of page breaks) and so forth.

`fo:external-graphic`

> The `fo:external-graphic` element type allows you to create a graphic that is formatted inline (between characters). You could use that for icons. The image is specified through a URI.

`fo:leader`

> The `fo:leader` element type creates a horizontal line. It has properties for changing the color, length, width and style (solid, dotted, dashed).

`fo:table`

> The `fo:table` element type is used for tables. It has a *table model* similar to (but not identical to) that used by HTML.

`fo:list-block`

> The `fo:list-block` element type represents a list. It can contain a sequence of `fo:list-item` elements, representing the list items, which are pairs of `fo:list-item-label`, `fo:list-item-body`

elements. The label/item pairs could be used for a dictionary; the words would be the labels and the definitions would be the items. The labels could also be used for bullets or numbers in unordered and ordered lists.

fo:basic-link

The fo:basic-link element type allows you to create hypertext links to a destination specified by a URI or to another element in the formatted document. This element type allows XLinks to be rendered.

fo:page-number

The fo:page-number element type generates a page number for printed documents.

Note   *There are over fifty formatting object types, so a complete discussion would take another book! The one we recommend is Ken Holman's Definitive XSL-FO, published in this series.*

61.5 | Conclusion

The XSL formatting object vocabulary is a powerful language that can describe the full complexity of paginated output. Even so, robust tools are available that implement the XSL-FO Recommendation. Our publisher has used XSL-FO for several years to produce titles in this book series.

Schema
Tutorials

- Datatypes
- XML Schema definition language (XSDL)
- Full specs on CD-ROM

Part Twenty-two

This part covers two parts of the XML Schema recommendation from the World Wide Web Consortium. Here too you'll need a pretty firm grasp of the material in Part 18, "XML Core Tutorials" before you tackle either of these.

Datatypes is a prerequisite for the XML Schema definition language (XSDL), but only the basics are needed before moving on.

Datatypes

- Datatype requirements
- Built-in datatypes
- User-derived datatypes
- Using datatypes in DTDs

Chapter

62

Perhaps the most widely used aspect of the W3C *XML Schema* project is the datatype work. It was made a separate Part 2 of the *XML Schema* spec, with the intention "that it be usable outside of the context of *XML Schema* for a wide range of other XML-related activities".

In this chapter, we describe the basic concepts of XML datatypes and show how they can be used both in the *XML Schema* definition language (XSDL – Part 1 of the spec) and in "other XML-related activities" such as XML DTDs and WSDL Web service descriptions.

62.1 | Understanding the problem

The DTD fragment in Example 62-1 shows the declaration for an attribute whose value is intended to be a year.

Example 62-1. Attribute declaration in a DTD

```
<!ATTLIST poem pubyear NMTOKEN #IMPLIED>
<!-- Publication year should be four-digits -->
```

Although the pubyear value is supposed to represent a year, XML's set of attribute types cannot say that directly. We've chosen the closest datatype built into XML but it is not very close. All of the pubyear values in the start-tags shown in Example 62-2 would be valid.

Example 62-2. Legal pubyear NMTOKEN values

```
<poem pubyear="1922">
<poem pubyear="0">
<poem pubyear="99999999999999999999999">
<poem pubyear="-3">
<poem pubyear="3.14159265">
<poem pubyear="Hello_World">
<poem pubyear=":">
<poem pubyear="----">
```

Wouldn't it be nice if the declaration for a pubyear attribute (or even for a pubyear element type) could specify that its value (or content) must be a four-digit number between 1000 and 2100?

This would make it easier to write robust applications that use that data. If your application must check whether this poem is in the public domain yet, it might add 75 to that pubyear value and compare the result with the current year to see if the poem is more than 75 years old.

You can only do this calculation reliably if you know that the value is an integer. You could do this by writing error-checking code, but one major goal of all schemas (including DTDs) is to reduce the need for custom error-checking code.

Programmers want to plug in an off-the-shelf, validating XML processor and have it check the mundane details of datatype conformance. When they get a weekly salary value out of a document they don't want to write code to make sure that it's a usable number before they subtract it from another number.

Most importantly, end users want to be able to do the checks with off-the-shelf processors also. By design, XML allows processing without validation – it doesn't even require schemas or DTDs! Some XML software may avoid validation for performance reasons, assuming the document was validated when it was created.

Datatypes answer important questions about the description and validation of element data content and attribute values.

With datatypes you could express things like "a date element should contain data that conforms to the syntax YYYY-MM-DD" or "an email address attribute value must be of the form xxxxxx@yyyyy.zzz".

62.2 | Datatype requirements

A system to support datatypes must meet three requirements:

- There must be a way to validate that the data really conforms to the restrictions of the datatype. There should be no February 30 in a date, every email address needs an @ symbol and so forth.
- There must be a way for an application to convert data from XML into programming language datatypes. For instance an attribute value might be the string "123" but the internal representation in a programming language would be a series of bits in an optimized format. Dates could be represented not as strings but as objects with properties representing years, months, days etc. In some systems, dates are represented in terms of the number of seconds that have passed since some event.
- There must be a way to define new datatypes. Just as XML allows you to define new element types, you would want to be able to define datatypes that are specific to your project. A geographer might define a latitude/longitude notation. A mathematician might define a notation for matrices.

XML Schema Datatypes is the standard that addresses these issues.

62.3 | Built-in datatypes

The *XML Schema Datatypes* spec defines two categories of datatype: primitive and derived. All primitive datatypes are defined in the spec and are therefore among the *built-in datatypes*. You may not create your own.

A derived datatype is defined in terms of one or more existing datatypes. It might be a specialized or extended version of another datatype. You may make your own derived datatypes. The spec also includes several among its built-in datatypes, which are therefore supported by every implementation. Figure 62-1 illustrates the built-in datatypes, showing the derivations.

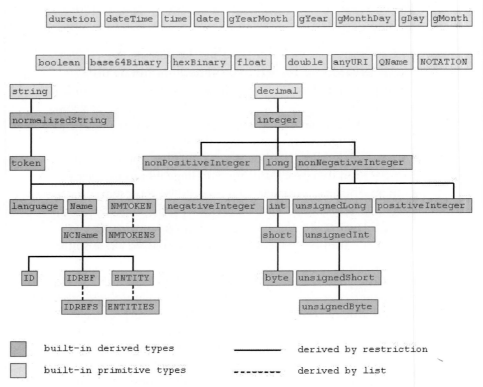

Figure 62-1   Built-in datatypes

62.3.1 *Primitive datatypes*

The *primitive datatypes* are the building blocks of all others. Most are also useful just by themselves.

62.3.1.1   Common programming datatypes

The first five we will cover include common datatypes in most programming languages and database management systems.

string
>   Equivalent to CDATA in a DTD – an arbitrarily long sequence of characters. You might use this for a `title` element's datatype.

boolean
>   True and false values. The data may be any one of the following strings: `false` or `0` for false values or `true` or `1` for true values. You might use this for a datatype that represented whether a checkbox in a graphical user interface should be turned on by default (true) or turned off by default (false).

decimal
>   Arbitrary precision decimal numbers. These can represent anything numerical: height, weight, financial amounts, etc. Decimal numbers may have a fractional part that follows a period as in `5.3`. Decimal numbers may be preceded by a plus (+) or minus (–) sign to represent whether they are negative or positive.

float
>   Single precision 32-bit floating point numbers. This is a form of number that is very efficient for numerical computation on 32-bit computers. Floats may have a fractional part and may also be preceded by a plus or minus sign. Compared to decimals, floats are less precise. They are an approximation. Sometimes the number you put into the computer will not be exactly the number you get out later![1]

double
>   Double precision 64-bit floating point numbers. These numbers are more precise than single-precision floats but are still approximations.[2]

---

1. If you do use them, they may have exponents (preceded by "e" or "E", as in "2.5E5") and may take the values "NaN", "INF" and "-INF".
2. And the same footnote applies!

62.3.1.2   XML datatypes

anyURI

This extremely important primitive datatype is used for URIs (typically URLs). These may include so-called *fragment identifiers* after a pound sign. For instance if the URI refers to an XML document the fragment identifier may be an XPointer.[3]

QName

This primitive datatype is based on the XML namespaces specification. It stands for a namespace-qualified name. In other words, a QName is a name that may have a colon in it. If it does, the text before the colon should be a namespace prefix for a namespace that has been declared. If it does not, the names should be interpreted as belonging to the default namespace. See Chapter 53, "Namespaces", on page 826 for more information on namespaces.

NOTATION

This datatype corresponds to the XML NOTATION attribute type.

62.3.1.3   Binary datatypes

There are two datatypes for representing binary data. The first is called hexBinary because it uses the *hex* notation, popular among practitioners of the occult and programmers of the UNIX operating system. There are sixteen hex digits.[4] The digits 0 through 9 represent the same thing they do in ordinary decimal numbers. The letter a represents 10, b represents 11 and so forth through f representing 15. Hex is popular not only because of its mystical powers but also because a few simple calculations can turn two hex digits into a value between 0 and 255, which is exactly the amount that can be held in a single byte.

The other datatype is called base64Binary because it represents base64-encoded data. Base64 is not as simple to translate into bytes without

---

3. See Chapter 64, "XML Pointer Language (XPointer)", on page 1052 for more information on XPointers.
4. In fact, hex is short for hexadecimal, which is the base-16 numbering system.

a computer but uses less space than hex. Hex doubles the size of the data. Base64 increases it by only a third, approximately.

62.3.1.4   Durations

The remaining primitive datatypes are all related to time: durations in this section and absolute dates and times in the next.

The duration datatype is based on the ISO 8601 date format standard. It represents a length of time, such as an hour or 3.56 seconds. Durations can be represented with a precision of seconds or fractions of a second. They can also span thousands of years.

A duration always starts with P; for example, P2Y. The 2Y that follows the P means two years (the gestation period for some elephants!).

Instead of measuring in years, you could measure in months: P3M would be three months (the amount of time it takes to get a new phone line installed in some cities).

You can also measure in years and months: P1Y3M means one year and three months (the shelf-life of a boy band). You can also count in days (with or without years or months): P3D (length of the Battle of Gettysburg).

But wait...that's not all. Durations can get as fine grained as a fraction of a second. If you want to deal in time units shorter than a day you use the designator T after you've listed all of the day/month/year parts (or directly after the P if you are interested only in hour/minute/second units).

For instance P1YT1M represents one year and one minute (which is the amount of time that a VCR with a P1Y warranty is likely to survive). As you can see, M represents both month and minute, which is why you must include the T designator that separates the date part from the time part. If you have an hour, a minute or a second part you must have the T.

In addition to minutes you may use H for hour and S for second. S is the only part of the duration that may have a fractional part. PT3M43.13S represents three minutes and 43.13 seconds (the world record for running a mile).

The different parts of the date and time must always come in the same order: P, years, months, days, T, hours, minutes, seconds. Remember that the P is always required and the T is required if there are hours/minutes/seconds. Everything else is optional.

62.3.1.5   Dates and times

The `date` datatype represents a specific calendar date in the form YYYY-MM-DD. For instance the date of the Beatles' debut on Ed Sullivan would be `1964-02-09` – February 9th, 1964.

Negative dates are also allowed, to represent BCE (BC) dates. For instance `-0133-06-01` represents the approximate date of a Roman slave revolt lead by a man called Aristonicus – June 1, 133 BCE.

The `time` datatype represents a time that recurs every day. Times have the form `hh:mm:ss`. The seconds may have a fractional part. So `14:12:34.843` represents 2:12 and 34.843 seconds in the afternoon. It is *not* legal to leave the seconds out, even if they are not relevant: `14:12:00`.

To indicate that the time is expressed in *coordinated universal time (UTC)*, also known as Greenwich mean time (GMT), add a `z` to the end of the time: `14:20:00Z`.

It is also possible (and a good idea!) to specify a time zone for a time, as an offset from GMT. Do this by appending a - or + sign and a number of hours and minutes in the form `hh:mm`, such as `08:15:00-08:00` (8:15 Pacific time) or `11:20:00+03:30` (11:20 Tehran time). The time zone is optional but if you leave it out then it will be impossible to compare times across time zones.

As you might guess, it is possible to combine a date and time into a `dateTime`. A `dateTime` has a `T` between the date and time parts: `1929-10-29T11:00:00-05:00`.

62.3.1.6   Recurring dates and times

The `gDay`, `gMonth` and `gMonthDay` datatypes represent a day that recurs every month (e.g. the first or fifteenth day of each month), a month that recurs every year (let's say July – or any other month!) and a particular date that recurs every year (such as Valentine's day). The `g` in their names indicates that they are based on the Gregorian calendar.

The `gDay` datatype is in the form `---DD`. There are three leading dashes, so the 8th of every month would be `---08`.

The `gMonth` datatype, `--MM`, is similar. However, there are only two leading dashes, so every June would be `--06`.

The gMonthDay datatype is in the form --MM-DD. For instance, Caesar's "Ides of March" (March 15th) would be --03-15 and a gMonth of --02 represents the month of February of every year.

These datatypes represent durations from the very first instant of the date to the very last. To improve precision, any of them may be followed by a time zone indicator.

The gYear and gYearMonth represent particular years or months in history or in the future. The year is a four-digit number and a gYearMonth is a four-digit number followed by a two-digit number: 2002-06. Either may be preceded by a negative sign (-) to represent BCE dates. They may also be followed by a time zone indicator.

62.3.2 *Derived datatypes*

The *derived datatypes* are based on the primitive ones. The *XML Schema Datatypes* spec defines some derived datatypes and provides facilities for users to define their own.

The ones defined in the spec are listed below. They fall into several categories.

62.3.2.1 Restricted numeric datatypes

These are numeric datatypes more specific (*restricted*) than the primitive datatypes.

62.3.2.1.1 *Integers*

integer
: Decimal number (no matter how large or small) with no fractional part.

positiveInteger
: Integer greater than zero

negativeInteger
: Integer less than zero.

`nonPositiveInteger`
> Integer less than or equal to zero.

`nonNegativeInteger`
> Integer greater than or equal to zero.

62.3.2.1.2 *Computer word lengths*

This group allows data to be restricted to values that specific computers can handle efficiently. Most modern computers handle everything from 8-bits to 32-bits well. A 64-bit computer handles `long` and `unsignedLong` most efficiently and other values less so.

`byte`
> 8-bit signed number (between -128 and 127)

`unsignedByte`
> 8-bit non-negative number (between 0 and 255)

`short`
> 16-bit number (between -32768 and 32767)

`unsignedShort`
> 16-bit non-negative number (between 0 and 65535)

`int`
> 32-bit number (between -2147483648 and 2147483647)

`unsignedInt`
> 32-bit non-negative number (between 0 and 4294967295)

`long`
> 64-bit number (between -9223372036854775808 and 9223372036854775807)

`unsignedLong`
> 64-bit non-negative number (between 0 and 18446744073709551615) (whew!)

62.3.2.2   Derived XML datatypes

Several derived datatypes are based on XML attribute types and other constructs.

62.3.2.2.1   *XML attribute types*

Some derived datatypes emulate XML attribute types. They are easy to recognize because they are the only built-in datatypes with upper-case names.

ID
> An identifier unique to a single element in a document.

IDREF
> A reference to a unique ID in the document.

IDREFS
> A whitespace-separated list of IDREF values.

ENTITY
> The name of an unparsed entity in the document.

ENTITIES
> A whitespace-separated list of ENTITY values.

NMTOKEN
> A string with certain character constraints (51.1.5, "Names and name tokens", on page 769) placed upon it.

NMTOKENS
> A whitespace-separated list of NMTOKEN values.

Note that some of these datatypes are single tokens and others are lists. The ones that are lists are created by *deriving by list* rather than *deriving by restriction*. We will show you how to do these yourself later on.

62.3.2.2.2   *Other XML constructs*

There are other datatypes for XML constructs.

Name

While XML has a "name" construct, (described in 51.1.5, "Names and name tokens", on page 769), the corresponding SGML NAME attribute datatype was a casualty of the minimalist XML design approach. NMTOKEN had been the closest, but now *XML Schema* has restored the datatype as Name (note the capitalization!).

language

The built-in, derived datatype called language accepts the same values as the xml:lang attribute discussed in 55.4, "Special attributes and newlines", on page 886.

NCName

Earlier we discussed the primitive datatype QName that is based on a concept from the XML namespaces specification. A QName is a name that may have a namespace prefix (and therefore a colon). There is a derived datatype that is the opposite of a QName called NCName. This stands for no-colon name which means (drum roll please...) a name with no colons in it. You can use this when you want to avoid namespace behavior in a datatype.

normalizedString

This datatype is for strings in which whitespace characters such as carriage return and tab characters should be replaced by spaces. If you use this datatype or derive from it, the schema processor will handle this normalization for you.

token

This datatype is for strings that collapse groups of adjacent whitespace into a single space and strip leading and trailing spaces. Many of the datatypes we have already discussed are derived from the token datatype in order to inherit its whitespace handling features. These are: language, Name, NMTOKEN and NCName, ID, IDREF and ENTITY.

62.4 | Defining user-derived datatypes

The XML Schema definition language (XSDL) provides a facility for defining user-derived datatypes, using the `simpleType` definition element.

The element must contain a child element for the desired form of derivation: `list`, `union`, or `restriction`.

derivation by list

Derivation by list is quite straightforward. You merely take an existing datatype (like `gYear`) and create a new datatype that accepts a list of them (we could call it `gYears`).

derivation by union

This sort of derivation merges two or more datatypes into one that supports values of either sort. For instance a datatype representing months might allow either `gMonth` integers or string names by deriving by union from `Name` and `gMonth`.

derivation by restriction

This form of derivation narrows down the values allowed by an existing datatype. For instance you could take the datatype `gYear` and restrict it to years in a particular century.

The child element might optionally be preceded by an `annotation` element, as shown in Example 62-3.

Note   Annotation elements can hold more than documentation, and XSDL elements in general have other properties that support self-documentation and application processing of schema definitions. As these facilities are not germane to deriving datatypes for general use, they are discussed in 63.3.2, "Schema components", on page 1036.

62.4.1 *Derivation by list*

You derive by list when you want to allow occurrences of the datatype in the document to contain multiple values rather than just one. For instance to

Example 62-3. A `simpleType` definition

```
<xsd:simpleType name="mynewType">
    <xsd:annotation>
        <xsd:documentation>Important new type</xsd:documentation>
    </xsd:annotation>
    <xsd:restriction base="someOtherType">
        ...
    </xsd:restriction>
</xsd:simpleType>
```

allow multiple dates you could derive a `dates` datatype[5] from the primitive `date` datatype as in Example 62-4.

Caution   Items in lists are always separated by whitespace. If a datatype allows embedded whitespace (such as `string`), deriving a list from it may produce unexpected results.

Example 62-4. Deriving a list from a named datatype

```
<xsd:simpleType name="dates">
  <xsd:annotation>
    <xsd:documentation>Multiple dates</xsd:documentation>
  </xsd:annotation>
  <xsd:list itemType="xsd:date"/>
</xsd:simpleType>
```

In Example 62-4, the list was derived from an existing named datatype. It is also possible to derive a list from a newly-defined anonymous datatype. Rather than putting an `itemType` attribute on the `list`, you would merely put a `simpleType` element in the `list` element content.

The embedded `simpleType` will be used just as if you had defined it elsewhere, given it a name and referred to it with the `itemType` attribute. Example 62-5 demonstrates.

---

5. XSDL would call this a simple type, rather than a datatype, but in this chapter it is clearer to call it a datatype.

Example 62-5. Deriving a list from an anonymous datatype

```
<xsd:simpleType name="pubDates">
  <xsd:list>
    <xsd:simpleType>
        ... derivation of pubDate ...
    </xsd:simpleType>
  </xsd:list>
</xsd:simpleType>
```

62.4.2 *Derivation by union*

Derivation by union is a way of combining existing datatypes into one datatype. For instance you might want to allow dates to be specified according to any one of:

- the built-in Gregorian date datatype,
- a notation based on the ancient Aztec calendar, or
- the Hebrew calendar.

If we define our datatypes so that they are syntactically distinct then we can easily create a union of them. One way to easily distinguish Aztec and Hebrew dates is to start them with the letters A and H, respectively, because we know that built-in dates start with a number. Example 62-6 demonstrates such a union datatype.

Example 62-6. Union datatype

```
<xsd:simpleType name="AnyKindaDate">
  <!-- we could put an annotation here -->
  <xsd:union memberTypes="myns:AztecDate myns:HebrewDate xsd:date">
      <!-- we could put another annotation here -->
  </xsd:union>
</xsd:simpleType>
```

If we carelessly defined our notations so that some Aztec dates could also be recognized as Hebrew or Gregorian dates, then the Aztec interpretation would win over the other ones because it is listed first in the memberTypes attribute.

Instead of – or in addition to – a memberTypes attribute, you could also put simpleType elements within the union to define anonymous in-line datatypes, just as we did for lists. Unlike lists, however, which are derived from a single datatype, we can define as many anonymous datatypes as we like. Each of them contributes to the union just as if it had been defined externally and referenced.

If we wanted to, we could define a union of two different kinds of lists. Perhaps we would allow a list of Hebrew dates or a list of Aztec dates. Conversely, we could define a list of a union datatype. For instance, a list derived from `AnyKindaDate` would be a list of a union.

Many complex combinations of different kinds of derivation are possible.

62.4.3 *Deriving datatypes by restriction*

Another way to derive a datatype is by restriction. In this case, you add constraints to an existing datatype, either built-in or user-derived.

By definition, a datatype derived by restriction is more constraining than its base datatype. Any value that conforms to the new derived datatype would also have to conform to the original base datatype.

Restrictions are created with the `restriction` element. You may have a single `restriction` as a child of the `simpleType` element. You can refer to a named base datatype with the `base` attribute, or define an anonymous base datatype by including a simple type in the content.

There is a fixed list of ways that you can constrain a given datatype. These are called *constraining facets*. There are twelve of them, each represented by a specific element type. They occur as sub-elements of the `restriction` element. The allowable ones depend on the base datatype.

They have several points in common:

- They all allow a single optional `annotation` sub-element and no other.
- Each has a required `value` attribute that specifies the constraining value. The exact meaning and allowable values of the attribute depend on the specific facet and the base datatype.
- They work together.

The last item requires some explanation.

If you define a datatype with a minimum value and then refine it by restriction to make a new datatype with a maximum value, the new datatype has *both* the minimum value constraint from the base datatype *and* the maximum value constraint from the derived datatype. If you defined yet a third datatype by restriction based on the new datatype, it would add still other restrictions.

This principle applies even when the same facet is applied at two different levels. So you could define a datatype that represents the set of numbers greater than 10,000 by setting a minimum value constraint. In a datatype derived from that you could set another minimum value constraint raising the minimum value to 20,000.

Values must now be both greater than 10,000 and greater than 20,000, which is the same as saying just that they must be greater than 20,000. In one sense both restrictions apply, but really the more constraining derived datatype overrides the base datatype.[6]

62.5 | Constraining facets

This section describes the twelve `facet` elements that are used when deriving by restriction. They fall into six categories: range, length, decimal digit, enumeration, white space, and pattern.

62.5.1 *Range restrictions*

The simplest kind of restriction available for numeric and date datatypes is a range restriction. For instance we might want to define a user-derived datatype called "publication year" as a year that must fall between 1000 and 2100. Example 62-7 defines a `pubYear` datatype with these characteristics.

The `minInclusive` element sets the minimum value allowed for the new `pubYear` datatype and the `maxInclusive` element sets the maximum value allowed.

Alternatively, we could use the `maxExclusive` and `minExclusive` elements. They also set upper and lower bounds, but the bounds exclude the

---

6. There is a way to prevent such overrides, but as it is rarely needed, we don't cover it here.

Example 62-7. Defining a restricted range integer datatype

```
<xsd:simpleType name="pubYear">
  <xsd:annotation>
    <xsd:documentation>A publication year</xsd:documentation>
  </xsd:annotation>
  <xsd:restriction base="xsd:gYear">
      <xsd:minInclusive value="1000"/>
      <xsd:maxInclusive value="2100"/>
  </xsd:restriction>
</xsd:simpleType>
```

named value. In other words, a `maxExclusive` value of 2100 allows 2099 but not 2100.

62.5.2 *Length restrictions*

There are three length constraining facets: `minLength` and `maxLength`, which work together or separately to set lower and upper bounds on a value's length, and a facet called simply `length` which requires a specific fixed length.

Length means slightly different things depending on the datatype that it is restricting.

list
> If the datatype is a list (e.g. `IDREFS`) then the length facets constrain the number of items in the list.

string
> If the datatype derives from string (directly or through multiple levels of derivation) then the length facets constrain the number of characters in the string.

binary
> Applied to a binary datatype, length facets constrain the number of bytes of decoded binary data.

62.5.3 *Decimal digit restrictions*

There are two facets that only apply to decimal numbers and types derived from them. These are `totalDigits` and `fractionDigits`.

The first constrains the maximum number of digits in the decimal representation of the number and the second constrains the maximum number of digits in the fractional part (after the `.`). For instance it would make sense when dealing with dollars to constrain the `fractionDigits` to two.

62.5.4 *Enumeration restrictions*

You can also define a datatype as a list of allowable values by using several `enumeration` elements. In Example 62-8, we define a `dayOfWeek` datatype.

Example 62-8. Defining an enumerated datatype

```
<xsd:simpleType name="workday">
  <xsd:restriction base="xsd:string">
   <xsd:enumeration value="Sunday"/>
   <xsd:enumeration value="Monday"/>
   <xsd:enumeration value="Tuesday"/>
   <xsd:enumeration value="Wednesday">
     <xsd:annotation>
       <xsd:documentation>Halfway there!</xsd:documentation>
     </xsd:annotation>
   </xsd:enumeration>
   <xsd:enumeration value="Thursday"/>
   <xsd:enumeration value="Friday">
     <xsd:annotation>
       <xsd:documentation>Almost done!</xsd:documentation>
     </xsd:annotation>
   </xsd:enumeration>
   <xsd:enumeration value="Saturday"/>
  </xsd:restriction>
</xsd:simpleType>
```

Note that an enumeration element, like all facet-constraining elements, may have an annotation sub-element.

Enumeration elements work together to restrict the value to one of the enumeration values. Enumeration elements are so strict that they supersede any of the base datatype's constraints. Where other constraints say things like "the value must be higher than X or look like Y", enumerations say: "the value must be one of these values and not anything else".

The enumeration values must be legal values of the base datatype. Therefore, if an enumeration datatype derives from another enumeration datatype, the derived datatype may only have values that the base datatype has.

62.5.5 The whiteSpace facet

The whiteSpace facet is a little bit different from the others. Rather than constraining the value of a datatype, it constrains the processing. The facet can have one of three values:

preserve
> The datatype processor will leave the whitespace alone.

replace
> Whitespace of any kind is changed into space characters.

collapse
> Sequences of whitespace are collapsed to a single space and leading and trailing whitespace is discarded.

The built-in datatypes all use the value collapse, except for string and types derived from it. Those types include normalizedString, which in turn is a base type for token. As we discussed in 62.3.2.2.2, "Other XML constructs", on page 1011, all of the datatypes that represent names of things (language, Name, NMTOKEN, etc.) derive from tokens.

62.5.6 The pattern facet

The most sophisticated and powerful facet is the pattern facet. Patterns have a value attribute that is a *regular expression*.

Variants of regular expression syntax are used in several aspects of XML. DTDs use one to describe content models.[7] The XML specification itself is written in terms of a grammar built of regular expressions.[8]

The regular expressions that constrain datatypes are based on those used in various programming languages. They have especially close ties to the Perl programming language which integrates regular expressions into its core syntax.

Note   *The full regular expression language is quite complicated because of deep support for Unicode. There are also shortcuts to reduce the size of regular expressions. We do not cover all of these. Instead we concentrate on those regular expression features that are used most of the time.*

Example 62-9 illustrates some interesting patterns. We'll explain what goes into them in the following sections.

Example 62-9. Pattern examples

```
<xsd:simpleType name="even-number">
    <xsd:restriction base="xsd:decimal">
        <xsd:pattern value="\d*[02468]"/>
    </xsd:restriction>
</xsd:simpleType>

<xsd:simpleType name="old-fashioned-domain-name">
    <xsd:restriction base="xsd:string">
        <xsd:pattern value="\w+\.(com|net|org|gov)"/>
    </xsd:restriction>
</xsd:simpleType>

<xsd:simpleType name="phone-number">
    <xsd:restriction base="xsd:string">
        <xsd:pattern value="(\d{3}-)?\d{3}-\d{4}"/>
    </xsd:restriction>
</xsd:simpleType>
```

---

7. See 52.5, "Content models", on page 804.
8. They are called "productions" and are discussed in Chapter 57, "Reading the XML specification", on page 904.

62.5.6.1   Constructing regular expressions

The simplest regular expression is just a character. `a` is a regular expression that matches the character "a". There is only one string in the world that matches this string.

If we put other letters beside the "a" then the regular expression will match them in order. `abcd` matches "a" and then "b" and then "c" and then "d". Once again there is only one string that matches that expression.

62.5.6.1.1   *Quantifiers*

A slightly more sophisticated regular expression will match one or more occurrences of the last letter "d": `abcd+`. Just as in DTD content models, the plus symbol means "one or more of this thing". "This thing" is whatever comes just before the plus symbol – typically a character. Just as in content models, there are also `?` and `*` symbols available. They stand for "zero or one of the thing" and "zero or more of the thing". We call these `quantifiers`.

There is another quantifier that is not available in DTD content models. It uses curly braces (`{}`) with one or two numbers between them. The quantifier `{3}` means that there should be three occurrences of the thing.

So `ba{3}d` matches "baaad". It is also possible to express a range: `ba{3,7}d` matches "baaad", "baaaad", "baaaaad", "baaaaaad" and "baaaaaaad". The lower bound can go as low as zero, in which case the item is optional (just as if you had used a question mark).

The upper bound can be omitted like this: `ba{3,}d`. That means that there is no upper bound. That expression is equivalent to `baaaa*d` which is itself equivalent to `baaa+d`. All three expressions match three or more occurrences of the middle letter "a".

We can put these ideas together. For instance `ab{2,5}c+d{4}` matches one "a" followed by two to five "b"s followed by one or more "c"s followed by exactly 4 "d"s. Example 62-10 demonstrates.

Example 62-10. Quantifiers in a regular expression

```
<xsd:simpleType name="reg-exp-example">
    <xsd:restriction base="xsd:string">
        <xsd:pattern value="ab{2,5}c+d{4}"/>
    </xsd:restriction>
</xsd:simpleType>
```

62.5.6.1.2 *Alternatives and grouping*

Regular expressions use the | symbol to represent alternatives just as DTD content models do.

Consider the regular expression yes+|no+. It matches "yes", "yess", "yesss", "no", "noo", "nooo" and so forth.

However, there is a big difference between content models and regular expressions. The primitive tokens in content models are elements. So in that context yes is judged as one "yes" element. In the world of regular expressions we are dealing with individual characters, so yes is three characters and yes+ repeats only the last character, not the rest.

If we do want to repeat the whole word yes, we can use parentheses (just as in content models). The regular expression (yes)+|(no)+ matches the strings "yes", "yesyes", "yesyesyes", "no", "nono", "nonono".

We can even use parentheses to group the whole expression: (yes|no)+. This expression allows us to match multiple occurrences of "yes" and "no". For example: "yes", "no", "yesyes", "yesno", "noyes", "nono", "yesyesyes", "yesnoyes" and so forth.

62.5.6.1.3 *Special characters*

There are ways to refer to function characters:

- \n represents the newline (or line-feed) character.
- \r represents the return character.
- \t represents the tab character.

So a\nb represents the letter "a" followed by a newline followed by "b".

There are also ways to refer to the characters that would normally be interpreted as symbols. For instance the + character might be necessary in a regular expression involving mathematics.

- Convert a symbol into an ordinary character by preceding it with the symbol \. So \? is translated into the ordinary character (not special symbol) ?.
- Convert a backslash symbol to a character like this: \\. Convert two of them like this: \\\\.
- The symbol characters you need to handle in this way are:

    \ | . - ^ ? * + { } ( ) [ ]

62.5.6.2   Character classes

It is often useful to be able to refer to lists of characters without explicitly listing all of the characters. For instance it would be annoying to need to enter (1|2|3|4|5|6|7|8|9|0) whenever you want to allow a digit.

Plus there are many Unicode characters that are considered digits that are not in this set. Examples include TIBETAN DIGIT ZERO, GUJARATI DIGIT TWO and DINGBAT NEGATIVE CIRCLED DIGIT NINE. It would not be internationally correct to ignore those!

These sets of reusable characters are known as *character classes*. They are represented by a backslash character followed by a letter.[9]

62.5.6.2.1   *Built-in character classes*

This particular character class, digits, is represented by \d. So \d+ means one or more digits, while \d+a\d{2,5} means one or more digits, and then the letter "a", and then two to five more digits. The opposite of this character class is indicated by an upper-case \D, meaning anything that is not a digit.

Another major character class is indicated simply by a period (.). It matches any character except a newline or linefeed character. So d.g matches "dig" and "dog" but also "d-g" and "d%g". The middle character could even be Kanji or Cherokee (both components of Unicode!).

The character class \s represents any whitespace character (space, tab, newline, carriage return). \S is its opposite. It represents any non-whitespace character.

\i represents the set of "initial name" characters – basically letters, the underscore and the colon.[10] \I is its opposite: anything that is not an initial name character. \c represents the set of all name characters. \C is its opposite.[11]

---

9. Note that the backslash does two different jobs. It turns symbol (punctuation) characters into ordinary characters and ordinary letters into character classes.

10. The class was renamed from the proper XML terminology of *name start characters* so that \n could have its common regular expression meaning of "newline".

11. See 51.1.5, "Names and name tokens", on page 769 for a refresher on both of these character classes.

\w represents what you might call "word" characters: basically letters, digits, and some symbols (e.g. currency, math). That is to say, characters that are not punctuation, separators or the like. \w+ will roughly match a word; \W represents the opposite – the characters that are not considered word characters.

62.5.6.2.2   *Constructing a character class*

You can also create character classes in your regular expressions (though you cannot give them fancy backslash-prefixed names!). The syntax to do this is called a *character class expression* and it uses square brackets ([]).

For instance to represent the first four characters in the alphabet you would say [abcd]. This simple example could just as easily be represented as (a|b|c|d) but the character class notation allows a couple of tricks that are difficult to emulate with the | symbol.

When you construct a character class expression you can specify ranges. For instance [a-z] represents the characters from "a" through "z" in Unicode (which are the same as in the English alphabet). You can even put multiple ranges together: [a-zA-Z0-9].

Inside square brackets, the characters *, +, (,), {, } and ? are just characters. They have no special meaning. Backslash (\) remains special because we use that to refer to the built-in character classes (\d for digits and so forth). Here is a character class that matches all of them and also matches Unicode digit and word characters: [*+(){}\d\w].

It is also possible to construct a "negative" character class which includes all of the characters that you do not list. You do this by starting your character class expression with a caret (^) symbol. So to match every character except "a" and "z", you would use the regular expression: [^az]. If you wanted to match everything except the characters *from* "a" *to* "z", you could do that like this: [^a-z].

62.6 | Using datatypes

Although *XML Schema* datatypes were originally designed for use with XSDL, they can also be used with DTDs and in other contexts. In fact several schema languages, such as RELAX NG, have chosen to use them. As the next section demonstrates, datatypes do not have to be used in schemas at all!

62.6.1 *Instance documents*

It is typical for a schema processor to infer the datatype of an element based on the element-type name and matching declarations in some schema. It is possible, however, for an element to explicitly declare its datatype using an attribute named type in the namespace:

    http://www.w3.org/2001/XMLSchema-instance

This namespace is conventionally given the prefix xsi so the attribute value typically has the qualified name xsi:type. Of course you may declare any prefix you like.

62.6.1.1 Built-in datatypes

This in-line datatype information is useful when your goal is not schema validation, but rather just informing applications about the data. The application can use this information to create appropriate object types in a programming language. Example 62-11 shows how datatype usage can be declared in a document instance that conforms to an XSDL schema definition.

Example 62-11. Instance syntax for built-in datatypes

```
<doc xmlns:xsi="http://www.w3.org/2001/XMLSchema-instance"
     xmlns:xsd="http://www.w3.org/2001/XMLSchema">
  <mynum xsi:type="xsd:decimal">409</mynum>
  <mystr xsi:type="xsd:string">You're so fine!</mystr>
</doc>
```

For other document instances, where the full XSDL namespace isn't needed, the second namespace declaration would be:

    xmlns:xsd="http://www.w3.org/2001/XMLSchema-datatypes

62.6.1.2 User-defined datatypes

There are two ways to package the simple type definitions for your derived datatypes:

- As simple type definitions within the full XSDL schema definition you are using for your documents; or
- As a set of simple type definitions to be used in conjunction with a DTD or schema definition written in another schema language. The definitions would be contained in an `xsd:schema` element and would be defined in a target namespace.[12]

If your schema defines datatypes in the namespace `http://www.myns.org/2000/datatypes` then you can refer to those datatypes using the syntax shown in Example 62-12.

Example 62-12. Instance syntax for user-defined datatypes

```
<doc xmlns:xsi="http://www.w3.org/2001/XMLSchema-instance"
    xmlns:dt="http://www.myns.org/2000/datatypes">
  <mynum xsi:type="dt:myType">3^2</mynum>
  <mystr xsi:type="dt:myOtherType">codeName</mystr>
</doc>
```

62.6.2 *Web Services Description Language (WSDL)*

The Web Services Description Language allows you to merge XSDL complex types and simple datatypes into your service descriptions. For instance you could say that the first element in a message must always be a `pubYear`. Example 62-13 demonstrates how you can embed a `schema` element with a datatype definition within a service description.

The example first initializes three namespaces, one that we will define ourselves (the one relating to publishing), one for *XML Schema* (so we have access to *XML Schema* datatypes) and one for WSDL itself. In the WSDL `types` element we embed a `schema` element containing the definition of the `pubYear` datatype. Then we use this datatype as a part of the WSDL message.

12.See 63.3.1, "Namespaces", on page 1036.

Example 62-13. Web service description

```
<!-- namespace declarations -->
<ws:definitions
  xmlns:pub="http://www.publisher.com"
  xmlns:xsd="http://www.w3.org/2001/XMLSchema"
  xmlns:ws="http://schemas.xmlsoap.org/wsdl/">
  <ws:types>
    <!-- embedded datatype definition -->
    <xsd:schema targetNamespace="http://www.publisher.com">
      <xsd:simpleType name="pubYear">
        ... definition here ....
      </xsd:simpleType>
    </xsd:schema>
  </ws:types>

  <!-- message based on datatype-->
  <ws:message name="publisherReport">
    <ws:part name="year" type="pub:pubYear"/>
    <ws:part name="title" type="xsd:string"/>
  </ws:message>
  ...
</ws:definitions>
```

62.6.3 *XML DTDs*

Since *XML Schema* datatypes were designed after DTDs[13], there is no built-in provision in DTD declarations for declaring the use of these datatypes. Instead, users and software developers have adopted a convention for making the association.

It is called *Datatypes for DTDs (DT4DTD)* and was first defined in the W3C Note at `http://www.w3.org/TR/dt4dtd`. A later version, which we use in this book, can be found at `http://www.xmlhandbook.com/dt4dtd`. That URI also serves as the namespace for two attribute names, which are declared with fixed values:

`dt4dtd:e`

> The datatype of the element's data content. The attribute is only needed when the data content is other than `string`.

---

13. About 30 years after, but who's counting.

`dt4dtd:a`

The datatypes of all the attributes that have datatypes. The attribute value is a list of pairs, each consisting of an attribute name followed by its datatype. The `dt4dtd:a` attribute is only needed when using a datatype that can't be declared with an XML attribute type (that is, a datatype other than `string` (declared as CDATA), NMTOKEN, ID, etc.).

If a datatype is not a built-in datatype, you can declare a namespace of the same name to reference its definition and use the namespace prefix to identify it uniquely.[14] An implementation can use the namespace URI to invoke the software that checks and/or processes the data.

In Example 62-14, the `dt4dtd:a` attribute declares the datatypes for the `pubyear` and `linecount` attributes. The datatype of `linecount` is built-in, but the datatype of `pubyear` is user-derived so there is a NOTATION declaration that references its definition.

Tip   There is open source software that supports DT4DTD. It is available on the CD-ROM and at `http://www.xmlhandbook.com/dt4dtd`.

Example 62-14. Declaring datatypes for attributes

```
<!ATTLIST poem
 xmlns:dt4dtd   CDATA #FIXED "http://www.xmlhandbook.com/dt4dtd/"
 xmlns:myTypes  CDATA #FIXED "file://datatypeDefs.xsd#pubYear"
 dt4dtd:a       CDATA #FIXED "pubyear   myTypes:pubYear
                              linecount nonNegativeInteger"
 pubyear        CDATA #IMPLIED
 linecount      CDATA #IMPLIED >
```

62.7 | Conclusion

XML Schema Datatypes provides a library of built-in datatypes and a facility for deriving your own from them. These datatypes can be used in XSDL schema definitions, in DTDs, and in non-XSDL schema languages.

14. In other words, exactly the same way it is done with XML Schema.

XML Schema (XSDL)

- *XML Schema* definition language

- Syntax and declarations

- Simple and complex types

- Locally-scoped elements

- Schema inclusion

Chapter

63

A n XML DTD is a specific case of a more general concept called a schema definition. The dictionary defines *schema* as a "general conception of what is common to all members of a class." A *schema definition* takes that "conception" and turns it into something concrete that can be used directly by a computer.

There are many types of schema in use in the computer industry, chiefly for databases. DTDs are different in that the class for which they declare "what is common to all members" is a class of XML documents.

The popularity of XML has brought DTDs to entirely new constituencies. The database experts and programmers who are taking to XML in droves are examining it from the standpoint of their own areas of expertise and familiar paradigms.

All of these creative folks have ideas about what could be done differently. The World Wide Web Consortium has incorporated these ideas into a design for an enhanced schema definition facility called the *XML Schema definition language (XSDL)*.

The name of the language is often shortened to "XML Schema", but we reserve that phrase for the name of the W3C spec. We call the language XSDL so you'll know when we are referring to the "schema definition language" as opposed to:

- a particular "schema definition",
- a conceptual "schema", or
- the *XML Schema* specification.

The words "XML schema", unfortunately, could refer to any of those four things.

Caution   The XML Schema spec is several times longer than the XML specification itself. It is also quite intricate and formal. This chapter will informally teach a subset that is sufficiently functional for most projects and yet simple enough that we can teach it all in one chapter.

63.1 | A simple sample schema

Let's start our explanation of XSDL by introducing a sample DTD and an equivalent schema definition and comparing the two.

63.1.1 *Sample DTD*

The sample DTD in Example 63-1 demonstrates some of the most important features of DTD declarations. Example 63-2 shows a document that conforms to that DTD.

Example 63-1. Poem DTD

```
<!ELEMENT   poem    (title, picture, verse+)>
<!ATTLIST   poem
  publisher CDATA       #IMPLIED
  pubyear   NMTOKEN     #IMPLIED
  xmlns:dt4dtd CDATA    #FIXED "http://www.xmlhandbook.com/dt4dtd/"
>
<!ELEMENT   title   (#PCDATA)>
<!ELEMENT   verse   (#PCDATA)>
<!ELEMENT   picture EMPTY>
<!ATTLIST   picture href        CDATA #REQUIRED
                    dt4dtd:a  CDATA #FIXED "href anyURI">
```

The DTD defines a `poem` element type that consists of a `title` element followed by a `picture` and one or more `verse` elements. The `poem` element type has two optional attributes: `publisher` and `pubyear`. It also has an `xmlns:dt4dtd` attribute to declare the namespace for attributes that assign datatypes.[1]

The `picture` element type's required `href` attribute is declared as a CDATA attribute. However, the `dt4dtd:a` attribute indicates that the value of `href` must have a URI datatype.

Example 63-2. Poem document

```
<!DOCTYPE poem SYSTEM "poem.dtd">
<poem xmlns="http://www.poetry.net/poetns"
    publisher="Boni and Liveright" pubyear="1922">
<title>The Waste Land</title>
<picture href="pic1.gif"/>
<verse>April is the cruellest month, breeding</verse>
<verse>Lilacs out of the dead land</verse>
</poem>
```

63.1.2 *Equivalent schema definition*

Example 63-3 is an XSDL definition for the poem document type. There are several notable differences between this example and Example 63-1.

- Perhaps the most obvious is that instead of using the syntax of DTD declarations, a schema definition is represented as an XML document.
- There is a dependency on namespaces, which are heavily utilized.[2] The `schema` element declares the prefix `xsd` for names defined in XML Schema and `poem` for names that are defined within this schema definition.
- There is a built-in syntax that can be used to declare datatypes: the `type` attribute. Actually, it is used for more than datatypes;

---

1. We use the "Datatypes for DTDs" convention (see 62.6.3, "XML DTDs", on page 1028). The namespace attribute is fixed in the DTD for reasons discussed in 53.3, "Namespaces and DTDs", on page 836.
2. Namespaces are discussed in Chapter 53, "Namespaces", on page 826.

Example 63-3. Poem schema definition in XSDL

```
<?xml version="1.0"?>
<xsd:schema xmlns:xsd="http://www.w3.org/2001/XMLSchema"
        xmlns:poem="http://www.poetry.net/poetns"
   targetNamespace="http://www.poetry.net/poetns">
  <xsd:element name="poem">
    <xsd:complexType>
      <xsd:sequence>
        <xsd:element ref="poem:title"/>
        <xsd:element ref="poem:picture"/>
        <xsd:element ref="poem:verse" maxOccurs="unbounded"/>
      </xsd:sequence>
      <xsd:attribute name="publisher" type="xsd:string"/>
      <xsd:attribute name="pubyear" type="xsd:NMTOKEN"/>
    </xsd:complexType>
  </xsd:element>
  <xsd:element name="title" type="xsd:string"/>
  <xsd:element name="verse" type="xsd:string"/>
  <xsd:element name="picture">
    <xsd:complexType>
      <xsd:attribute name="href" use="required" type="xsd:anyURI"/>
    </xsd:complexType>
  </xsd:element>
</xsd:schema>
```

it is arguably the most important concept in XSDL, as we'll soon see.

63.2 | Elements and types

Notice the four element elements[3] in Example 63-3: poem, title, verse and picture. They perform roughly the same task as the element-type and attribute-list declarations in a DTD, but they do it differently.

In a DTD, an element-type declaration and related attribute-list declaration declare the properties of a class of elements:

1. the element-type name;
2. the data structure of the content; and

---

3. Yes, element elements.

3. attributes provided for the class, including attribute types and default values.

In XSDL, a `complexType` element can define *and name* a data structure and attributes *independently of declaring an element type*. There is also a `simpleType` element, but it can define and name only the simplest data structures: various forms of character strings, such as datatypes.

The unqualified word *type* in XSDL is reserved for just these two types: complex types and simple types.[4]

An `element` element, then, declares the element-type name and data structure type of a class of elements. The type could be defined within the content of the `element` element, as in the case of `poem` in Example 63-3, in which case the type itself is not named.

Alternatively, if the type was defined and named elsewhere, the declaration could use a `type` attribute, as shown for the `title` element. As the `xsd` prefix in the attribute value suggests, the `string` type is not actually defined within this schema. XSDL automatically provides named simple type definitions for all of the built-in datatypes. Those names are in the *XML Schema* namespace.

The two methods of declaring data structure types for elements are equivalent, and are equally applicable to complex and simple types. That includes user-derived datatypes, which, as we saw in 62.4, "Defining user-derived datatypes", on page 1013, are actually simple types.

63.3 | Structure of a schema definition

A schema is defined by one or more *schema documents*. Their root element is a `schema` element. Its attributes can define applicable namespaces, and its content components include elements like those we have been discussing, plus annotation elements.

---

4. In fact the XSDL spec barely mentions any other types (element, attribute, data, etc.), perhaps to avoid confusion with the unqualified use of "type".

63.3.1   *Namespaces*

The `schema` element must have a declaration for the XML schema name-space, `http://www.w3.org/2001/XMLSchema`. It could either assign a prefix (`xsd` and `xs` are two popular ones) or it could make *XML Schema* the default namespace. The prefix (if any) is used both for schema component elements and in references to built-in datatypes.

To validate documents that use namespaces, you can specify a `targetNamespace` for the schema, as shown in Example 63-3. Components that are children of the `schema` element are called *global schema components*. They declare and define items in the schema's target namespace.

The example also declares the `poem` prefix for the schema's target name-space. It is used within the schema definition to refer to the elements, attributes and types declared (or defined) by global schema components.

The instance document in Example 63-2 utilizes the same namespace, `http://www.poetry.net/poetns`. However, as it is declared as the default namespace, no prefix is declared or used.

Note that the value of the `name` attribute of a component, such as a type definition or element declaration, does not have a namespace prefix. A component name always belongs to the target namespace. It is only when the declared or defined objects are referenced that the prefix may be used.

Within a namespace different kinds of components can normally have the same name. The exception is simple and complex types, as there are many places where they are treated interchangeably. Elements, however, are not types, so an element declaration component may use the same name as a complex or simple type. There is no more relationship between them than between a guy named Bob at your office and the guy named Bob on your favorite television show (unless you work in Hollywood!).

63.3.2   *Schema components*

The XSDL elements we have been discussing, such as `element` and `simpleType`, occur in the content of a `schema` element and are collectively known as *schema components*. Those, like `element`, that correspond to DTD declarations, are also called (surprise!) *declaration components*.

As XSDL schemas are themselves defined in XML documents, it was possible to provide techniques to make them self-documenting and capable of being processed by applications other than schema processors. These include unique identifiers, extension attributes, and annotation elements.

63.3.2.1   Unique identifiers

All schema components are defined with an optional `id` attribute. You can therefore assign unique identifiers to make the components easier to refer to using XPointers, XLinks and other hyperlinking techniques. Each value assigned to an `id` attribute must be different from any other assigned anywhere in the schema document.

63.3.2.2   Extension attributes

Schema components may be extended with arbitrary attributes in any namespace *other* than the *XML Schema* namespace. For instance you could add attributes from the XLink namespace or from the RDF namespace.

If you had software that helped you to visualize the schema, extension attributes could be used to store the graphical coordinates of the various elements. If you used software that converted XML schemas to a relational database schema, you might use the extension attributes to guide that process.

63.3.2.3   The `annotation` element

Any XSDL component may have an `annotation` element as its first sub-element. The `schema` element, however, goes above and beyond the call of duty! It may have as many `annotation` sub-elements as you like. It is good practice to have at least one annotation at the beginning as an introduction to the document type.

An `annotation` element may have zero or more `documentation` and `appinfo` children elements.

The `documentation` element is used to add user-readable information to the schema. Any elements are permitted; they needn't be defined in the schema. The benefit of using annotation elements rather than XML comments is that it is much easier to use rich markup such as XHTML or Docbook. Application software can extract this documentation and use it for online help or other purposes.

An `appinfo` element adds some information specific to a particular application. These are extension elements; they work like the extension attributes we discussed earlier. You may use them for the same sorts of tasks, but the elements can have an internal structure while attributes can only contain data characters. Your extension elements should be in a namespace that will enable your applications to recognize them.

63.3.3   *Complex types*

Example 63-4 shows the definition of an `address` type. It also shows two element declarations that utilize it.

Example 63-4. Elements built on an `address` type

```
<xsd:complexType name="address">
   <xsd:sequence>
     <xsd:element ref="myns:line1"/>
     <xsd:element ref="myns:line2"/>
     <xsd:element ref="myns:city"/>
     <xsd:element ref="myns:state"/>
     <xsd:element ref="myns:zip"/>
   </xsd:sequence>
   <xsd:attribute name="id" type="xsd:ID"/>
</xsd:complexType>
<xsd:element name="billingAddress" type="myns:address"/>
<xsd:element name="shippingAddress" type="myns:address"/>
```

In XSDL, types are defined independently of elements and may be associated with more than one element-type name. In the example, the `address` type is used by both `billingAddress` and `shippingAddress`.

This example shows some of the power of complex types: we can create structural definitions as reusable units that make element declaration and maintenance easier. Types are similar to the virtual or abstract classes used in object-oriented programming.

Types do not themselves define elements that will be used directly. Example 63-4 would not permit an `address` element in a valid document. Instead the type is a set of reusable constraints that can be used as a building block in element declarations and other type definitions.

XSDL does not require you to give every type a name. If you only intend to use a type once, you could put the definition for it right in an element declaration, as in Example 63-5.

Example 63-5. Inline type definition

```
<xsd:element name="address">
  <xsd:complexType>
   <xsd:sequence>
     <xsd:element ref="myns:line1"/>
     <xsd:element ref="myns:line2"/>
     <xsd:element ref="myns:city"/>
     <xsd:element ref="myns:state"/>
     <xsd:element ref="myns:zip"/>
   </xsd:sequence>
   <xsd:attribute name="id" type="xsd:ID"/>
  </xsd:complexType>
</xsd:element>
```

Example 63-5 was created from Example 63-4 by wrapping the complexType in an element and moving the name attribute. You could do the same with a simpleType. Note that the element declaration has no type attribute. You need to choose whether to refer to a named type or embed an unnamed type definition.

To create a type that allows character data in addition to whatever is specified in its content model, you may add a mixed="true" attribute value to the complexType element.

To declare the element-type empty, we could have left out the sequence element.

63.3.4   *Content models*

Just as in DTDs, content models allow us to describe what content is allowed within an element. Many of the concepts are very similar to DTDs. Just as DTDs allow you to express sequences and choice, so too does XSDL. Nevertheless, XSDL has a few more tricks up its sleeves.

63.3.4.1   Sequences

Sequences are equivalent to content models of the form A,B,C in DTDs. This one would indicate that there must be an A element followed by a B element followed by a C element. The XSDL equivalent is shown in Example 63-6.

Example 63-6. sequence element

```
<xsd:sequence>
    <xsd:element ref="myns:A"/>
    <xsd:element ref="myns:B"/>
    <xsd:element ref="myns:C"/>
</xsd:sequence>
```

An element element might declare things directly, or else indirectly by referencing an existing element declaration. The declarations in the example do the latter, as indicated by the use of ref attributes instead of name attributes. Note that an element reference must be prefixed if it lives in a namespace (which it will if declared in a schema with a targetNamespace).

63.3.4.2   Choices

DTDs also have a | operator that represents a choice rather than a sequence. A|B|C means A or B or C. Example 63-7 shows the XSDL equivalent.

Example 63-7. choice element

```
<xsd:choice>
    <xsd:element ref="myns:A"/>
    <xsd:element ref="myns:B"/>
    <xsd:element ref="myns:C"/>
</xsd:choice>
```

63.3.4.3   Nested model groups

For more complex content models, model groups can be nested. For example, we can duplicate the DTD content model (title,picture,verse+, (footnotes|bibliography)) with a `choice` element within a `sequence` element, as shown in Example 63-8.

Example 63-8. Sequence with nested choice

```
<xsd:sequence>
  <xsd:element ref="poem:title"/>
  <xsd:element ref="poem:picture"/>
  <xsd:element ref="poem:verse" maxOccurs="unbounded"/>
  <xsd:choice>
    <xsd:element ref="poem:footnotes"/>
    <xsd:element ref="poem:bibliography"/>
  </xsd:choice>
</xsd:sequence>
```

The declaration for `verse` states that it may have multiple occurrences through its `maxOccurs` attribute. There is a corresponding `minOccurs` that defaults to "1" – meaning at least one is required by default.

Inside of sequences and choices it is also possible to use `any` and `group` elements. `any` is like a DTD's `ANY`. It means that any content is allowed. It has various bells and whistles to allow you to narrow down what you mean by "any". Most document types do not require this feature so we will not go into any detail.

The `group` element allows you to refer to a named "model group definition". You can use these model group definitions to reuse parts of content models by referencing them.

63.3.4.4   `all` elements

There is an *and connector* (&) in SGML that is not included in XML DTDs because it is difficult to implement. It appears in XSDL in a simplified form. The `all` element specifies that all of the contained elements must be present, but their order is irrelevant. So you could enter "A B C", "A C B", "B A C" and all of the other combinations of the three. Example 63-9 demonstrates.

`all` must only be used at the top level of a complex type definition. `all` is also unique in that it may only contain `element` elements, not sequences, choices, groups etc.

Example 63-9. all element

```
<xsd:complexType name="testAll">
  <xsd:all>
    <xsd:element ref="myns:A"/>
    <xsd:element ref="myns:B"/>
    <xsd:element ref="myns:C"/>
  </xsd:all>
</xsd:complexType>
```

63.3.5 *Attributes*

The poem and picture element declarations in Example 63-3 both contain attribute declarations equivalent to those in our original DTD. Example 63-10 shows the declarations for the poem element's optional publisher and pubyear attributes.

Example 63-10. Attribute declarations

```
<xsd:attribute name="publisher" type="xsd:string"/>
<xsd:attribute name="pubyear" type="xsd:NMTOKEN"/>
```

They are optional because there is no use attribute in their definitions. You can also make them required with use="required".

Example 63-11 shows two attribute declarations. One uses a built-in datatype and the other a user-defined simple type.

Example 63-11. Built-in and user-defined types

```
<xsd:attribute name="href" use="required" type="xsd:anyURI"/>
<xsd:attribute name="pubdate" type="myns:pubyear"/>
```

Attribute declarations can also occur within a named attributeGroup element, which allows them to be reused in complex type definitions and in other attribute groups.

attribute elements have a default attribute that allows you to specify a default value for optional attributes. To supply a default value that cannot be overridden (just as you might use #FIXED in a DTD), supply it using the fixed attribute rather than the default attribute.

63.4 | Declaring schema conformance

How does an XML document tell a processor that it conforms to a particular XSDL schema definition? Usually it doesn't!

In theory, you can determine which schema definition to use from the root element type, file type, or other cues. In practice, the namespace is typically used.

There is a convention specified in the *XML Schema* specification to allow the document author to give a more explicit hint to the receiver. Example 63-12 demonstrates.

Example 63-12. Referring to a schema definition

```
<myns:mydoc
    xmlns:myns="http://www.myns.com/myns"
    xmlns:xsi="http://www.w3.org/2001/XMLSchema-instance"
    xsi:schemaLocation="http://www.myns.com/myns
                        http://www.mysite.com/myxsdl.xsd">

</myns:mydoc>
```

Note the declaration of the `xsi` namespace prefix. It identifies a namespace that is specifically for putting *XML Schema* information into instance documents. There is a global attribute in this namespace called `schemaLocation` that allows a document to point to an appropriate schema definition.

The attribute value is defined as a list of paired URIs. The first one in each pair is a namespace URI. The second one is the URI for a schema document. As the schema processor works its way through the instance document, it can find the applicable schema for an element or attribute by looking up its namespace.

The sender of a document may also provide the receiver with a schema through an API, command line, or graphical interface. Eventually, a trusted repository may supply the schema or DTD, as we describe in Chapter 66, "Public XML vocabularies", on page 1090.

Although there is nothing wrong with using these hints just to check whether a document is valid, often you want to check whether it validates against some particular schema. In that case you don't want your software to use hints, you want it to use the schema you've provided.

The manner in which you tell the software what schema to use for a particular namespace will depend on the software. One convention is merely to configure the software with a list of schemas. The software can read the schemas and collect the list of target namespaces from the `targetNamespace` attributes. Then, when it sees a particular namespace in a document it can use the appropriate schema to validate it. Because *you* provide the list of schemas in the beginning, you know exactly what schemas are being used to validate no matter what is in the document.

63.5 | Schema inclusion

DTDs can share text by means of external parameter entities. For example, the `common` parameter entity declared and referenced in Example 63-13 tells an XML processor to treat the DTD as if the two lines of Example 63-14 had been inserted at the fourth line.

Example 63-13. DTD with an external parameter entity reference

```
<!ELEMENT  book      (title,chapter+)>
<!ELEMENT  chapter (title,par+)>
<!ENTITY % common   SYSTEM "common.dtd">
%common;
```

Example 63-14. `common.dtd` file referenced in Example 63-13

```
<!ELEMENT title (#PCDATA)>
<!ELEMENT par    (#PCDATA)>
```

The *schema inclusion* facility works similarly. It allows a schema definition to treat another schema definition's contents as part of its own. Example 63-15 uses the `include` element to incorporate declarations from the schema in Example 63-16. The declarations are thenceforth treated as part of the `book.xsd` schema.

In addition to inclusion, XSDL also has support for importing and redefinition of other schemas. Importing is for combining schemas that describe different namespaces. A redefinition allows you to include another schema and override bits and pieces of the included schema. For instance you could redefine the type of an element or attribute that you are including.

Example 63-15. `book.xsd` schema definition including declarations from `common.xsd`

```
<xsd:schema xmlns:xsd="http://www.w3.org/2001/XMLSchema"
        xmlns:myns="http://www.myns.net/myns"
   targetNamespace="http://www.myns.net/myns">
  <xsd:include schemaLocation="common.xsd"/>
  <xsd:element name="book">
    <xsd:complexType>
      <xsd:sequence>
        <xsd:element ref="myns:title"/>
        <xsd:element ref="myns:chapter" maxOccurs="unbounded"/>
      </xsd:sequence>
    </xsd:complexType>
  </xsd:element>
  <xsd:element name="chapter">
    <xsd:complexType>
      <xsd:sequence>
        <xsd:element ref="myns:title"/>
        <xsd:element ref="myns:par" maxOccurs="unbounded"/>
      </xsd:sequence>
    </xsd:complexType>
  </xsd:element>
</xsd:schema>
```

Example 63-16. *common.xsd* schema definition

```
<xsd:schema xmlns:xsd="http://www.w3.org/2001/XMLSchema"
        xmlns:myns="http://www.myns.net/myns"
   targetNamespace="http://www.myns.net/myns">
  <xsd:element name="title" type="xsd:string"/>
  <xsd:element name="par" type="xsd:string"/>
</xsd:schema>
```

63.6 | Additional capabilities

So far we have pretty much just taken concepts from DTD declarations and represented them as XML elements conforming to the schema document type. Schemas get more interesting when they allow us to do things that are difficult or impossible in DTDs.

We'll now describe those additional functions briefly. We'll try to provide just enough detail to allow you to decide whether to investigate them further.[5]

63.6.1 *Locally-scoped elements*

Element-type names in a DTD are global; any element type can be referenced in any other element type's content model. So if you define `title` you can use it in chapters, sections and anywhere else you see fit.

Once you have defined your DTD, authors can use the `title` element in each of the contexts that you have specified. In each of those contexts the element type is exactly the same: it has the same name, attributes and allowed content.

XSDL has a facility that allows you to say that titles in one context should have a different attribute set and content model from titles in another – even if they are in the same namespace! In effect, you can declare two element types with the same name. The name is *bound* to a different element-type definition in each context.

You can do this by declaring an element type within the declaration for another element type. Example 63-17 shows two different title element types declared within the same schema. They each use a different user-derived datatype.

In documents conforming to this schema, a `title` element within a `book` element must conform to the `title` element declared within the `book` element declaration, complete with the required `ISBN` and `booktitle` attribute values.

A `title` element within an `employee` element, however, must conform to the `title` element declared inside the example's `employee` element declaration.

63.6.2 *Type derivation*

Type derivation is the creation of a new type as a variation of an existing one (or a combination of several existing ones). This is much like the way object-oriented classes inherit from other classes. The derived type will have a content model that is an extension of the base type's.

We discussed derivation of simple types in 62.4, "Defining user-derived datatypes", on page 1013. In Example 63-18 we see the derivation of a

---

5. For further information the spec is on the CD-ROM, but as we noted earlier, it's not a casual read!

Example 63-17. Two locally-scoped `title` declarations

```
<xsd:element name="book"><xsd:complexType>
  <xsd:sequence>
    <xsd:element name="title"><xsd:complexType>
      <xsd:attribute name="booktitle" use="required"
                     type="xsd:string"/>
      <xsd:attribute name="ISBN" use="required"
                     type="myns:ISBNFormat"/>
    </xsd:complexType></xsd:element>
    <xsd:element ref="myns:chapter"/>
  </xsd:sequence>
</xsd:complexType></xsd:element>

<xsd:element name="employee"><xsd:complexType>
  <xsd:sequence>
    <xsd:element name="empId"/>
    <xsd:element name="title"><xsd:complexType>
      <xsd:sequence>
        <xsd:element ref="myns:jobtitle"/>
        <xsd:element ref="myns:company"/>
      </xsd:sequence>
    </xsd:complexType></xsd:element>
  </xsd:sequence>
</xsd:complexType></xsd:element>
```

complex type, `internationalAddress`. It adds a new child element, called `countryCode`, to the `address` type we defined in Example 63-4.

Example 63-18. One type extends another

```
<xsd:complexType name="internationalAddr">
  <xsd:complexContent>
    <xsd:extension base="myns:address">
      <xsd:sequence>
          <xsd:element ref="myns:countryCode"/>
      </xsd:sequence>
    </xsd:extension>
  </xsd:complexContent>
</xsd:complexType>
```

With this definition, an `internationalAddr` is just like an `address`, but after specifying the details of the `address` you must also specify a `countryCode`.

You can also derive a type by *restriction*. That means that you add constraints, such as making an attribute or subelement required when it was previously optional. This is very similar to the equivalent concept for datatypes.

63.6.3 *Identity constraints*

There could be several elements in a document that logically represent a set. For example, records of the employees in a company might be represented as elements in an XML document.

Each element in a set must have a unique name or *key* that distinguishes it from all other elements in the set. For example, the employee records key could be an `empid` attribute or sub-element.

These *identity constraints* can get even more complicated: we might wish to declare that there must be no two customers with the same first name, last name, and address.

XSDL has sophisticated features for defining unique keys and the means of referencing them. It uses XPath for the purpose. For instance you could define the list of customers with one XPath expression and use a second to describe how each member of the set is unique.[6]

63.7 | Conclusion

XSDL is a sophisticated new tool in the toolbox of schema developers. It has the virtue of supporting modern ideas of inheritance, namespaces and schema lookup. At the same time it is somewhat controversial because it is so large and complex. The subset described in this chapter should be both useful and manageable.[7]

---

6. The discussion in 60.6.7, "Keys", on page 981 gives an idea of the problem and the approach to solving it.
7. For the whole story, we recommend Priscilla Walmsley's *Definitive XML Schema*, published in this series.

Navigation Tutorials

- Addressing and linking
- XML Pointer Language (XPointer)
- XML Linking Language (XLink)
- Full specs on CD-ROM

Part Twenty-three

This part covers navigation specifications from the World Wide Web Consortium. Again, you'll need a pretty firm grasp of the material in Part 18, "XML Core Tutorials" before you tackle them.

Part 20, "XPath Tutorials" is a prerequisite for both stylesheets and XPointers, but here too you won't need to master all the details before moving on.

XPointer isn't technically a prerequisite for XLink, though understanding XPointer will add to your appreciation of XLink's power.

XML Pointer Language (XPointer)

Friendly Tutorial

- Uniform Resource Identifiers (URI)
- Fragment identifiers
- XPointer framework
- xpointer() scheme
- element() scheme
- xmlns() scheme

Pointer allows authors to make references to specific fragments of XML documents, not just to documents as a whole.
There are many good reasons for doing so.

64.1 | XPointer: The reason why

There are many times when it is necessary to refer not just to another document but to a particular part of that document. We can use a simple URI to
refer to another document. Once we have a document it is possible to refer
to a particular node or set of nodes using XPath. The XPointer specification
allows the URI and the XPath to be combined into a *URI reference*. This
combination of document and node addressing is very powerful.

An XPointer-containing URI reference can be used almost anywhere that
an ordinary URI can be used. Not only can you put them in hypertext links
– you also put them on the sides of buses and in previews for movies!

You could type the URI reference into a compliant Web browser and
have the browser jump directly to a particular place in the document. In
some situations either the browser or the server could use an XPointer to
restrict your view to a particular section of the document.[1]

On today's Web, to quote a particular paragraph out of another document, you would need to go to that document and cut and paste the text into yours. If, in the future, the text on the Web changes, yours does not. If that is what you want, that is fine. But an XPointer application might allow you to construct a "living document" that quotes and refers to the very latest version of the paragraph. These sorts of applications already exist within particular organizations, but general purpose Web browsers are not yet this sophisticated.

Inter-document addressing is vital for precise linking. Using XPointer it is possible to link a single element in an XML document to a single character in another. The full power of XPath is available in XPointer. So it is also possible to link a set of nodes (e.g. element nodes) in one document to one or more nodes (e.g. attribute nodes) in another document.

Although XPointers are useful for linking, it is also important to remember that they can be used outside of Web pages. You might see an XPointer in a URI reference in the newspaper or in an email.

URIs are even common in MS Word or PDF documents. In the future it should be possible to use URI references with XPointers in these contexts. That will allow linking from deep in a Word document or PDF file to the middle of an XML document.

Let's take a closer look at URIs before we start tacking XPointers onto them.

64.2 | Uniform Resource Identifiers

The basic form of address on the Web is a *URI*, which stands for *Uniform Resource Identifier*. It comes in two flavors:

URL

Today's most common form of URI is the ubiquitous *URL* or *Uniform Resource Locator*. We'll discuss it in detail below.

---

1. Recent versions of Mozilla support XPointer but at this writing other mainstream browsers have yet to do so.

URN

A newer form of URI, *Uniform Resource Name (URN)*, isn't location-dependent and perhaps will reduce the number of broken links. However, it has yet to catch on because it requires more sophisticated software support. We'll say no more about it here.

64.2.1 *Uniform Resource Locators (URL)*

URLs are uniform, in that they have the same basic syntax no matter what specific type of resource (e.g. Web page, newsgroup) is being addressed or what mechanism is described to fetch it. They describe the locations of Web resources much as a physical address describes a person's location.

URLs are hierarchical, just as most physical addresses are. A surface mail address is resolved by sending a letter to a particular country, and from there to a local processing station, and from there to an individual. URLs are similar.

The first part of a URL is the *protocol*. It describes the mechanism that the Web browser or other client should use to get the resource. Think of it as the difference between Federal Express, UPS, and the other courier services. The most common such protocol is `http` which is essentially the "official" protocol of the World Wide Web. The `ftp` file transfer protocol is also widely used, chiefly for large downloads such as new browser versions.

After the protocol, there is a *hostname* and then a *datapath*. The datapath is broken into chunks separated by slash (/) characters, as you have no doubt seen in hundreds of URLs. Technically, a URL ends at that point. Since URLs are just the most common form of URI, it is also safe to say that the URI ends here.

> *Note*   There is another Three Letter Acronym that is relevant to our discussion of URIs. An Internationalized Resource Identifier (IRI) is a form of URI that allows non-ASCII characters. IRIs affect some details of escaping significant syntax characters that we don't discuss in this book, but in other respects are the same as URIs.

64.2.2 *Fragment identifiers*

There is yet another term that is confusingly similar to URI: *URI reference*. A URI reference is the combination of a URI (which could be a URL) and an optional *fragment identifier*. For instance you may have seen links into HTML documents that look like Example 64-1.

Example 64-1. Reference into HTML

```
http://www.megabank.com/banking#about
```

In the example, #about is a fragment identifier. It refers to a particular HTML anchor element, in this case <a name=about>.

XPointers are the form of fragment identifier developed for XML documents. They are much more flexible than HTML fragment identifiers, as we shall see, and there is a family of W3C specifications that define them.

64.3 | The XPointer specifications

Although the XML Pointer Language started life as a single W3C Recommendation, there are now several, reflecting an important change in the architecture. The foundation spec is *XPointer Framework*, so-called because multiple different addressing *schemes* can be plugged into it.

Two schemes have already been approved by the W3C and they are developing a third.

The most sophisticated of the W3C XPointer schemes is called (confusingly) the xpointer() scheme. It takes on the name of the entire language because it was the first to be conceived (though it is the only one that has not yet completed its W3C ratification process) and also because it is the most powerful. The scheme uses an extended form of XPath to address nodes, text strings, and ranges of nodes and strings.

The simpler element() scheme allows a subset of the xpointer() scheme's capabilities. It can address elements by their position in the XML document: "The fifth child of the fourth child of the seventh child of the root element."

Finally, the xmlns() scheme allows the declaration of namespaces for use by the other two schemes.

Let's look at the framework and schemes in more detail. We'll use the XML document in Example 64-2 as our target document and examine different ways to address its content. For our examples, we'll assume that the document is located at `http://www.hotdays.com/heatwave.xml`.

Example 64-2. Document located at
`http://www.hotdays.com/heatwave.xml`

```
<?xml version="1.0"?>
<!DOCTYPE HEATWAVES SYSTEM "heatwaves.dtd">
<HEATWAVES>
<WAVE ID="summer_92_info">
    <DURATION><FROM>July 22</FROM><TO>August 2</TO></DURATION>
    <TEMPERATURE>101 Degrees</TEMPERATURE>
</WAVE>
<WAVE ID="summer_94_info">
    <DURATION><FROM>July 12</FROM><TO>July 18</TO></DURATION>
    <TEMPERATURE>100 Degrees</TEMPERATURE>
</WAVE>
<WAVE ID="summer_96_info">
    <DURATION><FROM>June 15</FROM><TO>July 18</TO></DURATION>
    <TEMPERATURE>103 Degrees</TEMPERATURE>
</WAVE>
</HEATWAVES>
```

64.4 | XPointer Framework

The XPointer Framework Recommendation defines rules for constructing a form of fragment identifier that it calls a *pointer*. A pointer could either be based on addressing schemes (*scheme-based pointer*), or it could be the unique ID of an element (*shorthand pointer*).

64.4.1 *Shorthand pointer*

Example 64-3 shows three URI references with equivalent pointers. They all address the element whose ID is "summer_96_info".

Example 64-3. Equivalent pointers

```
http://www.hotdays.com/heatwave.xml#xpointer(id("summer_96_info"))
http://www.hotdays.com/heatwave.xml#summer_96_info
```

In each case, the pointer is the string that follows the pound sign (#). The first are scheme-based and take the ID as an argument, while the third is a shorthand pointer that consists of only the ID.

IDs are an excellent way to refer to an element because they are impervious to such changes to the document as re-ordering or adding elements.

64.4.2 *Scheme-based pointer*

A scheme-based pointer consists of one or more *pointer parts*, each consisting of a scheme name and a parenthesized string of *scheme data*. The two scheme-based pointers in Example 64-3 each consist of a single pointer part.

64.4.2.1   Multiple pointer parts

It is possible to string together several pointer parts to allow the system to attempt multiple addressing strategies. You may separate them with whitespace for clarity, as shown in Example 64-4.

As you study the example, don't worry about the syntax of the individual parts. We'll get to that later. The important thing is the relationship among them.

The pointer starts with an ID-based `element()` part because that is the most robust. This strategy might fail if the ID was deleted or changed, or if the processor does not support ID processing.

The example then uses an `xpointer()` part to try a string-search strategy, which could fail if the document had been edited to delete or change the target string. If so, the example falls back from there to a positional strategy in the final pointer part.

Example 64-4. Multiple pointer parts

```
http://www.hotdays.com/heatwave.xml#element(summer_96_info)
      xpointer(string-range('103 Degrees')/../..)
      xpointer(/HEATWAVES/WAVE[3])
```

With each strategy you are less and less sure that you have addressed the thing that you wanted to address, but it may be better to take that risk than to just give up if the ID can't be found. In a Web surfing situation, users may well tolerate the occasional mistake in exchange for fewer broken links overall.

64.4.2.2   New XPointer schemes

It is possible for anyone – not just the W3C – to extend XPointer by creating new XPointer schemes. For instance a vector graphics markup language might allow pointers that select ranges of the screen. A multimedia language might allow the selection of ranges of time.

Conflict among scheme names is avoided by qualifying them with namespaces.

64.5 | XPointer element() Scheme

The simplest form of `element()` pointer allows you to refer to a particular element named with an ID. This is also the most robust form, because it does not at all depend on the location of the referenced text within its document.

64.5.1   *Child sequence*

However, with the `element()` scheme you can also refer to a child or descendant element of some particular element, based on its position. For instance to refer to the first child of the `summer_96_info` element in Example 64-2 you would add a slash after the ID and follow that by an integer. Example 64-5 demonstrates.

Example 64-5. Child sequence

```
http://www.hotdays.com/heatwave.xml#element(summer_96_info/1)
```

This example refers to the first subelement of the WAVE element called `summer_96_info`. In our sample document, this is a DURATION element.

We can also refer to a subelement of a subelement (or subelement of a subelement of a subelement – you get the picture) by adding slash-separated numbers to the end. Example 64-6 addresses all of the elements within the element with ID `summer_96_info` and its children.

Example 64-6. Addressing elements of the summer of '96

```
http://www.hotdays.com/heatwave.xml#element(summer_96_info/1)
http://www.hotdays.com/heatwave.xml#element(summer_96_info/1/1)
http://www.hotdays.com/heatwave.xml#element(summer_96_info/1/2)
http://www.hotdays.com/heatwave.xml#element(summer_96_info/2)
```

These pointers refer (respectively) to DURATION, FROM, TO and TEMPERATURE elements.

64.5.2 *Rooted child sequence*

A child sequence need not be relative to a named element. It can be relative to the start of the document by starting the scheme data with "/1". The "/1" refers to the root (or document) element. The next number (if any) refers to one of its children. The number after that (if any) refers to a child of that child and so on.

Example 64-7 refers to the elements that apply to the earliest season on record. With the current data, they are within the element with ID `summer_92_info`. If the document grows to include more years and chronological order is maintained, the same pointer will continue to address whichever year is earliest.

Example 64-7. Addressing elements of the earliest year

```
http://www.hotdays.com/heatwave.xml#element(/1/3/1)
http://www.hotdays.com/heatwave.xml#element(1/3/1/1)
http://www.hotdays.com/heatwave.xml#element(/1/3/1/2)
http://www.hotdays.com/heatwave.xml#element(/1/3/2)
```

The "/1" refers to the root (document) element HEATWAVES. The "/1" in each pointer refers to the first child element of HEATWAVES, the WAVE with ID `summer_92_info`. The trailing numbers are as before.

64.6 | XPointer xpointer() Scheme

The xpointer() scheme is based upon XPath. Its scheme data is an XPath expression.

Caution   The xpointer() *scheme is still under development at the time of writing and is subject to change. The other two schemes we describe and the XPointer Framework, however, are approved W3C Recommendations.*

For example, we can refer to the second WAVE element in the document in Example 64-2 with the URI reference in Example 64-8.

Example 64-8. URI with xpointer() **scheme pointer**

```
http://www.hotdays.com/heatwave.xml#xpointer(id("summer_94_info"))
```

We are not restricted to XPath's id function. IDs are the most robust way to refer to elements but we can also refer to elements that do not have IDs. This is especially important if we do not control the document that we are referencing. Any XPath expression can be used.

Typically the expressions will be just like those defined in Chapter 59, "XML Path Language (XPath)", on page 924, but sometimes they will use extensions that are defined in the xpointer() scheme specification.

64.6.1 *Extensions to XPath*

The xpointer() scheme extends the XPath model to support two new concepts: *points* and *ranges*. Since a range is defined as the area between two points, we'll examine the point concept first.

XPath normally returns nodes, which represent actual pieces of a document. If you think of a row of boxes on a piece of graph paper, nodes are the boxes and points occur at the vertical blue lines that separate the boxes.

XPointer takes things even further, though. In addition to allowing points before and after a node, it also allows points between the characters of a text node.

Ranges represent an area that a user might select in a document. Just like a user interface selection, it starts at one point (between two characters of a text node or between two elements or other nodes) and goes to another point.

64.6.1.1   Ranges

Ranges can be addressed with a variety of functions introduced by XPointer's extensions to XPath.

64.6.1.1.1   range-to

The `range-to` function takes two XPaths and addresses a range from the point preceding the first XPath to a point following the second. For instance, if you had an element with ID "summer_92_info" and wanted to create a range that contained that element, an element named "summer_96_info", and everything in between, you could do so with the pointer in Example 64-9.

Example 64-9. range-to

```
xpointer(id("summer_92_info")/range-to(id("summer_96_info")))
```

The pointer takes the node addressed before the slash and generates a range to the node addressed after the slash.

64.6.1.1.2   string-range

The `string-range` function searches for a string in the text nodes representing the data content of an element or a set of elements, or in the values of any other node set.

The simplest form of this function takes an XPath as its first parameter and a string as its second parameter. It finds occurrences of the string in the values of the nodes and returns them as a list of ranges.

The XPath to address all title elements in a document is "//title". If we wanted to find all occurrences of the string "Extensible Markup Language" in the titles, we would do it through the pointer in Example 64-10.

Example 64-10. string-range

```
something.xml#xpointer(
  string-range( //title, "Extensible Markup Language" ))
```

You can also refer to a particular item in the list by appending an ordinary XPath predicate (Example 64-11).

Example 64-11. 11th occurrence

```
something.xml#xpointer(
  string-range( //title, "Extensible Markup Language" )[11])
```

Sometimes you want to address only a portion of long string. Perhaps you want to select the word "Markup" but only in the context of "Extensible Markup Language". To do this you would count into the string and find that the "M" in "Markup" is the twelfth character in the complete string.

In Example 64-12, we use "12" as the third argument to string-range. The final argument says how much of the string to select beyond the "M". The word "Markup" has six letters so we use "6" as the fourth parameter.

Example 64-12. range-slice

```
something.xml#xpointer(
  string-range( //title, "Extensible Markup Language", 12, 6 ))
```

These last two parameters are optional. If you do not specify them then you select the entire string. If you leave out the last parameter then you select to the end of the requested string.

64.6.1.1.3 `range-inside` *and* `range`

The `range-inside` function addresses a range that starts just inside the beginning of an element or other node or a set of nodes (including sets of elements) and goes to just inside the end.

For instance `range-inside(/book/title)` will select a range that includes everything inside of the `title` but does not include the `title` itself. If you visualize this in terms of the XML document string, it selects the content of the `title` element but not the `title` start- and end-tags.

A related function selects the content and the tags together. It is simply called `range`. This function is used to select an entire node or to address a set of ranges for a set of nodes. For instance `range(//title)` would select the ranges of each `title` element. If you visualize this in terms of the XML document string, it selects the ranges for the content and the tags of the elements.

Note the difference between `range(//title)` and `//title`. In the range case, the result is a list of ranges. In the straightforward XPath case, the result is a list of nodes.

64.6.1.2   Point functions

You can also select points without addressing a range. This capability could be used, for example, to position a cursor between characters or elements in a document.

The `start-point` function selects the point just before an element or range. For instance to create a point just before the string "XML" in a title you could use an expression like that in Example 64-13.

Example 64-13. start-point

```
foo.xml#xpointer(start-point(string-range(//title, "XML")[1]))
```

This would select the point just before the first occurrence of the string "XML" in any `title` in the document. If we change the function from `start-point` to `end-point` then we would select the point just after the "L" in "XML".

If you pass a node (typically an element) or list of nodes to the `start-point` function then it will select the first point within the node or in each of the nodes. Similarly, the `end-point` function will select the last point in the node or each of the nodes. If you want to select the point just before or after a node (not inside it) then you can combine one of these functions with the `range` function. For instance `start-point(range(//P[1]))` will select the point just before the first P element.

64.6.1.3   Other extension functions

XPointer adds some other functions to XPath which are unrelated to the new concepts of point and range.

The first new function is called `here`. It returns the node that contains the actual pointer text, if the pointer is in an XML document. This might be useful to find some other information that might be useful in computing the pointer. For instance, an attribute of the same element in the pointer source XML document might contain a string that should be matched in the target XML document.

The second new function is called `origin`. This function is useful only when XPointer is used with XLink[2] Outside of the XLink hyperlinking context, `origin` is not meaningful and not legal.

`origin` returns the element that was used to start traversal of the link. In the case of out-of-line (extended) links, this is not necessarily the element that contains the pointer.

64.6.2   *XPointer xmlns() Scheme*

An important reason for a multi-part pointer is to declare a namespace that will be used in an `element()` or `xpointer()` pointer part. The namespace is declared using an `xmlns()` scheme pointer part that precedes the actual reference.

Example 64-14 contains an `xpointer()` pointer part that precedes an XPointer reference to Example 64-15. Note that the namespace prefixes used (`pfx` and `blah`) are different. The prefixes are just local short-forms for the long namespace URI which is the same (`http://example.com/foo`) in both the document and the XPointer.

---

2. Discussed in Chapter 65, "XML Linking Language (XLink)", on page 1068.

Example 64-14. XPointer with a namespace

```
http://www.abcde.org#xmlns(pfx=http://example.com/foo)
                      xpointer(//pfx:local)
```

Example 64-15. Document referenced by Example 64-14

```
<blah:local xmlns:blah="http://example.com/foo"/>
```

64.7 | The role of XPointer

An important thing to note is that an XPointer does not *do* anything. It refers to something. Whether the object is included, hyperlinked, or downloaded depends completely on the context of the reference.

It is just like referring to a person by name. The act of referring to him doesn't really accomplish anything. You have to refer to someone before you can tell somebody to do something to him (hopefully something nice), but the reference is not the action.

For instance, you could use an XPointer in a document to create a cross-reference to something, or in a browser address window to download and display a particular element. It is also up to the software to decide whether the referenced element is returned alone, or in the context of its document.

A browser, for example, would probably present the whole document and highlight the referenced element. But if you use an XPointer in an inclusion link to include a paragraph, the software would probably take that paragraph out of its context and present it alone in the new context. The specific behavior depends on your link processor and stylesheet.

64.8 | Conclusion

XPointer is a framework for addressing XML documents and fragments of documents. Its `xpointer()` scheme allows extended XPaths to be used in URIs (including URLs). Its `element()` scheme allows simple, concise addressing of elements by their position. Using XPointer it is possible to make references deep into an XML document. This will allow new forms of commentary, annotation and information reuse.

XML Linking Language (XLink)

Friendly Tutorial

- Linking and addressing
- Simple links
- Extended links

H ypertext links are the backbone of the World Wide Web. Documents were shuffled around the Internet long before today's
Web existed, but it was the ease of moving from page to page
with hypertext links that made the Web into the mass market phenomenon it is today.

However, despite their centrality, Web links have many weaknesses. The
linking system that we use today is essentially unchanged from the earliest
version of the Web. Unfortunately, market inertia has prevented anything
more powerful from coming along ... until now.

The XML-family hyperlinking W3C Recommendation is called XLink.
It allows links that go far beyond those provided by HTML. XLinks can

have multiple end points, be traversed in multiple directions, and be stored in databases and groups independently of the documents they refer to.

Caution   XLink is not yet widely implemented. Although there are partial implementations in several products, they are not mainstream. That means that we can only talk about how it might be implemented, not how it is implemented in mainstream browsers.

65.1 | Basic concepts

The most important (and sometimes subtle) distinction in any discussion of hyperlinking is that of *linking* versus *addressing*. Linking is simply declaring a relationship between two (or more) things. If we say "George Washington and Booker T. Washington share a last name" then we have linked those two people in some way.

Addressing, on the other hand, is about describing how to find the two things being linked. There are many kinds of addresses, such as mail addresses, email addresses and URLs. When you create a link in XLink, you declare a relationship between two objects referred to by their addresses (URI References). We refer to these objects as *resources*. We discuss the addresses more in 64.2, "Uniform Resource Identifiers", on page 1054.

When you follow a link one way or another, we say that you have *traversed* the link. We call the process of doing so *traversal*.

The action that starts the traversal is called its *actuation*. The ringmaster lights the fuse that *actuates* the human cannonball's *traversal* across the circus arena to a vital net resource.[1]

If you have created Web pages before, you are probably familiar with HTML's simple A element. Whether or not you are familiar with HTML, that link is a good starting point for understanding hyperlinking in general.

The A stands for *anchor*. Anchor is the hyperlinking community's term for what the XLink spec calls a *participating resource*. An HTML link has two ends, termed the *source* and *destination*. When you click on the source

---

1. A 404 error would mean that more than the link was broken!

end, (designated with an A element and href attribute), the Web browser transports you to the other end. Example 65-1 shows how this works.

Example 65-1. An HTML (not XLink) link

```
<a href="http://www.mysite.com">Go to my site!</a>
```

In this case, the a element itself describes a link, and its href attribute points to one of the resources (the destination). As we know, links connect resources, so there must be at least one more resource involved. The other resource, the source, is actually the content of the a element itself! The XLink spec calls this a *local resource*. As we will see, XLink *simple* links also use the content of the linking element as one of the resources.

There is another pervasive type of link in HTML documents. Consider the HTML markup to embed an image (Example 65-2).

Example 65-2. HTML (not XLink) image-embedding link

```
<IMG SRC="http://www.hotpics.com/jalapeno.gif">
```

That may not seem like a link but it is.[2] It declares a relationship between the containing document and the embedded image: "that picture goes in this document." HTML element types that use href attributes to address Java applets and plug-in objects are also forms of link.

Note that the destination of a link does not necessarily know that it is a destination. If you want to link to the Disney home page, you do not need to inform Disney. If a particular document has fifty a elements with href attributes, then you know that it has fifty links out. But the Web provides no way to know how many links into it there are.

In the more general *extended* link case, we will link two things such that *neither* end will "know" that the two are being linked. The link exists in some third location. This is intuitive if you go back to the definition of linking as defining a relationship. In a real-world sense, I can "link" Jenny Jones and Oprah Winfrey just by speaking of them in the same sentence. Unless they are interested in careers as XML experts, they will probably

---

2. What it *isn't* is a *navigational* link. You don't click on it to go somewhere else. Instead, its traversal is actuated automatically, as we'll see later in this chapter.

never know. XLink provides a standardized way to express this relationship in markup.

We might even want to link something that is not explicitly labeled. For instance, we might want to link the third paragraph of the fourth sub-point of the second section of a legal document to the transcript of a relevant court case.

This is analogous to the real world situation where you can either send something to a labeled location ("Please take this to the White House.") or you can give directions to the destination. In hyperlinking terms, we would consider either one of these to be an "address." Obviously there must be some way of locating a resource from a link, but it could be either an address, a label or a combination of the two: "The building is 5 blocks down the street from the White House."

65.2 | Simple links

Although XLink allows more flexible links than does HTML, it also offers simple links that are not much more complicated than HTML's links are. This sort of link is referred to as a *simple link*. A simple link has two ends, a source and a destination, just like an HTML link. One end represents a resource (usually the source) and it refers to the other end through a URI as in Example 65-3.

Example 65-3. XLink simple link

```
. . . for more information, consult
<citation xlink:type="simple"
          xlink:href="http://www.uw.ca/paper.xml">
Biemans(1997)
</citation>
```

The biggest difference between this link and the HTML link is that this element is not designated a link by its element-type name. It is not called a or any special element-type name specified in the XML or XLink specification. You can call your linking elements whatever you want to. This is an important feature, because it allows you to have many different types of linking elements in a document, perhaps with different declarations, attributes and behaviors. Just as XML allows you to use any element-type name for paragraphs or figures, XLink allows you flexibility in your linking element-type names.

The link is actually designated an XLink link by its `xlink:type` attribute. The `xlink:type` attribute describes what kind of link is being described. In this case, it is a *simple* link. The `xlink:` prefix indicates that this attribute's allowed values and semantics are defined by the XLink specification.

Formally speaking, the attribute lives in the `xlink:` namespace. Namespaces are discussed in Chapter 53, "Namespaces", on page 826. This namespace should be declared in your document: probably in the document (i.e., root) element as shown in Example 65-4.

Example 65-4. Namespace declaration in root element

```
<yourdoc xmlns:xlink="http://www.w3.org/1999/xlink">
. . .
</yourdoc>
```

For documents that will be DTD-validated, it is best to declare the `xmlns:xlink` attribute in the DTD as a fixed attribute of the root element type, as shown in Example 65-5.

Example 65-5. Namespace declaration in DTD

```
<!ATTLIST yourdoc xmlns:xlink CDATA
                  #FIXED "http://www.w3.org/1999/xlink">
```

Note   *All of the examples in this chapter assume that the linking element is in the scope of a namespace declaration that sets up the* `xlink:` *namespace prefix.*

65.2.1 *Link roles*

In HTML, link resources are either sources or destinations. The linking element is always the source. The resource referred to is always the destination.

In XML, this rigid distinction is not hard-wired. An application can make either or both resources into sources or destinations.

Consider, for instance, if a Web browser made it possible to create notes about someone else's Web site and "stick" them on to it like Post-It notes. These *annotations* might be represented as XLink *extended* links as in Example 65-6.

Example 65-6. XLink annotations

```
<annotation xlink:type="extended"
        xlink:href="http://www.mynewspaper.com">
As usual, your editorial is filled with the kind of claptrap and
willywag that gives me the heebie-jeebies!
</annotation>
```

In this case, we actually want the application to make some form of clickable "hotspot" at the *other* end, on the newspaper's Web page. Of course we don't want them to have control of the actual linking element, or else they might just choose not to show our link. So we want the link to exist in one spot and create a "hotspot" at another. This is the opposite of traditional HTML links.

In order to reverse linking roles, we must somehow tell the application that we want it to do so. One way would be to use an element-type name that the application is hard-coded to understand as having that semantic. For instance an "annotation server" might only deal with `annotation` elements, or perhaps a few different variants, and would thus know exactly how to handle it.

Another way would be to use some form of stylesheet. But you would still need to have something special in the document that would differentiate annotations from other links (perhaps the annotation element-type name). The stylesheet would provide an extra level of translation to allow your private element-type names to be interpreted as annotations by software.

Yet another way to solve this problem would be to provide an attribute that describes the role of the link in the document and hypertext system. Any of these are valid approaches, and the XLink specification provides a special `xlink:role` attribute to handle the last case. Example 65-7 is an example of that attribute in action.

Example 65-7. Role attribute

```
<hlink xlink:role="http://www.annotation.com"
    xlink:type="extended"
    xlink:href="http://www.mynewspaper.com">
As usual, your editorial is filled with the kind of claptrap and
willywag that gives me the heebie-jeebies!
</hlink>
```

In this case, the role designation has moved from the element-type name (now `hlink` instead of `annotation`) to the role attribute. Which is more appropriate will depend on your DTD, your software and your taste. XLink could perhaps dictate one style or the other, but real world usage is not that simple. For instance you might need to extend an industry standard DTD and thus have no control over element-type names. In another application, you might need to constrain the occurrence of certain kinds of linking elements, and thus need to use element-type names and content models.

The role is a URI reference. XLink does not specify what sort of data (if any) must be available at the URI's location. The URI is abstract, just like a namespace URI. It is just a long, verbose name for something that is meant to be globally unique. The only thing that matters is that you control the URI so that someone else will not use it to mean something else.

65.2.2 *Is this for real?*

You might well ask whether all of this annotation stuff is likely to happen. After all, there are all sorts of social, technical and financial difficulties related to being able to annotate someone else's Web page. Imagine annotation spam: "Tired of reading this boring technical Web page? Click here for HOT PICS!!!"[3]

It turns out that early versions of the pre-Netscape Mosaic browser allowed remote annotations (using a proprietary linking scheme), and you could share your annotations with friends or co-workers, but not with everybody on the Web. There are various other experimental services and products that provide the same ability for the modern-day Web. However, each uses a distinct link description notation so that they cannot share.

---

3. We realize that spammers already do this, but they have to get by without the customization. That's because they have no standards!

We may or may not get to the point where everybody can publish annotations to the whole world, but we already have the technology to create annotations that can be shared by other people we know. Unfortunately, this technology has never been widely deployed.[4] Perhaps when XLink is finalized and third-party annotation products are able to interoperate, Web pages will become generally annotatable and even more linkable than they are today.

So what can you do without a world-wide link database? Well let's say that your organization was considering buying a very expensive software product. You and your co-workers might agree to submit your opinions of the product specifications published on the vendor's Website. You could make a bunch of external links from the vendor's text to your comments on it and submit that to your organizational link database. When your co-workers go to see the page, their browsers can fetch your links and actually display them as if they were part of the original document. When your co-workers click on them, the browser will take them to your annotations.

In fact, with a reasonably large link database, you could annotate any Web page you came upon in this manner. When others from your organization came upon the page, they would see your annotations. In one sense, you are editing the entire Web! Of course, the bigger your organization is, the more points of view you can see on each page. On the other hand, sometimes you might not want to share all of your comments with the entire company, so you might have a smaller departmental database which is separate, and only shared by your direct co-workers. And of course at the opposite end of the spectrum, there might be a database for everyone on the Web (if we can make link database software that scales appropriately and find someone to run it).

External links can be useful even without a link database. Without such a database, there is no easy way to distribute your links to other people, so you must communicate the links' existence in some other way. For instance, you could include a critique of a Web page as an attachment to an email. You could also build a document full of links that annotated one of your own Web pages with links to glossary and bibliographic information. The XLink specification terms such a collection a *link base*. Depending on which link base the reader used, he would get either the glossary links or the

---

4. One product that has recently taken another run at the problem is called Third Voice™.

bibliographic links or both sets of links overlapping. A link base is not a full database; it is an XML document that must be parsed before it can be used.

If it makes sense to "project" a link from your home computer onto an existing website, then surely it makes just as much sense to link two existing websites. For instance, we could make a link that is targeted towards members of the SGML newsgroup that links the World Wide Web consortium's XML Web page to a related page we know about on the Web. This link would still have two ends, but both could be sources and destinations at the same time. If so, we would term that link *bidirectional*, because you could *traverse* it from either end. Because the link would exist on your Web site, but link two other pages, we would call it a *third-party* link. And if it makes sense to link two pages, then why not three, or four, or five? Extended links allow this.

65.2.3 *Link behaviors*

XML authors usually go out of their way to avoid putting information about formatting and other types of document behavior into XML documents. We've already been through all of the benefits of keeping your information "pure". As we have said, if you just mark up your documents according to their abstractions, you can apply formatting and other behavior through stylesheets.[5]

Even though it is usually best to put behavioral information in a stylesheet, XLink provides a more direct mechanism. There are some link behaviors that are so common – almost universal – that the XML working group decided that it should provide some attributes so that users could easily specify them. This facility removes a level of indirection and thereby makes hyperlinking a little bit easier. Still, one should think thrice about adding rendition attributes to abstract documents. The stylesheet is usually the best place to describe behavior and other presentational issues.

The most interesting type of link behavior is traversal. When you click on a hyperlink, you are traversing it. If a link is intended to embed informa-

---

5. That is the theory, anyhow. At the time of writing, however, mainstream stylesheet languages did not support the recognition of XLinks or the execution of link behaviors. As we said in the introduction, XLinks are not quite there.

tion from one resource in another, then the process of actually accomplishing the embedding is a traversal.

The behavioral descriptions are still abstract enough to allow a variety of specific behaviors, depending on the situation. For example, a printer might interpret them differently from a Web browser. Although a printer might not seem like a machine that would care about hyperlinks, it might be useful to have one that could directly print Web pages and their annotations, and that could access the images to print by traversing XLinks in the Web pages.

65.2.3.1   Show

As the name implies, the `xlink:show` attribute describes how the results of a link traversal should be shown. When you click on a Web link, that is a link traversal – one initiated by your click. On the other hand, if you have ever been to a site where a Web page comes up and says: "You will be forwarded to another page in just a few seconds", then that is a link traversal that is automatic. Typically on the Web, when a link is traversed (manually or automatically) it replaces the previous document in the Web browser window. XLink allows an author to request this behavior with the `replace` value of the `show` attribute:

Spec Excerpt (XLink) 65-1. Replace

An application traversing to the ending resource should load the resource in the same window, frame, pane, or other relevant presentation context in which the starting resource was loaded.

For example see Example 65-8.

Example 65-8. A `replace` link

```
<A   xlink:type="simple"
     xlink:show="replace"
     xlink:href="http://www.gop.org/">
Click here to visit the GOP</A>
```

Sometimes you will also come across a link that actually opens a new window, so that after traversal there is a window for the new page in front of the window for the old page. XLink allows this through the new value of the show attribute.

Spec Excerpt (XLink) 65-2. New

An application traversing to the ending resource should load it in a new window, frame, pane, or other relevant presentation context.

Example 65-9 shows a link where the remote resource is launched into a new window.

Example 65-9. A new link

```
<A xlink:type="simple"
   xlink:show="new"
   xlink:href="http://www.democrats.org/">
Click here to launch a new window and visit the the Dems.</A>
```

As we have seen, a link can represent *any* relationship. We discussed the relationship between a document and an embedded graphic, but did not discuss the XLink syntax for it yet. We can say that one resource should be embedded in another using the embed option of the xlink:show attribute. Example 65-10 demonstrates.

Example 65-10. An embedded link

```
<MyEmbed xlink:type="simple"
   xlink:show="embed"
   xlink:href="http://www.democrats.org/platform.gif"/>
```

An embedded link can embed any datatype, not just graphics. You could embed a movie, sound or even another XML document:

Example 65-11. An embedded XML document

```
<MyEmbed xlink:type="simple"
   xlink:show="embed"
   xlink:href="somedata.xml"/>
```

Note that this is not like embedding text using text entities. When you use text entities, the entire behavior of those entities is defined by the XML specification. The parser manages the expansion of entities according to well-defined rules. In the case of embed, the embedding rules are dictated by the application (which might delegate the decision to a stylesheet or configuration file). Valid behaviors might include textual inclusion (as with text entities), image-like embedding in a square box or something in between. The application could also decide whether the inclusion inherits font properties.

To summarize: the big difference between embed-style links and text entities is who controls the embedding. Text entities are expanded by the XML parser and the application has no control over it. Embedded links must be expanded by the application (browser, editor, B2B engine, video game, whatever).

There are two other values for xlink:show: other and none. In both cases, the author is telling the application that it is free to determine the behavior that will accompany the traversal. With other, however, the author is saying that other markup present in the link should guide that determination. none implies that no behavior is really expected.

65.2.3.2   Actuate

The actuate attribute allows the author to describe when the link traversal should occur. For instance it could be user-triggered, such as by a mouse click or a voice command. Or else it could be automatic, such as the automatic embedding of a graphic, or an automatic forward to another Web page (e.g. "This page has moved. You will be directed to the new page momentarily.")

The onRequest value indicates that the traversal should be user-triggered. When it is combined with a a show attribute of replace, it is a typical, click-here-to-go-there link, at least in a graphical browser. On a text-based browser, it might be a type-this-number-to-go-there link. On a spoken-word browser it might be a say-this-number-to-go-there link.

When it is combined with a value of new it opens a new "context" (usually a browser window) at user command and leaves the old one open. When it is combined with a value of embed, the target resource is displayed embedded in the source, replacing the linking element.[6]

The onLoad value of the actuate attribute is used to specify that traversal should be done automatically when the document is loaded. For instance, most show="embed" links would specify automatic traversal. If you combine show="new" with actuate="onLoad", then you can create a Web page that immediately opens another Web page (like a popup advertisment). Perhaps with a stylesheet or other attribute, you could make them appear side by side. The final combination is show="replace" with actuate="onLoad". You would use this to set up a "forwarding" link, such as the one we have described, and thus forward users from one page to another.

65.3 | Extended links

In this section, we will discuss more features of *extended links*. One that we have already discussed is the ability to specify them in third-party documents. Extended links also allow for more link ends, more advanced link roles, and other good stuff. We will also be able to re-describe the simple links that we have already seen in the terminology of the more general extended link system.

65.3.1 *Locator elements*

The first extension we will undertake is links with more than two link ends. Consider, for example, that you are redirecting users to several different interpretations of a text. For instance if there were two competitive schools of thought on a topic, each hotspot in the document might allow traversal to a different interpretation of the topic. Now you have three link ends, one for the source and one for each of the interpretations of it. Just as in real life, XLink allows you to make logical links among two or more concepts.

The first big difference between simple links and extended links is that we need to figure out how to specify the address of more than one destination link. We do this by putting *locator* subelements into the extended linking element. Example 65-12 demonstrates.

---

6. In hypertext terms, this is called a *transclusion*.

Example 65-12. Multi-ended link

```
<commentary xlink:type="extended">
   <locator xlink:type="locator"
            xlink:href="roberts.xml"
            xlink:role="http://commentary.com/analysis"/>
   <locator xlink:type="locator"
            xlink:href="beam.xml"
            xlink:role="http://commentary.com/rebuttal"/>
   <locator xlink:type="locator"
            xlink:href="goodwin.xml"
            xlink:role="http://commentary.com/precis"/>
<P>My fellow Americans, this speech will go down in history...</P>
</commentary>
```

In this case, the three locators each address a resource. A sufficiently sophisticated browser displaying this document might represent each with an icon or supply a popup menu that allows access to each of the resources. It could even open a small window for each interpretation when the hot-spot is selected. This could be controlled by a stylesheet or a behavior attribute. As you can see, each locator can have a different role, but they could also share roles. The role just specifies a semantic for processing the resource when processing the link, not some sort of unique identifier.

Locators can also have some other associated attributes. They can have titles, specified through a `xlink:title` attribute. These provide information for human consumption. The browser does not act on them. It merely passes them on to the human in some way, such as a popup menu, or text on the status bar.

The locator's `xlink:label` attribute is used in combination with *arcs* (next section) to declare which resources can be the start of a traversable path and to which other resources the user can traverse.

65.3.2 *Arcs*

An extended link can link many resources. You may not want to allow traversal from every resource to every other resource. In other words, you may want to restrict some *traversal paths*. XLink has a feature called arcs to allow this.

An arc defines an allowed traversal path. An arc is an element that exhibits a `xlink:type` attribute with the value `arc`. Arcs go directly within the content of the extended link element itself. If you have no arcs then all paths are traversable. If you have one, then only the paths defined by that one arc are traversable, and so forth.

If you have three resources in your link then you can have between zero and six arc elements. For instance, if your links are to Peter, Paul and Mary (or to their home pages!) then you may or may not want to allow traversal from (1) Peter to Paul, (2) Peter to Mary, (3) Paul to Peter, (4) Paul to Mary, (5) Mary to Peter and (6) Mary to Paul.

Of course, resources do not have names like Peter, Paul and Mary. Well, actually they can! We can give names to resources by putting an `xlink:label` attribute on the locators. This is shown in Example 65-13.

Example 65-13. Extended links with labels

```
<extendedlink xlink:type="extended">
  <loc xlink:type="locator"
       xlink:label="Peter"
       xlink:href="..."/>
  <loc xlink:type="locator"
       xlink:label="Paul"
       xlink:href="..."/>
  <loc xlink:type="locator"
       xlink:label="Mary"
       xlink:href="..."/>
</extendedlink>
```

Now we can set up traversal paths between them. For instance if Peter and Paul have had a little fight, then they could both talk (traverse) to Mary but not to each other. Example 65-14 demonstrates.

Example 65-14. Peter and Paul traverse to Mary

```
<loc xlink:type="arc"
     xlink:from="Peter"
     xlink:to="Mary"/>
<loc xlink:type="arc"
     xlink:from="Paul"
     xlink:to="Mary"/>
```

It turns out that there is a shorter way to say the same thing. If we leave out the `xlink:from` attribute then an XLink processor is supposed to presume that all paths to the named resource are legal. See Example 65-15.

Example 65-15. Abbreviated form of Example 65-14

```
<loc xlink:type="arc"
     xlink:to="Mary"/>
```

In this case traversal from both Peter and Paul to Mary is allowed. We might also want to allow the opposite. In that case we would use an arc with a `xlink:from` attribute with a value of "Mary" and no `xlink:to` attribute. Just to round out our example, we might allow Peter to traverse to Paul but not the reverse. (Paul is a little sedentary). Example 65-16 shows what a complete extended link would look like in that case.

Example 65-16. Extended link with arcs

```
<extendedlink xlink:type="extended">
  <loc xlink:type="locator"
       xlink:label="Peter"
       xlink:href="..."/>
  <loc xlink:type="locator"
       xlink:label="Paul"
       xlink:href="..."/>
  <loc xlink:type="locator"
       xlink:label="Mary"
       xlink:href="..."/>
  <arc xlink:type="arc" xlink:from="Mary"/>
  <arc xlink:type="arc" xlink:to="Mary"/>
  <arc xlink:type="arc" xlink:from="Peter" xlink:to="Paul"/>
</extendedlink>
```

In this example, every path is traversable except Paul to Peter. You might wonder whether there is a more concise way to say this. For instance, you might expect an anti-arc element. There is no such thing. You always specify which paths are traversable. On the other hand, if you provide no arc elements at all, all paths are traversable.

Arcs may not have `xlink:role` attributes but they may have an equivalent attribute called `xlink:arcrole`. That attribute is a URL, just as `xlink:role` is.

65.3.3 *Simple links and extended links*

You can do anything with extended links that you can do with simple links. In fact, a simple link is a combination of a link, a locator, a resource and an arc. In fact, this is how they are defined in the XLink spec:

Spec Excerpt (XLink) 65-3. Simple links

The purpose of a simple link is to be a convenient shorthand for the equivalent extended link. A single simple linking element combines the basic functions of an extended-type element, a locator-type element, an arc-type element, and a resource-type element.

A simple link automatically defines an arc between the local resource (the linking element) and the remote resource (the target of the `xlink:href` attribute). You do not need to add an arc-type element inside of it and in fact you are not allowed to.

It is both useful and convenient that simple links combine these things, but it means that we must be careful to keep the ideas separate in our heads. The link describes a relationship. The locators say what resources are being related. A simple link uses the linking element itself as one resource and the target of its `xlink:href` attribute as the other.

65.4 | Linkbases

It is often useful to be able to process a group of hyperlinked documents all together. For instance, if one document contains some text and another contains a rebuttal of the text, the browser might want to show them "side by side". It could also allow link traversals in one window to trigger the correct portion of the rebuttal in the other.

Such processing can only work if the browser knows about both documents at the same time. Linkbases allow you to tell the browser about all of the documents that should be processed together.

A *linkbase* element is an arc that associates one XML document with another XML document that serves as a linkbase. The linkbase is used as a source of links in addition to those in the original XML document.

Linkbases are distinguished from other arcs with an `xlink:arcrole` attribute. That attribute must have the value: `http://www.w3.org/1999/xlink/properties/linkbase`

We said before that simple links automatically define an arc. So the simplest way to declare a linkbase is with a simple link, as in Example 65-17.

Example 65-17. Reference to a linkbase

```
<xlink
  xlink:type="simple"
  xlink:arcrole="http://www.w3.org/1999/xlink/properties/linkbase"
  xlink:href="http://www.xxx.com/mylinks.xml" />
```

This will instruct an XLink processor that there are additional links to be found in the `mylinks.xml` file.

65.5 | XML Base

XML documents may sometimes contain relative URLs ("`foo.xml`") instead of absolute ones ("`http://www.something.com/foo.xml`"). For brevity, many of the examples in this chapter were relative URLs. One nice thing about relative URLs is that they are concise. Another is that you can move around a package of related documents from computer to computer and keep the links the same.

On the other hand, sometimes you want to download a single document to your computer and have all relative links point to the original documents in their original (remote) location. One way to do this would be to rewrite all of the links. This is inconvenient, however. A second option is to use the `xml:base` construct.

XML Base is not part of XLink. It is a separate specification that may be used with XLink. When it is used, all relative URLs in a document are interpreted as being relative to a base URL specified in an `xml:base` attribute. Adding this one attribute is equivalent to re-writing all of the relative URLs in the document.

Example 65-18. XML Base example

```
<doc xml:base="http://www.mysite.com/base/">
    ....
    <citation xlink:type="simple"
          xlink:href="paper.xml">
    ....
</doc>
```

It is possible to declare the base on any element and have it apply to all sub-elements, but it is simplest to just declare a single base on the root element.

65.6 | Conclusion

XLink has the power to change the Web, and our lives, in unforeseeable ways. For more of the vision, see Chapter 34, "Extended linking", on page 546. For the full text of the W3C Recommendation, see the *XML SPECtacular* on the CD-ROM.

Resources

- Free XML software on the CD-ROMs
- XML specifications on the CD-ROMs
- Public XML vocabularies
- Acronyms and initialisms for XML
- Other XML-related books

Part Twenty-four

On the back cover of the first edition of this book, an inspired copywriter wrote: "The accompanying CD-ROM brings together an amazing set of XML resources."

As authors, we of course don't engage in such hyperbole, except on behalf of technologies that excite us. However, we feel obligated to make the purely factual observation that the CD-ROM for this edition is far superior to the first. In fact, there are two of them!

There are over 200 free XML software packages, compared to 55 in the first edition. Please note that we use the word "free" very precisely. We mean genuinely free use, XML-centric, no enforced time limit, uncrippled software, that is usable with your own documents.

In addition, the the Sponsor Showcase materials include more free software, plus trial versions of major commercial products for your evaluation, and white papers, demos, and examples.

This part includes an introduction to the CD-ROM resources, a directory of over 300 XML vocabulary projects, a dictionary of acronyms and initialisms, and for those who like to read actual books, a reader's guide to other books in this series.

Public XML vocabularies

Resource Description

- Schemas, DTDs and other specifications
- Industry vocabularies
- Vertical and cross-industry
- Over 300 Web links

Contributing experts: Lilia Prescod and Andrew Goldfarb

Chapter

66

There are so many XML projects in the world that it can be hard to find the ones that apply to you. Here's a guide.

The growth in XML activity has been so frantic that it seems as though there is now a vocabulary, or several, for every industry and application. We've prepared this chapter to help you find the ones that might apply to your situation. It lists over 300 vocabularies that were available when we wrote this book.

The list is not totally comprehensive. Even if it were, there are new vocabularies being created every day, so you'll want to know how to find them yourself. A good place to start is with one of the websites that accumulates XML vocabularies. We discuss them in 5.3, "Repository stories", on page 113.

We use the catch-all term *vocabulary* to refer to all sorts of element-type and attribute specifications. Some are DTDs, some use one of the schema definition languages, and some use informal English prose.

Some vocabularies define complete, self-contained document types, both POP-like and for messages. Some define only parts of the document because their designers expect them be augmented by other vocabularies that define the other parts.

In the following list, we've grouped the vocabularies into 77 categories, which are in turn grouped into eight super-categories. For each project, there is a URL. For your convenience, the list is also available on a page on the CD-ROM so you can let your browser link directly to the project sites. That list also includes a brief description of each vocabulary, derived from the project website.

66.1 | Business Systems

Application integration

Open Applications Group Interface Specification (OAGIS)
http://www.openapplications.org

Calendaring

iCalendar
http://www.imc.org/rfc2445
vCard and vCalendar
http://www.imc.org/pdi/

Catalog

Open Catalog Format (OCF)
http://www.martsoft.com/ocf/
Open Catalog Protocol (OCP)
http://www.martsoft.com/ocp/
Product Data Markup Language (PDML)
http://www.pdml.org/pdmlintro.html
eCatalog XML (eCX)
http://www.ecx-xml.org/

Commerce

BizTalk Framework 2.0
http://www.microsoft.com/biztalk/techinfo/framwork20.asp
Business Process Modeling Language (BPML)
http://www.bpmi.org/faq.esp
Business Rules Markup Language (BRML)
http://www.research.ibm.com/rules/commonrules-overview.html

CommerceXML (cXML)
http://www.cxml.org/
Common Business Library (xCBL)
http://www.xcbl.org/
Electronic Business XML Initiative (ebXML)
http://www.ebxml.org/geninfo.htm#what
Global Uniform Interoperable Data Exchange (GUIDE)
http://www.bizcodes.org/GUIDE/
Guideline XML
http://www.edifecs.com/b2b_resources_guideline.jsp
Internet Open Trading Protocol (OTP)(Trade)
http://www.ietf.org/html.charters/trade-charter.html
Marine Trading Markup Language (MTML)
http://www.mtml.org/
Network Trade Model (NTM)
http://www.risk.sungard.com/standards/index.php
Open Buying on the Internet (OBI)
http://www.openbuy.org/
RosettaNet
http://www.rosettanet.org
Small and Medium Sized Business XML (SMBXML)
http://www.netledger.com/portal/partners_5_4.jsp
Universal Commerce Language and Protocol (UCLP)
http://www.w3.org/TR/NOTE-uclp/
Visa XML Invoice Specification
http://www.visa.com/xml
eCo Framework
http://eco.commerce.net/
eXchangeable Routing Language (XRL)
http://tmitwww.tm.tue.nl/staff/wvdaalst/Workflow/xrl/

Customer information

Customer Profile Exchange Network (CPExchange)
http://www.cpexchange.org/
Unified Customer Reporting (UCR)
http://www.haifa.il.ibm.com/projects/software/ucr/index.html
eXtensible Customer Information Language (xCIL)
http://members.ozemail.com.au/~sakthi/dtd/dtd.html

eXtensible Name and Address Language (xNAL)
http://members.ozemail.com.au/~sakthi/dtd/dtd.html

Data mining

Predictive Model Markup Language (PMML)
http://www.dmg.org/pmmlspecs_v2/pmml_v2_0.html

Electronic data interchange (edi)

ACORD EDI (AL3)
http://www.acord.org/
ANSI ASC X12/XML
http://www.x12.org/
Formal Language for Business Communication (FLBC)
http://www-personal.umich.edu/~samoore/research/flbc/index.htm
l
TranXML
http://www.transentric.com/products/commerce/tranxml.asp
XML/EDI (Electronic Data Interchange)
http://www.xmledi-group.org/

Finance

Bank Internet Payment System (BIPS)
http://www.fstc.org/projects/bips/
Common Markup for micropayment per-fee-links
http://www.w3.org/TR/Micropayment-Markup/
eXtensible Business Reporting Language (XBRL)
http://www.xbrl.org/
FinXML
http://www.finxml.org/
Financial Information Exchange Markup Language (FIXML)
http://www.fixprotocol.org/cgi-bin/rbox/Welcome.cgi
Financial Information eXchange (FIX)
http://www.fixprotocol.org/cgi-bin/rbox/Welcome.cgi
FpML (Financial products Markup Language)
http://fpml.org/
Interactive Financial eXchange (IFX)

http://www.ifxforum.org/

Market Data Definition Language (MDDL)

http://www.mddl.org

Mortgage Industry Standards Maintenance Organization (MISMO)

http://www.mismo.org/mismo/Mismo_faq.cfm#1

Open Financial Exchange (OFX)

http://www.ofx.net/ofx/default.asp

Research Information Exchange Markup Language

http://www.rixml.org/faqs.html#gen

Straight Through Processing Markup Language (STPML)

http://www.stpml.org/

XMLPay

http://www.verisign.com/developer/xml/xmlpay.html

data link for intermediaries Markup Language (daliML)

http://www.dali1441.com/dali/dalihome.nsf/daliML?openframeset

swiftML

http://www.swift.com/

Human resources

HR-XML

http://www.hr-xml.org/channels/home.htm

Human Resources Markup Language (hrml)

http://www.hrml.com/

Human Resources XML (HR-XML)

http://www.hr-xml.org/channels/home.htm

Job Survey (JobSur) Markup Language (JSML)

http://www.codap.com/job_survey_jobsur.htm

XMLRèsumè Library

http://xmlresume.sourceforge.net/

Industrial automation

Machinery Information Management Open Systems Alliance (MIMOSA)

http://www.mimosa.org/

Virtual Instruments Markup Language (VIML)

http://nacimiento.com/VIML/

Product information

Product Definition eXchange (PDX)
http://www.pdxstandard.org/
StepML
http://www.stepml.org/index.html

Security

XML Key Management Specification (XKMS)
http://www.w3.org/TR/xkms/
Intrusion Detection Exchange Format (idwg)
http://www.ietf.org/html.charters/idwg-charter.html
Security Assertion Markup Language (SAML)
http://www.oasis-open.org/committees/security/docs/draft-sstc-
saml-spec-00.PDF
Signed Document Markup Language (SDML)
http://www.w3.org/TR/1998/NOTE-SDML-19980619/#SECTION00200
XML Access Control (XACL)
http://www.trl.ibm.com/projects/xml/xacl/index.htm
XML Key Information Service Specification (X-KISS)
http://www.w3.org/2001/07/xkms-ws/cfp.html
XML Key Registration Service Specification (X-KRSS)
http://www.w3.org/2001/07/xkms-ws/cfp.html
XML-Signature
http://www.w3.org/Signature/
eXtensible Access Control Markup Language (XACML)
http://www.oasis-open.org/committees/tc_home.php?wg_abbrev=xac
ml

Systems administration

ALURe (Aggregation and Logging of User Requests) XML Specification
http://www.alurexml.org/
DMTF Common Information Model (CIM)
http://www.dmtf.org/standards/standard_cim.php
DirXML
http://www.novell.com/products/nds/dirxml/quicklook.html
Extensible Log Format (XLF)

`http://www.docuverse.com/xlf/`
Log File Format
`http://communicator.sourceforge.net/logstandard/log-standard-v14.html#Introduction`
Log Markup Language (LOGML)
`http://www.cs.rpi.edu/~puninj/LOGML/`

Workflow

Simple Workflow Access Protocol (SWAP)
`http://www.isr.uci.edu/events/twist/wisen98/presentations/Swenson/`
Workflow Management Coalition (WfMC)
`http://www.wfmc.org/`

66.2 | Content management and distribution

Content management protocols

DAV Searching & Locating (DASL)
`http://www.webdav.org/dasl/protocol/draft-dasl-protocol-00.html`
HTTP Distribution and Replication Protocol (DRP)
`http://www.w3.org/TR/NOTE-drp-19970825.html`
WebDAV
`http://www.webdav.org/`

Content organization

Portable Site Information (PSI)
`http://www.xml.com/pub/2000/03/22/psi/index.html`
XEditor
`http://www.openhealth.org/editor/`

Metadata

BiblioML
http://www.culture.fr/BiblioML/
Common Warehouse Metadata (CWM)
http://www.cwmforum.org/
Dublin Core
http://dublincore.org/
Encoded Archival Description (EAD)
http://cidc.library.cornell.edu/xml/
Image Metadata Aggregation for Enhanced Searching (IMAGES)
http://www.diglib.org/pubs/news02_01/umnpv.htm
Jigsaw XML Format (JigXML)
http://www.w3.org/Jigsaw/Doc/Programmer/JigXML.html
XML representation of Lexicons and Terminologies (XLT)
http://www.ttt.org/oscar/xlt/dxlt.html
MAchine Readable Cataloging (MARC)
http://lcweb.loc.gov/marc/marc.html
MPEG-7 Description Definition Language
http://mpeg.telecomitalialab.com/standards/mpeg-7/mpeg-7.htm
Manuscript Access through Standards for Electronic Records (MASTER)
http://www.cta.dmu.ac.uk/projects/master/
Meta Content Framework Using XML (MCF)
http://www.w3.org/TR/NOTE-MCF-XML.html
Open Archives Metadata Set (OAMS)
http://www.openarchives.org/
Platform for Internet Content Selection (PICS)
http://www.w3.org/PICS/
Publishing Requirements for Industry Standard Metadata (PRISM)
http://www.prismstandard.org/index.asp
Resource Description Framework (RDF)
http://www.w3.org/RDF/
Resource Directory Description Language (RDDL)
http://www.openhealth.org/RDDL/#intro
Structured Graph Format (SGF)
http://www7.scu.edu.au/programme/fullpapers/416/416.html
Topic Maps (ISO/IEC 13250)
http://www.topicmaps.org/
Web Modeling Language (WebML)

```
http://www9.org/w9cdrom/177/177.html
```
XMLMARC
```
http://xmlmarc.stanford.edu/
```
XMLTV
```
http://www.doc.ic.ac.uk/~epa98/work/apps/xmltv/
```
bibteXML
```
http://bibtexml.sourceforge.net/
```

Mobile delivery

Open eBook
```
http://www.openebook.org/
```
SyncML
```
http://www.openmobilealliance.org/syncml/
```
Wireless Markup Language (WML)
```
http://www.wapforum.org/
```
XML DTD for Roaming Access Phone Book
```
http://rfc3017.x42.com/
```
XML Document Navigation Language (XDNL)
```
http://www.w3.org/TR/2000/NOTE-xdnl-20000323/#sec-intro
```

Rights management

Open Digital Rights Language (ODRL)
```
http://odrl.net/
```
eXtensible Media Commerce Language (XMCL)
```
http://www.xmcl.org/
```

Syndication

Channel Definition Format (CDF)
```
http://www.w3.org/TR/NOTE-CDFsubmit.html
```
Information and Content Exchange (ICE) Protocol
```
http://www.icestandard.org/
```
NITF (News Industry Text Format)
```
http://www.nitf.org/
```
NewsML
```
http://www.iptc.org/site/NewsML/brochurenml.html
```
Open Content Syndication (OCS)

`http://internetalchemy.org/ocs/index.html`
RDF Site Summary (RSS)
`http://www.oreillynet.com/topics/rss/rss`
XMLNews-Meta
`http://www.xmlnews.org/docs/xmlnews-meta.html`
XMLNews-Story
`http://www.xmlnews.org/docs/xmlnews-story.html`

Technical publishing

DocBook DTD
`http://www.oasis-open.org/docbook/`
Electronic Book Exchange (EBX)
`http://www.ebxwg.org/`
Institute of Electrical and Electronics Engineers Standard (IEEESTD)
`http://standards.ieee.org/resources/spasystem/dtd/`
ONIX International DTD
`http://www.editeur.org/onix.html`
OpenOffice.org XML project
`http://xml.openoffice.org`
Printing Industry Markup Language (PrintML)
`http://printml.org/index_en.htm`
Question and Answer Markup Language (QAML)
`http://www.ascc.net/xml/en/utf-8/qaml-index.html`
RFC2629
`http://www.faqs.org/rfcs/rfc2629.html`
Text Encoding Initiative (TEI)
`http://www.tei-c.org/`
eFirst XML for Scholarly Articles
`http://www.openly.com/efirst/`

Translation

OpenTag Format
`http://www.opentag.com/`
Translation Memory Exchange (TMX)
`http://www.lisa.org/tmx/tmx.htm`

66.3 | Content types

Forms

Extensible Forms Description Language (XFDL)
http://www.w3.org/TR/1998/NOTE-XFDL-19980902
XForms
http://www.w3.org/MarkUp/Forms/

Hypertext

HyTime
http://www.hytime.org/
Virtual HyperGlossary (VHG)
http://www.vhg.org.uk/home/index.html
XML Bookmark Exchange Language (XBEL)
http://www.python.org/topics/xml/xbel/
ibtwsh: Itsy Bitsy Teeny Weeny Simple Hypertext DTD
http://www.ccil.org/~cowan/XML/

Multimedia

DIG35
http://www.i3a.org/i_dig35.html
Image Markup Language (IML)
http://faculty.washington.edu/lober/iml/
MPEG-21 Multimedia Framework
http://www.cselt.it/mpeg/standards/mpeg-21/mpeg-21.htm
Multimodal Presentation Markup Language (MPML)
http://www.miv.t.u-tokyo.ac.jp/MPML/en/
Synchronized Multimedia Integration Language (SMIL)
http://www.w3.org/AudioVideo/Activity.html
XGL File Format Specification
http://www.xglspec.org/
XML Messaging Specification (XMSG)
http://www.w3.org/TR/xmsg/

Music

4ML
`http://fourml.sourceforge.net/`
Music Markup Language (MML)
`http://www.musicmarkup.info/`
MusicXML
`http://www.musicxml.org/default.asp`
eXtensible Score Language (XScore)
`http://grigaitis.net/xscore/`

Outlines

Outline Processor Markup Language (OPML)
`http://www.opml.org/`

Tables

CALS table
`http://www.oasis-open.org/specs/a502.htm`

Vector graphics

Extensible 3D (X3D)
`http://www.web3d.org/x3d.html`
Precision Graphics Markup Language (PGML)
`http://www.w3.org/TR/1998/NOTE-PGML`
Scalable Vector Graphics (SVG)
`http://www.w3.org/Graphics/SVG/Overview.htm8#intro`
Vector Markup Language (VML)
`http://www.w3.org/TR/NOTE-VML`

Voice

JSpeech Grammar Format (JSGF)
`http://www.w3.org/TR/jsgf/`
Java Speech Markup Language Specification (JSML)
`http://java.sun.com/products/java-media/speech/forDevelopers/J
SML/`

NISO Digital Talking Books (DTB)
http://www.loc.gov/nls/niso/dtd.htm
Natural Language Semantics Markup Language
http://www.w3.org/TR/2000/WD-nl-spec-20001120/
SABLE: A Synthesis Markup Language
http://www.w3.org/TR/voice-tts-reqs/
Speech Recognition Grammar Specification
http://www.w3.org/TR/speech-grammar/
Speech Synthesis Markup Language (SSML)
http://www.cstr.ed.ac.uk/projects/sable/
TalkML
http://www.w3.org/Voice/TalkML/
Voice eXtensible Markup Language (VoiceXML)
http://www.voicexml.org/

66.4 | Personal communication

Email

HTML Threading: Conventions for use of HTML in email
http://www.w3.org/TR/1998/NOTE-HTMLThreading-0105

Instant messaging

Common Profile for Instant Messaging (CPIM)
http://www.ietf.org/internet-drafts/draft-ietf-impp-im-03.txt
Instant Messaging and Presence Protocol (impp)
http://www.imppwg.org/
Jabber XML
http://www.jabber.org/

66.5 | Science

Astronomy and instruments

Astronomical Dataset Markup Language (ADML)
http://xml.gsfc.nasa.gov/
Flexible Image Transport System (FITS)
http://fits.gsfc.nasa.gov/fits_intro.html
Spacecraft Markup Language (SML)
http://www.interfacecontrol.com/sml/

Biology

BIOpolymer Markup Language (BIOML)
http://www.bioml.com/BIOML/index.html
Bioinformatic Sequence Markup Language (BSML)
http://www.bsml.org/
CellML
http://www.cellml.org/public/about/what_is_cellml.html
Gene Expression Markup Language (GEML)
http://www.rosettabio.com/products/conductor/geml/default.htm
Taxonomic Markup Language
http://www.albany.edu/~gilmr/pubxml/
The Systems Biology Markup Language (SBML)
http://www.cds.caltech.edu/erato/sbml/docs/index.html

Chemistry

CHEM ESTANDARDS
http://www.cidx.org/default_XML.asp?Level=2&SecondLevelURL1=/S
tandard/Standard.asp
Chemical Markup Language (CML)
http://www.xml-cml.org/

General science

Extensible Scientific Interchange Language (XSIL)
http://www.cacr.caltech.edu/SDA/xsil/
eXtensible Data Format (XDF)

`http://xml.gsfc.nasa.gov/XDF/XDF_home.html`
nanoML
`http://www.nanotitan.com/`

Geography

CaveScript XML
`http://www.speleonics.com.au/cavescript/`
Geography Markup Language (GML)
`http://www.opengis.net/gml/01-029/GML2.html`
LandXML
`http://www.landxml.org/over.htm`
Point Of Interest eXchange Language Specification (POIX)
`http://www.w3.org/TR/poix/`

Math

Mathematical Markup Language (MathML)
`http://www.w3.org/Math/`
Open Mathematical Documents (OMDoc)
`http://www.mathweb.org/omdoc/`

Meteorology

Weather Observation Definition Format (ODF)
`http://zowie.metnet.navy.mil/~spawar/JMV-TNG/XML/OMF.html`
WeatherML
`http://www.idealliance.org/XMLRoadmap/WEB/ts0/tp57.htm`

66.6 | Social

Economics

EcoKnowMICS ML
`http://www.ecoknowmics.com`

Game playing

Board Game Markup Language (BGML)
`http://www.vilab.com/bgml/home.html`
Caxton Chess XML (CaXML)
`http://www.chesscity.com/Caxton/caxton_xml.htm`
Chess Game Markup Language (ChessGML)
`http://www.saremba.de/chessgml/index.htm`
ChessML
`http://www.oliversick.de/chess/chessml/faq/`
Quest Markup Language (QML)
`http://www.outer-court.com/goodies/qml.htm`
Smart Game Format (SGF)
`http://www.red-bean.com/sgf/`

Geneology

GedML: Genealogical Data in XML
`http://users.iclway.co.uk/mhkay/gedml/`

Humor

Adult Entertainment Markup Language (XXXML)
`http://www.sdtimes.com/news/027/story7.htm`
ComicsML
`http://www.jmac.org/projects/comics_ml/`
Mind Reading Markup Language (MRML)
`http://www.jonzer.com/mrml.htm`

Linguistics

ATLAS (Architecture and Tools for Linguistic Analysis Systems) Interchange Format (AIF)
`http://www.nist.gov/speech/atlas/develop/aif.html`

Public interest

Human Markup Language (HumanML)
`http://www.humanmarkup.org/`

International Development Markup Language (IDML)
`http://www.idmlinitiative.org/`

Religion

Liturgical Markup Language (LitML)
`http://www.oremus.org/LitML/`
Theological Markup Language (ThML)
`http://www.ccel.org/ThML/`

66.7 | Software development

Artificial intelligence

Artificial Intelligence Markup Language (AIML)
`http://alicebot.org/alice/aiml.html`
DARPA Agent Markup Language (DAML)
`http://www.daml.org/`
Description Logic Markup Language (DLML)
`http://co4.inrialpes.fr/xml/dlml/`
Information Flow Framework (IFF)
`http://www.ontologos.org/IFF/IFF.html`
Knowledge Query and Manipulation Language (KQML)
`http://www.cs.umbc.edu/kqml/`
OML/CKML
`http://www.ontologos.org/`
Ontology Inference Layer (OIL)
`http://www.ontoknowledge.org/oil/`
Petri Net Markup Language (PNML)
`http://www.informatik.hu-berlin.de/top/pnml/`
Procedural Markup Language (PML)
`http://www.cc.gatech.edu/classes/cs7100_98_fall/projects/ram02`
`.html`
Relational-Functional Markup Language (RFML)
`http://www.relfun.org/rfml/`
XML Belief Network File Format (XBN)
`http://research.microsoft.com/dtas/bnformat/default.htm`

XML-Based Ontology Exchange Language (XOL)
`ftp://smi.stanford.edu/pub/bio-ontology/xol.doc`

Components

Bean Markup Language (BML)
`http://www.alphaworks.ibm.com/tech/bml`
Koala Bean Markup Language (KBML)
`http://www-sop.inria.fr/koala/kbml/kbmltech.html`
Koala Object Markup Language (KOML)
`http://www-sop.inria.fr/koala/XML/serialization/`
Open Software Description (OSD)
`http://msdn.microsoft.com/workshop/delivery/osd/overview/osd.asp`

Documentation

JavaDox
`http://www.creativepro.com/story/news/2953.html`
Object-Oriented Programing Meta-Language (OOPML)
`http://www.iro.umontreal.ca/labs/gelo/xml4se/oopml/Welcome.html`
Pattern Markup Language (PML)
`http://www.yy.ics.keio.ac.jp/~suzuki/project/uxf/`

Graph exchange

Graph eXchange Language (GXL)
`http://www.gupro.de/GXL/`
eXtensible Graph Markup and Modeling Language (XGMML)
`http://www.cs.rpi.edu/~puninj/XGMML/draft-xgmml.html`

Internationalization

Character Mapping Markup Language (CharMapML)
`http://www.unicode.org/unicode/reports/tr22/tr22-2.2.html`

Middleware

Mediation of Information Using XML (MIX)
http://www.npaci.edu/DICE/MIX/
Simple Object Access Protocol (SOAP)
http://www.microsoft.com/mind/0100/soap/soap.asp
Web Distributed Data eXchange (WDDX)
http://www.openwddx.org/faq/
Web Interface Definition Language (WIDL)
http://www.w3.org/TR/NOTE-widl
WebBroker: Distributed Object Communication on the Web
http://www.w3.org/TR/1998/NOTE-webbroker/
XML-RPC (Remote Procedure Calling)
http://www.xmlrpc.com/stories/storyReader$7

Modeling

Architecture Description Markup Language (ADML)
http://www.opengroup.org/onlinepubs/009009899/index.htm
CDIF XML-Based Transfer Format
http://www.eigroup.org/cdif/intro.html
OMG Model Driven Architecture (MDA)
http://www.omg.org/mda/
UML eXchange Format (UXF)
http://www.yy.cs.keio.ac.jp/~suzuki/project/uxf/
UML-Xchange
http://www3.sympatico.ca/rivardn/uml/umlxchng.html
XML Metadata Interchange Format (XMI)
http://www-4.ibm.com/software/ad/library/standards/xmi.html

Protocols

Blocks Extensible Exchange Protocol (BEEP/BXXP)
http://beepcore.org/beepcore/home.jsp
Common Name Resolution Protocol (CNRP)
http://www.ietf.org/html.charters/cnrp-charter.html
Media Object Server Communications Protocol (MOS)
http://www.mosprotocol.com/
Roaming Operations (roamops)

```
http://www.ietf.org/html.charters/roamops-charter.html
```
Voluntary Interindustry Commerce Standards (VICS) Collaborative Planning, Forecasting and Replenishment (CPFR) XML Messaging Model
```
http://www.cpfr.org/
```
XLANG
```
http://www.gotdotnet.com/team/xml_wsspecs/xlang-c/default.htm
```
XML DTD for ACAP - ACAP (Application Configuration Access Protocol) data interchange format
```
http://asg.web.cmu.edu/acap/
```
XML Encoding Rules (XER)
```
http://asf.gils.net/xer/concept.html
```
XML Encoding for SMS (Short Message Service) Messages
```
http://www.smsforum.net/
```
XML Inter-ORB Protocol (XIOP)
```
http://xiop.sourceforge.net/index.html
```
XML MIME Transformation Protocol (XMTP)
```
http://www.openhealth.org/documents/xmtp.htm
```
eXtensible Name Service (XNS)
```
http://www.xns.org/
```

Schema languages

Document Definition Markup Language (DDML)
```
http://www.w3.org/TR/1999/NOTE-ddml-19990119
```
RELAX
```
http://www.xml.gr.jp/relax/
```
RELAX NG
```
http://www.oasis-open.org/committees/relax-ng/
```
Schema for Object-Oriented XML 2.0 (SOX)
```
http://www.w3.org/TR/NOTE-SOX/
```
Schematron
```
http://www.ascc.net/xml/resource/schematron/schematron.html
```
W3C XML Schema
```
http://www.w3.org/XML/Schema
```

Theoretical computer science

Rule Markup Language (RuleML)
```
http://www.dfki.uni-kl.de/ruleml/
```

Turing Machine Markup Language (TMML)
`http://www.unidex.com/turing/tmml.htm`

User interface

Extensible User Interface Language (XUL)
`http://www.mozilla.org/xpfe/xptoolkit/xulintro.html`
User Interface Markup Language (UIML)
`http://www.uiml.org/intro/index.htm`
XML Binding Language (XBL)
`http://www.w3.org/TR/2001/NOTE-xbl-20010223/`

66.8 | Vertical industry

Advertising

Banner Mark-up Language (BannerML)
`http://www.idealliance.org/XMLRoadmap/WEB/BannerML.htm`
NAA Classified Advertising Standards Task Force and DTD
`http://www.naa.org/technology/clsstdtf/`

Agriculture

AgXML
`http://www.agxml.org/`

Application service providers

Information Technology Markup Language (ITML)
`http://www.itml.org/`

Architecture, engineering, and construction

Architecture, Engineering, and Construction XML Working Group (aecXML Working Group)
`http://www.iai-na.org/aecxml/mission.php`
Green Building XML (gbXML)

`http://www.idea-server.com/gbxml.htm`
Materials Property Data Markup Language (MatML)
`http://www.ceramics.nist.gov/matml/matml.htm`

Automotive

MSR MEDOC
`http://www.msr-wg.de/`
NaVigation Markup Language (NVML)
`http://www.w3.org/TR/NVML`
Standards for Technology in Automotive Retail (STAR)
`http://www.starstandard.org/`
XML for the Automotive Industry - SAE J2008
`http://www.xmlxperts.com/sae.htm#over`

Education

IMS Metadata Specification
`http://www.imsproject.org/metadata/index.html`
Learning Material Markup Language (LMML)
`http://www.lmml.de/`
NetQuest Tutorial Markup Language (TML)
`http://www.ilrt.bris.ac.uk/netquest/about/lang/`
Schools Interoperability Framework (SIF)
`http://www.sifinfo.org/`
Universal Learning Format (ULF)
`http://www.saba.com/standards/ulf/Overview/Frames/overview.htm`

Food services

Recipe Markup Language (RecipeML)
`http://www.formatdata.com/recipeml/index.html`

Government

Election Markup Language (EML)
`http://www.oasis-open.org/committees/election/index.shtml#documents`
ParlML

```
http://www.europarl.eu.int/docman/texts/TFDM(2000)0014EN(TOC)0
.htm
```
Triple-s Survey Interchange Standard
```
http://www.triple-s.org/index.htm
```

Hardware and electronics

Component Information Dictionary Specification (CIDS)
```
http://www.si2.org/si2_publications/ecix/CIDS/
```
Robotic Markup Language (RoboML)
```
http://www.roboml.org/
```
nanoML
```
http://www.nanotitan.com/
```

Healthcare

Clinical Data Interchange Standards (CDISC)
```
http://www.cdisc.org/
```
Health Level 7 (HL7)
```
http://www.hl7.org/
```
Template Definition Language (TDL) for Electronic Patient Records (EPR)
```
http://www.schattauer.de/zs/methods/2000/1/pdf/00010050.pdf
```

Hospitality

Hospitality Industry Technology Integration Standards (HITIS)
```
http://www.hitis.org/
```

Insurance

ACORD XML for Life Insurance
```
http://www.acord.org/standards/lifexml.aspx
```
Acord XML Property and Casualty
```
http://www.acord.org/standards/propertyxml.aspx
```

Legal

Digital Property Rights Language (DPRL)
```
http://citeseer.nj.nec.com/context/143250/0
```

Legal Electronic Data Exchange Standard (LEDES)
http://www.ledes.org/
Legal XML
http://www.legalxml.org/
XML Court Interface (XCI)
http://www.oasis-open.org/cover/xcidemo-20001002.html
XrML (eXtensible rights Markup Language)
http://www.xrml.org/

Manufacturing

Process Specification Language (PSL)
http://ats.nist.gov/psl/

Military

Defense Logistics Format (DLF)
http://milpac.com/specs/xml-dlf.pdf

Petrochemical

WellLogML
http://www.posc.org/ebiz/WellLogML
WellSchematicML
http://www.posc.org/ebiz/WellSchematicML/index.shtml

Real estate

Data Consortium Namespace (DCN) DTD
http://www.dataconsortium.org/documents.html
Real Estate Information Standards (REIS)
http://www.dataconsortium.org/
Real Estate Listing Management System (OpenMLS)
http://www.numerata.com/
Real Estate Transaction Specification
http://www.rets-wg.org/

Resource extraction

Epicentre XML Exchange Format (PEF XML)
`http://www.posc.org/ebiz/pefxml/ExchangeFormat.html#gen`
Equation of State ML (eosML)
`http://www.posc.org/ebiz/eosML/index.shtml`
GeophysicalML
`http://www.posc.org/ebiz/Geophysics/index.shtml`
Log Graphics Markup Language (LogGraphicsML)
`http://www.posc.org/ebiz/LogGraphicsML/v1.0/index.html`
PetroXML
`http://www.petroxml.org/`
ProductionML
`http://www.posc.org/ebiz/ProductionML/index.shtml`
eXploration and Mining Markup Language (XMML)
`http://www.ned.dem.csiro.au/XMML/`

Retail

Retail Enterprise Data in XML (REDX)
`http://www.nrf-arts.org/redx.htm`

Telecommunications

Call Policy Markup Language (CPML)
`http://www.coppercom.com/applications.asp`
Call Processing Language (CPL)
`http://www.bell-labs.com/mailing-lists/iptel/draft-ietf-iptel-cpl-00.txt`
XML-for-Fax (XML-F)
`http://www.vsi.com/pdf/xmlf-spec.pdf`
eXtensible Telephony Markup Language (XTML)
`http://www.pactolus.com/pcs-xtml.pdf`

The XML Handbook Acronym Guide

Resource Description

- Organizations
- Protocols
- Standards
- Jargon

Chapter

67

Every product, trend, and concept created by the high tech industry spawns a new vocabulary of impenetrable, redundant, and/or meaningless phrases. The industry then attempts to avoid using that vocabulary by coining a raft of equally impenetrable abbreviations. Or so it may seem to a newcomer faced with a flood of inimical acronymical initialisms (IAI). Here's our attempt to help.

I n this chapter you'll find the initialisms and acronyms used in the body of The XML Handbook.

67.1 | Where do acronyms come from?

Twisted minds!

We know because we've coined a few ourselves.[1] But here's an explanatory bit of pedantry:

abbreviation

A short way of saying something long, like "spec" instead of "specification".

initialism

An abbreviation composed of the initials of the something long, like "XML" instead of "Extensible Markup Language". (Did we mention that people don't always follow rules perfectly?)

---

1. But only four for this book: IEC, MOM, POP, and XDBMS.

acronym

> An abbreviation that would be an initialism except that it is pronounced like a word, rather than as separate letters. "PRISM" is an acronym; "XML" is an initialism.[2] "ISO" is both.[3]

67.2 | Acronyms and initialisms in *The XML Handbook*

The following table includes 289 acronyms and initialisms (including a few contractions and some words that look like acronyms but aren't). We think it has every one that has occurred in the body of the book since the Fourth Edition, which means:

- It includes even incidental ones that aren't vital to understanding the text. Fortunately, there are lots of these.
- It also includes initialisms and acronyms that don't occur directly but are used in the definition of other ones (like "ITU").
- It probably doesn't include any that might be used in the industry but aren't used in the book.[4]
- It probably doesn't include any that are defined and used in a single chapter of the book but aren't used in the industry.
- It probably does include some that have become obsolete.
- It doesn't include all of the acronyms and initialisms for XML vocabulary projects. You can find hundreds of those in Chapter 66, "Public XML vocabularies", on page 1090.
- It includes some that have no connection with XML, or even with computers. But we couldn't draw a reasonable line

---

2. Albeit a forced one.
3. And also a triumph of political correctness over sanity. It deliberately doesn't match the name "International Organization for Standardization" in order to be "language neutral". As a result, almost every English speaker calls ISO the "International Standards Organization".
4. That includes those coined for last month's hot trend. They'll probably be forgotten by next month anyway.

because if you don't understand an initialism, how can you know it isn't relevant?[5]

The table includes the spelled-out definitions of the abbreviations, but there is no attempt to explain them. In other words, this isn't a glossary. We've explained all the important terms in context in the body of the book; you can find them in the index.

---

5. So if you always wondered what "DNA" stood for, now you can find out!

Table 67-1	Acronyms and initialisms in *The XML Handbook*
AAA	American Arbitration Association
ACL	access control list
AI	artificial intelligence
aka	also known as
ANI	automatic number identification
ANSI	American National Standards Institute
AOL	America Online
ANI	automatic number identification
API	application program(ming) interface
APS	CGM Application Structure
APXL	Apple Presentation XML
ASCII	American Standard Code for Information Interchange
ASN.1	Abstract Syntax Notation 1
ASP	Active Server Pages
ASP	application service provider
AU	Unix audio file
AVI	Audio Video Interleave
B2B	business-to-business
B2Bi	business-to-business integration
B2C	business-to-consumer
BC	before Christ
BCE	before the Common Era
BLOB	binary large object

BMP	Basic Multilingual Plane
BMP	bitmap
BMS	Basic Mapping Support
BP	business process
BPA	business process automation
BPM	business process management
BSP	business service provider
CA	Certification Authority
CallXML	Call XML
CBL	common business library
CBR	content-based routing

CC/PP	Composite Capabilities/Preferences Profile
CD-ROM	compact disc read-only memory
CGI	Common Gateway Interface
CGM	Computer Graphics Metafile
CIA	US Central Intelligence Agency
CICS	Customer Information Control System
CJK	Chinese, Japanese, and Korean
CLOB	character large object
CML	Chemical Markup Language
CMS	content management system
COBOL	Common Business Oriented Language
COM	Component Object Model
CORBA	Common Object Request Broker Architecture
COTS	commercially available off-the-shelf
CPA	Collaboration-Protocol Agreement
CPP	Collaboration-Protocol Profile
CPU	central processing unit
CRM	customer relationship management
CSS	Cascading Style Sheets
CSV	comma-separated values
cXML	commerce XML
DB	database
DBMS	database management system
DCE	Distributed Computing Environment

DCOM	Distributed Component Object Model
DHCP	Dynamic Host Configuration Protocol
DHTML	Dynamic HTML
DMS	document management system
DNA	deoxyribonucleic acid
DNS	Domain Name System
DOM	Document Object Model
DSML	Directory Services Markup Language
DSO	Data Source Object
DSSSL	Document Style Semantics and Specification Language
DT4DTD	Datatypes for DTDs
DTD	document type definition
DTMF	Dual Tone Multi-Frequency
DTV	digital television
EAI	enterprise application integration
eBI	e-business integration
EBI	enterprise business integration
ebXML	Electronic Business XML
EDGAR	Electronic Data Gathering, Analysis, and Retrieval
EDI	electronic data interchange
EDIFACT	EDI for Administration, Commerce and Transport
EFT	electronic funds transfer
EIP	enterprise information portal
EJB	Enterprise JavaBeans

EMR	electronic medical records
EPS	Encapsulated PostScript
ERP	enterprise resource planning
FAQ	frequently asked question
FBI	US Federal Bureau of Investigation
FIDOM	Format-Independent DOM
FIXML	Financial Information Exchange ML
FNOC	franchised network operations center
FTP	File Transfer Protocol
GIF	Graphics Interchange Format
GM	General Motors
GML	Generalized Markup Language
GMT	Greenwich mean time
GPS	global positioning system
GUI	graphical user interface
HL7	Health Level Seven
HR	human resources
HTML	HyperText Markup Language
HTTP	Hypertext Transfer Protocol
HTTPS	HTTP over SSL
HyTime	Hypermedia/Time-based Structuring Language
IBM	International Business Machines
ICE	Information Content and Exchange
ID	identifier

IDE	integrated development environment
IDREF	identifier reference
IEC	integrated e-commerce
IEC	International Electrotechnical Commission
IETF	Internet Engineering Task Force
IFX	Interactive Financial Exchange
IIOP	Internet Inter-ORB Protocol
IP	Internet Protocol
IPTC	International Press Telecommunications Council
ISO	International Organization for Standardization
ISP	Internet service provider
IT	information technology
ITU	International Telecommunications Union
ITU-T	ITU telecommunication standardisation sector
IVR	interactive voice response
J2EE	Java 2 Platform, Enterprise Edition
JAXB	Java Architecture for XML Binding
JAXM	Java API for XML Messaging
JAXP	Java APIs for XML Processing
JDBC	Java Database Connectivity
JDOM	Java Document Object Model (unofficial meaning)
JPEG	Joint Photographic Experts Group
JSP	JavaServer Pages
JTC1	ISO/IEC Joint Technical Committee 1

KB	kilobytes
LaTeX	Lamport TeX
LAN	local area network
LCD	liquid crystal display
LDAP	Lightweight Directory Access Protocol
MAPI	Messaging API
MathML	Mathematical Markup Language
MCL	master component library
ML	markup language
MOM	machine-oriented messaging
MOM	message-oriented middleware
MPEG	Motion Picture Experts Group
MP3	MPEG 3
MRP	materials resource planning
MSMQ	Microsoft Message Queuing
MSP	managed service provider
MSXML	Microsoft XML Core Services
NDS	Netware Directory Services
NewsML	News Markup Language
NIST	US National Institute for Standards and Technology
OAG	Open Applications Group
OASIS	Organization for the Advancement of Structured Information Standards
OBI	Open Buying Initiative

OCR	optical character recognition
ODBC	Open Database Connectivity
OFX	Open Financial Exchange
OMG	Object Management Group
OPEC	Organization of Petroleum Exporting Countries
ORB	Object Request Broker
OS	operating system
PBX	private branch exchange
PC	personal computer
PCDATA	parsed character data
PDA	personal digital assistant
PDF	Portable Document Format
PDP	Policy Decision Point
PEP	Policy Enforcement Point
PHP	PHP: Hypertext Preprocessor
PIC	Pictor graphic file
PICS	Platform for Internet Content Selection
PIP	Partner Interface Process
PKI	public key infrastructure
PNG	Portable Network Graphics
PNOC	primary network operations center
POP	people-oriented publishing
POP	Post Office Protocol

POST	(not an acronym: an HTTP method with a case-challenged name)
PRISM	Publishing Requirements for Industry Standard Metadata
QIR	quarterly investment review
QoS	quality of service
RADIUS	Remote Authentication Dial-in User Service
RDBMS	relational DBMS
RDF	Resource Description Framework
RELAX	Regular Language Description for XML
RELAX NG	RELAX Next Generation
REST	Representational State Transfer
RMI	remote method invocation
ROI	return on investment
RPC	remote procedure call
RSS	RDF Site Specification
RTF	Rich Text Format
SAML	Security Assertions Markup Language
SAX	The Simple API for XML
SC34	ISO/IEC JTC1 Subcommittee 34
SCM	screen cam recording
SCM	supply chain management
SGML	Standard Generalized Markup Language
SIC	standard industry classification
SKU	stockkeeping unit

SME	small-to-medium enterprise
SMF	schema model file
SMIL	Synchronized Multimedia Integration Language
SMTP	Simple Mail Transfer Protocol
SNA	Systems Network Architecture
SNMP	Simple Network Management Protocol
SOA	service-oriented architecture
SOAP	Simple Object Access Protocol
SQL	Structured Query Language
SRP	standard retail price
SSL	Secure Sockets Layer
SVG	Scalable Vector Graphics
SyncML	Synchronization Markup Language
TCP	Transmission Control Protocol
TDCC	Transportation Data Coordinating Committee
TES	Total-e-Server
TeX	Tau epsilon Xi text formatter
TIFF	Tagged Image File Format
TLA	three-letter acronym
TMCL	Topic Map Constraint Language
tpaML	Trading Partner Agreement Markup Language
TREX	Tree Regular Expressions for XML
UBL	Universal Business Language
UBR	Universal Business Registry

UDDI	Universal Description, Discovery, and Integration
UI	user interface
ULF	Universal Listener Framework
UML	Unified Modeling Language
UN/CEFACT	United Nations Centre for Trade Facilitation and Electronic Business
URI	Universal Resource Identifier
URL	Universal Resource Locator
URN	Universal Resource Name
US	United States of America
USD	US dollars
UTC	coordinated universal time
UTF-8	8-bit Unicode Transformation Format
UUID	Universal Unique Identifier
VAN	value-added network
VAT	value-added tax
VBA	Visual Basic for Applications
VBScript	Visual Basic Scripting Edition
VoiceXML	Voice XML
VoIP	voice over IP
VPN	virtual private network
W3C	World Wide Web Consortium
WAN	wide area network
WAP	Wireless Application Protocol

WAV	wave audio file
WBXML	WAP Binary XML
WebDAV	Web Distributed Authoring and Versioning
WfMC	Workflow Management Coalition
WMF	Windows Metafile
Wi-Fi	Wireless fidelity
WML	Wireless Markup Language
WP	word processing
WSDL	Web Services Description Language
WWW	World Wide Web
WYSIWYG	what you see is what you get
X.25	ITU-T standard protocols for packet-switched networks
X.500	ITU-T standards for electronic directory services
X12	ANSI Accredited Standards Committee X12
XACML	Extensible Access Control Markup Language
XBRL	eXtensible Business Reporting Language
XCBF	XML Common Biometric Framework
xCBL	XML Common Business Library
XDK	XML developer's kit
XDBMS	native XML DBMS
XHTML	Extensible HyperText Markup Language
XKISS	XML Key Information Service Specification
XKMS	XML Key Management Specification
XKRSS	XML Key Registration Service Specification

XLink	XML Linking Language
XML	Extensible Markup Language
XML-DEV	XML Developers discussion group
XML-RPC	XML Remote Procedure Call
XMS	XML Information Management System
XPath	XML Path Language
XPointer	XML Pointer Language
XPP	XML Professional Publisher
XQuery	XML Query Language
XrML	Extensible rights Markup Language
xsd	XML Schema document
XSDL	XML Schema definition language
XSL	XML Stylesheet Language
XSL-FO	XSL formatting objects
XSLT	XSL Transformations
XSQL	XML SQL
XTM	XML Topic Maps
XXXML	Adult Entertainment Markup Language
Y2K	Year 2000

Other books on XML

- Program development with XML

- DTDs and schemas

- XML transformations

- Rendering XML

- XPath 2.0: The next generation

- Learning the foundations of XML

Chapter

68

Charles wrote this chapter using material from his award-winning website, *All the XML Books in Print*™, http://www.xmlbooks.com.

E d Mosher, Ray Lorie, and I invented the first structured mark-up language in 1969, IBM's Generalized Markup Language (GML). It led to SGML, HTML, XML, and countless applications and variations on the theme.

But strangely, considering that markup is for documents, for the first two decades in which the markup language concept was gaining its now universal acceptance, hardly any books were published on the subject.

Well, the last four years have more than made up for the first two decades. When we went to press my website, *All the XML Books in Print*, listed more than 400 titles. I won't repeat them all here, but I will describe the ones I recommend most highly.

These are books from the *Definitive XML Series* that I edit for Prentice-Hall PTR, in which *The XML Handbook* appears.

XML isn't HTML with a capital X. It isn't just a representation of Web content. It has become the *lingua franca* of inter-program communication, Web services, business integration, and electronic commerce. It is also the notation of choice for Web security, voice control, and even office suites.

The authors of these books understand XML and its uses and know how to share that understanding with you. I recruited them personally for my book series because I know they are genuine experts. We worked together to

1135

make their books accurate and clear, which is why I am able to recommend the books from personal knowledge.

Of course, the book you are now reading is my recommendation for an introduction to XML. It focuses on what XML is and what it can do for you, but it doesn't purport to tell you how to go about doing it. For that, there are more specialized books.

68.1 | Program development with XML

Contrary to misuse in the popular press, and by some experts who ought to know better, XML isn't a programming language. It is a markup language, of course, and that means it's a data description language. You use normal programming languages, including scripting languages, to develop XML applications. These books show you how.

68.1.1 *General principles and techniques*

Definitive XML Application Development
Lars Marius Garshol
ISBN 0130889024
For experienced developers, this book provides thorough and systematic coverage of XML application development: DOM, SAX, XSLT, XPath, schemas, and all the important APIs and techniques. The author was a designer of SAX and creator of the SAX Python translation.

68.1.2 *Specific applications*

XML in *Office 2003*: Information Sharing with Desktop XML
Charles F. Goldfarb, Priscilla Walmsley
ISBN 013142193X
Microsoft Office 2003 Professional Edition has finally brought XML to the rest of us. Thanks to its native support for custom XML schemas, developers can use the world's most popular office suite as a smart client and XML editor for business integration,

content management, and Web services. This book shows you step-by-step how to tap Office's power for your own applications.

Definitive VoiceXML

Adam Hocek, David Cuddihy

ISBN 0130463450

XML is not a spoken language, but thanks to VoiceXML, it is the language of choice for developing spoken interfaces. If you want to voice-enable your applications and Web sites, this book speaks *your* language.

68.2 | DTDs and schemas

Nature abhors a schema-less database equally as much as she abhors a vacuum. Create a data table in a spreadsheet and the program will immediately search for field names, and supply them even if you fail to. Although XML will let you create a document without an explicit formally-written schema (also known as a "document type definition"), the benefits of having one are enormous, whether you write it out using XML markup declarations or a schema definition language.

Definitive XML Schema

Priscilla Walmsley

ISBN 0130655678

The W3C's *XML Schema* is an incredibly powerful – and complex! – document schema language, with such new capabilities as strong typing, modularity, inheritance, and identity constraints. This book was written by one of the developers of the language. It carefully guides you through the complexity so you can tap that power for your own projects. The book has won 15 five-star reviews at Amazon, with universal praise for clarifying the near-incomprehensible W3C spec!

68.3 | XML transformations

The key to processing XML is being able to address its structures and data and transform them into a new XML document. XPath and XSLT are the W3C recommendations that govern this process. These technologies affect everything from programming to database design, and for many developers they require a new way of thinking about those problems. This book will help you down the XPath and transform your development experience!

Definitive XSLT and XPath

    G. Ken Holman
    ISBN 0130651966
    Nobody has taught XSLT and XPath to more people than Ken Holman, chair of OASIS's XSLT/XPath Conformance Technical Subcommittee and long-time leader in the XML community. In this book, he draws upon his popular live training materials that have been used by thousands of developers.

68.4 | Rendering XML

Definitive XSL-FO

    G. Ken Holman
    ISBN 0131403745
    The fact that you are reading this is proof – if anyone needs it – that people like to get information from books, with their proven page-oriented navigational tools and sophisticated formatting. XSL-FO is the W3C Recommendation that lets you do this job for your own data. Ken Holman has taught thousands how, using the examples and insights in this book.

68.5 | XPath 2.0: The next generation

The ubiquitous XPath is being extended to handle datatypes and other things. A new XSLT and an XML query language are being built on top of it. These books show you how to put these new languages to work.

XSLT 2.0 Web Development
  Dmitry Kirsanov
  ISBN 0131406353
  Most websites today are broken: they lack a consistent semantic and media-independent representation of content. XML helps solve that problem, and the key to applying XML to Web development has always been XSLT transformations. Now XSLT 2.0 has added powerful new capabilities to the repertoire of website developers. Dmitry Kirsanov is both a graphic artist and a programmer. He shares the insights of both professions as he shows you how XML and XSLT 2.0 can – literally! – transform your website.

Definitive XQuery
  Priscilla Walmsley
  ISBN 0131013750
  The data elements in XML documents are as well-defined and predictable as those in any database. The W3C has recognized this fact and XQuery is the result. XQuery tools currently in development will allow programmers to query document collections and extract information without writing custom code. Priscilla reveals the secrets of this important technology with the same clarity that made her *Definitive XML Schema* such a success.

68.6 | Learning the foundations of XML

XML is a proper subset of SGML and the XML Recommendation is much shorter than the SGML International Standard. But the subsetting isn't the only reason for the shorter document. The XML spec is written for parser implementors and deliberately doesn't discuss applications, philosophy, style, alternatives, and other usage issues. I don't claim that you need to learn SGML in order to use XML, but I think it would help you use it better.

The SGML Handbook
  Charles F. Goldfarb / Oxford University Press
  ISBN 0198537379

Here is the official ISO Standard, annotated by yours truly (who is also the Project Editor of the Standard). I've added a structured overview of the complete language that introduces every term and concept in context. This book has been in print for more than twelve years and was the essential reference used by the W3C Working Group when designing XML.

Tip   *You can find Charles' up-to-date list of All the XML Books in Print at* `http://www.xmlbooks.com.`

Free resources on the CD-ROM

▌ Over 200 free software packages

▌ IBM alphaWorks XML software suite

▌ XML SPECtacular

Contributing experts: Lars Marius Garshol, David A. Epstein, and Daniel Jue

Chapter

69

Do you really need 200 XML software packages? Not likely, but our two CD-ROMs will save a lot of download time while you decide which you do need. Most of the packages are described in this chapter, along with the W3C specifications that are on the CDs.

he two CD-ROMs that supplement *The XML Handbook* contain a wide variety of resources. There is free trial software, genuine freeware with no time limit, demos, white papers, markup and code samples, product information from our sponsors, and the full text of the most important standards and specifications.

We describe most of the free software and specs in this chapter, but not all of it; you'll need to dig into the discs for the rest.

Enjoy!

69.1 | Software featured on the covers

In this section, we briefly describe the free software and trialware that our sponsors feature on the covers of the book. We specify the platforms supported and, if it is trialware, the time limit or other usage description.

69.1.1 *Adobe FrameMaker XML/SGML editor/formatter*

FrameMaker is a tool for editing and formatting long, complex publications such as books, manuals, and catalogs. It can generate HTML and PDF output for publishing electronically and on the Web. The product offers both a WYSIWYG formatted interface and a document-tree structured interface; both can be used simultaneously.

The tryout version on the CD-ROM has a 30-day time limit and is fully functional. It is available for Microsoft® Windows® 98, Windows Millennium Edition, Windows 2000, Windows NT® 4.0, and Windows XP.

69.1.2 *Ontopia Omnigator topic map browser*

The Omnigator is a topic map browser written in Java. It lets you browse any conforming topic map and comes with eight of them.

Four are practical examples covering the *CIA World Factbook*, free XML tools, world languages, and Italian opera. The other four are tools for learning about topic maps, including a topic map of the relevant standards.

You can also use the Omnigator as a learning aid, a debugger, and a prototyping tool for topic maps you have written yourself.

The version on the CD-ROM can be used freely for personal use with no time limit. It runs on any system with Java 1.3 or higher and 30MB of free disk space.

69.1.3 *IBM alphaWorks XML software suite*

This suite of software has no built-in time restrictions or registration requirements and can be evaluated freely for 90 days. It contains a wide variety of programs, most of which will run on any Java platform. We'll describe them shortly, but first it's helpful to understand their origin.

69.1.3.1 The *alphaWorks* idea

IBM *alphaWorks* is a team dedicated to speeding emerging IBM technology to the marketplace, from fields as diverse as management and transaction functions, networking, security, and power management.

The *alphaWorks* website is a focal point for bidirectional communication with early adopters of strategic emerging technologies. At the site, users can download "alpha-code" implementations of those technologies. More importantly, they can also access and provide feedback to IBM's top researchers and developers, through the site's technology discussion forums.

alphaWorks serves as one of IBM's primary channels for the distribution of XML technology. You can find several different categories of XML technology at the site.

1. One of the main categories, which fulfills one of *alphaWorks'* primary goals, is implementations that track the important W3C Recommendations and other related XML specifications. One of the objectives in providing these implementations is to have them available in a timely manner, often the same day that Recommendations (proposed and final, and early Notes) become public.
2. In addition to these implementations of the important XML specifications, the site also serves as a distribution point for example applications that make use of these specifications.
3. *alphaWorks* also serves as a proving ground in which experimental new XML technologies are introduced and evaluated. User feedback is monitored directly by the research and development staff, and updated according to the comments supplied by users.
4. Finally, the site offers a variety of tools and components that provide a bridge between the XML and Java spaces.

69.1.3.2 XML at *alphaWorks*

The list of emerging XML technologies on *alphaWorks* is already quite long and growing almost daily. Rather than try to list all of them, we'll briefly describe a representative selection. They are all included on the accompanying CD-ROM.

Agent Building and Learning Environment

A Java framework, component library, and productivity tool kit for building intelligent agents using machine learning and reasoning.

BPWS4J

A platform for creating and executing BPEL4WS processes.

Data Wizard for Java

A tool for building a simple graphical user interface (GUI) that makes it easy to collect necessary data.

DEBA4WS

An asynchronous architecture and Java framework for Web services based on the Listener pattern.

IBM Lightweight Services

A J2EE application that provides an event-driven hosting environment for lightweight services.

IBM XML Forms Package

A toolkit consisting of software components designed to showcase the possibilities presented by XForms, an emerging W3C standard.

IBM XSL Formatting Objects Composer

A typesetting and display engine that implements the XSL FO language for typesetting, printing, or displaying any written language.

JROM

XML schema-based tool that provides a Java representation of structured information. In particular, XML instances typed according to XML Schema and SOAP messages.

SheetPages

A technology that provides a simple HTML front end for complex spreadsheets.

ToXgene

A template-based generator for complex, semantically-correlated collections of XML documents.

UDDI for Python

A Python package that allows the sending of requests to and processing of responses from the UDDI Version 2 APIs.

Web Services for Life Sciences

A collection of examples of Web services for life sciences: Pubmed, GenBank, BLAST, Phylogenic Tree, and ClustalW.

Web Services Outsourcing Manager

A framework that enables dynamic composition of Web service flow based on customer requirements.

Web Services Tool Kit for Mobile Devices

Tools and run-time environments that allow development of applications that use Web services on small mobile devices, gateway devices, and intelligent controllers.

XincaML

A package including the XincaML language specification and the XincaML Processor, which is a Java™ implementation package of the language parser and constraints checker.

XML for C++

Three shared C++ libraries with classes for parsing, generating, manipulating, and validating XML documents in over 150 different encodings.

XML for Tables

A tool that provides an XML view of relational tables and a query of those views as if they were XML documents.

XML Integrator

A tool for transforming data between data storage systems and XML.

XML Parser for Java

A validating XML parser, written in 100% pure Java, that easily enables applications to read and write XML data.

XML Processing Plus Plus

A typed and stream-based XML processing extension for Java.

XML Schema Quality Checker

Check for problems in W3C XML Schemas, and clearly identify any problems found.

XML Security Suite

A tool that provides security features such as digital signature, encryption, and access control for XML documents.

Tip   *You can visit the alphaWorks site,* `http://www.alphaWorks.IBM.com`, *to engage IBM researchers and developers at the earliest stages of development and to download the latest software.*

69.2 | An eXtravagance of free XML software

To make this list, software has to be genuinely free, worthwhile XML software. That means:

- It must have substantial XML-oriented functionality; no graphics packages, file utilities, or other general-purpose filler.
- It must let you do useful processing of your own documents. If you are taking the trouble to install and learn it, you should get some benefit from it.
- It can't have a time limit on its use. As above: you should be the one to decide when it's no longer interesting.

■ Most of all, it's got to be pretty good stuff! Some of it is proven code that rivals the best ever written for speed and stability. Other packages are promising newcomers.

On the CD-ROMs you'll find hyperlinks to the author's website for the latest versions of the programs that you like. The descriptions here are just to give you the flavor and, of course, they apply only to the version on the CDs.

69.2.1 *Parsers and engines*

XML parsers, parsing toolkits, HyTime engines and DSSSL engines.

69.2.1.1 Architectural forms engines

xmlarch

xmlarch is an architectural forms engine written in Python that works with any SAX 1.0 parser and offers a SAX 1.0 interface to the processed documents. It is also possible to receive architectural document events for several architectures in one parse pass.

69.2.1.2 XLink/XPointer engines

XML::XPath

XML::XPath is a Perl implementation of XPath. It can parse XPath expressions and resolve them against a document tree built by the XPath module from SAX events or the XML::Parser.

SAXPath

SAXPath is an event-based API for XPath parsers, that is, for parsers which parse XPath expressions. SAXPath is intended to be for XPath what SAX is for XML. Note that the SAXPath package only parses XPath expressions; it does not evaluate them, or even provide an object structure for representing them once they have been parsed.

Jaxen

Jaxen is an XPath implementation written in Java, which can parse XPath expressions, and evaluate them against XML tree representation. Jaxen currently supports DOM, dom4j, EXML, and JDOM.

Pathan

Pathan is an XPath engine built on top of the Xerces C++ DOM Parser. Pathan has full support for XPath.

69.2.1.3   XSL engines

Engines that support the XSL formatting objects specification.

FOP

FOP is a Java application that takes an XML document conforming to the XSL:FO 2000-11-21 Candidate Recommendation and produces PDF output. It also supports some parts of SVG. FOP can be used with any SAX 2.0 parser to produce PDF from XSL. FOP can be invoked from the command line and read from a file, or it can be given a DOM document or a SAX DocumentHandler at run-time. FOP uses XP through SAX 1.0 to parse the input document. FOP should be considered to be an alpha release. It is also possible to use FOP with XT as its XSLT engine to produce PDF directly from XML source and an XSL stylesheet. This provides better performance, by skipping a step in the process.

PassiveTeX

PassiveTeX is a TeX implementation of the XSL November 2000 WD and MathML which reads XML documents containing XSL formatting objects and MathML elements and uses LaTeX to produce formatted output. This can be used to produce well-formatted PDF, DVI or PostScript, and even supports bookmarks in the PDF output.

REXP

REXP is an XSL:fo to PDF file converter, based on the source of FOP 0.9.2. It supports a bit more of XSL than FOP does. A tiny bit of support for SVG is also there, and there will probably be more in the future.

jfor

jfor converts XSL:FO documents into RTF. jfor attempts to preserve the structure of the input document, and so may lose some formatting. jfor can be used both from the command-line as well as from within Cocoon.

69.2.1.4   XSLT engines

Engines that support the XSL Transformations specification.

SAXON

SAXON is a Java framework for processing XML documents optimized for XML to XML/SGML/HTML conversions. Essentially, it is an XSLT engine (1.0 recommendation) which can also be used as a Java development framework. The XSLT implementation is fast, fully conformant and provides many useful extensions. Through its API Java and XSLT code can be combined. SAXON is built on top of SAX 2.0 and DOM 1.0, and should work with any compliant implementation of these. It also supports the XSLT part of JAXP. The API of the XPath implementation can also be used independently. Through integration with FOP SAXON can produce PDF directly from XML. An improved version of Ælfred with validation support and SAX 2.0 drivers is included, as is a small application that can generate DTDs from sample input files.

XT

XT is an XSLT engine that implements the final XSLT recommendation, as well as the XPath recommendation. It does not support the full recommendation, but does have some useful extensions. It can be used with any SAX 1.0 parser and also as a servlet.

XML::XSLT

xslt-parser is a budding XSLT engine written in Perl. It is of alpha quality and not yet complete nor bug-free, but work is progressing.

Xalan-Java

Xalan-Java is an XSLT processor written in Java. It implements the entire final XSLT recommendation, and can produce both SAX and DOM output, with support for Java and JavaScript extensions. Xalan-Java uses Xerces-Java for XML parsing. Xalan has a JAXP API. Xalan can also compile XSLT stylesheets to Java bytecode.

Xalan-C++

Xalan-C++ is a C++ implementation of an XSLT processor, following the final XSLT recommendation. It can pre-parse documents, and precompile stylesheets. The XML parser used is Xerces.

Sablotron

The Sablotron is an XSLT processor written in C++ (as open source). The goal is to make the processor fast, compact and portable. The Sablotron has both a command-line and an API interface. Not all features of XSLT are currently implemented. The Sablotron uses expat for XML parsing.

MDC-XSL

MDC-XSL is an XSLT engine written in C++ as part of the Circare product developed by Minoru Development Corporation. The engine is open source and supports a subset of the XSLT specification. The engine has both an API and a command-line interface.

XSLTC

XSLTC compiles XSLT stylesheets to C++ code for faster execution. It is based on the TransforMiix XSLT engine and implements 95% percent of its functionality. XSLTC is currently an experimental release.

4Suite

4Suite is a collection of XML processing tools based on the Python XML-SIG package. It contains a complete XSLT implementation, an XPath implementation, a DOM implementation (level 1 and level 2), a persistent DOM implementation that stores documents in an object database, an RDF toolkit with persistence and schema support, an XPointer implementation an XLink processor, an XInclude processor, and an XUpdate processor.

libxslt

libxslt is an XSLT processor written in portable C, based on the libxml XML parser. It is not yet feature-complete, but work is progressing rapidly. It has both a command-line interface as well as an API. XML Catalog support is provided by libxml.

jd.xslt

jd.xslt is an XSLT processor implementing the 2000-12-12 XSLT 1.1 working draft. It claims to have a very high degree of conformance and good performance. The xsl:script element is supported and scripts can be written in many languages.

XML::LibXSLT

XML::LibXSLT is the Gnome XSLT Engine wrapped as a Perl module. The module is considered stable by its author.

Pyana

Pyana wraps the Xalan-C++ XSLT engine as a Python module, making it available to Python programs.

69.2.1.5   DSSSL engines

Jade

Jade is James Clark's excellent DSSSL engine, which is really a general SGML tool for conversion from SGML to other SGML DTDs or to output formats like RTF and TeX. Jade can process XML documents and can also output XML. Jade uses SP to parse the SGML/XML input.

OpenJade

OpenJade is a variant of James Clark's Jade DSSSL engine that has been extended and modified by an open source project.

69.2.1.6   SGML/XML parsers

SP

SP is an SGML/XML parser, and is fast, complete, highly conformant and very stable. SP has been the parser of choice for most of the SGML community for many years and has been embedded in lots of other applications. SP supports architectural forms as well as SGML Open catalogs. The SP package includes the SX program, which can convert arbitrary SGML documents to XML automatically.

SGMLSpm

SGMLSpm is a Perl script that reads ESIS output (from parsers like SP) and offers an event-based interface to the parser. As long as the parser can parse XML this also works for XML.

OpenSP

OpenSP is a variant of James Clark's SP SGML parser that has been extended and modified by an open source project. It supports more of SGML open catalogs, more of annex K to the standard, is internationalized among other things. Note that the page linked to is the OpenJade page. OpenSP seems to have no home page of its own, but the information can be found on the OpenJade page.

pysp

pysp wraps the SP SGML parser as a Python module and makes it easy to develop SGML processing applications in Python. pysp provides a simple event-based API to the SGML parser, the exact minimum of what is required in order to develop applications on top of the parser.

69.2.1.7   XML parsers

expat

expat is a non-validating parser written in C, and is the parser previously known as XMLTok. It is used in Mozilla 5.0 and in parser modules for several different scripting languages. It is very fast and highly conformant. expat does no validation, but can read external entities and aims to be a fully conforming well-formedness parser. It does not read the external DTD subset. XML namespaces are supported. expat supports Unicode, and through a callback the application can extend the number of encodings supported. expat is also designed to support multi-language error messages. Applications are also given access to the raw markup of the document, for the applications that need lexical information.

XP

XP is written to be fully-conforming and as fast as possible, with an emphasis is on server-side production use. There is no validation, only well-formedness checking. Even though 0.5 is a beta release it is stable, conformant and fast. A SAX 1.0 driver is included. XP supports several Unicode encodings.

Lark

Lark was one of the two first XML parsers to appear, written by XML spec co-editor Tim Bray, but was non-validating for a long time. Tim Bray has now added Larval, a validating parser, to the package. Lark is fast, small and thread-safe. Larval is in version 0.8 and not yet finished. The interface is non-standard, but there is a SAX 1.0 driver in the SAX driver package.

Ælfred

Ælfred is designed to be small and fast, especially intended for use in Java applets (it uses only two .class files). It has a non-standard interface. Ælfred reads the DTD, but does not validate the document. Note that an enhanced version is available in the GNU project's GNU JAXP package and there is also one in SAXON. The original Ælfred was written by David Megginson at Microstar and widely used, but has since disappeared with Microstar. The above three projects are all that remain.

xmlproc

xmlproc is a validating parser written in Python. It implements nearly all of the XML Recommendation, including XML namespaces. (The home page lists the deviations.) xmlproc provides access to DTD information and also offers a DTD parsing module. xmlproc supports SGML Open catalogs and XML Catalogs. xmlproc can report errors in Norwegian and English and can be extended to support other languages as well. xmlproc comes with a DTD-parsing module that it uses to do validation. This module is stand-alone and can be used separately by applications that need to parse DTDs and work on them. xmlproc has a non-standard interface, but a SAX 1.0 driver is available in the PyXML package.

RXP

RXP is a thread-safe validating parser written in C. It is distributed as C source and must be compiled before use. It supports Unicode and XML namespaces and comes with a command-line application that prints out the parsed document. It provides a non-DOM tree interface to the parsed document. RXP is also available as part of the LTXML package. RXP also supports the ISO 8859-1 to ISO 8859-9 character encodings.

Windows Foundation Classes

WFC is a collection of C++ classes for Windows programming. Included are a non-validating XML parser as well as other tools for working with XML documents. The parser has been tested on Unix too.

Expat Module for Ruby

This module wraps the expat parser (version 1.2) for access from within the Ruby interpreter. (Ruby is an object-oriented scripting language with similarities to Perl.) It also has a DOM 1.0 implementation and XPointer support.

XML Parser Component for Delphi

This is a validating XML parser written in Delphi that parses XML documents into a DOM element tree that can then be modified and traversed. The component also allows programs to build DOM trees and write them out as an XML document. The parser supports both 8-bit and 16-bit encodings.

CL-XML

CL-XML is an XML parser written in Common Lisp. The parser is validating, and contains a DOM implementation as well as object models representing the infoset and the XPath data model. It also provides access to DTD information, and supports XML namespaces, even in DTDs. The parser also contains an XPath module which can evaluate XPath expressions written in XPath or S-expression syntax against DOM trees. CL-XML also supports XML Query.

libxml

libxml is a validating XML parser written in C (also known as gnome-xml). It has an event-based (SAX-like) interface and can also build an in-memory DOM-like tree of the parsed document. It can use XML Catalog to resolve entity references. libxml has a full XPath implementation, and supports namespaces, XPointer, XInclude, SGML Open Catalogs, XML Catalog, RELAX-NG, and XML Schema 1&2. An HTML parser is also included. A DOM implementation is available through Gdome.

fxp

fxp is a validating XML parser written in Standard ML, a functional programming language in the ML family. fxp has a programming interface, and comes with some example command-line applications. It has only been tested with the Standard ML of New Jersey compiler under Unix, but might well work elsewhere as well. fxp supports XCatalog and Unicode.

Whisper

Whisper is a general-purpose application framework written in C++, Whisper contains (among many other things) a validating XML parser with support for Unicode. Whisper makes extensive use of C++ features like templates (parametric classes), multiple inheritance, the Standard Template Library and exceptions. The design uses something similar to Design by Contract. Whisper can build a document tree, but this does not follow the DOM recommendation, but is instead a non-standard tree structure.

Gobo Eiffel

Gobo Eiffel is a collection of Eiffel components, among which can be found the expat XML parser wrapped into the Eiffel programming language. (Eiffel is an industrial-strength object-oriented language with many features beyond what Java and C++ offer.) There is also a tree-building package on top of the wrapped expat parser. In addition to the expat wrapper can be found Nenie XML, which is a non-validating XML parser written in pure Eiffel. It passes 99% of the OASIS test cases, and so is highly conformant. The parser supports XML namespaces, and does read the DTD, although it does not use it for validation. The parser supports Unicode by passing data to the application as UTF-8-encoded strings. Nenie XML has both event-based and tree-based interfaces. These are not translations of SAX and the DOM, but specific to Nenie.

Perl libxml

The Perl libxml includes the Perl version of SAX 1.0, PerlSAX (a special Perl version of SAX), a SAX driver for XML::Parser, a SAX driver that can read ESIS output from SP and XML::Grove integration code.

Tony

Tony is a lightweight XML parser written in the functional programming language Objective CAML. It claims to be much smaller than most other XML parsers, but is not complete. Tony comes with an advanced configurable pretty-printer.

HaXml

HaXml is a collection of libraries for using XML in Haskell. This includes a non-validating XML parser, an HTML parser, a library for transforming XML documents (and generating HTML) and special modules for building Haskell data structures from XML documents and dumping them back out as XML. HaXml supports Unicode if the Haskell compiler does.

AdvXMLParser

AdvXMLParser is a small and simple to use non-validating XML parser written in C++, which accepts a subset of the XML specification. (The DOCTYPE declaration is not accepted.) The parser builds a tree structure and can be used to generate XML.

PXP

PXP is a complete validating XML parser written in Objective Caml, a functional programming language in the ML family with OO features. PXP has some advanced features for building customized XML document trees and also provides access to DTD information. It supports Unicode and can read documents in many different encodings.

XML Tools Scripting Addition

XML Tools Scripting Addition enables AppleScript programs to use expat to parse XML documents into a tree structure of records. It supports XML Namespaces.

GNU JAXP

This is a collection of various Java XML utilities, including an improved version of the Ælfred XML parser known as Ælfred2 with SAX 2.0 support, a DOM 2.0 implementation, and a JAXP implementation.

Xerces Java

Xerces Java is a validating XML parser with support for the DOM level 1 and 2, SAX 1.0 and 2.0, and the XML Schemas final recommendation. Xerces can be invoked through the JAXP API.

Xerces C++

Xerces C++ is a validating XML parser written in a portable subset of C++. It supports XML Namespaces, the DOM level 2, SAX 1.0, DOM level 2, SAX 2.0, and XML Schemas.

Xerces Perl

Xerces Perl is the validating Xerces C++ parser wrapped as a Perl module. It supports the DOM level 2, SAX 2.0, XML namespaces, and XML Schema.

XMLIO

XMLIO is a non-validating XML parser with a pull interface, where the application can take over parsing of element contents and elements from the parser. XMLIO can also be used to generate XML documents.

XDOM

XDOM is an open source XML parser with a DOM level 1 and level 2 (core and traversal) implementation written in Delphi. The implementation implements some convenience extensions and also deviates from the specification in a couple of places.

xmlparse

xmlparse is a validating XML parser written in C++ with full Unicode support. The parser has been tested on the OASIS conformance test suite and should be highly conformant (only 3 errors). It uses a SAX-like API and passes text to the application in UTF-8 encoding.

xml.lisp

CLOCC is an open source library of useful Common Lisp modules, which contains a non-validating XML parser known as xml.lisp. This parser originally came from the CLLIB library.

CenterPoint/XML

CenterPoint/XML is a SAX 2.0 and DOM 1.0 2.0 implementation built on top of expat.

xmlutils

xmlutils is a non-validating XML parser that reads the external subset and external entities (if desired) and produces a Lisp S-expression tree as a result of parsing. The parser supports both Unicode and XML Namespaces. According to the authors it fails only four cases on the OASIS conformance test, and those it fails due to the support for 4-byte Unicode code points.

XML Pull Parser

This XML parser has implementations in both Java and C++ and uses a rather unusual API design in that it does not have a tree-based or event-based API, but rather a pull API where the document is pulled as individual tokens from the parser. The parser is very small and it is also claimed to be fast.

HXML

HXML is a non-validating XML parser written in Haskell, with emphasis on space-efficiency through lazy evaluation. It is intended to be usable as a drop-in replacement for HaXml. It is currently of alpha quality.

SCEW

SCEW, Simple C Expat Wrapper, is a tree API to XML documents built on top of expat. SCEW lets you modify the trees once built, and also gives you access to the expat parser underneath to give full flexibility.

Arabica

Arabica provides SAX 2.0 support for a number of C and C++ XML parsers as well as a DOM level 2 implementation on top of the SAX 2.0 interfaces. Arabica has SAX 2.0 wrappers for Xerces, expat, libxml, and (on Windows) the MSXML parser.

SAXExpat

The SAXExpat package is a wrapper around the expat XML parser that makes it possible to use it within Delphi and Kylix. It also includes an interface for generating XML documents from programs.

Ælfred2 for Pascal

Ælfred2 for Pascal is a translation of David Megginson's (and later David Brownell's) Ælfred Java XML parser to Delphi. It supports a SAX-like interface and is validating, and has a high level of conformance against the XML Conformance test suite.

SKYRiX Libraries for XML Processing

The SKYRiX Libraries contains a SAX 2.0 translation to Objective C, and contains SAX drivers for a number of XML parsers. One is the CoreFoundation XML parser that is part of MacOS X, another is for the libxml parser, a third for expat, and there are some more. There is also a DOM implementation built on top of the SAX API.

Piccolo

Piccolo is a small high-performance XML parser for Java without validation, but with support for XML Namespaces. Piccolo have come out of several tests as the fastest XML parser tested, despite being created using automatic parser generators.

69.2.1.8   DOM implementations

Docuverse DOM SDK

The Docuverse DOM SDK is a Java implementation of the Document Object Model (DOM 1.0) that can use any SAX 1.0 to build the DOM document tree. The DOM builder part of the implementation is very general, so one can extend it to use other kinds of builders as well. The DOM SDK also supports the DOM HTML API, and included in the SDK is a SAX 1.0 driver for the Swing HTML parser and a DOMReader that can be used to read HTML documents into the HTML DOM. The Docuverse DOM SDK was previously called FREE-DOM and before that SAXDOM.

tDOM

tDOM is a C implementation of the DOM level 1 core using expat and tclexpat for parsing. tDOM also includes C implementations of XPath and . tDOM is written to be accessed from tcl. Bundled with tDOM are also a wrapped version of expat as well as tclXML.

GNU JAXP

This is a collection of various Java XML utilities, including an improved version of the Ælfred XML parser known as Ælfred2 with SAX 2.0 support, a DOM 2.0 implementation, and a JAXP implementation.

XDOM

XDOM is an open source XML parser with a DOM level 1 and level 2 (core and traversal) implementation written in Delphi. The implementation implements some convenience extensions and also deviates from the specification in a couple of places.

Gdome

Gdome is a DOM 2.0 implementation currently in development as part of the GNOME project. It is written to be used with the libxml parser. This implementation is currently experimental.

4Suite

4Suite is a collection of XML processing tools based on the Python XML-SIG package. It contains a complete XSLT implementation, an XPath implementation, a DOM implementation (level 1 and level 2), a persistent DOM implementation that stores documents in an object database, an RDF toolkit with persistence and schema support, an XPointer implementation an XLink processor, an XInclude processor, and an XUpdate processor.

domc

domc is a lightweight DOM level 1 and level 2 core implementation written in pure C. It uses expat to build DOM trees.

69.2.1.9 XML validators

Software for validating XML documents by other means than DTDs.

DSD Processor

DSD is an XML schema language developed by researchers at AT&T and the University of Aarhus. The developers claim that it is more powerful and readable than XML Schemas or DTDs. The DSD Prototype Processor is a prototype implementation of the

DSD schema language, which can also convert DTDs to DSD schemas.

XML Schema Validator

XSV is an XML validator that validates XML documents according to the XML Schemas Recommendation. Currently, the only interface is a command-line interface. The validator is based on the Python LTXML module, which you can also get by installing XED. XSV supports RDDL.

PyTREX

PyTREX is an implementation of the TREX schema language based on Pyexpat. It can be used to validate XML documents against TREX schemas.

Schematron

The Schematron is an innovative schema language for XML documents radically different from existing approaches. It can be used as a friendly validation language and for automatically generating external annotation (links, RDF, perhaps Topic Maps). Because it uses paths rather than grammars, it can be used to assert many constraints that cannot be expressed by DTDs or XML Schemas.

VBRELAXNG

VBRELAXNG is a RELAX NG implementation written in Visual Basic, which can validate XML documents against RELAX NG schemas.

Jing

Jing is a validator that allows XML documents to be validated against RELAX NG schemas. Jing is implemented as a SAX 2.0 ContentHandler, and so can be used with any SAX 2.0-compliant parser.

Schematron.NET

Schematron.NET is a C# implementation of the Schematron schema language instead of the usual approach, which is to implement the Schematron in XSLT. Reports indicate that

Schematron.NET is substantially faster than XSLT implementations of Schematron.

69.2.1.10   XML middleware

General software packages for making XML-aware applications of some form.

XML::Grove

XML::Grove uses XML::Parse to build a tree structure from the parsed document that programs can access and change. Similar to DOM, that is, but non-standard.

SAXON

SAXON is a Java framework for processing XML documents optimized for XML to XML/SGML/HTML conversions. Essentially, it is an XSLT engine (1.0 recommendation) which can also be used as a Java development framework. The XSLT implementation is fast, fully conformant and provides many useful extensions. Through its API Java and XSLT code can be combined. SAXON is built on top of SAX 2.0 and DOM 1.0, and should work with any compliant implementation of these. It also supports the XSLT part of JAXP. The API of the XPath implementation can also be used independently. Through integration with FOP SAXON can produce PDF directly from XML. An improved version of Ælfred with validation support and SAX 2.0 drivers is included, as is a small application that can generate DTDs from sample input files.

Parser Filters

The ParserFilters are classes that wrap SAX 1.0 parsers in classes that provide SAX 1.0 parser interfaces. This allows for the development of extra services layered on top of ordinary parsers. Included are two filters, one that adds attribute inheritance and one that implements XML namespaces. This should be considered an alpha release.

DOMParser

The DOM Parser is a SAX 1.0-compliant parser that turns a DOM Document into a SAX event stream, instead of parsing an XML document. This should be considered an alpha release.

XML::Writer

XML::Writer is a Perl module which makes it easier to generate correct XML output from Perl. It has intelligent support for XML namespaces and will automatically generate prefixes (although this can be controlled, if desired).

Python XML package

The Python XML package is a package of various Python XML tools that has been put together by the Python XML Special Interest Group, a group of volunteers led by Andrew M. Kuchling, for the convenience of Python XML developers. The package contains SAX for Python, a HOWTO document, Pyexpat, a SAX 2.0 implementation, 4DOM (which supports DOM 1.0 and DOM 2.0) and xmlproc. A module for serializing and deserializing Python objects into XML is also included, as well as a number of demos.

Cost

Cost is an old and well-known programming tool for writing SGML (and now XML) transformations in tcl. It can use both SP and expat as parsers.

LT PyXML

LT PyXML is a Python interface to the LT XML package parser and API, which provides Python with access to a fast validating parser and a powerful API.

Flute

Flute is a CSS2 parser written in Java that implements SAC. SAC is a standard event-based API for CSS parsers, closely modelled on the SAX API for XML parsers. This parser was earlier incorrectly listed here under the name SAC.

GPS

GPS is a general implementation of the grove data model (from the HyTime ISO-standard). It implements both groves and property sets, in two different implementations. One is an in-memory structure, the other uses the ZODB object database for persistence.

DT4DTD

DT4DTD supports schema-compatible datatyping in existing SAX or DOM implementations. After some modest 'wiring' it makes a set of routines available to the developer for use in accessing and validating datatypes such as numbers and dates in element and attribute information in forms other than simple strings. An extensible registry of types also permits developers to build libraries of custom datatypes that can be reused in various implementations.

Pyxie

Pyxie is a powerful XML processing library written in Python which can be used to develop XML processing software which is event-driven, tree-based or event-driven with tree access. Pyxie requires the Python XML package.

CSS2 Parser

This tool can parse CSS2 stylesheets into a DOM2 structure and also supports the SAC API.

SAX2

SAX is a simple event-based API for XML parsers. It is not an official standard, since it was developed by the participants of the xml-dev mailing list instead of a standards body. However, SAX is very much a de facto standard, since it is supported by most XML parsers and is used by lots of applications SAX2 is an extended version of the original SAX 1.0 API for XML parsers, which is now obsolete. SAX 2.0 adds support for XML namespaces, configurability as well as lexical and DTD information.

xmlBlaster

xmlBlaster is a pure Java publish/subscribe MOM server (message-oriented middleware) which exchanges XML-encoded messages between publishers and subscribers. Communication with the server is based on CORBA (using JacORB), RMI and XML-RPC, and subscribers can use XPath expressions to filter the messages they wish to receive. xmlBlaster uses the Sun XML parser for XML parsing.

Protégé 2000

Protégé is a very advanced knowledge-based framework for developing domain-specific systems. It has been developed and used by the medical informatics community for years and has lately been extended with support for RDF. So Protégé does much much more, but can also be used for generating editors for specific RDF applications. It understands both RDF and RDF schemas.

XML::Twig

XML::Twig is a module for writing tree-based XML processing applications that only build partial document trees, so as to allow them to work with much larger documents. XML::Twig uses XML::Parser for the actual parsing.

Relaxer

Relaxer is a Java tool that can read a RELAX schema and generates a set of Java classes that can represent the objects described by the schema in memory or in an RDBMS. Relaxer uses Xerces as its XML parser, but also supports SAX 2.0 and supports XML Namespaces and XBase. Relaxer also has a JSP tag library that can be used to build web applications based on RELAX.

JDOM

JDOM is an API for representing the XML document tree structure similar to the DOM, but much simpler and designed specifically for Java using the collections API. JDOM structures can be built from XML files, DOM trees and SAX events and can be converted to the same.

dom4j

dom4j is a Java toolkit for writing XML processing applications, with its own tree-based model for XML documents, inspired by the XPath data model. It has both event-based and tree-based modes, supports evaluation of XPath expressions against the document tree, and also has an implementation of its own tree model that supports the DOM. There is even alpha support for XML Schema data types. It uses Jaxen to provide XPath support.

BML

BML is a binary representation of XML (Binary Markup Language), and also a set of tools for working with BML. The BML tools have their own event-based and tree-based APIs similar to SAX and the DOM. BML can also convert back and forth between XML and BML representations of documents.

Simkin

Simkin is a scripting language that can be embedded in XML documents to store behaviour in the documents. It is intended to be used in XML somewhat like JavaScript is used in HTML. There is a Java interpreter for Simkin as well as a C++ one, allowing Simkin to be used with both languages.

XInclude.NET

XInclude.NET is an XInclude implementation (based on the Candidate Recommendation) written in C# for the .NET platform.

SAX for Pascal

SAX for Pascal is a translation of SAX to Pascal. Like the original SAX, SAX for Pascal defines a common interface to XML parsers, but in this case for Object Pascal, or Delphi, instead of Java.

69.2.1.11   RDF parsers

repat

repat is an RDF parser built on top of the expat XML parser. It uses a callback interface rather like the interface used by expat itself.

Redfoot

Redfoot is a framework for developing RDF-based applications, consisting of an RDF database with a query API, an RDF parser and serializer and a web interface for viewing and editing RDF. It also intends to support inter-database communications.

4Suite

4Suite is a collection of XML processing tools based on the Python XML-SIG package. It contains a complete XSLT implementation, an XPath implementation, a DOM implementation (level 1 and level 2), a persistent DOM implementation that stores documents in an object database, an RDF toolkit with persistence and schema support, an XPointer implementation an XLink processor, an XInclude processor, and an XUpdate processor.

Raptor

Raptor is an RDF parser written in C, designed to be used from the Redland RDF database system, but can also be used separately. It does not do XML parsing itself, but can use either expat or libxml to do XML parsing. Raptor is designed to be fast and robust, but at the moment it is of beta quality. The parser used to be called Rapier.

Jena

Jena implements an API that represents RDF models, that is, the RDF data model. With this API you can access RDF data in-memory, change it, navigate over it, store it in an RDBMS, and so on. Jena uses ARP to parse RDF documents, and can also export RDF models back to XML documents.

ARP

ARP is an RDF parser (the name is short for Another RDF Parser) that parses RDF XML documents into RDF triples. ARP is designed to be used as an RDF parser in Jena, but can also be used separately.

69.2.1.12   Topic map engines

tmproc

tmproc is a Python implementation of Topic Maps (ISO 13250), a standard for creating navigational indexes on large sets of documents. tmproc requires the PyXML package and can also be used with xmlarch if architectural processing is wanted.

TM4J

TM4J is an implementation of the XTM topic map standard. TM4J can read in topic maps encoded in XML using SAX 1.0 or the DOM and also generate XML topic maps. It provides a general API for manipulating topic maps, but no functionality directed towards end-users.

Perl XTM

XTM::Base is a topic map engine that supports XTM 1.0. It can load topic maps from XTM 1.0 documents, and provides a generic API for working with them. There is also a simple text-based interpreter, which can be used to query loaded topic maps, as well as support for XTMPath and LTM.

TmTk

TmTk is a generic topic map toolkit written in C, with a Python wrapper. It can import and export the XTM 1.0 syntax, can store topic maps in a native persistent backend, and has a built-in query language. The toolkit was previously known as GWTK.

TMTab

TMTab is a topic map engine and editor implemented as a Protege plug-in, which allows ontologies to be created and edited using the Protege editing interface. TMTab bases its topic map capabilities on TM4J.

GNOWSYS

GNOWSYS is a topic map engine developed using Zope. It is quite experimental, and does not yet support import from any topic map syntax.

69.2.1.13   Data binding engines

Software for easily binding XML documents to programming language objects for serialization and deserialization.

Java/XML Quick

Java/XML Quick is a tool for mapping between Java object models and XML documents. Quick has a markup language for describing Java object models, and from this it can generate serialization and deserialization code that can move data back and forth between XML and Java objects. The Java code is generated by Quick, and the XML representation is also defined by Quick from the object model definition.

JiBX

JiBX is an XML data binding framework which simplifies transferring data between domain-specific object structures and input XML documents. The binding is specified using a binding definition document, and JiBX uses a binding compiler to compile the definitions into Java bytecode for efficiency. JiBX is designed for high performance.

Digester

Digester is a simple XML data binding framework designed to make it easy to read data from XML configuration files to Java objects. It uses a configuration file defining mapping rules described using patterns that are designed to be implementable on top of SAX, while looking like XPath. If these patterns are not sufficient you can plug in the pattern engine of your choice. Digester uses JAXP to find a SAX 2.0 parser.

JaxMe

JaxMe is an XML data binding framework based on SAX 2.0, which makes it fast and memory-efficient. Based on a JaxMe schema (which shares a subset with W3C XML Schema) JaxMe generates Java classes for working with the XML data and loading into Java objects, EJB objects, and storing it in an RDBMS or writing it back out when modified. The next version of JaxMe (2.0) will support JAXB and XML::DB.

Skyron

Skyron simplifies reading XML data into Python objects though a "recipe" file, which describes the actions to be taken upon encountering specific pieces of XML data. The recipe files can have Python code and calls to Python methods interspersed, which allows Skyron to be used for XML data binding, but also for creating interpreters for active XML languages. This is the first Skyron release, and it is therefore of alpha quality.

gogoXML

Is based on the expat parser built into PHP, but uses it to build a tree representation of XML documents that can be modified and written back to XML. The tree API is not DOM, but deliberately designed to be easier to use.

Castor

Castor is a XML data binding framework with support for mapping both between XML and Java objects and between Java objects and relational databases. This makes it very suitable for loading XML into Java applications built on relational databases. Castor uses Java reflection to figure out how to map Java objects to XML, and to reverse the process. A mapping file can also be used to describe the mapping, but it cannot cover all cases. Castor can make use of an XML Schema to improve the mapping.

Zeus

Zeus is an XML data binding framework that generates Java classes from a DTD, and which can then load data from instances of that DTD to instances of the generated Java classes. It is also able to write data out from the Java objects back to an XML representation.

69.2.2 *Control information development*

Tools for creating, modifying and documenting DTDs, XSL style sheets etc.

69.2.2.1   CSS editors

css-mode

css-mode is a simple Emacs major mode (that is, an extension to the Emacs editor) for editing CSS stylesheets. It does syntax colouring, indentation and auto-completion of property names.

69.2.2.2   XSLT editors

xslide

xslide is a major Emacs mode for editing XSLT style sheets that has both syntax colouring, automatic indention, automatic completion and convenience functions to run XSLT engines. xslide was tested in Emacs 20.3.1.

XSL Tester

XSL Tester is an XSLT authoring tool that can be used to write XSLT stylesheets and test them on source documents, showing the results either as plain text or as HTML in a browser window.

XSLT-process

XSLT-process is an Emacs minor mode (that is, it can be used in combination with a major mode such as PSGML or xslide) that adds support for running XSLT processors and debugging the results of XSLT processing. It has quite powerful debugging support, including breakpoints, step-by-step running, and variable viewing.

FOA

FOA (short for Formatting Objects Authoring tool) is a graphical XSLT stylesheet editor designed for editing stylesheets that produce XSL-FO output. When using FOA you provide it with input XML files that are already written, and use FOA to create the XSLT stylesheet that will transform the files into XSL-FO documents. FOA can only work with stylesheets produced either by itself or by WH2FO.

XPath Visualizer

XPath Visualizer can be used to learn XPath and also debug XPath expressions. The visualizer can show an XML document in a tree view and then allows the user to execute an XPath expression against that document, and see which nodes were matched. XPath visualizer uses Xerces and Xalan for XML parsing and XPath evaluation.

69.2.2.3   XSL checkers

XSL Lint

XSL Lint is a Perl script that checks XSLT style sheets for mistakes. It is of alpha quality.

69.2.2.4   XSLT generators

WH2FO

WH2FO reads HTML files produced by Microsoft Word and converts them into an XML document, with two XSLT stylesheets: one for conversion back to HTML and one for conversion to XSL-FO.

69.2.2.5   DTD editors

ezDTD

ezDTD is a DTD editor that tries to make DTD editing a bit simpler. It stores DTDs in its own format (with metadata), but can import DTDs. It can export DTDs into HTML and save them as either SGML (with minimization info) or XML (without).

tdtd

This is an Emacs major mode for editing DTDs. It does syntax colouring, has some convenience macros for inserting commonly-typed constructs as well as ETAGS integration. It is a stand-alone mode, but works well together with PSGML.

69.2.2.6   DTD generators

SAXON

SAXON is a Java framework for processing XML documents optimized for XML to XML/SGML/HTML conversions. Essentially, it is an XSLT engine (1.0 recommendation) which can also be used as a Java development framework. The XSLT implementation is fast, fully conformant and provides many useful extensions. Through its API Java and XSLT code can be combined. SAXON is built on top of SAX 2.0 and DOM 1.0, and should work with any compliant implementation of these. It also supports the XSLT part of JAXP. The API of the XPath implementation can also be used independently. Through integration with FOP SAXON can produce PDF directly from XML. An improved version of Ælfred with validation support and SAX 2.0 drivers is included, as is a small application that can generate DTDs from sample input files.

xml2ddml

This is two OmniMark scripts that convert XML DTDs to DDML schema documents.

69.2.2.7   DTD documenters

perlSGML

perlSGML is a collection of Perl tools for working with SGML, but they also work with XML. Included are DTD documentation tools, a DTD diff tool and several useful related libraries.

DTDParse

DTDParse is a Perl module that can parse a DTD into an in-memory structure. This structure can then be used in various kinds of programs that need DTD information. It comes with several scripts that can produce DTD documentation using this module.

dtddoc

dtddoc is a Python tool that can be used to generate HTML and DocBook RefEntry documentation for XML DTDs. It reads the DTD (using xmlproc) and an XML documentation file (using SAX) and generates the documentation from that. The XML DTD for DTD documentation is available separately and is documented using dtddoc. If tmproc has been installed, dtddoc can also provide output in the form of a topic map.

LiveDTD

LiveDTD parses XML DTDs and generates HTML files from the DTDs with cross-links to element and parameter entity definitions. These HTML files can then be used as documentation, thanks to the links.

69.2.2.8   DTD parsers

xmlproc

xmlproc is a validating parser written in Python. It implements nearly all of the XML Recommendation, including XML namespaces. (The home page lists the deviations.) xmlproc provides access to DTD information and also offers a DTD parsing module. xmlproc supports SGML Open catalogs and XML Catalogs. xmlproc can report errors in Norwegian and

English and can be extended to support other languages as well. xmlproc comes with a DTD-parsing module that it uses to do validation. This module is stand-alone and can be used separately by applications that need to parse DTDs and work on them. xmlproc has a non-standard interface, but a SAX 1.0 driver is available in the PyXML package.

CL-XML

CL-XML is an XML parser written in Common Lisp. The parser is validating, and contains a DOM implementation as well as object models representing the infoset and the XPath data model. It also provides access to DTD information, and supports XML namespaces, even in DTDs. The parser also contains an XPath module which can evaluate XPath expressions written in XPath or S-expression syntax against DOM trees. CL-XML also supports XML Query.

DTDParse

DTDParse is a Perl module that can parse a DTD into an in-memory structure. This structure can then be used in various kinds of programs that need DTD information. It comes with several scripts that can produce DTD documentation using this module.

PXP

PXP is a complete validating XML parser written in Objective Caml, a functional programming language in the ML family with OO features. PXP has some advanced features for building customized XML document trees and also provides access to DTD information. It supports Unicode and can read documents in many different encodings.

DTDParser

DTDParser is a Java module for parsing XML DTDs separately from any XML document. The parser can parse from any kind of stream and builds an object structure representing the DTD. This structure can then be accessed to extract information about the DTD and also be modified.

DTD Parser

The DTD Parser can parse an internal or external subset in the form of a SAX InputSource and build a structure of non-standard objects representing the DTD, which can then be used to explore or modify the DTD. The package can also be used to convert between DTDs and the DDML schema language.

69.2.2.9   Schema converters

DTD2RELAX

DTD2RELAX converts a DTD into a RELAX schema module. The converter has both a command-line and a GUI interface. It uses XML4J 1.1.16 to parse the DTD. Output can be produced as SAX events.

dtd2xs

This tool converts DTDs into XML Schema instances. It knows about parameter entites in the DTD and translates those into equivalent constructs in the XML Schemas, which makes the resulting schemas much smaller than they would otherwise have been.

DTDInst

DTDInst can convert DTDs into an XML DTD developed especially for this tool that represents DTDs in XML syntax. DTDInst handles parameter entities well, and can even detect the semantic intent behind some parameter entities and convert these into XML elements representing higher-level semantic constructs.

69.2.3 *Electronic delivery*

Tools for electronic delivery and display of XML documents.

69.2.3.1   XML browsers

Amaya

Amaya is the W3C testbed browser, and is an HTML and XHTML browser (and editing tool) with CSS support. It supports the MathML 2.0 XML DTD and can edit and display presentational MathML graphically; Amaya can also display some SVG. There is support for simple XLinks. Amaya can read HTML documents written in XML, and save HTML documents as XHTML.

Mozilla

This is version 5 of Netscape Navigator, which can display XML documents with CSS style. It also has some support for MathML. Please note that this is a beta release.

eXchaNGeR

eXchaNGeR is an XML document manager, which categorizes XML documents in a tree display and allows them to be opened in browser or editor applications. It includes a simple text-based editor and a similar viewer, but can also connect to external services for particular elements. Some services for well-known vocabularies are already included. eXchaNGeR is based on the DOM4J XML processing toolkit.

69.2.3.2   Web publishing

Cocoon

Cocoon is a XML publishing framework that can be used to publish XML on the web as HTML. It is designed to be performant and flexible, using SAX pipelines and XSLT stylesheets. Over the years Cocoon has grown to become a large and powerful tool with support for many kinds of formats and data sources. The framework builds on several already known products such as the Xalan XSLT processor and the FOP XSL to PDF converter.

mod_xslt

mod_xslt is an Apache module useful for publishing XML documents using XSLT. It uses a configuration file that maps document element names to XSLT stylesheets and when an XML document is requested it automatically applies the XSLT stylesheet to the XML document to produce its output. The XSLT engine used is Sablotron.

maki

maki is a Python framework for publishing XML documents on the web using a combination of XSLT and Python. maki uses Sab-pyth and 4XSLT (you can choose which you want to use) to provide XSLT processing.

69.2.4 *Conversion*

Tools for scripted creation and modification of XML documents.

69.2.4.1 General X-converters

XML converters are tools for automated processing of XML documents.

SwiX

SwiX is an XML validator and normalization tool, which can be used to validate XML documents and also to normalize them. It can also parse and and normalize DTDs. SwiX is based on Xerces-J.

XPA

XPA, short for XML Processing for Antlr, is a toolkit for XML processing and transformation based on the Antlr parser generator for Java. It allows XML processing to be described using a declarative grammar syntax interspersed with Java code to perform actions at particular points in the parsing.

X-Tract

X-Tract is an interpreter for XML Script, an XML transformation language with XML syntax. XML Script can be seen as a non-standard version of XSLT, also using XPath, but with different syntax and based more on a traditional imperative programming model, rather than the functional model of XSLT. It uses the Xerces parser for XML parsing and Pathan for XPath.

MetaMorphosis

MetaMorphosis is a tree-based XML transformation tool that can be used to convert between SGML/XML applications, to publishing formats etc. MetaMorphosis has an architecture where several parsers and output generators are available (and more can be written in Visual Basic or C++ and plugged in). MetaMorphosis transformations are defined in a tool-specific declarative language based on the tree structure. It supports many Unicode encodings as well as many oriental character encodings.

Fxt

Fxt is an XML processing tool that combines XML pattern matching capabilities with the Standard ML programming language to create a language for XML processing. Fxt uses Fxp for XML parsing and Fxgrep for pattern matching.

XML::DT

XML::DT is a Perl package for simplifying down-translation from XML into some other format, for example LaTeX or HTML. XML::DT uses mapping rules that map element type names to Perl handler functions.

69.2.4.2   General N-converters

Non-XML converters are designed for converting to XML from multiple non-XML representations

Tidy

Tidy is a tool that can read your XML and HTML markup and detect and to some extent also fix errors in it. This can be used to clean up bad HTML and XML and also to convert from poor HTML to XML. Tidy can also pretty-print your markup, and has special features for dealing with the HTML produced by MS

Word '97 and 2000. It is to some extent also aware of ASP, JSP and PHP directives and will ignore these.

DB2XML

DB2XML is a tool for generating XML from database queries. It is a GUI-driven application written in Java, but can also be used as a servlet and as a command-line application. The XML generated is configurable, and metadata (types etc) can optionally be included, dates can be customized and currency representation can be localized. The generated XML can be processed with an XSLT stylesheet. DB2XML uses JAXP to get parsers and XSLT engines. DB2XML can generate external and internal DTDs for the XML produced, and can also handle binary data (either encoded in the generated XML file or externally). It can also handle different character encodings and primary keys. The generated XML is available as a stream, as a file or through a DOM interface.

JEDI

JEDI is a general tool for converting various kinds of text files (plain text, HTML, ...) into a structured form, which can be XML. It does this using an advanced rule language, and even has features for following HTML links and filling out forms. It can also be extended with Java code.

xmlizer

xmlizer can produce XML from database contents via JDBC, either using a simple generic mapping or using a rule set. The rule set can be created using a GUI from a DTD or an XML Schema. The product is divided into a server and a client, where the server maintains the configuration and the database connections, and the client connects to it to retrieve XML data.

TagSoup

TagSoup is an HTML parser which can parse HTML as it is found on the web (and not just valid HTML) and make it available through a SAX 2.0 interface. It attempts to emulate the behaviour of web browsers by correctly nesting elements, inferring missing tags, and adding default attribute values, and it never signals syntax errors.

CyberNeko HTML Parser

The CyberNeko HTML parser is an HTML parser built on the native interface of the Xerces XML parser. It adds missing parent elements, automatically closes elements, and can handle mismatched end tags.

69.2.4.3   Specific N-converters

Specific non-XML converters are designed for converting to XML from a particular non-XML representation

Majix

Majix is an RTF-to-XML converter written entirely in Java. It can handle RTF styles and also lets you customize it to fit your own XML DTDs.

RTF2XML

RTF2XML (formerly known as RTF2SGML) reads RTF files and converts them to an XML document corresponding to an XML DTD that comes with RTF2XML. RTF2XML supports Unicode RTF. RTF2XML is written in OmniMark and so requires OmniMark to run.

XML::Edifact

XML::Edifact is a set of Perl scripts for converting EDIFACT into an XML representation that mimics the original EDIFACT structure in an XML syntax. A DTD called edicooked.dtd describes the XML structure.

69.2.5 Document Storage and Management

Tools for document management, such as document databases and search engines.

69.2.5.1 XML document management utilities

xmldiff

xmldiff reads two XML documents and compares them using a tree comparison algorithm. xmldiff uses its own tree model, but can build instances of the model from both SAX and DOM2 sources. xmldiff depends on the Python XML-SIG package. xmldiff can output diff results both in a private notation, as well as in the form of an XUpdate document.

69.2.5.2 XML document database systems

Systems for persistently storing XML documents and providing access to their structure and individual parts.

XML-DBMS

XML-DBMS is a Java library that can be used to move data from XML to a relational database and also back again. Through the use of a mapping document the structure of the original document is preserved.

XDBM

XDBM is an open source XML database manager for storing XML documents in and modifying them while in the database. It's designed as a library to be linked into programs. XDBM also has searching functionality.

infozone

Ozone is an open source OODBMS written in Java, on top of which several XML tools have been built, loosely grouped under the name infozone. Prowler is a persistent DOM level 1 implementation which stores its nodes in Ozone. It also supports XPath. RelDOM supports storing XML documents persistently in an RDBMS. Lexus is an implementation of the XML Update language on top of Prowler. Schemox is a tool for generating input form for XML data.

RDFDB

RDFDB is a database that supports the RDF data model directly. It can load data from files or data can be inserted using the database API. It also supports an SQL-like query language.

Redfoot

Redfoot is a framework for developing RDF-based applications, consisting of an RDF database with a query API, an RDF parser and serializer and a web interface for viewing and editing RDF. It also intends to support inter-database communications.

4Suite

4Suite is a collection of XML processing tools based on the Python XML-SIG package. It contains a complete XSLT implementation, an XPath implementation, a DOM implementation (level 1 and level 2), a persistent DOM implementation that stores documents in an object database, an RDF toolkit with persistence and schema support, an XPointer implementation an XLink processor, an XInclude processor, and an XUpdate processor.

eXist

eXist is a lightweight XML database that supports fulltext search. It has two backends, one native and one using an RDBMS. The query language implemented is XPath. eXist provides an HTTP interface, an XML-RPC interface, and also implements the XML:DB Java API. eXist uses SAX to import XML documents.

XIndice

XIndice is a native XML database for storing XML documents in and running XPath queries against them. The update language used is XUpdate, and XIndice also implements the XML::DB API.

69.2.5.3   XML search engines

sgrep

sgrep is a general tool for searching and indexing text that supports XML (and SGML). It also has its own very powerful query language. sgrep supports Unicode.

Xtract

Xtract is a document search tool for with a query language loosely based on XQL. Xtract can handle both HTML and XML documents, but is currently at beta level.

XSet

XSet is an XML search engine oriented towards performance. It keeps its working set in memory (using paging to support large documents) and can be accessed through RMI. The query language is very simple.

Fxgrep

Fxgrep is a command-line tool for querying an XML document. Queries can be specified either in an XPath-like pattern language or using a more verbose (but also more powerful) grammar language. It is based on the fxp parser.

69.2.6   *Editing and composition*

Tools for interactive creation, modification and composition of XML documents.

69.2.6.1   XML editors

PSGML

Emacs is easily one of the most powerful (if not the most powerful) text editors in the world. It has an internal Lisp programming language, which means that it can be easily extended, and as a consequence Emacs has suppot for most programming languages ever invented, as well as a web browser with CSS support and a world-class news and mail reader. The user interface is quite unlike most modern editors, but Emacs comes with internal documentation which can help you out. This is an old SGML mode which has been patched to support XML. It reads the DTD, can use an external parser to validate documents, does syntax colouring as well as help you insert only the correct elements at your current location.

XED

XED is a simple XML editor written in C, Python and Tk. It tries to ensure that the author cannot write a document that is not well-formed and reads the DTD in order to be able to suggest valid elements to be inserted at any point in the document. The document is shown as text, not as a tree view. XED supports running external command-line validators and stepping through errors.

Amaya

Amaya is the W3C testbed browser, and is an HTML and XHTML browser (and editing tool) with CSS support. It supports the MathML 2.0 XML DTD and can edit and display presentational MathML graphically; Amaya can also display some SVG. There is support for simple XLinks. Amaya can read HTML documents written in XML, and save HTML documents as XHTML.

S-Link-S Editor

The S-Link-S Editor is an RDF editor. It is currently of alpha quality.

Protégé 2000

Protégé is a very advanced knowledge-based framework for developing domain-specific systems. It has been developed and used by the medical informatics community for years and has lately been extended with support for RDF. So Protégé does much much more, but can also be used for generating editors for specific RDF applications. It understands both RDF and RDF schemas.

xmloperator

xmloperator is a tree-based XML editor, which can make use of a DTD or a RELAX-NG schema to provide schema-driven editing. xmloperator is mainly suitable for data-oriented XML rather than document-oriented XML. The editor supports undo, and redo, comparison of documents, as well as conversion using XSLT. It is based on the Xerces-J XML parser and the Xalan-J XSLT engine.

xmltools

xmltools is a tree-based XML editor and browser written in Python using PyGtk for the graphical interface. It can read the DTD and use the DTD to guide editing of the document. It uses 4DOM, 4XPath and xmlproc.

debit

debit is an XML editor based on MSIE. It validates as you edit, uses XSLT to transform for preview and allows elements to be reordered (as permitted by the DTD). debit is more suitable for data-oriented XML than for document-oriented XML.

GenDoc

GenDoc is an open source XML editor for data-oriented applications which has a tree-view and a styled view. It has a plugin API that allows the editing of some elements to be customized for specific DTDs, and also allows publishing actions to be executed from the editor. GenDoc is based on the now defunct Merlot project, and was formerly known as GenDiapo.

Cooktop

Cooktop is an XML editor which shows a plain-text view of the XML documents being edited. It does syntax colouring of XML documents, DTDs, and XSLT stylesheets. It can check for well-formedness and validate documents, pretty-print via Tidy, and test XSLT stylesheets and XPath expressions inside the editor.

eXchaNGeR

eXchaNGeR is an XML document manager, which categorizes XML documents in a tree display and allows them to be opened in browser or editor applications. It includes a simple text-based editor and a similar viewer, but can also connect to external services for particular elements. Some services for well-known vocabularies are already included. eXchaNGeR is based on the DOM4J XML processing toolkit.

69.3 | The XML SPECtacular

The CD includes a collection of the relevant standards and specifications that you can browse, search, and print. There is a brief description of each.

For each document, we've included a link to a website where you can learn more about the underlying project and obtain the latest version of the spec. Where copyright and production considerations allowed, we've also included a browseable copy on the CD-ROM.

In this listing, we've only included brief summaries of specs for which the full text exists on the CD.

69.3.1 *W3C base specifications*

CSS: Cascading Style Sheets, level 2
CSS was the first style sheet standard to be implemented in browsers, and still the most widely supported style sheet language for XML. It is simple, but effective and elegant, and much used by XML editors for WYSIWYG display of XML documents being edited.

DOM: Document Object Model, level 2
The DOM is an important XML standard that is often used to implement many of the others. It describes a standardized API for accessing, manipulating and building XML and HTML document structures in memory, and is often the basis for implementations of XSLT, XPath, and many other standards. It is also intended to be used in browsers and editors.

Namespaces in XML
What this standard does is to enable XML element type names to be given globally unique names. This can be used in many ways,

such as to mix elements from different vocabularies in a single document as RDF and XSLT do. This standard is fundamental to the family of XML standards, and many believe it should have been part of XML 1.0 from the beginning.

Namespaces in XML 1.1

This version of XML Namespaces updates the previous very slightly, by internationalizing URIs, adding support for undeclaring prefixes, and incorporating the errata gathered since the publication of version 1.0.

OWL: Web Ontology Language

OWL extends RDF Schema to provide more constraints on RDF models and going beyond that to allow users to express advanced semantic constraints on their RDF data. This can be used to do logical inferencing and also advanced error detection.

RDF Schema

RDF promises to become an important part of the infrastructure of the Web in the future. It provides a framework for describing resources on the Web and as such holds great promise of providing new means of navigation on the Web and better guidance for Web robots. This RDF specification builds on the RDF syntax and data model specification and provides a schema syntax for RDF models.

RDF: Resource Description Framework - Model and Syntax Specification

RDF promises to become an important part of the infrastructure of the Web in the future. It provides a framework for describing resources on the Web and as such holds great promise of providing new means of navigation on the Web and better guidance for Web robots. Of the two RDF specifications this is the most basic one, which describes the syntax and data model of RDF.

XInclude: XML Inclusions

XInclude provides a means of including XML documents in other documents without having to use entities. XInclude uses elements and so operates at a higher level than entities, which for example means that where they can appear can be controlled by a DTD or schema.

XLink

XLink provides the means for defining hyperlinking in XML documents and takes major steps beyond the hyperlinking provided by HTML.

XML Base

XML Base is a very simple standard that provides a means for markup in XML documents to change the base URI of the document in parts of the document. This is more or less the same as what the BASE element in HTML does.

XML Infoset

This standard is much more important than it may seem at first glance. The XML recommendation itself only describes a syntax for representing the data in XML documents, but an actual data model for XML documents is not provided there. And, when you think about it, the only reason we have the syntax is to enable us to exchange documents and then recreate the data described by the document inside our systems and programs. And this is what the XML Information Set provides: a formal data model for XML documents.

XML Schema Part 0: Primer

This is not a standard, but a tutorial introduction to the XML Schema specification. Reading this before moving on to the specifications themselves may be a good idea.

XML Schema Part 1: Structures

This is perhaps one of the most important standards in the set of XML-related standards. XML 1.0 already has DTDs, which can be used to define what a particular type of XML documents can and cannot look like. Schemas go beyond the features offered by DTDs in order to offer functionality required in the many new areas where XML is currently being used. This specification provides the features used to define the structure of XML documents (which attributes are allowed where, which elements are allowed where etc).

XML Schema Part 2: Datatypes

This specification provides the features used to define the types of elements and attributes. This can be used to declare that an element contains dates, numbers or URLs, and similarly for attributes. Although datatypes are part of the work on schemas, they can also be used in DTDs, and several other schema languages, like RELAX-NG, also use them. (There is open source software on the CD-ROM that supports such use.)

XML: Extensible Markup Language 1.0, second edition

Here it is: the XML standard itself. For a standard it is mercifully short and readable, and clearly written. This is definitely recommended reading! Note that this is the second edition of the specification, where numerous errors and ambiguities have been fixed.

XML: Extensible Markup Language 1.1

XML 1.1 is a small update to XML 1.0 which for the first time since the XML Recommendation was published in February 1998 changes the definition of well-formed documents. The changes are, however, very small, and are motivated by the need to stay in sync with versions of the Unicode character set. What has changed is mainly what characters are allowed in names, and also what characters are allowed in XML documents at all.

XPath: XML Path Language

XPath provides an expression language that can be used to search XML documents, to filter them, to address into them and to compute values from them. It is an extremely versatile and useful standard, and it provides the foundation for both XSLT and XPointer. XPath is also seeing very usage as a simple, declarative query languages in a wide range of specifications and tools, and has now become a key XML standard.

XPointer Framework

XPointer is a language intended to be used in Web links for pointing into XML documents, even to parts of an XML document that may have no identifier. This part of XPointer defines a framework whereby different kinds of addressing schemes for addressing different kinds of content can be declared and used in a single language. The addressing schemes are defined in separate documents.

XPointer element() Scheme

This document defines an XPointer addressing scheme called element() which is a simple scheme for addressing XML elements either by identifiers or using a simple stepping algorithm down through the document.

XPointer xmlns() Scheme

This document defines an XPointer addressing scheme called xmlns() which does not itself address anything, but which can be used to define XML namespace prefixes to be used by other XPointer addressing schemes in the same XPointer.

XPointer xpointer() Scheme

This document defines an XPointer addressing scheme called xpointer() which defines an extensive language for addressing strings, points, and ranges in XML documents. It is based on XPath, but extends it with additional functionality to support addressing ranges, and also to provide additional addressing.

XQuery 1.0 and XPath 2.0 Data Model

XQuery is a query language for XML data, based on XPath. This specification formally defines the data model on which XQuery (and XPath 2.0) work. If you want an introduction to XQuery, don't start here.

XQuery 1.0 and XPath 2.0 Formal Semantics

XQuery is a query language for XML data, based on XPath. This specification formally defines the semantics of XQuery using mathemathics. If you want an introduction to XQuery, start with the specification above.

XQuery 1.0: An XML Query Language

XQuery is a query language for XML data, based on XPath. It extends XPath with many powerful features, such as for-let-where expressions, the ability to define functions, generate XML output, and much more. XQuery will become the query language of the new generation of XML databases, and as such is a very important member of the XML standards family. This specification defines the syntax and semantics of the query language, although only informally. A separate specification (below) contains the formal specification.

XSL: Extensible Stylesheet Language

This is another important standard which provides a means of rendering XML documents in a way that is optimized for end-users of the information. This can be as visually formatted documents or as aurally formatted documents destined for text-to-speech synthesis. This specification only describes how to specify the formatting of XML documents, not how to produce this formatting. That is left for XSLT.

XSLT: XSL Transformations

XSLT is an XML-based language for describing transformations on XML documents. It can be used to convert between XML document types, to HTML, or to XSL. This is one of the most common operations performed on XML documents, and so XSLT is a key standard in the XML standards family, and one which has contributed considerably to the success of XML. Note that XSLT builds on XPath (below).

69.3.2 *Non-W3C base specifications*

SAX: Simple API for XML 2.0

SAX is a general event-based API for XML parsers. Using SAX enables application programmers to write applications and utilities that are parser-independent. Today it is almost universally supported by XML parsers, and is probably the most widely used XML standard apart from XML itself. SAX is not presently being standardized by an official standards body. It is a de facto standard developed by the participants on the xml-dev mailing list.

69.3.3 *W3C XML applications*

SMIL: Synchronized Multimedia Integration Language 2.0
SMIL is an XML application that can be used to integrate a set of multimedia objects into a coherent presentation complete with hyperlinks and synchronization. SMIL can be integrated with XHTML and SVG.

XHTML: The Extensible HyperText Markup Language 1.1
XHTML is a reformulation of HTML 4.0 in XML syntax, and is intended to be the future of HTML. Its main benefits are that it is much easier to develop software for than HTML itself, and that it allows controlled integration with other vocabularies such as MathML, SVG, and SMIL.

MathML: Mathematical Markup Language 2.0
MathML is the long-awaited solution to a problem many scientists and teachers have struggled with: how to publish mathematical formulae on the Web. It also provides a solution for exchanging formulae between programs.

SVG: Scalable Vector Graphics 1.1
SVG is an XML application that can be used to describe two-dimensional vector graphics, text and raster images. This allows for styling images with style sheets, and hyperlinking into (and out of) images.

SOAP: Simple Object Access Protocol 1.2
SOAP is an XML-based system for making method and function calls across the network on top of the HTTP protocol. It could be described as a simpler and easier-to-use alternative to CORBA and RMI. SOAP is often considered crucial to the implementation of Web services.

XForms 1.0

XForms is the next generation of forms on the Web, designed to replace the much less powerful HTML forms. With XForms, forms-based applications will become much easier to develop and maintain. For large organizations, which typically have huge numbers of forms, this is likely to be a significant relief.

69.3.4 *Non-W3C XML applications*

XTM: XML Topic Maps 1.0

XML Topic Maps is the XML syntax for ISO 13250 Topic Maps, a standard for organizing and systematizing information. XTM makes it possible to use topic maps with XML and on the Web.

Index

LICENSE AGREEMENT AND LIMITED WARRANTY

READ THE FOLLOWING TERMS AND CONDITIONS CAREFULLY BEFORE
OPENING THIS SOFTWARE MEDIA PACKAGE. THIS LEGAL DOCUMENT IS
AN AGREEMENT BETWEEN YOU AND PRENTICE-HALL, INC. (THE
"COMPANY"). BY OPENING THIS SEALED SOFTWARE MEDIA PACKAGE, YOU
ARE AGREEING TO BE BOUND BY THESE TERMS AND CONDITIONS. IF YOU
DO NOT AGREE WITH THESE TERMS AND CONDITIONS, DO NOT OPEN
THE SOFTWARE MEDIA PACKAGE. PROMPTLY RETURN THE UNOPENED
PACKAGE AND ALL ACCOMPANYING ITEMS TO THE PLACE YOU OBTAINED
THEM FOR A FULL REFUND OF ANY SUMS YOU HAVE PAID.

1. GRANT OF LICENSE: In consideration of your payment of the license fee,
which is part of the price you paid for this product, and your agreement to abide
by the terms and conditions of this Agreement, the Company grants to you a
nonexclusive right to use and display the copy of the enclosed software program
(hereinafter the "SOFTWARE") on a single computer (i.e., with a single CPU) at
a single location so long as you comply with the terms of this Agreement. The
Company reserves all rights not expressly granted to you under this Agreement.

2. OWNERSHIP OF SOFTWARE: You own only the magnetic or physical media
(the enclosed CD-ROM) on which the SOFTWARE is recorded or fixed, but the
Company retains all the rights, title, and ownership to the SOFTWARE recorded
on the original CD-ROM copy(ies) and all subsequent copies of the SOFTWARE,
regardless of the form or media on which the original or other copies may exist.
This license is not a sale of the original SOFTWARE or any copy to you.

3. COPY RESTRICTIONS: This SOFTWARE and the accompanying printed
materials and user manual (the "Documentation") are the subject of copyright.
You may not copy the Documentation or the SOFTWARE, except that you may
make a single copy of the SOFTWARE for backup or archival purposes only. You
may be held legally responsible for any copying or copyright infringement which
is caused or encouraged by your failure to abide by the terms of this restriction.

4. USE RESTRICTIONS: You may not network the SOFTWARE or otherwise use
it on more than one computer or computer terminal at the same time. You may
physically transfer the SOFTWARE from one computer to another provided that
the SOFTWARE is used on only one computer at a time. You may not distribute
copies of the SOFTWARE or Documentation to others. You may not reverse
engineer, disassemble, decompile, modify, adapt, translate, or create derivative
works based on the SOFTWARE or the Documentation without the prior written
consent of the Company.

5. TRANSFER RESTRICTIONS: The enclosed SOFTWARE is licensed only to you
and may not be transferred to any one else without the prior written consent of

the Company. Any unauthorized transfer of the SOFTWARE shall result in the immediate termination of this Agreement.

6. TERMINATION: This license is effective until terminated. This license will terminate automatically without notice from the Company and become null and void if you fail to comply with any provisions or limitations of this license. Upon termination, you shall destroy the Documentation and all copies of the SOFTWARE. All provisions of this Agreement as to warranties, limitation of liability, remedies or damages, and our ownership rights shall survive termination.

7. MISCELLANEOUS: This Agreement shall be construed in accordance with the laws of the United States of America and the State of New York and shall benefit the Company, its affiliates, and assignees.

8. LIMITED WARRANTY AND DISCLAIMER OF WARRANTY: The Company warrants that the SOFTWARE, when properly used in accordance with the Documentation, will operate in substantial conformity with the description of the SOFTWARE set forth in the Documentation. The Company does not warrant that the SOFTWARE will meet your requirements or that the operation of the SOFTWARE will be uninterrupted or error-free. The Company warrants that the media on which the SOFTWARE is delivered shall be free from defects in materials and workmanship under normal use for a period of thirty (30) days from the date of your purchase. Your only remedy and the Company's only obligation under these limited warranties is, at the Company's option, return of the warranted item for a refund of any amounts paid by you or replacement of the item. Any replacement of SOFTWARE or media under the warranties shall not extend the original warranty period. The limited warranty set forth above shall not apply to any SOFTWARE which the Company determines in good faith has been subject to misuse, neglect, improper installation, repair, alteration, or damage by you. EXCEPT FOR THE EXPRESSED WARRANTIES SET FORTH ABOVE, THE COMPANY DISCLAIMS ALL WARRANTIES, EXPRESS OR IMPLIED, INCLUDING WITHOUT LIMITATION, THE IMPLIED WARRANTIES OF MERCHANTABILITY AND FITNESS FOR A PARTICULAR PURPOSE, EXCEPT FOR THE EXPRESS WARRANTY SET FORTH ABOVE, THE COMPANY DOES NOT WARRANT, GUARANTEE, OR MAKE ANY REPRESENTATION REGARDING THE USE OR THE RESULTS OF THE USE OF THE SOFTWARE IN TERMS OF ITS CORRECTNESS, ACCURACY, RELIABILITY, CURRENTNESS, OR OTHERWISE.

IN NO EVENT, SHALL THE COMPANY OR ITS EMPLOYEES, AGENTS, SUPPLIERS, OR CONTRACTORS BE LIABLE FOR ANY INCIDENTAL, INDIRECT, SPECIAL, OR CONSEQUENTIAL DAMAGES ARISING OUT OF OR IN

CONNECTION WITH THE LICENSE GRANTED UNDER THIS AGREEMENT, OR FOR LOSS OF USE, LOSS OF DATA, LOSS OF INCOME OR PROFIT, OR OTHER LOSSES, SUSTAINED AS A RESULT OF INJURY TO ANY PERSON, OR LOSS OF OR DAMAGE TO PROPERTY, OR CLAIMS OF THIRD PARTIES, EVEN IF THE COMPANY OR AN AUTHORIZED REPRESENTATIVE OF THE COMPANY HAS BEEN ADVISED OF THE POSSIBILITY OF SUCH DAMAGES. IN NO EVENT SHALL LIABILITY OF THE COMPANY FOR DAMAGES WITH RESPECT TO THE SOFTWARE EXCEED THE AMOUNTS ACTUALLY PAID BY YOU, IF ANY, FOR THE SOFTWARE.

SOME JURISDICTIONS DO NOT ALLOW THE LIMITATION OF IMPLIED WARRANTIES OR LIABILITY FOR INCIDENTAL, INDIRECT, SPECIAL, OR CONSEQUENTIAL DAMAGES, SO THE ABOVE LIMITATIONS MAY NOT ALWAYS APPLY. THE WARRANTIES IN THIS AGREEMENT GIVE YOU SPECIFIC LEGAL RIGHTS AND YOU MAY ALSO HAVE OTHER RIGHTS WHICH VARY IN ACCORDANCE WITH LOCAL LAW.

ACKNOWLEDGMENT

YOU ACKNOWLEDGE THAT YOU HAVE READ THIS AGREEMENT, UNDERSTAND IT, AND AGREE TO BE BOUND BY ITS TERMS AND CONDITIONS. YOU ALSO AGREE THAT THIS AGREEMENT IS THE COMPLETE AND EXCLUSIVE STATEMENT OF THE AGREEMENT BETWEEN YOU AND THE COMPANY AND SUPERSEDES ALL PROPOSALS OR PRIOR AGREEMENTS, ORAL, OR WRITTEN, AND ANY OTHER COMMUNICATIONS BETWEEN YOU AND THE COMPANY OR ANY REPRESENTATIVE OF THE COMPANY RELATING TO THE SUBJECT MATTER OF THIS AGREEMENT.

Should you have any questions concerning this Agreement or if you wish to contact the Company for any reason, please contact in writing at the address below.
Robin Short
Prentice Hall PTR
One Lake Street
Upper Saddle River, New Jersey 07458 USA

About the CD-ROMs

Our two CD-ROMs are packed with useful XML tools and information. A full description can be found in "Free resources on the CD-ROM" on pages 1142-1197.

There are three main areas, distributed over the two CD-ROMs:

- A hand-picked collection of genuine, productive, no-time-limit XML-centric free software. There are over 200 titles.
- A showcase for leading XML software and service providers. It features product and service information, white papers, XML samples, demos, and trialware.
- The XML SPECtacular, a collection of the relevant specifications that you can browse, search, and print.

How to use the CD-ROMs

A CD-ROM is just another drive on your Windows 95, 98, Me, 2000, NT, or Windows XP computer. No special installation is necessary. Just do this:

1. Start your Web browser.
2. Select "Open File" from the File menu.
3. Type "d:\index.htm" as the file name, where "d" is your CD-ROM drive.

License Agreement

Use of the CD-ROMs is subject to the terms of the License Agreement and Limited Warranty on the preceding pages.